George Chambers

A handy digest of more than 2750 cases relating to public health

and local government

George Chambers

A handy digest of more than 2750 cases relating to public health and local government

ISBN/EAN: 9783337281717

Printed in Europe, USA, Canada, Australia, Japan

Cover: Foto ©Andreas Hilbeck / pixelio.de

More available books at **www.hansebooks.com**

A

HANDY DIGEST

OF MORE THAN 2750

CASES

RELATING TO

PUBLIC HEALTH

AND

LOCAL GOVERNMENT

WITH MORE ESPECIAL REFERENCE TO THE POWERS AND DUTIES OF
LOCAL AUTHORITIES, INCLUDING COUNTY COUNCILS.

BY

GEORGE F. CHAMBERS, F.R.A.S.,

OF THE INNER TEMPLE, BARRISTER-AT-LAW;

AN ASSOCIATE OF KING'S COLLEGE, LONDON (ENGINEERING DEPARTMENT), AND

AN ASSISTANT BOUNDARY COMMISSIONER FOR ENGLAND AND WALES (1887).

Author of "A Digest of the Law relating to Public Health," "A Handbook of Public Meetings,"
and many other Works.

LONDON:

KNIGHT AND CO., 90 FLEET STREET.

1893.

PREFACE.

SOME years ago, when preparing for press the 8th Edition of my *Digest of the Law Relating to Public Health and Local Government*, I arrived at the conclusion that, owing to the immense increase in the number of the Cases on the subjects dealt with in that Work, which year by year were coming before the Superior Courts, the time was approaching when it would be expedient to gather those Cases into a separate volume. That time has, I think, now fully arrived, and hence the publication of the present Digest.

The classification of the Cases conforms in the main to that originally adopted, but the very large number of new Cases which have been reported since 1881 has rendered satisfactory classification very difficult, and good indexing more than ordinarily important. The indexes will I trust be found very full and therefore useful. Any one who has studied with attention the Cases which have come before the Courts of Law during recent years under the great stimulus given to Municipal matters in Town and Country alike, will readily understand how difficult is the task of drawing lines of demarcation between subject and subject. Having had occasion to exhibit Cases relating to Rates and Public Libraries in new editions of my Works on those subjects, questions relating to Rating and Libraries (including Museums, Parks and Recreation Grounds) will, as a rule, not be found in the present volume. Subject to this reservation, this work therefore is intended to exhibit generally all the Cases relating to Public Health and Local Government in the widest sense of those phrases.

Inasmuch as the Highway Cases and the Cases decided under the "Local Government Act, 1888," all hang very much together respectively, and readily yield to a comprehensive and convenient system of Classification, they have been put together in separate "Parts" (being Part II. and Part III. respectively), the 1st and principal "Part" containing all the Cases which may be said to cluster round the "Public Health Act, 1875," and its affiliated Acts, now very numerous and important. It ought to be added, however, that Cases decided under the "Municipal Corporations Acts," the "Poor Law Acts," and the "Burial Acts," are not included, unless they have some special bearing on the subject of Local Government generally, that is to say, on the powers and duties of County Councils, Local Boards, Boards of Guardians, &c., in their aspect of Local Administrative Authorities.

The reader is asked specially to bear in mind that this Digest has only a modest aim, namely, to serve as a sort of Encyclopædic Index to the Authorised Reports. A mere outline only of each Case has been attempted, the object aimed at being to give a clue to the general principles laid down rather than a detailed statement—to tell readers where to look for what they want without always professing to supply here in full what may be wanted. Within the limits of space prescribed much detail would have been quite impossible. For more explicit information respecting the principles on which the Digest has been put together, the reader is referred to the "Introduction." The references have been corrected by the several Reports up to November 15, 1892.

It only remains that I should tender my thanks to Mr. H. W. Fovargue, the able Town Clerk of the Borough of Eastbourne, for much useful help in the revision of the proof sheets, and generally.

G. F. C.

1 CLOISTERS, TEMPLE.
December, 1892.

CONTENTS.

PART I.

Public Health.

INTRODUCTION.

THE following explanations as to the objects aimed at in this Digest may conveniently be given as a guide to the reader consulting it.

Where a decision was appealed against, references to Reports of the Case in its earlier stages are usually omitted unless the facts and arguments were not set forth with satisfactory fulness at the final stage.

Much confusion often arises in citing references to periodicals running over a long term of years, where there exists an "Old" and a "New" Series of each. Having considered this matter in connection with the *Law Journal* and *Law Times*, and bearing in mind that the "New Series" of each of these periodicals has now been going on for many years, and that references to the "Old Series" are not only few, but cannot increase, it has been decided on reflection to suppress the letters "N. s." usually appended to references to the above-named periodicals, and to do the converse thing, that is, append the letters "O. s." to such references as apply to the "Old Series" of each respectively. This arrangement, it is to be understood, is limited to the *Law Journal* and *Law Times*, and does not extend to any other works, so that the *Common Bench Reports*, for instance, are cited in the usual way, "*Common Bench*" and "*Common Bench, New Series*," and so on in other instances.

The ample Index of subjects appended, coupled with a little ingenuity on the part of the reader, in always turning to more heads than one, will, it is hoped, render reference to the Cases a task free from serious difficulty.

Though the *Weekly Reporter* is not as a rule cited, many of the Cases will be found therein. The dates appended will facilitate search. The *Weekly Reporter* and the *Jurist* are usually only cited in instances where no other Report was to be had, but this has not been from any distrust of the *Weekly Reporter* at any rate, because that is a very trustworthy and useful publication. It was necessary, however, to draw the line somewhere, or there would have been a superfluity of references in many places. The *Times* is freely cited, for that Journal often reports Cases of importance not noticed elsewhere, and the periodical reprint of *Times* Cases has come to be looked upon as a very authentic and useful record.

Cases which are obsolete by reason of subsequent legislation, or because they have been overruled, are usually suppressed altogether. If in a few instances the titles of such Cases have been given with an asterisk prefixed, this has been done because it was judged convenient for some reason or other that these Cases should not be entirely lost from record.

It must of course be understood that the Cases have been taken very much as they were found reported. It has been no part of my duty to comment on them, still less, save in very exceptional instances, to attempt to reconcile contradictions, of which not a few will be found.

The reader who concerns himself with such details will find that great pains have been taken to exhibit the references not only correctly but methodically. Every reference has been specially verified and very carefully read at press.

Care has been taken in the Index to distinguish Cases of the same name from one another. In some few instances the same Case has been printed twice over where reasons of convenience seemed to render this expedient. Making allowance for this the total number of Cases here digested will be found to amount to more than 2750.

DIGEST OF CASE

PART I.—PUBLIC HEALTH.

1. ACCOUNTANT.

1858. [1]
Haigh v. *North Bierley Union.* A Board of Guardians by resolution employed an Accountant; his appointment was not by a contract under seal, but he was held entitled to recover for work done. (28 L. J., Q. B., 62 : E. B. & E., 873 : 31 L. T., (o. s.), 213.)

1857. [2]
Reg. v. *Worksop L. B.* Accountant—Held that the Court of Quarter Sessions was entitled to decide whether a Local Board was justified in incurring the expense of employing an accountant. (21 J. P., 451.)

2. ADOPTION OF "THE PUBLIC HEALTH ACT."

1857. [3]
Barber v. *Jessopp.* Validity of application of the "Public Health Act, 1848"—Inexact use by Inspector in his Report of the terms "parish," "town," and "township"—Application held valid—Highway Rate over the whole Parish held invalid. (26 L. J., Ex., 186 : 1 H. & N., 578 : 28 L. T., (o. s.), 306.)

1859. [4]
Bird, Ex parte. Adoption of the "Local Government Act, 1858"—Appeal to Secretary of State who confirmed the adoption—His Order held binding and conclusive and beyond the interference of the Court, and this though on the face of the Order it was doubtful whether it was good—*Mandamus* for a Poll of the Ratepayers refused as too late. (28 L. J., Q. B., 223 : 1 E. & E., 931 : 33 L. T., (o. s.), 162.)

1871. [5]
Driver v. *Kingston H. B.* Adoption of "Local Government Act, 1858"—Repair of highways—Outstanding contract with the Highway Board — Contractor held entitled to recover on his contract for work done during 2 months following Adoption of Act. (24 L. T., 480 : 20 W. R., 20.)

1870. [6]
Littleborough L. B., Ex parte. Meeting to adopt "Local Government Act, 1858"—Chairman

takes the show of hands, but if a Poll is demanded, the Summoning Officer is to conduct it. (22 L. T., 437.)

1862. [7]
Matlock Bath District, Ex parte. "Local Government Act, 1858," §§ 12, 14, and 16—Though a place has boundaries assigned to it, it cannot adopt the above Act until the parish in which it is situated has refused to do so—*Mandamus* to Secretary of State to publish boundaries, refused, because the parish meanwhile had resolved to adopt the Act. (31 L. J., Q. B., 177 : 2 B. & S., 543 : 6 L. T., 243.)

1864. [8]
Reg. v. *Bird.* Proposed adoption of the "Local Government Act, 1858"—If the Chairman has improperly refused to cause a Poll to be taken, the Meeting is abortive and a new Meeting is necessary—*Mandamus* refused. (39 L. T. Newsp., 286.)

1873. [9]
Reg. v. *Grasmere L. B.* "Local Government Act, 1858," §§ 12 and 17—Adoption—Place having "a known or defined boundary"—Township containing detached portion of other Townships—Order by Local Government Board for adoption held valid. (42 L. J., Q. B., 131 : [*Reg.* v. *Local Government Board*] L. R., 8 Q. B., 227.)

1868. [10]
Reg. v. *Hardy* (Secretary of State for the Home Department). Adoption of the "Local Government Act, 1858," by a Parish which included a Corporate Borough but not the whole of Parliamentary Borough of the same name—Adoption held valid. (38 L. J., Q. B., 9 : L. R., 4 Q. B., 117 : 9 B. & S., 926 : 19 L. T., 352.)

1866. [11]
Reg. v. *Northowram & Clayton Ratepayers.* "Local Government Act, 1858," §§ 12–14 and 16—Adoption—An Ecclesiastical District under 6 & 7 Vict., c. 37, is a place having "a known and defined boundary." (35 L. J., Q. B., 90 : L. R., 1 Q. B., 110 : 7 B. & S., 110.)

B

1861. [12]
Todmorden, In re. "Local Government Act, 1858," § 16 [Repealed]—*Certiorari* to quash Secretary of State's Order as to boundaries refused as applied for too late—*Per Cockburn, C.J.*: It is "very doubtful" whether it is competent for a Secretary of State to enlarge the boundaries suggested in a petition. (30 L. J., Q. B., 305 : 4 L. T., 509 : [*Smith, Ex parte*] 1 B. & S., 412.)

3. ADULTERATION OF FOOD.

1878. [13]
Barnes v. *Chipp.* "Sale of Food Act, 1875," §§ 14 and 20—It is a condition precedent to a summary conviction that the purchaser should notify to the vendor his intention to have the article analysed by the *public* analyst. (47 L. J., M. C., 85 : L. R., 3 Ex. D., 176 : 38 L. T., 570.)

1888. [14]
Betts v. *Armstead.* Proof that vendor had no knowledge that he was selling an adulterated article is no defence to a prosecution under the "Sale of Food Act, 1875." (L. R., 20 Q. B. D., 771 : 58 L. T., 811 : 52 J. P., 471.)

1892. [15]
Brown v. *Foot.* "Sale of Food Act, 1875," §§ 6, 25—Milk confessedly adulterated by vendor's servant—Held that vendor was liable to the penalty although he had taken special precautions to divest himself of all responsibility for improper conduct on the part of his servants. (61 L. J., M. C., 110 : 66 L. T., 649 : 56 J. P., 85.)

1883. [16]
Chappell v. *Emson.* Milk stated to be purchased for analysis—No offer to divide it into 3 parts under § 14 of the "Sale of Food Act, 1875"—Held nevertheless that Justices were entitled to hear the case, and conviction upheld. (47 J. P., 804.)

1890. [17]
Crane v. *Lawrence.* "Margarine Act, 1887," § 6—Margarine not duly labelled kept in a shop behind a screen, Held not "exposed for sale"; and therefore the want of the proper label was not under the circumstances an offence. (59 L. J., M. C., 110 : L. R., 25 Q. B. D., 152 : 63 L. T., 197.)

1890. [18]
Dixon v. *Wells.* "Sale of Food Acts, 1875 and 1879"—Informality in issue of summons as to milk—Computation of time—Conviction quashed. (59 L. J., M. C., 116 : L. R., 25 Q. B. D., 249 : 54 J. P., 725.)

1891. [19]
Dyke v. *Gower.* "Sale of Food Act, 1875," § 9—It suffices to prove that food has been altered by abstracting some part of it, and is so sold without notice of the alteration—It is not necessary to prove that it was so altered by the vendor with intent to sell it without notice. (61 L. J., M. C., 70 : L. R., [1892] 1 Q. B., 220 : 65 L. T., 760 : 56 J. P., 163.)

1890. [20]
Farmers & Cleveland Dairy Co. v. *Stevenson.* "Sale of Food Act, 1875," § 25—Defendant in a prosecution held exempt from penalty on proving that he bought milk of a Farm Company by whom its quality was guaranteed by means of a special label attached to their cans, the words used amounting to a warranty. (60 L. J., M. C., 70 : 63 L. T., 776 : 55 J. P., 407.)

1891. [21]
Fecitt v. *Walsh.* Sale of milk in pursuance of a contract—Several Informations in respect of one delivery—Held that though there was but one sale each day as between Appellant and his customer, yet each sale of a sample to a Police officer was a separate sale in respect of each of which a separate Information might be laid—Conviction affirmed. (60 L. J., M. C., 143 : L. R., 2 Q. B., 304 : 65 L. T., 82 : 55 J. P., 726.)

1892. [22]
Filshie v. *Evington.* "Sale of Food Amendment Act, 1879," § 3—Town in which consignee's railway station was situate, held to be the "place of delivery," and a conviction by Justices there held good. (L. R., 2 Q. B., 200 : 66 L. T., 199 : 56 J. P., 312.)

1873. [23]
Fitzpatrick v. *Kelly.* "Adulteration of Food Act, 1872," §§ 2-3 — Sale of adulterated butter — Guilty knowledge need not be proved. (42 L. J., M. C., 132 : L. R., 8 Q. B., 337 : 28 L. T., 558 : 38 J. P., 55.) [See No. 44.]

1883. [24]
Gage v. *Elsey.* "Sale of Food Act, 1875"—Vendor of gin adulterated with 40 per cent. of water, held not punishable under the Act, ample notice having been given that quality was not guaranteed. (52 L. J., M. C., 44 : L. R., 10 Q. B. D., 518 : 48 L. T., 226 : 47 J. P., 391.)

1892. [25]
Garforth v. *Esam.* "Sale of Food Act, 1875"—Gin with water added bought by servant of Inspector for his master — Held that the master who followed within one minute was the purchaser, and that Justices ought to have convicted the vendor. (56 J. P., 521.)

1891. [26]
Hale v. *Cole.* "Sale of Food Act, 1875," § 13—Where constable prosecutes it is not necessary to prove as a condition precedent that he was directed by the Local Authority to do so. (55 J. P., 376.)

1883. [27]
Harris v. *May.* Milk—Written *general* Warranty by farmer to dealer held not to protect the latter in a specified case of adulteration. (53 L. J., M. C., 39 : L. R., 12 Q. B. D., 97 : 48 J. P., 261.)

1889. [28]
Harris v. *Williams.* "Sale of Food Acts, 1875 and 1879"—Milk delivered wholesale to purchaser who took samples—Held that the former Act was inapplicable to wholesale

deliveries, and that proceedings should have been taken under the latter Act, and by the public officer—No public officer having acted, Held that the whole proceedings were void—Conviction quashed. (*Times*, May 16, 1889.)

1881.   [29]
Harrison v. *Richards*. "Sale of Food Act, 1875," §§ 6 and 21—Certificate by Analyst that certain milk was adulterated with 20 per cent. of Water—Nevertheless summons dismissed by Magistrate, partly because the milk was shown to have been standing some hours; can had been largely taken from at top: but sample analysed taken from near bottom, and therefore bottom portion might be expected to be thin without having been adulterated—Magistrate's decision held bad; he ought not to have ignored Analyst's Certificate. (45 J. P., 552.)

1892.   [30]
Hewson v. *Gamble*. Tin of coffee bought by Inspector, and then seized by vendor who refused to restore it—Held that the Justices were wrong in convicting the vendor of larceny of the Inspector's coffee. (56 J. P., 534.)

1886.   [31]
Higgins v. *Hall*. "Sale of Food Act, 1875," § 6—Coffee mixed with chicory, so labelled, and sold as a mixture—Conviction quashed. (51 J. P., 293.)

1880.   [32]
Horder v. *Meddings*. "Sale of Food Act, 1875," § 6—Coffee adulterated with 75 per cent. of chicory—"Coffee" asked for by purchaser—After sale but before delivery vendor labelled it "a mixture," &c.—On proof of which fact the Magistrate refused to convict—Case remitted to Magistrate because he had not found whether the statement of the mixture was for the purpose of concealing "fraudulent" increase in the "bulk" of the article—*Semble* that it was—Otherwise, vendor's defence good. (44 J. P., 234.) [See No. 40.]

1880.   [33]
Horder v. *Scott*. "Sale of Food Act, 1875," §§ 6, 12, 13—Although an Inspector employs a deputy to purchase samples for him and does not do it himself directly, yet the Inspector may in his own name summon the vendor—The purchaser need not himself deliver the sample to the Analyst. (49 L. J., Q. B., 78: L. R., 5 Q. B. D., 552: 42 L. T., 660: 44 J. P., 520.)

1891.   [34]
Hotchin v. *Hindmarsh*. "Sale of Food Act, 1875"—Sale by foreman of milk company of adulterated milk though the milk was guaranteed genuine by original vendor — Conviction held good because foreman had not taken steps under § 25, or otherwise, to protect himself against default on the part of the original vendor. (60 L. J., M. C., 146: L. R., 2 Q. B., 181: 65 L. T., 149: 55 J. P., 775.)

1879.   [35]
Hoyle v. *Hitchman*. (48 L. J., M. C., 97.) [The

Act 42 & 43 Vict., c. 30, terminates the conflict of opinion connected with this case.]

1891.   [36]
Kearley v. *Tonge*. "Sale of Food Act, 1875," §§ 6, 8—Adulterated lard sold without a label—A master is not responsible for unauthorised acts of servant, and therefore evidence that such acts were unauthorised should have been received by the Magistrate at the hearing of the summons. (60 L. J., M. C., 159: [*K.* v. *Tylor*] 65 L. T., 261: 56 J. P., 72.) [See No. 15.]

1885.   [37]
Kirk v. *Coates*. "Sale of Food Act, 1875," § 6 —To constitute an offence the false representation must be made at the time of sale—A false statement made previously does not suffice. (55 L. J., M. C., 182: L. R., 16 Q. B. D., 49: 54 L. T., 178: 50 J. P., 148.)

1885.   [38]
Knight v. *Bowers*. "Sale of Food Act, 1875 "— Selling an article totally different from that demanded by the purchaser is not an offence within § 6. (L. R., 14 Q. B. D., 845: 49 J. P., 614.)

1884.   [39]
Lane v. *Collins*. "Sale of Food Act, 1875 "— Skimmed milk held to be "milk," and Magistrate justified in refusing to convict. (54 L. J., M. C., 76: L. R., 14 Q. B. D., 193: 52 L. T., 257: 49 J. P., 89.)

1879.   [40]
Liddiard v. *Reece*. "Sale of Food Act, 1875," § 8—Appellant convicted of selling coffee adulterated with 40 per cent. of chicory—Held that though the package was labelled as a "mixture," yet it was not protected, the addition of the chicory being in fraud, because the full price of pure coffee was charged, and the purchaser's attention was not called to the label before the sale. (44 J. P., 233.)

1890.   [41]
Lush v. *Wilson*. "Sale of Food Act, 1879 "—Milk adulterated with water—Place of Delivery —Delivery to Railway Company—Carriage paid by purchaser—Conviction of consignor affirmed. (At Q. Sess.) (54 J. P., 73.)

1889.   [42]
Morris v. *Johnson*. Adulterated whiskey—Notices posted up in some rooms of a public-house but not in others; and not where the purchaser consumed the whiskey—Justices refused to convict—Held that if the purchaser knew otherwise than by the notices that diluted whiskey was sold in the house the decision of the Justices was right—Case remitted. (54 J. P., 612.)

1881.   [43]
Morton v. *Green*. "Sale of Food Act, 1875," § 6: "Amendment Act, 1879," § 2—Cream thinned with skim milk, and sold at a price obviously below the price of genuine cream— Held that no offence had been committed, the custom of selling such "cream" being well-known, and no deleterious ingredient being added. (8 Ct. of Sess. Cas., 4th Ser., Ct. of Justic., 36.)

1890.   [44]
Pain v. *Boughtwood.* "Sale of Food Act, 1875," § 9—In a prosecution under this Section it is unnecessary to prove guilty knowledge on the part of the seller. (59 L. J., M. C., 45: L. R., 24 Q. B. D., 353: 62 L. T., 284: 54 J. P., 469.)

1882.   [45]
Parsons v. *Birmingham Dairy Co.* "Sale of Food Act, 1875," § 14—This Section applies equally to a purchase by a private individual under § 12, and by the public officer mentioned in § 13. (51 L. J., M. C., 111 : L. R., 9 Q. B. D., 172: 46 J. P., 727.) [See comments in *Enniskillen* v. *Hilliard*, 14 L. R., Ir., 214.]

1876.   [46]
Pashler v. *Stevenitt.* "Sale of Food Act, 1875," § 6 — A customer asking for "Gin" held to demand Gin as ordinarily sold, not Gin weakened by water — Conviction affirmed. (35 L. T., 862: 41 J. P., 136.) [See now 42 & 43 Vict., c. 30, § 6.]

1874.   [47]
Pope v. *Tearle.* "Adulteration of Food Act, 1872," §§ 2-3—Admixture—A declaration of the bare fact suffices—The Vendor is not required to give details of the nature of the admixture. (43 L. J., M. C., 129: L. R., 9 C. P., 499: 30 L. T., 789.)

1877.   [48]
Reg. v. *Foster.* Indictment for false pretences—Adulterated tea—Three-fourths of the mixture not tea—Defence that it was simple exaggeration, and not misrepresentation of material fact—Conviction affirmed. (46 L. J., M. C., 128 : L. R., 2 Q. B. D., 301 : 41 J. P., 295.)

1890.   [49]
Reg. v. *Wakefield.* "Sale of Food Act, 1879," § 10—Summons alleged to be defective in the particulars given—It is for the Justices to decide if the particulars are sufficient. (54 J. P., 148.)

1879.   [50]
Reg. v. *White.* (4). "Public Health Act, 1875," §§ 116-7—Unsound meat seized and condemned—No notice to owner to appear before the Justice who condemned the meat—Nevertheless, conviction held good. (49 L. J., M. C., 19: [*W.* v. *Redfern*] L. R., 5 Q. B. D., 15: 41 L. T., 524: 44 J. P., 87.)

1874.   [51]
Roberts v. *Egerton.* "Adulteration of Food Act, 1872"—A custom of the trade to colour tea is not to be supposed to be known to the public — Conviction affirmed. (43 L. J., M. C., 135: L. R., 9 Q. B., 494: 30 L. T., 633.)

1892.   [52]
Rolfe v. *Thompson.* "Sale of Food Amendment Act, 1879," § 3—An Inspector is not bound to submit for analysis the whole of a sample taken by him—A portion of such portion may be a proper sample—This is a question of fact for the Justices. (L. R., 2 Q. B., 196: 67 L. T., 295: 56 J. P., 425.)

1878.   [53]
Rook v. *Hopley.* "Sale of Food Act, 1875,"

§ 6—Lard adulterated with 15 per cent. of water—Retail dealer held liable, and not protected by the "bought-note" invoice which he had with the lard, such invoice not being a written warranty within § 25. (47 L. J., M. C., 118: L. R., 3 Ex. D., 209: 38 L. T., 619: 42 J. P., 551.)

1880.   [54]
Rouch v. *Hall.* "Sale of Food Act, 1875:" "Amendment Act, 1879"—§ 14 of former Act does not apply to cases within § 3 of the latter Act. (50 L. J., M. C., 6: L. R., 6 Q. B. D., 17: 44 J. P., 748.)

1877.   [55]
Sandys v. *Markham.* "Sale of Food Act, 1875," § 6 (1)—Mustard "Condiment"—Case remitted to Justices to state more fully the facts as to usage with respect to mixing flour with mustard. (41 J. P., 52.)

1878.   [56]
Sandys v. *Small.* "Sale of Food Act, 1875," §§ 6 and 8—A publican who had put up a conspicuous notice "all spirits sold here are mixed" held protected. (47 L. J., M. C., 115: L. R., 3 Q. B. D., 449: 39 L. T., 118: 42 J. P., 550.)

1880.   [57]
Smith v. *Stace.* Adulterated butter purchased by Inspector's deputy, Inspector waiting outside — Purchase divided, notice given, and summons obtained by Inspector—Held that the proceedings were regular, and that it was not necessary for the Deputy to have taken the later steps. (44 J. P., 796.) [See No. 25.]

1890.   [58]
Somerset v. *Miller.* "Sale of Food Act, 1875," § 14—Diluted gin—Meaning of the word "forthwith"—It must be reasonably construed. (54 J. P., 614.)

1880.   [59]
Warren v. *Phillips.* "Sale of Food Act, 1875," § 3—Baking Powder held not an article of Food—Therefore, selling such powder with alum admixed is not selling an adulterated article of food. (At Q. Sess.) (44 J. P., 61.)

1881.   [60]
Warnock v. *Johnstone.* "Sale of Food Act, 1875," § 6 (4) — Butter-milk to which water had been added held not within the Act, such water being a necessary addition to render the milk available for butter-making in the first instance. (8 Ct. of Sess. Cas., 4th Ser., Ct. of Justic., 55.)

1877.   [61]
Webb v. *Knight.* "Sale of Food Act, 1875," § 6—Gin adulterated with 43 per cent. of water—Custom of the trade to adulterate "gin" set up as a defence—Held, that the question was one of fact what a purchaser buying "gin" would reasonably expect to receive — Conviction affirmed. (46 L. J., M. C., 264: L. R., 2 Q. B. D., 530: 36 L. T., 791: 41 J. P., 726.)

1892.   [62]
Wheat v. *Brown.* "Margarine Act, 1887," § 6—Margarine is exposed for sale if placed in a shop, albeit completely wrapped in paper—The offence was complete on proof that there

was no label of the statutory size on the packages. (66 L. T., 464 : 56 J. P., 153.)

1887. [63]
Wheeler v. Webb. " Sale of Food Act, 1875," § 14 —Held that to announce to a vendor that the " County Analyst " would be called upon to analyse a sample was a sufficient notice, though the Act uses the words " Public Analyst." (51 J. P., 212.)

1887. [64]
White v. Baywater. " Sale of Food Act, 1875 "— When a drug is asked for which has usually a certain strength specified in the *British Pharmacopœia* it is an offence against § 6 to sell a drug not of that strength. (L. R., 19 Q. B. D., 582 : 51 J. P., 340.)

4. AGGRIEVED PARTY.

1856. [65]
Harrop v. Bayley. Local Act—Right of appeal for " an aggrieved party "—A Commissioner present at a meeting and concurring in a resolution, is thereby debarred from claiming *quâ* ratepayer to be an aggrieved party. (25 L. J., M. C., 107 : 6 E. & B., 218.)

1858. [66]
*Hollis v. Marshall. (27 L. J., Ex., 236.) [See *Verdin* v. *Wray.*]

1876. [67]
Rockfort v. Atherley. " Public Health Act, 1875," § 253—Action for penalty without consent of the Attorney-General—Special circumstances —Held that the plaintiff, the late Clerk of a Board, was not an " aggrieved party." (L. R., 1 Ex. D., 511.)

1876. [68]
Smith v. Fieldhouse.—" Public Health Act, 1875," Sched. II. (1), 70.—The consent of the Attorney-General must be obtained before an Action for penalty under this enactment. (35 L. T., 602.) [Overruled in *Fletcher v. Hudson.*]

1877. [69]
Verdin v. Wray. " Public Health Act, 1875," § 253—Held that a defeated candidate was an " aggrieved party " entitled to proceed without the consent of the Attorney-General against a person for fabricating Voting-papers —*Per* Lush, J. :—" I think a candidate would be aggrieved by a fabricated vote being given against him, whether the election would have been turned by such fabricated vote or not." (46 L. J., M. C., 170 : L R., 2 Q. B. D., 608 : 35 L. T., 942 : 41 J. P., 484.)

5. APPOINTMENT OF OFFICERS.
** See also " Seal," (§ 67, *post*).

1874. [70]
Austin v. St. Matthew's, Bethnal Green, Guardians. Clerk to Master of Workhouse—Such an appointment must be under seal. (43 L J., C. P., 100 : L. R., 9 C. P., 91 : 29 L. T., 807 : 38 J. P., 248.)

1872. [71]
Dyte v. St. Pancras Guardians. Appointment of Medical Officer—An appointment of this character involves a contract which should be under seal. (27 L. T., 342.)

1861. [72]
Eales v. Cumberland Black Lead Mine Co. If Directors of a Company appoint one of themselves to a salaried office, such appointment is not void—*Quære*, Is it a breach of trust? (30 L. J., Ex , 141 : 6 H. & N , 481 : 3 L. T., 861.)

1838. [73]
Reg. v. Dolgelly Union. Election of a Clerk— Allegation that the successful candidate was elected by the votes of Guardians not themselves duly elected—*Mandamus* to admit the unsuccessful candidate as having the majority of valid votes, refused, no public inconvenience being shown. (7 L. J., M. C., 99 : 8 A. & E., 561 : 3 N. & P., 542.)

1851. [74]
Reg. v. Griffiths. (1). " Art. 155 of C. O., 1847 "— Election by Guardians of a Clerk — If a Guardian be present he must, whether willing or not, be counted in ascertaining if a " majority of the Guardians present " concur. (17 Q. B., 164.)

1857. [75]
Reg. v. Griffiths. (2). Appointment of an Officer in a certain month fixed by Statute—Held that an appointment some months later was good. (26 L. J., Q. B., 313 : 7 E. & B., 953 : 29 L. T., (o. s.), 196). [Glen relied on this case to show that a casual vacancy in a Local Board might (" Public Health Act, 1848." § 12) be filled up *after* a month had elapsed : *sed quære?*]

1847. [76]
Reg. v. Grimshaw. " Municipal Corporations Act, 1835," § 69—Meeting convened to appoint a Coroner—An appointment without any writing save the entry in the minutes, held good after the appointee had been in actual exercise of the office. (16 L. J., Q. B., 385 : 10 Q. B., 747 : 9 L. T., (o. s.), 221.)

1846. [77]
Reg. v. Welch. Salaried Treasurer to Board of Guardians under a Local Act—Held that such an appointment required a stamp. (2 C. & K., 296.)

1805. [78]
Rex v. Bedford Level Corporation. Election to an office—Majority made up of bad votes— *Mandamus* granted to admit another candidate who had a majority of good votes. (6 East., 356.)

1878. [79]
Richards, Ex parte. By-Law requiring a month's notice of a resolution to revoke or rescind a prior resolution—Clerk dismissed at a meeting convened in the usual way, but without a month's notice to the members of a motion to rescind his appointment—Held, nevertheless, that the dismissal was valid, he holding office only during pleasure, the motion to dismiss being an independent one, and not a rescinding motion—*Quo warranto* by the old Clerk against the new one—Such process not applicable to an office held during pleasure— *Rex v. Wrexham Roads Trustees* not followed. (47 L. J., Q. B., 498 : L. R., 3 Q. B. D., 368 : 38 L. T., 684 : [*Reg. v. Jones*] 42 J. P., 614.)

1856.   [80]
Smart v. *West Ham Union.* Poor Rate Collector —Action for poundage—Appointment not under seal—Guardians held not liable— Action should have been against the parish in default. (25 L. J., Ex., 210 : 10 Ex., 867 : 11 Ex., 867 : 3 C. L. R., 696 : 26 L. T., (o. s.), 285.)

6. APPORTIONMENT.

** See also "Paving Expenses," (§ 60, *post*).

The "Private Street Works Act, 1892," (if adopted) alters usual principles of Apportionment.

1888.   [81]
Bettesworth v. *Richer.* Sale of leasehold house charged with apportioned expenses under "Public Health Act, 1875," § 150—Final demand served after purchase ought to have been completed—Held that the expenses became a charge when the work was completed, and as between vendor and purchaser were payable by vendor. (L. R., 37 Ch. D., 535 : 58 L. T., 796 : 52 J. P., 740.)

1878.   [82]
Bradley v. *Greenwich B. W.* "Metropolis Management Amendment Act, 1862," § 52—Delay of eight years in apportioning the expenses of a sewer—Held nevertheless that the apportionment was good, the Statute containing no express limitation of time. (47 L. J., M. C., 111 : L. R., 3 Q. B. D., 384 : 38 L. T., 849 : 42 J. P., 725.)

1888.   [83]
Egg v. *Blayney.* Paving expenses apportioned under the "Metropolis Management Amendment Act, 1862," § 77, are not a charge on the property so that where a vendor sells, leaving the expenses unpaid purchaser can recover the amount under an implied covenant against incumbrances as in the "Conveyancing Act, 1881," § 7, (1 A.). (L. R., 21 Q. B. D., 107 : 59 L. T., 65 : 52 J. P., 517.)

1863.   [84]
Jacomb v. *Dodgson.* "Local Government Act, 1858," §§ 62 and 63 [="Public Health Act, 1875," § 257]—Sewering, &c., a street—Apportionment—Limitation—The time for proceeding summarily to recover apportioned expenses runs from the end of the three months within which the amount may be disputed. (32 L. J., M. C., 113 : 3 B. & S, 461 : 7 L. T., 674 : 27 J. P., 548.)

1880.   [85]
Mair v. *Greenwich B. W.* "Metropolis Management Act, 1855," § 227—Summonses for expenses of sewer—Notice of apportionment served in 1876—First demand for payment in December 1878—Held that the six months' limitation ran from December 1878, and therefore summons served in time. (44 J. P., 424.)

1870.   [86]
Sawyer v. *Paddington Vestry.* Sewers rate— Definition of new street—Apportionment— Owner held liable. (Metrop.) (40 L. J., M. C., 8 : L. R., 6 Q. B., 164 : 23 L. T., 662 : 34 J. P., 756.)

1880.   [87]
Shanklin L. B. v. *Miller.* "Public Health Act, 1875," §§ 150 and 257—Expenses apportioned —Alleged irregularities which might have avoided the apportionment—Held that apportionment not having been appealed against was binding and that the defendant was too late in raising his objections, inasmuch as he did not appeal within the statutory three months. (49 L. J., C. P., 512 : L. R., 5 C. P. D., 272 : 42 L. T., 738 : 44 J. P., 635.)

1876.   [88]
Sheffield v. *Fulham B. W.* New sewer—Non-compliance with statute as to division of expenses between Board and owner, and no charge apportioned upon owners at the ends of certain streets—Apportionment held bad. (L. R., 1 Ex. D., 395.)

1869.   [89]
St. Giles, Camberwell v. *Weller.* Sewering a "new street" where sewer rates have already been levied. (20 L. T., 756 : 17 W. R., 973.) [Dissented from in *Sawyer* v. *Paddington.*]

1883.   [90]
Wake v. *Sheffield, Mayor.* "Public Health Act, 1875," §§ 150, 268—Paving expenses apportioned—Works executed partly in a public street and partly on private land—Held, that the apportionment was in due form and Magistrate's decision regular, and that frontager's only remedy was appeal to Local Government Board under § 268. (L. R., 12 Q. B. D., 142.)

7. ARBITRATION.

** See the "Arbitration Act, 1889."

1868.   [91]
Barnett v. *Great Eastern Railway Co.* "Lands Clauses Act, 1845," § 76—Money payable under an Award—Defendants dissatisfied with Title, therefore *Mandamus* for payment into the Bank, granted. (18 L. T., 408 : 16 W. R., 793.)

1866.   [92]
Beckett v. *Midland Railway Co.* "Lands Clauses Act, 1845," § 68—Damages awarded by Arbitrator—Action on the Award—Plea, that Arbitrator had made a mistake and that no damage had been done—Plea held good in spite of the Award. (35 L. J., C. P., 163 : L. R., 1 C. P., 241 : 13 L. T., 672.) Again before the Court in 1868—It being shown by evidence that permanent injury had been caused to the freehold, damages held recoverable. (37 L. J., C. P., 11 : L. R., 3 C. P., 82 : 17 L. T., 499.)

1856.   [93]
Blagrave v. *Bristol Waterworks Co.* An arbitration clause in a Local Water Act held not to extend to a claim for compensation for damage caused by the interruption of a drain by the Company's works. (26 L. J., Ex., 57 : 1 H. & N., 369.)

1855.   [94]
Bradby v. *Southampton L. B. H.* "Public Health Act, 1848," § 144 [="Public Health Act, 1875," § 308]—Construction of a Sewer— Where a Local Board denies simply that

damage is done, this involves a dispute as to an amount and not as to liability, and therefore is a matter for arbitration. (24 L. J., Q. B., 239: 4 E. & B., 1014: 19 J. P., 644.)

1884.   [95]
Brierley Hill L. B. v. Pearsall. "Public Health Act, 1875," § 308—A person claiming compensation may insist on amount being decided by arbitration, even though a dispute exists as to the liability—A valid decision as to liability is not a condition precedent to arbitration as to amount—A Local Authority can raise the question of liability by defending an Action on the award. (54 L. J., Q. B. D., 25: L. R., 9 App. Cas., 595: 51 L. T., 577: 49 J. P., 84.)

1882.   [96]
Brighton Sewers Act, In re. Local Act—Duty of County Court Judge to act as Arbitrator. (L. R., 9 Q. B. D., 723.)

1872.   [97]
Buccleuch (Duke of) v. Metropolitan B. W. "Lands Clauses Act, 1845," § 68—Lands injuriously affected—Arbitration—Admissibility of the Umpire's Evidence as to what matters he had taken into consideration. (41 L. J., Ex., 137: L. R., 5 H. L., 418: 27 L. T., 1.)

1877.   [98]
Burgess v. Northwich L. B. (1). "Public Health Act, 1875," §§ 179-80, 308—Injury to private property by works of street improvement—Matter referred to arbitration—Refusal of the Board to take part therein—Award given against the Board—Motion to set aside the Award refused—If a Board should be dissatisfied with an Award on the ground of non-liability, they can raise that question when an Action on the Award is brought—Arbitrator's jurisdiction is not ousted by the other party denying liability and refusing to appear. (37 L. T., 355.)

1886.   [99]
Chesterfield Corporation v. Brampton L. B. "Public Health Act, 1875," §§ 179-80—Disputes as to Joint Sewerage Scheme referred to Arbitration—As the submission to arbitration had been made a Rule of Court the Taxing Master was bound to tax the costs on application. (50 J. P., 824.)

1851.   [100]
Collins v. South Staffordshire Railway Co. "Lands Clauses Act, 1845"— Arbitration — Award thereunder—Strict compliance with all the preliminary forms is not indispensable where the arbitration is by agreement and is not compulsory. (21 L. J., Ex., 247: 7 Ex., 5.)

1869.   [101]
East London Union v. Metropolitan Railway Co. "Lands Clauses Act, 1845," §§ 76-7—When the price of land taken compulsorily has been settled by Arbitration, the execution of the conveyance is a condition precedent to the right of Action for the purchase money. (38 L. J., Ex., 225: L. R., 4 Ex., 309.)

1888.   [102]
Gifford and Bury Town Council, In re. "Public Health Act, 1875," § 180—Arbitrators appointed one in due form, one not in due form not being in writing—Umpire appointed by them—Held that one of the original appointments being irregular the Umpire's appointment was therefore irregular and that his award could not be enforced, (57 L. J., Q. B., 181: L. R., 20 Q. B. D., 368: 52 J. P., 119.)

1863.   [103]
Holdsworth v. Wilson. "Public Health Act, 1848," §§ 125 and 127 [= "Public Health Act, 1875," § 140]—Appointment of Umpire not prompt—Per Erle, C.J.:—"We follow the rule . . . that Arbitrators 'may appoint an Umpire at any time, before the time for making the umpirage has expired' "—Costs awarded held recoverable notwithstanding the Non-Taxation thereof, no attempt having been made to dispute them. (32 L. J., Q. B., 289: 4 B. & S., 1: 8 L. T., 434.)

1867.   [104]
Hopper, In re. Though both Arbitrators must sign the appointment of an Umpire they need not sign at the same time—Circumstances which will avoid an Award on the ground of corruption. (36 L. J., Q. B., 97: L. R., 2 Q. B., 367.)

1874.   [105]
Jacomb v. Huddersfield Corporation. Local Act—The Act gave power to Corporation to take more land than was described in the Parliamentary Notice—Held that the Act was not controlled by the Notice—Compulsory purchase of land—Arbitration—Form of Notice to treat. (43 L. J., Ch., 748: 44 L. J., Ch., 96: L. R., 10 Ch. App., 92: 31 L. T., 466.)

1864.   [106]
Kellet v. Tranmere L. B. H. Arbitration under the "Public Health Act, 1848"—A Court cannot enlarge the time for making an award. (34 L. J., Q. B., 37: 11 L. T., 457.) [Dissented from in *Warburton v. Haslingden.*]

1892.   [107]
Kirkleatham L. B. In re, and Stockton Water Co. Purchase of Waterworks—Erroneous principle of valuation—Arbitrator ordered to state a case. (*Times,* Feb. 24, 1892.)

1875.   [108]
Leicester Waterworks Co. v. Cropstone Overseers. Disputed Assessment—Reference to Arbitration—If parties agree to abide by an Award but when they find it is against them refuse to be bound the Court will interfere to make them. (44 L. J., M. C., 92: 32 L. T., 567 and 752: 40 J. P., 165.)

1886.   [109]
Mackenzie and Ascot Gas Co. Arbitration, In re. In arbitrations under the "Public Health Act, 1875," time cannot be extended under the "Common Law Procedure Act, 1854," § 15. (55 L. J., Q. B., 309: L. R., 17 Q. B. D., 114.)

1876.   [110]
McBryde, Ex parte: Metropolitan Building Act, In re. "Metropolitan Building Act, 1855," § 85—The Court [and presumably the Local Government Board, under the "Public Health Act, 1875," § 180 (7)] has power to

appoint an umpire to act with surveyors appointed by "the building owner" and "the adjoining owner," on their refusal to nominate an umpire, notwithstanding that an Action is pending between the parties as to an ancient light in the party wall. (46 L. J., Ch., 153 : L. R., 4 Ch. D., 200 : 35 L. T., 543.)

1887. [111]
Peake v. *Finchley L. B.* "Public Health Act, 1875," § 180 (13)—An arbitrator must deal with the costs of a reference, and if he does not do so the Court will require him to do so. (W. N., 1887, p. 203 : 57 L. T., 882.)

1878. [112]
Rayner, Ex parte. Compulsory purchase of Land under the "Lands Clauses Act, 1845 "—Arbitration under the " Public Health Act, 1875," § 176—Award silent as to Costs—Landowner held entitled to his Costs under the former Act notwithstanding the "Public Health Act, 1875," § 180—The procedure in such cases is wholly governed by the first-named Act. (47 L. J., Q. B., 600 : L. R., 3 Q. B. D., 446 : 42 J. P., 807.)

1860. [113]
Reg. v. *Burslem L. B.* "Public Health Act, 1848," § 144 — Compensation — Denial of Liability — *Mandamus* — Arbitrator or Justices only to deal with disputes as to amount and not as to liability. (29 L. J., Q. B., 242 : 1 E. & E., 1077 : 2 L. T., 667.)

1878. [114]
Reg. v. *Darlington Corporation.* Proposed purchase of Land for Sewer—Notice to take compulsorily—Arbitration — Award — *Mandamus* to Corporation to take up Award—Return, that the notice to treat had been revoked, and that all subsequent proceedings had been under protest—Application for a Rule to take this return off the file as untrue and no answer, discharged with Costs. (*Times*, May 17 and June 8, 1878.)

1853. [115]
Reg. v. *Metropolitan Commissioners of Sewers.* Compensation for Damage—Arbitration *Ex parte*—Arbitration only applicable where amount is in dispute; not where liability is denied. (Metropolis.) (22 L. J., Q. B., 234 : 1 E. & B., 694 : 21 L. T., (O. S.), 58.)

1863. [116]
Reg. v. *West Midland Railway Co.* "Lands Clauses Act, 1845," § 25—Where a landowner has agreed to accept a definite sum as compensation in full for injury done to him, and has been paid the amount, he cannot afterwards have recourse to arbitration in respect of the same property—And if he only appoints an Arbitrator (the other party refusing to do so) and that Arbitrator proceeds *ex parte*, the other party cannot be compelled to take up the Award, which is void. (11 W. R., 857.)

1863. [117]
Ringland v. *Lowndes.* "Public Health Act, 1848," §§ 124-5 [= "Public Health Act,

1875," § 180] — Construction of Sewer — Damage — Arbitration — Attendance under protest—Held that an Award in such case cannot be enforced. (33 L. J., C. P., 25 and 337 : 17 C. B., (N. S.), 514.)

1874. [118]
Uttley v. *Todmorden L. B.* "Public Health Act, 1848," § 144—Land taken for Sewer—Powers of Arbitrator in assessing compensation—He is not only entitled but, *per* Lush, J., "bound " to take into consideration prospective as well as present damages. (44 L. J., C. P., 19 : 31 L. T., 445 : 39 J. P., 56.)

1888. [119]
Wakefield Corporation v. *Wakefield Union.* Local Act — Proposed sale of Water pipes and fittings—Arbitrator appointed by the Local Government Board at the instance of the Guardians of the Union, the proposed purchasers—Application by the Guardians for authority to revoke their submission—Application refused, on the ground that the Arbitrator had been appointed under the Powers of the Local Act, the terms of which were imperative. (*Times*, May 18, 1888.)

1884. [120]
Walker and Beckenham L. B. Arbitration. An Award in an Arbitration under § 308 of the "Public Health Act, 1875," for damages for carrying a sewer through lands is not enforceable by Motion—Claimant must bring an Action and prove his title to the lands injuriously affected. (48 J. P., 264.)

1879. [121]
Warburton v. *Haslingden L. B.* "Public Health Act, 1875," § 180—The reference to arbitration of a dispute as to compensation is a submission to arbitration by consent within the "Common Law Procedure Act, 1854," and the Court may (under § 8) remit the Award back to Arbitrator for consideration—But proposed remittance refused under the circumstances—*Kellett* v. *Tranmere* dissented from. (48 L. J., C. P., 451.)

8. ARTIZANS' DWELLINGS.
* * * See the " Housing of the Working Classes Act, 1890."

1881. [122]
Badham v. *Marris.* "Artizans' Dwellings Act, 1875," § 20—If any interference with ancient lights occurs in consequence of proceedings under this Act, compensation may be recovered from the Local Authority. (52 L. J., Ch., 237 : 45 L. T., 579.)

1890. [123]
Barlow v. *Ross.* "Artizans' Dwellings Act, 1875," § 20—This section must be taken to include nascent growing or inchoate rights which are capable of being measured by a money compensation. (59 L. J., Q. B., 183 : L. R., 24 Q. B. D., 381 : 54 J. P., 666.)

1882. [124]
Barnett v. *Metropolitan B. W.* "Metropolitan Building Act, 1855," § 80 : "Artizans' Dwellings Act, 1875,"—Notice to take certain dilapidated premises had been served on owner;

yet owner held liable for emergency repairs notwithstanding that proceedings for compulsory sale were pending, and were brought to a close only 3 days after the expenses were incurred. (46 L. T., 384 : 46 J. P., 469.)

1877.   [125]
Bouffler v. *St. Mary, Islington, Vestry.* Appeal against an Order of Vestry to demolish houses built on the site of a Burial Ground—Ground effectively concreted so as to be impervious to noxious gases—Probability that a settlement of the soil might hereafter impair the protection afforded by the concrete—Held that as it was not shown that there was any present injury to health to be feared the Order was bad. (*Times*, August 1, 1877.) Some comments on this case gave rise to an Action for Libel against the *Daily Telegraph*, but a verdict for the plaintiff Bouffler was set aside in the Q. B. D. on the ground of privilege. (*Times*, May 6, 1881.)

1880.   [126]
Carr v. *Metropolitan B. W.* "Artizans' Dwellings Act, 1875," Sched. sub-s. 8, 11, 12—Compensation to owner—Omission of owner's interest from provisional award—Powers of Arbitrator to award compensation. (49 L. J., Ch., 272 : L. R., 14 Ch. D., 807 : 42 L. T., 354.)

1871.   [127]
Flight v. *St. George's, Southwark, Vestry.* "Artizans' and Labourers' Dwellings Act, 1868," §§ 5-6—Held that under the particular circumstances, reports by Medical Officer and Surveyor might include a row of houses in one statement, all the houses being defective. (25 L. T., 24.)

1891.   [128]
Gough v. *Liverpool, Mayor.* Local Act—Insanitary houses condemned — Compensation awarded on basis of value of site and materials—Held that the houses should have been valued according to their condition and state of repair as they stood before demolition, but ignoring the stigma that they had been "presented" by a Grand Jury. (65 L. T., 512 : 56 J. P., 357.)

1889.   [129]
Hyde v. *Berners.* "Artizans' and Labourers' Dwellings Act, 1868," § 27—The expenses of repairs executed by a Local Authority held payable by a tenant in possession under a long lease. (53 J. P., 453.)

1880.   [130]
Jones, Ex parte. "Artizans' Dwellings Act, 1875,"—Purchase of Lands—Limitation of Costs payable by Local Authority in respect of moneys paid into Court. (L. R., 14 Ch. D., 624 : 43 L. T., 84 : W. N., 1880, p. 134.)

1892.   [131]
Pilgrove, Ex parte. "Housing of the Working Classes Act, 1890"—Conviction in respect of dangerous houses held good, though the notice was served only on the owner's agent notwithstanding that the owner's address was known. (*Times*, May 27, 1892.)

1887.   [132]
Reg. v. *St. Marylebone Vestry.* "Artizans' Dwellings Act, 1868," § 3 —Definition of "owner" —Test of ownership is by ascertaining who was owner when preliminary notice was served on tenant, not who was when Order to demolish was served. (L. R., 20 Q. B. D., 415 : 58 L. T., 180 : 52 J. P., 534.)

1884.   [133]
Shaw and Birmingham Corporation, In re. "Artizans' Dwellings Act, 1875"—Arbitration —Payment into Court of sum awarded—Appeal—Verdict of Jury for larger sum—Interest on difference. (L. R., 27 Ch. D., 614 : 51 L. T., 684.)

1892.   [134]
Stevenson, Ex parte. "Housing of the Working Classes Act, 1890," Sched. II., s. 26 (*a*)—Party dissatisfied with Award of Arbitrator —There is no appeal from refusal of Judge at Chambers for leave to submit question to Jury. (L. R., 1 Q. B., 609 : 61 L. J., Q. B., 492 : 66 L. T., 544 : 56 J. P., 501.)

1883.   [135]
Swainston v. *Finn & Metropolitan B. W.* "Artizans' Dwellings Act, 1875," § 20—Easement affecting Land purchased by Local Authority—No right of Action to restrain interference with easement, but compensation payable in respect thereof. (52 L. J., Ch., 235 : 48 L. T., 634 : W. N., 1883, p. 19.)

1889.   [136]
Walker v. *Hobbs.* "Housing of Working Classes Act, 1885," § 12—Action for damages caused by ceiling falling held sustainable, the statutory condition that the house was reasonably fit for habitation not having been complied with. (54 J. P., 199.)

1887.   [137]
Wigram v. *Fryer.* Local Acts—Artizans' Dwellings—Ancient Lights—Easement—Remedy, Claim for Compensation not Injunction. (Metrop.) (56 L. J., Ch., 1098 : L. R., 36 Ch. D., 87 : 57 L. T., 255.)

1883.   [138]
Wilkins v. *Birmingham Corporation.* "Artizans' Dwellings Act, 1875"—Publication under this Act of a Notice of intention to take property is analogous to a Notice under the "Lands Clauses Act," and after it is given the property cannot be dealt with by way of granting a new lease. (53 L. J., Ch., 93 : L. R., 25 Ch. D., 78 : 49 L. T., 468 : 48 J. P., 231.)

9. BANKRUPTCY.

1873.   [139]
Hardwicke v. *Brown.* "Municipal Corporations Act, 1835," § 52—Town Councillor—Disqualification *ipso facto* by bankruptcy—Not purged—Election void. (L. R., 8 C. P., 406 : 28 L. T., 502 : 37 J. P., 407.)

1879.   [140]
Leftley v. *Monnington.* "Metropolis Management Act, 1855," § 54—Member of Vestry *ex officio* as Churchwarden—Disqualification by Bankruptcy—Defendant held liable to

penalty for acting as member of Vestry.
(48 L. J., Ex., 513: L. R., 4 Ex. D., 307:
40 L. T., 850.)

1863.   [141]
Saberton, In re. "Bankruptcy Act, 1861," § 156
[Repealed]—Local Rates due from a bank-
rupt—Order made for the payment in full of
one year's Rates. (9 L. T., 267.) [See the
"Bankruptcy Act, 1883," § 40.]

10. BATHING.

1821.   [142]
Blundell v. Catterall. The King's subjects have
no Common Law right to bathe on the Sea-
shore and to pass over it for *that* purpose on
foot or in vehicles. (5 B. & Ald., 268 : Hall,
On Seashores, 2nd ed., p. 156.)

1864.   [143]
Mace v. Philcox. "Public Health Act, 1848 : "
Local Acts—A License for Bathing Machines
granted by a Board does not confer a right
to use a foreshore without the consent of the
owner of the soil. (33 L. J., C. P., 124 : 15
C. B., (N. S.), 600 : 9 L. T., 766.)

1871.   [144]
Reg. v. Read. To bathe so near a public footpath that exposure to passers-by is unavoid-
able renders a bather indictable for indecency.
(12 Cox, C. C., 1.)

1809.   [145]
Rex v. Crunden. It is an indictable offence to
bathe on the Seashore within distinct view of
inhabited houses. (2 Camp., 89.)

11. BATHS AND WASH-HOUSES ACTS.

1861.   [146]
Cowley v. Sunderland, Mayor. "Baths and Wash-
houses Acts"—Steam Wringing Machine
unfenced—Action for compensation maintainable. (30 L. J., Ex., 127; 6 H. & N.,
565; 4 L. T., 120.)

1859.   [147]
Mulholland v. Belfast Corporation. Baths and
Wash-houses — Site — Sub-lease —Proposed
purchase of site held a breach of Trust.
(9 Irish Chan. R., 204 and 292.) [This is an
Irish case, but cited because decided upon a
Section similar to 9 & 10 Vict., c. 74, § 27.]

12. BOROUGH FUND.

1887.   [147a]
A.-G. v. Blackburn Corporation. "Municipal
Corporations Act, 1882," §§ 15, 140-41, 143—
Action by certain Ratepayers to restrain
Corporation from applying any part of
Borough Fund towards Her Majesty's Ju-
bilee Festivities—Interlocutory Injunction
refused, there being no evidence of a threat
or intention on the part of the Corporation so
to apply the Borough Fund—*Quare*, whether
having regard to the unprecedented character
of the Festivities in question such an expenditure would not have been justifiable under
§§ 140-41. (57 L. T., 385.)

1878.   [148]
A.-G. v. Brecon, Mayor. "Municipal Corporations Act, 1835," § 92—Bill promoted by a
Market Company which infringed on the
Statutory privileges of the Corporation—
Held, that both under the Act of 1835 and
under the general law authorising trustees to
employ Trust funds in defence of their property, the Corporation were justified in the
action they took to resist the passing of the
Market Bill—The "Borough Funds Act,
1872," § 4, does not take away previously
existing powers. (48 L. J., Ch., 153 : L. R.,
10 Ch. D., 204 : 40 L. T., 52 : 43 J. P., 366.)

1880.   [148a]
Reg. v. Exeter Corporation. Borough Fund—Costs
of defending action—Action brought against
Chief Constable for a malicious prosecution
and a verdict recovered against him in re-
spect of an Information laid by direction of
Borough Justices—Held that as Justices had
no jurisdiction to order prosecution Town
Council had no power to order payment of
Chief Constable's Costs out of Borough Fund.
(L. R., 6 Q. B. D., 135 : 44 L. T., 101.)

1879.   [149]
Reg. v. Leamington Corporation. Held that the
proceeds of the sale of sewage ought to be
carried to the General District Rate, to relieve the Rate, and not to the Borough Fund.
(*Times*, Dec. 16, 1879.)

1872.   [150]
Reg. v. Liverpool, Mayor. "Municipal Corporations Act, 1835," § 82—Action by a Board's
officer for libel on him—Expenses paid out
of Borough Fund disallowed. (41 L. J.,
Q. B., 175 : [*Wilmer v. Liverpool*,] 26 L. T.,
101.)

1850.   [151]
Reg. v. Prest. Municipal Corporation—Salaried
Clerk also an Attorney—Irregular retainer
for extra services—Fees for obtaining Counsel's opinion—Borough Fund held chargeable. (20 L. J., Q. B., 17 : 16 Q. B., 32 : 16
L. T., (O. S.), 210.)

1868.   [152]
Reg. v. Tamworth, Mayor. "Municipal Corporations Act, 1835," § 92—Held, that the Costs
of litigation for the defence of corporate
rights incurred on reasonable grounds, might
be charged to the Borough Fund. (19 L. T.,
433 : 17 W. R., 231.)

1878.   [153]
Sunderland Corporation, In re. "Municipal Corporations Act, 1835"—Borough Fund and
Borough Rate charged with expenses for fire-
works, bell-ringing, &c., in connection with
the visit of a distinguished foreigner—The
resolution of the Town Council authorising
the charge quashed on *Certiorari* as *ultra
vires*, the Borough Rate having been drawn
upon in the absence of a surplus from the
Borough Fund; but Costs refused. (*Times*,
June 24 and July 2, 1878.)

1890.   [154]
Thompson, In re. Mortgages secured on a Borough
Fund and on a District Fund respectively,

held not charges on an interest in land and therefore that they might be given to charity. (59 L. J., Ch., 689 : L. R., 45 Ch. D., 161 : 63 L. T., 471.)

1887.   [155]
Ward v. *Sheffield, Mayor.* " Borough Funds Act, 1872," § 4—A Town Council is not bound to keep a Register of owners and proxies ready to use at any Poll that may be called for, but must make one under the Public Health Act, 1875, Sched. II., R. 19, as may be necessary, and must give sufficient time for claims to be made. (56 L. J., Q. B., 418 : L. R., 19 Q. B. D., 22.)

1873.   [156]
Wrexham and East Denbighshire Water Bill, In re. " Borough Funds Act, 1872," § 1—*Quære* whether every Sanitary Authority may promote or oppose Bills in Parliament. (1 Cliff. and Rick., 59.)

1892.   [157]
Yarmouth, Mayor, In re. "Municipal Corporations.Act, 1882," Sched. V., Part 1—Resolution duly passed by a Town Council to grant to the Mayor under the name of " Salary " a sum of money to be devoted by him to a purpose for which a grant could not legally be made directly—Resolution held good—*Certiorari* refused. (*Times*, Aug. 10, 1892.)

13. BORROWING.

1853.   [158]
Arnold v. *Rigge.* "Municipal Corporations Act, 1835," § 92—Powers of a Creditor against a Corporation in respect of an old debt. (22 L. J., C. P., 235 : [*A.* v. *Ridge*] 13 C. B., 745 : 21 L. T., (o. s.), 141.)

1889.   [159]
Crapp v. *East Stonehouse L. B.* Money advanced to Board's Clerk on Mortgage of Rates he having forged the chairman's signature—Subsequently he embezzled the money—Held that the Board was not liable to make good the loss, the Clerk having no authority to issue the mortgage or to receive the money. (*Times*, May 24, 1889.)

1889.   [160]
North British Railway Co. v. *Holme Cultram L. B.* Paving expenses defrayed by money borrowed—Repayment ordered to be spread over a term of years—Interest charged against the owner higher than the interest paid by the Local Authority—Held that the Justices had no power to allow such an objection or to revise the terms of interest, and that their order for payment was good. (54 J. P., 86.)

1850.   [161]
Pallister v. *Gravesend, Mayor.* "Municipal Corporations Act, 1835," § 92—Validity of a Bond securing money advanced to pay an old debt. (19 L. J., C. P., 358 : 9 C. B., 774 : 15 L. T., (o. s.), 253.)

1874.   [162]
Reg. v. *Wigan Churchwardens.* 5 Geo. IV., c. 36, § 1—Loan by Public Works Commissioners on security of Rates—Neglect by borrowers for 20 years to repay any Principal or In-

terest—Held that the Commissioners had lost their remedy. (L. R., 1 App. Cas., 611 : 35 L. T., 381 : 41 J. P., 132.)

1870.   [163]
Webb v. *Herne Bay Commissioners.* Assignment of Debentures of a Corporation—Corporation estopped from alleging that the Debentures had been illegally issued—*Mandamus* granted to compel moneys raised by Rates to be applied in discharge of the Debenture debt. (39 L. J., Q. B., 221 : L. R., 5 Q. B. 642 : 22 L. T., 745.)

14. BOUNDARY.

1854.   [164]
A.-G. v. *Chambers.* In the absence of evidence of particular usage the extent of the right of the Crown to the seashore landwards is *primâ facie* limited by the line of the medium high tides between the Spring and Neap high tides. (23 L. J., Ch., 662 : 4 De G. M. and G., 206 : 23 L. T., (o. s.), 238.)

1859.   [165]
Reg. v. *Gee.* "Nuisances Removal Act, 1855," § 6 [Repealed]—Where the seashore is the boundary of a Parish the part below high-water mark of Medium tides and low-water mark is " extra-parochial " within this section, and therefore within the jurisdiction of the Authority for Nuisance purposes. (28 L. J., Q. B., 298 : 1 E, & E., 1068 : 33 L. T., (o. s.), 183.) [See 31 & 32 Vict., c. 122, § 27, and various Rating Cases.]

1864.   [166]
Reg. v. *Strand B. W.* Paving expenses borne by two parishes—Where a highway is employed to define the boundary of a district, the *medium filum viæ* must (in the absence of contrary evidence) be deemed the actual boundary. (Metropolis.) (33 L. J., Q. B., 299 : 4 B. & S., 551 : 11 L. T., 183.)

1834.   [167]
Rex v. *Landulph Inhabitants.* When two Parishes are separated by a river the *medium filum* is the presumptive boundary between them. (1 Mood. and Rob., 393.)

15. BUILDING LINE.

1890.   [168]
A.-G. v. *Edwards.* "Public Health (Buildings in Streets) Act, 1888," § 3—In considering what is a "front main wall" of a building, and whether such building is " on either side of" or " in the same street" as a building in course of erection, all the circumstances must be taken into account. (L. R., [1891] 1 Ch., 194 : 63 L. T., 639.)

1872.   [169]
Auckland (Lord) v. *Westminster B. W.* Local Act—"Vacant Ground" does not include the site of buildings recently pulled down—Such a site must so far as a Building Line is concerned be treated as if still occupied by houses, and if line is required to be set back Local Authority must pay compensation. (41 L. J., Ch., 732 : L. R., 7 Ch. App., 598 : 26 L. T., 961.)

1886.   [170]
Barlow v. *St. Mary Abbott's, Kensington, Vestry.*
"Metropolis Management Act, 1862." § 75—
Building-Line of corner house—How the
Building-Line of a corner house is to be
determined. (55 L. J., Ch., 680: L. R., 11
App. Cas., 257: 55 L. T., 221: 50 J. P.,
691.)

1867.   [171]
Baumann v. *St. Pancras Vestry.* Building Line—
Held that the Magistrate had jurisdiction to
order demolition. (36 L. J., M. C., 127:
L. R., 2 Q. B., 528: 8 B. & S., 446.) [*St.
George's, Hanover Square, Vestry* v. *Sparrow*,
questioned, but sco *Simpson* v. *Smith*.]

1873.   [172]
Bermondsey Vestry v. *Johnson.* "Metropolis
Amendment Act, 1862"—Building Line—
There is no limitation of time for a complaint as to an infringement—§ 107 which
prescribes a limitation of 6 months for recovery of a penalty or forfeiture does' not
apply to an order for demolition under § 75.
(Metropolis.) (42 L. J., M. C., 67: L. R.,
8 C. P., 441: 28 L. T., 665: 37 J. P., 392.)
[*Brutton* v. *St. George's, Hanover Square,
Vestry*, commented on as regards the limitation of time for proceedings.]

1871.   [173]
Brutton v. *St. George's, Hanover Square, Vestry.*
Building Line—The owner or occupier ought
to be summoned for an infringement of a
Building Line if the work is completed—
Time limited for penalties runs from the dis-
covery of the offence and not from the com-
pletion. (41 L. J., Ch., 134: L. R., 13 Eq.,
339: 25 L. T., 552.) [But see *Bermondsey
Vestry* v. *Johnson*.]

1891.   [174]
City & South London Railway v. *London County
Council.* Provisions of Special Act at variance
with those of General Act—Held that the
latter must be deemed *pro tanto* repealed—
Magistrate therefore held to have no jurisdiction to compel the pulling down of projecting masonry. (56 J. P., 6, and see same
vol., p. 23.)

1861.   [175]
Ecclesiastical Commissioners v. *Clerkenwell Vestry.*
A Local Authority may control the Ecclesiastical Commissioners in the erection of a
Church at any rate as regards the infringement of a Building Line. (30 L. J., Ch.,
454: 3 De G., F. & J., 688: 4 L. T., 599.)

1882.   [176]
Elsdon, Ex parte. "Metropolis Management
Amendment Act, 1862," § 75—An Appeal to
Sessions in respect of any "Penalty or forfeiture" held not to extend to proceedings
for the demolition of an encroachment on a
Building-Line. (51 L. J., M. C., 94: 46 J. P.,
551: [*Reg.* v. *Middlesex*] L. R., 9 Q. B. D.,
41.)

1872.   [177]
Folkestone Corporation v. *Woodward.* Local Act,
18 & 19 Vict., c. cxlvii., § 50—Building Line
—Delay in prescribing the same—Injunction

refused—"House" includes a Church—A
Perpetual Curate in whom a site is vested is
an "owner" within the meaning of the Local
Act in question. (42 L. J., Ch., 782: L. R.,
15 Eq., 159: 27 L. T., 574: 37 J. P., 324.)

1878.   [178]
Fort William Commissioners v. *Kennedy.* 25 & 26
Vict., c. 101, § 162 (Scotch)—Forecourt proposed to be built upon—Railing removed—
The "railing" held not to be a building
within the Statute, and therefore, notwithstanding its removal, no right arose on the
part of the Commissioners to interfere with
the new works. (W. N., 1878, p. 177: 5 Ct.
of Sess. Cas., (II. L.), 4th Ser., 215.)

1891.   [179]
Fortescue v. *St. Matthew, Bethnal Green, Vestry.*
Conflict of Acts—General Line of Building
—Projections—Certain projecting pilasters,
held not unlawful. *St. Mary, Islington* v.
Goodman overruled. (60 L. J., M. C., 172:
L. R., 2 Q. B., 170: 65 L. T., 256: 55 J. P.,
758.)

1888.   [180]
Gilbert v. *Wandsworth B. W.* Corner house—
House facing one street but out of the Building Line of another Street—Held that Magistrate had power to order demolition for encroachment on Building Line of latter street
—*Barlow* v. *Kensington* distinguished. (Metrop.) (60 L. T., 149: 53 J. P., 229.)

1880.   [181]
Goldstraw v. *Duckworth.* 5 Vict., c. xliv., § 2—
Local Act prohibiting projections in or over
streets—Oriel window projecting 2½ ft. but
14 ft. above the ground, held not to contravene the Act, as such a window could not
inconvenience foot-pas-engers, the object of
the Section not being to secure free passage
of light and air. (49 L. J., Q. B., 73: L. R.,
5 Q. B. D., 275: 42 L. T., 411: 44 J. P.,
410.)

1877.   [182]
Inglis v. *St. Giles, Camberwell, Vestry.* Building
Line duly prescribed—Order by Magistrate
authorising Board to demolish an encroachment—Subsequent re-erection of the encroachment by the present plaintiff, and an
application by him for an Injunction to
restrain the Board from again interfering—
Application refused. (*Times*, April 17, 1877.)

1876.   [183]
Kerr v. *Preston Corporation.* "Public Health
Act, 1875," §§ 156 and 251—Wrongful encroachment on a Building Line by plaintiff
—Threat of proceedings against him—Injunction to restrain such possible proceedings
on the ground of acquiescence, refused—A
Local Authority has no power to acquiesce;
it can only give assent by writing—The
Court has no jurisdiction to restrain criminal
proceedings for breaches of the Statute Law.
(46 L. J., Ch., 409: L. R., 6 Ch. D., 463.)

1892.   [184]
London County C. v. *Cross.* "Metropolis Amendment Act, 1862," § 75—When a building is
erected beyond the general line the matter

of complaint arises so soon as the building shows above the ground to be projecting even though the line has not yet been certified. (61 L. J., M. C., 160: 66 L. T., 731: 56 J. P., 550.)

1887. [185]
Nankivell v. Bournemouth Commissioners. "Public Health Act, 1875," § 156—Question of a stable being or not being an "addition" to a house, and whether the house affected was or was not part of a "street"—Case stated sent back to be re-stated, it being defective, the justices not having sufficiently expressed their conclusions on the facts. (*Times*, Dec. 21, 1887.)

1881. [186]
Paddington Vestry v. Snow. "Metropolis Amendment Act, 1862," § 75—The Certificate of the Architect does not necessarily establish the Building Line, or the offence of building beyond such Line—Limitation of time—*Morant v. Taylor*, and *Wandsworth v. Hall* followed. (45 L. T., 475: 46 J. P., 87.)

1879. [187]
Poplar B. W. v. North Metropolitan Tramways Co. "Metropolis Amendment Act, 1862," § 75—It is an offence to encroach on the Building Line of a street, even although the street may not have been completely dedicated as a public highway. (Metropolis.) (43 J. P., 590.)

1889. [188]
Ravensthorpe L. B. v. Hinchcliffe. "Public Health (Buildings in Streets) Act, 1888," § 3—Buildings commenced in advance of a Building Line already sanctioned but not yet raised above the street level—Held that an offence had not yet been committed—*Semble* that a house 300 yards away cannot be said to be "on the side of" another house. (59 L. J., M. C., 19: L. R., 24 Q. B. D., 168: 61 L. T., 780: 54 J. P., 421.)

1876. [189]
Read v. Perrett. Projecting Sign-board—Held that the Magistrate was right in refusing to hear witnesses called to prove that the Sign-board was no obstruction—Conviction affirmed. (Metropolis.) (L. R., 1 Ex. D., 349: 41 J. P., 135.)

1890. [190]
Reg. v. Middlesborough Corporation. "Public Health (Buildings in Streets) Act, 1888,"—Old road with a few scattered houses at distant intervals—Held that an old house pulled down might be rebuilt on the same site and that the Corporation was not entitled to require the new house to be set back—A house 400 ft. off held not to be "on the side of" another house. (*Times*, July 7, 1890.)

1866. [191]
Reg. v. Nicholson. 24 & 25 Vict., c. 61, § 28 [Repealed = "Public Health Act, 1875," § 156]—Building Line—Erection of Porch—Verdict of "Not Guilty," directed, no actual nuisance or inconvenience to the public being proved. (41 *Law Times* Newspaper, 657.)

1874. [192]
Reg. v. Wolstenholme. 24 & 25 Vict., c. 61, § 28 [="Public Health Act, 1875," § 156]—Building Line—Erection of Shop front in a fore-court—Houses facing the sea—Defendant fined 100l. (*Loc. Gov. Chro.*, Oct. 31, 1874, and Jan. 16, 1875.)

1871. [193]
Simpson v. Smith. Building Line. (40 L. J., C. P., 89: L. R., 6 C. P., 87: 24 L. T., 100: 35 J. P., 310.)

1885. [194]
Spackman v. Plumstead B. W. Architect's definition of "Building Line" is final, and Magistrate cannot review it—*St. George's H. S. v. Sparrow*, and *Simpson v. Smith* disapproved. (54 L. J., M. C., 81: L. R., 10 App. Cas., 229: 53 L. T., 157: 49 J. P., 420.)

1864. [195]
St. George's, Hanover Square, Vestry v. Sparrow. Building Line—Held that it is for the Magistrate to decide whether a structure complained of is within the Act—Held also that the Architect's certificate as to the Line is not final. (Metropolis.) (33 L. J., M. C., 118: 16 C. B., (N.S.), 209: 10 L. T., 501.) [Questioned in *Bauman v. St. Pancras Vestry*, upheld in *Simpson v. Smith*, and disapproved of in *Spackman v. Plumstead.*]

1889. [196]
St. Mary's Islington, Vestry v. Goodman. Local Act: "Metropolitan Buildings Act, 1855"—Projection found by Vestry to be inconvenient —Order for removal held good. (58 L. J., M. C., 122: L. R., 24 Q. B. D., 154: 61 L. T., 44: 53 J. P., 372.) [Dissented from in *Fortescue v. St. Matthew, Bethnal Green.*]

1858. [197]
Tear v. Freebody. A Building Line need not be a strict mathematical line, but a substantially regular line suffices—"Old Building" defined to be a building the walls of which were carried higher than the footings—Voting at Meetings. (Metropolis.) (4 C. B., (N.S.), 228: [*Sear v. F.*] 31 L. T., (O. S.), 131.)

1878. [198]
Thomas v. Roberts. "Public Health Act, 1875," § 156—A road is none the less within the Section for the fixing of a Building Line merely because it is a Turnpike road. (43 J. P., 574.)

1868. [199]
Wandsworth B. W. v. Hall. A New Building must be erected within the existing Building Line if erected without consent, and this notwithstanding that the Building Line has not been prescribed—A Magistrate may order a Building thus improperly erected to be demolished. (Metropolis.) (38 L. J., M. C., 69: L. R., 4 C. P., 85: 19 L. T., 641.)

1891. [200]
Warren v. Mustard. "Public Health (Buildings in Streets) Act, 1888," § 3—Building Line—House "on either side"—Degree of proximity of neighbouring houses—Corner house—Whether in two streets a question of fact for

Justices—They having decided in a certain way the Court declined to interfere. (61 L. J., M. C., 18: 66 L. T., 26: 56 J. P., 502.)
1874. [201]
Wilson v. *Cunliffe.* Local Act—Building Line—A greengrocer's tray when let down had for 30 years projected beyond the wall of the house—Held that the line of the tray, and not the line of the wall, must be taken as the Building Line, and that, therefore, there was no encroachment. (29 L. T., 913: 38 J. P., 231.)
1892. [202]
Worley v. *St. Mary Abbott's, Kensington, Vestry.* "Metropolis Amendment Act, 1862." §§ 74–5 — General line of buildings — Buildings pulled down and site thrown into garden—Held that owner had abandoned his right of rebuilding although foundations never removed and garden never laid out—*Auckland* v. *Westminster* distinguished. (61 L. J., Ch., 601 : L. R., 2 Ch., 404 : 66 L. T., 747.)

16. "BUILDINGS," DEFINITION OF.

1854. [203]
Arnell v. *Regent's Canal Co.* Local Act—Repair of a Bridge over Canal—A parapet wall held not to be a "Building." (23 L. J., C. P., 155 : 14 C. B., 564: 23 L. T., (o. s.), 95.)
1863. [204]
Ashby v. *Woodthorpe.* Two adjacent houses with an opening in a party wall held to be one "Building" for the purposes of the building regulations of the Metropolitan Building Act. (33 L. J., M. C., 68 : 9 L. T., 400.)
1870. [205]
Bowes v. *Law.* Meaning of the word "Buildings" in a covenant not to erect "Buildings" —*Quære,* Is a wall a "Building?" *Semble* that it is, if of excessive height beyond what is necessary merely for boundary purposes. (39 L. J., Ch., 483: L. R., 9 Eq., 636: 22 L. T., 267.)
1890. [206]
Hall v. *Smallpiece.* "Metropolitan Building Act, 1855," §§ 6, 46 : 45 Vict., c. 14, § 13—Caravans, shooting gallery, and steam roundabouts held not to be "structures" or "erections," and therefore to be exempt. (59 L. J., M. C., 97 : 54 J. P., 710.)
1889. [206a]
Hibbert v. *Acton L. B.* Conservatory 15 ft. by 9 ft. held not a "building" which the Board was entitled to pull down under its Building By-Laws. (5 *Times* L. R., 274.)
1873. [207]
Hobbs v. *Dance.* By-Laws—Old Stable pulled down and re-built partly on a different site, held to be a "new Building"—Held also that the question was properly raised as one of law and was not merely one of fact. (43 L. J., M. C., 21 : L. R., 9 C. P., 30 : 29 L. T., 687: 38 J. P., 56.)
1879. [208]
Knight v. *Purssell.* "Metropolitan Building Act, 1855," 18 & 19 Vict., c. 122—Definition of "party" wall—A wall with a shed on one

side and closets on the other held to be a party wall to the extent in height and width that the closets and shed were conterminous. (48 L. J., Ch., 395: L. R., 11 Ch. D., 412: 40 L. T., 391: 43 J. P., 622. On appeal, appeal dismissed, W. N. 1880, p. 104. Costs; 49 L J., Ch., 120 : 41 L. T., 581.)
1892. [209]
London C. C. v. *Pearce.* Builder's Pay-office on wheels and moveable held not a "wooden structure or erection of a moveable or temporary character" so as to require a license. (L. R., 2 Q. B., 109 : 66 L. T., 685: 56 J. P., 324.)
1875. [210]
Manners (Lord) v. *Johnson.* The erection of a bay window held a breach of a covenant not to erect a "building"—Such a window may be an encroachment on a Building Line. (45 L. J., Ch., 404 : L. R., 1 Ch. D., 673.)
1891. [211]
Moir v. *Williams.* "Metropolitan Building Act, 1855," §§ 49, 51—Fourteen sets of Chambers under one roof, but with a common staircase —Held that only one fee was payable to the surveyor. (61 L. J., M. C., 33 : L. R., [1892] 1 Q. B., 264 : 66 L. T., 215 : 56 J. P., 197.)
1865. [212]
Morish v. *Harris.* "Reform Act, 1832," § 27—A roofed store-house with walls and door held to be a "building." (L. R., 1 C. P., 155.)
1858. [213]
Poplar B. W. v. *Knight.* A Marsh Wall held to be an essential part of the "Sewer" of a Level—A house built on the surface of the ground without any excavation is, nevertheless, a "Building" as to which notice must be given. (Metropolis.) (28 L. J., M. C., 37: E. B. & E., 408: 31 L. T., (o. s.), 175.)
1892. [214]
Reg. v. *Llandudno Improvement Commissioners.* Provisional Order under "Piers and Harbours Act, 1861"—Power to Pier Company to erect pier, &c.—"Shops, Saloons, bazaars" held not to include a theatre, and Commissioners not bound to sanction a theatre—*Mandamus* refused. (56 J. P., 85.)
1833. [215]
Rex v. *Gregory.* Local Act prohibiting a building within 10 ft. of a road—Footpaths declared to be part of the road—Held that a building within 10 ft. of the footpath was within the prohibition—Open shop erected on old foundations immediately adjoining a footpath and connected by a roof with a house behind which was beyond the statutory distance—Held that such open shop was a "building." (3 L. J., M. C., 25 : 5 B. & Ad., 555: 2 N. & M., 478.)
1891. [216]
Slaughter v. *Sunderland, Mayor.* "Public Health Act, 1875," § 157—An Advertising hoarding held not to be a "building"—The Building By-Laws cited point to a place with a roof and capable of affording protection or shelter. (65 L. T., 250: 55 J. P., 519.)

1859.   [217]
Stevens v. *Gourley.* A large and substantial wooden structure, though erected without footings or masonry foundations, held to be a "Building." (29 L. J., C. P., 1: 7 C. B., (N. S.), 99: 1 F. & F., 498: 1 L. T., 33.)

1847.   [218]
Watson v. *Cotton.* "Reform Act, 1832," § 27—Shed formed of six posts let into the ground —Tarpaulin roof—One side boarded up with boards nailed to the posts—Such shed held to be a "warehouse" or "other building." (17 L. J., C. P., 68: 5 C. B., 51: 2 Lutw., Reg. Cas., 53.)

17. BURIALS.

1867.   [219]
Foster v. *Dodd.* A dead body is under the protection of the public—An indecent disinterment, even by an order of a Secretary of State, is indictable. (37 L. J., Q. B., 28: L. R., 3 Q. B., 67: 8 B. & S., 842: 17 L. T., 614.)

1873.   [220]
Greenwood v. *Wadsworth.* "Burial Act, 1855," 18 & 19 Vict., c. 128, § 9—The prohibition of Burial Grounds within 100 yards of a house applies to all such grounds, whether public or private. (43 L. J., Ch., 78: L. R., 16 Eq., 288: 29 L. T., 88: 38 J. P., 116.)

1890.   [221]
Pitchforth v. *Acton L. B.* Action for Trespass in removing a coffin containing a dead body left unburied for an improper time, namely 15 days—Judgment for the Defendants. (*Times*, July 5, 1890.)

1880.   [222]
Reg. v. *Jacobson.* Disturbance of a disused unconsecrated Burial Ground with a view to building operations, by digging up same and indecently exposing human remains—Held that defendant was guilty of a "serious offence" against the law in submitting human remains to disturbance and indignity—Fine of 25l. inflicted. (*Times*, Dec. 21, 1880.)

1889.   [223]
Reg. v. *Kent Treasurer.* 48 Geo. III., c. 75—Burial of bodies cast ashore—A Magistrate's Order on County Treasurer to reimburse parish officers their expenses must be explicit in its terms as to the facts which led to its issue, or it will be bad. (58 L. J., M. C., 71: L. R., 22 Q. B. D., 603: 60 L. T., 426: 53 J. P., 279.)

1810.   [224]
Reg. v. *Stennett.* Held that the Overseers of a parish are not responsible for the burial of a pauper dying in a hospital. (10 L. J., M. C., 40: [*Reg.* v. *Stewart*] 12 A. & E., 773: 4 P. & D., 349.)

1881.   [224a]
Woolwich Overseers v. *Robertson.* 48 Geo. III., c. 75—"Sea" does not include a navigable tidal river—County Treasurer held not liable to Overseers of parish for expenses incurred in removing bodies. (50 L. J., M. C., 87: L. R., 6 Q. B. D., 654: 45 J. P., 237.)

1887.   [225]
Wright v. *Wallasey L. B.* "Burial Act, 1855" 18 & 19 Vict., c. 128, § 9—In calculating the distance of 100 yards within which no burial may take place the actual dwelling house and not the curtilage is to be taken as the *Terminus a quo.* (56 L. J., Q. B., 259: L. R, 18 Q. B. D, 783: 52 J. P., 4.)

18. BY-LAWS.
(1.) BUILDING.

1872.   [226]
Adams v. *Bromley L. B.* "Local Government Act, 1858," § 34 [="Public Health Act, 1875," §§ 157, 159]—By-Laws as to open space — Dwarf fence held to be an "erection" infringing the By-Law. (37 J. P., 662.)

1863.   [227]
Anderton v. *Birkenhead.* "Local Government Act, 1858," § 34—By-Laws—Breadth of open space in rear of a building to be everywhere at least the minimum specified. (32 L. J., M. C., 137: [*Anderton* v. *Rigby*] 13 C. B., (N. S.), 603.)

1877.   [228]
Baker v. *Portsmouth, Mayor.* "Local Government Act, 1858," § 34—By-Laws requiring notice of intention to lay out new street; and authorising the pulling down of work improperly erected—Street laid out and houses built without notice being given to the Local Authority—Whereupon, after notice, houses pulled down by the Authority—Held that the By-Law was valid, and that the pulling down was justifiable, provided that no unnecessary destruction of property took place —More force having been used than was shown to be necessary, a verdict for a small amount against defendant Corporation allowed to stand. (47 L. J., Ex., 289: L. R., 3 Ex. D., 157: 37 L. T., 822.)

1885.   [229]
Baxter v. *Bedford, Mayor.* Plaintiff, a builder, connected certain houses with Corporation sewer, without giving to Surveyor notice as required by By-Law—Whereupon Corporation severed the connexion—Action held not maintainable as plaintiff had broken the By-Law, and there had been no waiver by Surveyor—A Corporation cannot dispense with the Law, which is not for their benefit but for the benefit of the public. (1 *Times* L. R., 424.)

1889.   [230]
Bennett v. *Skegness L. B.* Plans deposited for a wooden structure—Plans rejected—Whereupon land fenced by owner with a wooden fence, and canvas stretched over it by his temporary tenant—Held that such a user of the land was not an offence against the Building By-Laws. (54 J. P., 469.)

1884.   [231]
Blashill v. *Chambers.* By-Law as to foundations of house—"Foundations" means ground actually covered and pressed upon by bottoms of walls—"Site" means the place which the building filled up and on which the house was erected. (L. R., 14 Q. B., 479: 53 L. T., 38: 49 J. P., 388.)

1887. [232]
Bovill v. *Gibbs*. Building with insufficient open space—Plans deposited in April; notice of insufficiency given in August; 6 months limitation for proceedings for default held to run from August. (Metrop.) (51 J. P., 485.)

1892. [233]
Bromley L. B. v. *Lloyd*. A Proposed new street of the required width would have opened on to a lane which was a public highway but which was not of the width required under the By-Law for the new street—Injunction granted to restrain landowner from making his new street until he was able and willing to provide an entrance of the full width—It made no difference that the mode of access to the new street was by means of a public street if such street was of less than the required width. (66 L. T., 462: 56 J. P., 278.)

1880. [234]
Brown v. *Edmonton L. B.* Breach of By-Law—Definition of "person erecting" a new building—Contractor summoned, though a subcontractor was the person actually guilty—Held that the contractor was not a proper party to be proceeded against. (45 J. P., 553.)

1862. [235]
Brown v. *Holyhead L. B.* "Local Government Act, 1858," § 34—Validity of a By-Law—Pulling down a wall alleged to have been erected in contravention of a By-Law—By-Law held invalid because *ultra vires* as regards the pulling down powers which it claimed for the Board. (32 L. J., Ex., 25 : 1 H. & C., 601 : 7 L. T., 332.)

1881. [236]
Bull v. *Southampton JJ*. Temporary wooden shed erected to shelter workmen and their tools, the former being at work on buildings close by, held not within the Building By-Laws of a Corporation—Conviction quashed. (At Q. Sess.) (45 J. P., 541.)

1864. [237]
Burgess v. *Peacock*. "Local Government Act, 1858," § 34—By-Law designed to apply to buildings erected before the constitution of the District, held invalid. (16 C. B., (N. S.), 624 : 10 L. T. 617.)

1887. [238]
Burton v. *Acton*. Erection of Tub-closets in the nature of privies on sites different from sites marked on deposited plans held a breach of By-Law. (51 J. P., 566.)

1885. [239]
Clark v. *Bloomfield*. "Public Health Act, 1875," § 158—Defendant gave a month's notice of his intention to build on part of an open space—Board came to no decision, and so he built—Held that proceedings for penalties could not be taken. (*Times*, March 5, 1885.)

1863. [240]
Cooper v. *Wandsworth B. W.* Statutory right to demolish on neglect by a builder to give notice of intention to build—On an alleged breach of a By-Law it is the duty of a Local Authority in all cases to give an offender an opportunity of being heard before pulling down his work. (Metropolis.) (32 L. J., C. P., 185 : 14 C. B., (N. S), 180 : 8 L. T., 278.)

1877. [241]
Crosby, Ex parte. "Public Health Act, 1875," §§ 157-8—Plans duly deposited—No decision given by the Local Authority within the statutory time—Approval eventually withheld, on the ground that the applicant was going to build on land that did not belong to him—Rule *Nisi* granted for a *Mandamus* to Local Authority to pass the plans—A Sanitary Authority has no jurisdiction to deal with questions of title in connection with building plans. (41 J. P., 740.)

1887. [242]
Elkington v. *Smee*. Tobogganing slide erected in the grounds of the Crystal Palace held a "building" within the "Metropolitan Building Act, 1855," and not exempt by reason of the "Crystal Palace Company's Act, 1881," § 21. (*Times*, Dec. 14, 1887.)

1863. [243]
Felkin v. *Berridge*. Legal proceedings to enforce Building By-Laws—Old By-Laws replaced by new ones—Sufficiency of notices. (15 C. B., (N. S.), 257 : 9 L. T., 333.)

1878. [244]
Fielding v. *Rhyl Improvement Commissioners.*—"Public Health Act, 1848 ": Local Act—Building By-Laws—A brick-kiln and a toolhouse, 12 yards square, both erected for the temporary convenience of a builder, held not "buildings" within the By-Laws, because *bonâ fide* temporary only—*Semble* that had the By-Laws been intended to apply to temporary as well as permanent structures, it would have been bad—*Quære*, How far an excessive delegation of the powers of a Local Authority to a town Surveyor would invalidate By-Laws conferring such powers? (L.R., 3 C. P. D., 272 : 38 L. T., 223 : 42 J. P., 311.)

1890. [245]
Foot v. *Hodgson*. "Metropolitan Building Act, 1855," Sched. I.—The "topmost storey" of a house need not be enclosed within 4 vertical walls, and rooms enclosed on 3 sides by vertical walls and in front by the slopin ; roof held to belong to a storey, and so within Building Rules. (59 L. J., Q. B., 313 : L. R., 25 Q. B. D., 160.)

1891. [246]
Gery v. *Black Lion Brewery Co.* Summons for building over an open space—The "building" was a boiler set in brickwork replacing a smaller boiler—Held that no breach of By-Law had been committed. (55 J. P., 711.)

1875. [247]
Hall v. *Nixon*. "Local Government Act, 1858," § 31—Building By-Law to enforce, under a penalty, the deposit of plans held good—

Justices ought to have convicted. (44 L. J., M.C., 51: L. R., 10 Q. B., 152: 32 L. T., 87: 39 J. P., 341.)

1866.   [248]
Hattersley v. Burr. (4 II. & C., 523.)

1889.   [249]
Hendon L. B. v. Pounce. Held that a proposed new street could not be legally constructed until an entrance of full width had been provided for it; and this though such an entrance could only be obtained by using land belonging to another party. (L. R., 42 Ch. D., 602: 61 L. T., 465.)

1876.   [250]
Hill v. Hall. "Chimney Sweepers Act," 3 & 4 Vict. c. 85: Local Act—Partition of chimney flue of insufficient thickness — Two Acts somewhat inconsistent—Held that the Local Act was not intended to over-ride the General Act. (45 L. J., M. C., 153: L. R., 1 Ex. D., 411: 35 L. T., 860: 41 J. P., 183.)

1890.   [251]
Hopkins v. Smethwick L. B. "Public Health Act, 1875," § 158 — This Section does not give a Board power to pull down a building alleged to contravene a By-Law without giving notice to the owner of the Board's intention so to do—*Cooper v. Wandsworth* and *Masters v. Pontypool* approved. (59 L. J., Q. B., 250: 62 L. T., 783: 54 J. P., 693.)

1888.   [252]
Horsell v. Swindon (New) L. B. "Public Health Act, 1875"—By-Law that no new house was to be inhabited until its drainage was complete and until a certificate to that effect was granted by Local Authority, held, good. (58 L. T., 732: 52 J. P., 597.)

1890.   [253]
Jagger v. Doncaster Union R. S. A. Building erected in breach of a By-Law pulled down by Local Authority—In such cases no excessive violence must be used nor danger caused. (54 J. P., 438.)

1884.   [254]
James v. Wyvill. "Public Health Act, 1875," §§ 157, 179—Whether works are "additions to an old building," or are a "new building," is a question of fact for Justices to decide. (51 L. T., 237: 48 J. P., 725.)

1857.   [255]
Jay v. Hammon. Building intended as a Militia Store-house held exempt. (Metrop.) (27 L. J., M. C., 25: 30 L. T., (o.s.), 133: [*Reg. v. Jay*] 8 E. & B., 469.)

1890.   [256]
Jones, Ex parte, West Cowes L. B., In re. Breach of By-Law by A. a member of the Board—Board unwilling to take proceedings—Application by a neighbouring owner for a *Mandamus* to the Board to enforce its By-Law—Rule *Nisi* granted. (*Times*, April 3, 1890.)

1887.   [257]
Jones v. Parry. In calculating the size of an "open space" at the back of a "new building" a public street is to be deemed the "opposite property" and is not to be taken into account to eke out the restricted dimensions of the owner's own space. (57 L. T., 492: 52 J. P., 69.)

1885.   [258]
Josolyne v. Meeson. "Metropolitan Building Act, 1855," § 3—An ambulance station is not necessarily a "public building." (53 L. T., 319: 49 J. P., 805.)

1891.   [259]
London County Council v. Candler. "Metropolis Management Act, 1882," § 13—During rebuilding of public-house temporary wooden structure erected for sale of liquors in garden—Such structure not exempt as being "erected by a builder for use." (55 J. P., 679.)

1892.   [260]
Manchester, Sheffield & Lincolnshire Railway Co. v. Barnsley Union. "Public Health Act, 1875," § 157—This exemption of Railway property does not apply to dwelling-houses erected for Railway servants on land near a station—Such are within the reach of Building By-Laws. (67 L. T., 119: 56 J. P., 679.)

1873.   [261]
Marshall v. Smith. Continuing offence. (42 L. J., M. C., 108.)

1878.   [262]
Masters v. Pontypool L. B. H. "Public Health Act, 1875," §§ 158 and 176 — House partly pulled down for rebuilding — Attempt by Board to acquire part of site compulsorily—Refusal to sell—Action to restrain Board from interfering after having approved the plan for rebuilding—Judgment for plaintiff on the ground that the Board had acquiesced in the rebuilding and took, too late, objections as to plans which might have been good if taken in time. (47 L. J., Ch., 797: L. R., 9 Ch. D., 677.),

1890.   [263]
Meadows v. Taylor. Local Act—Conservatory sanctioned by Local Authority as part of a house — Subsequently, conservatory partly pulled down so as to be reconstructed to form a bedroom—Proceedings for breach of Act—The Justices held that the bedroom did not when erected occupy any greater space than the conservatory and dismissed the summons—Held that the Justices were wrong; that the reason they gave for their decision was inadequate and that they must inquire whether what had been done amounted to such an addition to the original house as would require notice to be given. (59 L. J., M. C., 99; L. R., 24 Q. B. D., 717: 62 L. T., 658: 54 J. P., 757.)

1884.   [264]
Metropolitan B. W. v. Anthony. Temporary structure erected without licence—Held a continuing offence which might be made the subject of complaint at any time whilst structure existed. (54 L. J., M. C., 39: 49 J. P., 229.)

1885.   [265]
Metropolitan B. W. v. Nathan. Passage between Artisans' Dwellings—Laying out street for

C

foot traffic only—Held that consent of Board was not required. (54 L. T., 423: 50 J. P., 502.)

1858. [266]
North Kent Railway Co. v. *Badger.* Railway arches walled up and used as stables held exempt from the control of the Local Authority as being still Railway buildings. (Metropolis.) (27 L. J., M. C., 109: [*Badger, In re.*] 8 E. & B., 728: 30 L. T., (o. s.), 285.)

1879. [267]
Parsons v. *Timewell.* "Metropolitan Building Act," § 46—Skating Rink sanctioned on condition that owner removed it within 2 years—Undertaking to do this given by owner—On breach of the undertaking, held that no summary power was vested in a Magistrate to order its removal as an unauthorised building—The statutory powers to that effect only applied to buildings which were in course of erection and without due authority. (44 J. P., 296.)

1891. [268]
Payne v. *Wright.* "Metropolitan Building Act, 1855," § 19—A roof covered with woven iron wire which was coated with a material which would easily catch fire held not covered with an "incombustible material." (61 L. J., M. C., 7: L. R., 1 Q. B., 104: 65 L. T., 612: 56 J. P., 120.) No appeal from decision of Q. B. D. on Case stated. (61 L. J., M. C., 114: 66 L. T., 148.)

1865. [269]
Pearson v. *Kingston-upon-Hull L. B. H.* "Local Government Act, 1858," § 34: Local Act—Building before plans were approved—Using a building without the consent of the Board—Meaning of "back-yard or other vacant ground or area" as used in the Local Act. (35 L. J., M. C., 36: 3 H. & C., 921: 13 L. T., 180.)

1888. [270]
Quinby v. *Liverpool, Mayor.* Local Act—By-Law prohibiting any open space left at rear or side of a dwelling-house from ever after being built upon without the consent of the Local Authority, held bad as regards rear of premises. (53 J. P., 213.)

1886. [271]
Reay v. *Gateshead, Mayor.* Building without depositing plans—Continuing offence—By-Law made before 1875 held *ultra vires*—Conviction quashed, as more than 6 months had elapsed since offence committed. (55 L. T., 92: 50 J. P., 805.)

1864. [272]
Reg. v. *Carruthers.* "Metropolitan Building Act, 1855," § 30—Rules under Act as to the construction of Public Buildings—Church held exempt from such Rules and the subject of special discretion. (Metropolis.) (33 L. J., Ex., 107: 4 B. & S., 804: 9 L. T., 825.)

1891. [273]
Reg. v. *Goole L. B.* "Public Health Act, 1875," §§ 4, 157 (1)—Passages at back of houses giving access to the ashpits and privics of

such houses come within the definition of "street," and are therefore subject to Building By-Laws. (60 L. J., Q. B. 617: L. R., 2 Q. B., 212: 64 L. T., 595: 55 J. P., 535.)

1870. [274]
Reg. v. *London Commissioners of Sewers.* Local Act—Application for a license to erect a hoarding round a work likely to occupy 2 years, and abutting on 4 streets—Conditions that there must be 4 licenses: that their duration was to be limited to 2 months, and that no bills were to be posted—All held unreasonable—The duration of a license should be proportionate to the magnitude of the works. (22 L. T., 582.)

1889. [275]
Reg. v. *Newcastle, Mayor.* Local Act—A proposed new building did not violate any existing By-Law, but Corporation judged it a building unsuitable to the locality—Held that valid plans could not be disallowed merely on sentimental grounds. (60 L. T., 963: 53 J. P., 788.)

1887. [275a]
Reg. v. *Preston Corporation.* Building plans disapproved of because designed to occupy a site once proposed and authorized for a new street—Corporation not entitled to reject plans for such a reason—*Mandamus* to consider and approve of the plans granted. (3 *Times* L. R., 665.)

1881. [276]
Reg. v. *Thompson.* By-Law that every new street should be 30 ft. wide—Plans deposited and sanctioned for 8 new houses, plan shewing a 30 ft. new street therewith—Houses built within 9 ft. of owner's boundary and no provision made by him for a 30 ft. roadway—Conviction for breach of By-Law—Conviction quashed—*Semble*, that a man building an isolated row of houses is not bound in all cases to shew a roadway of full width appurtenant to the houses, but that the width of the roadway must stand over till some one else proposes to build opposite to the houses. (45 J. P., 420: *Times*, June 16, 1881.)

1856. [277]
Reg. v. *Tunstall Turnpike Road Trustees.* "Public Health Act, 1848," § 53 [Repealed]: Turnpike Act—Erection of a Toll-house—Held that the Trustees were subject to the provisions of the first named Act as regards Building and Sanitary matters. (27 L. T., (o. s.), 184: [*Tunstall &c.* v. *Lowndes*] 20 J. P., 374.)

1885. [278]
Richardson v. *Brown.* Local Act—Wooden structure on wheels, 30 ft. long, used as a butcher's shop held a "new building." (49 J. P., 661.)

1890. [279]
Roberts v. *Richards.* "Public Health Act, 1875," § 157—By-Law requiring any new street to be at least 30 ft. wide held reasonable. (54 J. P., 693.)

1859.   [280]
Robins v. *Merry*. Building unlawfully erected on a fore-court at the time when the main building was being re-erected, held lawfully pulled down by a Board. (Metropolis.) (32 L. T., (o. s.), 256.)

1883.   [281]
Robinson v. *Barton L. B.* "Public Health Act, 1875," § 156—"New street" is not confined to streets formed for the first time out of grass or other vacant land, but may include old rural roads which by having become occupied by buildings have become popularly "streets." (53 L. J., Ch., 226: L. R., 8 App. Cas., 798: 50 L. T., 57: 48 J. P., 276.)

1875.   [282]
Robshaw v. *Leeds, Mayor*. Local Act—By-Laws —Houses back to back—Restrictions on number to be erected in a block—Insufficient open space—Conviction affirmed. (39 J. P., 149.)

1884.   [283]
Rudland v. *Sunderland, Mayor*. "Public Health Act, 1875," § 157—By-Law requiring kerbing to be laid in new street before erection of new building held unreasonable and void. (52 L. T., 617: 49 J. P., 359.)

1882.   [284]
Rumball v. *Schmidt*. "Public Health Act, 1875," § 156—Continuing offence—An offence to which the penalty is applicable continues so long as the addition to the house is maintained after written notice from the Authority, notwithstanding that the addition was completed before the notice—*Marshall* v. *Smith* distinguished. (L. R., 8 Q. B. D. 603: 46 L. T. 661; 46 J. P., 567.)

1877.   [285]
Scott v. *Legg*. "Metropolitan Building Act, 1855," §§ 27-8, 106—By-Law that no building should comprise more than 216,000 cubic ft. without a party wall, but this not to apply to old buildings—Held that adding a wing to an old building, whereby the joint content of the whole would be greater than 216,000 ft., was not within the prohibition, because the addition was by itself less than 216,000 ft. (46 L. J., M. C., 267: L. R., 10 Q. B. D., 236: 36 L. T., 456: 41 J. P., 773.)

1890.   [286]
Shaw v. *Solihull Union*. "Public Health Act, 1875," § 157—Houses commenced with mortar of bad quality ordered to be pulled down —Builder heard in his defence—Subsequently, walls pulled down by the officers of the Local Authority—Held that the By-Laws were valid, and the Local Authority justified in the course taken. (*Times*, July 4, 1890.)

1861.   [287]
Shiel v. *Sunderland, Mayor*. "Local Government Act, 1858," § 34—By-Law—Coach-house and stables appurtenant to an hotel pulled down in order that an additional wing to be tacked on to the hotel might occupy the site—Held that such erection was not a "New Building"—Back Street. (30 L. J., M. C., 215: 6 H. & N., 796: 25 J. P., 647.)

1863.   [288]
Slee v. *Bradford, Mayor*. "Local Government Act, 1858," § 34—Building By-Laws — Setting back line of street—Approval of plans—Injunction granted under the circumstances to restrain the defendants from interfering with the plaintiff's building—After a Local Authority has sanctioned plans for rebuilding premises, and the premises have been pulled down, it cannot insist on conditions as to an alteration of the Building Line. (4 Giff., 462: 8 L. T., 491.)

1880.   [289]
Sunderland, Mayor v. *Brown*. New street—Infringement of By-Law prescribing minimum width—Held on the facts that the owner was the person who had "laid out" the street, and that as the builder of the houses had had nothing to do with the laying out a summons against him for alleged breach of the By-Law was rightly dismissed. (43 L. T., 478: 44 J. P., 831.)

1861.   [290]
Tucker v. *Rees*. "Local Government Act, 1858," § 34—By-Law requiring an open space of a stated area to be left belonging to a building, held bad as regards old buildings—Conviction quashed. (7 Jur., (N. S.), 629.)

1867.   [291]
Waite v. *Garston L. B. H.* "Local Government Act, 1858," § 34—By-Law that no house should be erected without a back roadway communicating with some adjoining public street, held unreasonable. (37 L. J., M. C., 19: L. R., 3 Q. B., 5: 17 L. T., 201.)

1891.   [292]
Wallasey L. B. v. *Gandy Belt Co.* Question whether an old country lane had by virtue of certain building operations become liable to be treated as a "new street"—Summons against defendants for non-compliance with By-Law applicable to New Streets dismissed by Justices—Case insufficiently stated and therefore sent back. (*Times*, Dec. 4, 1891.)

1880.   [293]
Watson v. *Gray*. Adjacent owners—Meaning of the word "Party wall"—The most ordinary and primary meaning is a wall of which the two adjoining owners are tenants in common. (49 L. J., Ch., 243: L. R., 14 Ch. D., 192: 42 L. T., 294: 44 J. P., 537.)

1886.   [294]
West Hartlepool Commissioners v. *Levy*. Local Act—Dwelling-house altered to Workshop by permission on conditions—Premises sold and altered back by purchaser who was ignorant of the conditions—Conviction held good, Act being retrospective as regards existing buildings. (50 J. P., 196.)

1874.   [295]
Weston v. *Arnold*. Local Act—Party Wall—Ancient lights—Held that a wall might be a party wall near its base and an outer wall above, each portion having its own legal attributes independent of the other. (43 L. J., Ch., 123: 22 W. R., 284.)

C 2

1883. [296]
Williams v. *Powning.* Cottages built in a lane—Held that there was no evidence that builder was liable for not having proceeded as if laying out a new street. (48 L. T., 672 : 47 J. P., 486.)

1886. [297]
Williams v. *Wallasey L. B.* " Public Health Act, 1875," § 156—" Bringing forward " a house —This does not include new buildings on land never built upon. (53 L. J., M. C., 133 : L. R., 16 Q. B. D., 718 : 55 L. T., 27 : 50 J. P., 582.) [See now the " Public Health (Buildings in Streets) Act, 1888."]

1887. [298]
Woodhill v. *Sunderland, Mayor.* Local Act—By-Law—Notice given by builder of his intention to lay out a new street—Houses built before more than a part of such street had been sewered, &c., as required by the Local Act—Conviction affirmed, consent of Local Authority not having been given. (57 L. T., 303 : 52 J. P., 5.)

1879. [299]
Workington L. B., In re. " Public Health Act, 1875," § 158—Plans for new street in a certain direction duly deposited under a Building By-Law—Disapproval by Local Authority, and refusal to state the grounds on which the disapproval was based, otherwise than that the Board wished the proposed street to run in a different direction—*Mandamus* granted to compel the Board to give its reasons, but doubts expressed by the Court (1) whether the Act required reasons to be assigned by the Board for its refusal; and (2) whether the Board could insist on the direction of a street being altered. (*Times,* April 9, 1879.)

1864. [300]
Young v. *Edwards.* " Local Government Act, 1858," § 34—Local Act—Building By-Laws —By-Law respecting non - compliance with the requirements of the Board, held *ultra vires,* and a conviction under it bad. (33 L. J., M. C., 227 : 11 L. T., 424.) [Questioned in *Hall* v. *Nixon.*]

(2.) MARKET.

1885. [301]
Collins v. *Wells Corporation.* " Markets and Fairs Clauses Act, 1847 " — By-Law forbidding sales by Auction on Market Days till after a certain hour held good. (*Times,* March 9, 1885.)

1864. [302]
De Caux v. *Powley.* By-Law—Market Place—Leaving a cart there for an unreasonable period—Conviction. (28 J. P., 806.)

1863. [303]
Savage v. *Brook.* " Markets and Fairs Clauses Acts, 1847," § 42—By-Laws restricting the deposit of articles, held good, notwithstanding a long-existing local usage. (33 L. J., M. C., 42 : 15 C. B., (N. S.), 264 : [*Savage* v. *Savage*] 9 L. T., 334.)

1886. [304]
Strike v. *Collins.* By-Law prescribing what part of a Market shall be used for wholesale and what for retail trade held good. (50 J. P., 741.)

(3.) VARIOUS.

1845. [305]
Calder and Hebble Navigation Co. v. *Pilling.* By-Laws must be within the scope of the Act under which they are made. (14 L. J., Ex. 223 : 14 M. & W., 76.)

1890. [306]
Cotterill v. *Lempriere.* Where a Statute or By-Law creates two distinct offences in the alternative an Information or Conviction grounded on such Statute or By-Law must point out which offence is intended to be charged. (59 L. J., M. C., 133 : L. R., 24 Q. B. D., 634 : 62 L. T., 695 : 54 J. P., 583.)

1884. [307]
Ellwood v. *Bullock.* By-Law—Fair—A By-Law prohibiting the erection of a Booth without the licence of the Mayor; and that any such license given, save in respect of Fair-time, might be revoked at the instigation of householders, is unreasonable and therefore bad, although the By-Law was duly published and not disallowed by the Secretary of State. (13 L. J., Q. B., 330 : 6 Q. B., 383 : 8 J. P., 473.)

1824. [308]
Harrison v. *Williams.* Corporate Town—A resident inhabitant has a right even though he be not a member of the corporation, to inspect and have a copy of a By-Law for a breach of which an Action against him is pending—*Mandamus* granted. (4 D. & R., 820.)

1839 and 1841. [309]
Hopkins v. *Swansea, Mayor.* Municipal Corporation—Annual distribution of rents—By-Law. (8 L. J., Ex., 121 : 4 M. & W., 621 : Affirmed 8 M. & W., 901.)

1886. [310]
Johnson v. *Croydon, Mayor.* " Municipal Corporations Act, 1882," §. 23—By-Law prohibiting street music on Sundays held unreasonable and *ultra vires.* (55 L.J., M. C., 117 : L. R., 16 Q. B. D., 708 : 54 L. T., 295 : 50 J. P., 487.)

1887. [311]
Macdonald v. *Lochrane.* "Municipal Corporations Act, 1882," § 23—A By-Law prohibiting children unless of a certain age selling articles in a street after a certain hour held *ultra vires.* (51 J. P., 180.)

1875. [312]
Mayer v. *Burslem L. B.* "Public Health Act, 1848," § 87 [= " Public Health Act, 1875," § 207, &c]—District divided for rating purposes—Subsequent By-Law that resolutions of the Board should not be altered, except (1), after one month's notice, and (2), unless as many members were present when the resolution was altered, as when it was

originally passed — Rating arrangements altered without the month's notice—Rate held therefore bad. (39 J. P., 437.) [*Quære*, Is Condition No. 2 now invalid in consequence of Sched. I. (1), 7, of " Public Health Act, 1875 "?]

1887.   [313]
Munro v. *Watson*. Street obstruction by Salvation Army procession—By-Law prohibiting street music generally held *ultra vires*—A proper By-Law might easily be framed. (57 L. T., 366 : 51 J. P., 180.)

1840.   [314]
Poulters' Co. v. *Phillips*. An omission in a By-Law may be supplied by implication from the subject-matter of the By-Laws—A By-Law is to receive a reasonable construction. (9 L. J., C. P., 190: 6 Bing., (N. S.), 314 : 4 Jur., 124.)

1862.   [315]
Reg. v. *Lundie*. Local Act—Common—A By-Law, unreasonable in part, may be divisible and may be good as to that part which is not unreasonable. (31 L. J., M. C., 157 : 5 L. T., 830.)

1884.   [316]
Reg. v. *Powell* (2). "Municipal Corporations Act, 1835," § 90 — By-Law prohibiting use of Musical Instruments in a street after notice to desist for a reasonable cause, held valid—Salvation Army captain convicted—Conviction affirmed. (51 L. T., 92: 48 J. P., 740.)

1855.   [317]
Reg. v. *Rose*. Local Boards have no *general* powers to make By-Laws, but may only make such By-Laws as are authorised by Statute. (24 L. J., M. C., 130 : [*Reg.* v. *Wood*] 5 E. & B., 49 : 3 C. L. R., 1134 : [*Reg.* v. *Staffordshire JJ.*] 25 L. T., (O. S), 127.)

1810.   [318]
Rex v. *Ashwell*. A municipal By-Law may be repealed by the Body which made it. (12 East., 22.)

1799.   [319]
Rex v. *Faversham Fishermen*. A By-Law may be good in part and bad in part, if the two parts are entire and distinct. (8 T. R., 352 and 356.)

1867.   [320]
Ryde Pier Co. v. *Porter*. Local Act—By-Laws to control persons using the pier held reasonable and of general application. (31 J. P., 355.)

1834.   [321]
Shaw v. *Poynter*. Municipal By-Law — When a person is sued for breach of a By-Law to which there is a proviso making certain exemptions, it is unnecessary to aver that the case was not within the exceptions : such fact if it exist must be proved by the Defendant by way of excuse. (3 L. J., K. B., 110 : 4 N. & M., 290 : 2 A. & E., 312.)

1840.   [322]
Sills v. *Brown*. Evidence of a practice in contravention of a By-Law is not admissible by way of defence at proceedings for an alleged breach of the By-Law. (9 C. & P., 601.)

1888.   [323]
Slattery v. *Naylor*. In determining whether or not a By-Law is reasonable it is material to consider the relation of its framers to the locality affected by it, and the Authority by which it is sanctioned. (57 L. J., P. C., 73 : L. R., 13 App. Cas., 446 : 59 L. T., 41.)

1882.   [324]
Torquay L. B. v. *Bridle*. "Public Health Act, 1875," § 164—By-Laws to regulate a Pleasure Ground—Owner of fowls which had strayed into Ground fined under By-Law for the trespass—By-Law held *ultra vires*—Conviction quashed. (47 J. P., 183.)

19. CLERK.

1869.   [325]
Deeks v. *Bailey*. "Public Health Act, 1848," § 138 : "Sanitary Act, 1866," § 46 [=" Public Health Act, 1875," § 7]—A Clerk to a Local Board must answer a Bill in Chancery in his official capacity if made defendant. (21 L. T., 581.)

1888.   [326]
Edwards v. *Salmon*. "Public Health Act, 1875," § 193—Acceptance by Clerk of Local Board of a special fee for special services to his Board held not within this Section. (58 L. J., Q. B., 571 : L. R., 23 Q. B. D , 531: 54 J. P., 180 : *59 L. T., 416.)

1879.   [327]
Meredith v. *Radcliffe L. B.* Law stationers employed by Local Board Clerk to do certain work which, as Clerk, it was his duty to do himself—Plaintiffs held not entitled to recover from the Board, there being no proof of agency. (43 J. P., 819.)

1879.   [328]
Newington L. B. v. *Eldridge*. Defendant a solicitor and late Clerk to Local Board—Defendant being dismissed, refused to deliver up various papers, claiming a lien on them in respect of an unpaid Bill of Costs—Ordered that the Board should pay into Court 1000*l.*, which done, defendant was to have the same lien, if any, on the money as upon the papers, but that the latter must be delivered up to plaintiffs. (L. R., 12 Ch. D., 349.)

1886.   [328a]
Reg. v. *Petticrew*. "Towns Improvement (Ireland) Act, 1854," § 30—A Town Clerk having received 3 months' notice and been directed to advertise for a successor did so—Held that he had acquiesced in his own dismissal— Moreover *Quo Warranto* not applicable, the office being one held during pleasure. (18 L. R., Ir., 342.)

1874.   [329]
Reg. v. *Wilts & Berks Canal Co.* Application by a Shareholder for a *Mandamus* to allow inspection of Books—Objected, that the Shareholder was Clerk of a Local Board against

which a suit had been instituted by the Company—*Mandamus* granted with Costs. (30 L. T., 498.)

1890. [330]
Salford, Mayor v. *Lever.* A Town Clerk held privileged from answering Interrogatories seeking information on matters which were within his knowledge in his official capacity as Solicitor of the plaintiff Corporation—*Swansea* v. *Quirk* distinguished. (59 L. J., Q. B., 248 : L. R., 24 Q. B. D., 695 : 54 J. P., 519.)

1879. [331]
Swansea, Mayor v. *Quirk.* Interrogatories—Corporation answering by their Town Clerk as Solicitor—Privilege—Held that under the circumstances the privilege claimed for the Town Clerk could not be allowed. (49 L. J., C. P., 157 : L. R., 5 C. P. D., 106 : 41 L. T., 758 : 44 J. P., 378.)

20. COAL DUTY.

1891. [332]
Fletcher v. *Fields.* "Metropolitan Streets Act, 1867," § 15—Unloading of "coal" an offence—Coke is not coal—Conviction quashed. (55 J. P., 502.)

1876. [333]
Margate Pier Co. v. *Perry.* Local Act dating from 1812, authorising a duty on all coals brought into the district—Held that railwayborne coal was not exempt. (*Times*, March 18, 1876.)

1891. [334]
North Eastern Railway v. *Kingston-upon-Hull, Mayor.* Coal conveyed into a Borough for carrier's own use and not for sale—Held, a "dealing" with coal, and tonnage payable accordingly—*Wilson* v. *Hull* followed. (55 J. P., 518.)

1873. [335]
Vaux v. *Chapman.* Local Act—Coal Duty—Drawback authorised on coal landed but sent beyond the town limits—Held that the drawback did not apply to coal sold in the town by retail although for consumption outside. (27 L. T., 758.)

1866. [336]
Wilson v. *Hull L. B. H.* Local Act—Coals—To convey coals in one vessel and tranship them into another for coal-owner's use within the jurisdiction of a taxing Authority is evidence of "dealing with" them so as to render them taxable. (12 Jur., (N. S.), 706 : 14 W. R., 638.)

21. COMPENSATION.

⁎⁎⁎ See also "Lands Clauses Act, 1845," (§ 44, *post.*)

1876. [337]
Baker v. *St. Marylebone Vestry.* Local Acts—Road raised to detriment of Houses—Held that under the circumstances no compensation was payable—*Semble*, that the Legisla-

ture committed an oversight. (Metropolis.) (35 L. T., 129.)

1873. [338]
Bigg v. *London Corporation.* New street constructed under Parliamentary powers—Held that compensation was payable for the direct injury to a cellar by an unauthorised interference therewith, but not for the indirect injury resulting from a diversion of the traffic. (L. R., 15 Eq., 376 : 28 L. T., 336 : 37 J. P., 564.)

1857. [339]
Bold v. *Williams.* "Public Health Act, 1848," § 68 [="Public Health Act, 1875," § 149] —Altering the level of a highway—Damages for private injury held not recoverable. (21 J. P., 84.)

1824. [340]
Boulton v. *Crowther.* Powers under a Turnpike Act—Raising and lowering a road with the result that the access of the plaintiff to his property was interfered with—Held that the Turnpike Trustees were not liable they not having exceeded their powers, and Parliament not having created any right to compensation. (2 L. J., K. B., (o. s.), 139 : 2 B. & C. 703 : 4 D. & R., 195.)

1858. [341]
Bradford L. B. H. v. *Hopwood.* "Public Health Act, 1848," § 123 [="Public Health Act, 1875," §§ 179-80]—Compensation for damage done by works—§ 123 of the aforesaid Act cannot be distinguished from § 25 of the "Lands Clauses Act, 1845." (22 J. P., 561.)

1880. [342]
Burgess v. *Northwich L. B.* (2). "Public Health Act, 1875," §§ 144, 149, 179, 308—Highway —Houses abutting—Road raised by Board to obviate inconvenience from floods—Houses raised by owners—Compensation for cost of this not payable by Board as the alteration in the level of the road had not been done under the "Public Health Act"—§ 308 refers to powers created by that Act and not to powers created under the "Highway Act, 1835," and merely transferred. (50 L. J., C. P. D., 219 : L. R., 6 Q. B. D., 264 : 44 L. T., 154 : 45 J. P., 256.)

1882. [343]
Caledonian Railway Co. v. *Walker's Trustees.* Direct access to premises cut off by new railway —Such an injury fit matter for compensation, although no land taken—Principles on which compensation is payable where works are executed which injure private property. (L. R., 7 App. Cas., 259 : 46 L. T., 826 : 46 J. P., 676.)

1883. [344]
Drew v. *Metropolitan B. W.* Office abolished— Salary small but increased by extras—How extras to be taken into account. (50 L. T., 138).

1880. [345]
Essex v. *Acton L. B.* Where part of an estate is taken for a Sewage Farm the Owner can not

only claim compensation for the value of the land taken, but for the depreciation of the remainder not taken. (58 L. J., Q. B., 594 : L. R., 14 App. Cas., 153 : 61 L. T., 1 : 53 J. P., 756.)

1880.   [346]
Grainger v. Dudley, Mayor. "Public Health Act, 1875 "—Subsidence of road and of house abutting thereon — Road raised again by Local Authority to same level as before the building of the house—House only 10 years old — Action on an award — Held that no compensation was payable Local Authority being entitled to restore road to level existing before house was built. (Times, Nov. 11, 1880.)

1876.   [347]
Great Western Railway Co. v. Smith. "Railways Clauses Act, 1845," § 78—Coal Mine—Compensation paid to lessee for loss of right to work—Compensation held not payable to reversioner. (45 L. J., Ch., 235: L. R., 2 Ch. D., 235: 31 L. T., 267.)

1867.   [348]
Hall v. Bristol, Mayor. "Public Health Act, 1848," § 144 [="Public Health Act, 1875," § 308]—Construction of Sewer—In order to be entitled to compensation a person must show actionable damage—"Damage" does not include inconvenience. (36 L. J., C. P., 110: L. R., 2 C. P., 322: 15 L. T., 572.)

1889.   [349]
Huddersfield, Mayor v. Shaw. Local Act—Land taken for sewer — Compensation and costs awarded—Held that the Justices were at liberty to award costs. (54 J. P., 724.)

1889.   [350]
Jersey (E. of) v. Neath Union. Grant of Land for Sewers, minerals reserved—Held that brickearth and clay were within the reservation, and such materials having been disturbed in laying the sewers compensation was payable in respect thereof. (58 L. J., Q. B., 373 : L. R., 22 Q. B. D., 555; 53 J. P., 404.)

1851.   [351]
Lawrence v. Great Northern Railway Co. Injury to property by works constructed—The compensation covers all damage known or contingent which was apparent and capable of being ascertained and estimated when the compensation was awarded, but does not include contingent damage which could not have been foreseen — Action for further damages held sustainable notwithstanding that compensation had once been paid. (20 L. J., Q. B., 293 ; 16 Q. B., 643.)

1837.   [352]
Lister v. Lobley. Compulsory purchase of premises—Compensation is payable to a lessee as well as to the freeholder. (6 L. J., K. B., 200 : 7 A. & E., 124 : 6 Nev. & M., 340 : 2 Harr. & Woll., 12.)

1891.   [353]
McIntosh and Pontypridd Improvements Co., In re. Compulsory sale of premises for Street Improvements — Compensation—Re-erection with modifications—Arbitration as to compensation—Though plans may be passed by a Local Authority yet such Authority is not entitled to sanction breaches of its own By-Laws, nor is it an Arbitrator to take into account matters based upon such breaches. (61 L. J., Q. B., 164.)

1865.   [354]
Pentney v. Lynn Paving Commissioners. "Towns Improvement Clauses Act, 1847," §§ 22 and 25—Tidal Watercourse illegally arched over by Commissioners in excess of their powers—This done, plaintiff held entitled to compensation, the facts not disclosing any acquiescence on his part. (12 L. T., 818.)

1865.   [355]
Pettiward v. Metropolitan B. W. Land taken for a sewer by a Board—Supersession of that Board by another Board—Transfer of liabilities—The making of compensation held not to be a condition precedent to the taking of land, but to be an obligation incurred after the act is done. (31 L. J., C. P., 301: 19 C. B., (N. S.), 489 : 12 L. T., 764.)

1865.   [356]
Reg. v. Darlington L. B. H. "Public Health Act, 1848," §§ 45 and 144 [="Public Health Act, 1875," §§ 15, 16, 18, 308]: "Local Government Act, 1858," § 73 [=Ibid., § 332] —Construction of Sewer—Injury by abstraction of water—Held that as the work complained of had been done without proper authority the remedy was by Action at Law and not by proceedings for compensation under the first named Act. (35 L. J., Q. B., 45: 6 B. & S., 562: 29 J. P., 419.)

1845.   [357]
Reg. v. Lancaster & Preston Railway Co. 7 Will. IV. & 1 Vict., c. xxii.—A jury summoned to assess compensation are entitled to find that no damage has been done. (14 L. J., Q. B., 84: 6 Q. B., 759.)

1876.   [358]
Reg. v. Postmaster-General. Compensation for loss of office—"Emolument"—What is a subject for compensation—Principle of computation in determining the pension value of a lost salary. (45 L. J., Q. B., 609: L. R., 1 Q. B. D., 658: 35 L. T., 241.)

1869.   [359]
Reg. v. Wallasey L. B. H. "Public Health Act, 1848," §§ 69 and 144 [="Public Health Act, 1875," §§ 150, 308]—When a Local Board executes works on default of an owner and causes damage, compensation is payable in the usual way to that owner. (38 L. J., Q. B., 217: L. R., 4 Q. B., 351: 10 B. & S., 428: 21 L. T., 90.)

1826.   [360]
Rex v. Watts. Nuisance—Indictment—Conviction—Local Act—Compensation held not payable for the compulsory removal under a Statute of a noxious trade, there being a Common Law Nuisance clearly proved to arise at the place where it had been

previously carried on, and which rendered it at any time liable to removal after an Indictment. (2 C. & P., 486.)

1876. [361]
Rhodes v. *Airedale Drainage Commissioners.*
Local Act, 24 & 25 Vict., c. clx.—Arbitration —"Sustaining any damage"—Interpretation of a Statute which made special provision for the assessment of compensation for damage done under it. (45 L. J., C. P., 861: L. R., 1 C. P. D., 402: 35 L. T., 46.)

1857. [362]
Stainton v. *Woolrych.* Interference with Water-Works planned by public Boards may be executed, though they tend to inflict injury on property—Compensation payable—Injunction refused. (26 L. J., Ch., 300: 23 Bea., 225: 23 L. T., (o. s.), 333.)

1888. [363]
Thirsk v. *Beverley, Mayor.* Action for obstruction of light and air to certain buildings erected by the Corporation, the plaintiff being a member of the Corporation and some time chairman of the Committee responsible for the erection of the buildings — The facts showing that the plaintiff did not know beforehand that his property would be injured it was held that he had not forfeited his right to claim compensation in his private capacity, and was entitled to the £80 awarded him by an arbitrator. (*Times*, Oct. 26, 1888.)

1892. [364]
Walton-on-the-Hill L. B. In re, Serjeant, Ex parte. Local Act — Notice to treat for land for sewage farm—Board alarmed at high price asked for, refused to go on with negociation —Hold that the Board could not recede but must take its chance that the Jury would cut down the price—Rule *Nisi* granted for *Mandamus* to Board to take steps for having the compensation assessed. (*Times*, Feb. 19, 1892.)

22. CONTRACT.

* See also "Seal," (§ 67, *post.*)

1858. [365]
Bateman v. *Ashton-under-Lyne, Mayor.* Water supply — Engineer's plans — Validity of a Contract entered into by a Corporation—Generally speaking, a Corporation is as much bound by its contract as an individual where the seal is affixed in a binding manner. (27 L. J., Ex., 458: 3 H. & N., 323: 31 L. T., (o. s.), 290.)

1892. [366]
Bottems v. *York, Mayor.* Sewers—A contractor is not entitled to abandon his contract merely because as the work proceeds difficulties connected with the subsoil involving enormous expense disclose themselves, which could not have been foreseen by either party. (*Times*, July 18, 1892.)

1886. [367]
Botterill v. *Ware Guardians.* Contract for construction of sewers—Default by contractor to

complete—Certificate withheld by Engineer —There being no proof of fraud on the part of the Engineer, held that contractor could not recover balance due. (*Times*, May 14, 1886.)

1852. [368]
Clark v. *Cuckfield Union.* Erection of Water-closets — Contract not under seal — Action held to be maintainable—*Per* Wightman, J.: "Goods purchased and work done in accordance with the legitimate objects of a Corporation must be paid for even where there is no sealed contract to pay." (21 L. J., Q. B., 349: 1 Bail Ct. Cas., 81: 19 L. T., (o. s.), 207.) [Decision questioned and Wightman's remarks dissented from by the Judges in *Smart* v. *West Ham.*]

1860. [369]
Cobham v. *Holcombe.* "Public Health Act, 1848," § 138 — Contract "on behalf of" a Local Board—Suit by Clerk for the enforcement of the Contract held maintainable. (8 C. B., (N. S.), 815.) [See now "Public Health Act, 1875," § 259.]

1833. [370]
Curling v. *Johnson.* Contract with a Board—Condition that the Contractor should pay the Law expenses thereof—Held that when the Contractor refused to pay unreasonable charges the Clerk suing *quâ* Clerk could not recover, his remedy being personal against the Contractor. (10 Bing., 89: 3 Moo. & S., 496.)

1853. [371]
Davies v. *Swansea, Mayor.* "Public Health Act, 1848," § 139 [="Public Health Act, 1875," § 264]—Neglect to complete Works—Construction of a Contract as regards the right to enforce a forfeiture clause — Notice of Action held not necessary as regards contracts; only in cases of Tort. (22 L. J., Ex., 297: 8 Ex., 808: 21 L. T., (o. s.), 143.)

1885. [372]
Eastbourne L. B. v. *Jackson.* Contract to build sea wall—Part of wall washed away—Default by contractor to rebuild and finish—Wall finished by Board—Board held entitled to recover damages and excess of cost beyond contract. (*Times*, Feb. 19, 1885.)

1880. [373]
Eaton v. *Basker.* "Public Health Act, 1875," § 174—Contract not under seal between Local Authority and Medical Man to attend fever patients at so much a head—Doctor's Bill eventually exceeded 50l. and payment resisted by the Local Authority—Held that the Section did not apply for the said contract when entered into did not amount to 50l. and therefore the Local Authority was liable. (50 L. J., Ex., 444: L. R., 7 Q. B. D., 529: 44 L. T., 703: 45 J. P., 616.)

1878. [374]
Ellis v. *Aberystwith, Mayor.* Action by contractor against a Corporation for labour and materials provided for street paving—Rise in price of materials, and contract completed at a loss—Verdict for the defendant Corporation

on the ground that it had not consented to any release of the contract terms. (*Times*, June 25, 1878.)

1865.   [375]
Goodyear v. *Weymouth, Mayor.* Building Contract for a Market—Extras—Architect's certificate held final. (35 L. J., C. P., 12 : Harr. & Ruth., 67.)

1884.   [376]
Hanson v. *Halifax, Mayor.* Motion for Injunction to restrain affixing of Seal to contract for coals alleged to be improvident—Motion refused—A Corporation is elected to deal with such matters: they are too trivial for the Court—Where the "Municipal Corporations Act" and the "Public Health Act" are inconsistent, a Corporation is at liberty to proceed under either Act. (*Loc. Gov. Chron.*, Feb. 2, 1884.)

1874.   [377]
Harrison v. *Enfield L. B. H.* Contract for 25 years to receive sewage—Sewage alleged to be worthless because too watery—Motion for a decree to keep back subsoil water, refused, (*Times*, Mar. 27, 1874.)

1878.   [378]
Hunt v. *Wimbledon L. B.* "Public Health Act, 1875," §§ 173-4—Employment of Architect by Board's surveyor on the authority of the Board—Plans for offices duly prepared but not used, and not paid for—Action held not maintainable, the amount exceeding 50*l.* and there being no contract under seal—§ 174 is imperative and not directory. (48 L. J., C. P., 207 : L. R., 4 C. P. D., 48 ; 40 L. T., 115 ; 43 J. P., 284.)

1873.   [379]
Kidderminster, Mayor v. *Hardwick.* Market Tolls let by auction—A Contract not under seal nor signed by an Agent [expressly appointed under seal for the purpose, cannot be enforced—Payment of a month's rent is not such part performance as would support a Bill for specific performance. (43 L. J., Ex., 9 : L. R., 9 Ex., 13; 29 L. T., 611.)

1854.   [380]
Kingston-upon-Hull Guardians v. *Petch.* Tender for supplies—Held that an acceptance by Guardians of a Tender was not binding until a written agreement had been signed, there having been a stipulation that there was to be such an agreement. (24 L. J., Ex., 23 : 10 Ex., 610.)

1892.   [381]
Kingston-upon-Hull, Mayor v. *Harding.* Powers of Local Authority to recover from sureties of a Contractor where work scamped, but scamping successfully concealed till after contract moneys all paid. (L. R., 2 Q. B., 494.)

1848.   [382]
Kirk v. *Bromley Union.* Erection of a Workhouse—Builder's Contract — Extras — Absence of written contract held fatal. (2 Phillips, 640 ; 11 L. T., (o. s.), 429.)

1849.   [383]
Lamprell v. *Billericay Union.* Corporation—Parol Contract with a Builder—Held that the Architect had no authority to cause the erection of additional works. (18 L. J., Ex., 282 : 3 Ex., 283 : 12 L. T. (o. s.), 593.)

1891.   [384]
Law v. *Redditch L. B.* Contract for Works—Sums to be payable on failure to complete works by a specified day—Default—Held that on the default occurring the sums payable became liquidated damages, not penalties. (61 L. J., Q. B., 172 : L. R., 1 Q. B., 127 ; 66 L. T., 76 : 56 J. P., 292.)

1883.   [385]
Lawson v. *Wallasey L. B.* Contract for Works—Powers of a Board's Engineer to authorise delays and additional Works, and so compromise his employers. (52 L. J., Q. B., 302 : L. R., 11 Q. B. D., 229 : 48 L. T., 507 : 47 J. P., 437.)

1885.   [386]
Melliss v. *Shirley L. B.* "Public Health Act, 1875," §§ 174, 193—Contract—§ 193 has a specified effect, and debars an officer from suing on a contract. (55 L. J., Q. B., 143 : L. R., 16 Q. B. D., 446; 53 L. T., 810.)

1874.   [387]
Mountstephen v. *Lakeman.* Construction of Sewer by a Contractor—Verbal Contract with the Chairman of the Board—Judgment for the plaintiff (the contractor) against the Chairman in his *private* capacity. (43 L. J., Q. B., 188 : 30 L. T., 437 : L. R., 7 H. L., 17 : 38 J. P., 452.)

1892.   [388]
McDonald v. *Workington Corporation.* Contract to construct Sewers—Contract incapable of execution by reason of Water in sub-soil—Contract abandoned by contractor—Held, there being no certificate of Engineer, that the contractor had no claim in regard either as to the whole or as to any part of the moneys agreed to be paid had the contract been carried out. (*Times*, Nov. 1, 1892.)

1866.   [389]
Nicholson v. *Bradfield Union.* Purchase money of necessaries (*e.g.* coals) held recoverable, although there was no contract under seal. (35 L. J., Q. B., 176 : L. R., 1 Q. B., 620 : 7 B. & S., 774 : 14 L. T., 830.)

1854.   [390]
Nowell v. *Worcester, Mayor.* "Public Health Act, 1848," § 85 [= "Public Health Act, 1875," §§ 173-4]—Contract—Condition precedent—A Contract duly entered into may be enforced, although no estimate or report from the Surveyor has been previously obtained—This omission, however, might affect the levy of a Rate. (23 L. J., Ex., 139 : 9 Ex., 457 ; 2 C. L. R., 981 : 22 L. T., (o. s.), 244 : 18 J. P., 88.)

1846.   [391]
Paine v. *Strand Union.* Contract with a Surveyor under seal—Additional work not under seal—Payment for the latter item held not recoverable. (15 L. J., M. C., 89 ; 8 Q. B., 326.)

1855. [392]
Pauling v. *Dover, Mayor.* Construction of sewerage works—Defective work—A particular notice to contractor to cancel his contract held sufficiently specific in its indications as to what was expected of the plaintiff. (24 L. J., Ex., 128 : 10 Ex., 753.)

1870. [393]
Roberts v. *Bury Improvement Commissioners.* Contract for a Cemetery—Right to determine the same on an unfavourable certificate from Architect—One of 2 contracting parties is exonerated from the performance of a contract when the performance is prevented or rendered impossible by the wrongful act of the other. (39 L. J., C. P., 129 : L. R., 5 C. P., 310 : 22 L. T., 132.)

1865. [394]
Russell v. *Trickett.* Contract with Local Board—Specification acted upon although unsigned—Contractor's Sureties held not released. (13 L. T., 280.)

1861. [395]
Rutledge v. *Farnham L. B. H.* Contract to employ an Engineer at a salary—Board held not liable for extra work not contracted for by deed. (2 F. & F., 406.)

1846. [396]
Sanders v. *St. Neot's Union.* Erection of necessary gates—Contract not under seal—Notwithstanding this, Action held maintainable. (15 L. J., M. C., 104 : 8 Q. B., 810.) [See however the remarks of Parke, B., in *Smart* v. *West Ham Union.*]

1858. [397]
Scott v. *Liverpool Corporation.* Construction of Waterworks—Contract — Engineer's certificate withheld—Contract determined—When a contract refers possible disputes to the decision of a particular person, no rights, enforceable in law, arise, till he has spoken. (28 L. J., Ch., 236 : 3 De G. & J., 334 : 32 L. T., (o. s.), 265.)

1869. [398]
South of Ireland Colliery Co. v. *Waddle.* A Contract with Corporation may be enforceable even if it be not under seal, if the subject-matter is closely related to the functions of the Corporation in the way of trade. (38 L. J., C. P., 338 : L. R., 4 C. P., 617 ; 18 L. T., 405, affirmed on appeal.)

1875. [399]
Thorn v. *London, Mayor.* A Local Authority in entering into a contract based on certain plans and estimates, does not thereby so guarantee that the plans are capable of execution as that a contractor has a remedy against the Authority if the contract cannot be carried out according to the plans. (44 L. J., Ex., 62 : L. R., 10 Ex., 112 : 31 L. T., 455.)

1890. [400]
Trehearne, In re, Ealing L. B., Ex parte. Bankruptcy of Board's contractor — Garnishee order served on Board—Duty of Board under such circumstances. (60 L. J., Q. B., 50 : 63 L. T., 798.)

1877. [401]
Waghorn v. *Wimbledon L. B.* Resolution of Board that its Surveyor should procure tenders for works—Plaintiff employed by Surveyor as a "quantity surveyor"—Tenders not accepted by Board—Held that the plaintiff had impliedly been employed by the authority of the Board, and that he was entitled to be paid his proper fees. (*Times,* June 4, 1877.)

1880. [402]
Wakefield, &c., Banking Co. v. *Normanton L. B.* Contract for Reservoir to be paid for by instalments after certificate by Engineer—Reservoir found faulty and further payments refused—Action by Contractor against Board for balance—The debt assigned to a Bank—Action by Bank against Board—Defence that the original certificates had been obtained by fraud and conspiracy—This being proved, held that the Board was not liable to the assignees of the debt. (44 L. T., 697 : 45 J. P., 601.)

1862. [403]
Worthington v. *Sudlow.* "Public Health Act, 1848," § 69 [= "Public Health Act, 1875," § 150]—Contract between a Local Board and a Paving Contractor—Condition that payment was to be made as the money was recovered from the owners—No money recovered—Held that under the circumstances the Contractor could recover from the Board irrespective of the condition. (31 L. J., Q. B., 131 : 2 B. & S., 508 : 6 L. T., 283.)

23. CONTRACT, DISQUALIFICATION FROM.

1853. [404]
Boyce v. *Higgins.* "Public Health Act, 1848," §§ 19 and 133 [= "Public Health Act, 1875," scheds. and §§ 253–4]—Member of a Local Board voting on a matter affecting a Company in which he was interested—Action for Penalty—Consent of A.-G. not obtained—Action held not maintainable. (23 L. J., C. P., 5 : 14 C. B., 1 : 22 L. T., (o. s.), 103.) [The authority of this case has been much shaken by later cases, especially by *Fletcher* v. *Hudson.*]

1884. [405]
Burgess v. *Clark.* "Public Health Act, 1875," § 193—Clerk of Local Board receiving rent for rooms let to Board, held liable to penalty. (L. R., 14 Q. B. D., 735 : 49 J. P., 388.) [See now 47 & 48 Vict., c. 74.]

1890. [406]
Cox v. *Ambrose.* Municipal Election — Two Partners contractors to a Town Council—Partnership dissolved and contracts assigned to one of the late partners—Held that this did not render the other partner eligible as the liability under the contracts remained—Votes given to a candidate notoriously disqualified are thrown away, and next candidate will be entitled to the seat. (60 L. J., Q. B., 114 : 55 J. P., 23.)

1874. [407]
Davies v. *Harvey.* "Poor Law Amendment Act, 1834," § 77—Guardian held liable to a penalty for the supply of goods to a Relieving Officer by Guardian's partner. (43 L. J., M. C., 121: L. R., 9 Q. B., 433: 30 L. T., 629 : 38 J. P., 661.)

1866. [408]
Dyer v. *Best.* Local Act—Commissioner interested in a Contract—Action for penalties—An Action by a common informer must be brought within one year. (35 L. J., Ex., 105: L. R., 1 Ex., 152: 4 H. & C., 189: 13 L. T., 753.)

1880. [409]
Fletcher v. *Hudson.* "Public Health Act, 1875," § 253, Sched. II. (1.), Rules 64, 70—Member disqualified by participation in profits of work done for Board—The Rule in question is an "express provision" of the Act within the Section in question, so that *any person* may sue for the penalty mentioned in Rule 70 without consent of the A.-G. [But see remarks of Brett, L.J.] (49 L. J., Ex., 793 : L. R., 5 Ex. D., 287: 43 L. T., 404: 45 J.P., 5.) Penalty held payable even though member had resigned. (51 L. J., Q. B D., 48: L. R., 7 Q. B. D., 611: 46 L. T., 125: 46 J. P., 372.)

1853. [410]
Foster v. *Oxford, Worcester, & Wolverhampton Railway Co.* "Companies Clauses Consolidation Act, 1845," §§ 85-6—A Contract with a Director is not void because he is interested therein, but he vacates his office. (22 L. J., C. P., 99: 13 C. B., 200: 20 L. T., (o. s.), 224.)

1861. [411]
Greenhow v. *Parker.* 55 Geo. III., c. 137, § 6 : "Poor Law Amendment Act, 1834," § 51—A Guardian supplying goods for a Workhouse is liable even although the Master gives the order in his own discretion without the authority of his Board. (31 L. J., Ex., 4: 6 H. & N., 882: [*Greenough* v. &c.] 4 L. T., 473.)

1883. [412]
Hunnings v. *Williamson.* "Metropolis Management Act, 1855," §§ 54, 60—Member interested in contract between Board and his brother by having lent his brother money and taken an assignment of the contract as security—Member held liable to penalty—Evidence of acting as member. (L. R., 11 Q. B. D., 533: 49 L. T., 361: 48 J. P., 132.)

1885. [413]
Lea v. *Facey.* Where Improvement Commissioners became the Urban Authority under the "Public Health Act, 1875," they acquired all the rights and privileges usually appertaining to Urban Authorities constituted directly under the Act—Defendant proceeded against for certain penalties held entitled to Notice of Action under § 264. (56 L. J., Q. B., 536: L. R., 19 Q. B. D., 352: 58 L. T., 32: 50 J. P., 295.)

1854. [414]
Le Feuvre v. *Lankester.* A contract with a Town Council acting as a Sanitary Authority, operates as a disqualification under the "Municipal Corporations Act"—But a Contractor may purchase of a member without by so doing causing that member to be disqualified. (23 L. J., Q. B., 254: 3 E. & B., 530: 2 C. L. R., 1426: 22 L. T., (o. s.), 87.)

1876. [415]
Lewis v. *Carr.* "Municipal Corporations Act, 1835," § 28—Goods bought over the counter at the shop of an Alderman, the order being given when the defendant was not present—Held that there was no continuing contract, and that he was not disqualified from being re-elected, and having been re-elected was not liable to the penalty. (46 L. J., Ex., 314: L. R., 1 Ex. D., 484: 36 L. T., 44: 40 J. P., 692.)

1862. [416]
Nicholson v. *Fields.* "Commissioners Clauses Act, 1847," § 9—Bills receipted by the defendant held to be evidence of his being concerned in a Contract with a Board—Defendant further held to be disqualified thereby, and liable to a penalty. (31 L. J., Ex., 233: 7 H. & N., 810.)

1889. [417]
Nutton v. *Wilson.* "Public Health Act, 1875," Sched. II. (1.), Rules 64, 70—Defendant, a member of a Local Board, employed by a man to whom the Board had given a contract—Held that Defendant was "interested" and therefore liable to the penalty. (58 L. J., Q. B., 443: L. R., 22 Q. B.D., 744: 53 J.P., 644.)

1880. [418]
Reg. v. *Gaskarth.* "Public Health Act, 1875," Sched. II., (1.), Rule 64—Annual Election of Local Board—One successful candidate the lessee of Board's sewage farm—Whereupon the Returning Officer refused to declare him duly elected—*Mandamus* granted to Returning Officer to do so—A lessee as aforesaid is not to be deemed interested in a contract with the Board, or the holder of a place of profit even though the lease contains covenants by Board to supply him with the sewage; on the contrary, he is within the exceptions specified in the Rule. (49 L. J., Q. B., 509 : L. R., 5 Q. B. D., 321 : 42 L. T., 688 : 44 J. P., 507.)

1837. [419]
Rex v. *St. Margaret's, Westminster, Paving Commissioners.* Commissioners accepting a tender put in by one of themselves—Held that the Contract arising was not of necessity void—*Mandamus* to advertise for new tenders refused. (1 Jur., 104.)

1885. [420]
Roberts v. *Priestley.* "Public Health Act, 1875," Sched. II. (1.), Rule 70—Defendant, member of a Local Board—Contract between Board and defendant's son—Action held, on the evidence, not maintainable. (At *Nisi Prius*.) (49 J. P., 328.)

1875.   [421]
Tanfield v. Reynolds. "Education Act, 1870," §§ 20 and 34—Member of a Board interested in a printing contract relating to the Board held rightly convicted, though the contract was not made with the Board but with the Mayor as statutory Returning Officer. (39 J. P., 293.)

1884.   [422]
Todd v. Robinson. "Public Health Act, 1875," § 193—Defendant, Clerk of Local Board and Director of Gas Company—Contract between Board and Company—Defendant held liable to penalty—Yet not a "convicted offender" within 22 Vict., c. 32, so that Treasury could remit penalty. (51 L. J., Q. B. D., 47: L. R., 14 Q. B. D., 739: 49 J. P., 278: *50 L. T., 298.)

1826.   [423]
Towery v. White. "General Turnpike Act, 1822," § 65—A Turnpike Trustee who let a horse and cart to a Contractor, held liable to a penalty as a person interested—Where a Notice of Action is required it must be given in strict form. (4 L. J., (o. s.), Q. B., 61: 5 B. & C., 125: 7 D. & R., 810.)

1822.   [424]
West v. Andrews. 55 Geo. III., c. 137, § 6—Master of a Workhouse purchasing goods from a Guardian—Guardian held liable to the penalty. (2 D. & R., 184: 1 B. & C., 77: 5 B. & Ald., 128.)

1887.   [425]
Whiteley v. Barley. (1.) "Public Health Act, 1875," § 193—In an action for penalty against an officer for being interested in a contract he cannot be compelled to produce documents which he swears by affidavit may incriminate him. (W. N., 1887, p. 212.)

1856.   [426]
Woolley v. Kay. Local Act—Disqualification by reason of interest in a Contract—Defendant contracted to sell Land to a Board of which he afterwards became a member, before the completion of the purchase—Held that he was not disqualified, for the Contract was not of a continuing character. (25 L. J., Ex., 351: 1 H. & N., 307: 27 L. T., (o. s.), 205.)

24. DANGEROUS STRUCTURES.

1875.   [427]
Cheetham v. Manchester, Mayor. Local Acts—Dangerous structure—Value of repairs executed at the instance of the Town Clerk recovered from the plaintiff—Action by plaintiff to recover back the amount, the building falling down in spite of the repairs—Judgment for the defendants, it being held that the Surveyor's certificate was conclusive—Notice as to a building held to be good for adjoining premises with which there was internal communication. (44 L. J., C. P., 249: L. R., 10 C. P., 249: 32 L. T., 28: 39 J. P., 343.)

1858.   [428]
Labalmondiere v. Addison. "Metropolitan Build-

ing Act, 1855," 18 & 19 Vict. c. 122, §§ 73, 97—Dangerous structure—Expenses chargeable on Owner—Time runs from the demand of re-payment and not from the completion of the works. (Metropolis.) (28 L. J., M. C., 25: 1 E. & E., 41: 23 J. P., 26.)

1859.   [429]
Labalmondiere v. Frost. "Metropolitan Building Act, 1855," 18 & 19 Vict. c. 122, § 73—Dangerous structure—What an Order for Removal ought to show on its face—When proceedings are taken to recover expenses due under an Order, the Justices to whom the application is made may consider whether the Order is valid. (Metropolis.) (28 L. J., M. C., 155: 1 E. & E., 527.)

1861.   [430]
Mourilyan v. Labalmondiere. "Owner"—"Lessee"—Expenses relating to a "dangerous structure" held to be recoverable from a lessee for 21 years. (Metropolis.) (30 L. J., M. C., 95: 1 E. & E., 533: [*Reg. v. Mourilyan*] 3 L. T., 668.)

25. DISQUALIFICATION.

*** See also "Contract, Disqualification from," (§ 23, *ante.*)

1834.   [431]
Charlesworth v. Rudgard. Local Act—Action for a penalty against a Commissioner alleged to be interested—Held that proof of the defendant speaking in favour of a footpath opposite his own house was evidence for a jury of *acting* as a Commissioner, although interested, and disqualified accordingly. (4 L. J., Ex., 89: 1 C. M. & R., 498: 4 Tyr., 824.)

1814.   [432]
Dumelow v. Lees. Local Act—Pecuniary qualification of a Commissioner—The words "above all charges and incumbrances" do not mean beyond payment of debts, but only apply to specific charges on the property in respect of which he claims his qualification—As regards the latter, the *onus probandi* lies upon the person impugning the candidate's qualification. (1 C. & K., 408.)

1877.   [433]
Goodhew v. Williams. Election of Vestryman—Qualification by rating—Candidate not rated, elected and acting—Subsequent offer to be rated and to pay Rates accepted by the Rate Collector—Held, that the candidate had been duly convicted of acting without a qualification—The decision of the Returning Officer held not to be conclusive. (Metrop.) (47 L. J., Q. B., 313: L. R., 3 C. P. D., 382: 37 L. T., 454: 42 J. P., 199.)

1878.   [434]
Reg. v. Turmine. "Education Act, 1870," § 12—Member becoming disqualified from neglecting to attend for 6 months—Resulting vacancy filled up—Same person elected again on another vacancy—*Quo Warranto* to question the validity of his re-election refused, it being clear that no perpetual disqualification

attached to a man disqualified once merely by efflux of time, but re-elected. (48 L. J., Q. B., 5 : L. R., 4 Q. B., 79 : 43 J. P., 6 : [*Re Turmine*] 39 L. T., 255.)

1853. [435]

Tupper v. *Newton*. Alleged disqualification of a member of a Board—Held that the defendant was not bound to prove that he had taken the oath, the oath not being part of the qualification. (14 C. B., 114 : 22 L. T., (O. S.), 103.)

26. DISTANCES, MEASUREMENT OF.

1856. [436]

Jewel v. *Stead*. A distance of "three miles" named in a Turnpike Act, means three miles in a straight line. (25 L. J., Q. B., 294 : 6 E. & B., 350 : 27 L. T., (O. S.), 101.)

1855. [437]

Lake v. *Butler*. A distance of "20 miles," named in an Act of Parliament, means 20 miles measured in a straight line. (24 L. J., Q. B., 273 : 5 E. & B., 92 : 3 C. L. R., 1124 : 25 L. T., (O. S.), 128.)

1872. [438]

Mouflet v. *Cole*. Trade covenant—"Half-a-mile" means half-a-mile in a straight line, measured from the point of nearest approach, in a straight line as on a map. (42 L. J., Ex., 8 : L. R., 8 Ex., 32 : 27 L. T., 678.)

1846. [439]

Reg. v. *Saffron Walden Inhabitants*. "Ten miles" in a Statute means ten miles measured in a straight line. (15 L. J., M. C., 115 : 9 Q. B., 76 : 2 New Sess. Cas., 360.)

1854. [440]

Stokes v. *Grissell*. A distance of "20 miles" named in an Act of Parliament, means 20 miles measured in a straight line. (23 L. J., C. P., 141 : 14 C. B., 678 : 2 C. L. R., 729 : 23 L. T., (O. S.), 114.)

27. DITCH.

1864. [441]

Felkin v. *Herbert (Lord)*. Suit by a Local Board for filling up a ditch and obstructing an ancient easement—Bill dismissed, the proper remedy being under the "Public Health Act, 1848," § 63. [Since repealed.] (11 L. T., 173.) [A contempt by a newspaper arising out of this matter is reported 33 L. J., Ch., 294 : 12 W. R., 241 and 332 : 10 Jur., (N. S.), 62.]

1873. [442]

Tutill v. *West Ham L. B.* Ditch adjoining a highway—Dispute as to Board's right to fill up the same—Judgment for the plaintiff, presumption being that the ditch was his. (L. R., 8 C. P., 447 : 28 L. T., 597 : 37 J. P., 455.)

28. DIVISION OF DISTRICTS.

18—. [443]

Farr v. *Boston*. "Public Health Act, 1848," § 89 [="Public Health Act, 1875," §§ 210-11] —Division of a District and Assessment on part thereof. (Glen, 205, 8th Ed.)

29. DRAINS.

1858. [444]

Austin v. *St. Mary's, Lambeth, Vestry*. "Metropolis Management Act, 1855," 18 & 19 Vict., c. 120, § 76—Drain pipes—Vestry entitled to prescribe pattern—Injunction to restrain removal by Vestry of pipes not according to pattern, refused. (Metropolis.) (27 L. J., Ch., 388 and 677 : 4 Jur., (N. S.), 274 and 1032 : 30 L. T., (O. S.), 300.)

1875-7. [445]

Baker v. *Wisbeach, Mayor*. Drain pipes laid through private land maliciously broken by the land-owner—Conviction for malicious injury affirmed—Such a mode of questioning the acts of a public Board held highly improper. (*Times*, Nov. 18, 1875.) Again before the High Court (Ch. Div.) on a motion for Injunction to restrain flow of sewage so as to be nuisance to a water-course—Injunction granted—No Notice of Action required. (W. N., 1877, p. 56.)

1874. [446]

Bolingbroke (Lord) v. *Swindon L. B.* Sewage Farm—Trespass by Manager on plaintiff's land to pare away edges of a ditch between the two properties—Master and Servant— Verdict for the defendants held good, it not being within the scope of the manager's employment, and therefore there being no implied authority to him to commit a trespass. (43 L. J., C. P., 287 : 30 L. T., 723.)

1879. [447]

Bowes v. *Watson*. "Land Drainage Act, 1847," 10 & 11 Vict. c. 38, §§ 14-5—The words "drain, stream, or water-course," include an underground drain, and are not necessarily limited to an open drain. (42 L. T., 27 : 44 J. P., 364.)

1856. [448]

Cawkwell v. *Russell*. Obstruction of a Drain— Plea, limited right of use only, whereas the plaintiff had sought to assert an absolute right. (26 L. J., Ex., 34.)

1844. [449]

Coulton v. *Ambler*. "Public or Parish Drain"— Navigable river or cut held not to be a "drain." (14 L. J., Ex., 10 : 13 M. & W., 403 : 3 Rail. Cas., 724, n.)

1861. [450]

Ewart v. *Cochrane*. Adjacent properties held by one owner drained by one drain—On severance a grant of an easement as to the drain held to go with the Conveyance of the property though not actually named. (4 Macq., H. L. Cas., 117 : 5 L. T., 1 : 10 W. R., 3.)

1875. [451]

Finlinson v. *Porter*. "Public Health Act, 1848," § 49 : [="Public Health Act, 1875," §§ 23, 25] : "Local Government Act, 1858," § 34, [=Ibid. §§ 157, 159]—Conveyance of rights as to a drain—Drain altered by defendants on the demand of the Local Board—Action of Trespass—Judgment for the defendants, the conveyance operating to give them an interest in the drain which they had not alterd in any material manner. (44 L. J., Q. B., 56: L. R., 10 Q. B., 188: 32 L. T., 391: 39 J. P., 661.)

1877. [452]
Humphries v. *Cousins.* Easement—Drain—Injury to plaintiff's goods by overflow of sewage from defendant's premises—Held that the plaintiff was entitled to recover, although the defendant was only tenant, and did not know that some part of the drain passed under the plaintiff's premises, and was out of repair. (46 L. J., C. P., 438: L. R., 2 C. P. D., 239: 41 J. P., 280.)

1857. [453]
Pyer v. *Carter.* Rights of the owners of 2 adjacent houses to a Drain common to each—Easement. (26 L. J., Ex., 258: 1 H. & N. 916: 28 L. T., (o. s.), 371.) [Not accepted as of authority by Westbury, C., in *Suffield* v. *Brown*, (33 L. J., Ch., 249.) But Lord Westbury's views dissented from by James and Mellish, L.JJ. in *Watts* v. *Kelson*, (40 L. J., Ch., 126.) "*Pyer* v. *Carter* is good sense and good law."]

1842. [454]
Russell v. *Shenton.* Nuisance—The cleansing and repair of drains is *primâ facie* the duty of the occupier and does not devolve on the owner merely as such. (11 L. J., Q. B., 269: 3 Q. B., 449: 2 G. & D., 573.)

1882. [455]
Stannard v. *St. Giles, Camberwell, Vestry.* Dispute as to drain interfered with by plaintiff—Proceedings before Justices—Injunction to restrain such proceedings refused, no intention to commit a trespass being shown. (51 L. J., Ch., 629: L. R., 20 Ch. D., 190: 46 L. T., 243.)

30. ELECTION BUSINESS.

1875. [456]
Aberdare L. B. H. v. *Hammett.* Filling up of a voting-paper by voter's wife with his authority—Held that this was not "fabricating" a voting-paper, and therefore that no offence had been committed. (44 L. J., M. C., 49: L. R., 10 Q. B., 162: 32 L. T., 20: 39 J. P., 598.)

1789. [457]
Anthony v. *Seger.* Parochial Election—Show of hands—Poll—One candidate elected, afterwards declared disqualified—Effect of this decision on the other candidates. (1 Hagg., C. C. C., 13.)

1879. [458]
Bell v. *Morson.* Filling up voting-paper without Voter's authority—Held that though there might have been evidence to convict of fabricating the voting-paper, the Appellant was wrongly convicted of assuming to act, as it was not proved that the voter did not afterwards agree to what had been done. (40 L. T., 128: 43 J. P., 638.)

1867. [459]
Bennett v. *Brumfitt.* The use by a person of a *fac-simile* stamp of his signature in place of

affixing his signature with a pen held good. (37 L. J., C. P., 25: L. R., 3 C. P., 28: 17 L. T., 213.)

1888. [460]
Bowden v. *Besly.* Municipal Election—Nomination paper—A Burgess's ordinary signature suffices provided the initials signed tally with the initials of the Christian names printed in full on the Roll. (L. R., 21 Q. B. D., 309: 59 L. T., 219.)

1862. [461]
Buckmaster v. *Reynolds.* "Metropolis Management Act, 1855," § 21—Riotous conduct in a room where a poll is being taken is within the words "by a contrivance attempting to obstruct." (13 C. B., (N. s.), 62.)

1836. [462]
Campbell v. *Maund.* Parochial Election—The Common Law right to demand a poll can only be abrogated by express Law or custom. (6 L. J., M. C., 145; 5 A. & E., 865: 1 N. & P., 558: 2 H. & W., 457.)

1872. [463]
Davies v. *Stone.* Election of Guardians—Filling up a marksman's paper otherwise than according to his wishes—Conviction for "Fabrication" held good. (36 J. P., 390.)

1861. [464]
Easton v. *Alce.* Local Act—Qualification depending on being "rated by one or more Rate or Rates" to a specified minimum amount, held to refer to the annual rateable value, and not to the money payable annually. (31 L. J., Ex., 115: 7 H. & N., 452: 5 L. T., 323.)

1874. [465]
Fox v. *Dally.* 30 & 31 Vict. c. 132, § 3—A Militia Sergeant held to occupy not as "tenant"—Vote disallowed. (44 L. J., C. P., 42: L. R., 10 C. P., 285: 31 L. T., 478.)

1889. [466]
Gledhill v. *Crowther.* "Local Government Act, 1888:" "Municipal Corporations Act, 1882," Sched. III., part ii.—The signature "James Sykes, jun." held good although voter only registered as "James Sykes." (58 L. J., Q. B., 327: L. R., 23 Q. B. D., 136: 60 L. T., 866: 53 J. P., 677.)

1892. [467]
Gordon v. *Williamson.* "Metropolis Management Act, 1855," § 6: 19 & 20 Vict., c. 112, § 8—Qualification of £40 Rating prescribed—A person occupying property rated at £125 sublet a portion, retaining a portion clearly worth more than £40, but no separate rating—Held qualified. (L. R., 2 Q. B., 459: 56 J. P., 456.)

1889. [468]
Harding v. *Cornwell.* Municipal Election—A nomination paper signed with the correct name of an assenting Burgess held good, though it did not tally with the name entered on the Burgess Roll, the latter having been erroneously printed. (60 L. T., 959.)

1883. [469]
Henry v. *Armitage.* "Municipal Elections Act, 1875," § 1, (2)—Nomination paper in which

" William " was represented by " Wm." held good. (53 L. J., Q. B. D., 111: L. R., 12 Q. B. D., 257 : 48 J. P., 424.)

1876. [470]
Howes v. Turner. "Municipal Elections Act, 1875," 38 & 39 Vict., c. 40—A contraction in signing a nomination paper, thus " Fred^k " for " Frederick " held not to invalidate the paper. (45 L. J., C. P., 550: L. R., 1 C. P. D., 670 : 35 L. T., 58.)

1856. [471]
Howitt v. Manfull. "Public Health Act, 1848 " —Local Board—Three members were disqualified by non-attendance, and the Board decided that they should be the members to retire by rotation—Held that a Rate subsequently made by the Board re-constituted was good. (25 L. J., Q. B., 411 : 6 E. & B., 736 : 27 L. T., (o. s.), 183.)

1872. [472]
Jones, In re. School Board Election—The Returning Officer a Solicitor—Bill of Costs, which included business connected with both Election and Meeting of the Board, sent in by him in the form of a Solicitor's Bill— Held that as he had by the form of his account treated himself as Solicitor of the Board the Bill was liable to taxation. (41 L. J., Ch., 367 : L. R., 13 Eq., 336 : 20 W. R., 395.)

1887. [473]
Knighton Election Petition: Gough v. Murdoch. "Public Health Act, 1875," Sched. II. (1.), Rule 69—For a candidate to insert in the margin of a voting-paper a voter's initials on behalf of himself in the presence of the Voter is no offence. (57 L. T., 308 : 51 J. P., 471.)

1862. [474]
Lambe v. Grieves. Vestry—In calculating the votes to which a voter is entitled his assessments must be taken in the aggregate and not singly. (8 Jur., (N. S.), 288.)

1876. [475]
Mather v. Brown. "Municipal Corporations Act, 1835," § 142 : "Municipal Elections Act, 1875"—Held that in signing a name, where a Christian name is required to be mentioned, the initial thereof is not sufficient. (45 L. J., C. P., 547: L. R., 1 C. P. D., 596: 34 L. T., 869 : 40 J. P., 616.)

1856. [476]
Metcalfe, Ex parte. "Public Health Act, 1848," § 30 [="Public Health Act, 1875," Sched. II., (1), 67]—A Local Board has an absolute discretion as to the remuneration to be paid to a Returning Officer. (6 E. & B., 287 : 27 L. T., (o. s.), 78.)

1885. [477]
Mogg v. Clarke. "Poor Rate Assessment Act, 1869," § 3—Qualification by rating—Action for penalties. (Metrop.) (55 L. J., Q. B., 69 : L. R., 16 Q. B. D., 79: 53 L. T., 890 : 50 J. P., 342.)

1885. [478]
Moorhouse v. Linney. " Municipal Corporations Act, 1882," § 241—Nomination paper signed by burgess with his correct Christian names, though one Christian name was omitted from Burgess Roll—Paper held void for uncertainty. (L. R., 15 Q. B. D., 273: 53 L. T., 313 : 49 J. P., 471.)

1885. [479]
Newhaven L. B. v. Newhaven School Board. Lapse of Local Board—Powers of minority of members to fill up vacancies—General powers of Board so reconstituted. (L. R., 30 Ch. D., 350: 53 L. T., 571.)

1887. [480]
Pritchard v. Bangor, Mayor. The Returning Officer at a Municipal Election has no power to decide whether a candidate is eligible— His duty is to count the votes and pronounce on their validity—The eligibility of a candidate must be questioned by Petition and in no other way. (57 L. J., Q. B., 313 : L. R., 13 App. Cas., 241: 58 L. T., 502 : 52 J. P., 564.)

1852. [481]
Reg. v. Avery. "Municipal Corporations Act, 1835," § 32—A Voting-paper signed with the Voter's usual signature is good : e.g. Initials and Surname. (21 L. J., Q. B., 428; 18 Q. B., 576: 19 L. T., (o. s.), 161.)

1866. [482]
Reg. v. Backhouse. An Election of a Local Board conducted in the usual manner, save that the Chairman was absent and no deputy was appointed, is void, and his certificate of the result a nullity. (36 L. J., Q. B., 7 : L. R., 2 Q. B., 16 : 7 B. & S., 911 : 15 L. T., 240.)

1858. [483]
Reg. v. Beckwith. Election of Guardians—Forgery of Voting-papers—Practice at Trial as to reply by Counsel. (7 Cox, C. C., 505.)

1866. [484]
Reg. v. Blanshard. "Public Health Act, 1848," §§ 28 [="Public Health Act, 1875," Sched. II., (1), 68 ; §§ 253-4 and 133]—Local Board Election—Prosecution of a Returning Officer by a member of a Board, but without the consent of the A.-G. or Local Board—Held that the Justices had no jurisdiction to convict. (30 J. P., 280.)

1866. [485]
Reg. v. Blizard. Municipal Corporation—*Quo Warranto*—Where a successful candidate is not qualified, he cannot by resigning his seat deprive of his rights an opponent who claims his seat. (36 L. J., Q. B., 18 : L. R., 2 Q. B., 55 : 7 B. & S., 922 : 15 L. T., 242.) [See *Reg. v. Tewkesbury, Mayor.*]

1861. [486]
Reg. v. Bradley. "Municipal Corporations Act, 1835," § 14—A contraction of a Christian name which is well known and in ordinary use may be employed in a Voting-paper. (30 L. J., Q. B., 180 : 3 E. & E., 634 : 3 L. T., 853.)

1864. [487]
Reg. v. Briggs. Local Act—*Quo Warranto* against a Commissioner—Interest of Relator—An owner of rateable property held qualified to be a Relator—Promise by agent of candidate

to pay the Rates of ratepayers in arrear does not render their votes good if Act requires actual pre-payment. (11 L. T., 372 : 29 J. P., 423.)

1880. [488]
Reg. v. *Clerk of Bury Guardians.* 7 & 8 Vict. c. 101, § 15—A Clerk of Guardians sitting to revise a list of voters is not entitled to insist on a claimant appearing in person if he sends a suitable representative or agent. (44 J. P., 216.)

1876. [489]
Reg. v. *Collins.* Local Board Election—Error in casting up votes discovered some time after the declaration of the Poll—*Quo Warranto*— A Chairman's certificate is not conclusive as to mere mechanical errors of casting up, but it is conclusive as regards the validity of votes —Bad votes not rejected at the proper time cannot afterwards be questioned. (46 L. J., Q. B., 257 : L. R., 2 Q. B. D., 30 : 36 L. T., 192.)

1886. [490]
Reg. v. *Cooban.* "Public Health Act, 1875," Sched. II. (1.), Rules 5, 65—What constitutes a "composition" with creditors—"Six weeks" is to be computed from the day when the retiring member goes out of office, and not from the day on which an election to fill his place is held. (56 L. J., M. C., 33 : L. R., 18 Q. B. D., 269 : 51 J. P., 500.)

1851. [491]
Reg. v. *Coward.* "Municipal Corporations Act, 1835," § 142—A Candidate long resident in one street and well known, moved to a new address a few days before an election—Old address given in the Voting-papers—Held a fatal variance and Candidate not duly elected —*Quo Warranto* issued. (20 L. J., Q. B., 359 : 16 Q. B., 819 : 17 L. T., (o. s.), 71.)

1852. [492]
Reg. v. *Cross.* "Public Health Act, 1848"— A Returning Officer exercises judicial functions; his certificate is, therefore, conclusive and cannot be questioned under a *Quo Warranto*—The defendant may be a witness on his own behalf. (19 L. T., (o. s.), 35 : 16 J. P. 215.) [See *Reg.* v. *Collins.*]

1844. [493]
Reg. v. *Deighton.* Municipal Corporations Act, 1835"—*Quo Warranto*—Election of Alderman—To describe a Candidate as of a place where he daily transacts business, instead of giving his residence, is a misdescription sufficient to avoid his election. (13 L. J., Q. B., 241 : D. & M., 682 : 5 Q. B., 896.)

1858. [494]
Reg. v. *Eddows.* Local Act—Qualification by Rating—Candidate rateable but not rated, held ineligible. (28 L. J., Q. B., 84 : 1 E. & E., 330.)

1880. [495]
Reg. v. *Ellis*(1). Local Board Election—Candidate elected who was not qualified because not rated passed over by Returning Officer who returned candidate who was in minority—

Rule for *Quo Warranto* against minority candidate discharged; and Returning Officer exonerated. (44 J. P., 748.)

1872. [496]
Reg. v. *Franklin.* A contractor held disqualified from being elected member of a Corporation, even though he had, before the election (but without the privity of the Corporation), purported to assign his contract to a third person —A vote given for a disqualified person is not a mere nullity unless the voter had notice of the disqualification; and therefore if a disqualified candidate has a majority of votes a defeated candidate cannot claim the seat by means of a scrutiny. (6 L. R., Ir., 239.)

1864. [497]
Reg. v. *Hague.* "Municipal Corporations Act, 1859," § 9—The offence of personation is complete when a person not the voter hands in a nomination-paper to the officer—The conviction need not show that the election was duly held. (33 L. J., M. C., 81 : 4 B. & S., 715 : 9 Cox, C. C., 412 : 9 L. T., 648.)

1852. [498]
Reg. v. *Hammond.* "Municipal Corporations Act, 1835," § 32—Voting-papers—A Candidate's place of business, if he does not reside there, is not his "place of abode"—*Quo Warranto*—Election void. (21 L. J., Q. B., 153 : 17 Q. B., 772 : 19 L. T., (o. s.), 21.)

1873. [499]
Reg. v. *Harrald.* "Municipal Corporations Act, 1835," § 44—*Quo Warranto*—If a Voter votes in two wards, his first vote is to stand and the second is a nullity. (42 L. J., Q. B., 211 : L. R., 8 Q. B., 418 : 28 L. T., 767 : 38 J. P., 40.)

1853. [500]
Reg. v. *Hartshorn.* "Public Health Act, 1848," § 25 [="Public Health Act, 1875," Sched. II., (1), 45]—Held that to fill up Voting-papers on behalf of marksmen, with their consent, but without obtaining their marks and attesting the same, is not forgery at Common Law—*Quære,* Is this an indictable misdemeanour? (6 Cox, C. C., 395.)

1877. [501]
Reg. v. *Hazley.* "Commissioners Clauses Act, 1847," § 19—Casual vacancy in a Board filled up by names being written on slips of paper thrown into a hat and then counted— The papers destroyed, and no scrutiny possible—The Court intimated an opinion that such a mode of election was invalid, but no formal order made, the parties consenting to a new election. (11 L. R., Ir., 360 : 26 W. R. Digest, 242.)

1838. [502]
Reg. v. *Hiorns.* "Municipal Corporations Act, 1835"—*Semble* that where an unqualified person is a candidate, notice of disqualification must be given at the time of election, or votes recorded for such candidate cannot be deemed thrown away. (7 A. & E., 960 : 3 N. & P., 148.)

1868. [503]
Reg. v. *Ireland.* "Municipal Corporations Act, 1835," § 9 (1)—*Quo Warranto*—Parochial relief to a father is not relief to a son, so as to disqualify the latter. (37 L. J., Q. B., 73 : L. R., 3 Q. B., 130 : 9 B. & S., 19 : 17 L. T., 466.)

1861. [504]
Reg. v. *Kirby.* "Vestries Act, 1818," § 3—Right to vote as Executor—Claim held good—Held also that it was immaterial that the claimant was not entered by name as an Executor ; and that the testator's property was available for adding to the executor's private property so as to confer additional votes. (31 L. J., Q. B., 3 : 1 B. & S., 647 : 5 L. T., 280.)

1866. [505]
Reg. v. *Lofthouse.* "Public Health Act, 1848," § 24 [="Public Health Act, 1875," Sched. II. (1), 43]—A Voting-paper issued without the number of Votes allotted being stated thereupon is not on that account invalid—A relator who has acquiesced in the mode of voting to which he afterwards objects is disqualified from applying for a *Quo Warranto.* (35 L. J., Q. B., 145 : L. R., 1 Q. B., 433 : 7 B. & S., 447 : [*Reg.* v. *Lockhouse*] 14 L. T., 359.)

1871. [506]
Reg. v. *Morgan.* "Public Health Act, 1848," § 24 [="Public Health Act, 1875," Sched. II. (1), 40]—A Voting-paper need not state any qualification for the Nominator—*Quo Warranto*—Relator held not entitled to costs, the office of member of Local Board not being within 9 Anne, c. 20. (41 L. J., Q. B., 55 : L. R., 7 Q. B., 26 : 25 L. T., 950 : 37 J. P., 105 : [Question of Costs] 26 L. T., 790.)

1859. [507]
Reg. v. *Owens.* "Municipal Corporations Act, 1835," § 25, &c.—A Mayor, if a Returning Officer, cannot be a Candidate. (28 L. J., Q. B., 316 : 2 E. & E., 86 : 33 L. T., (o. s.), 257.)

1867. [508]
Reg. v. *Parkinson.* Municipal Corporation—Ward Election—A Nominator must be entitled to vote in the Ward for which he nominates, or a nomination by him will be invalid. (37 L. J., Q. B., 52 : L. R., 3 Q. B., 11 : 8 B. & S., 769 : 17 L. T., 169.)

1869. [509]
Reg. v. *Plenty.* "Municipal Corporations Act, 1835," § 32—*Quo Warranto*—A Voting-paper naming the Candidates only by their Initials and Surnames is good. (38 L. J., Q. B., 205 : L. R., 4 Q. B., 346 : 9 B. & S, 386 : 20 L. T., 521.)

1876. [510]
*Reg. v. *Rippon.* "Public Health Act, 1848," § 23 [="Public Health Act, 1875," Sched. II., (1), 36, 66]—Ordinary vacancies and a casual vacancy filled up at one election, no notice being given as to a distinction—Election held to be void. (45 L. J., Q. B., 188 : L. R., 1 Q. B. D., 217 : 34 L. T., 444 : 40

J. P., 536.) [Effect of decision met by "Public Health Act, 1875," Sched. II. (1), 65.]

1890. [511]
Reg. v. *Soutter.* "Metropolis Management Act, 1855," § 6—*Quo Warranto*—A person is not qualified under this Section unless he occupies the premises in respect of which he is rated—*Mogg* v. *Clark* followed : *Rex* v. *St. Pancras* distinguished. (60 L. J., Q. B., 71 : L. R., 1 Q. B., 57 : 64 L. T., 40 : 55 J. P., 229.)

1857. [512]
Reg. v. *St. Pancras Inspectors of Votes.* Parochial Election—A Returning Officer is not to return an unqualified Candidate even though he have a majority of votes. (7 E. & B., 951 : [*Ross, Ex parte*] 26 L. J., Q. B., 312 : 29 L. T., (o. s.), 197.)

1872. [513]
Reg. v. *Strachan.* Municipal Election—Stamp Act—Held that a Voting-paper used at an election of Alderman does not require a stamp. (41 L. J., Q. B., 210 : L. R., 7 Q. B., 463 : 26 L. T., 835.)

1859. [514]
Reg. v. *Tart.* "Municipal Corporations Act, 1835," § 32—A Voting-paper must be properly signed, so as to connect the Voter's address with his name. (28 L. J., Q. B., 173 : 1 E. & E., 618 : 32 L. T., (o. s.), 314.)

1868. [515]
Reg. v. *Tewkesbury, Mayor.* "Municipal Corporations Act, 1835," § 35—Though the vote of an elector knowingly and wilfully voting for a disqualified candidate is lost, yet knowledge of facts that constitute a legal disqualification is not necessarily knowledge that the candidate is legally disqualified, so as to give the candidate next on the poll a "majority of good votes." (37 L. J., Q. B., 288 : L. R., 3 Q. B., 629 : 9 B. & S., 683 : 18 L. T., 851.)

1853. [516]
Reg. v. *Thwaites.* "Municipal Corporations Act, 1835," § 142—A voter named *Joseph* O. was entered on the Burgess Roll as *James* O. and therefore signed his name as *James* O. though it was not correct—Vote held good—*Semble* that the vote would also have been good had he signed as *Joseph* O., the misnomer being capable of rectification under the Statute. (22 L. J., Q. B., 238 : 1 E. & B., 704 : 21 L. T., (o. s.), 72.)

1874. [517]
Reg. v. *Tong Street L. B.* Neglect to hold the customary annual election — *Mandamus* granted to compel the Board to do so six months after the proper time. (38 J. P., 756.)

1868. [518]
Reg. v. *Tugwell.* "Municipal Corporations Act, 1835"—*Quo Warranto*—Defective Voting-paper—A Burgess rated in two wards may vote in either without selecting one in which to be enrolled. (37 L. J., Q. B., 275 : L. R., 3 Q. B., 704 : see also 38 L. J., Q. B., 12 : 9 B. & S., 367.)

D

1873. [519]
Reg. v. Ward. (1) " Public Health Act, 1848," § 21 [=" Public Health Act, 1875," Sched. II., (1), 32]—Local Board Election—When the Chairman is a Candidate, he ought to take no part in the conduct of an election even during the preliminary stages—But a *Quo Warranto* refused under the particular circumstances. (42 L. J., Q. B., 126: L. R., 8 Q. B., 210: 28 L. T., 118: 37 J. P., 453.)

1867. [520]
Reg. v. White. (3) "Municipal Corporations Act, 1835," § 36—*Quo Warranto*—Delegation by Mayor of his duties as Returning Officer when he is a candidate, valid. (36 L. J., Q. B., 267: L. R., 2 Q. B., 557: 8 B. & S., 587: 16 L. T., 828.)

1885. [521]
Reg. v. Wigan, Mayor. "Municipal Corporations Act, 1882," § 36—A Town Councillor wrote a letter resigning his office—Held that the letter was final, and that writer could not withdraw it even with the concurrence of the Council. (54 L. J., Q. B., 338: L. R., 14 Q. B. D., 908: 52 L. T., 435: 49 J. P., 372.)

1836. [522]
Rex v. Arnold. "Municipal Corporations Act, 1835," § 35—Inspection of Voting-papers—Extent of the discretion vested in Town Clerk to restrict applicants in their operations —He may make such regulations to control applicants as may be necessary to obviate confusion and delays. (5 L. J., M. C., 54: 4 A. & E., 657: 6 N. & M., 152.) [Obsolete: *See* now " Ballot Act, 1872."]

1829. [523]
Rex v. London, Mayor. Change of Returning Officer during an election—Successor can complete predecessor's unfinished work. (9 B. & C., 1.)

1855. [524]
Robinson, Ex parte. " Public Health Act, 1848 " —Alleged void Election—Rule *Nisi* for *Quo Warranto.* (19 J. P., 724.) [Rule absolute: 26 L. T., (o. s.), 105, *nom., Reg. v. Robinson*: but this Report useless.]

1877. [525]
Soper v. Basingstoke, Mayor. "Municipal Elections Act, 1875 "—Address of a nominator—Name of street lately changed—Old name on nomination paper; new name on Burgess Roll — Nomination paper held improperly rejected. (46 L. J., C. P., 422: L. R., 2 C. P. D., 440: 36 L. T., 468: 41 J. P., 535.)

1868. [526]
Summerhill v. Coley. " Public Health Act, 1848 " — Attestation of Voting-papers — Voting-papers held valid. (32 J. P., 821.)

1857. [527]
Tozer v. Child. An Action does not lie against a Returning Officer for rejecting a vote unless it be proved that the vote was maliciously rejected. (26 L. J., Q. B., 151: 7 E. & B., 377: 28 L. T., (o. s.), 309.)

1872. [528]
Turner, Ex parte. Local Board Election—Accidental neglect to add up votes on the proper day—Held that it might be done on a subsequent day. (36 J. P., 744.)

1891. [529]
Unwin v. McMullen. "Municipal Corporations Act, 1882," §§ 9, 11—Joint occupation—Qualification of councillor. (L. R., 1 Q. B., 694: 56 J. P., 582.)

1854. [530]
Westbury-on-Severn Union, In re. Election of Guardians—Delivery of a Nomination Paper on a Sunday treated as a delivery on the day following. (4 E. & B., 914: 18 J. P., 758: [*Reg. v. Poor Law Commissioners*] 1 Jur., (N. s.), 251: 24 L. T., (o. s.), 156.)

1868. [531]
Whitely v. Chappell. 14 & 15 Vict., c. 105, § 3— Voting at an Election of Guardians in the name of a deceased Voter is not personating anyone "entitled to vote." (38 L. J., M. C., 51: L. R., 4 Q. B., 147: 9 B. & S, 1019: 19 L. T., 355: 33 J. P., 244.)

31. ESTIMATE.

1857. [532]
Cunningham v. Wolverhampton L. B. H. " Public Health Act, 1848," §§ 85 and 69 [=" Public Health Act, 1875," §§ 173-4; § 150]—Execution of Works—Estimate and Report from Surveyor are only requisite when a Local Board will have hereafter to maintain works which it may execute. (26 L. J., M. C., 33: 7 E. & B., 107: as to Costs, 28 L. T., (o. s.), 252.)

32. FENCES.

1850. [533]
Barnes v. Ward. Occupier bound to fence an excavation near a public way; on default and an accident happening, "Lord Campbell's Act" (9 & 10 Vict. c. 93) is applicable. (19 L. J., C. P., 194: 2 C. & K., 661: 9 C. B., 392.)

1855. [534]
Cornwell v. Metropolitan Commissioners of Sewers. An ancient tidal sewer running along a highway—Held that the right to the highway was subject to the sewer, and the owner of the sewer was not bound to fence. (10 Ex., 771: 3 C. L. R., 417: 19 J. P., 313.)

1878. [535]
Firth v. Bowling Iron Co. Iron fence which defendants were bound to maintain, allowed to become defective and decayed—Fragment thereof eaten by plaintiff's cow, which died —Action held maintainable—The defendants were acquainted with the bad condition of their fence. (47 L. J., C. P., 358: L. R., 3 C. P. D., 254: 38 L. T., 568: 42 J. P., 470.)

1868. [536]
Wilson v. Halifax, Mayor. "Towns Improvement Clauses Act, 1847," § 83: "Public Health Act, 1848," §§ 68 and 139 [=" Public Health

Act, 1875," §§ 149, 264]—An ancient open water-course alongside a public foot-path is not a "hole or other place near a street" which a Local Board is bound to fence—Duty as to erection of posts or rails—The alleged cause of Action being the continued non-performance of a duty imposed by the "Public Health Act, 1848," and therefore a thing "done or intended to be done" under the Act, the defendants were entitled to Notice of Action. (37 L. J., Ex., 44 : L. R., 3 Ex., 111 : 17 L. T., 660.)

33. FIRE-ENGINE.

1873.   [537]
Drighlington L. B. H. v. *Bower.* "Towns Police Clauses Act, 1847," § 32—Claim for use of Fire-Engine within the District—Held that a Local Board could not recover more than the amount paid out of pocket for hire of men—The power to charge for extinguishing fires outside a District impliedly negatives the right to charge within it. (W. N., 1873, p. 220: 22 W. R., 165: 38 J. P., 73.)

1881.   [538]
Joyce v. *Metropolitan B. W.* A Fire Brigade in the exercise of its duty took possession of the plaintiff's premises and consumed wine and other goods—Held that the Board was liable to make good the damage done by its servants. (44 L. T., 811 : 45 J. P., 667.)

1875.   [539]
Lewis v. *Arnold.* "Towns Police Clauses Act, 1847," § 33 — Expenses of Fire-Engine attending a hay-stack on fire—Held that the owner of the stack, being the occupier of the land, was to be deemed for the purpose of the Act, "the owner of the land."—A hay-stack is not a "building." (44 L. J., M. C., 69 : L. R., 10 Q. B., 245 : 32 L. T., 553 : 39 J. P., 519.)

34. FOOD, UNWHOLESOME.

1891.   [540]
Barlow v. *Terrett.* "Public Health Act, 1875," §§ 116-17—An owner of meat who knowing it to be unsound sends it to a salesman cannot be convicted as being the owner of unsound meat unless such meat has been actually "sold or exposed for sale." (65 L. T., 148 : 55 J. P., 632.)

1847.   [541]
Burnby v. *Bollitt.* A public dealer is criminally liable for selling unwholesome food : not so a private person selling. (17 L. J., Ex., 190 : 16 M. & W., 644.)

1886.   [542]
Barton v. *Bradley.* "Public Health Act, 1875," §§ 116-17—In seeking for a Justice to condemn unsound meat, reasonable diligence must be used, but it need not necessarily be on the same day as the seizure. (51 J. P., 118.)

1870.   [543]
Daly v. *Webb.* "Nuisances Removal Act, 1863," § 2 [="Public Health Act, 1875," §§ 116-7] —A cart conveying diseased meat is "a place"—Meat so being conveyed to a Food Factory is being "exposed for sale." (4 I. R., Ir., 309 : [*Webb* v. *Daly*] 18 W. R., 631.)

1862.   [544]
Emmerton v. *Matthews.* The sale of meat in a market does not imply a warranty that it is sound and fit for human food—A purchaser has no remedy against a vendor in the absence of fraud. (31 L. J., Ex., 139 : 5 L. T., 681.)

1862.   [545]
Hartley, In re. "Public Health Act, 1848," § 63 [="Public Health Act, 1875," §§ 116-7]—Unwholesome meat—The Court has no discretion to refuse a Rule to issue distress warrants if the proceedings are regular. 31 L. J., M. C., 232 : [*Reg.* v. *Hartley, In re Over Darwen*] 26 J. P., 438.]

1890.   [546]
Mullinson v. *Carr.* "Public Health Act, 1875," § 116—A person in possession of unsound meat intended for human food may be convicted although he has not exposed the meat for sale. (60 L. J., M. C., 34 : L. R., 1 Q. B., 48 : 63 L. T., 459 : 55 J. P., 102.)

1880.   [547]
Moody v. *Leach.* "Public Health Act, 1875," §§ 116-7, 119—These sections include live animals — But in the particular case the evidence was held sufficient to show that a live cow found in a building adjacent to a slaughter-house was not placed there intended to be killed for food. (At Q. Sess.) (44 J. P., 459.)

1888.   [548]
Newton v. *Monkcom.* "Public Health Act, 1875," § 117—An under-bailiff held not the "owner" of certain diseased meat—Conviction quashed. (58 L. T., 231 : 52 J. P., 692.)

1879.   [549]
Reg. v. *Blount.* "Public Health Act, 1875," §§ 116-7—Summons against a butcher for exposing unsound meat for sale—Summons dismissed on proof that defendant did not know the meat had been brought upon his premises—Whereupon second summons for the offence of having the meat on his premises—Conviction—Conviction quashed as irregular, the offence charged under each summons being substantially the same. (43 J. P., 383.)

1862.   [550]
Reg. v. *Crawley.* A person is not indictable for sending unwholesome meat to market if he does not intend it to be sold for human food, nor send it for that purpose. (3 F. & F., 109.)

1862.   [551]
Reg. v. *Jarvis.* A carrier can be indicted and convicted at Common Law for knowingly taking to market meat unfit for human food. (3 F. & F., 108.)

D 2

1862.   [552]
Reg. v. *Stephenson.* A meat salesman can bo
indicted and convicted at Common Law for
knowingly sending or exposing meat for sale
in a public market as fit for human food
which was not so. (3 F. & F., 106.)

1875.   [553]
Shillito v. *Thompson.* By-Law under "Municipal
Corporations Act, 1835," § 90—Exposure for
sale of putrid cheese is a nuisance at Common
Law—By-Law held good, and therefore conviction affirmed. (45 L. J., M. C., 18 : L. R.,
1 Q. B. D., 12 : 33 L. T., 506 : 40 J. P., 535.)

1878.   [554]
Smith v. *Baker.* In a sale of butcher's meat in a
market there is no warranty, and therefore if
meat proves to be unsound a purchaser has
no remedy where there is no fraud—*Caveat
Emptor.* (*Times,* Dec. 20, 1878.)

1882.   [555]
Vinter v. *Hind.* "Public Health Act, 1875,"
§§ 116-7—These sections only apply where a
seizure and condemnation has taken place
on intending vendor's premises—A person
only becomes liable to penalty under § 117,
when the formalities of § 116 have been
complied with. (52 L. J., M. C., 93 : L. R.,
10 Q. B. D., 63 : 48 L. T., 359 : 47 J. P.,373.)

1885.   [556]
Waye v. *Thompson.* "Public Health Act, 1875,"
§ 117—Where meat alleged to be unwholesome has been condemned *ex parte* by a
Justice, the owner if prosecuted is entitled
to be heard and to give evidence in contra-
diction. (54 L. J., M. C., 140 : L. R., 15
Q. B. D., 342 : 53 L. T., 358 : 49 J. P., 693.)

1882.   [557]
Williams v. *Narberth S. A.* Meat sold in July
condemned by Medical Officer but not till
next day, and after it had been sent home—
Conviction quashed—The "Public Health
Act, 1875," §§ 116-7, only authorises seizure
when food is exposed for sale, and a Conviction when it is found at once to be unsound.
(*Times,* Dec. 7, 1882.)

35. FOOTPATH.

*** See also "Obstruction of Highways,"
              (Part II., § 6, *post.*)
1879.   [558]
Reg. v. *Wigan JJ.* Conviction by Justices of a
householder for obstructing a footway by
furniture—Allegation that no part of the
public footway was obstructed ; merely an
open forecourt—Conviction quashed by *Certiorari.* (43 J. P., 220.)

36. GAS COMPANY, POWERS, &c.,
              OF.

*** See also "Pollution of Water by Gas,"
              (§ 81 (i.), *post.*)
1868.   [559]
A.-G. v. *Cambridge Consumers' Gas Co.* Breaking

up streets for gas pipes without authority—
Injunction refused, under the circumstances
—The disturbance of a pavement by a Gas
Company without authority, for laying pipes
is not a nuisance so serious that a Court of
Equity will prevent it. (38 L. J., Ch., 94 :
L. R., 4 Ch. App., 71 : 19 L. T., 508.)

1877.   [560]
A.-G. v. *Gas-Light and Coke Co.* "Gasworks
Clauses Act, 1847," § 29—Nuisance from gas
refuse during its removal from place to place
—No defence to proceedings for abatement
of nuisance to allege that gas cannot be made
of requisite purity without creating such
nuisance—Injunction granted to restrain the
Company from carrying on their operations
so as to be a nuisance. (47 L. J., Ch., 534 :
L. R., 7 Ch. D., 217 : 37 L. T.,716 : 42 J. P.,
391.)

1853.   [561]
A.-G. v. *Sheffield Gas Consumers' Co.* Breaking
up of Streets—Held not to be such a nuisance
as to afford sufficient ground for an Injunction—For a continuing nuisance the Court
will not refuse an Injunction merely because
the actual damage is slight. (22 L. J., Ch.,
811 : 3 De G. M. & G., 304 : 21 L. T., (o. s.),
49.)

1879.   [562]
Birmingham Corporation, In re. Gasworks
Undertaking extending over the districts of
several Local Authorities sold to one Local
Authority, with a right to each Authority
affected to repurchase its own portion—
Principle of valuation for such repurchase.
(*Times,* May 30, 1879.)

1870.   [563]
Burrows v. *March Gas & Coke Co.* Escape of
gas from a defective meter pipe supplied by
the defendants—Explosion caused by the
act of a third party—Held that the defendants were liable for the consequential
damage. (39 L. J., Ex., 33 : L. R., 5 Ex.,
67 : 22 L. T., 24.)

1875.   [564]
Commercial Gas Co. v. *Scott.* "Gasworks
Acts, 1847, 1860, 1871 "—Unjustifiably cutting off
supply of gas — Penalty — Company held
rightly convicted. (44 L. J., M. C., 171 :
L. R., 10 Q. B., 400 : 32 L. T., 765 : 40 J. P.,
214.)

1891.   [565]
Dillon v. *Haverfordwest Corporation.* Local
Act—Gasworks carried on by Corporation
for purposes of public supply and private
supply—Corporation held not entitled to
make deductions for expenses involved in
public supply before estimating their profits
(under the Income Tax Acts) arising out of
the supply to private consumers. (60 L. J.,
Q. B., 477 : L. R., 1 Q. B., 575 : 64 L. T.,
202 : 55 J. P., 392.)

1855.   [566]
Dover Gaslight Co. v. *Dover, Mayor.* A permission to break up a Street for a specified

purpose of public advantage should receive a wide construction. (7 De G. M. & G., 545 : 1 Jur., (N. s.), 812 : 25 L. T., (O. s.), 277.)

1874.   [567]
Edgware Highway Board v. *Harrow Gas Co.* Agreement for permission to the defendants to open a road, they to make good the same or pay money—Action for breach—Defence that the agreement was invalid as authorising a nuisance—Judgment for the plaintiffs (44 L. J., Q. B., 1 : L. R., 10 Q. B., 92 : 31 L. T., 402.)

1853.   [568]
Ellis v. *Sheffield Gas Consumers' Co.* Company without Parliamentary powers—Contractor —Digging a trench in a street—Where a person is employed to do an unlawful act by which an injury is done to a third party, the employer is liable, although he himself is not the immediate author of the injury. (23 L. J., Q. B., 12 : 2 E. & B., 767 : 22 L. T., (O. s.), 84.)

1876.   [569]
Gas-light & Coke Co. v. *Mead.* Special Act— Out-going and in-coming tenant—Payment for good-will—Held that the Company had no remedy against the incoming tenant. (45 L. J., M. C., 71 : 33 L. T., 729 : 40 J. P., 662.)

1872.   [570]
Gas-light & Coke Co. v. *St. George's, Hanover Square, Vestry.* Local Acts—Quality of Gas —Interpretation of Statutes imposing conditions. (42 L. J., Q. B., 51 : 28 L. T., 281.)

1887.   [571]
Gas-light & Coke Co. v. *South Metropolitan Gas Co.* Powers of Gas Company restricted in its limits of sale to sell for consumption within the limits of a rival company. (56 L. J., Ch., 858 : 57 L. T., 557.)

1888.   [572]
Gosport Gas Co. v. *Alverstoke L. B.* "Gasworks Clauses Act, 1847," § 49 : "Public Health Act, 1875," § 157—Gas Companies established before the last-named Act are nevertheless subject to its Sanitary Provisions and the erection of new buildings by such companies is subject to the By-Laws of an Urban Authority. (2 *Municip. Corp., Assoc. Month. Circular*, 11.)

1872.   [573]
Hawkins v. *Robinson.* "Highway Act, 1835," § 72—Injury to a highway by a Gas Company not established by Act of Parliament unlawfully opening the same to lay gas pipes—Held that the consent of the Local Board was no answer ; such consent being *ultra vires*. (37 J. P., 662.)

1877.   [574]
Hill, Ex parte ; Roberts, In re. "Gasworks Clauses Act, 1847" : Special Act : "Bankruptcy Act, 1869"—Warrant of Distress issued for non-payment of gas "rent" after notice that debtor had filed a petition—Held that the Company were not landlords to

whom "rent" was due within the "Bankruptcy Act, 1869," § 34, notwithstanding that the word "rent" was used in the Special Act. — Injunction to restrain proceedings granted. (37 L. T., 46 : 25 W. R., 784.)

1883.   [575]
Hornby v. *Liverpool United Gas Co.* "Gas-Works Clauses Act, 1847," § 6—Company's servant lawfully breaking up a street caused a fragment of concrete to break a plate-glass window—Company held liable. (47 J. P., 231.)

1860.   [576]
London Gas-light Co. v. *Chelsea Vestry.* Contract for Street Lights—Alleged breaches— Judgment for the plaintiffs, on the ground that the performance of all the several stipulations by the plaintiffs was not a condition precedent to their right to receive the money. (8 C. B., (N. s.), 215 : 2 L. T., 217.)

1862.   [577]
Meek v. *Langdon.* A Local Board cannot fix a Gas-lamp to a private tenement without leave. (37 *Law Times* Newspaper, 181.)

1864.   [578]
Mose v. *Hastings & St. Leonard's Gas Co.* Action for damages—A Gas Company is bound to keep up such a systematic inspection of its mains as shall enable it to detect a serious escape of gas likely to lead to an explosion— Verdict for the plaintiff. (4 F. & F., 324.)

1882.   [579]
Normanton Gas Co. v. *Pope.* "Gas-Works Clauses Acts, 1847 and 1871" : Special Acts—Plaintiffs held entitled to be protected against the consequences of injury to highway resulting from Defendant's mining operations. (52 L. J., Q. B. D., 629 : 49 L. T., 798 : W. N., 1883, p. 108.)

1873.   [580]
Pudsey Coal Gas Co. v. *Bradford, Mayor.* Rival Gas Companies—Invasion by one (a Municipal Corporation) of the district of the other —Whereupon Injunction sought—Demurrer for want of Equity, allowed. (42 L. J., Ch., 293 : L. R., 15 Eq., 167 : 28 L. T., 11 : 37 J. P., 340.)

1877.   [581]
Reg. v. *Colne Valley Gas Co.* Indictment for obstructing highway by making trenches—Verdict of "Guilty"—Rule absolute for a new trial on the ground that the Judge had misdirected the jury as to the effect of *Reg.* v. *Longton Gas Co.* (*Times*, May 19, 1877.)

1862.   [582]
Reg. v. *Lambeth Vestry.* Private Bridge Act— Bridge transferred to a public Board—Whereupon the Board became liable for the lighting. (31 L. J., Q. B., 252 : 3 B. & S., 1 : 6 L. T., 644.)

1860.   [583]
Reg. v. *Longton Gas Co.* Obstruction to highway— Commissioners for Lighting possessed powers to lay down mains for public lighting but not for private supply—Held that a Company

---

which, possessing no Parliamentary powers, had under the authority of the Commissioners properly laid down mains for public purposes, had no power to obstruct the highways for the purpose of supplying private persons. (20 L. J., M. C., 118 : 2 E. & E., 651 : 8 Cox, C. C., 317 : 2 L. T. 14.)

1853.   [584]
Reg. v. *White.* (2). Fraudulent consumption of gas by means of pipe surreptitiously affixed between main and meter—Prisoner held rightly convicted of larceny. (22 L. J., M. C., 123.)

1877.   [585]
Thompson v. *Sunderland Gas Co.* "Gasworks Clauses Act, 1847," § 6—Laying of pipes under a highway—Damage to arches belonging to plaintiff—Held that an arch was a "building," and that compensation was payable. (46 L. J., Ex., 710 : L. R., 2 Ex. D., 429 : 37 L. T., 30 : 42 J. P., 198.)

1885.   [586]
Wood v. *West Ham Gas Co.* "Gas-works Clauses Act, 1847," § 18—One pipe substituted for another—No fraud, waste, or misuse—Held nevertheless that the offence contemplated by the Statute had been committed. (52 L. T., 817 : 49 J. P., 662.)

1873.   [587]
Worksop Gas Co., In re; Worksop L. B. H. Ex parte. Local Gas Act—*Mandamus* to Gas Co. to erect lamps, &c., refused, as it would be necessary to lay 738 yards of otherwise unproductive main—Compulsion limited to 25 yards. (Q. B., Jan., 1873; MS.)

37. GUARDIANS, BOARD OF.

1888.   [588]
Dearle v. *Petersfield Union.* "Poor Law Act, 1859," 22 & 23 Vict., c. 49, § 1 : "Public Health Act, 1875," § 9—The limitation of time as to payment of Debts by Guardians contained in the former Act are not relaxed by the last-named Act. (57 L. J., Q. B., 640 : L. R., 21 Q. B. D., 417 : 60 L. T., 85 : 53 J. P., 102.)

1877.   [589]
Luckraft v. *Pridham.* Local Poor Law Act—The "Mortmain Act" has a general application, and Guardians of the Poor are incapable of taking officially the benefit of a gift by will of land. (46 L. J., Ch., 744 : L. R., 6 Ch. D., 205 : 37 L. T., 204.)

1839.   [590]
Reg. v. *St. Andrews, Holborn, Guardians.* The validity of an election of Guardians cannot be questioned on a *Mandamus* to enforce a Contribution. (10 A. & E., 736.)

1873.   [591]
Walker v. *Nottingham Guardians.* Guardians acting officially are entitled to Notice of Action in respect of official acts, unless it be shown that they have acted *mala fide*—The presumption is to be that they have acted *bonâ fide.* (28 L. T., 308.)

38. HACKNEY CARRIAGES.

1871.   [592]
Allen v. *Tunbridge.* Unlicensed Hackney Carriage, to wit, a Brougham, plying for hire in a Railway Station—Magistrate ought to have convicted for plying for hire without a license. (Metropolis.) (40 L. J., M. C., 197 : L. R., 6 C. P., 481 : 24 L. T., 796 : [*A.* v. *Trowbridge*] 35 J. P., 695.)

1891.   [593]
Banton v. *Davies.* "Towns Police Clauses Act, 1847"—Hackney Carriage driven without a license—Requirement that applicants for licenses must attend in person held reasonable, and that defendant who declined to attend, and drove without any license ought to have been convicted. (56 J. P., 294.)

1874.   [594]
Bateson v. *Oddy.* Local Act—Hackney Carriage —License duly revoked—A Carriage is a Hackney Carriage if it is offered for common use for any one who chooses to engage it, even though it actually stands in a private place—Held that there ought to have been a conviction. (43 L. J., M. C., 131 : 30 L. T., 712 : 38 J. P., 598.)

1859.   [595]
Blackpool L. B. H. v. *Bennett.* "Public Health Act, 1848"—Local Act—A By-Law need not specify the exact localities of Hackney Carriage Stands—The sea-shore between high and low water mark was held to be within the jurisdiction of the Board. (28 L. J., M. C., 203 : 4 H. & N., 127 : 23 J. P., 198 : [*Reg.* v. *Bennett*] 32 L. T., (o. s.), 299.)

1870.   [596]
Bocking v. *Jones.* Hackney Carriages—Flag inscribed with Fares. (Metropolis.) (40 L. J., M. C., 19 : L. R., 6 C. P., 29 : 23 L. T., 739.)

1864.   [597]
Buckle v. *Wrightson.* A Hackney Carriage license under "Towns Police Clauses Act," §§ 37 and 45, is necessary in a Local Board District, notwithstanding that a proprietor holds a Revenue license. (34 L. J., M. C., 43 : 5 B. & S., 854 : 11 L. T., 341 : 29 J. P., 326.)

1869.   [598]
Case v. *Storey.* Hackney Carriage—A Railway Station is not a "Public Street" or "Place." (Metropolis.) (38 L. J., M. C., 113 : L. R., 4 Ex., 319 : 20 L. T., 618 : 33 J. P., 470.) [After this decision the law as regards the Metropolis was altered by the Act 32 & 33 Vict., c. 115, § 4 ; hence later decisions to a different effect.]

1871.   [599]
Clarke v. *Stanford.* Unlicensed Hackney Carriage plying for hire in a Railway Station—Conviction affirmed. (Metropolis.) (40 L. J., M. C., 151 : L. R., 6 Q. B., 357 : 24 L. T., 389 : 35 J. P., 662.)

1865.   [600]
Cousins v. *Stockbridge.* "Towns Police Clauses Act, 1847," § 38—A Local Act provided that the Section of the above-named General Act

should apply also to Stage Coaches, &c., but it was held that the proviso in the General Act defeated such application, there being no express exception. (30 J. P., 166.)

1872. [601]
Curtis v. *Embrey.* " Towns Police Clauses Act, 1847," §§ 45 and 3—Hackney Carriages—A vehicle when on the premises of a Railway Company is not "plying for hire" in a "Street," a "Street" being a place over which the public have a right of passage—Conviction quashed. (42 L. J., M. C, 39: L. R., 7 Ex., 369.)

1877. [602]
Foinett v. *Clark.* Private vehicle plying for hire at a Railway Station—Hiring effected by negotiation at an office—Summons for plying for hire without a license—Conviction affirmed. (41 J. P., 359.)

1872. [603]
Foulger v. *Steadman.* Hackney Carriage—Railway Station—Driver refusing to leave at the request of the Company held to be a trespasser—Claim of Right. (42 L. J., M. C., 9: L. R., 8 Q. B., 65: 26 L. T., 395: 37 J. P., 660.)

1880. [604]
Marks v. *Ford.* Cab plying for hire on an open space visibly forming part of a public street but legally belonging to an hotel adjacent—Driver in employ of hotel-keeper held properly convicted of plying for hire not at an appointed stand. (45 J. P., 157.)

1866. [604a]
Player v. *Jenkens.* Municipal By-Law limiting the number of Hackney Carriages to ply for hire in a town held good, although in restraint of trade ; an unlimited number would have so blocked the streets as to have stopped all traffic. (Siderfin, 284.)

1856. [605]
Powles v. *Hider.* Hackney Carriage—Loss of Luggage—Proprietor held liable on the facts for driver's negligence. (25 L. J., Q. B., 331 : 6 E. & B., 207 : 27 L. T., (o. s.), 77.)

1812. [606]
Rex v. *Cross.* (1). It is an indictable offence for stage carriages to loiter about in the public streets for an unreasonable time—" The King's Highway is not to be used as a stable-yard." (3 Camp., 224.)

1826. [607]
Rex v. *Rawlinson.* Local Act empowering Commissioners to " direct and regulate" Hackney Carriage Stands—Held that this included a power to appoint stands, and to declare that any place in their judgment unsuitable for the purpose should not be used as a stand. (6 B. & C., 23: 9 D. & R., 7.)

1853. [608]
Rogers v. *Macnamara.* A Stage Carriage Proprietor has no right to depreciate the license of a Conductor in his employ by endorsing it with words injurious to the Conductor's character. (Metropolis.) (23 L. J., C. P., 1: 14 C. B., 27 : 2 C. L. R., 569.)

1872. [609]
Skinner v. *Usher.* Hackney Carriage plying for hire on an open space which was private property—Conviction held bad. (Metropolis.) (41 L. J., M. C., 158: L. R., 7 Q. B., 423: 26 L. T., 430 : 36 J. P., 693.)

39. "HOUSE," DEFINITION OF.

1845. [610]
Daniel v. *Coulsting.* 2 Will. IV., c. 45, § 27. " House "—The word, " House," may include a building capable of being used as a dwelling-house, though not so used. (14 L. J., C. P., 70 : 7 M. & G., 122 : 8 Scott, N. R., 949.)

1881. [611]
Esdaile v. *Metropolitan, &c., Railway Co.* " Lands Clauses Act, 1845 "—*Per* Cave, J.:—"A house is an enclosed space, with walls, a roof, and an entrance capable of being closed." (46 J. P., 103.)

1866. [612]
Halligan v. *Gauly.* Irish Local Act—Non-resident landlord of small tenements held to be the "keeper" of a Common Lodging-house. (19 L. T., 268.)

1867. [613]
Hole v. *Milton Commissioners.* Local Act—Rating of " House "—" House " includes curtilage, &c. (31 J. P., 804.)

1877. [614]
Langdon v. *Broadbent.* " Public Health Act, 1875 "— Lodging-house receiving lodgers, chiefly hawkers and pedlars, at 6d. a night— Held, a house which ought to have been registered as a " common" lodging-house— Whether a house is kept as a common lodging-house so as to require registration is a question of fact for the determination of Justices on proceedings under § 86. (L. J. *Notes of Cases*, 1877, p. 203: 37 L. T., 434 : 42 J. P., 56)

1869. [615]
Marson v. *London, Chatham, & Dover Railway Co.* " Lands Clauses Act, 1845," § 92—Curtilage—A strip of ground in front of a Public-house held part of the house. (37 L. J., Ch., 483: 38 L. J., Ch., 371 : L. R., 6 Eq., 101, and 7 Eq, 546: 18 L. T., 317)

1844. [616]
Nunn v. *Denton.* Stable with living rooms over held to be a " house," within 2 Will. IV., c. 45, § 27. (14 L. J., C. P., 43 : 8 Scott, N. R., 794.)

1851. [617]
Rey. v. *Warwickshire JJ.* Local Act—Paving expenses—Stables held part of a " house " and therefore chargeable. (17 L. T., (o. s.), 183 : 15 J. P., 417.)

1886. [618]
Roots v. *Beaumont.* " Public Health Act, 1875," § 99—A Lodging-house is a house let in lodgings; and Lodging-house By-laws apply even if only one family of lodgers come in. (51 J. P., 197.)

1845. [619]
Surman v. *Durley.* Local Act—"House" *primâ facie* means "dwelling-house" — Theatre held not rateable. (14 L. J., M. C., 145: 14 M. & W., 181.)

40. INCOME TAX.

1871. [620]
A.-G. v. *Black.* Coal dues levied under a Local Act by a Municipal Corporation held chargeable with Income Tax. (40 L. J., Ex., 89 and 194: L. R., 6 Ex., 78 and 308: 24 L. T., 370.)

1884. [620a]
Paddington Burial Board v. *Inland Revenue.* Circumstances under which Income Tax is payable by a public Board carrying on work which yields a profit. (53 L. J., Q. B., 224: L. R., 13 Q. B. D., 9: 50 L. T., 211: 48 J. P., 311.)

41. INFECTIOUS DISEASES, HOSPITALS, MORTUARIES.

1881. [621]
A.-G. v. *Fulham B. W.* Motion for Injunction to restrain the erection of a temporary Small-Pox Hospital—Motion to stand over, the balance of public convenience being in favour of the hospital—Liberty to plaintiffs to apply again to the Court after the Hospital was opened—Undertaking by defendants not to receive more than 50 patients at a time. (*Times*, May 23, 1881.)

1882. [622]
A.-G. v. *Strand B. W.* (1.) Action to restrain use of disinfecting chamber and premises at hours likely to involve danger to the children of an adjoining day-school—Arrangement agreed on that all clothes taken to the chamber should be partially disinfected previously, and hours of user restricted to before 8.30 a.m., after 8 p.m., and during school hours. (*Times*, May 25, 1882.)

1883. [623]
A.-G. v. *Strand B. W.* (2.) Proceedings by London School Board to restrain defendants from disinfecting clothes of scarlet fever patients at a place in a crowded neighbourhood — Injunction refused, the evidence showing that all reasonable care was being exercised. (*Times*, May 2, 1883.)

1752. [624]
Baines v. *Baker.* Proposed construction of a Small-Pox Hospital near inhabited houses—A nuisance must be a nuisance at Law and not a mere fear—Injunction refused. (Amb., 159: Atk., 750.)

1887. [625]
Bendelow v. *Wortley Union.* Motion to restrain erection of a Small-pox Hospital—Distance between the properties less than 50 yards—Question of risk referred to a medical arbitrator—His opinion being that the hospital would be a nuisance and dangerous to the healthiness of the plaintiff's property, In-

junction granted.—*Fleet* v. *Metrop. Asyl. Bd.* followed. (57 L. J., Ch., 762: 57 L. T., 849.)

1883. [626]
Benthal v. *Kilmorey,* (E. of). Action by resident Medical Officer to restrain Hospital Committee from dismissing him—There being a Trust Deed and plaintiff having proceeded without the sanction of the Charity Commissioners (16 & 17 Vict. c. 137, § 17), held that he was without remedy. (53 L. J., Ch., 298: L. R., 25 Ch. D., 39: 50 L. T., 137.)

1872. [627]
Best v. *Stapp.* Liability for taking into a Lodging-house a person suffering from an infectious disease whereby the plaintiff's children became diseased—Verdict for the plaintiff. (*Times*, Nov. 7, 1872: L. R., 2 C. P. D., 191 n.)

1882. [628]
Booker v. *Taylor.* "Public Health Act, 1875," § 124—Infectious case—Where a medical man issues a Certificate for the removal, and a Magistrate issues an Order, and the removal is obstructed, on a summons for the obstruction other Magistrates cannot review the validity of the Certificate and Order, but must convict for the obstruction, if the evidence suffices. (*Times*, Nov. 21, 1882.)

1879. [629]
Bramwell v. *Lacy.* A covenant not to carry on any trade, business, or dealing whatsoever, in a house, is broken by using such a house as a hospital for out-patients. (48 L. J., Ch., 339: L. R., 10 Ch. D., 691: 40 L. T., 361.)

1881. [630]
Chambers v. *Metropolitan Asylums Board.* Application for Injunction to limit the area from which small-pox patients were to be received into the hospital of defendants, in order to minimise the danger likely to arise from the concentration of large numbers of patients—Injunction granted. (*Times*, December 3, 1881.)

1882. [631]
Dalton v. *St. Mary Abbots, Kensington, Guardians.* Action to restrain use of house as Small-pox Hospital—Plaintiff's interest in the property alleged to be injured had ceased, but he was willing that one B. should be joined as co-plaintiff—Sanction of Court refused—The Injury being personal, the Remedy was also personal. (47 L. T., 348.) Action compromised, Guardians not to use Hospital except on emergency, after sanction of Local Government Board. (*Times*, Feb. 17, 1883.)

1886. [631a]
Fleet v. *Metropolitan Asylums Board.* Camp Hospital for small-pox patients established within 685 yards of plaintiff's house—Injunction to restrain the continuance of the same refused. (2 *Times* L. R., 361.)

1885. [632]
Gibbons v. *Chambers.* "Disused Burial Grounds Act, 1884"—Rent payable under a building agreement held irrecoverable, the agreement itself being contrary to Law. (1 Cab. & Ellis, 577: *Times*, June 11, 1885.)

1878. [633]
Hansard v. *St. Matthew, Bethnal Green.* Application by Vicar and Churchwardens for Faculty to erect a Mortuary and Rooms for Coroner's Inquests on a part of a closed Churchyard opposed by a Non-resident Freeholder of neighbouring property as contrary to Ecclesiastical Law—Application granted. (L. R., 4 P. D., 46.)

1880. [634]
Marjrie v. *Westminster (Duke of).* Application by one Churchwarden for Faculty to erect a Mortuary in a disused London Churchyard—Application opposed by the Rector, the other Churchwarden, and an adjacent landowner, on the ground that the proposed site was too near inhabited houses—Decision on the main question postponed to enable suggested alternative sites to be considered. (Consist. Ct. Lond.) (*Times*, Aug. 23, 1880 : July 26, 1881.)

1887. [635]
Matthews v. *Sheffield Corporation.* Motion for Injunction to restrain the erection of a Convalescent small-pox hospital — Injunction refused, the balance of evidence showing that the convalescent was not a particularly dangerous stage of the disease, and that good precautions would be taken by defendants to secure isolation, and the protection of the approaches to the hospital. (*Times*, Oct. 6, 1887.)

1881. [636]
Metropolitan Asylums Managers v. *Hill.* "Metropolitan Poor Act, 1867," 30 Vict., c. 6—Infectious Hospital built under the Act, and at the instance of Local Government Board—Action by adjacent landowners—Held that the Act did not make the defendants irresponsible agents exempt from liability—And that they were not exempt on the ground that they only obeyed the directions of the Local Government Board, and acted *bonâ fide* in the discharge of a duty cast upon them by Statute. (50 L. J., Q. B. 353 : L. R., 6 App. Cas., 193 : 44 L. T., 653 : 45 J. P., 664. (Case 1); 47 L. T., 29 : 47 J. P., 148.)

1879. [637]
Portman (*Visct.*) v. *Home Hospitals Association.* Covenant in lease not to use premises for carrying on any art, trade, or business, occupation or calling, held to prohibit user of house for hospital purposes, even although without a view to profit to the managers. (W. N., 1879, p. 196.)

1815. [638]
Rex v. *Burnett.* Indictment for exposing in a Street a child suffering from Small-pox—Conviction. (4 Maule & S., 272.)

1815. [639]
Rex v. *Vantandillo.* Carrying a Child suffering from Small-pox along a Highway—Offender held indictable—Three months' imprisonment. (4 Maule & S., 73.)

1888. [639a]
Roberts v. *Falmouth S. A.* School closed by order of Urban Authority, owing to outbreak of infectious disease, whereby Master lost various fees, and claimed compensation under the "Public Health Act, 1875," § 308—Compensation held not payable, the power to close being given under the Education Code, 1886, and not by the "Public Health Act, 1875." (52 J. P., 741.)

1881. [640]
Robinson v. *Fulham B. W.* Proposed small-pox hospital—Conflict of medical evidence as to whether such a building was necessarily dangerous to the health of a neighbourhood —Held that as the reality of the nuisance was not clearly established, and as interference might be productive of more mischief than non-interference, an Interlocutory Injunction ought not to be granted. (3 *Municip. Corp. Assoc. Month. Circular*, 129 : *Times*, May 11 and 14, 1881.)

1886. [641]
Saunders v. *New Windsor, Mayor.* Motion for interlocutory Injunction to restrain continuance of tents used for Small-pox Patients—On its being shown that the site was isolated, the patients few, and the whole arrangement temporary, Injunction refused with costs. (*Times*, Sept. 13, 1886.)

1879. [642]
St. George's Hanover Square Burial Board v. *Hall.* Application by Burial Board for faculty to erect Mortuary and *Post Mortem* Room in consecrated Burial Ground closed for Burials—Application granted subject to conditions, as to use of disinfectants, hours of reception, &c. (L. R., 5 P. D., 42.)

1882. [643]
St. Luke's Chelsea, In re. Application for a Faculty to erect Mortuary on part of a closed Burial-ground — Mortuary intended to comprise rooms for infectious as well as ordinary cases —Some grave-stones to be moved—Application granted, subject to a short delay, to enable parties interested in the grave-stones to appear. (*Times*, Jan. 24, 1882.)

1886. [644]
St. Saviour's Trustees and Oyler. "Disused Burial Grounds Act, 1884," §§ 3–5—Right to build on disused Burial Ground—Contract held not enforceable. (55 L. J., Ch., 269 : L. R., 31 Ch. D., 412 : 54 L. T., 9 : 50 J. P., 325.)

1888. [645]
Tod-Heatly v. *Benham.* The establishment of a *non-infectious* Hospital held a breach of covenant not to carry on a business calculated to be an "annoyance" to neighbours. (58 L. J., Ch., 83 : L.R., 40 Ch. D., 80 : 60 L. T., 241.)

1877. [646]
Tunbridge Wells L. B. v. *Bisshopp.* "Public Health Act, 1875," § 126—A medical man walking with a patient through a public street in order to secure his admission to a Hospital, held not in charge of the person suffering, so as to be liable to penalties for exposing him. (46 L. J., C. P., 314 : L. R., 2 C. P. D., 187.)

1880. [647]
Warwick Sanatorium Committee v. *Spicer.* The parent of a patient is not liable for expenses incurr d in respect of a child. (70 *Law Times* Newspaper, 157.)

1880. [648]
Watson v. *Leamington College.* Proposed conversion of a villa into a Sanitorium—Covenant in lease not to do anything which should be a "nuisance" or "annoyance" to the neighbourhood—Held that to use a house as a Sanitorium would be to make it, if not a "nuisance," certainly an "annoyance"—Injunction granted. (*Times*, Nov. 8, 1880.)

42. JURISDICTION.

1844. [649]
Flight v. *Clarke.* Local Act—A Local Authority can only take cognizance of nuisances within its own district. (13 L. J., Ex., 309: 13 M. & W., 155.)

1858. [650]
Reg. v. *Warner.* "Nuisances Removal Act, 1855," § 22 [Repealed]—A Local Authority has no power to assess property outside its jurisdiction, even although such property derives benefit from the sewer in respect of which a rate is contemplated. (27 L. J., M. C., 144: [*Reg.* v. *Tatham*] 8 E. & B., 915: [*Hornsey* v. *Middlesex JJ.*] 30 L. T., (o. s.), 272.)

43. LANDLORD AND TENANT.

1886. [651]
Aldridge v. *Ferne.* Held that under a Covenant to pay all outgoings payable either by landlord or tenant a tenant must pay his lessor's proportion of paving expenses. (Metrop.) (55 L. J., Q. B., 587: L. R., 17 Q. B. D., 212.)

1888. [652]
Badcock v. *Hunt.* A Covenant by Landlord to pay "all rates, taxes, and impositions, whether Parliamentary or Parochial, or imposed by the Corporation of . . . London, or otherwise howsoever" does not include the payment of Water Rates. (58 L. J., Q. B., 134: L. R., 22 Q. B. D , 145: 53 J. P., 340.)

1889. [653]
Batchelor v. *Bigger.* "Metropolis Amendment Act, 1862," § 96—Covenant by Tenant to pay all Rates, &c., "and outgoings of every description," held to include Paving Works. (60 L. T., 416 : W. N., 1889, p. 51.)

1868. [654]
Bird v. *Elzes.* Landlord and Tenant—Agreement by Landlord to pay "Rates" and "Charges"—Foul Mud in Pond—Expenses under "Nuisances Removal Act, 1855," § 19 [= "Public Health Act, 1875," § 104]—Tenant held liable, such expenses not being a "Charge." (37 L. J., Ex., 91 : L. R., 3 Ex., 225 : 18 L. T., 727 : 32 J. P., 694.)

1884. [655]
Bird v. *Greville (Lord).* Recent case of infectious disease in furnished house—The fact not disclosed to intending tenant—Held that landlord could not enforce agreement to hire—*Per* Field, J.:—In a contract for letting a furnished house it is implied that the house is "in a fit state for occupation at the commencement of the tenancy." (1 Cab. & Ellis, 317 : *Times*, May 21, 1884.)

1882. [656]
Buck v. *Hurlock.* Action by Tenant against Landlord to recover 400*l.*, losses and expenses attendant on an outbreak of typhoid fever alleged to have arisen from use of well found polluted by sewage—Judgment for defendant, there being no proof that he had warranted the water, or that it was impure when the house was taken. (At *Nisi Prius.*) (*Times*, March 31, 1882.)

1879. [657]
Budd v. *Marshall.* "Public Health Act, 1875," § 104—Plaintiff charged as landlord with the expenses of certain drain communications —Action against tenant under a lease, to refund—Covenant to pay "all Taxes, Rates, Duties and Assessments"—Held that under the Covenant of the lease the tenant was liable. (50 L. J., C. P., 24 : L. R., 5 C. P. D., 481 : 42 L. T., 792 : 44 J. P., 584)

1886. [658]
Bunn v. *Harrison.* Unfurnished house verbally warranted by house agent found after entry to be defective as to drains, water supply, and ventilation, whereupon tenant went out and refused to pay any rent—Judgment for tenant—*Per* Lord Esher, M.R.:—"A statement made at the time of a verbal contract, and for the purposes of the contract, must be taken to be part of the contract." (*Times*, Dec. 3, 1886.)

1879. [659]
Castleberg v. *Kenyon.* House with defective drains and water supply—Notices to abate nuisance served by Local Authority on occupier, and proceedings against same—Work done by occupier, who claimed repayment from owner in County Court—Occupier held entitled to reimbursement by owner. (*Times*, June 16, 1879.)

1889. [660]
Charsley v. *Jones.* Landlord and tenant—It is not enough that a landlord letting a furnished house honestly believes it fit for habitation : it must reasonably be so in fact. (53 J. P., 280.)

1885. [661]
Crawley, In re. "Metropolis Management Act, 1855," § 73—Certain drainage expenses imposed by Local Authority held rightly deducted by Trustee of a will from income payable to tenant for life. (54 L. J., Ch., 652 : 49 J. P., 598.)

1874. [662]
Crosse v. *Raw.* "Sanitary Act, 1866," § 10 [= "Public Health Act, 1875," § 23]—Landlord and Tenant—Covenant that the

tenant should pay all "outgoings" held to include the expense of making a drain for which the "owner" might have been made liable. (43 L. J., Ex., 144 : L. R., 9 Ex., 209.)

1877.   [663]
Devonshire (Duke of) v. *Barrow Hæmatite Steel Co.* "Rating Act, 1874," § 8—Lease dated 1864, in which Lessees covenanted to pay all Rates—Held that the clause in the lease was not "a specific contract" within the exemption in § 8, and that the defendants as Lessees were entitled to make a deduction from their rent and royalties in consideration of the new burden imposed by the "Rating Act, 1874." (46 L. J., Q. B., 435 : L. R., 2 Q. B. D., 286 : 36 L. T., 355.)

1869.   [664]
Ecclesiastical Commissioners v. *Merral.* A tenant of corporate property holding under an agreement for a demise for years, to which the Common Seal had not been attached, is to be considered a yearly tenant. (38 L. J., Ex., 93 : L. R., 4 Ex., 162 : 20 L. T., 573.)

1864.   [665]
Gandy v. *Jubber.* Accident owing to a defective street grating—*Semble* that to allow a tenant to remain such, year after year, on a yearly tenancy, is not equivalent to a re-letting so as to make the reversioner liable as for letting premises with a nuisance existing at the time of letting. (9 B. & S., 15 : 13 W. R., 1022.) [*See* No. 677.]

1883.   [665a]
Gardner v. *Furness Railway Co.* "Public Health Act, 1875," § 150—Covenant by Lessee to pay all outgoings—Held that paving expenses under this section were an outgoing payable by Lessee. (47 J. P., 232.)

1892.   [666]
Gebhardt v. *Saunders.* "Public Health (London) Act, 1891," §§ 4, 11—Owner held liable for expenses incurred by tenant who under a Notice from the Local Authority abated a nuisance. (L. R., 2 Q. B., 452.)

1886.   [667]
Harrison v. *Malet.* Furnished house found defective as to drains, &c.—Illness of inmates from sewer gas—Judgment for defendant (the tenant) on the counter-claim ; damages 40l. (*Times*, Nov. 1, 1886.)

1879.   [668]
Hartley v. *Hudson.* "Public Health Act, 1848," § 69 [= "Public Health Act, 1875," § 150] —Covenant to pay Rates, Taxes, Charges and Assessments charged on the premises or on any person in respect thereof—Plaintiff lessor of premises—Notice to him to pave, &c.—On default, work done by Local Board and recovered from plaintiff—Held that the outlay was one which the landlord was entitled to recover from his tenant under covenants in the lease. (48 L. J., C. P., 751 : L. R., 4 C. P. D., 367 : 43 J. P., 784.)

1885.   [669]
Hugall v. *M'Lean.* Landlord and tenant—Both parties ignorant of defect in drains—Land-

lord held not liable. (53 L. T., 91 : *Times*, May 2, 1885.)

1851.   [670]
Keates v. *Cadogan (Earl of).* There is no implied duty in the owner of a house which is in a ruinous or unsafe condition to inform a proposed tenant that it is unfit for habitation ; and no Action will lie against him for an omission to do so in the absence of express warranty or active deceit. (20 L. J., C. P., 76 : 10 C. B., 591 : 15 Jur., 428.)

1881.   [671]
Kinnaird v. *Smith.* House hired by plaintiff, on defendant's guarantee that the drains were carried outside and were in good order— After entry drains found to run inside and to be choked with sewage causing serious illness to inmates—Action to rescind contract of hiring and for damages in respect of defendant's misrepresentations — Agreement set aside by the Court and damages to be assessed. (*Times*, May 16, 1881.)

1858.   [672]
Lee v. *Stevenson.* Landlord and tenant—Power reserved by lease to former to make a covered Sewer across the demised land—Right of the landlord to the exclusive use of a Sewer upheld by the Court. (27 L. J., Q. B., 263 : E. B. & E., 512.)

1880.   [673]
May v. *Verity.* Action by assignor of a lease against intending assignee for specific performance of agreement to take a house— Defence that the drains were defective ; and that the house was subject to an easement not clearly disclosed in the lease, to wit a duty to receive and transmit the drainage of adjoining houses—Judgment for defendant on last-named ground. (*Times*, Dec. 22, 1880).

1879.   [674]
Midgley v. *Coppock.* Vendor and purchaser— Agreement to pay outgoings up to date of completion—Sewering and paving expenses demanded after completion, but in respect of works executed before, held to be an "outgoing" which the vendor was liable to pay under his agreement. (48 L. J., Ex., 674 : L. R., 4 Ex. D., 309 : 40 L. T., 870 : 43 J. P., 683.)

1881.   [675]
Muspratt v. *Hussey.* Action for damages—House taken on lease by plaintiff of defendant— Allegations that verbal guarantees were given about drains being in good order—Subsequently, bad smells, followed by typhoid fever, after about a year's possession—Drains found partly obstructed, presumably however by negligence of plaintiff's household—Verdict for defendant. (At *Nisi Prius.*) (*Times*, June 17, 1881.)

1844.   [676]
Payne v. *Burridge.* Paving Expenses under a Local Act held, on the construction of a covenant in a lease, to be payable by a tenant. (13 L. J., Ex., 190 : 13 M. & W., 727.)

44. "LANDS CLAUSES ACT, 1845."

*** See also "Arbitration," (§ 7, *ante*) ; and "Compensation," (§ 21, *ante*).

compensation under § 68 of "Lands Clauses Act." (44 L. J., Ch., 549: L. R., 20 Eq., 353: 33 L. T., 156.)

1886. [694]
Benington v. *Metrop. B. W.* "Lands Clauses Act, 1845," § 92—Place of business as distinguished from manufactory—No liability on Board to take two properties. (54 L. T., 837: 50 J. P., 740.)

1863. [695]
Bourne v. *Liverpool, Mayor.* "Lands Clauses Act, 1845"—Local Act—Street Improvement—Principle of assessing compensation for a Public-House owned by a Brewer and leased with a restrictive covenant—Special compensation held payable. (33 L. J., Q. B., 15: 8 L. T., 573.)

1857. [696]
Broadbent v. *Imperial Gas Co.* "Lands Clauses Act, 1845," § 68—"Injuriously affected by the execution of the works" means by the actual construction of such works, not the user thereof. (26 L. J., Ch., 276: 7 De G. M. & G., 436: 28 L. T., (o. s.), 329.)

1886. [697]
Burgess v. *Bristol Urban A.* A Local Authority is not bound to proceed with a notice to take lands under the "Public Health Act, 1875," even though a Provisional Order has been granted and confirmed. (50 J. P., 455.)

1886. [698]
Bygrave v. *Metropolitan B. W.* Contract for sale of premises for street improvement—On a difficulty arising and possession on payment into Court being claimed, held that not having proceeded under "Lands Clauses Act" the Board must stand or fall by their contract. (55 L. J., Ch., 602: L. R., 32 Ch. D., 147: 54 L. T., 889: 50 J. P., 788.)

1874. [699]
Clark v. *London School Board.* In the case of lands purchased under compulsory powers, unpurchased easements to which they are subject are the subject of compensation. (43 L. J., Ch., 421: L. R., 9 Ch. App., 120: 29 L. T., 903.)

1870. [700]
Cranwell v. *London, Mayor.* "Lands Clauses Act, 1845," § 121—A Tenant from year to year is entitled to compensation. (Metropolis.) (39 L. J., Ex., 193: L. R., 5 Ex., 284: 22 L. T., 760.)

1863. [701]
Croft v. *London & North-Western Railway Co.* "Lands Clauses Act, 1845," § 68—When in proceedings for compensation points entitling to compensation are left out of consideration through want of forethought no redress can be had subsequently by Action for damages, or *semble* in any other way. (32 L. J., Q. B., 113: 3 B. & S., 436: 7 L. T., 741.)

1867. [702]
Delaney v. *Metropolitan B. W.* "Metropolis Management Amendment Act, 1862"—Sewerage Works—Claim for compensation—Award under the "Lands Clauses Act"

—Such proceedings are not within § 106 of the first-named Act so as to be subject to the "6 months" limit there mentioned. (37 L. J., C. P., 59: L. R., 3 C. P., 111: 17 L. T., 262.)

1874. [703]
Dowling v. *Pontypool, &c., Railway Co.* Deposited plans of land—Construction of the word "delineated." (43 L. J., Ch., 761: L. R., 18 Eq., 714.)

1879. [704]
Eccleshill L. B., In re. Land let to tenants purchased for sewage farm—Price settled by Jury—Possession not taken until termination of existing tenancies—Held that interest was payable from date of Jury's verdict. (49 L. J., Ch., 214: L. R., 13 Ch. D., 365.)

1871. [705]
Edwards, Ex parte; Marylebone Improvement Act, 1868, In re. "Lands Clauses Act, 1845," § 68—An interest in property created by an agreement entered into by an owner after a notice to treat has been served on him does not confer on his tenant any right to compensation. (40 L. J., Ch., 697: L. R., 12 Eq., 380: 25 L. T., 149.)

1873. [706]
Falkner v. *Somerset & Dorset Railway Co.* "Lands Clauses Act, 1845," §§ 92–3—Market garden with cottage—Severance by tunnel—Extent of liability to purchase—Premises held not to be within a "town" although within the Municipal boundary. (42 L. J., Ch., 851: L. R., 16 Eq., 458.)

1869. [707]
Ferrar v. *Commissioners of Sewers of London.* Local Act incorporating parts of "Lands Clauses Act, 1845"—Compensation—Construction of Local Act. (38 L. J., Ex., 102: L. R., 4 Ex., 227: 21 L. T., 295.)

1884. [707a]
Fowell v. *Normanton L. B.* Rule granted for a Prohibition to restrain Board from taking a portion only of certain lands the whole of which had been notified for taking for sewage works. (*Times*, July 18, 1884.)

1874. [708]
Great Western Railway Co. v. *May.* "Lands Clauses Act, 1845," § 127—"Lands acquired . . . . but not required for the purposes" for which they were acquired—"Required" means "necessary," and when the land ceases to be necessary it becomes "superfluous land." (43 L. J., Q. B., 233: L. R., 7 H. L., 283: 31 L. T., 137.)

1857. [709]
Grosvenor (Lord) v. *Hampstead Junction Railway Co.* "Lands Clauses Act, 1845," § 92—Alms-houses partly built—Compulsory purchase of whole of site—Land held to be part of a house. (26 L. J., Ch., 731: 1 De G. & J., 446: 29 L. T., (o. s.), 319.)

1874. [710]
Harvie v. *South Devon Railway Co.* "Lands Clauses Act, 1845," § 92—Held that a pair of semi-detached Villas could not be treated as one House, so as to involve purchase of both. (32 L. T., 1.)

1865. [711]
Herring v. *Metropolitan B. W.* "Lands Clauses Act, 1845"—Damage caused by the erection of a temporary hoarding for a public purpose, *e.g.*, during the construction of a sewer, is not such damage as will carry compensation. (Metrop.) (34 L. J., M. C., 224: 19 C. B., (N. S.), 510.)

1877. [712]
Hooper v. *Bourne.* "Lands Clauses Act, 1845," § 127—Superfluous lands—Progressive increase in the traffic of a railway, such as to render it probable that the whole of the surplus land would at no distant period be required for the purposes of the undertaking —Held, on the evidence, that the adjoining owners were not entitled to recover possession of their land—Burden of proof that land is superfluous lies on claimant—*G. W. R.* v. *May* distinguished. (49 L. J., Q. B., 370 : L.R.,5 App. Cas.,1 : 42 L.T.,97: 44 J.P.,327.)

1882. [713]
Huddersfield, Mayor, Ex parte; Dyson, In re. "Lands Clauses Act, 1845," § 85—Practice as to repayment of Deposit where the property has been purchased in due course after the Deposit has been paid. (46 L. T., 730.)

1878. [714]
Littler v. *Rhyl Improvement Commissioners.* "Lands Clauses Act, 1845," § 92—Notice to treat for land—Lapse of and subsequent revival of the compulsory powers—House built on land after the lapse and before new notice to treat was given—Held nevertheless that the position of matters at the time of the first notice fixed the relative rights of the parties, and that the Commissioners could not be required to take more than they originally gave notice for, namely, a certain plot of land as unenclosed and unbuilt on— Second notice held unnecessary. (W. N., 1879, p. 30.)

1885. [715]
Lynch v. *Commissioners of Sewers of London.* Local Act—Compulsory powers for acquisition of land—Notice to treat — Alleged estoppel by conduct. (55 L. J., Ch., 409: L. R., 32 Ch. D., 72 : 54 L. T., 699 : 50 J. P., 548.)

1864. [716]
Macey v. *Metropolitan B. W.* "Lands Clauses Act, 1845"—Injury to a Wharf-owner by construction of an embankment—Practice. (33 L. J., Ch., 377: 10 L. T., 66.)

1874. [717]
M'Carthy v. *Metropolitan B. W.* "Lands Clauses Act, 1845," § 68—Private Dock injuriously affected by the formation of an embankment —Compensation held payable. (43 L. J., C. P., 385: 31 L. T., 183: 38 J. P., 820.)

1869. [718]
Metropolitan B. W. v. *Metropolitan Railway Co.* "Lands Clauses Act, 1845"—Damage to Sewer—Right to lateral support of adjoining land—Action held not maintainable. (38 L.J., C. P., 172: L. R., 4 C. P., 192: 19 L. T., 714.)

1878. [719]
Morgan v. *Swansea Urban Authority.* "Land Transfer Act, 1875," § 48—Purchase of land by a Local Authority—Death of vendor—A trustee with a beneficial interest in the Trust estate is not a "bare trustee." (L. R., 9 Ch. D., 5s2.)

1859. [720]
North London Railway Co. v. *Metropolitan B. W.* Construction of sewer through land not scheduled for purchase, held *intra vires* (28 L. J., Ch., 909 : 1 Johns., 405 : 33 L. T., (o. s.), 383.)

1854. [721]
Pinchin v. *London & Blackwall Railway Co.* "Lands Clauses Act, 1845," § 92—*Quære*, Is an easement "land"? [*Semble*, that it is not. See *Macey* v. *Met. B. W.*] (24 L. J., Ch., 417: 5 De G. M. & G., 851 : 24 L. T., (o. s.), 196.)

1882. [722]
Pullen and Liverpool Corporation, In re. "Lands Clauses Act, 1845," §§ 23, 31—The period of 3 months within which an umpire must make his Award is to be calculated from the date of his appointment, and not from the time when the awarding power of the arbitrator came to an end. (51 L. J., Q. B , 285 : 46 L. T., 391 : 46 J. P., 468.)

1874. [723]
Quinton v. *Bristol, Mayor.* "Lands Clauses Act, 1845" — Street Improvement — An Urban Sanitary Authority empowered to acquire lands, &c., compulsorily may take whatever it includes in its notice, whether required or not : the restrictions put upon a railway company do not apply. (43 L. J., Ch., 783 : L. R., 17 Eq., 524 : 30 L. T., 112 : 38 J. P., 516.)

1848. [724]
Ramsden v. *Manchester, South Junction & Altrincham Railway Co.* "Lands Clauses Act, 1845 "—Trespass—A public body must make compensation *before* entry, whether they purchase the land itself, or permanently occupy it. (1 Ex. 723: 5 Rail. Cas., 552 : 10 L. T., (o. s.), 464.)

1862. [725]
Reddin v. *Metropolitan B. W.* "Lands Clauses Act, 1845," § 92—The sorting place of a Dust Contractor is not such "a part" of a "Manufactory" as to come within this Section. (31 L. J., Ch., 660: 4 De G. F. & J., 532 : 7 L. T., 6.)

1863. [726]
Reg. v. *Combe.* "Lands Clauses Act, 1845," § 121—Compensation to annual Tenant— Justices may decide verbally and need not put their decision into writing. (32 L. J., M. C., 67 : [*Combe* v. *L. C. D. R.*] 11 W. R., 441.)

1876. [727]
Reg. v. *Great Northern Railway Co.* "Lands Clauses Act, 1845," §§ 68 and 121—A tenancy which, whatever may have been the term, has less than one year to run is to be

treated as a tenancy for less than a year.
(46 L. J., Q. B., 4: L. R., 2 Q. B. D., 151:
35 L. T., 551: 41 J. P., 197.)

1874.   [728]
Reg. v. *Hannay.* "Lands Clauses Act, 1845"—
Injury prospective because land not actually
yet taken—An adjudication of two Justices
under § 22 is not an order to pay money
within 11 & 12 Vict. c. 43, § 11, and a summons to determine compensation is not out
of time if issued after 6 months from notice
to treat being given. [*R.* v. *Leeds, &c.,* distinguished and somewhat questioned.] (44
L. J., M. C., 27: 31 L. T., 702.)

1852.   [729]
Reg. v. *Leeds and Bradford Railway Co.* "Lands
Clauses Act, 1845," §§ 22 and 24—"Jervis's
Act." § 11—Compensation under 50l.—Order
of Justices—Limitation of time—Order bad
if based on complaint made more than
6 months after cause of complaint arose.
(21 L. J., M. C., 193: 19 L. T., (o. s.), 86:
16 J. P., 631: [*Edmundson, In re*] 17 Q. B.,
67.)

1869.   [730]
Reg. v. *Metropolitan B. W.* (2). "Lands Clauses
Act, 1845," § 68 — Premises injuriously
affected—Injury to a public landing-place,
and obstruction of access to a public place
where there was a right to dip for water—
Held that neither injury was a case for compensation. (38 L. J., Q. B., 201: L. R.,
4 Q. B., 358: 10 B. & S., 391.)

1872.   [731]
Reg. v. *St. Luke's, Chelsea, Vestry.* (2). Raising
level of a Street—When a Local Act incorporates the whole of the "Lands Clauses Act,
1845," the right of compensation to parties
whose lands are taken follows as a matter of
course. (41 L. J, Q. B., 81: L. R., 7 Q. B.,
148: 25 L. T., 914.)

1878.   [732]
Richards v. *Swansea Improvement Company.*
"Lands Clauses Act, 1845," § 92—Establishment consisting of cottages, yards, shops,
bakery, corn-mills, stables, &c., all within a
circumscribed ambit, and with internal communication and in one occupation, and user,
held to be a "house," so that the whole
property must be purchased if the owner
required it. (L. R., 9 Ch. D., 425: 38 L. T.,
833: 43 J. P., 174.)

1867.   [733]
Rickett v. *Metropolitan Railway Co.* "Lands
Clauses Act, 1845," § 68—Construction of
Works—A temporary obstruction of Highway although involving loss of trade, does
not entitle to compensation—There must be
an injury to land or to an interest in land.
(36 L. J., Q. B., 205: L. R., 2 H. L., 175:
16 L. T., 542.)

1885.   [734]
Shepherd v. *Norwich Corporation.* "Lands
Clauses Act, 1845," §§ 18, 19, 25, 27, 30—
Service of notice—Counter notice. (54 L. J.,
Ch., 1050: L. R., 30 Ch. D., 553: 53 L. T.,
251.)

1873.   [735]
Souch v. *East-London Railway Co.* "Lands
Clauses Act. 1815"—A cul-de-sac dedicated
to the public is for this purpose a public
street, and there need be neither notice nor
compensation. (42 L. J., Ch., 477: L. R.,
16 Eq., 108.)

1882.   [736]
Spencer v. *Metropolitan B. W.* "Lands Clauses
Act, 1815"—Local Act—Land may be said to
be "taken" for a public purpose although
possession is not actually entered upon.
(52 L. J., Ch., 249: L. R., 22 Ch. D., 142:
47 L. T., 459.)

1870.   [737]
Stebbing v. *Metropolitan B. W.* "Lands Clauses
Act, 1845"—Closed graveyard—Compensation is payable on the actual value of land
considered as depreciated by the purpose to
which it is applied, and is not to be estimated
at what would be the value of such land
supposing it had been secularised. (40 L. J.,
Q. B., 1: L. R., 6 Q. B., 37: 23 L. T., 530.)

1877.   [738]
Syer v. *Metropolitan B. W.* "Lands Clauses
Act, 1845," § 18—A quarterly tenant held
not entitled to compensation. (W. N., 1877,
p. 41: 33 L. T., 277.)

1885.   [739]
Teulière v. *St. Mary Abbots, Kensington, Vestry.*
Local Act—Powers as to taking part of
premises for widening a street—Owners
willing to sell part but not the whole—Held
that Vestry could not insist on taking the
whole—*Gard* v. *Commissioners of Sewers*
considered. (55 L. J., Ch., 23: L. R , 30
Ch. D., 612: 53 L. T., 422: 50 J. P., 53.)

1871.   [740]
Tyson v. *London, Lord Mayor.* "Lands Clauses
Act, 1845," § 121—Compensation—Tenant's
interest in property is to be computed according to what it was when the notice was
given. (41 L. J., C. P., 6: L. R., 7 C. P., 18:
25 L. T., 640.)

1858.   [741]
Ware v. *Regent's Canal Co.* "Lands Clauses
Act, 1845"—Compensation—An occasional
flooding of lands caused by the proper execution of Parliamentary powers is within § 68.
(28 L. J., Ch., 153: 3 De G. & J., 212: 32 L.T.,
(o. s.), 136.)

1862.   [742]
Wedmore v. *Bristol, Mayor.* Local Acts incorporating the "Lands Clauses Act, 1845"—
Raising of footway—Injunction to stop the
alterations refused, as Corporation was only
carrying out its statutory powers, but the
plaintiff to have damages awarded him.
(1 New Rep., 120 and 187: 7 L. T., 459:
11 W. R., 136.)

1880.   [743]
Wells v. *Chelmsford L. B.* "Lands Clauses
Act," §§ 76-7—Action by vendors for specific
performance of agreement for purchase of
Lands by a Board—Complicated state of
facts—Failure of vendors to make a good
title to part of the land whereupon de-

fendant executed a Deed Poll under § 77—
Payment of the whole purchase money into
Court held under the circumstances improper and specific performance decreed
under conditions. (49 L. J., Ch., 827 : L. R.,
15 Ch. D., 108 : 43 L. T., 378 : 45 J. P., 6.)

1877.   [744]
Wombwell v. *Barnsley Corporation.* "Lands
Clauses Act, 1869," § 1—Proposal to purchase land referred to arbitration—Settlement before the Award—Terms that the
Corporation should pay the costs—Held that
there having been a special contract the
Section did not apply as regards Taxation ;
but that the costs might be taxed in Chancery
under 6 & 7 Vict. c. 73, § 38. (36 L. T., 708 :
41 J. P., 502.)

45. LEGAL PROCEEDINGS.

(1.) GENERAL.

1874.   [745]
Andrews v. *Ryde, Mayor.* "Local Government
Act, 1858," § 24 [="Public Health Act,
1875," Scheds.] — Municipal Corporation
acting as a Local Board—Action for work
and labour as a professional witness—Held
that as the action was against the Corporation *quâ* Local Board, the Corporation was
liable without being otherwise or more expressly described. (43 L. J., Ex., 174 : L. R.,
9 Ex., 302.)

1883.   [746]
A.-G. v. *Bermondsey Vestry.* Practice—Costs—
Action against Corporation—When Costs are
not asked for against a Corporation it is
irregular to make individual members defendants solely for the purpose of saddling
them with the Costs of the main proceedings.
(52 L. J., Ch., 567 : L. R., 23 Ch. D., 60 :
48 L. T., 445 : 47 J. P., 453.)

1846.   [747]
A.-G. v. *Pearson.* Circumstances under which
the costs and damages in an Action against
Officers of a Parish Trust may be defrayed
out of the Trust Funds. (2 Coll., Ch. C.,
581 : 10 Jur., 651.)

1890.   [748]
Baker v. *Fleetwood Commissioners.* Action on
behalf of Urban Authority brought in the
County Palatine Court of Lancaster which
might have been brought in the County
Court—Action dismissed—Whereupon defendants refused to pay the plaintiff's Bill of
Costs—Held that they were bound to do so,
and that plaintiff had not been guilty of
actionable negligence in not instituting the
proceedings in the County Court. (62 L. T.,
831 : 54 J. P., 711.)

1857.   [749]
Bedford v. *Sutton Coldfield Society.* Local Inclosure Act—A Rent-charge held not recoverable by Action against the landowner. (27
L. J., C. P., 105 : 3 C. B., (N. S.), 449.)

1865.   [750]
Bermondsey Vestry v. *Brown.* Vestry empowered
by Statute to indict or take other proceed-

ings as to obstructed rights of way—Held
that it must nevertheless indict in the name
of the Queen and sue in Equity in the name
of the Att.-Gen. (L. R., 1 Eq., 204 : 35
Bea., 226 : 13 L. T., 574.)

1873.   [751]
Bolingbroke (Lord) v. *Townsend.* If a plaintiff
by inadvertence sues the Clerk of a Local
Board instead of the Board, the writ may be
amended. (42 L. J., C. P., 255 : L. R., 8
C. P., 645 : 29 L. T., 430 : 38 J. P., 7.)

1862.   [752]
Brine v. *Great Western Railway Co.* Negligent
execution of works sanctioned by Parliament
—Action held maintainable. (31 L. J., Q. B.,
101 : 2 B. & S., 412 : 6 L. T., 50.)

1884.   [753]
Bristol, Mayor v. *Cox.* Opinion of Counsel taken
by a Town Council is a privileged document,
and Council may refuse inspection even to
Ratepayers — *Semble* that a confidential
Report by a Committee is similarly privileged. (53 L. J., Ch. D., 144 : L. R., 26 Ch. D.,
678 : 50 L. T., 719.)

1879.   [754]
Bryant v. *Lefever.* Easement—Obstruction of
air by adjacent building—Prescription—The
free circulation of air round a chimney is
not a privilege which the law protects, and
an obstruction thereto is not actionable—
Observations by the Court on Rights of air.
(48 L. J., C. P., 380 : L. R., 4 C. P. D., 172 :
40 L. T., 579 : 43 J. P., 478.)

1836.   [755]
Cane v. *Chapman.* Annuity chargeable on Rates
under a Local Act — Form of Action on
failure to make a quarterly payment that
was due. (6 L. J., K. B., 49 : 1 N. & P., 104 :
5 A. & E., 647 : 2 H. & W., 355.)

1862.   [756]
Caswell v. *Cook.* "Markets and Fairs Clauses
Act," § 13—Local Act—Construction—Costs
not given against the appellant in an argu-
able case. (31 L. J., M. C., 185 : 11 C. B.,
(N. S), 637 : [Costs] 12 C. B., (N. S.), 242.)

1878.   [757]
Day v. *Brownrigg.* A person may give his house
any name he pleases, even although his next
door neighbour has made use of the same
name for many years previously.—*Per* Jessel,
M.R.:—"In our law, in order to support an
Action, there must be injury as well as
damage ; the two things must co-exist."
(48 L. J., Ch., 173 : L. R., 10 Ch. D., 294 :
39 L. T., 553.)

1866.   [758]
Derriman's Settlement, In re. Local Act—"Public Health Act, 1848"—A Local Board which
has taken land compulsorily, must pay the
costs of a petition for payment out of Court
of the purchase money of such land where
it is settled property. (W. N., 1866, p. 269.)

1852.   [759]
Edwards v. *Lowndes.* Local Act—Special Trust
—Statutory payment in arrear—Action by
an organist against a Local Board—Action

held not maintainable, the remedy being in Equity. (22 L. J., Q. B., 104: 1 E. & B., 81: 25 L. T., (o. s.), 154.)

1853.   [760]
Egginton, Ex parte. "Municipal Corporations Act, 1835," § 60.—Where an Officer refuses to account, his commitment is in the nature of a Civil process and his arrest on a Sunday illegal, but he may be detained at the instance of a third party under a *ca. sa.* subsequently issued. (23 L. J., M. C., 41: 2 E. & B., 717: 2 C. L. R., 385: 22 L. T., (o. s.), 118.)

1871.   [761]
Gill v. *Bright.* Seizure of Liquors.—A man's property must not be declared forfeited until he has had an opportunity of being heard. (41 L. J., M. C., 22: 25 L. T., 591.) [See observations on this case in 42 J. P., 401.]

1878.   [762]
Glossop v. *Heston L. B.* A witness giving evidence by affidavit may supplement orally his evidence in chief if he is in Court, unless the agreement between the parties that the evidence shall be taken by affidavit says "by affidavit only." (47 L. J., Ch., 536: 26 W. R., 433.)

1844.   [763]
Hall v. *Swansea, Mayor.* An Action lies against a Corporation aggregate to recover moneys wrongfully received by it in respect of fees payable to the holder of an office improperly abolished. (13 L. J., Q. B., 107: 5 Q. B., 526: D. & M., 475.)

1867.   [764]
Harring v. *Stockton, Mayor.* Violation of a By-Law — Convicting Justices held not to be disqualified because members of the Board —Held also that the Information did not require to be laid by a person appointed under seal, and by consent of the Attorney-General. (31 J. P., 420.)

1854.   [765]
Harrison v. *Southampton, Mayor.* 8 & 9 Vict., c. 43, extended by 13 & 14 Vict., c. 65 [and further extended by 18 & 19 Vict., c. 70].—A Statute authorising a devise of land for a public purpose will be taken to include a bequest of money for the purchase of land —The Court will put a liberal construction on an Act which legalises the gift of property for laudable purposes. (23 L. J., Ch., 919: 2 Sm. & G., 387: 23 L. T., (o. s.), 330.)

1883.   [766]
Holder v. *Margate, Mayor.* "Public Health Act, 1875," § 264—Notice of Action is not required in proceedings for the recovery of land. (52 L. J., Q. B. D., 711: [*Foat* v. &c.] L. R., 11 Q. B. D., 299: 47 J. P., 535.)

1858.   [767]
Itchen Bridge Co. v. *Southampton L. B. H.* The Common Law right of a Judge to change the Venue in an Action, is not taken away by the "Public Health Act, 1848," § 139. (27 L.

J., Q. B., 128: 8 E. & B., 803 (n): 30 L. T., (o. s.), 151.) An Action may be supported against a Local Board for a tort, notwithstanding the compensation clause of the above Act, § 144. (28 L. J., Q. B., 41: 8 E. & B., 801: 30 L. T., (o. s.), 256.)

1873.   [768]
Jolliffe v. *Wallasey L. B.* Negligence—Management of a landing stage vested in Local Board—The plaintiffs might have recovered damages if they had not omitted to give the Notice of Action required by the "Public Health Act." (43 L. J., C. P., 41: L. R., 9 C. P., 62: 29 L. T., 582: 38 J. P., 40.)

1891.   [769]
Lee Conservancy Board v. *Tottenham L. B.* Joint Committee formed by two Local Boards for management of sewers—The control of the sewers having passed to such Committee under statutory powers, it was held that one constituent Board could not be proceeded against for a nuisance. (64 L. T., 198: 55 J. P., 343.)

1886.   [770]
Martin v. *Treacher.* "Public Health Act, 1875" —In action for penalty for acting as member when not qualified plaintiff cannot administer interrogatories in order to prove his own case. (L. R., 16 Q. B. D., 507: 50 J. P., 356.)

1860.   [771]
Mason v. *Birkenhead Improvement Commissioners.* Negligence of Servants—Commissioners held entitled to Notice—Attorney's letter not a sufficient Notice. (29 L. J., Ex., 407: 6 H. & N., 72: 2 L. T., 632.)

1842.   [772]
Maund v. *Monmouthshire Canal Co.* Trespass as well as Trover lies against a Corporation aggregate for an act done by their agent within his authority. (11 L. J., C. P., 317: 4 M. & G., 452: 3 Rail. Cas., 159: 5 Scott, N. R., 457.)

1875.   [773]
Mill v. *Hawker.* "Highway Act, 1862," § 9 (6) and § 16—Obstruction—Liability of members of a Board for acts that are *ultra vires*— Officer obeying orders of that character— Certain members of a Highway Board, and the Surveyor, held liable personally for a trespass. (44 L. J., Ex., 49: L. R., 10 Ex., 92: 33 L. T., 177: 39 J. P., 181.)

1882.   [774]
Prestney v. *Culchester, Mayor.* Place at which valuable Corporation documents should be produced in connection with pending legal proceedings. (52 L. J., Ch., 346: 48 L. T., 353.)

1885.   [775]
Reg. v. *Aspinall.* Local Act similar to the "Metropolitan Building Act" — Houses "presented" as unfit for habitation—Owners refused a hearing—Presentment held invalid because owners had not been heard against it—Rule *Absolute* for a Certiorari. (*Times*, July 4, 1885.)

E

1857.   [776]
Reg. v. *Fairie.* 16 & 17 Vict., c. 128, § 1—Nuisance
—Smoke—Evidence of a prior summary conviction is not receivable on an Indictment.
(8 E. & B., 486: 8 Cox, C. C., 66: 30 L. T.,
(o. s.), 131.)

1875.   [777]
Reg. v. *Foulkes.* The son of a Clerk to a Local
Board living at home and receiving no salary
held duly convicted of embezzling the
moneys of the Board although not directly
employed by the Board. (44 L. J., M. C., 65:
L. R., 2 C. C. R., 150: 39 J. P., 501.)

1856.   [778]
Reg. v. *Halifax L. B. H.* Damage to premises by
drainage works—Compensation—A public
body should be careful not to spend money
recklessly—If two legal remedies are available the less expensive should be chosen.
(20 J. P., 51.)

1871.   [779]
Reg. v. *Lovibond.* "Metropolis Management
Amendment Act, 1862 "—Building Line—
Encroachment—Indictment—Held that an
Indictment did not lie, for the Statute had
prescribed a particular remedy. (24 L. T.,
357: 36 J. P., 20: 19 W. R., 753.)

1864.   [780]
Saunders v. *Slack.* Local Act—Action against
the Clerk of Commissioners—Judgment and
fi. fa.—Rule *Nisi* to set aside the same discharged on the ground that the Commissioners if in the right might obtain redress
otherwise, *e.g.* by Action of Trespass. (11 L.
T., 484.)

1876.   [781]
Scarborough, Mayor v. *Scarborough Union.*
"Public Health Act, 1875," § 91 — Town
refuse deposited in a field in the Rural District with the consent of a farmer—Nuisance
—Order on Corporation to "discontinue and
abate"—Order held good as regards discontinuance, but bad as regards abatement,
Corporation possessing no power to enter in
order to abate. (L. R., 1 Ex. D., 344: 34 L.
T., 768: 40 J. P., 726.)

1876.   [782]
Skeet v. *Bishop Stortford L. B.* Suit pending as
to the rights of a Board—Abusive language
by the Clerk and a member towards a witness
—Alleged contempt—Circumstances under
which the Court would interfere. (*Times,*
June 24, 1876.) Proceedings to try a right
of way. (*Times,* June 5, 1877.)

1875.   [783]
Small v. *Bickley.* "Nuisances Removal Act,
1863," § 3 [="Public Health Act, 1875,"
§ 118]—Search for diseased meat—Held that
refusing to send a key ½ mile to admit an
Inspector was not an offence within the Act,
as such refusal did not amount to obstructing
an officer. (32 L. T., 726: 40 J. P., 119.)

1889.   [784]
Smith v. *Finchley L. B.* Successful Action by
plaintiff against Board for balance due under
a contract—Subsequently, a letter addressed
to the Board was discussed publicly and

handed to the press and published—Application for an attachment against 6 members
and the clerk—Application refused—*Per*
Lopes, J.:—"It would be ridiculous to grant
this application." (*Times,* May 9, 1889.)

1878.   [785]
St. Leonard's, Shoreditch, Guardians v. *Franklin.*
Action for penalties—A Corporation cannot
sue as a common informer unless expressly
authorised by Statute to do so. (47 L. J.,
C. P., 727: L. R., 3 C. P. D., 377: 39 L. T.,
122: 42 J. P., 727.)

1859.   [786]
Ward v. *Lowndes.* "Public Health Act, 1848,"
§ 89 [="Public Health Act, 1875," §§ 210-11]
—Action by an Architect for work done, &c.,
for an Authority whose powers had been
transferred to another Authority—Claim of
Mandamus to levy a Rate—Plea of Limitation
of time—Judgment for the plaintiff. (29 L.
J., Q. B., 40: 1 E. & E., 940: 1 L. T., 268.)

1864.   [787]
Wednesbury L. B. H. v. *Stephenson.* "Public
Health Act, 1848," § 38 [="Public Health
Act, 1875," § 192]; "Local Government
Act, 1858," § 63 [= Ibid., § 257]—Appeal to Q. B.—Judgment for appellants—
Held that though the respondent did not
appear, yet he was liable for the Costs of the
appeal—Surveyor interested in a patent for
bricks—Held that notwithstanding this, he
was entitled to represent the Board which
was suing for Paving expenses. (33 L. J.,
M. C., 111: [*Reg.* v. *Wednesbury*] 9 L. T.,
731: 27 J. P., 741.)

1885.   [788]
Westbury-on-Severn Sanitary A. v. *Meredith.*
"Public Health Act, 1875," § 257—Action
in Chancery Division to declare that £6 odd
expended on premises shall be charged on
them—Held that such an action being for
less than £10 could not be maintained in the
Chancery Division. (L. R., 30 Ch. D., 387:
42 L. T., 838.)

1865.   [789]
Williams v. *Golding.* Local Act—Persons entitled to Notice of Action—The words "district surveyor or other persons" mean "other
official persons" and do not include a builder
guilty of negligence. (Metrop.) (35 L. J.,
C. P., 1: L. R., 1 C. P., 69: 13 L. T., 291.)

1865.   [790]
Wootton v. *Harvey.* "Militia Act, 1802," 42 Geo.
III., c. 90, § 61—Distress Warrant may issue
after a single demand even though there
may have been an appeal to Sessions
against the demand and the appeal have
been dismissed.—A person who is bound to
pay money to another is required to find out
his creditor, if in England, and to tender
him the money. (6 East, 75.)

(ii.) "CERTIORARI."

1857.   [791]
Reg. v. *Dickenson.* "Municipal Corporations Act,
1835," § 132—By-Law—Projection of a Shop
Front—By consent of the parties, the Court

may have cognizance of a Special Case, although *Certiorari* has been taken away. (26 L. J., M. C., 204: 7 E. & B., 831: 29 L. T., (o. s.), 180.)

1860.   [792]
Reg. v. *Gosse.* "Nuisances Removal Act, 1855," § 39 [="Public Health Act, 1875," § 262] —If Justices have acted without jurisdiction, *Certiorari* may be had notwithstanding § 39. (30 L. J., M. C., 41: 3 E. & E., 277: 3 L. T., 404.)

1867.   [793]
Reg. v. *Staffordshire JJ.* "Public Health Act, 1848," § 63 [="Public Health Act, 1875," §§ 116-17]—A conviction can only be removed by *Certiorari* where there is excess or refusal of jurisdiction—The "Railway Clauses Consolidation Act, 1845," is so incorporated with the "Towns Improvement Clauses Act, 1847," as to take away *Certiorari*. (16 L. T., 430.)

(iii.) COUNTY COURT.

1877.   [794]
Hall v. *Pritchett : Huddersfield Corporation, Garnishees.* Judgment summons for debt obtained in County Court against defendant, a Medical Officer of Health—Garnishee summons on the Corporation (his employers) set aside on the ground that the current instalment of the officer's salary before it was actually payable was not a debt due or owing or accruing at the time when the summons was issued, within the County Court Rules, 1875, Order XXIV., Rule 4. (47 L. J., Q. B., 15: L. R., 3 Q. B. D., 215: 37 L. T., 671.)

1887.   [795]
Leeds, Mayor, v. *Robshaw.* Local Acts—A certain (local) limitation of time for recovery of expenses held not to apply when proceedings were taken in the County Court. (51 J. P., 441.)

1879.   [796]
Reg. v. *Harrington.* Nuisance—Jurisdiction of County Court—A County Court Judge, where he can entertain an Action for damage owing to a nuisance, has power to grant an Injunction to restrain such nuisance, and can enforce it by Attachment. (43 J. P., 429.)

1855.   [797]
Taylor v. *Crowland Gas & Coke Co.* A Corporation may be sued in a County Court, and "dwells" at the place where its business is carried on. (24 L. J., Ex., 233: 11 Ex., 1: 3 C. L. R., 865: 24 L. T., (o. s.), 118.)

1876.   [798]
Tottenham L. B v. *Rowell.* (1). "Public Health Act, 1848," §§ 69 and 129 [="Public Health Act, 1875," § 150, 251]—The limitation of 6 months in 11 & 12 Vict., c. 43, § 11, applies to proceedings in County Courts as well as to proceedings before Justices. (46 L. J., Q. B., 432: L. R., 1 Ex. D., 514: 35 L. T., 837.)

1876.   [799]
West Ham L. B. v. *Muldums.* "Public Health Act, 1848," § 69 [=Public Health Act, 1875," § 150]: 24 & 25 Vict., c. 61, § 24 [=Ibid., § 261] —Paving expenses recoverable summarily or

in a County Court—The limitation of 6 months for proceedings applies also in a County Court. (33 L. T., 809: 40 J. P., 470.)

(iv.) "ELEGIT."

1891.   [800]
Jersey (Earl of) v. *Uxbridge R. S. A.* Injunction granted to restrain pollution of stream—Costs taxed—Writ of *Elegit* sued for—Where certain lands are held in trust for a certain parish they cannot be taken in execution for a judgment debt not chargeable exclusively against that parish—Held also that the costs in question were "general expenses"—Held also that the judgment could only be enforced against property acquired out of the Common Fund. (60 L. J., Ch., 833: L. R., 3 Ch. D., 183; 64 L. T., 858.)

1866.   [801]
Worral Waterworks Co. v. *Lloyd.* Land conveyed to a Local Board for the purposes of the "Public Health Acts" held liable to be taken under an *Elegit.* (L. R., 1 C. P., 719.)

(v.) EVIDENCE.

1889.   [802]
Caton v. *Hamilton.* An Ordnance map is receivable in evidence to prove the position of a boundary line at the time when the Survey was made, but it cannot be used as any proof of title. (53 J. P., 504.)

1845.   [803]
Doe d. Hopley v. *Young.* Acting in an official capacity may be proved by evidence of the person having exercised the office before or after. (15 L. J., Q. B., 9 : 8 Q. B., 63.)

1836.   [804]
Meeker v. *Van Keusselaer.* Parol evidence of the acts of a Board of Health in directing the abatement of nuisances is not admissible: written minutes or orders should be produced. (15 Wendell, 397.) [American.]

1838.   [805]
Merrick v. *Wakley.* "Poor Law Amendment Act, 1834," § 15—A register of attendances kept by a Medical Officer in obedience to an order of the Poor Law Commissioners is not admissible in evidence on behalf of the author as a public official book. (7 L. J., Q. B., 190 : 8 A. & E., 170 : 8 C. & P., 283.)

1846.   [806]
Slater v. *Hodgson.* A Workhouse is not an improper repository for documents belonging to a parish within the Union so as to make them inadmissible in evidence when produced from thence. (2 New Sess. Cas., 488: 9 Q. B., 727: 8 L. T., (o. s.), 160.)

1879.   [807]
Weymouth L. B. H., In re. Nuisance on property belonging to a Town Council—Proceedings against Council—Appeal dismissed, proceedings being informal, it being shown that the Council were not owners *qua* Local Board and did not occupy. (*Times,* May 27, 1879.)

F. 2

1876.   [808]
Witney v. *Wycombe Union.* "Public Health Act, 1875"—"Special" Expenses—A well, constructed by private individuals for public use, repaired by the Local Authority—Held, that this evidence justified the enforcement of a precept for money. (40 J. P., 149.)

(vi.) INJUNCTION.

1866.   [809]
A.-G. v. *Staffordshire Copper Extracting Co.* Nuisance under the "Nuisances Removal Act, 1855"—Bill filed by a Local Board of Health—Question as to the frame of the suit. (W. N., 1866, p. 258.)

1867.   [810]
Cooke v. *Forbes.* Where an accidental escape of noxious vapour on 3 occasions inflicted injury on a neighbouring manufacturer, held that an Injunction was not an appropriate remedy. (37 L. J., Ch., 178: L. R., 5 Eq., 166: 17 L. T., 371.)

1877.   [811]
Flower v. *Leyton L. B.* Action for damage to crops by overflow of sewage, and application for Injunction to restrain—Held, that application for an Injunction was the chief part of the plaintiff's case and the claim for damages only subsidiary, and therefore that the Board was not entitled to Notice of Action under § 264 of the "Public Health Act, 1875." (46 L. J., Ch., 621: L. R., 5 Ch. D., 347: 36 L. T., 760.) Action brought; damages assessed by the Court. (W. N., 1878, p. 91.)

1883.   [812]
Foster v. *Bristol Corporation.* Local Act—Formation of new street through part of disused Burial ground—Allegation that works were being carried out indecently—Injunction granted in form of an admonition to defendants to take precautions not to disturb human remains. (*Times*, June 12, 1883.)

1865.   [813]
Grindley v. *Booth.* Action for nuisance—Boiling offal—*Ex parte* Injunction under the "Common Law Procedure Act, 1854," § 82, granted pending the trial—Practice as to costs. (34 L. J., Ex., 135: 3 H. & C., 669: 12 L. T., 469.)

1875.   [814]
Hardinge v. *Southborough L. B.* Pollution of Stream by Sewage—Injunction granted against a Board, though all the members had resigned office. (W. N., 1875, p. 78: 32 L. T., 250.)

1865.   [815]
Lingwood v. *Stowmarket Co.* The right to an Injunction is founded on the fact of injury, and this must, therefore, be averred. (L. R., 1 Eq., 77: 13 L. T., 540.)

1834.   [816]
Ripon (Earl of) v. *Hobart.* Fen Drainage—Anticipated damage to banks of river—Injunction refused on the ground that there was no antecedent certainty of a nuisance arising. (3 L. J., Ch., 145: 3 Myl. & K., 169.)

1864.   [817]
Swaine v. *Great Northern Railway Co.* Nuisance—Railway Sidings used for Manure Trucks—An Injunction will not be granted against a temporary and occasional nuisance. (33 L. J., Ch., 399: 4 De G. J. & S., 211: 9 L. T., 571 and 745.)

1873.   [818]
Thorpe v. *Brumfitt.* Street Obstruction by carts loading and unloading—The Court will restrain a nuisance caused by several persons, though the mischief caused by any one of them would by itself be inappreciable. (L R., 8 Ch. App., 650: 37 J. P., 742.)

(vii.) JUSTICES.

1880.   [819]
Debenham v. *Metropolitan B. W.* Default in taking down dangerous party wall ordered by Magistrate to be taken down by owner—Whereupon wall removed by contractor employed by the Board for the purpose—Refusal by owner to reimburse Board on ground that the Board had incurred needless expense—Held that a Magistrate had no power to review the reasonableness of the outlay, but that on proof of the fact that it had been incurred he must order owner to refund. (50 L. J., M. C., 29: L. R., 6 Q. B. D., 112: 43 L. T., 596: 45 J. P., 190.)

1877.   [820]
Diss Urban Authority v. *Aldrich.* "Public Health Act, 1875," § 305—Application to Justices for an Order to enter premises to make a sewer. (46 L. J., M. C., 183: L. R., 2 Q. B. D., 179: 36 L. T., 663: 41 J. P., 549.) [See now 42 & 43 Vict., c. 49, § 33.]

1863.   [821]
Hargreaves v. *Taylor.* "Public Health Act, 1848," § 54 [="Public Health Act, 1875," §§ 40-1]—Nuisance—The nature and extent of the works to be done are in the discretion of a Local Board—At proceedings before Justices for the recovery of penalties, such Justices cannot review the determination of the Board. (32 L. J., M. C., 111: 3 B. & S., 613: 8 L. T., 149.)

1892.   [822]
Harvey v. *Gibb.* Summons for discharging refuse into a river—One of the magistrates a member of the Fishery Committee which instituted the prosecution—*Per* Wills, J.:—"We will not give costs against the magistrate personally; but, if in this last decade of the 19th century magistrates will not learn the elementary rule of law that they must not adjudicate or appear to adjudicate in cases in which they are interested, we shall have to do so in future." (*Times*, May 17, 1892.)

1862.   [823]
Leamington L. B. H., Ex parte. Complaint to Justices on behalf of a Local Board by a Superintendent of Police—Justices not bound to adjudicate unless the Clerk appears either in person, or by Counsel or Attorney. (26 J. P., 84.) [See "Public Health Act, 1875," § 259.]

1876.   [824]
Morant v. *Taylor.* Local Act—Order to demolish building—Limitation of time—11 & 12 Vict. c. 43, § 11—Held that all kinds of Orders are subject to the 6 months' limitation. (45 L. J., M. C., 78 : L. R., 1 Ex. D., 188 : 34 L. T., 139 : 40 J. P., 501.)

1851.   [825]
Newbold v. *Coltman.* 2 & 3 Vict., c. 84, § 1—Order on Overseers for contribution—Consideration of the circumstances which will justify refusal to pay. (20 L. J., M. C., 149 : 6 Ex., 189 : 15 J. P., 372.)

1860.   [826]
Newman v. *Baker.* "Metropolitan Building Act, 1855," § 46—"Street"—There being no question of Law involved, the Magistrate's decision held not liable to be reviewed. (8 C. B., (N. S.), 200.)

1863.   [827]
Reg. v. *Brodhurst.* "Public Health Act, 1848," §§ 2, 129, and 148 [="Public Health Act, 1875," §§ 251, 306]—"Justices acting for the place" means, in the case of a County, acting and also sitting within the Petty Sessional Division in which the case arises—Justices not so acting or sitting have no jurisdiction. (32 L. J., M. C., 168 : 11 W. R., 425.) [But see Paley, *Summary Convictions*, 6th ed., 1879, p. 38.]

1881.   [828]
Reg. v. *Deal JJ.* Justices, annual subscribers to local Branch of Society managed in London, held not disqualified from adjudicating on a charge preferred by the London Committee —Payment of a subscription is merely a mode of expressing an opinion—Allegation of bias too remote. (45 L. T., 439 : 46 J. P., 71.)

1892.   [829]
Reg. v. *Gainford.* A Justice attended a Vestry and proposed a resolution for removal of a nuisance caused by S. on a summons taken out against S. by Surveyor—The Justice sat and convicted him, further deciding that the materials complained of should be sold for the benefit of the Rates—Held that there was thus a double disability attaching to the Justice—Conviction quashed. (61 L. J., M. C., 50 : L. R., 1 Q. B., 381 : 56 J. P., 247.)

1880.   [830]
Reg. v. *Gibbon.* Local Act—Interest of Justices —Information laid before a Justice who was a member of Corporation prosecuting— Penalty payable to Corporation—Held that the Justice had an interest sufficient to disqualify him, and therefore *Mandamus* to 2 other Justices to hear the summons issued by the first Justice refused though they were not interested—*Reg.* v. *Weymouth JJ.* extended. (L. R., 6 Q. B. D., 168 : 29 W. R., 442.)

1881.   [831]
Reg. v. *Handsley.* "Public Health Act, 1875," § 258—A Justice though member of Body which prosecutes is not on that account disqualified from acting as a Justice : he is only disqualified when he has such a substantial

interest in the result as to make bias likely —*Reg.* v. *Gibbon* disapproved of. (51 L. J., M. C., 137 : L. R., 8 Q. B. D., 383 : 46 J. P., 119.)

1845.   [832]
Reg. v. *Hertfordshire JJ.* If a Justice hearing a case at Sessions is interested in the result the Court is improperly constituted—No answer, that there was a majority without counting the interested party—Nor that he withdrew before the decision if he had assisted in discussing the matter. (14 L. J., M. C., 73 : 6 Q. B., 753 : 1 New. Sess. Cas., 470.)

1879.   [833]
Reg. v. *Huntingdon JJ.* "Dogs Act, 1871"— Three Justices, Members of a Town Council, having assisted in making an Order, afterwards sat to hear a complaint of non-observance of the Order—Held that they had no such interest as to oust their jurisdiction. (L. R., 4 Q. B. D., 522 : 43 J. P., 767.)

1862.   [834]
Reg. v. *Jenkins.* "Nuisances Removal Act, 1855," § 14 [="Public Health Act, 1875," § 98]—When a penalty is imposed under this Section and remains unsatisfied, the Justices, before they can enforce it, must summon the defendant. (32 L. J., M. C., 1 : 3 B. & S., 116 : 7 L. T., 272.)

1880.   [835]
Reg. v. *Lancashire JJ.* (3). Justices members of an Urban Sanitary Authority held justified in declining to hear an Information laid before them for breach of a law in the vindication of which they were *ex officio* interested. (*Times*, Dec. 22, 1880.)

1882.   [836]
Reg. v. *Lee.* (3). "Public Health Act, 1875," §§ 116, and 275—Conviction—One of the convicting Justices Chairman of the Committee which directed the prosecution—Conviction quashed —§ 258 does not apply to such a manifest case of bias. (L. R., 9 Q. B. D., 394 : 30 W. R., 750 : 47 J. P., 118.)

1891.   [837]
Reg. v. *London C. C.* "Local Government Act, 1888," § 3—Application for renewal of a license—Refusal by Committee—Fresh application—Opposition by sitting Councillors— Disqualification by bias. (Metrop.) (61 L. J., M. C., 75 : L. R., 1 Q. B., 190 : 66 L. T., 168 : 56 J. P., 8.)

1875.   [838]
Reg. v. *Meyer.* Alleged default by two Sanitary Authorities ; a third party prosecutes H. who is convicted ; one of the Justices present at the conviction was chairman of one of the Sanitary Authorities concerned—Conviction quashed on the ground of interest in one of the Justices though he took no active part in the conviction. (L. R., 1 Q. B. D., 173 : [*Reg.* v. *Myers*] 34 L. T., 247 : 40 J. P., 645.)

1866.   [839]
Reg. v. *Pollard.* (1). A defendant charged with obstructing the works of a Local Board is not necessarily entitled to have the case dismissed by Justices because he justifies the obstruc-

tion by claim of private right—Justices required to state a Case. (14 L. T., 599.)

1873. [840]
Reg. v. *Pollard.* (2). "Nuisances Removal Act, 1855" [Repealed]—Proceedings for abatement of a nuisance—Defence that a public sewer must first be made—Complaint dismissed on the ground that construction of a sewer was a condition precedent to making of an Order of abatement—Justices ordered to state a Case on this point. (37 J. P., 309.)

1870. [841]
Reg. v. *Pratt.* (2). Costs awarded by Sessions in respect of an appeal and which are enforceable by distress and commitment are within the exception in § 4 (2) of the "Debtors Act, 1869," and the defaulter may therefore be imprisoned. (39 L. J., M. C., 73 : L. R., 5 Q. B., 176: [*Cole, Ex parte*] 21 L. T., 750.)

1885. [842]
Reg. v. *Priestley.* Non-compliance with Building By-Laws—Limitation of time—Justices held bound to state a Case. (49 J. P., 148.)

1866. [843]
Reg. v. *Rand.* A Justice pecuniarily interested is disqualified from acting judicially; but possibility of bias does not suffice. (35 L. J., M. C., 157 : L. R., 1 Q. B., 230 : 7 B. & S., 297.)

1877. [844]
Reg. v. *Trimble.* "Public Health Act, 1875," § 96 —Nuisance from stagnant water—Nuisance caused by A., but actually occurring on the land of his neighbour B.—Order to abate involving an entry by A. on the land of B. held bad. (36 L. T., 508 : [*Reg.* v. *Cumberland*] 41 J. P., 454.)

1879. [845]
Reg. v. *Weymouth JJ.* "Public Health Act, 1875," § 258 — Proceedings by a Local Authority against a person for a nuisance—Conviction—Of the Magistrates sitting on the Bench when the case was heard, 2 were members of the Local Authority—Held that they were interested—Accordingly, Rule absolute for *Certiorari* to quash the conviction. (48 L. J., M. C., 139 : [*Reg.* v. *Milledge*] L. R., 4 Q. B. D., 332: 40 L. T., 748: 43 J. P., 606.)

1882. [846]
Reg. v. *Winchester JJ.* Building By-Laws—Certain members of an Urban Authority, being also Justices, took part in a meeting whereat it was resolved that a roof was to be pulled down—Some of the same Justices heard the case, and ordered Builder in default to be fined—Order quashed on *Certiorari*, and the Justices who acted in both capacities to pay the Costs. (46 J. P., 724.)

1833. [847]
Rex v. *Cheshire JJ.* When Justices have signed and sealed an Order they cannot afterwards amend it. (5 B. & Ad., 439: 2 N. & M., 827.)

1865. [848]
Wakefield L. B. H. v. *West Riding & Grimsby*

Railway Co. Summary Conviction—If a Justice is interested, the parties may waive the objection ; if this is done, the proceedings will not on that account be afterwards avoided by the Superior Court. (L. R., 1 Q. B., 84: 6 B. & S., 794: 10 Cox, C. C , 162 : 13 L. T., 590.)

1858. [849]
Yorkshire Tyre and Axle Co. v. *Rotherham L. B. H.* Case stated under 20 & 21 Vict., c. 43, § 2—Material document omitted to be set out—Case sent back for amendment before it came on for argument. (27 L. J., C. P., 235 : 4 C. B., (N. S.), 362.)

(viii.) "MANDAMUS."

1857. [850]
Ham L. B., In re ; Bassett, Ex parte. "Nuisances Removal Act, 1855," § 14 [="Public Health Act, 1875," § 98]—If a Sanitary Authority does not think fit to enforce an Order of Justices obtained by its own officer, it cannot be made to do so by *Mandamus.* (26 L. J., M. C., 64 : 7 E. & B., 280 : [*Reg.* v. *Ham*] 28 L. T., (O. S.), 267.)

1876. [851]
Harrogate Medical Officer v. *Harrogate L. B. H.* Application for *Mandamus* to compel a Board to allow a duly appointed officer to discharge his duties—Application refused—*Mandamus* only the remedy for non-performance of public duties—A Board not being required to perform medical officer's duties, *Mandamus* does not lie—His remedy under the circumstances is an Action for non-payment of salary. (*Times,* Nov. 22, 1876.)

1864. [852]
Reg. v. *Boteler.* 2 & 3 Vict., c. 84, § 1—Contribution Order on an Overseer—On refusal to pay, application to Justices to issue Warrant —On their refusal, *Mandamus*—The discretion of Justices in such cases is not absolute ; they must not refuse to act merely for frivolous reasons. (33 L. J., M. C., 101 : 4 B. & S., 959 : 8 L. T., 514.)

1859. [853]
Reg. v. *Burleigh* [*Burley*] *L. B.* Payment made by a Board under the protection of a *Mandamus,* which was deemed necessary because of long delay—On a further delay in asking for Costs, Costs refused. (1 L. T., 92.)

1875 and 1876. [854]
Reg. v. *Keighley Guardians.* Refusal to enforce vaccination—Rule absolute for *Mandamus* at the instance of Local Government Board. (39 J. P., 309 and 360.) [Subsequently an application to quash the *Mandamus* was refused : and see the Return thereto discussed, 40 J. P., 70. Finally a Rule *Absolute* was granted for an Attachment against the Guardians for disobeying the *Mandamus. Times,* July 4, 1876.]

1875. [855]
Reg. v. *Peterborough, Mayor,* "Borough Funds Act, 1872 "—Application for *Mandamus* for a Poll refused, applicant, though a ratepayer, being personally interested as Solicitor for

the Bill, respecting which he desired a Poll
—On such an application it is essential to
show who is the real applicant, and that he is
bonâ fide interested. (44 L. J., Q. B., 85 :
23 W. R., 343.)

1862.   [856]
Reg. v. *St. Luke's, Chelsea, Vestry.* (1). "Metropolis Management Act, 1855," § 69—*Mandamus* ordering the construction of a sewer
held defective—It should have shown some
particular reason why one locality was to be
singled out, and that the Metropolitan Board
had given its consent. (31 L. J., Q. B., 50 :
1 B. & S., 903 : 5 L. T., 744.)

1837.   [857]
Rex v. *Nottingham Old Water-works Co.* Interference with Water rights—A *Mandamus*
will only be issued when there is a specified
legal right and an absence of an effectual
remedy ; or if there is a doubt whether there
be a remedy. (6 L. J., K. B., 89 : 1 Nov.
& P., 480 : 6 A. & E., 355 : W. W. & D.,
166.)

1891.   [858]
Schofield, Ex parte. "Public Health Act, 1875,"
§ 91—Conviction for black smoke—Order to
abate made—Refusal by Magistrate to state
a case—*Mandamus* to compel him to do so,
refused—No appeal lies in such case to the
Court of Appeal. (56 J. P., 4.)

1865.   [859]
Worthington v. *Hulton.* Where a Judgment has
been obtained against a Local Board on a
contract, a *Mandamus* may be issued within
6 months of the Judgment, though the Action
was more than 6 months after the claim
accrued, if the delay is explained. (35
L. J., Q. B., 61 : L. R., 1 Q. B., 63 : 6 B. &
S., 943 : 13 L. T., 463.)

(IX.) SESSIONS.

1882.   [860]
Eaglesfield v. *Teasdale.* "Public Health Act,
1875," § 117—Charge of having diseased
meat dismissed by Justices—Held that no
appeal against such dismissal lay to Quarter
Sessions. (At Q. Sess.) (46 J. P., 744.)

1876.   [861]
Reg. v. *Barnet Union.* "Public Health Act,
1875," §§ 48 and 269—Appeal "within 14
days"—The "14 days" must be computed
from the date of the Order of Justices. (45
L. J., M. C., 105 : L. R., 1 Q. B. D., 558 :
[*Reg.* v. *St. Albans*] 35 L. T., 362 : 41
J. P., 6.)

1862.   [862]
Reg. v. *Hampshire JJ.* "Nuisances Removal
Act, 1855," § 40 [="Public Health Act,
1875," § 269]—Where an Order of Quarter
Sessions is removed to the Q. B. and quashed
generally, a Court of Quarter Sessions cannot afterwards order the costs to be taxed.
(32 L. J., M. C., 46 : [*Isle of Wight Ferry Co.*
v. *Ryde Commissioners*] 7 L. T., 391 : 25
J. P., 454.)

1881.   [863]
Reg. v. *Middlesex JJ.* (2). Prosecution of Local

Board by Thames Conservators for alleged
pollution of River Colne by sewage—Complaint dismissed by Justices—Whereupon
Conservators appealed to Sessions—Prohibition issued to Sessions forbidding the Appeal
being heard—Only where there has been a
conviction can there be an Appeal—An
unsuccessful prosecutor has no right of
Appeal. (45 J. P., 420.)

(X.) "QUO WARRANTO."

1871.   [864]
Bradley v. *Sylvester.* Clerk of School Board
alleged to have been improperly elected—In
the case of any Office held at the pleasure of
a Board, application should be made to the
Board itself to remedy an impropriety in
Election, before applying for a *Quo Warranto.*
(25 L. T., 459.)

1846.   [865]
Darley v. *The Queen.* *Quo Warranto* will lie for
usurping any Office of a public nature. (12
C. & F., 520.)

1851.   [866]
Haydock, Ex parte. "Public Health Act, 1848"
—Election—Allegation that votes had been
improperly admitted and rejected—*Quo Warranto.* (15 J. P., 384.)

1891.   [867]
Reg. v. *Burrows.* This writ will lie to inquire
into the election of a Vestry Clerk under
13 & 14 Vict., c. 57, §§ 6-7. (61 L. J.,
Q. B., 88 : L. R., 1 Q. B., 399 : 66 L. T., 25 :
55 J. P., 725.)

1854.   [868]
Reg. v. *Coaks.* "Municipal Corporations Act,
1835," § 51—Election of Councillor—*Quo
Warranto.* (23 L. J., Q. B., 133 : 3 E. & B.,
249 : 2 C. L. R., 947 : 22 L. T., (o. s.), 230.)

1873.   [869]
Reg. v. *Cousins.* *Quo Warranto*—Annual Office
—Application delayed for 8 months—Application refused it not being shown that the
result of the election would probably have
been different had a better mode of election
been adopted. (42 L. J., Q. B., 124 : L. R.,
8 Q. B., 216 : 28 L. T., 116 : 37 J. P., 470.)

1869.   [870]
Reg. v. *Diplock.* Election of Coroner—A declaration by Returning Officer of the name
of the successful candidate cannot be disturbed by *Quo Warranto.* (38 L. J., Q. B.,
297 : L. R., 4 Q. B., 549 : 10 B. & S., 613 :
21 L. T., 24.)

1865.   [871]
Reg. v. *Hampton.* "Poor Law Amendment Act,
1834"—*Quo Warranto* is applicable to the
office of Guardian. (6 B. & S., 923 : 13
L. T., 431)

1873.   [872]
Reg. v. *Jones.* The Chairman as such of a
Vestry declared himself elected a member of
a Burial Board, but afterwards refrained
from acting on the Board—*Quo Warranto* is
not applicable where a person has neither
acted in an office nor claimed to do so. (28
L. T., 270 : 37 J. P., 453.)

1887. [873]
Reg. v. *Langton.* Town Commissioner—Acquiescence by Relator in illegal practices, is not a bar to an application for *Quo Warranto* in respect of an office vacated by a statutable illegality, as the Court cannot on any consideration of personal objections allow an office to remain full which a statute says shall be vacant. (20 L. R., Ir., 46.)

1891. [874]
Reg. v. *Morton.* "Municipal Corporations Act, 1882," §§ 6, 60, 87, 225—Election of Alderman—Mayor as Chairman voted for himself, and then gave a casting vote to the same effect—Held that *Quo Warranto* would not lie, though a petition might do so. (61 L. J., Q. B., 39: L. R., [1892] 1 Q. B., 39: 65 L. T., 611: 56 J. P., 105.)

1851. [875]
Reg. v. *St. Martin's-in-the-Fields Guardians.* Quo Warranto lies in respect of the office of Clerk of Guardians—*Mandamus* not appropriate. (20 L. J., Q. B., 423: 17 Q. B., 149: 15 J. P., 371.)

1867. [876]
Reg. v. *Staples.* Adoption of the "Local Government Act, 1858"—Application by an individual for a *Quo Warranto* against all the members of a newly formed Board, refused—The Att.-Gen. should have intervened. (9 B. & S., 928, n.)

(xi.) TAXATION OF COSTS.

1883. [877]
Cowdell, In re. Arbitration under the "Public Health Act, 1875"—Powers of Local Board to control Taxation of Costs to which they were liable. (51 L. J., Ch., 246: 31 W. R., 335: W. N., 1883, p. 18.)

1849. [878]
Lumb v. *Simpson.* Action for injury to a watercourse—Costs of scientific experiments disallowed on Taxation. (18 L. J., Ex, 377: 4 Ex., 85: 13 L. T., (o. s.), 260.)

46. LIABILITY FOR ACCIDENTS, &c.

*** See also " Gas Company," (§ 36, *ante*); "Water Company," (§ 80, *post*); "Obstruction of Highways," (Part II., § 6, *post*.)

1845. [879]
Allen v. *Hayward.* Navigation Commissioners—Failure of an earth-work—Contractor and not the Commissioners held under the circumstances liable for damage caused by negligent construction. (15 L. J., Q. B., 99: 7 Q. B., 960: 4 Rail. Cas., 104.)

1854. [880]
Alston v. *Grant.* Landlord and Tenant—Bursting of a Sewer improperly constructed—Damage to goods—Verdict for the Lessee in an Action against his Landlord. (23 L. J., Q. B., 163: 3 E. & B., 128: 2 C. L. R., 993: 22 L. T., (o. s.), 221.)

1857. [881]
Arthy v. *Coleman.* "Public Health Act, 1848," § 140 [="Public Health Act, 1875," § 265] —A contractor employed by a Local Board on a highway held liable to a third party for his negligence. (30 L. T., (o. s.), 101: 6 W. R., 34.)

1861. [882]
Backhouse v. *Bonomi.* Excavations under houses causing sinkage and damage—Statute of Limitations held to run not from date of excavation but date of actual injury becoming manifest. (34 L. J., Q. B., 181: 9 H. L. C., 503: 4 L. T., 754.)

1885. [883]
Barham v. *Ipswich Dock Commissioners.* Local Act—Highway maintainable by Commissioners broken up by Railway Company under Statutory powers—Highway not properly reinstated—Accident—Commissioners held not liable. (54 L. T., 23.)

1879. [884]
Bathurst, Borough of v. *Macpherson.* "New South Wales Acts"—Non-repair of highway —Accident to horse—Many English cases reviewed and commented on. (48 L. J., P. C, 61: L. R., 4 App. Cas., 256: 41 L. T., 778: 43 J. P., 827.)

1882. [885]
Blackmore v. *Mile End Vestry.* Flap placed in street to protect water meter used by Vestry —Accident—Held that Vestry was liable for the negligent non-repair of the flap, the flap not being used by Vestry *quâ* Highway Authority — *White* v. *Hindley* approved. (51 L. J., Q. B. D., 496: L. R., 9 Q. B. D., 451: 46 L. T., 869.)

1863. [886]
Blake v. *Thirst.* Construction of sewer—Absence of fence and lights—Accident—Defendant, the contractor, held liable though a subcontractor was the party in default. (32 L. J., Ex., 188: 2 H. & C., 20: 8 L. T., 251.)

1607. [887]
Blyth v. *Topham.* An Action will not lie for digging a pit in a Common, wherein a stray mare tumbles and perishes, the mare being unlawfully on the Common—It was held to be a case of *damnum absque injuriâ.* (Croke, Jac. I., 158.)

1876. [888]
Bower v. *Peate.* Rebuilding of a house—Defective shoring—Damage to adjacent land— Held that the contractors employed were liable. (45 L. J., Q. B., 446: L. R., 1 Q. B. D., 321: 35 L. T., 321: 40 J. P., 789.)

1879. [889]
Box v. *Jubb.* Water stored in reservoir—Overflow of, on neighbour's premises, from causes beyond owner's control, namely the act of a third party—Owner held not liable for the damage done—*Fletcher* v. *Rylands* distinguished: *Nicholls* v. *Marsland* followed. (48 L. J., Ex., 417: 41 L. T., 97.)

1792. [890]
British Cast Plate Manufacturers v. *Meredith.*

Paving Commissioners acting *intra vires* held not liable for consequential damage. (4 T. R., 794.)

1889.   [891]
Brown v. *Eastern and Midland Railway Co.*   A horse shied at a heap of materials placed on land of Defendants adjoining highway—Cart upset and Plaintiff injured—Proof that other horses had shied at the same heap, was good evidence that the heap was a public nuisance and that Plaintiff was entitled to recover. (58 L. J., Q. B., 212 : L. R., 22 Q. B. D., 391 : *60 L. T., 266 : *53 J. P., 342.)

1858.   [892]
Brown v. *Sargent.*   Bursting of a sewer constructed by a Local Board whereby a Bakehouse was damaged—Plea that an extraordinary storm was the cause—Evidence to support such a plea must extend over a considerable range of years—Proof of compensation having been paid on former occasions, with proof (even slight) of negligent construction will suffice to show liability—Verdict for plaintiff. (1 F. & F., 112.)

1862.   [893]
Clothier v. *Webster.*   "Metropolis Management Act, 1855," §§ 135, 220—Construction of a sewer—Negligence of a Contractor—Statutory provision as to compensation—If negligence can be shown a party is not tied down to a statutory remedy designed to afford compensation for injury necessarily inflicted by the due execution of works. (Metropolis.) (31 L. J., C. P., 316 : 12 C. B., (N. S.), 790 : 6 L. T., 461.)

1866.   [894]
Cox v. *Wise.*   Drainage Commissioners—Negligence—Bursting of a Sluice—Commissioners liable for the default of their servants. (37 L. J., Q. B., 262 : L. R., 1 Q. B., 711 : 7 B. & S., 831 ; 14 L. T., 891.)

1869.   [895]
Collins v. *Middle Level Commissioners.*   Local Act 7 & 8 Vict., c. cvi.—Circumstances under which a public body are liable for negligence where the act of a third party done to obviate some of the consequences of the negligence is the immediate cause of the injury to the plaintiff—Plaintiff held entitled to sue the Commissioners. (38 L. J., C. P., 236 : L. R., 4 C. P., 279 : 20 L. T., 442.)

1891.   [896]
Cox v. *Paddington Vestry.*   Leaky water pipe laid bare in making a sewer—Road imperfectly made good—Leakage, and consequent injury to roadway whereby van overturned—Held the Vestry was liable because knowing the condition of the water pipe no special care was taken to guard against the consequences of it leaking. (64 L. T., 566.)

1860.   [897]
Cracknell v. *Thetford, Mayor.*   Local Navigation Act—Duty to dredge—Liability for injury from the overflowing of a river—Corporation not being the owners of the soil of the river, held not liable. (38 L. J., C. P., 353 : L. R., 4 C. P., 629.)

1891.   [898]
Crumbie v. *Wallsend L. B.*   "Public Health Act, 1875," § 264—Injury to foundations of house by negligent construction of sewer—6 months held to run from commencement of visible injury, not from completion of works which caused tho injury. (60 L. J., Q. B., 392 : L. R., 1 Q. B., 503 : [*Crumlie* v. *W.*] 55 J. P., 421.)

1881.   [899]
Dewsbury Corporation v. *Batley Corporation.*   Accident to culvert maintained jointly by 2 united Authorities—Action by Landowner against them—Union dissolved by Act of Parliament after the accident but before the Action—Held that the one Corporation which had bought out the other could not recover contribution, the matter not having been brought before the Arbitrator who settled accounts at the dissolution. (*Times*, June 4, 1881.)

1881.   [900]
Dixon v. *Metropolitan B. W.*   Flood-gates of Sewer opened to permit the flow of a great quantity of storm water—Damage to plaintiff's wharf and barges by the sudden rush of water—Held that the Board had not exceeded its statutory powers and had only used the sewer-gates as it was entitled to do. (L. R., 7 Q. B. D., 418 : 45 L. T., 312 : 46 J. P., 4.)

1882.   [901]
Duke v. *Courage.*   Nuisance to highway—Refuse from brewery removed by contractor—Some spilt on highway—Accident to Plaintiff—Brewer held liable. (46 J. P., 453.)

1887.   [902]
Evans v. *Rhymney L. B.*   Action under "Lord Campbell's Act"—Accident to plaintiff's husband through falling down a steep embankment or causeway leading to a bridge unfenced and unlighted, and which had been an old way diverted—Judgment for the plaintiff, damages £150 and costs. (*Times*, Nov. 17, 1887.)

1871.   [903]
Foreman v. *Canterbury, Mayor.*   "Public Health Act, 1848," § 117—Highway—Obstruction by stones—A Local Board is liable for an injury caused by its servants negligently leaving a heap of stones on a highway. (40 L. J., Q. B., 138 : L. R., 6 Q. B., 214 : 24 L. T., 385 : 35 J. P., 629.)

1884.   [904]
Fowler v. *East London Waterworks Co.*   Street Plug allowed to project above general level of street—Accident to plaintiff's cart and injury to plaintiff—Defendants held liable : damages, £125. (*Times*, July 9, 1884.)

1885.   [905]
Gas-light and Coke Co. v. *St. Mary Abbot's, Kensington, Vestry.*   Action for damage to mains by steam roller, and for Injunction to restrain future use of roller so as to endanger mains—Judgment for plaintiffs, and Injunction granted—Consideration of the rights of the parties. (54 L. J., Q. B., 414 : L. R., 15 Q. B. D., 1 : 53 L. T., 457 : 49 J. P., 469.)

1878.   [906]
Geddis v. *Bann Reservoirs Proprietors.* Local Water Act—Persons possessing statutory powers to execute works likely to cause inconvenience and injury to others may be treated as under an obligation to take from time to time measures to prevent the occurrence of such inconvenience and injury.— *Cracknell* v. *Thetford* distinguished (L. R., 3 App. Cas., 430.)

1870.   [907]
Gibson v. *Preston, Mayor.* "Public Health Act, 1848," § 68—A Local Board is not liable to an Action for injuries received owing to the non-repair of a highway. (39 L. J., Q. B., 131: L. R., 5 Q. B., 218: 10 B. & S., 942: 22 L. T., 293: 34 J. P., 342.)

1865.   [908]
Gordon v. *St. James's, Westminster, Vestry.* Leakage of water from a drain into a cellar—Conflicting evidence of negligence—Judgment for the defendants. (13 L. T., 511.)

1864.   [909]
Gray v. *Pullen.* "Metropolis Management Act, 1855," §§ 77, 110–11—Construction of Drain resulting in injury to a highway—Accident to a foot passenger—A person is liable for an injury arising through negligent performance of a statutory obligation, whether performed by himself or by a contractor employed by him. (34 L. J., Q. B., 265: 5 B. & S., 970 : 11 L. T., 560.)

1875.   [910]
Gwinnell v. *Eamer.* Injury to plaintiff from the giving way of a defective coal-grating in a public highway—Premises under lease—Lessee to repair—Held that the plaintiff had no right of Action against the defendant as Lessor. (L. R., 10 C. P., 658: 32 L. T., 835.)

1877.   [911]
Hall v. *Batley, Mayor.* "Public Health Act, 1875," § 23—Damage to a wall owing to negligence in making excavations for drains—Verdict for the plaintiff notwithstanding that the work was being done at the request of the plaintiff, he having waived his right to do it himself. (47 L. J., Q. B., 148: 42 J. P., 151.)

1824.   [912]
Hall v. *Smith.* Local Act—Commissioners acting gratuitously held not individually liable for injury caused by the negligence of their workmen. (2 L. J., C. P., (o. s.), 113 : 9 Moo., 226: 2 Bing., 156.)

1874.   [913]
Hammond v. *St. Pancras Vestry.* Overflow of a sewer vested in defendants—Damage to property—Held that a public body is not liable for omissions to fulfil its duty unless negligence can be shown—When a Statute imposes a duty on a public body in terms by no means clear, such duty is not absolute, but reasonable care is implied. (43 L. J., C. P., 157: L. R., 9 C. P., 316: 30 L. T., 296.)

1892.   [914]
Hardcastle v. *Bielby.* "Highway Act, 1835," §

56—Highway obstructed by stones left there at night unguarded—Accident to horse and cart—Action against Surveyor—The stones had been put where they were by a Foreman unknown to the Surveyor—Surveyor held not liable. (61 L. J., M. C., 101 : L. R., 1 Q. B., 709 : 66 L. T., 343: 56 J. P., 549.)

1888.   [915]
Harding v. *Barker.* "Metropolis Management Act, 1855," § 207—The owner of a van is not liable for accidental damage done by his driver to a street lamp. (Metrop.) (53 J. P., 308.)

1862.   [916]
Hartnell v. *Ryde Commissioners.* "Towns Improvement Clauses Act," §§ 47 and 49—Non-repair of a Highway—Commissioners held liable to an action at the suit of a person who had suffered damage—The provisions of the "T. I. C. Act" herein differ from those of the "Public Health Act, 1848," § 68. [Repealed, but re-enacted as regards this detail in the same words; see § 149.] (33 L. J., Q. B., 39 : 4 B. & S., 361: 8 L. T., 574.)

1891.   [917]
Hendra v. *Chelsea Waterworks Co.* "Waterworks Clauses Act, 1847," § 38 — Old-fashioned fire-plug fixed in trunk of wood—Accident to foot passenger—Held that such a plug was not necessarily likely to be the cause of accidents— Judgment for defendants. (*Times*, Nov. 30, 1891.)

1868.   [918]
Hill v. *New River Co.* Spouting up of water from a main, whereby plaintiff's horses were frightened and fell into an unfenced excavation in a highway made by a contractor for sewers—Held that the water company and not the contractor was liable—The misuse of the water main was the *causa causans.* (9 B. & S., 303: 18 L. T., 355.)

1861.   [919]
Holliday v. *St. Leonard's, Shoreditch, Vestry.* (30 L. J., C. P., 361.) [Overruled by *Mersey Docks* v. *Gibbs*—Blackburn, J.; in *Foreman* v. *Canterbury.*]

1868.   [920]
Hyams v. *Webster.* Construction of Sewer—Subsidence of soil of road—Injury to a horse—Contractor held not liable, he having finished off the job and left it in proper condition. (38 L. J., Q. B., 21: L. R., 4 Q. B., 138: 9 B. & S., 1016: [In Court below, affirmed on appeal] 16 L. T., 118: 31 J. P., 439.)

1885.   [921]
Jones v. *Liverpool, Mayor.* Corporation water-cart used with hired horse and driver—Accident—Corporation held not liable for driver's negligence. (54 L. J., Q. B., 345: L. R., 14 Q. B. D., 890: 49 J. P., 311.)

1881.   [922]
Kennett v. *East London Water Co.* Stand-pipe erected during frost—Negligence in fixing whereby great quantities of water escaped on to surface of highway and froze—Accident

to plaintiff in crossing the highway—Verdict for plaintiff; damages £200. (At *Nisi Prius*.) (*Times*, April 2, 1881.)

1882. [923]
Kent v. *Worthing L. B.* Ground round water-valve in highway worn lower than top of valve—Accident to horse—Board held liable *quâ* Water Authority for negligence in not repairing the road.—Questioned in *Moore* v. *Lambeth.* (52 L. J., Q. B. D., 77: L. R., 10 Q. B. D., 118: 48 L. T., 362: 47 J. P., 23.)

1812. [924]
Leslie v. *Pounds.* Entrance to cellar from highway left uncovered, whereby plaintiff fell into cellar and was hurt—Landlord held liable for negligence of workpeople employed by him to execute repairs to the house. (4 Taunt., 649.)

1874. [925]
Letts v. *Oldbury L. B. H.* Alleged obstruction of highway with heaps of road material—Accident to a vehicle—Man killed—Verdict for the defendants. (38 J. P., 203.)

1830. [926]
Lloyd v. *Wigney.* Local Act requiring certain Actions to be brought within 6 months—Injury to house by negligent construction of sewer, to meet which, in part, the house was shored up by Local Authority—Action brought more than 6 months after cracks commenced, but within 6 months of the shore standing—Plaintiff nonsuited; the action was in respect of the cracks, and not of the shores, and the plaintiff was barred by time in respect of the cracks, they not being a "continuing damage," for the damage was the same at the end of the 6 months as at the beginning. (8 L. J., (o. s.), 161 : 6 Bing., 489 : 4 M. & P., 222.)

1860. [927]
Meek v. *Whitechapel B. W.* A Board held liable for a Sewer becoming choked, whereby it overflowed into the premises of the plaintiff. (2 F. & F., 144.) [See the observations of Brett, J., in *Hammond* v. *St. Pancras.*]

1883. [928]
Mellor v. *Heywood, Mayor.* Accident by carriage being driven against an unlighted street lamp—Action for damages held not maintainable, there being no duty to light the lamp, only a power to do so. (48 J. P., 149.)

1866. [929]
Mersey Docks & Harbour Board v. *Gibbs.* A Corporation created by a Statute for certain purposes is liable for the negligent acts of its servants, though deriving no benefit from the execution of its powers. (35 L. J., Ex., 225 : L. R., 1 H. L., 93 : 14 L. T. 677.)

1886. [930]
Moore v. *Lambeth Water Co.* Water Company held not liable for accident due to road being worn away round plug, plug itself being in good order—*Kent* v. *Worthing* questioned. (55 L. J., Q. B., 304 : L. R., 17 Q. B. D., 462 : 55 L. T., 309 : 50 J. P., 756.)

1888. [931]
Morgan v. *Hart.* Sign board blown down and plaintiff injured—Held that there being no evidence of negligence in the erection and fastening of the sign board, plaintiff could not recover damages. (*Times*, Nov. 27, 1888.)

1882. [932]
Murley v. *Grove.* Private road—Accident to trespasser by falling into a hole—Landowner held not liable to any person using the road without a license. (46 J. P., 360.)

1855. [933]
Newton v. *Ellis.* "Public Health Act, 1848," § 139 [= "Public Health Act, 1875," § 264] —Digging a Well—Injury—Negligence—A Contractor to a Local Board held entitled to Notice of Action. (24 L. J., Q. B., 337 : 5 E. & B., 115 : 25 L. T., (o. s.), 140.) [But see *Stringer* v. *Barker.*]

1876. [934]
Nichols v. *Marsland.* Overflow of reservoir owing to an unprecedented flood held to be an instance of *vis major*, for the injurious consequences of which the owner was not liable, all reasonable ordinary precautions having been taken. (46 L. J., Ex., 174 : L. R., 2 Ex. D., 1 : 35 L. T., 725 : 41 J. P., 500.)

1856. [935]
Ogilvy v. *Caledonian Railway Co.* Indirect damage to property by public works — Damage common to all the Queen's subjects is not a matter for which any individual legal remedy exists. (2 Macq., H. L. C., 229.)

1852. [936]
Overton v. *Freeman.* Contract for Paving—Stones left in street by a sub-contractor—Accident—Held that the Action was not rightly brought against defendant (the head contractor.) (21 L. J., C. P., 52 : 11 C. B., 867 : 18 L. T., (o. s.), 224.)

1853. [937]
Peachey v. *Rowland.* If A. employs B. to do a lawful act, and B. in doing it commits a nuisance, A. is not liable—Defendants contracted with one Ansell that he should fill in an opening in a highway made to permit a drain to be connected with a sewer—The earth was left by Ansell heaped up so as to be a nuisance, and plaintiff in driving suffered hurt—Held that defendants were not liable for Ansell's negligence. (22 L. J., C. P., 81 : 13 C. B., 182 : 20 L. T., (o. s.), 208.)

1875. [938]
Pendlebury v. *Greenhalgh.* Partial obstruction of a highway during repairs—Accident—Defendant, the Surveyor of Highways, held liable—Surveyor had only given the contractor part of the duty, and the duty of lighting and fencing by night remained with the Surveyor—*Taylor* v. *Greenhalgh* distinguished. (45 L. J., Q. B., 3 : L. R., 1 Q. B. D., 36 : 33 L. T., 372 : 40 J. P., 36.)

1878. [939]

Pocock v. Brighton, Mayor. Fracture of gas and water pipes in a street by the passage of a steam roller—Accident — Gas explosion—Verdict for the plaintiff, on the ground that the street and the roller being alike under the management of the Corporation, they had the means of preventing a roller of dangerous weight being sent along the street, and failed to do so. (*Times*, March 11, 1878.)

1867. [940]

Poulsum v. Thirst. Construction of Sewer—Injury to house—Contractor when sued held entitled to Notice of Action. (Metropolis.) (36 L. J., C. P., 225 : L. R., 2 C. P., 449 : 16 L. T., 324.)

1888. [941]

Ramsden v. Lancashire & Yorkshire Railway Co. Pump-house close to road—Nuisance caused by noise and steam—Accident to horse, the driver of which knew of the pump-house, and that it was dangerous to drive some horses past it—Action held not maintainable, there being nothing to show negligence or breach of duty. (53 J. P., 183.)

1851. [942]

Reg. v. Pocock. Trustees under a Local Paving Act are not chargeable with manslaughter if one of their roads be out of repair and a person using it is accidentally killed in consequence, such a case not being one of personal negligence. (17 Q. B., 34 : 17 L. T., (o. s.), 91.)

1880. [943]

Reg. v. Ware Guardians. Sewer grating improperly laid—Injury to a horse—Claim of compensation—*Mandamus* to Board to pay compensation awarded by Arbitrator—Held that the injury was not a matter for compensation at all, the facts disclosing neglect which was actionable, not a mischance arising necessarily from carrying out statutory powers. (*Times*, March 15, 1880.)

1877. [944]

Reid v. Darlington H. B. Wall of bridge out of repair repaired by Board's contractor—Stones left by him in highway—Accident to plaintiff —Held that there was no evidence of negligence against the Board's Surveyor. (41 J.P., 581.)

1889. [945]

Rochford v. Cheshunt L. B. Accident to horse caused by the unsafe state of a highway, in which the Board's contractor had recently constructed a sewer, and the surface not properly made good—Judgment for plaintiff against the defendants, and then for the defendants against the contractor as third party. (*Times*, Nov. 20, 1889.)

1860. [946]

Rowell v. Hartlepool B. H. Accident at a Sewer —Man killed—*Mandamus* granted to levy a Rate to provide compensation to widow (34 *Law Times* Newspaper, 232.)

1858. [947]

Ruck v. Williams. Negligent construction of a

Sewer—Damage to property—Paving Commissioners under Local Act held liable, great negligence being proved. (27 L. J., Ex., 357 : 3 H. & N., 308 : 31 L. T., (o. s.), 167.)

1882. [948]

Scott v. Huddersfield Corporation. Corporation held liable for accident to horse passing along a road newly asphalted, and therefore unusually slippery. (*Times*, Dec. 7, 1882.)

1857. [949]

Scott v. Manchester, Mayor. Laying of Gas Pipes —Accident — Compensation held payable, a Corporation being liable for the negligence of its workmen. (26 L. J., Ex., 132 and 406: 2 H. & N., 204: 29 L. T., (o. s.), 233.)

1888. [950]

Silverton v. Marriott. Two adjacent properties laid out for building—Roads over each in same line barred by lawful boundary wall—Wall gradually pulled down by trespassers, so that only stump left—Owner of wall held liable for accident to horse, the driver of which, supposing the two roads to be one, drove at and over the stump of wall. (59 L.T., 61 : 52 J. P., 677.)

1891. [951]

Smith v. Bailey. Owner of traction engine let on hire for 3 months held not liable for accident caused by hirer's negligence. (60 L. J., Q. B., 779 : L. R., 2 Q. B., 403 : 56 J. P., 116.)

1834. [952]

Smith v. Birmingham & Staffordshire Gas-light Co. A Corporation is liable for the tortious act of its agent, though not appointed by seal, if such act be an ordinary service—If the Corporation adopt the act, a jury may infer agency. (1 A. & E., 526 : 3 N. & M., 771.)

1878. [953]

Smith v. West Derby L. B. Sewers laid along a road by the Contractor of a Board—Subsequent subsidence of the road—Accident to a vehicle—Held that the Board was liable for the negligent restoration of the road in its joint capacity as Highway Authority and Sewer Authority—What particulars in a statutory Notice of Action are sufficient. (47 L. J., C. P., 607 : L. R., 3 C. P. D., 423: 38 L. T., 716: 42 J. P., 615.)

1881. [954]

Southard v. Eton Urban Authority. Accident to a horse through falling into a hole in a road caused by sinkage of surface into a cavity—Cavity apparently connected with a drain—Verdict for plaintiff. (*Times*, June 23, 1881.)

1891. [955]

Steel v. Dartford L. B. Road opened by C. for a drain connection to be made in pursuance of notice served by the Board—Trench imperfectly made good—Accident to plaintiff's cart—Board held not liable as the Sewer Authority, C. not being their agent ; nor as the Highway Authority, an action not lying for non-repair of a highway. (60 L. J., Q. B., 256.)

1879. [956]

Stringer v. Barker. "Public Health Act, 1875,"

§ 264—Sewer constructed by contractor—Accident to horse—Contractor held not entitled to Notice of Action because not an officer or person acting in his aid—The enactment in question is narrower in its tenour than the corresponding enactment in the "Public Health Act, 1848." (W. N., 1879, p. 127.)

1889.   [957]
Strute v. *Southwark Water Co.* Stop-cock box over a communication pipe negligently left open by consumer, and therefore plaintiff injured—New trial ordered, as there was evidence of negligence on the part of the defendants. (53 J. P., 424.)

1815.   [958]
Sutton v. *Clarke.* Persons who execute public functions without pay, and act to the best of their judgment, and without malice, are not liable for consequential damage. (6 Taunt., 29: 1 Marsh., 429.)

1876.   [959]
Tarry v. *Ashton.* Fall of a lamp projecting over a footway and injury to a passer-by—Held that it was the duty of the owner to keep it in repair, and that he was liable to anybody suffering hurt in consequence of its non-repair. (45 L. J., Q. B., 260: L. R., 1 Q. B. D., 314: 34 L. T., 97.)

1874.   [960]
Taylor v. *Greenhalgh.* "Highway Act, 1835," § 56—Highway—Negligence by a contractor in carrying out repairs—Held that no Action lay against Surveyor. (43 L. J., Q. B., 168: L. R., 9 Q. B., 487: 31 L. T., 184: 38 J. P., 599.)

1860.   [961]
Todd v. *Flight.* An Action lies against the owner of premises who lets them on lease when in a dangerous condition, and permits them to remain so until by reason of the want of repair they fall and injure the property of an adjoining owner. (30 L. J., C. P., 21: 9 C. B., (N. S.), 377.)

1888.   [962]
Tucker v. *Axbridge H. B.* Heap of stones negligently left projecting on to a highway—Accident and death—Action under "Lord Campbell's Act" held maintainable, although the party who actually was guilty of negligence was a contractor under the defendants. (53 J. P., 87.)

1884.   [963]
Wackerbath v. *St. Giles's B. W. and Mowlem.* Accident caused by Steam Roller—Liability of Board or Contractor—Verdict for Plaintiff—New Trial granted on points of evidence. (*Times*, June 21, 1883.)

1857.   [964]
Ward v. *Lee.* Metropolitan Commissioners of Sewers—Contractors held not personally liable for damage done by them in executing works; the liability, if any, was on the Commissioners as a body—Expenses of defending action. (26 L. J., Q. B., 142: 7 E. & B., 426: 28 L. T., (O. S.), 355.)

1864.   [965]
West Riding & Grimsby Railway Co. v. *Wakefield L. B. H.* "Railway Clauses Consolidation Act, 1845," § 58—Damage to Road by the carts of a Railway Contractor—Held that the Justices had power to make an Order on the Company which employed the Contractor. (33 L. J., M. C., 174: 5 B. & S., 478.)

1875.   [966]
White v. *Hindley L. B.* Street grating out of repair—Accident to a horse—Board held liable, it being a case of non-repair of sewer, not non-repair of highway. (44 L. J., Q. B., 114: L. R., 10 Q. B., 219: 32 L. T., 460: [W. v. *Wigan*] 39 J. P., 533.)

1857.   [967]
Whitehouse v. *Birmingham Canal Co.* An action for injury arising out of the ordinary user of works constructed under an Act of Parliament must be founded on negligence. (27 L. J., Ex., 25: 30 L. T., (O. S.), 156.)

1861.   [968]
Whitehouse v. *Fellows.* "General Turnpike Act, 1822," § 147—Negligent formation of a drain by the side of a road—Trustees held liable for consequential damage though they had acted *bonâ fide*—Where a Statute limits a time for Actions such time runs from the act done, unless there be a continuing trespass or a consequential injury, in which latter cases the time runs only from the cessation of the trespass, or the happening of the injury. (30 L. J., C. P., 305: 10 C. B., (N. S.), 765: 4 L. T., 177.)

1877.   [969]
Whiteley v. *Pepper.* Negligent opening of a coal-plate in a highway—Accident—Defendant, the coal merchant, held liable for the negligence of his carman. (46 L. J., Q. B., 436: L. R., 2 Q. B. D., 276: 36 L. T., 588.)

1868.   [970]
Whitman v. *Pearson.* Contractor under a Board—Accident owing to horse being left unattended and running away with a cart during driver's dinner-hour, driver having also disobeyed orders in driving home for his dinner—Master held liable, nevertheless—Notice of Action not required. (Metropolis) (37 L. J., C. P., 156: L. R., 3 C. P., 422: 18 L. T., 290.)

1872.   [971]
Winch v. *Conservators of the Thames.* Negligence—Towing-path out of repair—Accident to horses—Defendants held liable. (41 L. J., C. P., 241: L. R., 7 C. P., 458: 27 L. T., 95.)

1891.   [972]
Woodall v. *Nuttall.* "Towns Improvement Clauses Act, 1847," § 79—Hoarding erected so as to duly protect an excavation but rather too near to the rails of a tramway—Tramway passenger injured by contact with hoarding—Defendant who had erected the hoarding held not liable; no duty lay on him to block more of the street than was necessary for his own purposes. (56 J. P., 150.)

47. LIBEL.

1842. [973]
A.-G. v. *Compton.* To pay out of the Poor Rate the Law expenses of a medical officer of a Board of Guardians who had been libelled held to be a breach of trust. (1 Younge & Coll., Ch., 417.)

1881. [974]
Baldry v. *Fletcher.* Action of Libel by an assistant overseer—Libel contained in letter from one ratepayer to another, imputing to plaintiff long habit of mismanaging accounts —Defence: (1) No Libel; (2) Privilege, (3) No Malice—Verdict in favour of plaintiff held good by Divisional Court, and afterwards by the Court of Appeal. (MS.)

1877. [975]
Hariland, Ex parte. Alleged libel on a Poor Law Medical Officer—Whereupon a correspondence between the parties—Rule for a Criminal Information refused—*Per* Cockburn, C. J. :—" If a party chooses, instead of coming direct to this Court, to enter into a correspondence, and receive explanations, it is not usual for this Court to give leave to file a Criminal Information.' (41 J. P., 789.)

1879. [976]
Keight v. *Hill.* Complaint in writing to Guardians by the defendant, their Clerk, that the plaintiff, an assistant clerk, had neglected his duty—Whereupon plaintiff dismissed—Action of slander—Held that the complaint made by the defendant was a privileged communication if he was acting in the course of his duty, and without malice. (43 J. P., 176.)

1890. [977]
Manchester, Mayor v. *Williams.* A Municipal Corporation cannot sustain an action for libel in respect of a letter charging the Corporation with corruption—It is only individuals and not a Corporation in its corporate capacity that can be guilty of such an offence. (60 L. J., Q. B., 23 : L. R, 1 Q. B., 94 : 63 L. T., 805 : 54 J. P., 712.)

1862. [978]
Popham v. *Pickburn.* Action for Libel—A newspaper in giving an account of a Vestry Meeting at which there is read a Medical Officer's Report containing libellous matter, is not justified in reprinting such Report. (31 L. J., Ex., 133 : 7 H. & N., 891 : 5 L. T., 846.) [But see now 44 & 45 Vict., c. 60.]

1877. [979]
Purcell v. *Sowler.* Action by Medical Officer of a Union against a newspaper for libel, the libel being a report of a meeting of Guardians where libellous words were spoken—Action held maintainable, such report not being privileged. (46 L. J., C. P. D., 308 : L. R., 2 C. P. D., 215 : 36 L. T., 416, 41 J. P., 789.) [But see now 44 & 45 Vict., c. 60.]

1881. [980]
Reg. v. *Furrant.* Letter published by dismissed Medical Officer of Health imputing "individual and collective immorality, commercial and otherwise," to the Town Council, his former employers — Defendant pleading "Guilty" to a Criminal Information was fined £100. (In the Q. B. D., June, 1881. MS.)

48. LICENSES.

1872. [981]
Antony v. *Brecon Markets Co.* "Towns Improvement Clauses Act," §§ 125 and 129—Interpretation of Statutes—A consent to erect a slaughter-house held to carry with it a license to use it when erected—Local Act. (41 L. J., Ex., 201 : L. R., 7 Ex., 399 : 26 L. T., 979.)

1887. [982]
Blake v. *Kelly.* "Public Health Act, 1875," § 88—Registered lodging-house kept as a disorderly house—Whereupon Local Authority withdrew license—Held that there was no power to withdraw a license except on some one or more of the grounds specified in the Statute. (52 J. P., 263.)

1890. [983]
Booth v. *Ferrett.* Night Refuge and Lodging-house supported by charitable subscriptions —Held that the Magistrate was wrong in treating such an establishment as liable to registration &c. under the " Common Lodging-houses Acts," 14 & 15 Vict., c. 28; and 16 & 17 Vict., c. 41, it not being carried on for profit. (59 L. J., M. C., 136 : L. R., 25 Q. B. D., 87 : 63 L. T., 346 : 55 J. P., 7.)

1867. [984]
Brighton L. B. H. v. *Stenning.* Extent of a slaughter-house License—Alteration of premises—Held on the facts that the License as granted was sufficiently extensive to authorise the premises being used as they were used after the alterations. (15 L. T., 567.)

1884. [985]
Coles v. *Fibbens.* Resolution passed to license common lodging-house not acted upon by Local Board Clerk—Summons for keeping unlicensed house—Decision of Magistrates not to convict, upheld—Defendant held entitled to consider himself licensed although no license had been issued. (52 L. T., 358 : 49 J. P., 308.)

1876. [986]
Hanman v. *Adkins.* Licensed slaughter-house pulled down and rebuilt—Held that a new license was not necessary. (40 J. P., 744.)

1862. [987]
Howarth v. *Manchester, Mayor.* Local Act—Slaughter-house License—A resolution of a committee communicated to an applicant operated as a license. (6 L. T., 683.)

1867. [988]
Liverpool New Cattle Market Co. v. *Hodson.* "Public Health Act, 1848," § 64 [="Public Health Act, 1875," §§ 112-13]—"Newly establishing" the business of slaughtering Cattle—Conviction affirmed, the company allowing its premises to be used by others,

though not using them by its own servants. (36 L. J , M. C., 30 : L. R., 2 Q. B., 131 : 8 B. & S., 194 : 15 L. T., 534)

1889.   [980]
Openshaw v. *Oakeley*. "Hawkers Act, 1888,"— Local Act—General Act held not to dispense with the duty of a hawker to take out a license under the Local Act. (60 L. T., 927 : 53 J. P., 741.)

1866.   [990]
Reg. v. *Heyworth*. "Towns Improvement Clauses Act, 1847," § 126—A slaughter-house license applies to a place ; not to a person—A person who pays the owner for leave to use an unlicensed place cannot himself be convicted. (14 L. T., 600 : 30 J. P., 423.)

49. "LIGHTING ACT, 1833."

1812.   [991]
Beechey v. *Quentery*. "Lighting Act, 1833," §§ 9 and 18—A Majority of Two-Thirds is required under § 9 at the original meeting to determine on the adoption of the Act—But when the Act has been duly adopted a bare majority (either in Vestry or on a Poll) suffices to determine the amount to be raised —*Semble*, that the Parish being bound for 3 years by the adoption of the Act, the amount voted must not be merely nominal. (11 L. J., Ex., 420 : 10 M. & W., 65.)

1840.   [992]
Eynsham Ratepayers, In re. "Lighting Act, 1833," § 7—Where a Statute requires a definite proportion of those present, to render valid an act, there must be the specified proportion of those present voting : those who, being present, refuse to take any part cannot in such a case as this be deemed absent. (18 L. J., Q. B., 210 : 12 Q. B , 398, n. : New Sess. Cas., 507.)

1850.   [993]
Peto v. *West Ham Parish*. "Lighting Act, 1833," § 33—Wet Dock held rateable at the higher amount as being *ejusdem generis* with houses and buildings. (28 L. J., M. C., 240 : 2 E. & E., 144.)

1864.   [994]
Potton Churchwardens v. *Brown*. "Lighting Act, 1833," adopted for part of a Parish—Rate made purporting to be a Rate on the whole Parish but actually embracing only the names of Ratepayers within the limited area —Held, that as the Rate purported to be one for the whole Parish and as there was no power to make such a Rate, it was invalid. (10 L. T., 525.)

1860.   [995]
Quick v. *St. Ives Churchwardens*. "Lighting Act, 1833" : "Municipal Corporations Act, 1835," § 88—Powers of Lighting Inspectors under the former Act accepted by a Town Council under the latter Act—Subsequent relinquishment by the Town Council of its Lighting functions which were resumed by the Vestry—Held that such resumption was

invalid—When a Town Council adopts the Act it cannot afterwards abandon it. (2 L. T., 214 : 8 W. R., 414.)

1854.   [996]
Reg. v. *Deverell*. "Lighting Act, 1833," § 15— Notice of the adoption of the Act need not be affixed to the doors of Dissenting Meeting-Houses, they not b.ing "Chapels"—"Forthwith" means in a reasonable time. (23 L. J., M. C., 121 : 3 E. & B , 372 : [*Reg.* v. *Warblington*] 22 L. T., (o. s.), 304.)

1857.   [997]
Reg. v. *Dunn*. "Lighting Act, 1833," § 16— Meeting to adopt the Act—Decision against —Another meeting within a year—Decision in favour—Rate made and payment thereof refused by S., who on being summoned before Justices pleaded that the Rate was invalid because the second meeting was invalid being held within a year of the first—The Justices took this view and refused to issue a Distress Warrant—*Mandamus* to them to do so refused, they having acted within their jurisdiction, although perhaps their decision was erroneous, there being some evidence that the second meeting had reference to a different area from the first—The fact that S. had paid a previous Rate did not deprive him of the right to raise the objection as to the valid'ty of the adoption of the Act. (26 L. J., M. C., 74 : 7 E. & B., 220 : [*Reg.* v. *Sussex*] 28 L. T., (o. s.), 252.)

1854.   [998]
Reg. v. *Kingswinford Overseers*. "Lighting Act, 1833"—Adoption by a District Chapelry— Nullity of proceedings—Distress. (23 L. J., Q. B., 337 : 3 E. & B., 689 : 23 L. T., (o. s.), 91.)

1854.   [999]
Reg. v. *Lambert*. The owners of small tenements held liable to be assessed in respect of them to Rates under the "Lighting Act, 1833," where the Owners of such tenements were assessed to the Poor Rate under the "Small Tenements Rating Act, 1850" [repealed], but only on the reduced scale prescribed by that Act. (2 C. L. R., 883 : [*Reg.* v. *Oxfordshire*] 22 L. T., (o. s.), 219.)

1853.   [1000]
Reg. v. *Middlesex JJ.* (1). "Lighting Act, 1833" —Neither adoption nor a Rate is invalid because made at a Vestry presided over by a Chairman who is not a ratepayer—A Lighting Rate is a "Parochial Rate," the non-payment of which disqualifies a person from acting as Chairman of, or voting at, a meeting under the Act. (22 L. J., M. C., 106 : 1 Bail Ct. Cas., 156 : 21 L. T., (o. s.), 131.)

1875.   [1001]
Reg. v. *Midland Railway Co.* A Railway is none the less rateable as land because rails are laid on it, and signal posts and huts are erected on it—Possibly, however, the huts might be rateable as buildings. (44 L. J., M. C., 137 : L. R., 10 Q. B., 389 : 39 J.P., 359 : [*Midland R.* v. *Great Wigston*] 32 L. T., 753.)

1871.   [1002]
Reg. v. *Neath Canal Co.* "Lighting Act, 1833,"
§ 33—Canal, Towing Path, and Dry Dock
held to be "land," and therefore rateable at
the lower amount. (40 L. J., M. C., 193;
L. R., 6 Q. B., 707: [*Neath Canal v. Neath*]
24 L. T., 871.)

1861.   [1003]
Reg. v. *Rye JJ.* "Lighting Act, 1833," § 33—
The word "Overseers" here includes
"Churchwardens" although the Parish is
divided and each part has Overseers of its
own, the division not being under 13 & 14
Car. II., c. 12, or 59 Geo. III., c. 134—Orders
under § 32 for a Rate can only be questioned
by appeal under § 66. (13 W. R., 142.)

1858.   [1004]
Reg. v. *Somersetshire JJ.* "Lighting Act, 1833"
—Rating of houses and land—"Three times
greater" is to be taken "liter.lly." (31 L.
T., (o. s.), 215: 22 J. P., 431.)

1843.   [1005]
Reg. v. *Whipp.* "Lighting Act, 1833," § 33—
Publication of a Rate on one Church in a
Parish containing 3 Churches, held insuffi-
cient. (12 L. J., M. C., 64: 3 G. & D., 372:
4 Q. B., 141: 7 J. P., 656.)

1842.   [1006]
Reg. v. *Wilkinson.* Indictment for non-payment
of Costs in obedience to an Order of Sessions
—"Lighting Act, 1833," §§ 32, 33, and 66—
Appeal to Sessions against an Order on Overseers dismissed on the ground that Notice of
Appeal had not been served on the Justices
who made the Order as well as on the Inspectors—The Sessions cannot under these
circumstances award Costs to the respondent
because there has been no hearing and determining of the Appeal within the meaning of
§ 66—Present defendant acquitted. (2 Mood.
& R., 431.)

1844.   [1007]
Wilkinson v. Gray. "Lighting Act, 1833"—It
is competent for a part of a Parish to adopt
the Act so far as that part is concerned
though a Meeting of the whole Parish within
a year before rejected the adoption as for the
whole Parish—But the second meeting must
be substantially different from the first, and
not a mere evasion of the Section which pro-
hibits the re-discussion of the question within
a year of its rejection. (9 J. P., 71.)

50. LOCAL GOVERNMENT BOARD, &c.

1856.   [1008]
Arnold v. *Gravesend, Mayor.* "Municipal Corporations Act, 1835," § 94—The Consent of
the Treasury is sufficiently expressed by a
letter signed by the Secretary. (25 L. J.,
Ch., 776: 2 K. & J., 574: 27 L. T., (o. s.),
97.)

1867.   [1009]
A.-G. v. *Manchester, Bishop.* Remarks by
Stuart, V. C., on the Acts of a Public De-
partment [such as Local Government Board].
(L. R., 3 Eq., 436, 455: 15 L. T., 646, 650.)

1881.   [1010]
Barker v. *King's Norton Rural Sanitary A.*
Application for Injunction to stay drainage
scheme—Demurrer allowed on the ground
that the Local Government Board had full
power to deal with the plaintiff's case when
the Local Inquiry was held. (W. N., 1882,
p. 14.)

1882.   [1011]
Bexley L. B. v. *West Kent Sewerage Board.* Local
Act—Dispute between two Authorities—
The Local Government Board is not empowered to state Special Cases for the opinion
of the High Court, under the "Common Law
Procedure Act, 1854." (51 L. J., Q. B. D.,
456: L. R., 9 Q. B. D., 518: 47 L. T., 192:
46 J. P., 519.)

1870.   [1012]
Darlington Town Council v. *Secretary of State for
the Home Department.* "Sanitary Act, 1866,"
§ 49 [= "Public Health Act, 1875," § 299]—
Failure to provide sewerage—On default,
Order by Secretary prescribing the execution
of works, to wit, the establishment of a sewage
farm—Order quashed by con.ent, the A.-G.
on behalf of the Secretary admitting that it
was *ultra vires*. (*Times*, Nov. 15, Rule *nisi*,
afterwards *absolute*. MS.)

1838.   [1013]
Frewin v. *Lewis.* Remarks by Cottenham, C.,
on the jurisdiction of the Courts to review
the acts of a Public Department, in this case
the Poor Law Board. (4 Myl. & C., 249.)

1885.   [1014]
*Local Government Board, In re; Kingstown
Commissioners, Ex parte.* "Public Health
(Ireland) Act, 1878," § 214 (5)—*Semble* that
the Board in exercising its functions as to
Provisional Orders, is not a Court; nor are
purely legislative powers nor powers of promoting legislation subject to prohibition—
Quære whether a usurpation of jurisdiction
of Judicial character by the Board under
colour of exercising such functions might not
be the subject of prohibition. (18 L. R., Ir.,
500.)

1884.   [1015]
Reg. v. *Cheshunt L. B.* Default of Board for
several years to provide sewerage—*Mandamus*
issued at instance of Local Government Board
under "Public Health Act, 1875," § 299.
(*Times*, Jan. 22, 1884.)

1871.   [1016]
Reg. v. *Cockerell.* "Sanitary Act, 1866," § 49
[= "Public Health Act, 1875," § 299]—
Default of Sewer Authority—Order of Secre-
tary of State held valid. (40 L. J., M. C.,
153: L. R., 6 Q. B., 252.)

1876.   [1017]
Reg. v. *Lincoln Corporation.* "Public Health
Act, 1875," § 299—Neglect to execute Order
of Local Government Board as to drainage
works—*Mandamus* granted against Corporation. (*Times*, Feb. 23, 1876.)

1873.   [1018]
Reg. v. *Local Government Board.* (1). Local Act
Salaried Solicitor—Right to compensation

on abolition of office, (43 L. J., Q. B., 49 : L. R., 9 Q. B., 148: 29 L. T., 769: 38 J. P., 165.)

1878.   [1019]
Reg. v. *Local Government Board* (2). Default of Sanitary Authority to provide Sewerage—Refusal of Local Government Board to issue an Order under the "Public Health Act, 1875," § 299—Proceedings at the instance of an adjoining Authority prejudiced by the default alike of the Local and of the Central Authority—*Mandamus* refused, the Court being unwilling to interfere, without strong cause, with the discretion of the Local Government Board. (In the Q. B. D., March 4, 1878. MS.)

1882.   [1020]
Reg. v. *Local Government Board & Taylor.* "Public Health Act, 1875," §§ 150, 257, and 268 — Paving expenses — Apportionment— Notice of demand—Decision by Local Authority—Appeal by Party aggrieved—Time for appeal—Memorial to Local Government Board — Grounds of Appeal — Prohibition held not to lie, under the circumstances— *Semble* that it would, where Local Government Board was exceeding its powers. (52 L. J., M. C., 4 : L. R., 10 Q. B. D., 309 : 48 L. T., 173 : 47 J. P., 228.)

1878.   [1021]
Reg. v. *Local Government Board, Ireland.* "Towns Improvement Act, 1854" — An Order constituting a District may be quashed by *Certiorari* if it appears that the District ought not to have been constituted because not falling within the Statute. (2 L. R., Ir., 316 : 26 W. R., Dig., 242.)

1837.   [1022]
Reg. v. *Poor Law Commissioners.* Powers of the Commissioners [now Local Government Board]—An Order held invalid. (6 A. & E., 1 : 6 L. J., K. B., 41.)

1851.   [1023]
Reg. v. *Robinson.* An Order of the Poor Law Commissioners [now Local Government Board] may be quashed in part on *Certiorari* if the parts are sufficiently divisible. (17 Q. B., 466.)

1875.   [1024]
Reg. v. *Walker.* "Epping Forest Act, 1872"— Waste by digging marl and clay, &c.— Order issued by Commissioners acting under Statute—Disobedience—Held that the defendant by disobeying an Order duly made was guilty of a misdemeanour. (L. R., 10 Q. B., 355: 33 L. T., 167.)

1830.   [1025]
Teather, In re. "Poor Law Amendment Act, 1834," § 48—Poor Law Commissioners may remove a Relieving Officer at their discretion, without giving him notice, or hearing him—Where there is a discretionary power to remove, they may remove without assigning grounds, or calling on the party to defend himself—*Reg.* v. *Darlington School* (6 Q. B., 682) followed. (19 L. J., M. C., 70 : 1 L. M. & P., 7.)

1864.   [1026]
Wallington v. *Willes.* "Public Health Act, 1848," §§ 69 and 129 : "Local Government Act, 1858," §§ 62, 65, and 81 [= "Public Health Act, 1871," §§ 150, 251, 257, 294-5] —Paving expenses—Appeal to the Secretary of State—The adjudication of the Secretary of State may cover both claim and interest. [*Wallingford* v. *W.*] (33 L. J., M. C., 233 : 16 C. B., (N. S.), 797 : 10 L. T., 784.)

51. MARKETS.

1889.   [1027]
Abergavenny Improvement Commissioners v. *Straker.* "Markets and Fairs Clauses Act, 1847," § 13 : Local Act—Extension of exemptions from liability for infringement of first-named Act—Interpretation of Statutes. (58 L. J., Ch., 717: 60 L. T., 756: 53 J. P., 421.)

1869.   [1028]
Ashworth v. *Heyworth.* "Markets and Fairs Clauses Act, 1847," § 13—"Dwelling-place or shop"—Infringement of Market—Question of fact. (38 L. J., M. C., 91: L. R., 4 Q. B., 316: 10 B. & S., 309: 20 L. T., 439 : 33 J. P., 565.)

1863.   [1029]
A.-G. v. *Aberavon Corporation.* Powers of a Corporation as to letting on lease its Market rights. (3 De G. J. & Sm., 637 : 2 N. R., 564: 9 L. T., 187.)

1873.   [1030]
A.-G. v. *Cambridge, Mayor.* Local Act—Held that under powers to "enlarge and improve" a market it might be extended to streets not actually forming parts of its original sides. (L. R., 6 H. L., 303.)

1884.   [1031]
A.-G. v. *Horner.* Interpretation of a Charter granted in 1683—Question as to extent of area to which Charter applied. (55 L. J., Q. B., 193: L. R., 14 Q. B. D., 245: 54 L. T., 281 : 50 J. P., 564.)

1882.   [1032]
A.-G. v. *Norwich Corporation.* Application for an Injunction to restrain Corporation from letting a part of its Market land as a site for an Agricultural Hall, refused, it not being shown that the proposal was objectionable. (*Times,* May 22, 1882.)

1860.   [1033]
Black v. *Sackett.* Local Act—Tolls duly paid by wholesale dealer—Re-sale in a street held to be an infringement of Market. (10 B. & S., 639: 33 J. P., 420.)

1858.   [1034]
Bourne v. *Lowndes.* "Markets and Fairs Clauses Act, 1847," § 13—Infringement of Market— Sale outside Market limits of an article chargeable, but delivery within—Conviction quashed. (31 L. T. (O. S.), 114 : 22 J. P., 354.)

1862.   [1035]
Brecon, Mayor v. *Edwards.* Evidence of the sale by sample in a Shop near a Corn Market of Corn on a Market Day is not *per se* evidence of an infringement of the Market. (31 L. J., Ex., 368 : 1 H. & C., 51 : 6 L. T., 293.)

F

1839.   [1036]

Bridgland v. *Shapter*. An owner of sheep having taken them to a public-house within 40 yards of a market went into the market in search of customers; finding some he took them back to the public-house and there sold the sheep to them—Held that this was a fraud upon the market. (5 M. & W., 375.)

1870.   [1037]

Carter v. *Parkhouse*. Local Act—Market Tolls—Selling goods without paying the toll is an offence which cannot be condoned by a subsequent payment, and Justices should have convicted. (22 L. T., 788 : 34 J. P., 438.)

1876.   [1038]

Collier v. *Worth*. Local Act—Sale in a part of a town not built when the Act was passed—Held nevertheless, that a prohibition against selling in a town applied to the town as extended in course of time. (L. R., 1 Ex. D., 464 : 40 J. P., 808 : [C. v. *North*] 35 L. T., 345.)

1836.   [1039]

De Rutzen v. *Lloyd*. Infringement of Market—A market may be moved without loss of exclusive rights, for it is not a necessary legal inference that an immemorial market within a manor is limited to any particular place. (5 L. J., K. B., 202 : 5 A. & E., 456: 6 N. & M., 764.)

1869.   [1040]

Dorchester, Mayor v. *Ensor*. Disturbance of Market—A Corporation does not forfeit its ancient right of Market merely by moving the Market to a new site in the new part of the Borough when an extension of the municipal boundaries takes place. (39 L. J., Ex., 11 : L. R., 4 Ex., 335: 21 L. T., 115: 34 J. P., 167.)

1861.   [1041]

Draper v. *Sperring*. "Nuisances Removal Act, 1855," § 12 [="Public Health Act, 1875," § 95]—Owner of a Market held liable for a Nuisance arising from sheep droppings. (30 L. J., M. C., 225: 10 C. B., (N.S.), 113 : 4 L. T., 365.)

1885.   [1042]

East Retford, Mayor v. *Williams*. Injunction granted to restrain sale of dead meat in Market leased by defendant, but not intended for sale of such meat. (*Times*, March 21, 1885.)

1886.   [1043]

Edinburgh Magistrates v. *Blackie*. Held that where a Market legally existed under an Act of Parliament the public could not be excluded from a covered portion during market hours in order that such portion might be used for other than market purposes. (L. R., 11 App. Cas., 665.)

1858.   [1044]

Elias v. *Nightingale*. "Markets and Fairs Clauses Act," § 19 : Local Act—Held that to slaughter cattle on private premises, unless for *sale* as human food, is no offence within the Act—Definition of "slaughter-

house." (27 L. J., M. C., 151: 8 E. & B, 698 : 30 L. T., (O. S.), 285.)

1861.   [1045]

Ellis v. *Bridgenorth Corporation*. A Corporation which owns a Market may at Common Law move the same, but if it sets up a new Market under the "Local Government Act, 1858," § 50 [="Public Health Act, 1875," § 166], it must abide by the restrictions of that Act —A right of Stallage must be decided at Law before an Injunction will be granted to restrain an interference therewith, the right not being admitted. (2 Johns. & H., 67 : 4 L. T., 112.)

1863.   [1046]

Ellis v. *Bridgenorth, Mayor*. Disturbance of Market—Removal held to be illegal having regard to the proviso in the "Local Government Act, 1858," § 50—Judgment for the plaintiff. (32 L. J., C. P., 273 : 15 C. B., (N.S.), 52 : 8 L. T., 668.)

1879.   [1047]

Elwes v. *Payne*. Exclusive market rights vested in plaintiff and predecessors in title for 150 years and longer—Interlocutory Injunction to restrain proposed weekly sales by auction in same place, but on a different day, refused on the ground of the difficulty in ascertaining the compensation to which defendant would be entitled if successful at the trial; but defendant to keep an account of his sales till the trial of the Action. (48 L. J., Ch., 831 : 41 L. T., 118: L. R., 12 Ch. D., 468.)

1877.   [1048]

Exeter, Mayor v. *Heaman*. Local Market Act—Infringement of market—Carcases delivered at purchaser's door, and then and there weighed and paid for—Plea, that this transaction was in fulfilment of a contract entered into on a previous day—Summons therefore dismissed by Justices—Held that, as these facts showed a distinct breach of the Local Act, the Justices ought to have amended the date of the summons and have convicted. (37 L. T., 534 : 42 J. P., 503.)

1872.   [1049]

Fearon v. *Mitchell*. "Markets and Fairs Clauses Act, 1847," § 13—"Own dwelling-place or shop" within the limits of a Market—A large Agricultural Hall not such—Setting up a business with the sanction of a Local Board confers no "right, power, or privilege," within the "Local Government Act, 1858," § 50. (41 L. J., M. C., 170 : L. R., 1 Q. B., 690 : 27 L. T., 33: 36 J. P., 804.)

1858.   [1050]

Fox v. *Palmer*. Local Act—"Towns Police Clauses Act, 1847," § 21—Market—Obstruction caused by exposing horses for sale in a street. (22 J. P., 449.)

1883.   [1051]

Great Eastern Railway Co. v. *Goldsmid*. Market established by Railway Co. in connection with a Goods Station, held an infringement of Plaintiff's Market under Royal Letters Patent. (54 L. J., Ch., 162 : L. R., 9 App. Cas., 927 : 52 L. T., 270: 49 J. P., 260.)

1812. [1052]
Hill v. *Smith*. Sale by sample—Where samples are brought into a market tolls cannot be levied on bulk which is not brought in. (4 Taunt., 520.)

1877. [1053]
Hooper v. *Kenshole*. " Markets and Fairs Clauses Act, 1847," § 13: Local Act—Infringement of market by sale in covered skittle-ground—Held that such a place was not a " shop," and that the defendant ought to have been convicted. (46 L. J., M. C., 160: L. R., 2 Q. B. D., 127 : 36 L. T., 111 : 41 J. P., 182.)

1885. [1054]
Horner v. *Whitechapel B. W.* Approaches to a Market—Interference with Market Rights by erection of posts. (55 L. J., Ch., 298 : 53 L. T., 842.)

1875. [1055]
Howard v. *Lupton*. "Markets and Fairs Clauses Act, 1847," § 13: "Pedlars Act, 1871," § 6—Held that a licensee under the second Act was exempt from penalties under the first Act. (44 L. J., M. C., 150 : L. R., 10 Q. B., 598: 40 J. P., 7.)

1877. [1056]
Hughes v. *Trew*. "Markets and Fairs Clauses Act, 1847," § 19: Local Act—Slaughter-houses—Consent of Local Authority how to be signified—Copy of a minute sent appended to a letter by the Clerk held to convey a valid consent—Consent to one site particularly named, held not to cover another site to which the slaughter-houses had been removed —Summons for infringement of exclusive rights held properly dismissed. (36 L. T., 585: 41 J. P., 453.)

1878. [1057]
Lax v. *Darlington Corporation*. Plaintiff a stall-holder in Corporation Market—Iron railing there dangerous to restive cattle—Accident to cow—Judgment for the Plaintiff, on the ground that a market is a place to which the public are invited, and which therefore must be kept in a reasonably safe condition. (49 L. J., Q. B., 105 : L. R., 5 Ex. D., 28 : 41 L. T., 489: 44 J. P., 312.)

1860. [1058]
Llandaff & Canton District Market Co. v. *Lyndon*. Local Act—Infringement of Market—A horse is an "article." (30 L. J., M. C., 105: 8 C. B., (N. S.), 515: 2 L. T., 771.)

1890. [1059]
Loftos v. *Gleave*. Local Act—Hat-guards held not tollable articles and Corporation license not necessary. (54 J. P., 401.)

1890. [1060]
Loftos v. *Higgins*. Local Act—Hawker selling fish from a cart held not required to take out a Corporation license for the sale of a tollable article out of market. (54 J. P., 404.)

1879. [1061]
London, Mayor v. *Low*. Ancient Market—New Market— Disturbance — Smithfield Market removed under Parliamentary authority, but all privileges preserved—Held on the facts proved that the defendant's system of sales was an infringement of the plaintiff's rights. (49 L. J., Q. B. D., 144 : 42 L. T., 16.)

1882. [1062]
Manchester, Mayor v. *Lyons*. Market established by Statute—Old Market rights thereby extinguished—Sale of fish, &c., in shop not an Infringement of Market. (L. R., 22 Ch. D., 287: 47 L. T., 677.)

1875. [1063]
McHole v. *Davies*. Local Act incorporating " Markets and Fairs Clauses Act," 1847, § 13 —Infringement of market—Held that, for the purposes of the Act, a yard adjoining a dwelling-house was not included under " dwelling-place or shop " — Conviction affirmed. (45 L. J., M. C., 30 : L. R., 1 Q. B. D., 59 : 33 L. T., 502 : 40 J. P., 548.)

1889. [1064]
McIntosh v. *Romford L. B.* " Market and Fairs (Weighing of Cattle) Act, 1887," § 4—Plaintiffs, the Market Authority, held not only entitled, but bound to provide a weighing machine, even at the risk of interfering with the highway vested in the Defendant Board. (61 L. T., 185.)

1875. [1065]
Morgan v. *Kingdon*. Local Act—Market— Alleged infringement—Held that gingerade was not a "marketable commodity," within the meaning of the Act. (39 J. P., 471.)

1877. [1066]
Newtownards Commissioners v. *Woods*. "Markets and Fairs Clauses Act, 1847," § 13—A sale of goods on Market day within " prescribed limits " is not within the Statute unless the bulk of the goods sold is at time of the sale, also substantially within said limits. (11 L. R., Ir., 506.)

1746. [1067]
Northampton, Mayor v. *Ward*. Erecting a stall in a market is not of common right, and Trespass is the proper remedy for so doing. (2 Stra., 1238.)

1878. [1068]
Penryn, Mayor v. *Best*. Alleged right of a Corporation to levy on market days a toll or stallage, not only on inhabitants who sell in market, but on those who sell in their shops —Verdict for plaintiffs held good there being ample evidence of the prescriptive right claimed. (48 L. J., Ex., 103 : L. R., 3 Ex. D., 292 : 38 L. T., 805 : 42 J. P., 629.)

1873. [1069]
Perkins v. *Arber*. Local Market Act—Infringement of Market by selling pigs in the yard of an Inn not belonging to the Vendor— Conviction affirmed. (37 J. P., 406.)

1865. [1070]
Pope v. *Whalley*. "Markets and Fairs Clauses Act, 1847," § 13—Points to be taken into consideration in order to determine whether a place is a person's "own shop." (34 L. J., M. C., 76 : 6 B. & S., 303 : 11 L. T., 769: 29 J. P., 134.)

1837. [1071]
Rex v. *Starkey*. Right of Market on a Highway —Town market removed to a new site—Re-

moval held improper on the ground that the rights enjoyed by the public on the new site were less than those on the old—Old site on the King's Highway held still available for a lawful market. (6 L. J., K. B., 202: 7 A. & E., 95.)

1884.   [1072]
Shepherd v. *Folland.* Infringement of market—Potatoes held *ejusdem generis* with " corn, grain, meat, fish, poultry, or other provisions." (49 J. P., 165.)

1891.   [1073]
Spurling v. *Bantoft.* "Markets and Fairs Clauses Act, 1847," § 13: "Public Health Act, 1875," § 166—A cattle salesman leased land of a Corporation — Afterwards the Corporation established a public market—Held that the lessee had thereby lost his right to sell cattle unless he paid toll. (L. R., 2 Q. B., 384: 65 L. T., 584: 56 J. P., 133.)

1872.   [1074]
Swindon Market Co. v. *Panting.* Market held under Royal Letters Patent in open street—Claim of stallage held not maintainable. (27 L. T., 578.)

1841.   [1075]
Thompson v. *Gibson.* Action for continuing a nuisance to the plaintiff's Market by a building which excluded the public from a part of the space on which the Market was lawfully held—Held that the defendants were liable for continuing the nuisance although they had no right to enter on the land to remove it—Action therefore maintainable. (10 L. J., Ex., 330 ; 7 M. & W., 456.)

1883.   [1076]
Torquay Market Co. v. *Burridge.* Local Act—Person living and selling outside Market limits for delivery inside, held guilty of Infringement of Market. (48 J. P., 71.)

1875.   [1077]
Webber v. *Adams.* Local Act—Corn sold at an office, but not brought within the market limits, held not liable to toll. (Irish.) (11 L. R., Ir., 304.)

1821.   [1078]
Wells v. *Miles.* There can be no toll for goods not actually brought into market. (4 B. & Ald., 559.)

1861.   [1079]
Wiltshire v. *Baker.* " Markets and Fairs Clauses Act, 1847 :" Local Act — Exemption in favour of a "Dwelling-house, or shop attached to *any* dwelling-house"—Held that a Vessel in a canal, moored to a wharf, was not a "Shop." (31 L. J., M. C., 10 (n.) ; 11 C. B., (N. S.), 237 : 5 L. T., 355.)

1861.   [1080]
Wiltshire v. *Willett.* "Markets and Fairs Clauses Act, 1847" — Local Act — Exemption in favour of a " Dwelling-house or shop attached to *any* dwelling-house "—Held that a sale (even by auction) in a shop was lawful, although the dwelling-house to which the shop was attached did not belong to the

seller. (31 L. J., M. C., 8 : 11 C. B., (N. S.), 240 : 5 L. T., 355 : 26 J. P., 312.)

1869.   [1081]
Wortley v. *Nottingham L. B.* "Markets and Fairs Clauses Act, 1847," § 42 : " Local Government Act, 1858," § 50 [="Public Health Act, 1875," § 166.] Removal of part of a Market to another locality held legal—By-Law unduly restrictive held invalid. (21 L. T., 582 : 33 J. P., 806.)

1862.   [1082]
Yarmouth, Mayor v. *Groom.* Market—Stallage held payable on a wicker basket, which, having a lid was convertible into a sort of table—Any erection designed to facilitate the sale of goods is a "stall;" whether it be fixed or not is immaterial. (32 L. J., Ex., 74: 1 H. & C., 102: 7 L T., 161.)

52. MINUTE BOOK.

1871.   [1083]
A.-G. v. *Whitwood L. B.* A Minute Book ordered to be produced for the inspection of the Agent of a plaintiff. (40 L. J., Ch., 592 : 19 W. R., 1107.)

1853.   [1084]
Taylor v. *Addyman.* Account Books &c. wrongfully detained—A County Court has jurisdiction under the "County Court Acts," in Actions of *Detinue.* (22 L. J., C. P., 94 : 13 C. B , 309.)

53. MORTGAGE.

1840.   [1085]
A.-G. v. *Daniel.* Moneys raised by different classes of Rates mixed into a general fund—Proposal of Vestry to borrow for the purposes of one Rate and mortgage as security other Rates—Injunction granted. (9 L. J., Ch., 394.)

1858.   [1086]
De Winton v. *Brecon, Mayor.* Local Act—Power to mortgage land does not extend to surplus land when surplus land has been directed by Statute to be sold—Power to borrow on debentures—Default in payment of interest—Appointment of Receiver. (28 L. J., Ch., 598 : 26 Ben., 533 : 33 L. T., (O. S.), 296.)

1876.   [1087]
Derby Municipal Estates, In re. " Lands Clauses Act, 1845," § 69 : " Baths and Washhouses Act, 1847," § 21—Circumstances under which moneys received by a Municipal Corporation for sale of lands may be used to redeem mortgages. (L. R., 3 Ch. D., 289 : 24 W. R., 729.)

1883.   [1088]
Ford v. *Honiton Corporation.* Local Act : " Public Health Act, 1875," §§ 207, 210, 227 — Priority secured to Mortgagees of Rates—Held that the effect of the last-named sections was that if the Funds raised under the Local Act were insufficient for the sanitary purposes of the Corporation,

the Local Act might be disregarded and any funds really necessary raised. (5 *Municip. Corp. Assoc. Month. Circular*, 161.)

1858. [1089]
Payne v. *Brecon, Mayor*. Though a mortgage to secure money advanced to a Municipal Corporation may be void, yet a covenant therein to pay is good. (27 L. J., Ex., 495: 3 H. & N., 572: 31 L. T., (o. s.), 328.)

1883. [1090]
Rochdale Building Society v. *Rochdale Corporation*. Local Act—Definition of "owner"—Private Improvement Rate made on an owner at a time when the Property was mortgaged—6 years afterwards mortgagees took possession after death of owner—3 years afterwards Distress Warrant issued—Held that as Mortgagees were neither owners nor in possession when the Rate was made Justices had no power to issue Warrant—Warrant moreover void because not issued within 6 months of Rate being payable as required by "Jervis's Act." (51 J. P., 134.)

54. NOTICES.

1868*. [1091]
Amys v. *Creed*. (38 L. J., M. C., 22.)

1864. [1092]
Bayley v. *Wilkinson*. "Public Health Act, 1848," § 69 [="Public Health Act, 1875," § 150]—Notice to pave—Held that a Notice which, though vague in itself, yet stated where particulars of the work to be done could be ascertained, was good and sufficient. (33 L. J., M. C., 161: 16 C. B., (N. s.), 161: 10 L. T., 543.) [*Quære* not now applicable having regard to the language of the "Public Health Act, 1875," reading § 150 with Sched. IV., Form G.]

1874. [1093]
Caballero v. *Lewis*. "Public Health Act, 1848," § 76 [="Public Health Act, 1875," § 62]; "Local Government Act, 1858," § 51—Non-compliance with an Order to lay on water—An informality in the delivery of a Notice held cured by an admission that the Notice had reached the defendant. (38 J. P., 614.)

1869. [1094]
Corker v. *Cardwell*. "Nuisances Removal Act, 1860," § 13 [="Public Health Act, 1875," § 105]—There is no necessity for a Notice to be given by an inhabitant before he lays a complaint. (39 L. J., M. C., 28: L. R., 5 Q. B., 15: 10 B. & S., 797: 21 L. T., 457.)

1827. [1095]
Cook v. *Leonard*. Local Act requiring Notice of Action for anything done under the Act—Held that Notice was necessary only in cases in which the defendant-designate had reasonable ground for supposing himself entitled to act as ;he had done—Where there is a total absence of authority to do what has been done, the party is not entitled to the protection of a Statute. (6 C. B. & C., 351: 9 D. & R., 339.)

1827. [1096]
Curtis v. *Kent Waterworks Co.* Service of a Notice addressed to a Corporation by personal delivery of the same publicly at a meeting to the authorised chairman thereof, held good. (7 B. & C., 714.)

1855. [1097]
Danvers v. *Morgan*. "Metropolitan Police Act," 2 & 3 Vict., c. 47—Plaintiff given into custody for throwing down oyster shells in a thoroughfare by defendant a person employed to keep the place clean—Held that in an Action for false imprisonment he was entitled to Notice of Action. (1 Jur., (N. s.), 105.)

1869. [1098]
Doust v. *Slater*. A person who having received notice to drain, commits a trespass on another's land, is not entitled to Notice of Action before being sued for the trespass. (38 L. J., ¡Q. B., 159: 10 B. & S., 400: 20 L. T., 525.)

1880. [1099]
Edwards v. *St. Mary, Islington, Vestry*. "Metropolis Management Amendment Act, 1862," § 106—Plaintiff a driver employed by firm which had contracted to horse the Defendants' Water Carts—Accident owing to defective axle—Held that Defendants were entitled to Notice of Action. (58 L. J., Q. B., 165: L. R., 22 Q. B. D., 338: 53 J. P., 180: 60 L. T., 725.)

1886. [1100]
Farnworth L. B. v. *Compton*. Paving expenses under the "Public Health Acts"—The service of Notices is a condition precedent to the statutory liability of frontagers—Notices never served on existing owners, nor on their predecessors, but predecessors had made payments—Held that such payments did not operate as a waiver of the Notices, so as to make existing owners liable for unpaid balances. (34 W. R., 334.)

1883. [1101]
Freeman v. *Newman*. Registration of Parliamentary voters—Notices served in 1883 on old printed forms, dated 1880—Nobody misled or inconvenienced—Held nevertheless that the notices were bad; and that Overseers could not waive the objection and accept the notices—A notice which requires to be dated must be correctly dated. (53 L. J., Q. B., 108: L. R., 12 Q. B. D., 373: 51 L. T., 396.)

1869. [1102]
Hall v. *Potter*. "Public Health Act, 1848," § 69 [="Public Health Act, 1875," § 150]—A Notice to an owner to pave, &c., a street which is not a highway, if valid as regards part of a property specified therein and invalid as regards the rest, may be enforced *pro tanto*. (39 L. J., M. C., 1: 21 L. T., 454.)

1886. [1103]
Hardy v. *Yorkshire N. R. JJ.* 11 & 12 Vict., c. 44—The building of a Police Station is an act done by Justices in the execution of their

office—If sued for negligence in the building or maintaining of such Station, or for damage arising therefrom, they are entitled to Notice of Action under the above enactment. (At *Nisi Prius*.) (50 J. P., 663.)

1843. [1104]
Jones v. *Williams*. Nuisance—Trespass—An entry without notice on land to abate a nuisance is lawful, if the owner of the land is the original wrongdoer. (12 L. J., Ex., 249: 11 M. & W., 176.)

1878. [1105]
Lewis v. *Cardiff Urban Authority*. "Public Health Act, 1875," § 150—Notice to owners to pave—Notice endorsed by an owner that he wished the Local Authority to do the work at his expense—Held that by such endorsement the owner waived the necessity of the Local Authority proving compliance with the preliminaries to the Notice—But such waiver would not have conferred jurisdiction if none had legally existed. (47 L. J., M. C., 101.)

1874. [1106]
Lewis v. *Evans*. A Notice served by Post will not be deemed to be duly served "in the ordinary course of Post" if it be shown that the intended receiver lives where there is no delivery of letters by the P. O. Authorities, and that he has to fetch his letters from an office at some other place. (44 L. J., C. P., 41: L. R., 10 C. P., 297: 31 L. T., 487.)

1857. [1107]
Liverpool, Mayor, Ex parte. (27 L. J., M. C., 89.)

1892. [1108]
Madden v. *Kensington Vestry*. Non-repair of a "grid"—Accident—A Notice of Action held not bad merely because the place where the act complained of was done was incorrectly stated, if defendants were in fact not misled. (66 L. T., 347: 56 J. P., 470.)

1864. [1109]
Mason v. *Bibby*. "Public Health Act, 1848," §§ 69 and 150 [="Public Health Act, 1875," §§ 150, 267]—Service of a Notice at the owner's place of business by reading it and delivering it to his Clerk, held good—"Place of abode" for this Statute includes "Place of business," and a Clerk is an "inmate." (33 L. J., M. C., 105: 2 H. & C., 881: 9 L. T., 692.)

1858. [1110]
Parkinson v. *Blackburn, Mayor*. Local Act—A Notice to repair or pave a Street must specify the required works. (33 L. T., (o. s.), 119: 22 J. P., 418.) [And see 1 E. & E., 71.] [See now "Public Health Act, 1875," Sched. IV., Form G.]

1846. [1111]
Rawlins v. *West Derby Overseers*. Where a certain day of the month is fixed as the latest day for the delivery of a Notice, and that day happens to be a Sunday, a Notice served on that day is good. (15 L. J., C. P., 70: 2 C. B., 72.)

1853. [1112]
Read v. *Coker*. Things done "in pursuance of" or "in the execution of" a Statute—It is not necessary that a defendant who under a Statute is entitled to a Notice of Action should when he does the things complained of be conscious of his right to a Notice. (22 L. J., 201: 13 C. B., 850: 1 C. L. R., 746.)

1852. [1113]
Reg. v. *Shurstone Inhabitants*. Notices served by Post are to be considered as in time if they would have been in time but for default on the part of the Post Office. (21 L. J., M. C., 145: 18 Q. B., 388: 19 L. T., (o. s.), 105.)

1885. [1114]
St. Leonard's, Shoreditch, Vestry v. *Holmes*. Notice to repair drains served by Inspector—No formal Report to, or authority by, Vestry—Work done by Inspector on Owner's default—Notice held insufficient, and amount paid not to be recoverable. (50 J. P., 132.)

1848. [1115]
Watson v. *Pitt*. 6 Vict., c. 18, § 17—Service of a Notice by thrusting it into a house between 9h. and 10h. p.m., without any personal interview with an inmate held insufficient, the mode and time being unreasonable. (17 L. J., C. P., 143: 5 C. B., 77: 10 L. T., (o. s.), 418.)

55. NUISANCES.

(i.) ANIMALS.

1881. [1116]
Banbury Sanitary Authority v. *Page*. "Public Health Act, 1875," § 47—Pigs evidently kept so as to be a nuisance—Proof of injury to health not necessary in order to sustain a conviction so long as there is a "nuisance" in the Common Law meaning of the term. (51 L. J., M. C., 21: L. R., 8 Q. B. D., 97: 45 L. T., 759: 46 J. P., 184.)

1858. [1117]
Digby v. *West-Ham*. "Public Health Act, 1848," § 59 [="Public Health Act, 1875," §§ 47, 49]—Keeping of Pigs so as to be a nuisance—Conviction held good, the evidence shewing a Nuisance. (22 J. P., 304.)

1861. [1118]
Everett v. *Grapes*. A Municipal By-Law imposing a Fine for keeping Pigs within a Borough held bad. (3 L. T., 669: 25 J. P., 644.) [Virtually overruled by *Wanstead L. B.* v. *Wooster*.]

1884. [1119]
Heap v. *Burnley Union*. "Public Health Act, 1875," §§ 44, 276—By-Law forbidding Pigs being kept within 50 ft. of a dwelling-house, in a rural district, held unreasonable. (53 L. J., M. C., 76: L. R., 12 Q. B. D., 617: 48 J. P., 359.)

1884. [1120]
Lutton v. *Doherty*. "Public Health (Ireland) Act, 1878," § 57—By-Law prohibiting the keeping of Pigs within 21 ft. of a dwelling-house or building used for trade purposes held bad. (16 L. R., Ir., 493.)

1705. [1121]
Reg. v. *Wigg.* Keeping swine in a city is a nuisance at Common Law. (Salk., 460.)

1874. [1122]
Tong Street L. B. v. *Seed.* By-Law—Dung—Default as to removal—Held that the Justices ought to have convicted. (39 J. P., 278.)

1873. [1123]
Wanstead L. B. v. *Wooster.* "Local Government Act, 1858," § 34 [="Public Health Act, 1875," §§ 157,159]—By-Laws prohibiting the keeping of pigs within 100 ft. of a house, and requiring special provision to be made for the removal of dung and refuse, held reasonable. (38 J. P., 21.)

(ii.) BRICK-BURNING.

1862. [1124]
Bamford v. *Turnley.* Nuisance—Burning of Bricks—If nuisance be sufficiently great, an Action will lie, although carefulness be shown. (31 L. J., Q. B., 286 : 3 B. & S., 62 : 6 L. T., 721.)

1870. [1125]
Bareham v. *Hall.* Nuisance—Burning of Bricks—Injunction granted. (22 L. T., 116.)

1862. [1126]
Beardmore v. *Tredwell.* Nuisance—Burning of Bricks in such a place as unnecessarily to injure the plaintiff's trees — Injunction granted. (31 L. J., Ch., 892 : 3 Giff., 683 : 7 L. T., 207.)

1863. [1127]
Cavey v. *Lidbetter.* Nuisance—Burning of Bricks—Allegation of convenient place no answer to an Action. (32 L. J., C. P., 104 : 13 C. B., (N. S.), 470 : 3 F. & F., 14.)

1861. [1128]
Cleeve v. *Mahany.* Nuisance—Burning of Bricks—Whether a nuisance or not, depends on circumstances—No general rule as to distance can be laid down. (25 J. P., 819.)

1876. [1129]
Crawford v. *Hornsea Steam Brick Co.* Nuisance—Bill for Injunction ; damages not asked for—Held that the plaintiff might nevertheless have damages instead of an injuction, the award to be endorsed on the title-deeds to protect defendants from future proceedings. (45 L. J., Ch., 432 : W. N., 1876, p. 132 : 34 L. T., 923.)

1867. [1130]
Evans v. *Smith.* Nuisance—Burning of Bricks—*Per* Wood, V.C.:—It is now clearly settled that the fumes of a brick kiln are, if they reach dwelling-houses, a nuisance, which the Court will restrain without requiring any scientific evidence. (*Times,* June 7, 1867.)

1858. [1131]
*Hole v. *Barlow.* (27 L. J., C. P., 207.) [Overruled by *Bamford* v. *Turnley.*]

1867. [1132]
Luscombe v. *Steer.* Nuisance—Burning of Bricks—The nuisance must be a material injury, either to property or to personal comfort—Injunction refused. (17 L. T., 229 : 15 W. R., 1191.)

1868. [1133]
Roberts v. *Clarke.* Nuisance—Burning of Bricks at a distance of 240 yards — Injunction granted. (18 L. T., 49.)

1881. [1134]
Smith v. *Taylor* (1). Burning of Bricks in a Rural locality where manufacturing processes were not usual—Comfort of occupiers of houses interfered with and therefore Injunction granted. (*Times,* May 6, 1881.)

1881. [1135]
Smith v. *Taylor* (2). Nuisance—Burning of Bricks—Promise that nuisance was only temporary—Circumstances under which apparent acquiescence in a nuisance will not disentitle an aggrieved party to redress. (*Times,* Dec. 3, 1881.)

1851. [1136]
Walter v. *Selfe.* Nuisance—Burning of Bricks—Injunction granted. (20 L. J., Ch., 433: 4 DeG. & Sm., 315 : 17 L. T., (o. s.), 103.)

1863. [1137]
Wanstead L. B. v. *Hill.* "Public Health Act, 1848," § 64 [="Public Health Act, 1875," §§ 112-13]—Brick-making is not necessarily within this section. (32 L. J., M. C., 135: 13 C. B., (N. S.), 479 : 7 L. T., 744.)

(iii.) NOXIOUS TRADES.

1874. [1138]
A.-G. v. *Francis.* Nuisance—Smoke and Vapour from Lime and Cement Works—Held that it was sufficient if substantial discomfort were proved to arise—Injunction granted. (*Times,* Nov. 10, 1874.)

1875. [1139]
A.-G. v. *Hyde Chemical Co.* Nuisance—Chemical Works—Sulphuretted hydrogen — Injunction granted. (*Times,* Dec. 4, 1875.)

1891. [1140]
A.-G. v. *Logan.* Action, with Local Board as relators, against owners of Smelting Works for injury to Park vested in Board held maintainable. (L. R., 2 Q. B., 100 : 65 L. T., 162 : 55 J. P., 615.)

1882. [1141]
A.-G. v. *Metropolitan Railway Co.* Action for nuisance from mineral oil gas-works, nuisance comprising foul smells and chemical deposits —Injunction granted. (*Times,* Jan. 14, 1882.)

1860. [1142]
Bankart v. *Houghton.* Nuisance—Copper Smoke—A person who acquiesces in the erection of works where a noxious trade is to be carried on, does not forfeit his right to prevent such subsequent extension as will cause serious injury. (28 L. J., Ch., 473 : 27 Bea., 425.)

1876. [1143]
Bigsby v. *Dickinson.* Nuisance from Chemical Works — Injunction granted — Reported on points of practice, but see the Judgment, which reviews the facts. (46 L. J., Ch., 280 : L. R., 4 Ch. D., 24 : 35 L. T., 679.)

1838. [1144]
Bliss v. *Hale.* Nuisance —Tallow-melting—Action—Plea, that defendant possessed his mes-

suage and carried on his business before plaintiff acquired the adjoining messuage—Plea, held bad—The plaintiff came to his house with all the rights which the Common Law affords, and wholesome air is one of such rights — The Defendant could only justify his nuisance by proving a prescriptive right. (7 L. J., C. P., 122 : 4 Bing., N. C., 183 : 5 Scott, 500 : 6 Dowl., P. C., 442.)

1884. [1145]
Braintree L. B. H. v. *Boyton.* "Public Health Act, 1875," § 112—The frying of fish, although an offensive trade is not within the Section, not being *ejusdem generis* with the trades there mentioned. (52 L. T., 99 : 48 J. P., 582.)

1878. [1146]
Brooke v. *Wigg.* Nuisance from Chemical Works—Order by Vice-Chancellor on the appeal of the plaintiff that the case should be tried before himself without a Jury, held good on appeal — Subsequently, Injunction granted, the evidence of nuisance being very conclusive, but no order for inquiry as to damage, as damage had arisen from other works besides the defendant's. (47 L. J., Ch., 749 : L. R., 8 Ch. D., 510: 38 L. T., 549 and 732: and *Times*, July 29, 1878.)

1875. [1147]
Cardell v. *Newquay L. B.* The business of a manure merchant is not necessarily an offensive trade under the "Public Health Act." (39 J. P., 742.)

1890. [1148]
Cardiff Manure Co. v. *Cardiff Union.* "Public Health Act, 1875," § 112—The steaming of dry bones in sealed cylinders is not "bone-boiling" within the Act. (54 J. P., 661.)

1879. [1149]
Flux v. *Cumming.* Two tenants occupying a house with a common staircase—Application for an Injunction by the upper tenant against the lower one (a bath proprietor) to restrain the discharge of noxious fumes and hot vitiated air, which ascended the staircase and caused a nuisance—Injunction granted. (*Times*, Aug. 5, 1878.) Subsequently, question at issue sent to a Jury—*Per* Coleridge, J. : "The trade being a lawful one, in a lawful place, it was for plaintiff to prove that it was exercised in an unlawful way"—Verdict for defendant—New trial refused. (*Times*, May 30 and June 24, 1879.)

1860. [1150]
Houghton v. *Bankart.* Nuisance—Copper Smoke—Damage to farm—Principle of valuation. (3 L. T., 266 and 666: 8 W. R., 689.)

1885. [1151]
Houldershaw v. *Martin.* "Public Health Act, 1875," § 114—Nuisance from frying of fish — Medical certificate that process was a "nuisance" held sufficient without stating also that it was "injurious to health"—Justices should have convicted. (*Times*, March 4, 1885.)

1869. [1152]
Knight v. *Gardner.* Nuisance—Manufacture of

Manure from night-soil—Injunction granted. (19 L. T., 673.)

1879. [1153]
Malton Urban S. A. v. *Malton Farmers Manure Co.* "Public Health Act, 1875," §§ 112 and 114—An offensive trade causing effluvia is within § 114 if the effluvia though not injurious to persons in sound health cause sick persons to become worse—*Per* Stephen, J. :—"It is not necessary in order to bring a nuisance within this section to prove injury to health"—*G. W. R.* v. *Bishop* considered. (49 L. J., M. C., 90 : L. R., 4 Ex. D., 302: 40 L. T., 755: 44 J. P., 155.)

1879. [1154]
Passey v. *Oxford L. B.* "Public Health Act, 1875," § 112—A place where bones were deposited after collection held within the Act, on proof of offensive smells proceeding therefrom, notwithstanding that the bones were not subjected to any manufacturing process—Conviction affirmed. (43 J. P., 622.)

1861. [1155]
Pinckney v. *Ewens.* Action for Nuisance—Fellmonger's trade—Verdict for the plaintiff. (4 L. T., 741.)

1851. [1156]
Reg. v. *Garland.* Nuisance—Arsenic Works—Evidence of death of cattle held admissible in support of an Indictment charging noisome smells. (5 Cox, C. C., 165 : 15 J. P., 260.)

1878. [1157]
Reg. v. *Wallace* (1). Nuisance from Chemical Works—Indictment—Bankruptcy of Defendant—Fine of £3000 imposed, to include the prosecutor's costs — Fine not to be levied unless default were made in the payment of the costs, or the Works creating the nuisance were resumed. (*Times*, Nov. 15, 1878.)

1826. [1158]
Rex v. *Cross* (2). Nuisance—Slaughter-house—If a man sets up a noxious trade remote from habitations and roads, and afterwards houses are built and roads made, he may continue his trade, though it be a nuisance. (2 C. & P., 483.) [But see *Bliss* v. *Hale.*]

1805. [1159]
Rex v. *Davey.* Nuisance—Coke ovens—An offensive trade to be indictable as a nuisance must be destructive to health or render dwelling-houses uncomfortable or untenantable—Defendant acquitted. (5 Esp., 217.)

1826. [1160]
Rex v. *Neil.* Nuisance—Varnish Factory—To support an Indictment for a nuisance it is not necessary that the smells should be injurious to health: it suffices that they are offensive to the senses. (2 C. & P., 485.)

1791. [1161]
Rex v. *B. Neville.* Nuisance—Grease Melting—A man setting up a noxious business in a neighbourhood where such business has long been carried on is not indictable unless the nuisance is much increased — Defendant acquitted. (Peake, 91.)

1791. [1162]
Rex v. *S. Neville.* Nuisance—Grease Melting—

As the noxious trade had been carried on for "near 50 years," Kenyon, C.J., directed an acquittal. (Peake, 93.) [In *Weld* v. *Hornby* (7 East., 199), Lord Ellenborough laid it down that though an acquiescence of 20 years may determine private rights, "yet the public have an interest in the suppression of public nuisances though of longer standing."]

1827.   [1163]
Rex v. *Watts.* Nuisance—Horse Boiling—A man carrying on a long established noxious business is nevertheless indictable if the mischief is increased by alterations in the manner in which the business is carried on; but an increase of mischief due simply to an increase of business will not justify a conviction—Defendant convicted. (Moody & M., 281.)

1874.   [1164]
Salvin v. *North Brancepeth Coal Co.* Nuisance—Coke ovens—Nature and extent of damage necessary to sustain suit—Injunction refused. (44 L. J., Ch., 149: L. R., 9 Ch. App., 705: 31 L. T., 154.)

1876.   [1165]
St. Helen's Chemical Co. v. *St. Helen's Corporation.* "Nuisances Removal Act, 1855," § 12 [= "Public Health Act, 1875," § 95]—Discharge through separate drains of chemicals which, when they became mixed in the public sewers, emitted noxious fumes—Defence that the Corporation had not flushed the sewer—Held that the appellants were rightly convicted. (45 L. J., M. C., 150: L. R., 1 Ex. D., 196: 34 L. T., 397: 40 J. P., 471.)

1875.   [1166]
Umfreville v. *Johnson.* Nuisance—Cement Works—Bill filed by two plaintiffs in respect of properties at unequal distances from the Works—Injunction granted as to one plaintiff, but refused as to the other—Bill filed before the Works were open, and therefore when the nuisance was only in anticipation. (44 L. J., Ch., 752: L. R., 10 Ch. App., 580.)

1881.   [1167]
Verco v. *Morris.* "Public Health Act, 1875," § 112—The fact that bone-boiling is mentioned in this Section is not conclusive evidence that it is a nuisance, but only a point to be considered. (4 *Municip. Corp. Assoc. Month. Circular*, 181: *Times*, Dec. 17, 1881.)

(iv.) SMOKE.

1872.   [1168]
Barnes v. *Akroyd.* "Sanitary Act, 1866," § 19 [= "Public Health Act, 1875," § 91 (7)]—Black smoke from chimney—Master is liable although his servant is in default. (41 L. J., M. C., 110: L. R., 7 Q. B., 474: 26 L. T., 692: 37 J. P., 116.)

1876.   [1169]
Barnes v. *Norris.* "Public Health Act, 1875," § 91—Nuisance—Smoke—Several chimneys—Summons dismissed by Justices on the ground that the particular chimney complained of should have been specified—Held

that the Justices were wrong; they ought to have heard the case on the merits. (41 J. P., 150.)

1889.   [1170]
Chisholm v. *Doulton.* 16 & 17 Vict. c. 128, § 1—Smoke from furnace properly constructed—Negligence of stoker—Master held not liable. (58 L. J., M. C., 133: L. R., 22 Q. B. D., 736: 60 L. T., 966: 53 J. P., 550.)

1867.   [1171]
Cooper v. *Woolley.* "Towns Improvement Clauses Act, 1847," § 108: Local Act—To consume "as far as possible all" Smoke, means "consistently with carrying on the trade in which the furnace is employed." (36 L. J., M. C., 27: L. R., 2 Ex., 88: 15 L. T., 539.)

1867.   [1172]
Crump v. *Lambert.* Nuisance—Smoke without noise or noxious vapour; noise alone; and offensive odours alone, though not injurious to health, may severally constitute a nuisance—The material question is whether the annoyance materially interferes with the ordinary comfort of human existence—Injunction granted. (L. R., 3 Eq., 409: Affirmed on Appeal, 17 L. T., 133.)

1875.   [1173]
Eddleston v. *Barnes.* "Nuisances Removal Act, 1855," §§ 12-14 [= "Public Health Act, 1875," §§ 95-8]—Separate Orders for abatement and for prohibition of nuisance—Convictions on two Informations, the offence constituting the breach of both Orders being but one offence—Held that only one conviction could stand. (45 L. J., M. C., 73: L. R., 1 Ex. D., 167: 34 L. T., 497: 40 J. P., 88.)

1874.   [1174]
Gaskell v. *Bayley.* "Sanitary Act, 1866," § 19 [= "Public Health Act, 1875," § 91 (7)]—Nuisance—Smoke—If the quantity of dense black smoke evolved is great, a conviction may be had—It is not necessary to prove direct injury to health. (30 L. T., 516: 38 J. P., 293.)

1870.   [1175]
Higgins v. *Northwich Union.* "Nuisances Removal Act, 1855," §§ 13-14: "Sanitary Act, 1866," § 19—Nuisance—Black smoke from Salt-works—Order for abatement—Disobedience thereto—Conviction affirmed—The existence of a nuisance is a question of fact peculiarly within the province of a Court of Summary Jurisdiction. (22 L. T., 752: 34 J. P., 806.)

1874.   [1176]
Hutton v. *Lancashire & Yorkshire Railway Co.* Nuisance—Smoke from Locomotive Engine—31 & 32 Vict., c. 119, § 19—Prosecution by a passenger—Defendants convicted. (38 J. P., 731.)

1859.   [1177]
Manchester, Sheffield & Lincolnshire Railway Co. v. *Wood.* 8 Vict., c. 20, § 114—Nuisance from smoke—Held that the penalty only attaches where the engine is not constructed so as to consume its own smoke; and, there-

fore, where an engine is duly constructed as aforesaid, and the nuisance is due only to careless user, there is no liability under the Section. (29 L. J., M. C., 29 : 2 E. & E., 344 : 1 L. T., 31 : 24 J. P., 38.)

1890.   [1178]
Niven v. *Greaves.* "Public Health Act, 1875," § 91—Nuisance from black smoke—On proof that the nuisance was due to the default of the men in charge of the furnaces belonging to the defendants, the owners, the furnaces being duly constructed, the Justices dismissed the summons—Held that they were wrong; that the owners were liable for the default of their servants. (54 J. P., 548.)

1872.   [1179]
Norris v. *Barnes.* "Sanitary Act, 1866," §§ 14 and 19 : Proviso in the "Nuisances Removal Act, 1855," § 44 [= "Public Health Act, 1875," §§ 91 (7), 332, 334]—Black smoke—Manufacture of Bichrome—Held that Justices had no jurisdiction to order abatement. (41 L. J., M. C., 124 : L. R., 7 Q. B., 537 : 26 L. T., 122 : 37 J. P., 246.)

1892.   [1180]
Patterson v. *Chamber Colliery Co.* "Public Health Act, 1875," §§ 91, 334—§ 91 may (subject to § 334) apply to the chimneys of coal mines if they send forth black smoke—Case remitted to Justices to hear and determine on the facts. (56 J. P., 200.)

1872.   [1181]
Reg. v. *Waterhouse.* "Sanitary Act, 1866," § 19 (3)—Black smoke—19 Summonses on the same person—Held that the convictions were right. (41 L. J., M. C., 115 : L. R., 7 Q. B., 545 : 26 L. T., 761 : 36 J. P., 471.)

1812.   [1182]
Rex v. *Dewsnap.* Proceedings by Indictment—Persons dwelling near a smoke nuisance and specially affected are parties grieved so as to be entitled to special consideration. (16 East, 194.)

1757.   [1183]
Rex v. *White.* Nuisance—Sulphur Works—An Indictment lies for impregnating the air near a highway with noisome and offensive stinks : it is not necessary that they should be unwholesome. (1 Burr., 333.)

1847.   [1184]
Rich v. *Basterfield.* Nuisance from smoke emanating from a chimney—Action against landlord on the ground that as he built the chimney and let the premises with the chimney which caused the nuisance, he was liable—Action held not maintainable. (16 L. J., C. P., 273 : 4 C. B., 783.) [Commented on and distinguished in *Harris* v. *James.*]

1872.   [1185]
Savile v. *Kilner.* Nuisance—Smoke and vapour from Glass-works—Injunction granted. (26 L. T., 277.)

1856.   [1186]
Simpson v. *Savage.* Nuisance from smoke of Factory chimney—Causing smoke to issue from a chimney (the erection of the chimney itself not being a nuisance) is not ground for

an Action by the reversioner of adjoining premises, though his tenants have given notice to quit in consequence, and the saleable value of his premises is deteriorated—To entitle a reversioner to maintain an Action for injury to his reversion the injury must be of a permanent character. (26 L. J., C. P., 50 : 1 C. B., (N. S.), 347.)

1877.   [1187]
Smith v. *Midland Railway Co.* Nuisance from smoke and soot of Locomotive engines—Engines cleaned and lighted in the open air —Held that the Statutes authorising the working of the railway gave no authority for the continuance of a nuisance not necessarily connected with the working of the railway : the engine-shed might be moved to a better place—Injunction granted. (W. N., 1877, p. 200 : 37 L. T., 224 : 25 W. R., 861.)

1865.   [1188]
St. Helen's Smelting Co. v. *Tipping.* Nuisance—Copper Smoke—A distinction is to be drawn between mere personal discomfort and material injury to property—Verdict for plaintiff (deft. in error). (11 H. L. C., 642 : 12 L. T., 779.) [An Injunction was afterwards granted by the Court of Chancery, *Nom. Tipping* v. *St. Helen's, &c.* L. R., 1 Ch. App., 66.]

1885.   [1189]
Weekes v. *King.* "Public Health Act, 1875," § 91—Black smoke from Brewery—Held that the 2nd Proviso only applied to the 1st nuisance mentioned in the 7th Sub-section, and that evidence as to construction of furnace was rightly rejected. (53 L. T., 51 : 49 J. P., 709.)

(v.) VARIOUS.

1885.   [1190]
Andrews v. *Mansfield.* Market garden—Deposits of dust and refuse causing a nuisance held actionable : perpetual Injunction also granted. (*Times*, March 6, 1885.)

1866.   [1191]
A.-G. v. *Bradford Canal Proprietors.* Nuisance — Appeal at Law pending — Injunction granted. (35 L. J., Ch., 619 : L. R., 2 Eq., 71 : 14 L. T., 248 : 15 L. T., 9. For the proceedings at Law, see 34 L. J., Q. B., 191 : 6 B. & S., 631.)

1867.   [1192]
Bazendale v. *McMurray.* Nuisance—Discharge into a Stream of Refuse from a Paper Mill—The onus lies on the plaintiff of proving an increase in the amount of the pollution. (L. R., 2 Ch. App., 790 : 16 W. R., 32.)

1874.   [1193]
Benjamin v. *Store.* Obstruction of highway by vans—Action by occupier of adjoining house, because of the interference with his trade—In actions for damage from a public nuisance, the plaintiff must show that the injury is (1) particular, special : (2) direct, not merely consequential ; and (3) substantial, not merely temporary or evanescent—Evidence of unpleasant smells admitted. (43 L. J., C. P., 162 : L. R., 9 C. P., 400 : 30 L. T., 362.)

1882. [1194]

Bishop Auckland L. B. v. *Bishop Auckland Iron Co.* "Public Health Act, 1875," § 91, (4) —To constitute an offence it suffices if the accumulation interferes with the personal comfort of the neighbours though not injurious to their health—*G. W. R.* v. *Bishop* distinguished; *Malton* v. *Malton, and Banbury* v. *Page* followed. (52 L. J., M. C., 38: L. R., 10 Q. B. D., 138 : 48 L. T., 223 : 47 J. P., 389.)

1879. [1195]

Brown v. *Biggleswade Union.* "Public Health Act, 1875," §§ 91, 97-8—House unfit for habitation—Order of Justices that the Local Authority might abate the nuisance (the owner having failed to do so)—Whereupon Authority pulled down the house—Action in County Court by owner against the Authority —Nonsuit—Held that the Authority was justified in pulling down the house on the Justices being satisfied that it was unfit for habitation, and the owner refusing to repair. (*Times,* May 19, 1879.)

1868. [1196]

Brown v. *Bussell.* "Nuisances Removal Act, 1855," § 12 [="Public Health Act, 1875," § 95]—Nuisance caused by one person but visibly arising on the premises of another person—Order for abatement rightly made on the former. (37 L. J., M. C., 65 : L. R., 3 Q. B., 251 : 18 L. T., 19: 32 J. P., 196.)

1835. [1197]

Dawson v. *Moore.* In an Action for nuisance where the Defendant pleads Not Guilty the Plaintiff must not only prove the existence of the nuisance but that the Defendant caused it. (7 C. & P., 25.)

1884. [1198]

De La Torre v. *Kensington JJ.* "Nuisances Removal Act, 1855," § 8 [="Public Health Act, 1875," § 91]—Large numbers of cats and dogs in a private house held a "nuisance" within the Act. (At Q. Sess.) (48 J. P., 503.)

1613. [1199]

Dewell v. *Saunders.* The erection of a new pigeon-house by a Freeholder of a Manor is not a common nuisance inquirable at the leet; but if the pigeons fly abroad to the damage of the King's subjects, the Judges of Assize may take cognisance of it. (Cro. Jac., 490.)

1845. [1200]

Fay v. *Prentice.* Erection of a cornice which projected over plaintiff's garden so as to throw rain water into the garden — Held that the cornice might be assumed to be a nuisance in respect of which the plaintiff might maintain an Action. (14 L. J., C. P., 298; 1 C. B., 828.)

1839. [1201]

Flight v. *Thomas.* Action for nuisance from offensive manure heap—Plea, 20 years' right of user—Held, nevertheless, that plaintiff was entitled to judgment for the plea did not state that the stench complained of had

for 20 years passed over plaintiff's land. (8 L. J., Q. B., 337: 10 A. & E., 590: 2 P. & D., 591 : 7 Dowl., P. C., 741.)

1868. [1202]

Francomb v. *Freeman.* "Nuisances Removal Act, 1855," § 12 [="Public Health Act, 1875," § 95]—Watercourse fouled by sewage conveyed thither by a drain from certain cottages belonging to the appellant, but nuisance not on appellant's land—Held that he was nevertheless rightly convicted. (37 L. J., M. C., 65: L. R., 3 Q. B., 251 : 18 L. T., 19 : 32 J. P., 196.)

1872. [1203]

Great Western Railway Co. v. *Bishop.* Rainwater dripping through a Bridge not a nuisance under one of the "Sanitary Acts" [="Public Health Act, 1878," § 91]— because not a nuisance injurious to health. (41 L. J., M. C., 120; L. R., 7 Q. B., 550: 26 L. T., 905: 37 J. P., 5.)

1876. [1204]

Harris v. *James.* A landlord who lets premises for a purpose which may be expected to be a nuisance is liable for the nuisance jointly with his tenant. (45 L. J., Q. B., 545: 35 L. T., 240.)

1868. [1205]

Hendon Guardians v. *Bowles.* "Nuisances Removal Act, 1855," § 12 [="Public Health Act, 1875," § 95]—Joint and several liability for nuisance—Person "by whose act, default, or sufferance"—Held that an Order might be made upon each party whose sewage assisted in causing the nuisance. (17 L. T., 597: 16 W. R., 510 : 20 L. T., 609.)

1888. [1206]

Herbert v. *Leigh Mills Co.* "Factories (Steam Whistles) Act, 1872"—A whistle formerly blown by steam but now by compressed air held within the Act. (53 J. P., 679 : 5 *Times* L. R., 449.)

1855. [1207]

Hertford Union v. *Kimpton.* (25 L. J., M. C., 41.)

1876. [1208]

Home v. *Kelso Local Authority.* "Public Health (Scotland) Act, 1867," 30 & 31 Vict. c. 101, § 1, subs. F.—Nuisance from overcrowding— Where a landlord lets a cottage which comes under the control of the tenant, without restriction, the landlord is not, in the sense of the Statute, the author of the nuisance, nor jointly liable for the act or default of his tenant in allowing overcrowding on the part of a sub-tenant. (3 Couper, 239.)

1888. [1209]

Kirkheaton L. B. v. *Beaumont.* Nuisance from overflow from public sewer, the nuisance actually arising on defendant's land—Held however that, as he was not the author of the nuisance, remedial measures could not be enforced against him. (52 J. P., 68.)

1881. [1210]

Learoyd v. *Halifax Corporation.* Action to restrain slaughter-houses being carried on so as to create a nuisance—On undertaking

being given that system should be changed,
Motion for Injunction directed to stand over
till trial of Action. (*Times*, July 8, 1881.)

1823. [1211]
Lonsdale (Earl of) v. *Nelson.* *Per* Best, J.—"The
security of lives and property may sometimes
require so speedy a remedy as not to allow
time to call on the person on whose property
the mischief has arisen to remedy it. In
such cases an individual would be justified
in abating a nuisance from omission without
notice." (2 B. & C., 302 : 3 D. & R., 556.)

1857. [1212]
Reg. v. *Bateman.* 12 & 13 Vict. c. 45—Indictment for nuisance—§ 18 of this Act for
removing Orders of Quarter Sessions for the
purpose of enforcing them by Attachment
does not apply to an Order to abate a
nuisance of which a defendant has been
found guilty on an Indictment which can be
enforced in the ordinary way. (27 L. J.,
M. C., 95 : 8 E. & B., 584 : 30 L. T., (o. s.),
157.)

1880. [1213]
Reg. v. *Parlby.* "Public Health Act, 1875,"
§§ 91-6—These sections are not available
against a Local Authority to obtain an abatement of Nuisances arising from sewage
works constructed under § 27 by the Local
Authority ; and a Court of Summary Jurisdiction has therefore no power to make an
Order under § 96 against such Authority—
The remedy is by Information in the name
of the Attorney-General. (58 L. J., M. C.,
49 : L. R., 22 Q. B. D., 521 : 60 L. T., 422 :
53 J. P., 327.)

1703. [1214]
Reg. v. *Watts.* Where a house is so ruinous that
it is likely to fall down on a highway, the
occupier may be indicted for a nuisance
irrespective of the owner. (1 Salk., 357 :
[*R.* v. *Watson*] 2 L. Raym., 856.)

1835. [1215]
Rex v. *Curwood.* Pollution of river by gas refuse
—A prosecutor in an Indictment for nuisance
may be compelled to give a particular statement of the acts of nuisance intended to be
relied on. (3 A. & E., 815 : 5 N. & M., 369 :
1 H. & W., 310.)

1802. [1216]
Rex v. *Lloyd* (1). An Indictment will not lie for
that which is a nuisance only to a few inhabitants of a particular place—Indictment
for a nuisance affecting only 3 houses—
Lord Ellenborough said that the defendant
must be acquitted for the nuisance was not
sufficiently general. (4 Esp., 200.)

1832. [1217]
Rex v. *Pease.* Where Parliament authorises a
nuisance an Indictment against its authors
will not lie. (2 L. J., M. C., 26 : 4 B. & Ad.,
30.)

1868. [1218]
Richmond Union v. *St. Paul's, Dean and Chapter
of.* "Nuisances Removal Act, 1855," § 12
[="Public Health Act, 1875," § 95]—Pond

which had become a nuisance on a Common
managed by Conservators—Respondents held
not liable, because not the parties by whose
act, default, permission, or sufferance, the
nuisance arose. (18 L. T., 522 : 32 J. P.,
374.)

1875. [1219]
Rye Union v. *Paine.* "Sanitary Act, 1866," § 19
[="Public Health Act, 1875," § 91 (5)]—
Overcrowding—Held that this enactment
extends the "Nuisances Removal Act, 1855,"
and that there may be a conviction for overcrowding though only one family be concerned. (44 L. J., M. C., 148 : W. N., 1875,
p. 119 : 32 L. T., 757 : 40 J. P., 166.)

1863. [1220]
Smith v. *Waghorn.* Local Act—Nuisance from
Stable Dung—Conviction. (27 J. P., 744.)

1865. [1221]
Tomlins v. *Great Stanmore Nuisances Removal
Committee.* "Nuisances Removal Act, 1855,"
§§ 13-14 [="Public Health Act, 1875,"
§§ 97-8]—An owner who does not comply
with an Order to abate a nuisance may be
fined, although the Order was directed not
only to him, but also to the Nuisances Committee. (12 L. T., 118 : 29 J. P., 117.)

1887. [1222]
Wallasey L. B. v. *Gracey.* "Public Health Act,
1875," § 107—This section does not enable
a Board to sue in its own name for abatement
of a nuisance in any case where by Common
Law the proceedings must be by Information
in the name of the A.-G. (56 L. J., Ch.,
739 : L. R., 36 Ch. D., 593 : 57 L. T., 51 :
51 J. P., 740.) Subsequently, Injunction
granted. (*Times*, July 23, 1887.)

1874. [1223]
White v. *Jameson.* Brick-burning—Where an
occupier grants a license to another to do
certain acts on the land, and the licensee
commits a nuisance, the occupier may be
made a co-defendant in a suit to restrain the
nuisance, for he is bound to see that his
property is so managed that other persons
are not injured. (L. R., 18 Eq., 303 : 22
W. R., 761.)

1887. [1224]
Winter v. *Baker.* Nuisance and annoyance to
the occupier of a dwelling-house by the use
of a yard for steam circus, organ, swings,
roundabouts, shooting galleries, and other
sports—Injunction granted with costs, the
existence of the nuisance being clearly
proved. (*Times*, April 22, 1887.)

56. "OCCUPIER," DEFINITION OF.

1870. [1225]
Roads v. *Trumpington Churchwardens.* Poor
Rate—Exclusive occupation—Land let from
year to year under reservation of right of
entry for inspection—Minerals—Tenant to
be deemed "Occupier." (40 L. J., M. C., 35 :
L. R., 6 Q. B., 56 : 23 L. T., 821.)

57. "OWNER," DEFINITION OF.

⁎ See also "Paving Expenses," (§ 59, *post*).

1890. [1226]

Bacup Corporation v. *Smith.* "Public Health Act, 1875," § 4—The definition of "Owner" does not include a Receiver appointed by the Court, and so service of notice under § 150 on such Receiver is invalid. (59 L. J., Ch., 518 : L. R., 44 Ch. D., 395 : 63 L. T., 195.)

1863. [1227]

Blything Union v. *Warton.* "Nuisances Removal Act, 1855," §§ 2 and 19 [="Public Health Act, 1875," § 104]—Order of Justices —Meaning of "Owner"—Execution of Works —Issue subsequent to the execution of the works, of a Power of Attorney to receive rents—Attorney not liable—No personal liability attaches to one who becomes owner after the making of the Order. (32 L. J., M. C., 132 : 3 B. & S., 352 : 7 L. T., 672.)

1871. [1228]

Bowditch v. *Wakefield L. B. H.* "Public Health Act, 1848," §§ 2 and 69 [="Public Health Act, 1875," § 150]—"Owner"—Paving a Street—Trustees of a School-house and Buildings held liable. (40 L. J., M. C., 214 : L. R., 6 Q. B., 567 : 25 L. T., 88.)

1871. [1229]

Cancell v. *Hanson.* "Owner"—Fees payable to Surveyor—On default of owner his successor in title held not liable. (Metropolis.) (41 L. J., M. C., 8 : [*Caudwell* v. *H.*] 25 L. T., 595 : L. R., 7 Q. B., 55.)

1842. [1230]

Chorlton-upon-Medlock Constables v. *Walker.* Local Paving Act charging the owners of "hereditaments," &c.—Church built and consecrated—Various rents and profits assigned to defendant by the Incumbent in satisfaction of a debt—Held that the defendant as mortgagee was not rateable, not being an "Owner." (12 L. J., Ex., 88 : 10 M. & W., 742.)

1872. [1231]

Cook v. *Montague.* "Nuisances Removal Act, 1855," § 2—A Leaseholder for 21 years who sub-let, and not the Freeholder held to be "Owner," where the sub-tenant was author of the nuisance. (41 L. J., M. C., 149 : L. R., 7 Q. B, 418 : 26 L. T., 471 : 37 J. P., 53.)

1863. [1232]

Cowen v. *Phillips.* A tenant, having only an equitable interest under an agreement for a lease, held to be "adjoining owner" and privileged accordingly. (Metropolis.) (33 Bea., 18 : 8 L. T., 622.)

1858. [1233]

Evelyn v. *Whichcord.* Surveyor's Fees—Held that a lessee for 81 years was the "Owner" liable, and not the freeholder. (27 L. J., M. C., 211 : E. B. & E., 126 : 31 L. T., (o. s.), 96.)

1890. [1234]

Fillingham v. *Wood.* "Metropolitan Building Act, 1855," § 85 (1)—A tenant in posses-

sion of part of a house under an agreement for a greater interest than as tenant from year to year is an "adjoining owner." (L. R., [1891] 1 Ch., 51 : 64 L. T., 46.)

1867. [1235]

Holland (Lady) v. *Kensington Vestry.* Paving new street—Land agreed to be let on building leases but leases not actually executed— "Owner"—Construction — Freeholder held liable. (Metropolis.) (96 L. J., M. C., 105 : L. R., 2 C. P., 565 : 17 L. T., 73.)

1865. [1236]

Hunt v. *Harris.* Expense of repairing a dangerous party wall—Premises sub-let—Lessee for 99 years held to be an "Owner." (Metropolis.) (34 L. J., C. P., 249 : 19 C. B., (N. s.), 13 : 12 L. T., 421.)

1863. [1237]

Peek v. *Waterloo and Seaforth L. B. H.* "Public Health Act, 1848," § 69 [="Public Health Act, 1875," § 150]—Service of a notice on a person who *de facto* receives the rent is service on the "Owner." (33 L. J., M. C., 11 : 2 H. & C., 709 : 9 L. T., 338.)

1878. [1238]

Reg. v. *Lee (2).* "Metropolitan Building Act, 1855," 18 & 19 Vict., c. 122—Church in dangerously dilapidated state—Certain urgent repairs executed by the Local Authority, who thereupon sought to recover from the Incumbent, as being the "Owner" within the Statute—*Mandamus* to Magistrate to issue a Distress Warrant for these expenses refused, for the Incumbent had no such beneficial interest in the fabric as to make him an "Owner" within the Statute. (48 L. J., M. C., 22 : L. R., 4 Q.' B. D., 75 : 39 L. T., 605 : 43 J. P., 302.)

1879. [1239]

Reg. v. *Swindon L. B.* "Public Health Act, 1875," §§ 153 and 257—When works are executed by a Local Authority because the owner makes default in complying with an Order, and the property changes hands during the proceedings, the Owner at the time when the works are completed is the person to be sued—Practice as to Appeals. (49 L. J., Q. B., 522 : L. R., 4 Q. B. D., 305 : [*Hinton* v. *S.*] 42 L. T., 614 : 44 J. P., 505.)

1883. [1240]

St. Helen's Corporation v. *Riley.* "Public Health Act, 1875," § 150 : Local Act—Paving expenses—Definition of "Owner." (47 J. P., 471.)

1885. [1241]

St. Helen's, Mayor v. *Kirkham.* Local Act—Definition of "Owner"—"Agent" employed to collect rents held to be an "owner" in respect of collection of Improvement Expenses (L. R., 16 Q. B. D., 403 : 54 J. P., 647.)

1891. [1242]

Tendring Union v. *Dowton.* "Public Health Act, 1875," §§ 157, 257—"Owner" does not include a person who has the benefit of a covenant restricting the use of the premises in respect of which expenses for street improvement have been incurred—Therefore where a Local Authority had obtained a charge on certain land which was subject to a restrictive covenant as to building it was not entitled to an order for sale free of the covenant. (61 L. J., Ch., 82 : L. R., 3 Ch., 265 : 65 L. T., 434.)

1870.   [1243]

Tubb v. *Good.* Surveyor's Fees—By whom payable—"Owner." (Metropolis.) (39 L. J., M. C., 135 : L. R., 5 Q. B., 443 : 22 L. T., 885.)

58. PARLIAMENTARY EXPENSES.

[Some of the Cases which follow need to be considered in connection with the "Borough Funds Act, 1872" (35 & 36 Vict., c. 91), and with the Cases decided thereunder.]

1850.   [1244]

A.-G. v. *Andrews.* Improvement Commissioners—Application of Rates to defray the expenses of a Bill in Parliament to extend Powers—Injunction granted. (20 L. J., Ch., 467 : 2 Mac. & G., 225 : 2 Hall & T., 431 : 15 L. T., (o. s.), 322.)

1853.   [1245]

A.-G. v. *Eastlake.* Proposed application of moneys raised for defined Paving, &c., purposes to the cost of promoting a Bill in Parliament—Proposal held improper. (2 Eq. R., 145 : 11 Hare, 205.)

1878.   [1246]

A.-G. v. *Hull, Mayor.* "Borough Funds Act, 1872"—Alleged irregularities in the statutory public meeting which authorised a Parliamentary opposition to a Dock Bill—Held that, under the circumstances, the Corporation ought not to be restrained by Injunction—*Semble,* that the Act is an enlarging Act, and does not interfere with the ordinary powers of Municipal Corporations to spend money in Parliamentary contests. (*Times,* March 18, 1878.)

1888.   [1247]

A.-G. v. *Lambeth Vestry.* Action to restrain Vestry from applying the Rates to the promotion of a Bill in Parliament—Injunction granted so far as the application of the Rates was concerned, but the promotion of the Bill held not to be *ultra vires.* (*Times,* Jan. 31, 1888.)

1879.   [1248]

A.-G. v. *Lower Thames Valley Sewerage Board.* Board constituted under Provisional Order—Funds raised under aforesaid powers employed in expenses of a Bill in Parliament to extend powers—*Per* Jessel, M.R. :—Funds intrusted by Parliament to a public body for a definite purpose must not be used for another purpose only auxiliary or incidental to the specific purpose—Held that Defendant Board had no right to apply to Parliament without the sanction of the Local Government Board—Injunction granted to restrain application of funds to payment of Parliamentary expenses. (*Times,* July 19, 1879.)

1851.   [1249]

A.-G. v. *Norwich, Mayor.* Payment of expenses

of application to Parliament for a Bill out of Borough Fund—Injunction granted. (21 L. J., Ch., 139 : 16 Simons, 225 : 18 L. T., (o. s.), 58.)

1849.   [1250]

A.-G. v. *Southampton Guardians.* Proposed payment out of the Poor Rate of the expenses of a rejected Bill in Parliament—Injunction granted. (18 L. J., Ch., 393 : 17 Simons, 6 : 13 L. T., (o. s.), 503.)

1872.   [1251]

A.-G. v. *Tottenham L. B. H.* Costs of promoting a Bill in Parliament—Certain members held personally liable—But a member who proved he had not concurred was exonerated. (27 L. T., 440 : W. N., 1872, p. 205.)

1870.   [1252]

A.-G. v. *West Hartlepool Improvement Commissioners.* Local Act—Proposed payment out of the Rates, of the expenses of a Bill in Parliament to extend the District and powers of Commissioners—Injunction granted. (39 L. J., Ch., 624 : L. R., 10 Eq., 152 : 22 L. T., 510.)

1854.   [1253]

A.-G. v. *Wigan, Mayor.* Proposed payment of expenses of a partially successful opposition to a Bill in Parliament out of surplus of Borough Fund—Such payment held not a proceeding to be restrained by an interlocutory Injunction. (23 L. J., Cb., 429 : Kay, 268 : 5 De G. M. & G., 52 : 23 L. T., (o. s.), 43.)

1858.   [1254]

Bailey v. *Cuckson.* Action against four members of a Local Board for services in opposing, on behalf of the Board, a Gas Bill in a case where a Rate out of which plaintiff would have been paid had been declared void—Held that the plaintiff could not recover against individual members. (32 L. T., (o. s.), 124 : 7 W. R., 16.)

1883.   [1255]

Birmingham Town Council, In re. "Birmingham Improvement Act, 1851," § 63—Poll of Ratepayers as to promotion of Bill in Parliament—A 4 days' poll, between 9 a.m. and 4 p.m. each day, held to afford sufficient facilities for voting although population of Borough, 400,000. *Per* Huddleston, B.:—"There is no trace of any authority, in Cases reported now for 200 years, for any right in Ratepayers to insist upon a scrutiny against the decision and discretion of the presiding officer." (*Times,* March 22, 1883.)

1869.   [1256]

Bower v. *Sligo Commissioners.* A Corporation is justified, if acting *bonâ fide,* in applying funds in opposing Parliamentary Bills which would affect their existence, and materially injure their powers as a Corporation, even though no such power is expressly given by their incorporating Act. (4 Ir., R., C. L., 489.)

1847.   [1257]

Brighton v. *North.* Application of Trust Funds held by Commissioners for maintenance of river banks towards opposing a Bill in Parliament which threatened to injure the property of the Trust held legal. (16 L. J., Ch., 255: [*Bright* v. *North*] 2 Phillips, 216 : 8 L. T., (o. s.), 154, in the Court below.)

1886.   [1258]
Cleverton v. *St. German's Union.* "Public Health Act, 1875," §§ 51-70—Although it is the duty of a Sanitary Authority to procure a supply of water, this duty does not confer power to apply to Parliament for a Bill to enable them to do so if their ordinary powers prove insufficient. (56 L. J., Q. B., 83: 3 *Times* L. R., 43.) [This decision must not be pushed too far.]

1887.   [1259]
Reg. v. *Dover Corporation.* Order by Town Council for payment of costs of promoting a Bill in Parliament — Application for *Certiorari* to set aside the Order on the ground that the meeting of Ratepayers did not sanction the expenditure—Meeting duly convened and held, and resolution declared carried : long pause : no poll demanded : chair vacated by chairman : then poll demanded and not granted : no steps taken for 9 months—Held on these facts that it was too late to question the validity of the meeting, and *Certiorari* refused. (*Times*, Dec. 19, 1887.)

1873.   [1260]
Reg. v. *Liverpool, Mayor.* "Municipal Corporations Act, 1835," § 92—Tramway Bill opposed in Parliament—Terms suggested and accepted including an offer by Corporation to pay the expenses of the Bill—No available surplus in the Borough Fund during the current year—Held that the surplus accruing during the next year might be made available without an express Resolution. (37 J. P., 773.)

1850.   [1261]
Reg. v. *Norfolk Commissioners of Sewers.* Cost of opposing a Bill in Parliament likely to injure the property of a Board held payable out of the Board's funds. (15 Q. B., 549: 15 L. T., (o. s.), 391.)

1871.   [1262]
Reg. v. *Sheffield Corporation.* "Municipal Corporations Act, 1835," § 92—Expenses incurred in certain Legal and Parliamentary proceedings held not chargeable to the Borough Fund. (40 L. J., Q. B., 247 : L. R., 6 Q. B., 652 : [*Roberts* v. *Sheffield, &c.*] 24 L. T., 659.) [But see now 35 & 36 Vict., c. 91.]

1884.   [1263]
Reg. v. *Sibley.* Overseers of the Poor held justified in defraying out of the Poor Rate their "reasonable and moderate" expenses in resisting a Bill in Parliament in a case where it was intended to charge on the Poor Rate of their Parish the interest on the share capital of a proposed undertaking. (54 L. J., M. C., 23 : [*Reg.* v. *White*] L. R., 14 Q. B. D., 358 : 52 L. T., 116 : 47 J. P., 404 : 49 J. P., 291.)

1817.   [1264]
Vauxhall Bridge Co. v. *Spencer (Earl).* Securities given in consideration of withdrawing an opposition to a Bill in Parliament, are, on grounds of public policy, illegal. (2 Maddock, 356.)

59. PAVING EXPENSES.

1886.   [1265]
Acton L. B. v. *Lewsey.* "Public Health Act, 1875," § 150—On non-compliance by owner with notice to pave, &c., Board did the work, but in a cheaper manner—Held, nevertheless, that they could recover the apportioned expenses *pro ratâ.* (55 L. J., Q. B., 404 : L. R., 11 App. Cas., 93 : 54 L. T., 657 : 50 J. P., 708.)

1832.   [1266]
Allum v. *Dickinson.* "Metropolis Management Amendment Act, 1862," § 96—Paving Expenses held not a "Rate" but a Capital outlay, and therefore not recoverable by the Landlord from his Tenant in spite of covenants in Lease that Tenant was to pay all "Rates," &c. (52 L. J., Q. B., 190 : L. R., 9 Q. B. D., 632 : 47 L. T., 493 : 47 J. P., 102.)

1868.   [1267]
Angell v. *Paddington Vestry.* Paving new street—Church and land appurtenant not rateable. (Metropolis.) (37 L. J., M. C., 171 : L. R., 3 Q. B., 714 : 9 B. & S., 496 : 32 J. P., 742.)

1877.   [1268]
A.-G. v. *Wandsworth B. W.* Paving expenses paid by mistake 3 years previously out of a Rate, when they ought to have been charged to owners—Held that the Court could interfere and order the Board to levy on the owners, and recoup the current Rate with the proceeds. (46 L. J., Ch., 771 : L. R., 6 Ch. D., 539.)

1871.   [1269]
Bermondsey Vestry v. *Ramsay.* Local Act—An unsatisfied judgment against a former owner is no bar to an Action for Paving expenses against a tenant under a succeeding owner. (Metrop.) (40 L. J., C. P., 206 : L. R., 6 C. P., 247 : 24 L. T., 429.)

1876.   [1270]
Birkenhead Improvement Commissioners v. *Sansom.* Local Act—Making and sewering of street laid out and thrown open to the public 17 years previously but not formally dedicated as a highway—Held that the defendant, a frontager, was, nevertheless, liable. (34 L. T., 175 : 40 J. P., 406.)

1881.   [1271]
Birmingham Corporation v. *Baker.* "Public Health Act, 1875," § 257—The charge created by this Section is a charge not on the interest of any particular owner, but on the total ownership, *i.e.*, on the respective interest of every owner for the time being in proportion to the value of his interest—Therefore the charge affects the interest of mortgagee and takes priority over his mortgage. (L. R., 17 Ch. D., 782 : 46 J. P., 52.)

1886.   **[1272]**
Blackburn Corporation v. *Micklethwaite.* Local
Act—Mortgagee in possession held a "suc-
cessive owner." (54 L. T., 539: 50 J. P.,
550.)

1858.   **[1273]**
Blackburn, Mayor v. *Parkinson.* "Towns Improvement Clauses Act," §§ 149 and 210:
Local Act—Paving a Street—Recovery of
"damages"—Action not maintainable, but
proceedings to be before Justices. (28 L. J.,
M. C., 7: 1 E. & E., 71: 32 L. T., (o. s.), 91.)

1883.   **[1274]**
Bolton v. *Bolton Corporation.* "Public Health
Act, 1875," § 150—Evidence to prove dedication of highway. (At Q. Sess.) (47 J. P.,
505.)

1880.   **[1275]**
Boor v. *Hopkins.* "Public Health Act, 1875,"
§ 257—Charge on property—Date of commencement of charge—On death of father,
son became liable personally where no summary proceedings had been taken against
father. (58 L. J., Ch., 285: L. R., 40 Ch. D.,
572: 53 J. P., 467.)

1875.   **[1276]**
Bowles v. *St. Mary's, Islington.* Paving expenses
—Definition of " new street"—This is a ques-
tion of fact for the Sessions. (39 J. P., 757.)

1881.   **[1277]**
Caiger v. *St. Mary's Islington, Vestry.* "Metropolis Management Act, 1855," §§ 105, 250—
"Baptist Chapel" on leasehold land held a
"house," there being no dedication of it in
perpetuity as a place of Worship—Trustees
liable for Paving expenses. (50 L. J., M. C.,
59: 44 L. T., 605: 45 J. P., 570.) [See now
the " Private Street Works Act, 1892."]

1870.   **[1278]**
Chelsea Vestry v. *Evans.* Paving expenses—Held
that if the necessary formalities had been
complied with, the Magistrate could not
consider the expediency or excessive cost of
the work. (35 J. P., 23.)

1871.   **[1279]**
Cook v. *Ipswich L. B. H.* "Public Health Act,
1848," § 69 : " Local Government Act, 1858,"
§ 64 [="Public Health Act, 1875," §§ 150,
181]—Apportionment of Paving expenses—
If a Surveyor's apportionment is found to be
bad, he has a right to make another one—
Neither arbitrators nor Justices are entitled
to enquire whether an amount alleged to
have been expended has actually been so
expended—The remedy would be by a
memorial to Local Government Board. (40
L. J., M. C., 169: L. R., 6 Q. B., 45: 24
L. T., 579.)

1869.   **[1280]**
Dodd v. *St. Pancras Vestry.* Liability of Owner
—Back Alley held to be a New Street.
(Metropolis.) (34 J. P., 517.)

1876.   **[1281]**
Dryden v. *Putney Churchwardens.* An old public
highway gradually built upon and made into
a new street—Held that it was technically a
"new street" and that the paving expenses

must be charged at the outset on the Owners.
(Metropolis.) (L. R., 1 Ex. D., 223: 34
L. T., 69: 40 J. P., 263.)

1886.   **[1282]**
Eccles v. *Wirral R. S. A.* "Public Health Act,
1875," § 150—At proceedings for recovery of
paving expenses Justices must consider
whether street or no street: their functions
are not merely ministerial. (55 L. J., M. C.,
106: L. R., 17 Q. B. D., 107: 50 J. P., 596.)

1889.   **[1283]**
Evans v. *Newport S. A.* "Public Health Act,
1875," § 150—Ancient footpath or highway
altered, widened and added to and with new
houses abutting on it held to be a new street
and repairable by the frontagers—The last
clause of § 150 is conclusive. (59 L. J., M.
C., 8 L. R., 24 Q. B. D., 264: 61 L. T., 684:
54 J. P., 374.)

1891.   **[1284]**
Fenwick v. *Croydon R. S. A.* "Public Health
Act, 1875"—Urban powers conferred in
Rural District under § 276—A certain road
declared by Local Government Board to be a
"street" within § 150—This declaration
held not to be necessarily conclusive, but the
road held to be a "street" within § 4—
Portsmouth v. *Smith* and *Jowett* v. *Idle* followed ; *Reg.* v. *Burnup* doubted. (60 L. J.,
M. C., 161 : L. R., 2 Q. B., 216 : 65 L. T.,
645: 55 J. P., 470.)

1888.   **[1285]**
Field, In re. "Metropolis Amendment Act,
1862," § 77—Will—Question as to liability
for paving works completed after death of
tenant for life—Held that though Will silent
as to throwing burden on remaindermen, yet
as the Section gave Board right to recover
from Owner in possession when works were
completed, remaindermen must pay. (W. N.,
1888, p. 36: 84 *Law Times* Newspaper,
p. 297 : 32 *Law Journal,* 257.)

1881.   **[1286]**
Gould v. *Bacup L. B. H.* "Public Health Act,
1848," § 69 [="Public Health Act, 1875,"
§ 150]—Paving, &c., expenses—Notice by
Board that it intends to treat unpaid expenses as Private Improvement Expenses
binds the Board so that it cannot recover
afterwards by summary process. (50 L. J.,
M. C., 44: 44 L. T., 103: 45 J. P., 325.)

1883.   **[1287]**
Great Eastern Railway Co. v. *Hackney B. W.*
Railway Company which had built a bridge
across its line held liable to contribute to the
paving of the roadway, such roadway being
a "new street," and the Company owners of
land "abutting on such new street." (52 L.
J., M. C., 105 : L. R., 8 H. L., 687: 49 L. T.,
500.) [See now the "Private Street Works
Act, 1892."]

1877.   **[1288]**
Grece v. *Hunt.* "Local Government Act, 1858,"
§ 62 [="Public Health Act, 1875," § 257]
—Paving expenses—A notice of apportionment is not a "demand," and is essentially
different from a "demand"—The Section
contemplates that some document be served

which shall pointedly remind the person in default that such is the case, and time runs from the service of this Notice. (46 L. J., M. C., 202: L. R., 2 Q. B. D., 389: 36 L. T., 404: 41 J. P., 356.)

1888.   [1289]
Hackney B. W. v. Martin. A street once ordered to be paved—Expenses apportioned—Some irregularities—Held nevertheless that the Board had exhausted its powers and could not set up another apportionment. (52 J. P., 708.)

1881.   [1290]
Hall v. Bootle Corporation. Building Land—Intended road marked out—6 houses built abutting thereupon—Abandonment by landowner of her intentions, and rest of property, including site of proposed road, sublet for other purposes—Road occasionally used by the public for 15 years—Notice by Local Authority to landowner to sewer, pave, &c.—Notice ignored, whereupon Local Authority did the Work—Held that the mere setting out of an intended road is not such an irrevocable act as that the person who does it is to be deemed to have dedicated the road to the Public; and therefore Paving, &c., Expenses held not recoverable from Lessee. (44 L. T., 873: 29 W. R., 862.)

1875.   [1291]
Healey v. Batley Corporation. "Public Health Act, 1848," § 69—Piece of land alleged to be a street which the Corporation was entitled to have paved—Injunction granted against the Corporation doing any paving—Circumstances which amount to an interruption to prevent a right of way being acquired by user. (44 L. J., Ch., 912: L. R., 19 Eq., 375.)

1873.   [1292]
Hesketh v. Atherton L. B. "Public Health Act, 1848," § 69—Paving expenses—In a dispute as to an apportionment the question of liability remains open, even though notice has not been given within 3 months, but the apportionment is conclusive as to amount. (43 L. J., M. C., 37: L. R., 9 Q. B., 4: 29 L. T., 530: 38 J. P., 149.)

1872.   [1293]
Higgins v. Harding. Paving expenses—Strips of land abutting on a street and used only to facilitate the repair of Railway Arches, held chargeable. (Metropolis.) (42 L. J., M. C., 31: L. R., 8 Q. B., 7: 27 L. T., 483: 37 J. P., 677.)

1890.   [1294]
Hornsey L. B. v. Brewis. "Public Health Act, 1875," § 150—"Owner"—Building used as a Chapel but also for a School and Institute, and for Bazaars and Concerts held not exempt. (60 L. J., M. C., 48: [*Brewis v. H.*] 64 L. T., 288: 55 J. P., 389.)

1889.   [1295]
Hornsey L. B. v. Monarch Building Society. "Public Health Act, 1875," § 257—Paving Expenses apportioned 11 years after execution and proceedings taken to enforce same 13 years after date held barred. (59 L. J., Q. B., 105: L. R, 24 Q. B. D., 1: 61 L. T., 867: 54 J. P., 390.)

1859.   [1296]
Illingworth v. Montgomery. "Public Health Act, 1848," § 69—Street dedicated to the public—Long user—Owners held not liable for Paving expenses, for the facts showed a dedication to, and adoption by, the Public. (2 L. T., 726: 24 J. P., 101.)

1870.   [1297]
Jarrow L. B. v. Kennedy. A Local Board cannot recover apportioned Paving expenses unless it can prove the service of the preliminary notice required by the "Public Health Act." (L. R., 6 Q. B., 128: 19 W. R., 275.)

1888.   [1298]
Jowett v. Idle L. B. "Public Health Act, 1875"—Circumstances under which a private alley or court is to be deemed a "street" within § 150—And this is a question of Law, not of fact—The definition of "street" in § 4 must be read into § 150, according to the method of construction laid down in *Portsmouth v. Smith* —*Reg. v. Burnup* disapproved. (57 L. T., 928: W. N., 1888, p. 87: 36 W. R., 530.)

1887.   [1299]
Kershaw v. Sheffield Corporation. "Public Health Act, 1875," § 150—A Local Authority is not disentitled to recover apportioned expenses merely because it does the work more economically than was originally contemplated. (51 J. P., 276.)

1885.   [1300]
Lightbound v. Higher Bebington L. B. "Public Health Act, 1875," § 150—Land separated from street by wall which, with ground on which it stood, belonged to a different owner—Owner of first mentioned land held not liable for Paving expenses. (55 L. J., M. C., 94: L. R., 16 Q. B. D., 577: 50 J. P., 500.)

1878.   [1301]
Lister v. Hebden Bridge L. B. Order of Justices for the payment of apportioned Paving expenses quashed by the Quarter Sessions as void because it adjudged the defaulter to be imprisoned for 6 months with hard labour in event of insufficient distress—Whereupon new Information and new Order omitting the words "hard labour"—Held that the first Order having failed on a technical point, and being a nullity, the Justices might properly make a new Order, and that no Prohibition lay. (42 J. P., 119.)

1868.   [1302]
London & North Western Railway Co. v. St. Pancras Vestry. Local Act—Paving Expenses—Owners of a Railway in a cutting contiguous to a street held liable. (17 L. T., 654.) [See now the "Private Street Works Act, 1892."]

1879.   [1303]
London, Brighton & South Coast Railway Co. v. St. Giles, Camberwell, Vestry. "Metropolis Management Amendment Act, 1862," § 77—Land "abutting" on "new street"—Held under the circumstances that the Railway Company were not liable to contribute to the paving of the new public road by reason

G

of being owners of the slopes of the cutting.
(48 L. J., M. C., 184 : L. R., 4 Ex. D., 293 :
41 L. T., 162.) [Overruled by *Hackney B.W.
v. G. E. R.*]

1875.   **[1304]**
London School Board v. *St. Mary's, Islington,
Vestry.* Paving expenses—School-house not
fronting a street, but connected therewith by
a passage held chargeable according to its
assessment, and not according to the frontage
of the passage. (45 L. J., M. C., 1 : L. R., 1
Q. B. D., 65 : 33 L. T., 504 : 39 J. P., 741.)

1886.   **[1305]**
Manchester Corporation v. *Hampson.* "Public
Health Act, 1875," §§ 150, 257—Summons
for Paving expenses dismissed by Magistrate
—On second summons, held, that the matter
was not *res judicata* on the question of liability—Held also that the Local Authority
could make a second apportionment under
§ 150 and proceed under § 257 and make such
second apportionment a charge on the premises. (35 W. R., 334, 591.)

1868.   **[1306]**
Manchester, Mayor, v. *Chapman.* Local Act—
Owner of ground at the end of a street which
was a *cul-de-sac*, held liable for Paving expenses. (37 L. J., M. C., 173 : 18 L. T., 640 :
32 J. P., 582.)

1890.   **[1307]**
Middlesborough Corporation v. *Walton.* Highway
improved by construction of footpath—Held
that as to such footpath and the houses adjoining it the powers of the "Public Health
Act, 1875," § 150 might be put in force. (12
Municip. Corp. Assoc. Month. Circular, 361.)

1886.   **[1308]**
Midland Railway Co. v. *Watton.* "Public Health
Act, 1875," § 150—Private street with bars—
Evidence held sufficient to disprove "public
highway" repairable, &c. (55 L. J., M. C.,
99 : L. R., 17 Q. B. D., 30 : 54 L. T., 482 :
*50 J. P., 405.)

1883.   **[1309]**
Midland Railway Co. v. *Withington L. B.* Paving
expenses wrongly charged in respect of a
lane found afterwards to be a public highway
—Action to recover the money so paid by mistake—Action held not maintainable because
the limitations of time prescribed by "Public Health Act, 1875," § 264, had not been
observed. (52 L. J., Q. B., 689 : 49 L. T.,
489 : 47 J. P., 789.)

1876.   **[1310]**
Mile End Vestry v. *Whitechapel Union.* "New
Street"—A Decision to pave half a street in
width is valid, but the expenses must be
charged on premises on both sides. (Metrop.)
(46 L. J., M. C., 138 : L. R., 1 Q. B. D., 680 :
35 L. T., 354 : 41 J. P., 20.)

1854.   **[1311]**
Mills v. *Rydon.* Local Act making Churches,
&c., liable to Paving Rates—Newly-erected
District Church liable though the War-
dens had no funds. (23 L. J., Ex., 305 :

10 Ex., 67 : 2 C. L. R., 1015 : 23 L. T., (o. s.),
221.)

1888.   **[1312]**
Montagu v. *Goole L. B.* Lane 40 ft. wide with a
narrow public footway along it, the remainder
not being public—Held that when circumstances rendered it expedient for the lane to
be treated as a new street it could be so
treated—Order to pave, &c, held good. (52
J. P., 84.)

1882.   **[1313]**
Newington L. B. v. *Wright.* Paving expenses—
Capital outlay duly paid, but payment of
interest refused—Interest and Costs of the
Action ordered to be a "Charge" on the pre-
mises, under §§ 150 and 257 of the "Public
Health Act, 1875." (*Times*, Jan. 23, 1882.)

1882.   **[1314]**
Newport Urban A. v. *Graham.* "Public Health
Act, 1875," § 150—Back of premises held to
"abut" on a new street although inaccessible
from that street owing to a difference of
level of 5 ft. (L. R., 9 Q. B. D., 183 : 47 L. T.,
98 : 47 J. P., 133.)

1875.   **[1315]**
Nisbet v. *Greenwich B. W.* Paving Expenses—
An apportionment by a District Board is conclusive, and a Magistrate cannot review the
principle on which it is made. (Metrop.)
(44 L. J., M. C., 119 : L. R., 10 Q. B., 465 :
32 L. T., 762 : 39 J. P., 582.)

1880.   **[1316]**
Paddington v. *Bramwell.* House with back
garden bounded by dead wall—New street
made at back of house to which the garden
dead wall became an abutting wall—Held
that the garden so abutted on the new street
that the Owner became liable for share of the
Paving expenses of the new street. (44 J. P.,
815.)

1875.   **[1317]**
Plumstead B. W. v. *British Land Co.* Paving
expenses—Land set out for roads—Ownership of land at the intersection of streets
bounding properties. (44 L. J., Q. B., 38 :
32 L. T., 94 : 39 J. P., 376.)

1891.   **[1318]**
Plumstead B. W. v. *Ecclesiastical Commissioners.*
Land conveyed to Commissioners for site of
Church held to vest in Incumbent when
Church was consecrated, and this though
some portion was not consecrated and was
not used—Commissioners he'd not liable for
Paving expenses. (L. R., 2 Q. B., 361 : 64
L. T., 830 : 55 J. P., 791.)

1873.   **[1319]**
Plumstead B. W. v. *Ingoldby.* Paving expenses
—Apportionment—Expenses held chargeable
on the land and therefore recoverable against
present or future Owners, as the case may be.
(Metropolis.) (42 L. J., Ex., 50 and 136 :
L. R., 8 Ex, 174 : 29 L. T., 375 : 37 J. P.,
759 : [*Plumstead B. W.* v. *Planet Building
Society*] 27 L. T., 656.)

1874.   **[1320]**
Poplar B. W. v. *Love.* Paving expenses—Under
this head a Board may include such incidental

matters as the cost of serving notices and the cost of advertisements—"Owner." (Metropolis.) (29 L. T., 915: 38 J. P., 246.)

1871.   [1321]
Pound v. Plumstead B. W. An old narrow lane repairable as such by the public may under certain circumstances become a "New street," so that adjacent Owners may become liable for Paving expenses. (Metropolis.) (41 L. J., M. C., 51: L. R., 7 Q. B., 183: 25 L. T., 461: 36 J. P., 468.)

1889.   [1322]
Prescott v. Nicholson. Paving expenses made payable by instalments — Demand — When necessary — Time within which summary proceedings must be taken runs from the instalment falling due. (Metrop.) (60 L. T., 563: 53 J. P., 597.)

1882.   [1323]
Read v. Bullen. Building land—Covenant by vendor to form a road—Successful proceedings by Highway Authority against purchaser, in respect of further works—Vendor held not bound under his covenant to recoup purchaser the charges levied by the Highway Authority for further improvements to the road. (46 J. P., 259.)

1886.   [1324]
Reg. v. Burnup. "Public Health Act, 1875," § 150 —This Section applies only to streets which are in the popular sense of the word "streets": the word "street" does not here necessarily include every meaning given to it in § 4—In summary proceedings to recover expenses Justices may consider the attendant circumstances in deciding whether a given thoroughfare is a street.—(50 J. P., 598.) Doubted in *Fenwick v. Croydon* and *Jowett v. Idle.*

1889.   [1325]
Reg. v. Holt. Charges on land created under the "Public Health Act, 1875," § 257, do not require registration under the "Lands Registration and Charges Act, 1888." (59 L. J., Q. B., 113: 54 J. P., 120: [*Reg. v. Vice-Registrar*] L. R., 24 Q. B. D., 178: 62 L. T., 117.)

1881.   [1326]
Reg. v. Hutchins. "Public Health Act, 1875," § 150—Summons for apportioned expenses dismissed on the ground that the street was a highway repairable by the public—5 years after, an additional outlay, a second apportionment, and a second summons against the same party—Whereupon Justices made the Order to pay—Held that they were entitled to make the Order if they thought fit, for the first decision that the street was a highway involved a declaration which the former Justices had no juris lictiou to make ; and that therefore the matter was not *res judicata.* so that the legal character of the street might not again be considered. (50 L. J., M. C., 35: L. R., 6 Q. B. D., 300: 44 L. T., 364: 5 J. P., 504.)

1870.   [1327]
Reg. v. Livesey. "Public Health Act, 1848," § 69—Held that an owner on whom a Notice

to pave was served, and who had not given notice of objection, was estopped from showing that the Street was a highway repairable by the public. (22 L. T., 470: 34 J. P., 645.) [But see *Hesketh v. Atherton L. B.*, which is at variance with this case.]

1891.   [1328]
Reg. v. Marsham. "Metropolis Management Amendment Act, 1862," § 77—On a summons to enforce apportioned paving expenses the Magistrate is bound to hear evidence alleging that the sum claimed has not been actually and duly expended — Refusal to listen amounts to a declining of jurisdiction —*Mandamus* granted. (61 L. J., M. C., 520: L. R., 1 Q. B., 371: 65 L. T., 778: 56 J. P., 164.)

1863.   [1329]
Reg. v. Newport L. B. H. "Public Health Act, 1848," § 69—Railway alongside of Road—Expenses are to be apportioned according to frontage, even when there is no direct access from the road to the land charged. (32 L. J., M. C., 97: 3 B. & S., 341.)

1883.   [1330]
Reg. v. Sheffield, Recorder. "Public Health Act, 1875"—Bad notice to pave—Justices not on that account without jurisdiction to enforce paving expenses—Persons wrongly charged should have appealed (53 L. J., M. C., 1: 47 J. P., 504: [*Wake v. S.*] L. R. 12 Q. B. D., 142: 50 L. T., 76.)

1888.   [1331]
Richards v. Kessick. "Public Health Act, 1875," § 150—If a road repairable by the public is voluntarily widened by landowner he may be called upon under § 150 to pave, &c., the strip added by him to the old highway. (57 L. J., M. C., 48: W. N., 1888, p. 92: 59 L. T., 318: 52 J. P., 756.)

1873.   [1332]
Rolls v. St. Mary's, Newington, Vestry. Notice to pave private forecourts in front of houses voluntarily set back by Owner—Injunction granted on the ground that there had been no dedication of such forecourts to the public. (W. N., 1873, p. 168.)

1846.   [1333]
Salford, Mayor, v. Ackers. Local Act—Default in paving a street—Proof of Notice to pave held a condition precedent to an Action. (16 L. J., Ex., 6: 16 M. & W., 85.)

1892.   [1334]
Sandgate L. B. v. Keene. "Public Health Act, 1875," § 150—Any dispute arising out of a Surveyor's apportionment must be settled by arbitration—*West v. Downman* disapproved of in part. (L. R., 1 Q. B., 831: 66 L. T., 741: 56 J. P., 484.)

1881.   [1335]
Simcox v. Handsworth. "Public Health Act, 1875," § 257—Paving expenses—Information laid within the statutory 6 months, but summons not issued till 13 months afterwards—Held that the Information having been laid in time, payment of the expenses could be

G 2

enforced. (51 L. J., Q. B., 168 : L. R., 8 Q. B. D., 39 : 46 J. P., 260.)

1892.   [1336]
St. Giles, Camberwell, Vestry v. Crystal Palace Co. "Metropolis Management Act, 1855," § 105 : "Amendment Act, 1862," § 112—An old road held nevertheless to have become a "new street," and adjacent owners chargeable with Paving expenses. (L. R., 2 Q. B., 83 : 66 L. T., 840.)

1887.   [1337]
St. Giles, Camberwell, Vestry v. Greenwich B. W. Street in more than one District—Procedure —Paving Expenses to be recovered in such cases from Frontagers as if the whole street were in the District of the one Vestry which manages it. (Metrop.) (56 L. J., Q. B., 636 : L. R., 19 Q. B. D., 502.)

1887.   [1338]
St. Giles, Camberwell, Vestry v. Hunt. When a street has been paved once by owners, a Local Authority cannot put in force its powers a second time. (Metrop.) (56 L. J., M. C., 65 : 52 J. P., 132.)

1860.   [1339]
Stockport, Mayor, v. Cheetham. Local Acts— Action for Paving Expenses—Plea that the street was a common highway held, under the circumstances, bad, it being the evident intention that the Local Acts should apply to all highways. (1 L. T., 541 : 24 J. P., 196.)

1888.   [1340]
Stotesbury v. St. Giles's Vestry. "Metropolis Management Amendment Act, 1862," § 77 —Differential charges—As no principle of apportionment is prescribed the Vestry is not bound to follow any principle, and its apportionment cannot be questioned in the absence of caprice or mala fides. (57 L. J., M. C., 114 : W. N., 1888, p. 141 : 59 L. T., 473 ; 53 J. P., 5.)

1889.   [1341]
Strutt v. St. Mary Abbots, Kensington, Vestry. Houses abutting at their backs on a street but having no entrances into the street charged with one-sixth of the paving expenses—Such a method of apportionment held legal and not unreasonable. (Times, March 13, 1889.)

1882.   [1342]
Sunderland Corporation v. Alcock. "Public Health Act, 1875," § 257—Paving Expenses remain a charge on premises, and may be enforced against the owner for the time being, even though the premises have changed hands, and no summary proceedings were taken against the owner, who was such when the works were completed. (51 L. J., Ch., 546 : 46 L. T., 377.)

1853.   [1343]
Sunderland, Mayor v. Herring. "Public Health Act, 1848," §§ 68–9 ; 15 & 16 Vict. c. 42, § 13 —Paving expenses—Highway repairable by the public at large—Judgment for the plaintiff. (22 L. T., (o. s.), 98 : 17 J. P., 741.)

1880.   [1344]
Tottenham L. B. H. v. Rowell. (2). Rate for works

of sewering—Delay of several years in enforcing payment—Action to make the amount a charge on the property under the "Public Health Act, 1875"—Held that this power was independent of the summary remedy, and that the statutory limitation of 6 months for summary proceedings did not apply to this remedy, but that the Board could only enforce the charge in respect of unpaid instalments—Wilson v. Bolton distinguished. (50 L. J., Ch., 99 : L. R., 15 Ch. D., 378 : 43 L. T., 616.)

1879.   [1345]
Tunbridge Wells L. B. v. Akroyd. "Public Health Act, 1875," §§ 150, 257—Paving expenses apportioned, and defendant's share paid— Subsequently another Owner appealed against the apportionment with the result, inter alia, that the arbitrator found the defendant under-charged—On proceedings to compel the defendant to make a supplementary payment of the difference—Held that he was not bound to pay the extra amount, not having been a party to the later proceedings. (49 L. J, Ex., 403 : L. R., 5 Ex. D., 199 : 42 L. T., 640 : 44 J. P., 504.)

1876.   [1346]
Wakefield L. B. H. v. Lee. "Public Health Act, 1848," § 69—Premises separated from an unpaved street by a small stream but accessible from the street by a private bridge, held chargeable. (45 L. J., M. C., 54 : L. R., 1 Ex. D., 336 : 35 L. T., 481 : 41 J. P., 154.)

1880.   [1347]
Wakefield Urban Authority v. Mander. "Public Health Act, 1875," § 150—Foot pavement on one side of street made good in the terms of the Statute, and expenses apportioned only on owners on that side to the entire exemption of owners on the other side—Held that such restricted apportionment was good. (L. R., 5 C. P. D., 248 : 28 W. R., 922 : 44 J. P., 522.) [This case is to be distinguished from Mile End v. Whitechapel, and Whitchurch v. Fulham, the Statutes differing somewhat.]

1889.   [1348]
Wallsend L. B. v. Murphy. "Public Health Act, 1875," § 150—Notice to "owner or occupier" —Change of ownership before notice—Notice served on former owner—Held that the person on whom the notice was served (the former owner) was not liable for paving expenses, as not being the owner at the date of the notice. (61 L. T., 777.)

1891.   [1349]
Walthamstow L. B. v. Staines. "Public Health Act, 1875," §§ 150, 257, 268—Action against frontager and mortgagees to enforce a charge for paving expenses : items for legal expenses and collection included in charge—Held that the question whether such items were properly included was a matter which related not to the jurisdiction of the Local Board but to a defect in the exercise of its jurisdiction, and that therefore the appeal should have been to the Local Government Board under § 268, and not to the High Court—Bayley v.

Wilkinson, Cook v. *Ipswich, Reg.* v. *L. G. B.*, and *Wake* v. *Sheffield* approved—*Quære*, whether the items alluded to were properly included. (60 L. J., Ch., 738 : L. R., 2 Ch., 606 : 65 L. T., 430.) [At the first trial some remarks were made by the Judge at the time and expense wasted by the line of defence adopted. (*Times*, July 18, 1890.)]

1880.   [1350]
West v. *Downman.* "Public Health Acts "— Expenses of repairing roads—Death of owner —Demand on executors—Refusal by them to pay on ground that the roads were highways and the amount excessive—Arbitration—Refusal by executors to attend—Held that as the executors disputed their liability as well as the amount claimed, the Board's proper remedy was by Summons before Justices, who in such a case had jurisdiction as to the amount—Summary proceedings not having been resorted to within the time limited by "Jervis's Act " all remedy was gone. (L. R., 14 Ch. D., 111 : 42 L. T., 340.) [See No. 1334.]

1888.   [1351]
West Ham, Mayor v. *Grant.* Special Act, to be read with "Public Health Act, 1875 "— Held that only expenses actually incurred could be recovered; not the larger amount "estimated." (58 L. J., Ch., 121 : L. R., 40 Ch. D., 331 : 60 L. T., 17.)

1866.   [1352]
Whitchurch v. *Fulham B. W.* Paving Expenses —Street divided into sections—Apportionment of each section on the owners thereof —Apportionment held invalid : the street should have been dealt with as a whole. (Metropolis.) (35 L. J., M. C., 145 : L. R., 1 Q. B., 233 : 7 B. & S., 212 : 13 L. T., 631 : 30 J. P., 229.)

1884.   [1353]
Williams v. *Wandsworth B. W.* Owner of a strip of land 4 inches wide and 2·5 ft. long held a frontager, and as such, liable for paving expenses. (Metrop.) (53 L. J., M. C., 187 : L. R., 13 Q. B. D., 211 : 48 J. P., 439.)

1871.   [1354]
Wilson v. *Bolton, Mayor.* "Public Health Act, 1848," § 69—Paving Expenses — Where a Local Board apportions expenses and treats the amount as a debt, cannot turn round and proceed as for Private Improvement Expenses—Limitation of time. (41 L. J., M. C., 4 : 25 L. T., 597 : 36 J. P., 405.) [For the converse of this see *Gould* v. *Bacup.*]

1891.   [1355]
Wilson v. *St. Giles, Camberwell, Vestry.* "Metropolis Management Act, 1855," § 105 : "Amendment Act, 1862," § 112—Footway repairable as of old by Parish, but roadway undoubtedly a "new street"—Held that the two must be taken together, and that appellant, a frontager, was liable. (Metrop.) (61 L. J., M. C., 3 : L. R., [1892] 1 Q. B., 1 : 65 L. T., 790 : 56 J. P., 167.)

1886.   [1356]
Wortley v. *St. Mary, Islington, Vestry.* Proceedings for Paving Expenses begun in 1872

dropped—Fresh proceedings in 1885 against a succeeding owner—Expenses held recoverable, and Statute of Limitations not applicable. (51 J. P., 166.)

1885.   [1357]
Wright v. *Ingle.* A leasehold Dissenting Meeting-house held liable for Paving Expenses. (Metrop.) (55 L. J., M. C., 17 : L. R., 16 Q. B. D., 379 : 50 J. P., 436.)

60. PETROLEUM.

1871.   [1358]
Beck v. *Stringer.* "Petroleum Act, 1868 "— Method of testing—Method adopted h ld a compliance with the Act. (40 L. J., M. C., 174 : L. R., 6 Q. B., 497 : 25 L. T., 122.)

1873.   [1359]
Burslem L. B. v. *Shropshire Union Railway Co.* Storage of petroleum in illegal places and quantities. (37 J. P., 154.)

1879.   [1360]
Coleman v. *Goldsmith.* (43 J. P., 718.) [Effect of decision set aside by 44 & 45 Vict., c. 67.]

1871.   [1361]
Jones v. *Cook.* "Petroleum Act, 1868 "—Keeping without a license—Conviction affirmed—All Petroleum proper is within the Act. (40 L. J., M. C., 179 : L. R., 6 Q. B, 505 : 24 L. T., 806.)

61. POUND.

1860.   [1362]
Bignell v. *Clarke.* Distrainor bound to provide a proper pound. (5 H. & N., 485 : 2 L. T.,'189.)

1877.   [1363]
Dargan v. *Davies.* Cruelty to animals in a pound, arising from neglect to feed them— The distrainor and not the pound-keeper held liable. (46 L. J., M. C., 122 : L. R., 2 Q. B. D., 118 : 35 L. T., 810 : 41 J. P., 468.)

1883.   [1364]
Little Bowden H. B. v. *Wandly.* Action against Lord of Manor for appropriating materials belonging to a pound, held not to lie although Parish had occasionally repaired pound. (47 J. P., 772.)

62. POWERS OF LOCAL AUTHORITIES.

. See also "Parliamentary Expenses," (§ 58, *ante.*)

1883.   [1365]
A.-G. v. *Dartmouth.* Lands conveyed on Trust for "repair of a Church. . . . and the charitable. needful and necessary uses for the town " held not available for purposes of general utility. (48 L. T., 933.)

1880.   [1366]
A.-G. v. *Leeds Corporation.* Local Acts—Powers to exclude the public on a certain number of days from a public park held legally exercised. (*Times*, May 12, 1880.). [See now the "Public Health Acts Amendment Act, 1890," § 44.]

1881.   [1367]
A.-G. v. *Loughborough L. B.*   When a Recreation
Ground is acquired by a Local Board for
public purposes the Board has no power to
let it to private individuals for special
festivities to which the public will only have
access by payment—Injunction granted.
(*Times,* May 31, 1881.)

1884.   [1368]
A.-G. v. *Lyne.*   Harbour Commissioners had
expended or were about to expend sums in
providing portraits for two of themselves to
be hung up in Board Room; and in enter-
taining friends at an Inspection of the
Harbour with Wine, Cigars, &c.—Held that
such expenditure was improper, and ought
to be restrained. (*Times,* Feb. 15, 1884.)

1855.   [1369]
Dorling v. *Epsom L. B. H.* "Public Health Act,
1848," § 89 [="Public Health Act, 1875,"
§ 211 (4)]—The division of a District for
Rating purposes is a matter for the discretion
of the Board—All persons liable whether
their property receives benefit or not. (24
L. J., M. C., 152 : 5 E. & B., 471 : [*Reg.* v.
Dorling] 3 C. L. R., 945.)

1884.   [1370]
Gooding v. *Ealing L. B.*   A builder had signed a
notice which said "See Regulations over,"
and one was that deposited plans should
become the property of Board—Board held
therefore entitled to retain plans even though
they might be disapproved and not be carried
out. (1 Cab. & Ellis, 359 : *Times,* Nov. 14,
1884.)

1881.   [1371]
Haworth v. *Oswaldtwistle L. B.*   Money lent to
Board on security of Bonds forged by the
Clerk—About 200 Actions against Board
and about 150 Actions against individual
members for recovery of various sums amounting to about £40,000—All Actions except 8
"Test" Actions to be stayed pending reference of these to Arbitrator; he to decide all
questions of liability in these "Test" Actions,
costs in each case to abide the event and be
apportioned in his discretion. (*Times,* June
25, 1881.) [Compromise entered into ratified
by Special Act (45 & 46 Vict., c. cxvii.).]

1883.   [1372]
Hewitt's Estate, In re.   Gift to Corporation of
money, the interest to be applied in "acts of
hospitality or charity," held void for uncertainty. (53 L. J., Ch., 132 : [*Hewitt* v.
Hudspeth] 49 L. T., 587.)

1881.   [1373]
Holyhead L. B. v. *London & North-Western
Railway Co.*   Application by Board to Rail-
way Commissioners to order erection of a
foot-bridge, refused—The "Railway and
Canal Traffic Act, 1854," § 2, is not available
to support such an application. (4 Browne
& Mac., 37.)

1882.   [1374]
Hyde, Mayor v. *Bank of England.*   "Public
Health Act, 1875," § 310—Local Board

replaced by Municipal Corporation—Bank
Annuities held to pass to the new Authority.
(51 L. J., Ch., 747 : L. R , 21 Ch. D., 176 :
46 L. T , 910.)

1888.   [1375]
Kyle v. *Barber.* "Public Health Act, 1875,"
§ 259—A Local Board cannot delegate to
the Police its own powers to institute prosecutions, the Police not being officers of a
Local Board. (58 L. T., 229 : 52 J. P.,
725.)

1892.   [1376]
London C. C. v. *London School B.*   Building
erected under statutory powers which infringed the general Building Law of the
County Council—Held that the Special Act
must prevail over the General Act. (L. R.,
2 Q. B., 606.)

1878.   [1377]
Newington L. B. v. *North Eastern Railway Co.*
Application by a Local Board to the Railway
Commissioners for an Order to compel a
Railway Company to erect a station where
none existed—Judgment in part for the
Board, with half the costs. (*Times,* Nov. 27,
1878 : 23 *Solicitors' Journ.,* 301.)

1884.   [1378]
Ramsdale, Ex parte.   Local Board District about
to be merged in adjoining Municipal Borough
—Peremptory *Mandamus* to Board to make
a Rate before the extinction of the Board, to
repay a debt duly incurred. (*Times,* March
25, 1884.)

188–.   [1379]
Reg. v. *Bideford Corporation.*   Sums paid for
expense of yearly dinners to Juries of a
manor acquired by Corporation held illegal
payments. (*Municip. Corp. Assoc. Digest,*
col. 87.)

1883.   [1380]
St. Helen's Corporation v. *St. Helen's Colliery Co.*
"Public Health Act, 1875," § 227 : Local
Act—Special exemptions as to limit of
Borough Rate held not to apply so as to
restrict amount of Rates under the "Public
Health Act, 1875." (48 J. P., 39 : Affirmed
on Appeal, *Times,* June 28, 1884.)

1890.   [1381]
Winsford L. B. v. *Cheshire . Lines Committee.*
Proceedings by a Local Board to require a
Railway Company to resume working passenger traffic over a disused line—Held that
the Railway and Canal Commissioners had
jurisdiction. (59 L. J., Q. B , 372 : L. R.,
24 Q. B. D., 456 : 62 L. T., 268.)

63. PROVISIONAL ORDER.

1887.   [1382]
Burr v. *Wimbledon L. B.*   An Action brought to
enforce an obligation arising under a Provisional Order is not governed by the ordinary Rules applicable to Actions for specific
performance, and can be maintained without
joining the Trustee under the liquidation of
a tenant for life, if land taken compulsorily.
(56 L. T., 329 : 35 W. R., 404.)

1856. [1383]

Clayton v. *Fenwick.* "Public Health Act, 1848" —Provisional Order—Local Act—Powers of Local Boards as to Turnpike Gates. (25 L. J., Q. B., 226: 6 E. & B., 114: 27 L. T., (o s.), 119.)

1851. [1384]

Elmer v. *Norwich L. B. H.* "Public Health Act, 1848": Local Acts—Several parishes united to form a Local Government District —Effect of Provisional Order—Repair of Streets—District Rates. (23 L. J., Q. B., 203: 3 E. & B., 517: 2 C. L. R., 886.)

1865. [1385]

Freiren v. *Hastings L. B.* "Public Health Act, 1848," § 73: "Local Government Act, 1858," § 75 [= "Public Health Act, 1875," §§ 154, 176]—A Provisional Order has no validity till confirmed by Parliament, and cannot be removed by *Certiorari* with a view to its being quashed. (34 L. J., Q. B., 159: [*Reg.* v. *H.*] 6 B. & S., 401: 12 L. T., 346: 29 J. P., 711.)

1867. [1386]

Freiren v. *Hastings L. B. H.* Extent of the authority conferred by a Provisional Order for the acquisition of land. (16 L. T., 553.)

1875. [1387]

Morley, In re. "Tramways Act, 1870"—The Costs of Solicitors employed in obtaining a Provisional Order are to be on the Chancery, not the Parliamentary, Scale. (L. R., 20 Eq., 17: 32 L. T., 524.)

1868. [1388]

North Eastern Railway Co. v. *Tynemouth, Mayor.* A Provisional Order applying the "Public Health Act, 1848," but excepting so much of § 88 [repealed, and not *as a whole* re-enacted in the "Public Health Act, 1875," § 211] as provided that Railways, &c., should only be assessed at one-fourth, &c., held void. (37 L. J., M. C., 183: L. R., 3 Q. B., 723: 9 B. & S., 616: 32 J. P., 822.)

64. SALARY, &c.

1852. [1389]

Addison v. *Preston, Mayor.* A Salary chargeable on the Borough Fund cannot be recovered by Action of Debt, but possibly a *Mandamus* might lie to make a Rate for the purpose. (21 L. J., C. P., 146: 12 C. B., 108: 19 L. T., (o. s.), 184.)

1851. [1390]

Bagg v. *Pearse.* Commissioners under a Local Act—Appointment of Officer not a contract —Salary to be paid out of Rates—Refusal to pay Salary—Remedy not by *Indebitatus* Action, but by *Mandamus*, or Action on the case. (20 L. J., C. P., 99: 10 C. B., 534: 16 L. T., (o. s.), 462.)

1862. [1391]

Bush v. *Beavan.* Salary of Clerk in arrear—A claim for a *Mandamus* under the "Common Law Procedure Act, 1854," § 68, is not sustainable if any other equally effectual remedy is available. (32 L. J., Ex., 54: 1 H. & C., 500: 7 L. T., 106.)

1863. [1392]

Bush v. *Martin.* Salary of a Clerk in arrear—A report by a Committee is not such an acknowledgment as would take a case out of the Statute of Limitations. (33 L. J., Ex., 17: 2 H. & C., 311: 8 L. T, 509.)

1868. [1393]

Hall v. *Taylor.* Local Act—Action by an attorney against Commissioners for his salary as Clerk to be paid out of the Rates held maintainable. (27 L. J., Q. B., 311: E. B. & E., 107: 31 L. T., (o. s), 151: 23 J. P., 20.)

1863. [1394]

Mellish, Ex parte. Local Act—A gratuity paid out of the Rates to a Vestry Clerk held illegal. (8 L. T., 47.) [*Sed aliter as regards* Poor Law Officers if the sanction of the Local Government Board be had. (C. O., 1847, Art. 172.)]

1859. [1395]

Reg. v. *Gloucester, Mayor.* "Public Health Act, 1848"—*Certiorari*—Gratuity to Surveyor for special services auxiliary to, but beyond the scope of his prescribed duties as Surveyor held legal. (33 L. T., (o. s.), 145: 23 J. P., 709.)

1838. [1396]

Reg. v. *Norwich, Mayor.* (1). "Municipal Corporations Act, 1835," § 66—Office not legally held for life, but usually so held and accepted on that understanding—Compensation for loss of office held payable accordingly on a higher scale. (8 A. & E., 633.)

1871. [1397]

Reg. v. *Poor Law Board.* Dissolution of Union —Loss of office of Clerk of Guardians— Profits made by an officer in performing extra duties authorised by his employers held properly taken into account as enhancing the value of his office. (41 L. J., M. C., 16: L. R., 6 Q. B., 785.)

1878. [1398]

Slattery v. *Bean.* "Metropolis Management Act, 1855"—Action by a member of a Board of Works against the Board's Surveyor for accepting from the Board fees for special services over and above his salary—Held that no Action lay, the fees not being received from private parties. (Metropolis.) (*Times*, April 11, 1878.)

65. SCAVENGING.

1884. [1399]

Andrews v. *West Ham L. B.* Injunction granted to restrain a nuisance caused by the deposit of dust and refuse by Board and its contractor. (*Times*, July 12, 1884.)

1879. [1400]

Collins v. *Paddington Vestry.* "Metropolis Management Act, 1855," § 125—Contract with Local Authority that plaintiff should remove "Dust" and "Refuse"—Miscellaneous metal and other articles of value abstracted from the dust-carts by the dustmen, and retained by them for their own profit—Held that such articles were not *ejusdem generis* with "dust," &c., which the contractor was entitled to have, or for the detention of which he was entitled to compensation. (48 L. J., Q. B., 345 : 40 L. T., 843 : 43 J. P., 367 : See also 49 L. J., Q. B., 612 : L. R., 5 Q. B. D., 368 : 42 L. T , 573.)

1883. [1401]
Corrie v. *Reddin.* Action by Freeholder for damage done to his estate by a Leaseholder excavating soil and filling up the holes with scavenger's refuse—Damages awarded, £2000; and Injunction to remove the refuse and restore good soil. (*Times*, June 26, 1883.)

1892. [1402]
Ellis v. *Strand B. W.* "Metropolis Management Act, 1855," § 125—Neglect of Board duly to empty dust-bin—Held that no Action lay against the Board because it had exercised the alternative conferred by Statute of entering into a contract for the removal of dust, and that the Action should have been brought against Contractor. (67 L. T., 307.) [See now "Public Health (London) Act, 1891," § 30.]

1837. [1403]
Filby v. *Combe.* Scavenging—Refuse—A Scavenger cannot claim dust, ashes, &c., which the owner does not desire to get rid of. (Metropolis) (2 M. & W., 677 : 1 Jur., 721.)

1877. [1404]
Gay v. *Cadby.* Ashes from engine at a Piano Factory held to be trade refuse notwithstanding that they were simply coal ashes unmixed with any foreign material. (46 L. J.. M. C., 260 : L. R., 2 C. P. D., 391 : 36 L. T.. 410 : 41 J. P., 503.)

1880. [1405]
General Ice Well Co. v. *Clerkenwell Vestry and Stubbs.* Premises used by defendants for storage of Dust, Refuse, and Manure—Injunction to restrain such user refused, it being shown that every possible precaution had been taken to avoid a nuisance, and it not being shown that any nuisance did exist —Plaintiffs left to their remedy by Action. (*Times*, Oct. 7, 1880.)

1883. [1406]
Goodacre v. *Watson.* Injunction granted at suit of neighbours to restrain land from being used for deposit of house refuse, and before being built upon—*Per* Fry, *J.*:—"It was nothing short of horrible to think that persons should seek to place foul vegetable and animal matter as foundations for buildings, and then come into Court to defend such conduct." (*Times*, Feb. 23, 1883.)

1876. [1407]
Holborn Guardians v. *St. Leonard's, Shoreditch, Vestry.* Workhouse rated by Statute at a specially low figure—Held that this did not disentitle the Guardians to have their dust removed just as an ordinary householder. (46 L. J., Q. B., 36 : L. R., 2 Q. B. D., 145 : 35 L. T., 400 : 40 J. P., 740.)

1848. [1408]
Law v. *Dodd.* Ashes from a brass-founder's furnace are not claimable by a Scavenger. (Metropolis.) (17 L. J., M. C., 65 : 1 Ex, 815 : 10 L. T., (o. s), 286, 809.)

1892. [1409]
London & Provincial Laundry Co. v. *Willesden L. B.* "Public Health Act, 1875," §§ 4, 42 —Clinkers produced from boilers at a Steam Laundry held not "house refuse," although a dwelling-house for the manager formed part of the premises—The definition of "house" in § 4 is not to be read into § 42. (L. R., 2 Q. B., 271 : 56 J. P., 696.)

1879. [1410]
London General Omnibus Co. v. *Mead.* Action against a scavenger for storing and sifting dust and refuse so as to be a nuisance— Proceedings before Jessel, M.R., abandoned on defendant undertaking not to carry on his business so as to be a nuisance, and agreeing to pay costs. (*Times*, Dec. 10, 1879.)

1857. [1411]
Lyndon v. *Standbridge.* "Towns Improvement Clauses Act, 1847," § 87—Commissioners held not bound to remove ashes and rubbish produced at a manufactory. (26 L. J., Ex., 386 : 2 H. & N., 45 : 29 L. T., (o. s.), 111.)

1869. [1412]
Margate Pier Co. v. *Margate L. B. H.* "Nuisances Removal Act, 1855," § 12 [= "Public Health Act, 1875," § 95]—Nuisance—Seaweed— Held that the Company was an "occupier" and bound to remove drifted seaweed. (20 L. T., 564 : 33 J. P., 437.)

1884. [1413]
Metropolitan B. W. v. *Eaton.* "Metropolis Management Act, 1855," § 205—Scavenger who had swept mud into sewer held duly convicted of an offence against the Act. (50 L. T., 634 : 48 J. P., 611.)

1890. [1414]
Reg. v. *Bridge.* "Metropolis Management Act, 1855," § 129—A Magistrate held that ashes and clinkers from a furnace which provided an hotel with electric light were not trade refuse, and he refused to state a case on the ground that the matter was one of fact and not of law—Held that he was bound to state a case. (59 L. J., M. C., 49 : L. R., 24 Q. B. D., 609 : 62 L. T., 297 : 54 J. P., 629)

1890. [1415]
St. Martin's Vestry v. *Gordon.* "Metropolis Management Act, 1855," § 128—Clinkers from the Boilers of an Hotel held not to be trade Refuse—*Gay* v. *Cadby* considered. (60 L. J., M. C., 37 : L. R., [1891] 1 Q. B., 61 : 64 L. T., 243 : 55 J. P., 437.)

1858. [1416]
Sinnot v. *Whitechapel B. W.* Scavenging contract—Transfer of powers of Commissioners —Action properly brought against the substituted Authority. (Metropolis.) (27 L. J., C. P., 177 : 3 C. B., (N. S.), 674 : 31 L. T., (o. s.), 84.)

1879. [1417]
Williamson v. *St. Mary's, Islington, Vestry.* Contract to remove house-refuse at stated intervals—One condition, a fine for every instance of default, the Vestry being sole judges—Such fines to be deducted from contract money—Held that on the evidence the Vestry was entitled to enforce the penalties for breach of contract. (*Times,* June 19, 1879.)

66. SEAL.

*** See also "Accountant" (§ 1, *ante*); "Appointment of Officers" (§ 5, *ante*); and "Contract" (§ 22, *ante*).

1882. [1418]
A.-G. v. *Gaskill.* "Public Health Act, 1875"—An agreement between a Board and a person that a pending Action should be settled by his undertaking not to do a certain thing, and to pay the Costs of the Action, is not a contract under § 173 requiring to be sealed under § 174, and therefore may be enforced though unsealed. (52 L. J., Ch. 163: L. R., 22 Ch. D., 537: on a point of Practice, 51 L. J., Ch., 870.)

1867. [1419]
Barnsley L. B. v. *Sedgwick.* Appointment of committees by a Local Board—Neither the recommendations of a Committee, if acted upon by the Board, nor the Acts of the Board generally, need to be sealed and signed by five Members. (36 L. J., M. C., 65 : L. R., 2 Q. B., 183: 8 B. & S., 202: 15 L. T., 569 : 31 J. P., 165.) [As regards the signatures this question could not now arise since the passing of the "Public Health Act, 1875," § 7.]

1884. [1420]
Bournemouth Commissioners v. *Watts.* — Non-compliance with notice to pave—Thereupon Board employed contractor to do the work, but had no contract with him under seal—They paid him, and on suing the frontager he set up as defence that the paving contract was void—Held no defence for him. (54 L. J., Q. B., 93 : L. R., 14 Q. B. D., 87 : 51 L. T., 823 : 49 J. P., 102.)

1888. [1421]
Dartford Union v. *Trickett.* Contract intended to be under seal verbally altered by one party the other party assenting : held enforceable when duly sealed. (59 L. T., 754 ; 53 J. P., 277.)

1858, 1861. [1422]
Freud v. *Dennet.* "Public Health Act, 1848," § 85 [= "Public Health Act, 1875," §§ 173-4]—A contract by a Local Board is void if not under seal—All contracts under a Statute must be made in the mode prescribed by the Statute—Powers to be strictly construed. (27 L. J., C. P., 314 : 5 C. B., (N. s), 576: In Equity, 5 L. T., 73.)

1830. [1423]
Ludlow, Mayor v. *Charlton.* A contract by a Municipal Corporation to pay money out of the Corporate Funds for Improvements must

be under seal. (6 M. & W., 815 : 9 C. &. P., 242 : 10 L. J., Ex., 75.)

1887. [1424]
Merchants of the Staple of England v. *Bank of England.* Negligence as to custody of Corporate Seal—Pecuniary loss by unauthorised use—Stock wrongfully sold and transferred—Held that the Plaintiffs were entitled to maintain the Action to compel the Bank to replace the Stock. (57 L. J., Q. B., 418 : L. R., 21 Q. B. D., 160 : 52 J. P., 580.)

1882. [1425]
Reg. v. *Norwich, Mayor.* (2). "Municipal Corporations Acts": "Public Health Act, 1875," § 174—Street paved, several tradesmen supplying materials—No contracts under seal—Separate amounts under 50l. with one exception—The work being useful and the prices reasonable, the Court held that there would be no misapplication of the Borough Fund. (46 J. P., 308 : W. N., 1882, p. 74 : 30 W. R., 752.)

1870. [1426]
Smith v. *Hirst.* "Public Health Act, 1848," § 149—The seal of a Local Board is only needed to acts which sanction the acts of others—Appointments of officers need not be under seal. (23 L. T., 665 : 35 J. P., 247)

188-. [1427]
Stevens v. *Hounslow Burial B.* "Burial Act, 1852," § 31—Contract for repairs under seal—During progress of works several additional minor repairs became evidently necessary, and were done under the direction of the Board's Surveyor—Held that such further repairs ought also to have been done under a sealed contract, and not having been so done could not be recovered. (61 L. T., 839 : 54 J. P., 309.)

1864. [1428]
Sutton v. *Spectacle-Makers Co.* A retainer of an Attorney by a Corporation to conduct an opposition to a Bill in Parliament must be under the common seal. (10 L. T., 411 : 12 W. R., 742.)

1888. [1429]
Tunbridge Wells Commissioners v. *Southborough L. B.* Agreement between 2 Boards for transfer of land to be formed into a highway—Petition under seal to Local Government Board for requisite powers, but no agreement under seal between the Boards—Held that therefore the contract could not be enforced ; and that even if it had been in due form as regards seal the whole proposed bargain was *ultra vires.* (60 L. T., 172.)

1885. [1430]
Wandsworth B. W. v. *Heaver.* Negotiations by letter for the sale of land—The negotiations not having been brought to a head by an agreement under seal, Held that plaintiffs could not enforce the alleged contract. (*Times,* Dec. 1, 1885.)

1875. [1431]
Wells v. *Kingston-upon-Hull, Mayor.* Circumstances under which a contract with a Cor-

poration need not be under seal set out with some fulness. (44 L. J., C. P., 257: L. R., 10 C. P., 402 : 32 L. T., 615.)

1882. [1432]
Young v. *Leamington Corporation*. Contract under seal to construct Waterworks—On default of contractor new contract not under seal with Plaintiffs to finish the job—Job finished to the satisfaction of defendant's Engineer and various sums paid—Contracts made by a Town Surveyor within the scope of his authority are not binding on his employers unless under seal in accordance with the "Public Health Act, 1875," § 174, and therefore the unpaid balance claimed for extras, &c., held not recoverable. (L. R., 8 App. Cas., 517 : 49 L. T., 1 : 47 J. P., 660.)

67. SEA-SHORE.

1880. [1433]
A.-G. v. *Tomline*. Injunction granted to restrain removal of shingle on sea-shore, so as to endanger land—An obligation lies on every subject to do nothing to destroy the natural banks of a river or of the sea—Redress may in such cases be obtained by an adjacent owner prejudiced. (49 L. J., Ch., 377 : L. R., 14 Ch. D., 58 : 42 L. T., 880 : 44 J. P., 617.)

1866. [1434]
Bridgewater Trustees v. *Bootle-cum-Linacre Surveyors of Highways*. Assessment of Docks—In the absence of evidence it is not to be presumed that land between the high and low water mark of a tidal river belongs to the adjoining parish. (36 L. J., Q. B., 41 : L. R., 2 Q. B., 4 : 15 L. T., 351.) [But the Act 31 & 32 Vict., c. 122, § 27, passed since this case was decided, provides that the soil as far as low water mark inclusive, shall be deemed to belong to the adjacent parish.]

1860. [1435]
Embleton v. *Brown*. The sea-shore between high and low water mark is within the jurisdiction of Justices of the adjoining County. (30 L. J., M. C., 1 : 3 E. & E., 234.)

1886. [1436]
Fobbing Commissioners of Sewers v. *Reg.* 3 & 4 Will. IV., c. 22, §§ 13, 46 : "Land Drainage Act, 1861," § 33—Duties of Owners of Lands fronting a Sea Wall to keep same in repair against ordinary Storms and against extraordinary Storms. (56 L. J., M. C., 1 : L. R., 11 App. Cas., 449 : [*F.* v. *Abbott*] 55 L. T., 493 : 51 J. P., 227.)

1880. [1437]
Laird v. *Briggs*. Action to restrain removal of sand, shingle, and chalk from a Foreshore, and the use of the same as a Bathing-machine station—Practice—Statute of Limitations—A Tenant of a Reversioner suing within 3 years of death of Reversioner, held nevertheless not entitled to Judgment, being merely the owner of an easement. (45 L. T., 238 : L. R., 8 Q. B. D., 22.)

1880. [1438]
London & North Western Railway Co. v. *Fleet-*

wood L. B. Application for Injunction to restrain defendants from removing stones and shingle from a harbour shore—Dispute as to jurisdiction over the *locus in quo*—Order by consent; plaintiffs to supply defendants on demand annually with a prescribed maximum quantity of stones from other sources; defendants not to interfere with the *locus in quo*. (*Times*, Dec. 8, 1880.)

1884. [1439]
Plimmer v. *Wellington, Mayor*. License from Crown to erect jetty on foreshore in tidal water—Jetty afterwards extended at the request and for the use of the Government—Held that the license had, after 30 years, become irrevocable, constituting for the plaintiff an estate in the land and a proper subject of compensation under Local Acts. (53 L. J., P. C., 105 : L. R., 9 App. Cas., 699 : 51 L. T., 475.)

1878. [1440]
Reg. v. *Commissioners of Sewers for Sussex.* 3 & 4 Vict., c. 22—Sea-bank partly washed away —Default of Commissioners to repair, on the ground that the cost would be out of all proportion to the public benefit—*Mandamus* granted for the Commissioners to repair, the merits of the case to be argued on the return of the writ. (*Times*, June 25, 1878.)

68. SEWER.

1884. [1441]
Acton L. B. v. *Batten.* "Public Health Act, 1875," §§ 4, 13—A drain in new street laid by owner of houses to drain these houses and other houses is not a "sewer made for profit"—"Sewer" in said Act should receive largest possible interpretation—A drain is a "sewer" when more than one house has been connected with it. (54 L. J., Ch. D., 251 : L. R., 28 Ch. D., 283 : 52 L. T., 17 : 49 J. P., 357.)

1882. [1442]
A.-G. v. *Acton L. B.* "Public Health Act, 1875," §§ 15 and 23—An existing right to send the sewage of one district into the sewers of another is subject to limitations; the quantity cannot be increased except by consent. (52 L. J., Ch., 108 : L. R., 22 Ch. D., 221 : 47 L. T., 510.)

1876. [1443]
A.-G. v. *General Sewage Co.* Sewage works leased from a Local Board by a Company—Default in performance of covenants to remove sewage. (*Times*, July 28, 1876.)

1891. [1444]
A.-G. v. *St. James and St. John, Clerkenwell, Vestry.* A claim for Injunction by the B. Local Authority for nuisance arising within the district of the C. Local Authority by reason of sewage overflowing from the latter into the former, through communications sanctioned in time past by the C. Authority—Held that C. could not stop up communications which it had sanctioned; that it could not proceed against owners within the C. limits; that it could not proceed against

by Injunction (*A.-G.* v. *Dorking*); and that (*Glossop* v. *Heston*) no Injunction could be granted against the C. Board on any other grounds—On C. undertaking not to sanction any new communications, Injunction refused. (60 L. J., Ch., 788 : L. R., 3 Ch., 527 : 65 L. T., 312.)

1882.   [1445]
Baker v. *St. Pancras Vestry.* Injunction to restrain erection of urinal, refused—*Per* Jessel, M.R. :—"A wide street is a much more suitable place for a urinal than a narrow quiet street." (*Times*, July 29, 1882.)

1877.   [1446]
Barrow v. *Yorkshire, W. R., JJ.* "Public Health Act, 1875," §§ 94-6 and 255—Dispute between an owner and a tenant as to the right to use a private sewer—An existing connection cut by former—Stoppage of the sewage, and a nuisance the result—Order for abatement of the nuisance by renewing the connection held good. (41 J. P., 716.)

1886.   [1447]
Bateman v. *Poplar B. W.* (1). "Metropolis Management Act, 1855," § 250 — Action against Board for nuisance arising from smells—" Drain " or " sewer "—Ownership. (56 L. J., Ch., 149 : L. R., 33 Ch. D., 360 : 55 L. T., 374.)

1887.   [1448]
Bateman v. *Poplar B. W.* (2). "Metropolis Management Act, 1855," § 72—Circumstances under which the duty of keeping sewers vested in a Board free of nuisance is not an absolute duty, but only a duty to use all reasonable care and diligence—*Hammond* v. *St. Pancras* followed. (57 L. J., Ch., 579 : L. R., 37 Ch. D , 272 : 58 L. T., 720.)

1889.   [1449]
Bathard v. *City Commissioners of Sewers.* Local Act—Such an expression as " nearest common sewer " means not necessarily the sewer which is actually the nearest, but the nearest sewer which a house-owner exercising his ordinary proprietary rights can get access to. (54 J. P., 135.)

1863.   [1450]
Biddulph v. *St. George's, Hanover Square, Vestry.* Erection of a urinal—Injunction refused, the evidence not showing a probable nuisance, or any excess of powers, or improper motive. (33 L. J., Ch., 411 : 8 L. T., 558 : 2 N. R., 212.)

1883.   [1451]
Bird v. *Brentford Union.* Application for Injunction to restrain entry on land to lay a sewer under the " Public Health Act, 1875," § 16, no proper statutory notice having been previously given—On it being shown that a notice had been given 5 days after the entry, and that no real inconvenience had been caused, Injunction refused. (*Times*, July 2, 1883.)

1885.   [1452]
Birkenhead, Mayor v. *London & North Western Railway Co.* Embankment formed over sewer rendering access to sewer for repairs

very difficult—Held that Corporation could not claim compensation from Railway. (55 L. J., Q. B., 48 : L. R., 15 Q. B. D., 572 : 50 J. P., 84.)

1887.   [1453]
Bonella v. *Twickenham L. B.* "Public Health Act, 1875," § 150—The powers of § 150 must be exercised within a reasonable time—If a sewer large enough for its work when constructed becomes inadequate, and a larger one is needed, the Local Authority must pay for it. 57 L. J., M. C., 1 : L. R., 20 Q. B. D., 63 : 58 L. T., 299 : 52 J. P., 356.)

1887.   [1454]
Burton v. *Acton.* "Local Government Act, 1858," § 34—Tub closets are " privies " within the " Public Health Act, 1875 "—By-Laws requiring deposit of plans, and rendering it an offence to deviate from them, held good. (51 J. P., 566.)

1866.   [1455]
Chambers v. *Reid.* "Metropolis Management Act, 1855," §§ 88 and 106—Erection of a urinal at joint cost of Defendant and a Local Authority against plaintiff's wall—Action for trespass—Defendant held entitled to Notice of Action as a person acting under the direction of the Local Authority. (Metropolis.) (13 L. T., 703 : 14 W. R., 370.)

1859.   [1456]
Clarke v. *Paddington Vestry.* Construction of a Sewer along a New Street by a landowner under a misapprehension of his liability—No obligation on him to extend the length of such Sewer when he extends the length of the Street. (Metropolis.) (32 L. T., (o. s.), 238 : 5 Jur. (N. s.), 138.)

1866.   [1457]
Cleckheaton Industrial S. H. Society v. *Jackson.* "Public Health Act, 1848," § 45 [= " Public Health Act, 1875," § 16]—Construction of Sewer—Notice as to an intended sewer is " reasonable " when it specifies the object and describes the direction to be taken—Map not necessary. (14 W. R., 950.)

1874.   [1458]
Clegg v. *Castleford L. B. H.* Bricking up of a Sewer to stop passage of refuse from Malt Kilns — Injunction to remove obstruction granted—"it was a wanton and outrageous act." (W. N., 1874, p. 229.)

1887.   [1459]
Darenth Sewage B. v. *Dartford Union.* "Public Health Act, 1875," §§ 229-30, 283-4—A Joint Board must apportion contributions according to the rateable value of the properties in the component districts according to the Valuation Lists ; and lands, &c., are to be taken at the full value so appearing and not at the one-fourth value. (56 L. J., Q. B., 615 : L. R., 19 Q. B. D., 270 : 57 L. T., 233.)

1869.   [1460]
Derby (Earl of) v. *Bury Improvement Commissioners.* "Nuisances Removal Act, 1855," § 22 [= " Public Health Act, 1875," § 16]—A Local Authority in laying down a new

Sewer is not bound to follow the line of an old water-course. (38 L. J., Ex., 100 : L. R., 4 Ex., 222 : 20 L. T., 927.)

1881.   [1461]
Dudley Corporation, In re. "Public Health Act, 1875," §§ 15, 16, 175, 308—A Local Authority taking a sewer through private lands is entitled to subjacent support for such sewer, but must compensate the landowner for the consequent interference with his freedom to work minerals lying underneath—But compensation not payable for prospective injury by percolation. (51 L. J., Q. B., 86 : L. R., 8 Q. B. D., 86: [*Dudley, Mayor* v. *Dudley Trustees*] 45 L. T., 733 : 46 J. P., 340.)

1878.   [1462]
Ellissen v. *Lawrie.* Action against an architect for neglect properly to superintend, in accordance with an agreement, the erection of sewer pipes, &c.—Pipes improperly laid by builder—Escape of foul gas—Illness of family—Expenses incurred by owner in further repairs and for medical attendance—Verdict for the plaintiff. (*Times*, Feb. 19, 1878.)

1889.   [1463]
Fairbrother v. *Bury R. S. A.* Injury to house caused by excavations in making a sewer—Held that though more than 6 years had elapsed yet as negligence was proved and the damage was both gradual and continuing the plaintiff was not deprived of his remedy. (*Times*, April 3, 1889.)

1881.   [1464]
Fleming v. *Manchester, Mayor.* Bursting during a storm of an old sewer, out of repair, whereby cellars under a house were flooded, foundations were undermined, and house fell down—Verdict for plaintiff held good, the evidence showing that the Local Authority had entirely neglected to inspect the sewer and that due inspection would have disclosed before the accident the imminency of the danger—Remarks by the Court on the duty of inspecting sewers from time to time. (44 L. T., 517 : 45 J. P., 423.)

1876.   [1465]
Fulham B. W. v. *Goodwin.* Public Sewer constructed at the cost of owners, taken up after the lapse of years and reconstructed—Held that the subsequent outlay could not be apportioned on the adjacent owners, but must be charged to the Rates. (L. R., 1 Ex. D., 400: 35 L. T., 907: 41 J. P., 131.)

1879.   [1466]
Glossop v. *Heston and Isleworth L. B.* Stream polluted by sewage, which it was alleged that the Local Authority ought to have excluded from the stream by sewers constructed for the purpose—Injunction to restrain the continuance of the user of the stream as a sewage outfall refused, the Board itself being done nothing to create or increase the nuisance—The plaintiff might have proceeded by way of application for a Prorogative *Mandamus* to enforce the construction of sewers. (49 L. J., Ch., 89 : L. R., 12 Ch. D., 102 : 40 L. T., 736 : 44 J. P., 36)

1892.   [1467]
Graham v. *Newcastle-on-Tyne Corporation.* Square held by Corporation subject to a Covenant to keep it "open and unbuilt upon"—To erect a half-sunken Urinal held not a breach of covenant—A Urinal is not necessarily a "nuisance"—Injunction refused. (67 L. T., 260.)

1859.   [1468]
Hayward v. *Lowndes.* A Local Board has no power to go out of its District to make Sewers. (28 L. J., Ch. 400: 4 Drew., 454 : 32 L. T., (o. s.), 366.) [Such a power is, however, for purposes of outfall or distribution, now given by the "Public Health Act, 1875," § 16.]

1870.   [1469]
Holt v. *Rochdale, Mayor.* Local Act—New Sewer—A Corporation prohibited from making a new sewer into a river is not permitted to enlarge an old one—Injunction granted, (39 L. J., Ch., 761 : L. R., 10 Eq., 354 : 23 L. T., 43 : 35 J. P., 6.)

1861.   [1470]
Hughes v. *Metropolitan B. W.* When forming a sewer a Board need not of necessity do more than make compensation to the landowner—Purchase of land or of easement is not essential. (Metrop.) (4 L. T., 318 : 9 W. R. 517.)

1891.   [1471]
Kirkheaton L. B. v. *Ainley.* (1). "Public Health Act, 1875"—§ 17 does not affect the right conferred by § 21 upon an owner, &c., to drain into an existing public Sewer : it is for the Local Authority to see that its sewers are so arranged as not to contravene § 17. (60 L. J., Ch., 734.)

1880.   [1472]
Lamacraft v. *St. Thomas's Rural Sanitary Authority.* "Public Health Act, 1875," §§ 16, 19, 27, 305—Proposed sewer—Refusal by plaintiff, a landowner, to permit entry—Whereupon forcible entry—Injunction to restrain works granted, it being shewn that such works when finished must of necessity create a nuisance—§ 305 allowing entry under Justice's Order does not apply to entry to construct sewers under § 16. (42 L. T., 365 : 44 J. P., 441.)

1855.   [1473]
Maidenhead L. B. H., In re. Application for *Mandamus* to make sewers refused, as there had been no formal demand upon or refusal by the Board. (26 L. T. (o. s.), 104.)

1876.   [1474]
Mason v. *Wallasey L. B.* Proposed erection of urinal—Injunction to restrain refused, no *mala fides* being shown—A Local Board must be considered as elected to settle such questions, and to be well able to know what is requisite. (L. J., *Notes of Cases*, 1876, p. 212 : *Times*, Dec. 9, 1876.)

1892.   [1475]
Meader v. *West Cowes L. B.* "Public Health Act, 1875," §§ 13, 15, 19—Several houses drained into one cess-pit, the overflow from

which crossing, without licence, the land of a neighbour eventually reached a river—Overflow blocked by neighbour and sewage dammed back on to plaintiff's land—Held that the neighbour had acted within his rights; that plaintiff himself was in default and could not make the board responsible for the overflow pipes as being a public "sewer." (61 L. J., Ch., 561 : L. R., 3 Ch., 18.)

1883.　　　　　　　　　　　　　[1476]
Merrett v. Bridges. Grant of lands subject to a rent-charge in respect of use of roads and sewer—Effect of roads and sewer becoming vested in a Local Authority—Rent-charge held still in force. (47 J. P., 775.)

1881.　　　　　　　　　　　　　[1477]
Metropolitan B. W. v. London & North-Western Railway Co. "Metropolis Management Amendment Act, 1862," § 61—Houses outside the jurisdiction of a Board allowed to use the sewers of the Board—Held that this privilege did not extend to new buildings erected subsequently, although forming part of the first-named block—Injunction granted—*Semble,* that if Board had given written consent and fixed the size of the drain, the defendants might then have used it to the full extent of its capacity. (50 L. J., Ch., 409 : L. R., 17 Ch. D., 246 : 44 L. T., 270.)

1881.　　　　　　　　　　　　　[1478]
Metropolitan B. W. v. Willesden L. B. Rights of Local Authorities just outside the Metropolis as to user of Metropolitan sewers. (*Times*, Aug. 9, 1884.)

1888.　　　　　　　　　　　　　[1479]
Mogg v. Bocken. Motion to restrain the erection of a "kiosk" urinal at the junction of 2 roads on a site granted by the Vestry—Injunction refused, no adequate proof being forthcoming that the premises would be a nuisance.—*Sed quære,* Has a Metropolitan Vestry power under 18 & 19 Vict. c. 120, § 88, to delegate to a commercial firm its powers of erecting public conveniences? (*Times*, Nov. 1, 1888.)

1889.　　　　　　　　　　　　　[1480]
Molloy v. Gray. "Public Health (Ireland) Act, 1878," §§ 15, 17, 21, 23—Householders have a right to use water-closets, and the obligation cast upon a Sanitary Authority to construct "effectual" sewers includes sewers fit to carry away matter from water-closets, which otherwise would be apt to create a nuisance. (24 L. R., Ir., 258.)

1884.　　　　　　　　　　　　　[1481]
National Model Dwellings Co. v. St. George's, Southwark, Vestry. Proposed erection of Urinal at junction of two streets—Injunction to restrain erection refused, it not being shown that any special nuisance was to be anticipated. (*Loc. Gov. Chron.*, Feb. 9, 1884.)

1883.　　　　　　　　　　　　　[1482]
New River Co. v. Ware Union. "Public Health Act, 1875," § 16—This section must be read as if some such words as "after giving reasonable notice, &c.," were at the end thereof—Reasonable notice to owner or occupier is a

condition precedent to the right of a Local Authority to construct a sewer elsewhere than along a public highway. (18 L. J., *Notes of Cases*, 20.)

1879.　　　　　　　　　　　　　[1483]
Newington L. B. v. Cottingham L. B. Agreement dated 1874 between two Local Boards that the sewage of the C. District should be allowed to enter the sewers of the N. District, subject to the restriction that no sewage from any third district should be admitted—Claim by outside landowners to use the C. sewers in accordance with the provisions of the "Public Health Act, 1875," § 22—Held that they might do so, § 22 operating to repeal the conditions of the agreement of earlier date. (48 L. J., Ch., 226 : L. R., 12 Ch. D., 725 : 40 L. T., 58.)

1875.　　　　　　　　　　　　　[1484]
Nuneaton L. B. v. General Sewage Co. Lease of Sewage and Works to a Public Company——Neglect to perform the Covenants—Injunction granted to restrain the Defendants from keeping Sewage matter in the Town Sewers, followed by a second Injunction to restrain them pouring Sewage into a river. (44 L. J., Ch., 561 : L. R., 20 Eq., 127.)

1858.　　　　　　　　　　　　　[1485]
Parsons, Ex parte. Alleged necessity that a sewer ought to be constructed—*Mandamus* to a Local Board refused—Applicant to make a simple demand that a duty be discharged. (22 J. P., 68.)

1887.　　　　　　　　　　　　　[1486]
Pinnock v. Waterworth. "Public Health Act,1875," §§ 4, 13, 15, 19—A line of pipes with cesspool at end receiving drainage of several houses is a "Sewer"—Such a sewer constructed by a builder as the best and quickest mode of drainage is not a "Sewer made for purposes of profit"—Held, therefore, that under § 13 such pipes and cesspool were vested in the Local Authority, which became liable to maintain and cleanse same. (3 *Times* L. R., 563.)

1879.　　　　　　　　　　　　　[1487]
Reg. v. Clutton Union. "Public Health Act, 1875," § 35—Whether rebuilt cottages shall each have a separate privy, or whether one shall be deemed sufficient for 2 cottages, is a fit matter for the discretion of Justices. (48 L. J., M. C., 135 : 43 J. P., 332 : [*Clutton v. Pointing*] L. R.,4 Q. B. D., 340 : 40 L. T., 845.)

1866.　　　　　　　　　　　　　[1488]
Reg. v. Godmanchester L. B. H. Natural Watercourse, receiving a little sewage held not to be a "Sewer" within the "Public Health Act, 1848," § 43 [="Public Health Act, 1875," § 13]—*Mandamus* under §58 [repealed] held not enforceable, as it did not show that the person causing the nuisance had failed to comply with a notice to abate it. (35 L J., Q. B., 125 : L. R., 1 Q. B., 328 : 5 B. & S., 936 : 14 L. T., 104.)

1884.　　　　　　　　　　　　　[1489]
Reg. v. Greenwich B. W. A District Board cannot withhold sanction from new sewers to be

constructed by a landowner by way of compelling him to pay a sum for supervision of such sewers. (Metrop.) (1 Cab. & Ellis., 236.)

1890.   [1490]

Reg. v. *Paddington Vestry.* "Metropolis Management Act, 1855." § 85—4 houses using one drain—Order of Vestry that each house should be separately connected with the main sewer —Held that the Vestry must make the connections at its own expense. (55 J. P., 52.)

1888.   [1491]

Reg. v. *Staines L. B.* A Lo al Board has only a qualified property in the sewers within its district, and cannot prevent persons who have acquired a prescriptive right to u-c them from doing so unless it finds other sewers equally effectual. (60 L. T., 261 : 53 J. P., 358.)

1883.   [1492]

Reg. v. *Wandsworth B. W.* "Metropolis Management Amendment Act, 1862," §§ 47-8— Deposit of plans of proposed sewers—Duty of District Board. (49 J. P., 806)

1879.   [1493]

Riddell v. *Spear.* "Public Health Act, 1875," §§ 91-111—Sewer constructed by landlord through land lease1 by him to tenant, but without tenant's consent, and without compensation being made to him—Sewer became vested in Local Authority—Sewer stopped up by tenant—Nuisance thereupon created—Held that the tenant was rightly convicted as the person by whose act the nuisance arose or continued, and this, although the *locus in quo* of the nuisance was elsewhere, (40 L. T., 130 : 43 J. P., 317.)

1877.   [1494]

Roderick v. *Aston L. B.* "Public Health Act, 1875," § 16—Held that the words "into, through, or under" entitled a Local Authority to carry a sewer along an artificial embankment above the ground level—Injunction refused—Remedy, proceedings for compensation. (46 L. J., Ch., 802 : L. R., 5 Ch. D., 328 : 36 L. T., 328 : 41 J. P., 516.)

1883.   [1495]

Sandgate v. *Lenney.* Sewer carried through private land—Covenant in Deed granting Board access to Sewer held not broken by defendant merely by building over a portion of the ground, seeing that reasonably convenient access to sewer could still be had at all time. (*Times,* Aug. 2, 1883 : L. R., 25 Ch. D., 183, n.)

1877.   [1496]

Scarle v. *Barnet L. B.* Forcible entry on land by workmen of a Local Board in order to connect the drain of a house with a public sewer— Allegation that, owing to the carelessness of the workmen, a well of good water had been injured—Action for damages—Verdict for plaintiff, the owner of the house and land. (*Times,* Dec. 1, 1877.)

1883.   [1497]

Sellers v. *Matlock Bath L. B.* "Public Health Act, 1875," § 39—Urinal erected by Board partly on highway and partly on private

land, ordered to be removed—Board not entitled to say that Plaintiff's remedy was compensation under § 308—Notice of Action under § 264 not necessary—Board held entitled to place kerb-stones on highway even though they were some hindrance to persons approaching plaintiff's property (an inn). (L. R., 14 Q. B. D., 928 : 52 L. T., 762.)

1882.   [1498]

Selous v. *Wimbledon L. B.* Use of land for sewage farm—Alleged nuisance—Conflict of evidence —The Court will hesitate to grant an Injunction against a public Body entrusted by Statute with important duties, especially where the granting of such Injunction might be prejudicial to the public by breeding pestilence. (*Times,* Aug. 8 and 9, 1882.)

1886.   [1499]

Serff v. *Acton L. B.* Right of way over land taken compulsorily for sewage works. (55 L. J., Ch., 569 : L. R., 31 Ch. D., 679 : 54 L. T., 379.)

1885.   [1500]

Soady v. *Wilson.* Sewers Rate—Properties may be liable even though the benefit may not be immediate. (3 A. & E., 248 : 4 N. & M., 777 : 1 H. & W., 256.)

1886.   [1501]

St. John, Hampstead, Vestry v. *Cotton.* Sewer in disturnpiked road—Held that owner of land abutting thereon was not chargeable— *St. Giles, Camberwell* v. *Weller,* and *Sheffield* v. *Fulham* followed : *Sawyer* v. *Paddington* dissented from. (56 L. J., Q. B., 225 : L. R., 12 App. Cas., 1 : 56 L. T., 1 : 51 J. P., 340.)

1885.   [1502]

St. John, Hampstead, Vestry v. *Hoopel.* "Metropolis Management Act, 1855," § 78 : " Amendment Act, 1862," § 112—Connection of private drains with sewers—Right of Vestry to do the work in street virtually a highway though not taken over. (54 L. J., M. C., 147 : L. R., 15 Q. B. D., 652 : 49 J. P., 741.)

1865.   [1503]

St. Marylebone Vestry v. *Viret.* Unnecessary New Sewer and connections — Board and not owner held liable for the expenses. (34 L. J., M. C., 214 : 19 C. B., (N. S.), 424 : 12 L. T., 673.)

1879.   [1504]

Swanston v. *Twickenham L. B.* Sewer construct d along public road with man-hole on plaintiff's land—Man-hole erected without leave, and yielding noxious smells—If such a structure is necessary, the Board may construct it without purchasing a site for it, the landowner being entitled to compensation only— A man-hole is part of a " Sewer." (48 L. J., Ch., 623 : L. R., 11 Ch. D., 838 : 40 L. T., 734.)

1867.   [1505]

Thornton v. *Nutter.* A sewer is merely an easement, and to make it, proceedings under the "Lands Clauses Act, 1845," to acquire land are not requisite. (31 J. P., 419.)

1880.   [1506]

Vernon v. *St. James's Vestry.* Action to restrain erection of a urinal on a site alleged to be detrimental to plaintiff's property—Injunction granted. (50 L. J. Ch., 81: L. R. 16 Ch. D., 449: 44 L. T., 229.)

1885. [1507]
Walthamstow L. B. v. Jones. An agreement by tenant of sewage farm to receive "water, sewage and other matter" held to include storm water. (*Times*, May 8, 1885.)

1892. [1508]
Wandsworth B. W. v. Bird. "Metropolis Amendment Act, 1890," § 6—Permission to excavate soil of new street for construction of sewer refused—Held, that the only power vested in a District Board in such a case was to impose conditions, not to veto absolutely a necessary excavation. (61 L. J., M. C., 97: L. R, 1 Q. B., 481: 66 L. T., 376: 56 J. P., 280.)

1891. [1509]
Welstead v. Paddington Vestry. Local Act—Powers of Vestry to order and enforce alterations in a urinal. (Metrop.) (66 L. T., 194: 56 J. P., 295.)

1885. [1510]
Wheatcroft v. Matlock L. B. "Public Health Act, 1875"—Sewage passing through a sewer and then along an open watercourse—Held that under the circumstances such water-course was a "sewer" within § 4. (52 L. T., 356.)

1877. [1511]
Whitford L. B. v. Castleford L. B. Agreement between two Boards for joint sewerage works —Injunction granted to delay the cutting off of the sewer connections. (Jan. 1877.)

1884. [1512]
Windsor, Mayor v. Stovell. "Public Health Act, 1848," § 48 [Repealed]: "Public Health Act, 1875," § 22—Contract by Corporation to receive sewage from houses hereafter to be erected—Observance of the contract eventually burdensome to Corporation—Held that such a Contract having been good in Law could not be evaded by the Corporation. (54 L. J., Ch., 113: L. R., 27 Ch. D., 665: 51 L. T., 626).

1887. [1513]
Woburn Union v. Newport Pagnell Union. "Public Health Act, 1875," § 48—Order on plaintiffs (appellants) to cleanse a ditch receiving sewage from their district held good, although the ditch was wholly within the defendants' district. (51 J. P., 694.)

1834. [1514]
Woodward v. Cotton. Local Act—Construction of drain smaller in size than the Local Authority required and authorized—Action for penalty—Verdict for the plaintiff—Where one man directs another to commit a misdemeanour the other does so, both are equally guilty. (3 L. J., Ex., 300: 1 C. M. & R., 44: 4 Tyr., 689.)

69. STATUTES, INTERPRETATION OF.

1859. [1515]
A.-G. v. Birmingham Council. (1). Public Works ordered by Statute must not be executed so as to interfere with private rights—Injunction granted. (4 K. & J., 528: 22 J. P., 561.)

1846. [1516]
A.-G. v. Worcester Corporation. The way to apply an Interpretation Clause is, when the word is used in other enactments, to follow the direction of the Interpretation Clause and according to the subject-matter to read it as if it contained the other words, which by the Clause it is meant to include. (15 L. J., Ch., 398, at p. 399.)

1876. [1517]
Barnes v. Eddleston. "Public Health Act, 1875," § 343—Offence punishable under an Act repealed during the progress of the proceedings—Held that the repealed Act remained available. (45 L. J, M. C., 162: L. R., 1 Ex. D., 102: 33 L. T., 822: 40 J. P., 663.)

1871. [1518]
Bath, Mayor v. Commissioners of Inland Revenue. "Public Health Act, 1848," § 151 [repealed] —Exemptions from Stamp Duty—Construction of Local Act. (40 L. J., Ex., 181: 25 L. T., 28.)

1876. [1519]
Bentley v. Rotherham L. B. H. Local Act "extended" by subsequent Act—Where the operative part of a Statute is clear it is not to be controlled by the recitals, but where it is ambiguous the recitals may be referred to. (46 L. J., Ch. 284: L. R., 4 Ch. D., 588.)

1882. [1520]
Birkenhead Corporation v. Crowe. Special Act altering the general Law as to the incidence of Paving Expenses—Held that though the date for the alteration to come into force had (unknown to the defendants) been postponed whilst the Bill was in Parliament, yet the defendants could not claim the benefits which the Bill as originally drawn would have conferred on them. (46 J. P., 551.)

1883. [1521]
Burton v. Salford Corporation. "Highway Act, 1835," § 109: "Public Health Act, 1875," § 264—Limitation of time prescribed by former Act held available by way of defence, and Action not maintainable— *Taylor v. Meltham* distinguished. (52 L. J., Q. B., 668: L. R., 11 Q. B. D., 286: 49 L. T., 43: 47 J. P., 614.)

1859. [1522]
Cardiff, Mayor v. Cardiff Waterworks Co. Construction of the word "Port" used in a Local Act —Held to be not necessarily identical with a "Port" as defined for Customs purposes, but limited by the general context of the Act. (33 L. T., (o.s.), 104: 5 Jur., (n.s.), 953.)

1790. [1523]
Castle v. Burditt. Where computation of time is to be made from an act done the day on which it is done is to be included in the reckoning—Therefore in the case of a month's Notice of Action the month begins with the day on which the notice is served. (3 T. R., 623.)

1862. [1524]
Clarke v. Higgins. "Towns Police Clauses Act, 1847," § 28—"Wilful and wanton" disturbance by ringing a Door Bell—"Wanton"

means "without reasonable cause." (11
C. B., (N. S.), 545.)

1862.   [1525]

Daw v. Metropolitan B. W. Right to alter numbers on houses—If two Acts contain inconsistent provisions the later is to prevail.
(31 L. J., C. P., 223 : 12 C. B., (N. S.), 161 :
6 L. T., 353.)

1881.   [1526]

Ettrick, The. Where a public Body possesses powers to the same effect under 2 different Statutes it may proceed under whichever it deems most advantageous. (L. R., 6 P. D., 127.)

1861.   [1527]

Fitzgerald v. Champneys A Local Act is not in the absence of expressed intention on the part of the Legislature repealed or superseded by a Public General Act. (30 L. J.,
Ch., 777 : 2 Johns. & H., 31 : 5 L. T., 233.)

1860.   [1528]

Gough v. Hardman. Local Act—Unqualified person acting as a Commissioner—Two Local Acts to be read together when the one amends the other. (1 L. T., 375 : 5 H. & N., 112.)

1866.   [1529]

Hereford, Mayor v. Morton. Damage to gas-lamp —A corporation held to be within the designation of "person or persons" used in a Local Gas Act. (15 L. T., 187 : 15 W. R.,110.)

1841.   [1530]

Home v. Grimble. Merely to ring gently for a business purpose a front door bell accessible from a public street is not within the words "wilfully and wantonly" ringing a door bell used in the "Metropolitan Police Act," 2 & 3 Vict., c. 47, and does not warrant the person ringing being given into custody for creating a disturbance. (Carr. & M., 17.)

1885.   [1531]

Killmister v. Fitton. Local Act—"Town" held to include outlying districts void of population when the Act was passed. (53 L. T., 959.)

1856.   [1532]

London & Blackwall Co. v. Limehouse B. W. Powers conferred for an object of public benefit by a Special Act are not affected by a subsequent Act giving for another public purpose general powers inconsistent with them. (26 L. J., Ch., 161 : 3 K. & J., 123 :
28 L. T., (O. S.), 140.)

1886.   [1533]

Maddock v. Wallasey L. B. "Gasworks Clauses Act, 1847," §§ 3, 6, 7—Shore of an estuary traversed by the public held not a "highway or public place." (55 L. J., Q. B., 267 : 50 J. P., 404.)

1885.   [1534]

Portsmouth, Mayor v. Smith. "Towns Improvement Clauses Act, 1847," § 53 : Local Acts—Right of Action for Paving expenses—Effect of repeals in Local Acts—Defendant held not liable—*Maude v. Baildon* disapproved.
(54 L. J., Q. B., 483 : L. R., 10 App. Cas.,
364 : 53 L. T., 394 : 49 J. P., 676.)

1840.   [1535]

Queen (The) v. Burrell. "Municipal Corporations Act, 1835," § 48 [which the "Public Health

Act, 1875," § 247 (5) resembles]—Omission of Overseer's Signature from Burgess List—Penalty for omission, held incurred though the neglect was neither wilful nor corrupt—"Neglect is the omission to do some duty which the party is able to do." (9 L. J., Q. B., 337 :
[*King v. Burrell*] 12 A. & E. 460.)

1860.   [1536]

Reg. v. Bodkin. "Nuisances Removal Act, 1855," § 22 [Repealed as to the point here raised] —Sewerage — Division into Districts—Reassessment on an extension of the Sewerage —Defendant held chargeable as an occupier of a house "using" the sewer. (30 L. J.,
M. C., 38 : 3 E. & E., 271.)

1863.   [1537]

Reg. v. Epsom Union. "Nuisances Remova Act, 1855," § 22 [= "Public Health Act, 1875," § 15]—Requisition to "repair" does not cover reconstruction *de novo* of a work defectively made originally — Return to a *Mandamus* that sewer was defectively made and could not be repaired, held good. (8 L. T., 383 : 11 W. R., 593.)

1858.   [1538]

Reg. v. Rotherham L. B. H. "Public Health Act, 1848," § 89 [Public Health Act, 1875," §§ 210-11]—"Charges and Expenses"—A judgment against a Local Board is a "Charge," to defray which a Rate may be made—"Six months" runs from date when execution might first have issued, even in cases where execution has been stayed by consent—*Mandamus* granted. (27 L. J., Q. B.,
156 : 8 E. & B., 906 : 30 L. T., (O. S.), 271.)

1889.   [1539]

Reg. v. Vice-Registrar of Land Registry. "Public Health Act, 1875," § 257—Charges on property under such enactments as this are not "land charges" within the "Land Charges Registration and Searches Act, 1888," so as to require registration under that Act. (59 L. J., Q. B., 113 : L. R., 24 Q. B. D., 178 :
62 L. T., 117 : 6 *Times* L. R., 104.)

1759.   [1540]

Rex v. Robinson. Where a Statute creates a new offence, and appoints a specific remedy, that and no other must be pursued. (2 Burr.,
799 and 803.)

1825.   [1541]

Rex v. Washbrook Inhabitants. Private Inclosure Act—Award found to be at variance with statutory newspaper advertisement of boundaries—Order of Sessions based on the award, quashed—Where a special limited authority is given by Statute, it must be pursued strictly throughout all its conditions and qualifications, and is not to be considered merely directory. (4 B. & C., 732 : 7 D. & R., 221.)

1866.   [1542]

Smith v. Redding. 3 & 4 Vict., c. 61, § 15—Meaning of the words "Parish or place"—Held that a Hamlet within a Parish was not a "place" so as to govern a qualification depending on number of population. (35 L. J., M. C., 202 : L. R., 1 Q. B., 489 : 6 B. & S.,
617 and 621 : 14 L. T., 358.)

1876.   [1543]
Stone v. *Yeovil, Mayor.* Local Act: "Waterworks Clauses Act, 1847," §§ 6 and 12: "Lands Clauses Act, 1845," § 9—A word which makes a statute unintelligible may be disregarded. (46 L. J., C. P., 137: L. R., 2 C. P. D., 99: 36 L. T., 279: 42 J. P., 212.)

1866.   [1544]
Swinford v. *Keble.* "Municipal Corporations Act, 1835," § 142—A Local Board under the "Public Health Act, 1848," are not Paving, &c., Trustees within the meaning of the "Municipal Corporations Act." (35 L. J., Q. B., 185: L. R., 1 Q. B., 549: 7 B. & S., 573: 14 L. T., 770.)

1876.   [1545]
Taylor v. *Oldham Corporation.* Local Act—Powers of a Local Authority to construct a sewer under a private road—"Street" in the Local Act interpreted to include any "road".—The preamble of an Act cannot be resorted to in order to ascertain its intention unless there is an ambiguity in its enacting part—General provisions do not override special provisions—Clauses in Local Acts vesting sewers in a Local Authority confer an absolute property in the subsoil occupied by the sewers, not a mere easement. (46 L. J., Ch., 105: L. R., 4 Ch. D., 395: 35 L. T., 696.)

1870.   [1546]
Thorpe v. *Adams.* A General Act is not to be construed as repealing a previous Local Act, unless there are express words; or unless there is a necessary inconsistency in the two Acts standing together. (40 L. J., M. C., 45: L. R., 6 C. P., 125: 23 L. T., 810.)

1866.   [1547]
Triggs v. *Lester.* Local Act—Carrying cattle in a van is not "driving or conducting" cattle. (L. R., 1 Q. B., 259: 13 L. T., 701: 30 J. P., 228.)

1879.   [1548]
Walsall Overseers v. *London & North Western Railway Co.* "Public Health Acts, 1872 and 1875"—Local Acts—Rating privilege created by Statute — Statute repealed in part, but no mention made of the Rating privilege in question—A privilege granted by Statute ought not to be deemed to be taken away without a direct repeal of the Statute, or an inference so strong as to authorise a Court to say that the 2 Statutes cannot stand together—Rule quashed. (48 L. J., M. C., 166: L. R., 4 App. Cas., 467: 41 L. T., 106: 43 J. P., 748.)

1876.   [1549]
Williams v. *Evans.* Per Grove, J.:—"Statutes are to be construed according to the strict grammatical meaning of the language used, unless such a construction leads to an absurd result." (L. R., 1 Ex. D., 277: 35 L. T., 864: 41 J. P., 151.)

1868.   [1550]
Young v. *Gattridge.* "Nuisances Removal Act, 1863" [= "Public Health Act, 1875," §§ 116-18]—Seizure of diseased meat—A

butcher's yard held to be a "place." (38 L. J., M. C., 67: L. R., 4 Q. B., 166.)

70. STREET.

⁎ See also "Building Line," (§ 15, *ante*); and "Lands Clauses Act," (§ 44, *ante*).

1885.   [1551]
Anderson v. *Dublin Corporation.* "Towns Improvement Clauses Act, 1847," § 64: Local Act—Decision of Corporation to change name of street against wishes of householders —Held that § 64 gave no power to change an established name; that supposing it did the Court had jurisdiction to restrain the change if satisfied that it would be injurious to the owners or occupiers—Members of the Corporation specially active in promoting the change made to pay the costs of the action. (15 L. R., Ir., 410.)

1847.   [1552]
Baddeley v. *Gingell.* Local Act—A Yard having a frontage on a Street, and the sole access thereto being from such Street, is "within the Street" for rating purposes. (1 Ex., 319: 10 L. T., (o. s.), 114.)

1874.   [1553]
Ball v. *Ward.* "Towns Police Clauses Act, 1847," § 28—Obstruction of street, owing to persons crowding round a caravan lawfully placed away from the street—Held that the proprietor ought not to have been convicted. (33 L. T., 170: 40 J. P., 213.) [Cf. *Rex* v. *Carlile*.]

1857.   [1554]
Bearer v. *Manchester, Mayor.* Construction of a bridge—Plea of justification under a Statute —A "bridge" may be a street within the meaning of a Statute. (26 L. J., Q. B., 311: 8 E. B., 44: 29 L. T., (o. s.), 226.)

1830.   [1555]
Bouverie v. *Miles.* Local Act—Powers of a Board with respect to projections over a public way. (8 L. J., (o. s.), K. B., 338: 1 B. & Ad., 31.)

1842.   [1556]
Bradbee v. *London, Mayor.* Rebuilding of a House in a street—Hoarding to inclose materials— Powers of a public Authority to sanction such an inclosure—Action by adjoining owner suffering injury held maintainable only for injury accruing from negligence in the work of pulling down. (11 L. J., C. P., 209: 5 Scott, (N. S.), 79: 4 M. & G., 714.)

1851.   [1557]
Brown v. *Clegg.* Lowering the level of a new street under a provision in a Local Act similar to "Towns Improvement Clauses Act," § 51—Proceedings of Commissioners held *ultra vires.* (16 Q. B., 681: 17 L. T., (o. s.), 122.)

1864.   [1558]
Cary v. *Kingston-upon-Hull.* "Public Health Act, 1848," § 69—The power of a Local Board to compel the levelling, &c., of a Street is limited to work needed in a particular Street looked at as an isolated one, and does not extend to work needed to bring that Street

H

to a level with other adjoining Streets. (34 L. J., M. C., 7: [*Caley* v. *K.*] 5 B. & S., 815: 11 L. T., 339: 29 J. P., 116.)

1875.   [1559]
Challenger v. *Bristol Corporation.* "Tramways Act, 1870," § 9: "Public Health Act, 1848," § 68 [= "Public Health Act, 1875," § 149]—Alleged evasion of former enactment—Injunction to restrain the widening of a roadway at the expense of the adjacent footway, refused. (*Times*, Feb. 10, 1875.)

1845.   [1560]
Davey v. *Warne.* "Metropolitan Paving Act," 57 Geo. III., c. 29, § 75—Held that a Surveyor had no right to remove a ladder placed against a house by a whitewasher; the section only applied to the erection of hoards or posts or rails, &c., by which an inclosure is made. (15 L. J., Ex., 253: 14 M. & W., 199.)

1890.   [1561]
Daw v. *London County Council.* "Metropolis Management Amendment Act, 1862," § 98—Width of new Street—Barrier erected at end—Continuing penalty adjudged. Conviction affirmed. (59 L. J., M. C., 112: 62 L. T., 937: 54 J. P., 502.)

1884.   [1562]
Fulham B. W. v. *Smith.* Local Acts—Obstruction of street by costermonger's barrow. (48 J. P., 375.)

1859.   [1563]
Gabriel v. *St. James's, Westminster, Vestry.* "Metropolis Management Act, 1855," § 119—Projecting Lamp-iron—Whether such be an annoyance justifying a conviction or not, is a fit matter for the discretion of a magistrate. (23 J. P., 372.)

1866.   [1564]
Galloway v. *Commonalty of London; Metropolitan Railway Co. London* v. *Galloway.* The powers entrusted to Public Bodies for purposes of Public Improvements are not subject to a strict and restrictive construction—The word "street" means not a mere roadway, but "a thoroughfare with houses on both sides." (35 L. J., Ch., 492: L. R., 1 H. L., 34: 14 L. T., 865.)

1885.   [1565]
Gard v. *Commissioners of Sewers.* Local Act—Powers to take premises for widening a street restricted—*Thomas* v. *Daw* and *Galloway* v. *London* distinguished. (54 L. J., Ch., 698: 52 L. T., 827.)

1888.   [1566]
Grosvenor v. *Sutton L. B.* Injunction granted restraining Board from permanently occupying part of a highway as a depot for road material, so as to interfere with plaintiff's access to her property—Nevertheless Injunction not to preclude some moderate use of the highway as far as might be lawful under any Statute or authority vested in Board. (W. N., 1888, p. 223.)

1874.   [1567]
Hoare v. *Metropolitan B. W.* "Metropolitan Commons Act, 1866," 29 & 30 Vict., c 122, § 15—Long existent right to maintain a

Sign-post in front of a Public-house—Held that such a post was renewable from time to time, and that no offence had been committed by replacing a dilapidated post by a new one. (43 L. J., M. C., 65: L. R., 9 Q. B., 296: 29 L. T., 804: 38 J. P., 535.)

1887.   [1568]
Holden v. *St. Mary, Islington, Vestry.* Old road with houses and footpath on one side held nevertheless a "new street." (Metrop.) (*Times*, Jan. 31, 1887.)

1858.   [1569]
Le Neve v. *Mile End Old Town Vestry.* Open space between houses and pavement used for the deposit of goods by a shopkeeper—Held that such space was not part of a "street," so as to render the shopkeeper guilty of an obstruction. (Metropolis.) (27 L. J., Q. B., 208: 8 E. & B., 1054: 31 L. T., (o. s.), 81.)

1868.   [1570]
London, Chatham & Dover Railway Co. v. *London, Mayor.* Local Acts—The strict meaning of the word "street" is confined to the roadway and footways. (19 L. T., 250.)

1892.   [1571]
London C. C. v. *Edmondson.* Local Acts—New Street—Laying out—Through communication. (66 L. T., 200: 56 J. P., 343.)

1877.   [1572]
Mackett v. *Herne Bay Commissioners.* Local Act —Project for laying out land for building and for roads—Question of title—Injunction granted to restrain the defendants interfering with the sites of the roads, except in a few cases where dedication was shown. (W. N., 1877, p. 221: 37 L. T., 812.) [In connection with this case an Injunction was granted to restrain a Commissioner from preaching a sermon on it *pendente lite.* 24 W. R., 845.]

1883.   [1573]
Maude v. *Baildon L. B.* Whether a place is a "street" within the "Public Health Act, 1875," § 150, is a question of fact for Justices: they are not bound by definition of "street" in § 4. (L. R., 10 Q. B. D , 394: 48 L. T., 875: 47 J. P., 644.) [Disapproved of in *Portsmouth* v. *Smith.*]

1868.   [1574]
Metropolitan B. W. v. *Clever.* "Metropolis Management Amendment Act, 1862," § 98—Laying out road for building—Width of Street—Fence set back—Held that the landowner had not, by what he had done, brought himself within the Section. (Metropolis.) (37 L. J., M. C., 126: L. R., 3 C. P., 531: 18 L. T., 723.)

1865.   [1575]
Metropolitan B. W. v. *Cox.* An enactment that a roadway shall not be laid out for building, unless at least 40 ft. wide, held not to apply where the buildings abutted *in the rear* on an old lane of less than the width in question. (Metropolis.) (19 C. B., (N. S.), 445.)

1884.   [1576]
Metropolitan B. W. v. *Lathey.* Notices of intention to lay out new street held good and proceedings barred by time. (49 J. P., 245.)

1881. [1577]
Metropolitan B. W. v. *Steel.* "Metropolis Management Amendment Act, 1862," § 98—Street not open at both ends held to contravene the Act, although of the specified width. (51 L. J., M. C., 22 : L. R., 8 Q. B. D., 445 : 45 L. T., 611 : 46 J. P., 199.)

1873. [1578]
Milward v. *Redditch L. B.* "Public Health Act, 1848," § 68 [= "Public Health Act, 1875," § 149]—Alteration of Street level—Accumulation of storm water—Damage to premises—Mandatory Injunction granted—Paving not to remain in such a condition that water was necessarily dammed up against plaintiff's house. (21 W. R., 429.)

1876. [1579]
Montreal, Mayor v. *Drummond.* Canadian Law—The permanent closing of one end of a street, whereby access to houses was rendered inconvenient, held no such interference with the rights of the owners as to entitle them to compensation. (45 L. J., P. C., 33 : L. R., 1 App. Cas., 384 : 35 L. T., 106.)

1864. [1580]
Reg. v. *Fullford.* 24 & 25 Vict. c. 61. § 28 [= "Public Health Act, 1875," § 156]—Misdemeanour—Indictment for bringing forward a house in a Street without the consent of a Local Board—Meaning of the word "Street"—Street seems only to apply to a row of houses in some degree continuous, but this is a question of fact for a Jury. (33 L. J., M. C., 122 : 10 L. T., 346 : 9 Cox, C. C., 453 : 28 J. P., 357.)

1859. [1581]
Reg. v. *Great Western Railway Co.* "Towns Improvement Clauses Act, 1847," § 53—Paving of Street—The word "theretofore" refers to any time before the passing of the Special Act—A street which was a public highway at the passing of the Special Act, and had been but was not then sufficiently paved, was not within the Section. (28 L. J., M. C., 246 : [G. W. R. Co.] v. *West Bromwich Commissioners*] 1 E. & E., 806.)

1873. [1582]
Reg. v. *Hackney B. W.* "Metropolis Management Act, 1855," § 105—Barrier erected by owners in a New Street—When a Board compels owners to form a New Street, the Board is bound to repair notwithstanding the barrier —*Mandamus* granted. (42 L. J., M. C., 151 : L. R., 8 Q. B., 528.)

1852. [1583]
Reg. v. *Ingham.* Projection in Street—*Mandamus* —Costs. (Metropolis.) (21 L. J., M. C., 125 : 17 Q. B., 884 : 18 L. T., (o. s.), 303.)

1877. [1584]
Reg. v. *Metropolitan B. W.* (3). Local Act embodying an Agreement with a Landowner that a "Roadway" should be made 25 ft. wide—Question whether this meant 25 ft. of carriage-way, exclusive of footways, or 25 ft. of roadway, inclusive of footways—Held that "roadway" meant "carriage-way," and that

the width of the footways would have to be added to the 25 ft. (*Times*, Nov. 13, 1877.)

1858. [1585]
Reg. v. *St. Mary's, Islington, Vestry.* A certain unfinished road held not to be a "Street" which the Vestry was bound to light. (E. B. & E., 743 : 22 J. P., 383.)

1884. [1586]
Reg v. *Sheil.* "Metropolis Management Acts, 1855, 1862"—Meaning of "street"—Magistrate found that a certain lane was not a "street"—Held that this was a question not of Law but of fact—*Mandamus* to state a case refused. (50 L. T., 590 : 49 J. P., 68.)

1859. [1587]
Reg. v. *Sidebotham.* Local Act—Width of Street —A prescribed minimum distance between houses held not to apply to houses not in a street. (28 L. J., M. C., 189 : Bell, C. C., 171 : 33 L. T., (o. s.), 187.)

1697. [1588]
Rex v. *Webb.* To rebuild a house on a larger scale whereby the street becomes darker than before is not a public nuisance. (1 Ld. Raym., 737.)

1858. [1589]
St. Mary, Newington, Vestry v. *South London Fish Market Co.* Company formed to construct a market and make, under penalties, new streets as approved—Failure of Market scheme—Action against promoters for penalties in respect of the new streets—Defence that the street improvements were subsidiary to the market, and that as the latter was not established the duty of making the new streets did not arise—Held, no defence, and promoters liable to the penalties. (52 J. P., 292.)

1860. [1590]
Sarrett v. *Bradshaw.* "Highway Act, 1835"—Obstruction to street by hoarding authorised by a Surveyor appointed under the "Local Government Act, 1858"—Conviction on the ground that the hoarding projected unnecessarily, affirmed, the Court being inclined to be equally divided. (*Times*, May 3, 1860.)

1884. [1591]
Sheffield v. *Heath.* Covenants by defendants to bear certain expenses until the roads upon a certain building estate "used in common" by occupiers on the estate were taken over by Parish—Roads used by public generally but not yet taken over—Held that the roads were not "used in common" by the occupiers within the meaning of the covenant, and defendants therefore not liable. (*Times*, July 8, 1884.)

1889. [1592]
Sunderland, Mayor v. *Skinner.* Old house with shop front abutting on lane—Plan deposited by owner showing lane widened and new house set back—Subsequently he rebuilt an old site—Held that no offence had been committed as regards width of street. (53 J. P., 660.)

1867. [1593]
Taylor v. *Metropolitan B. W.* "Metropolis

H 2

Management Amendment Act, 1862," § 98—Removal of an old fence and erection of a permanent wall held to be "laying out" of a new road so that widening to the dimensions prescribed by the Act became obligatory. (36 L. J., M. C., 53: L. R., 2 Q. B., 213: 31 J. P., 581.)

1866.   [1594]
Thomas v. *Daw.* Local Act, 57 Geo. III., c. xxix., § 80—Improvement of Street—Commissioners held entitled to take only so much of a site as was necessary for their purpose. (36 L. J., Ch., 201 : L. R., 2 Ch. App., 1 : 15 L. T., 200.)

1889.   [1595]
Tod-Heatley v. *Foakes.* "Metropolis Management Act, 1855," §§ 105, 250 : "Amendment Act, 1862," §§ 77, 112—Magistrate found that so many changes had been made and new buildings erected as to render the place practically a new street—Held that there was sufficient evidence to justify this conclusion—The powers of a Local Authority are not confined to the part of the road on which new buildings are put up—No test of a road being or not being a "new street" that buildings are continuous—*Semble*, that wherever maintenance of pathway and footway have not been assumed by Local Authority there may be a "new street." (53 J. P., 772.)

1884.   [1596]
Wandsworth B. W. v. *Postmaster-General.* "Telegraph Act, 1878"—Decision by Railway Commissioners as to places where wires ought to be put overhead, and where they ought not to be so put—Rule laid down that distance between supports ought not to exceed 100 yards. (*Times,* May 21, 1884.)

1884.   [1597]
Wandsworth B. W. v. *United Telephone Co.* Street vested in a Board—Injunction to restrain the maintenance of telephone wires across a street refused, there being no sufficiently exclusive rights. (53 L. J., Q. B., 449 : 51 L. J., 148 : 48 J. P., 676.)

71. SURETY.

1852.   [1598]
Benham v. *United Guarantee & Life Assurance Co.* Consideration of what would vitiate a policy of guarantee obtained by the employer of a clerk. (21 L. J., Ex., 317 : 7 Ex., 744 : 19 L. T., (o. s.), 206.)

1862.   [1599]
Black v. *Ottoman Bank.* Principles of Law respecting the liability or the non-liability of a Surety—A Surety guarantees the honesty of the person employed, and he is not entitled to relief from his obligation merely because the employer fails to use all means in his power to provide against the dishonesty of the person in respect of whom the bond is given. (15 Moo., P. C., 472 : 6 L. T., 763.)

1892.   [1600]
Cosford Union v. *Grimwade.* Union Treasurer partner in a Bank which failed—Question whether the money deposited belonged to the Guardians directly as customers of the Bank or was dealt with by the Treasurer on his own responsibility—Latter view held by the Court, and surety therefore liable. (*Times,* Aug. 5, 1892.)

1875.   [1601]
Hawkins v. *Aldershot School Board.* Contract by builder—Bankruptcy of Builder—Substituted contractor—Contract varied—Original surety held released. (*Times,* April 22, 1875.)

1870.   [1602]
Malling Union v. *Graham.* 7 & 8 Vict., c. 101, § 61-2—Principal and Surety—Acceptance of a new office—Sanction of Poor Law Board obtained—Held nevertheless that the surety was discharged. (39 L. J., C. P., 74 : L. R., 5 C. P., 201 : 22 L. T., 789.)

1872.   [1603]
Phillips v. *Foxall.* Surety—Dishonesty—If a master finds his servant dishonest and condones the offence, he cannot afterwards call upon the surety to make good a subsequent loss. (L. R., 7 Q. B., 666 : 27 L. T., 231 : 37 J. P., 37.)

1873.   [1604]
Sanderson v. *Aston.* Neglect by an employer to dismiss a servant found guilty of irregularities which would justify dismissal discharges the Surety. (42 L. J., Ex., 64 : L. R., 8 Ex., 73 : 28 L. T., 35.)

1867.   [1605]
Skillet v. *Fletcher.* Collector of Poor Rate—Additional duties—Bond of Surety held not void because of the alteration of office. (36 L. J., C. P., 206 : L. R., 2 C. P., 469 : 16 L. T., 426.)

1869.   [1606]
Stiff v. *East-Bourne L. B.* Sewerage Works—Bond—Failure of Contractor—*Semble* that a Surety from whom a material fact has been concealed is not liable. (19 L. T., 408 : 20 L. T., 339 : 17 W. R., 68 and 428.)

1862.   [1607]
Towle v. *National Guardian Assurance Society.* Bond of Suretyship—Numerous inaccuracies in the answers to preliminary questions—Bond held void. (30 L. J., Ch., 900 : 5 L. T., 193.)

72. SURVEYOR.

1888.   [1608]
Lewis v. *Weston-super-Mare L. B.* "Public Health Act, 1875," §§ 54 and 16—The Surveyor must determine the "necessity" of every case, and if his decision is given *bonâ fide* it cannot be set aside—Held that a person appointed to act as Surveyor during the Surveyor's illness is not the Surveyor contemplated by the Act—Only an officer appointed under § 189 can act. (58 L. J., Ch., 39 ; L. R., 40 Ch. D., 55 : 59 L. T., 769.)

1873.   [1609]
Metropolitan B. W. v. *Flight.* Dangerous premises—Fees of Surveyor chargeable to the

Owner—An Item in the Board's Bill "office expenses, 2s. 6d." disallowed. (Metropolis.) (43 L. J., M. C., 46 : L. R., 9 Q. B., 58 : 29 L. T., 608 : 38 J. P., 503.)

1872.   [1610]
Power v. *Wigmore.* Surveyor's Fees—Fifty-one Arches held to be so many separate buildings, on each of which a fee was payable. (Metropolis.) (L. R., 7 C. P., 386 : 27 L. T., 148.)

1889.   [1611]
Reg. v. *Ramsgate Corporation.* Borough Surveyor employed on other work and specially remunerated—Proceedings against him for penalties—Decision subsequently of Corporation to defray his expenses held *ultra vires.* (58 L. J., Q. B., 352 : L. R., 23 Q. B. D., 66 : 61 L. T., 333 : 53 J. P., 740.) Subsequent proceedings to make the members concerned in the illegal resolutions liable for the Costs of the *Certiorari.* (*[Reg.* v. *Whiteley]* 58 L. J., M. C., 164 : 61 L. T., 253 : *[Reg.* v. *Vaile]* 54 J. P., 134.)

1863.   [1612]
Westwick, Ex parte; Nottingham Corporation, In re. Surveyor appointed by order of Borough Justices to value property required for a street improvement—Order quashed by *Certiorari* on the ground of interest, the Justices being ratepayers. (38 *Law Times* Newspaper, 203.)

1887.   [1613]
Whiteley v. *Barley.* (2.) "Public Health Act, 1875," § 193—A Local Authority employed their Surveyor to superintend a contract for drainage works and paid him a percentage for his services independently of his official salary—Held that he was liable to penalty as "concerned or interested" in a contract. (57 L. J., Q. B., 643 : L. R., 21 Q. B. D., 154 : 60 L. T., 87 : 52 J. P., 595.) [See *Reg.* v. *Ramsgate* for further references to this case.]

73. TIME, COMPUTATION OF.

1863.   [1614]
Baker v. *Billericay Union.* An action against Guardians for money due, where no extension has been obtained from Local Government Board, must be commenced within the current half-year or within 3 months afterwards. (33 L. J., M. C., 40 : 2 H. & C., 642 : 9 L. T., 486.)

1846.   [1615]
Beenlen v. *Hockin.* In notices and documents required to be dated, mention of the year is an essential part of such date. (16 L. J., C. P., 49 : 4 C. B., 19 : 8 L. T., (o. s.), 143.)

1860.   [1616]
Eddleston v. *Francis.* "Public Health Act, 1848," §§ 51 and 129 [="Public Health Act, 1875," §§ 35–6, 251]—Proceedings for the recovery of money due for works executed must be commenced within 6 months of the completion of the works, and not within 6 months of the demand for payment—*Quære,*

Is a Receiver appointed by the Court of Chancery an "owner"? (7 C. B., (N. S.), 568 : 3 L. T., 270 : 25 J. P., 135.)

1803.   [1617]
Glassington v. *Rawlings.* Where time is to be computed from an act done the day in which it is done is to be included. (3 East, 407.)

1878.   [1618]
Kay v. *Atherton L. B.* Local Board acting as Surveyors of highways—Accident to plaintiff through negligent deposit of stones in a road —The limit of time within which a plaintiff must bring his Action against a Local Board is not the 3 months prescribed by the "Highway Act, 1835," § 109, but the 6 months prescribed by the "Public Health Act, 1875," § 264. (42 J. P., 792.)

1879.   [1619]
Migotti v. *Colville.* A sentence of one calendar month expires on the day preceding the same numerical day in the following month : if the following month has not sufficient days, then on the last day of the following month—Such a sentence passed on October 31 expires on November 30. (48 L. J., C. P., 695 : L. R., 4 C. P. D., 233 : 40 L. T., 747 : 43 J. P., 620.)

1829.   [1620]
Pellew v. *Wonford Inhabitants.* General principles of computing limits of time named in Statutes. (7 L. J., (o. s.), M. C., 84 : 9 B. & C., 134 : 4 M. & R., 130.)

1891.   [1621]
Radcliffe v. *Bartholomew.* 12 & 13 Vict., c. 92, § 14—Complaint to be made "within one calendar month after the cause . . . shall arise"—Offence committed on May 30; complaint laid on June 30 held laid in time. (61 L. J., M. C., 63 : 65 L. T., 677.) [See notes on this case in 55 J. P., 809, and 56 J. P., 19.]

1858.   [1622]
Reg. v. *Middleton Nuisances Committee.* "Nuisances Removal Act, 1855," § 16 [="Public Health Act, 1875," § 99]—§ 16 refers only to the abatement of Nuisances on private premises. (28 L. J., M. C., 41 : 1 E. & E., 98 : 32 L. T., (o. s.), 124.)

1838.   [1623]
Reg. v. *Shropshire JJ.* Where an act is to be done so many days *at least* before a given event, the time must be reckoned excluding both the day of the act and that of the event itself. (7 L. J., M. C., 56 : 8 A. & E., 173 : 2 N. & P., 286 : 1 W. W. & H., 158.)

1833.   [1624]
Rex v. *Yorkshire, W. R., JJ.* Where a Statute requires "Ten days' notice" of an appeal, one day is to be inclusive and the other exclusive. (4 B. & Ad., 685.)

1859.   [1625]
Simpkin, Ex parte. "Nuisances Removal Act, 1855," § 40 [="Public Health Act, 1875," § 269]—Circumstances under which Sunday will be counted against an appellant who

seeks to enter into a recognizance. (29 L. J., M. C., 23 : 2 E. & E., 392 : [*Reg.* v. *Leicester-shire JJ.*) 1 L. T., 92.)

1859.   [1626]
Swire v. *Burley L. B. H.* "Public Health Act, 1848," § 89 [= "Public Health Act, 1875," §§ 210-11]—Judgment debt due to a Contractor—Six months to be calculated from Judgment, not from date of debt—*Mandamus* to make a Rate granted. (33 L. T., (o. s.), 222 : 23 J. P., 420.)

1821.   [1627]
Zouch v. *Empsey.* "Fourteen days at least" means 14 clear intervening days. (4 B. & Ald., 522.)

74. "TOWN," DEFINITION OF.

1879.   [1628.]
Deards v. *Goldsmith.* The meaning of the word "Town" considered. (40 L. T., 328.)

1848.   [1629]
Elliott v. *South Devon Railway Co.* "Railway Clauses Act, 1845," § 11—"Town" here means a collection of inhabited houses so near each other that they may reasonably be said to be continuous; and the term will include a space of open ground surrounded by houses; and, *Semble*, all open spaces occupied as mere accessories to such houses, although not so surrounded. (17 L. J., Ex., 262 : 2 Ex., 725 : 5 Rail Cas., 500.)

1870.   [1630]
London & South-Western Railway Co. v. *Blackmore.* "Lands Clauses Act, 1845," § 128—Definition of "Town" : Continuous occupancy of ground by houses. (38 L. J., Ch., 713 : L. R., 4 H. L., 610 and 615 : 23 L. T., 504.)

1867.   [1631]
Milton Commissioners v. *Faversham Highway Board.* Local Act—Held that the word "town" meant not as it existed when the Act was passed, but as extended from time to time—A highway is within a town where there is a continuous series of contiguous houses. (10 B. & S., 548, n.: 31 J. P., 341.)

1851.   [1632]
Reg. v. *Charlesworth.* "Beerhouse Act, 1840," § 15—Definition of the word "place" : "An aggregation of houses and inhabitants which has received a separate name"—And this where the "place" in question had no defined boundaries or legal rights of its own. (20 L. J., M. C., 181.)

1851.   [1633]
Reg. v. *Cottle.* Local Act—A "town" is a spot "surrounded by houses so reasonably near that the inhabitants may be fairly said to dwell together"—The fact that the houses are separated by gardens is not of importance. (20 L. J., M. C., 162 : 16 Q. B., 412, 416 : 17 L. T., (o. s.), 15.)

1872.   [1634]
Rice v. *Slee.* "Beerhouse Act, 1840," § 15—Definition of the word "place"—*Reg.* v. *Charlesworth* followed. (L. R., 7 C. P., 378.)

75. "TOWNS POLICE CLAUSES ACT, 1847."

1859.   [1635]
Martin v. *Pridgeon.* "Towns Police Clauses Act, 1847," § 29—"Drunk" and "riotous"—Latter charge not proved—Justices convicted for simple drunkenness under 21 Jas. I., c. 7 [Repealed]—Conviction quashed, the charge being under one Statute and the punishment under another. (28 L. J., M. C., 179: 1 E. & E., 778 : 33 L. T., (o. s.), 119.)

1888.   [1636].
Reg. v. *Long.* "Town Police Clauses Act, 1847," § 28—Foot Pavement blocked up by rowdies walking abreast up and down—Held no offence within this section. (59 L. T., 33 : 52 J. P., 630.)

1891.   [1637]
Reg. v. *Williams.* "Towns Police Clauses Act, 1847," § 28—Four men walking abreast on a footway and causing passengers to go off the footway held not punishable under this section for obstructing the footway—*Reg.* v. *Long* followed. (55 J. P., 406.)

76. TRAMWAYS.

1891.   [1638]
Aldred v.*West Metropolitan Tramway Co.* "Tramways Act, 1870," §§ 28, 29—Where a Tramway Company contracts with a Road Authority for the repair of a road by the latter, the liability for non-repair which under § 28 attaches to the Tramway Co. is transferred to the Road Authority. (L. R. 2 Q. B., 398 : 65 L. T., 138 : 55 J. P., 824.)

1890.   [1639]
Badcock v. *Sankey.* "Tramways Act, 1870": "Public Health Act, 1875 " : "Towns Police Clauses Act, 1847," § 68—Regulation prohibiting overcrowding — An incommoded passenger held entitled to prosecute. (54 J. P., 564.)

1887.   [1640]
Bell v. *Stockton Tramway Co.* The "Highway Act, 1878 " does not apply to steam-engines used on a tramway, although the tramway is laid on a highway. (51 J. P., 804: 3 *Times* L. R., 511.)

1890.   [1641]
Bristol Trams Co. v. *Bristol, Mayor.* An Urban Authority may alter the material used in paving a street without the sanction of a Tramway Company whose lines run along it —§ 33 of the "Tramways Act, 1870," is not applicable to such a case, but § 60 is. (59 L. J., Q. B., 441 : L. R., 25 Q. B. D., 427 : 63 L. T., 177: 55 J. P., 53.)

1886.   [1642]
Davis v. *Loach.* Regulation of Board of Trade prohibiting emission of smoke or steam from Engines used on Tramway so as to constitute any reasonable ground of complaint—Held that emitting smoke was not the less an offence because steam was mixed with it. (51 J. P., 118.)

1884.   [1643]
Devonport, Mayor v. *Plymouth, Devonport, &c.,
Tramways Co.* Special Act—Breach of conditions imposed by Parliament—Mayor held
entitled to sue for Injunction. (52 L. T., 161 :
49 J. P., 405.)

1873.   [1644]
Edinburgh Street Tramways Co. v. *Black.* "Tramways Act, 1870": Special Act—General Act
varied by special Act — Held that the aggrieved parties had no legal redress—When
an Act directs compliance with deposited
plans and sections, they are to be regarded
as embodied in the Act. (L. R., 2 Sc. App.
Cas., 336.)

1885.   [1645]
Hartley v. *Wilkinson.* Board of Trade By-Law
forbidding the emission of steam from Tramway Engines so as to constitute any reasonable ground of complaint—By-Law held
imperative and that proof of the fact of
em ssion sufficed to prove the offence —
Defence that driver could not help what had
happened, held no answer to the charge.
(49 J. P., 726.)

1883.   [1646]
Howitt v. *Nottingham Tramways Co.* "Tramways Act, 1870," §§ 28–9, 55—Where a
Tramway Co. contracts with a Road Authority for latter to repair road for an annual
payment, the Road A. becomes liable for
accidents due to non-repair. (53 L. J.,
Q. B., 21 : L. R., 12 Q. B. D., 16 : 50 L. T., 99.)

1876.   [1647]
Liverpool Tramways Co. v. *Toxteth Park L. B.*
Arbitrary powers to remove a tramway—
Private Act—Injunction to restrain Board
from requiring the removal of the tramway,
refused. (W. N., 1876, p. 145.)

1879.   [1648]
Murdoch v. *London Street Tramways Co.* "Tramways Act, 1870," § 56: Special Act, "London Street Tramways Act, 1877," 40 & 41
Vict. c. ccxix., § 24—Tramway out of repair
—Held that a private individual could not
sue for the penalty. (*Times*, May 30, 1879.)

1887.   [1649]
Over Darwen, Mayor, v. *Lancashire JJ.* (2.).
"Tramways Act, 1870," § 28 : Special Act—
Agreement between Tramway Company and
Road Authority for repair by latter of roads
the liabilities as to which rested upon the
company—Held that such an agreement was
binding upon the County Authority, which
was therefore liable to pay the statutory half
of the expense incurred by the Road Authority, though this Authority was voluntarily
relieving the Tramway Company of some of
its burden. (58 L. T., 51 : 36 W. R., 140.)

1885.   [1650]
Oxford L. B. v. *Oxford Tramways Co.* Action
for specific performance by Company of agreement to relay tramway in a certain manner
to wit, in the centre of a bridge. (*Times*,
Feb. 10, 1885.)

1886.   [1651]
Reg. v. *Croydon & Norwood Tramways Co.* On
non-compliance by Tramway Co. with conditions as to Paving prescribed by Local
Authority, the remedy is a Reference to the
Board of Trade under § 33 of the "Tramways Act, 1870," not a *Mandamus* to remove
the paving. (56 L. J., Q. B., 125 : L. R., 18
Q. B. D., 39 : 56 L. T., 78 : 51 J. P., 420.)

1891.   [1652]
St. Helen's Tramway Co. v. *Wood.* Local Act—
Breach of Board of Trade Regulations as to
Lights on Engine—Company held liable for
Engine-driver's neglect. (60 L. J., M. C.,
141 : 56 J. P., 70.)

1876.   [1653]
St. Luke's Vestry v. *North Metropolitan Tramways
Co.* "Tramways Act, 1870," §§ 26 and 28—
Merely to raise and readjust the level of rails
is not an act needing the "superintendence"
of the Vestry. (L. R., 1 Q. B. D., 760 : 35
L. T., 529 : 40 J. P., 806.)

1883.   [1654]
Smith v. *Butler.* "Tramways Act, 1870," §§ 46,
48—A Local Authority may make By-Laws
which may be valid although not assented to
by the Lessees. (L. R., 16 Q. B. D., 349 : 50
J. P., 260.)

1886.   [1655]
Steward v. *North Metropolitan Tramways Co.*
"Tramways Act, 1870," §§ 28–9—Action
against Company for neglect to repair—More
than 6 months after cause of Action accrued
Company applied to amend their defence by
pleading a contract with Vestry that Vestry
should repair—Held too late because plain-
tiff had thus lost his chance of suing the
Vestry — *Howitt* v. *Nottingham* doubted.
(L. R., 16 Q. B. D., 556 : 54 L. T., 35 : 50
J. P., 324.)

1879.   [1656]
Val de Travers Asphalt Co. v. *London Tramways
Co.* Contract between Asphalt Co. and
Parish to keep road in repair for a term of
years—Road damaged by tramways—Suit
by Asphalt Co. against Tramway Co.—It
being doubtful whether the former body was
entitled to sue, the Court allowed the Parish
to be added as plaintiffs, though the Parish
had not consented, Parish, however, to be
fully indemnified against the costs. (48
L. J., C. P., 312 : 40 L. T., 133 : 43 J. P.,
402.)

1883.   [1657]
Wallasey Tramway Co. v. *Wallasey L. B.* Conviction under Tramway By-Laws held bad
where they had not been confirmed by Q.
Sess. (47 J. P., 821.)

1886.   [1658]
Wolverhampton Tramways Co. v. *Great Western
Railway Co.* "Tramways Act, 1870," § 32—
Railway Company bound by Statute to maintain a highway (being a bridge and its approaches) is a "Road Authority" within
§ 32. (56 L. J., Q. B., 190 : 56 L. T., 892.)

77. TREASURER.

1881.   [1659]
Capital & Counties Bank v. *Ventnor L. B.*
Manager of Branch Bank the Treasurer of
the Local Board—Cheque belonging to Board
passed to Treasurer, who, turning it into
money at his Bank, absconded with the proceeds—Held that Board must bear the loss
on the ground that the cheque and the money
was in Treasurer's hands *quâ* Treasurer—
Verdict for Plaintiffs for amount of cheque
and interest. (At *Nisi Prius.*) (*Times,*
May 26, 1881.)

1829.   [1660]
Delane v. *Hillcoat.* Treasurer to a Board—An
office is an "office of profit" if it is capable
of yielding a profit irrespective of whether
the holder chooses to make it do so or not.
(9 B. & C., 310: 4 M. & R., 175.)

1875.   [1661]
Halifax Union v. *Wheelwright.* Negligence in
drawing Cheques—Alteration of amounts—
Cheques payable to Order—Forged Endorse-
ments—Held that the defendant as Treasurer and Bank Manager, was not liable.
(44 L. J., Ex., 121 : L. R., 10 Ex., 183 : 32
L. T., 802 : 39 J. P., 823.)

1839.   [1662]
Hawkings v. *Newman.* Local Act somewhat
similar to "Public Health Act, 1875," §§ 189
and 192—Clerk's Clerk made Assistant Treasurer—Action for penalties. (8 L. J., Ex.,
82 : 4 M. & W., 613.) [§ 192 as it now
stands probably meets the evasion attempted
in this case.]

1832.   [1663]
Rex v. *Pattison.* 12 Geo. II., c. 29, § 6—*Quo
Warranto*—Appointment of an Alderman as
Treasurer — Held that an appointment of
Treasurer was complete though the appointee
had not given security. (2 L. J., K. B., 33 :
4 B. & Ad., 9.)

78. TURNPIKE.

1840.   [1664]
Northam Bridge Co. v. *London & Southampton
Railway Co.* A road on which Toll-gates
are erected and tolls lawfully taken is a
"Turnpike Road." (9 L. J., Ex., 165 : 6
M. & W., 428 : 1 Rail. Cas., 665.)

1868.   [1665]
Sims v. *Matlock Bath L. B.* "Towns Police
Clauses Act, 1847"—§ 45 applies to offences
on a Turnpike Road within the district under
the Act, although the road is not under the
management of the Local Board. (32 J. P.,
134.)

1858.   [1666]
Swinburne v. *Robinson.* Local Act—Agreement
between 2 Turnpike Trusts for the repair of
a Turnpike Road held not affected by the
adoption of the "Public Health Act, 1848."
(28 L. J., Q. B., 4 : 1 E. & E., 80 : 32 L. T.,
123.)

79. WATER COMPANY, POWERS, &c., OF.

1887.   [1667]
Allan v. *Hamilton Waterworks Commissioners.*
Barracks supplied with water by agreement
—Income Tax held payable on the amount
received for such supply—*Glasgow* v. *Miller*
followed. (51 J. P., 727.)

1877.   [1668]
Atkinson v. *Newcastle & Gateshead Waterworks
Co.* "Waterworks Clauses Act, 1847," § 42
—Water Company held not liable in damages
for not keeping their pipes duly charged
with water, whereby plaintiff's premises
were burnt down—In such a case a Company
is only subject to a penalty for its neglect.
(46 L. J., Ch., 775 : L. R., 2 Ex. D., 441 :
36 L. T., 761 : 42 J. P., 183.)

1892.   [1669]
Barnstaple Water Co. v. *Tucker.* Special Act—
Differential charges in respect of different
levels. (*Times,* May 26, 1892.)

1860.   [1670]
Bayley v. *Wolverhampton Waterworks Co.* Non-
repair of a fire-plug—Horse lamed—Plugs
belonging to a Board, but kept in order by
the Water Company—Held that the Company was liable. (30 L. J., Ex., 57 : 6 H. & N.,
241.)

1881.   [1671]
Bingham v. *Sheffield Waterworks Co.* Dispute as
to whether Company could insist on a certain
scale of payment for baths or that otherwise
their customers must pay by meter—On
plaintiff refusing to erect meter at his own
expense Company gave notice that water
would be cut off—Motion to restrain cutting
off granted till Action tried : meanwhile
account to be kept on Company's scale,
excess to be refunded if decision at trial
adverse. (*Times,* Sept. 12, 1881.) [See Cases
1725 and 1726.]

1856.   [1672]
Blyth v. *Birmingham Waterworks Co.* Bursting
of a fire-plug during an extraordinary frost
—Damage to cellar—Company held not
liable—The frost was severe beyond what
was to be expected and no negligence was
shewn. (25 L. J., Ex., 212 : 11 Ex., 781 :
26 L. T., (o. s.), 261.)

1889.   [1673]
Bristol Water Co. v. *Bristol, Mayor.* Special Act
—Duty to provide water pipes in public
places—Dock quay held to be a "public
place"—Alterations of level having been
made by Corporation, held that Corporation
must pay the cost of consequential alteration
of pipes. (*Times,* June 5, 1889.)

1885.   [1674]
Bristol Waterworks Co. v. *Uren.* Special Act—
"Gross sum assessed to the Poor Rate" held
to mean "gross estimated rental," not "rateable value"—Tap in garden. (54 L. J.,
M. C., 97 : L. R., 15 Q. B. D., 637 : 52 L. T.,
655 : [*Uren* v. *B.*] 49 J. P., 564.)

1888.   [1675]
British Empire Assurance Co. v. Southwark Water Co. " Waterworks Clauses Act, 1847," § 72 —Special Act—Rating of unoccupied houses. (59 L. T., 321: 52 J. P., 758.)

1858.   [1676]
Busby v. Chesterfield Waterworks & Gas-light Co. Supply of water—The use of water for a horse and carriage in the stable of a private Dwelling-house is a "domestic use." (27 L. J., M. C., 174: E. B. & E., 176: 31 L. T., (O. S.), 98.)

1875.   [1677]
Bush v. Trowbridge Waterworks Co. Abstraction of Water—"Waterworks Clauses Act, 1847," § 8—An owner's remedy for loss of water is compensation under the "Lands Clauses Act, 1845," § 68—He cannot compel the purchase of a portion of a stream. (44 L. J., Ch., 645: L. R., 10 Ch. App., 459: 33 L. T., 137: 39 J. P., 660.)

1872.   [1678]
Campbell v. East London Waterworks Co. Statutory duty to supply Water—Failure—Fire—Plea that another fire occurring contemporaneously for which water was being taken was the cause of a deficiency—Plea good. (26 L. T., 475.)

1888.   [1679]
Chelsea Water Co. v. Paulet. "Water Companies Act, 1887," 50 & 51 Vict., c. 21—Where an occupier occupies without title and after notice to quit from his landlord, to cut off water is not an offence. (52 J. P., 724.)

1885.   [1680]
Coleman v. West Middlesex Waterworks Co. Special Act—Domestic supply chargeable at so much per cent.: trade supply by agreement—Public-house—Fact of license in force to be taken into account: also that £7500 had been paid as premium—Latter amount to be capitalised and part of interest to be treated as rent. (54 L. J., M. C., 70 : L. R., 14 Q. B. D., 529 : 52 L. T., 579.)

1884.   [1681]
Colne Valley Water Co. v. Treharne. "Public Health Act, 1875": "Public Health (Water) Act, 1878"—§ 62 of the former Act is not repealed by § 3 of the latter Act: the latter applies to cases which do not come within the former. (50 L. T., 617: 48 J. P., 279.)

1889.   [1682]
Cooke v. New River Co. "Waterworks Clauses Act, 1847," § 53: Special Act—Water wanted to supply a Lift held not wanted for a "Domestic purpose" — *Semble*, that any house in which water is required for Domestic purposes is a "Dwelling-house" within the "New River Act, 1852," § 35, though no person sleeps or takes meals there. (59 L J., Ch., 333: L. R., 14 App. Cas., 698: 61 L. T., 816: 54 J. P., 260.)

1882.   [1683]
Dobbs v. Grand Junction Water Co. Special Acts —Held that the Water Rate was to be computed on the "Rateable Value" of the premises, as appearing from the Poor Rate

Assessment.   (53 L. J., Q. B., 50: L. R., 9 App. Cas., 49: 49 L. T., 541: 48 J. P., 5.)

1892.   [1684]
East London Water Co. v. Kellerman. "Water Companies (Powers) Act, 1887," § 4—The purchaser of the freehold of a dwelling-house is liable for arrears of Water Rate which accrued before the date of purchase. (L. R., 2 Q. B., 72: 67 L. T., 319.)

1886.   [1685]
East London Water Co. v. St. Matthew, Bethnal Green, Vestry. "Waterworks Clauses Act, 1847," §§ 28-34: "Metropolis Water Act, 1881"—Company held entitled to place stop-valves in public footway. (55 L. J., Q. B., 571 : L. R., 17 Q. B. D., 475 : 54 L. T., 919: 50 J. P., 820.)

1892.   [1686]
East Molesey L. B. v. Lambeth Water Co. "Waterworks Clauses Act, 1847," § 28—Injunction granted against Water Company on the ground that the Act contemplated the submission to the Road Authority of a definite "plan," which required approval, and that a mere notice of intention to break up a road was not a "plan"—*Edgware v. Colne Valley* followed. (*Times*, Aug. 9, 1892.)

1877.   [1687]
Edgware Highway Board v. Colne Valley Water Co. "Waterworks Clauses Act, 1847": Local Act—Injunction granted to restrain the opening of roads by the Company before furnishing to the Highway Authority "plans" of the proposed works, although notice had been given—A "plan" held to mean not merely a statement of the general manner in which it was proposed to lay the mains, but something in the nature of a map of the line intended to be followed. (46 L. J., Ch., 889 : W. N., 1877, p. 154.)

1885.   [1688]
Elliott v. Chesterfield Rural S. A. Defendants had purchased a Water Company's rights subject to the Company's Special Act, which contained a condition that a certain minimum quantity of water was always to be left in a brook for the use of plaintiff, a mill-owner—Injunction granted to restrain defendants from doing anything in derogation of plaintiff's rights under the Act. (*Times*, Dec. 4, 1885.)

1883.   [1689]
Ferens v. O'Brien. Water stored in a Water Main may be the subject of a Larceny at Common Law. (52 L. J., M. C., 70 : L. R., 11 Q. B. D., 21 : 47 J. P., 472.)

1889.   [1690]
Folkestone, Mayor v. Downing. Injunction granted to restrain the occupier of a house from breaking up pavement in front thereof in order to attach to his service-pipe certain fittings—Held that such an act would be a trespass on the Corporation's property which only the Waterworks Company had a legal right to commit. (*Times*, Aug. 3, 1889.)

1886. [1691]
Glasgow Corporation Water Commissioners v.
Miller. Profits on Sale of Water by a Public
Body are chargeable with Income Tax. (50
J. P., 503.)

1868. [1692]
Glover v. *East London Water Co.* "Waterworks
Clauses Act, 1847," § 52—House-owner
breaking up Street to allow Company to
connect—Owner held liable for careless re-
instatement of Street—"Pavement" includes
roadway. (17 L. T., 475 : 16 W. R., 310.)

1874. [1693]
Goodson v. *Richardson.* Water-pipes laid in soil
of highway without consent of owner of soil
—Injunction to restrain continuance of pipes
granted, although no inconvenience or damage shewn to arise to owner. (43 L. J.,
Ch., 790 : L. R., 9 Ch. App., 221 : 30 L. T.,
142.)

1861. [1694]
Gwatkin v. *Chepstow Waterworks Co.* Private
Act—Tariff of Charges—Construction of
terms. (25 J. P., 180.)

1889. [1695]
Hancocks v. *Southwark & Vauxhall Water Co.*—
Fire-plug—Liability for bursting of. (W. N.,
1889, p. 198.)

1891. [1696]
Harrison v. *Southwark & Vauxhall Water Co.*
"Waterworks Clauses Act, 1847," § 12—
Sinking of a shaft by pumps, &c., which
caused vibration and temporary annoyance,
held not a legal nuisance—Where a Statute
authorises the execution of certain works,
that authority includes everything reasonably necessary for the execution of the works.
(60 L. J., Ch., 630 : 64 L. T., 864.)

1884. [1697]
Hayward v. *East London Water Co.* "Waterworks Clauses Act, 1847," § 68—Circumstances under which an Injunction to restrain
cutting off of water will or will not be
granted. (54 L. J., Ch., 523 : L. R., 28
Ch. D., 138 : 52 L. T., 175 : 49 J. P., 452.)

1885. [1698]
Henderson v. *Folkestone Waterworks Co.* Water
Rate—Excessive payment. (*Times*, March 9,
1885.)

1860. [1699]
Hildreth v. *Adamson.* "Waterworks Clauses
Act, 1847," § 59 : Local Act—Special charge
for persons keeping horses—Held that a
person who, to evade this charge, habitually
took horses to a public Drinking Fountain,
kept up for a limited purpose, ought to have
been convicted by Justices. (30 L. J., M. C.,
204 : 8 C. B., (N. S.), 587 : 2 L. T., 359.)

1892. [1700]
Hill v. *Wallasey L. B.* "Waterworks Clauses
Act, 1847," § 29 : "Public Health Act,
1875," §§ 4, 16, 54, 57—A Local Board has no
power to break up a private road to lay water
mains, without the consent of the owner.
(L. R., 3 Ch., 117 : 67 L. T., 49 : 56 J. P., 469.)

1890. [1701]
Holliday v. *Wakefield, Mayor.* "Waterworks
Clauses Act, 1847"—Apprehended injury to
mines—Compensation held not payable in
respect of coal in certain positions in a mine.
(60 L. J., Ch., 361 : L. R., 1 App. Cas., 81 :
64 L. T., 1 : 55 J. P., 325.)

1887. [1702]
Jackson v. *Farnham Water Co.* A water company contracting to supply water only
engages to do its best, and in the absence of
proof that it failed to do its best the consumer has no remedy for the supply being
short. (*Times*, May 19, 1887.)

1886. [1703]
Kidwelly, Mayor v. *Richardson.* Pipes laid to
receive a water supply and used for several
years — Negociations with landowner for
lease broken off, and supply stopped—Held
that Corporation had acquired no right to
be deemed perpetual licensees, and had no
redress for their outlay having been rendered
nugatory. (*Times*, Feb. 4, 1886.)

1892. [1704]
Kirkleatham L. B. v. *Stockton & Middlesborough
Water Board.* Circumstances under which
a Water Authority will be restrained from
cutting off the supply to a Local Board
within the Water District. (*Times*, Feb. 27,
1892.)

1885. [1705]
Lea v. *Abergavenny Improvement Commissioners.*
"Waterworks Clauses Act, 1847," § 68 :
Special Act—Justices may determine a dispute as to annual value of premises when
hearing summons to enforce Rate — Two
separate proceedings unnecessary. (55 L. J.,
M. C., 25 : L. R., 16 Q. B. D., 18 : 53 L. T.,
728 : 50 J. P., 165.)

1878. [1706]
Leamington Corporation v. *Oldham.* Contract for
the supply to a town of filtered water—Neglect to filter some of the water so supplied—
Action properly commenced, and defendants
to pay the costs. (*Times*, February 22, 1878.)

1888. [1707]
Lewis v. *Swansea, Mayor.* Local Acts—Water
Supply powers conferred upon Corporation
with the duty of sending a minimum daily
quantity down certain streams for the use of
Riparian owners—Default—Action for penalties—Held that though any owner could
proceed, only one penalty could be recovered
in respect of each day's default. (*Times*,
July 24, 1888.)

1881. [1708]
Liskeard Union v. *Liskeard Waterworks Co.*
Guardians held entitled to demand a supply
of Water for their workhouse as for a
"domestic use," the workhouse being a
"house," and the officers and inmates a
"family" within the special Act. (L. R.,
7 Q. B. D., 505 : 45 J. P., 780.)

1875. [1709]
Low v. *Lambeth Water Co.* Bill to restrain the
defendant Company from cutting off water
used in a garden—Bill dismissed, the proper

remedy being at Law, and watering a garden not a " domestic purpose." (*Times*, July 7, 1875.)

1889.   [1710]
M'Colla v. *Clacton-on-Sea Gas Co.* Supply—Remedy available to consumers for withholding. (5 *Times* L. R., 690.)

1877.   [1711]
Metropolitan B. W. v. *New River Co.* Special Act, 15 & 16 Vict., c. clx., § 41—Claim of Board to be supplied at statutory low rate with water for watering streets—Judgment for the Company. (37 L. T., 124 : 41 J. P., 790.)

·1886.   [1712]
Milnes v. *Huddersfield, Mayor.* A Water Company is not liable for injury to the health of a customer merely because its water, otherwise pure and wholesome, is of such a nature as to take up an abnormal quantity of lead in passing through leaden pipes. (56 L. J., Q. B., 1 : L. R., 11 App. Cas., 511 : 55 L. T., 617 : 50 J. P., 676.)

1875.   [1713]
New River Co. v. *Mather.* " Waterworks Clauses Act, 1847," § 68 : Special Act—Held that as the " annual value " was disputed, no Court had jurisdiction until 2 Justices had determined the value — Decision reversed. (44 L. J., M. C., 105 : L. R., 10 C. P., 442 : 32 L. T., 658 : 39 J. P., 614.)

1882.   [1714]
Newhaven Water Co. v. *Newhaven L. B.* " Public Health Act, 1875," § 52—Action to restrain the Board from constructing Waterworks—Company formed, but no works in operation —The evidence showing a *bonâ fide* probability that the Company would be able to fulfil its promises, Injunction granted. (*Times*, Jan. 21, 1882.)

1883.   [1715]
Ossalinsky (Countess) and the Manchester Corporation, In re. Compulsory purchase of land for Waterworks—Principles of valuation—An arbitrator may take into consideration as an element of value, the natural adaptability of the land, but not the increased value in consequence of the powers conferred by the special Act. (*Loc. Gov. Chron.*, June 9, 1883.)

1868.   [1716]
Piercy v. *Harding.* " Waterworks Clauses Act, 1847," § 42—A Water Company is liable to a penalty for not keeping fire-plugs supplied at high pressure even though no notice to do so may have been served on Company. (32 J. P., 630.)

1881.   [1717]
Piercy v. *Pope.* " Waterworks Clauses Act, 1847," § 59 : *Ib.* 1863, § 20—Water drawn from tap in an empty house by daughter of person paying the Water-rent and therefore entitled to draw in his own house but not in an empty house—Such an offence (if an offence at all) held not within § 59. (45 L. T., 477 : 46 J. P., 102.)

1885.   [1718]
Preston, Mayor v. *Fullwood L. B.* Corporation

supplying water outside their District, without Parliamentary Powers—Breaking up of streets held *ultra vires*. (53 L. T., 718 : 50 J. P., 228.)

1861.   [1719]
Purnell v. *Wolverhampton Waterworks Co.* Special Act antecedent to the " Waterworks Clauses Act, 1847 " : Second Special Act—Water at high-pressure held not obligatory. (10 C. B., (N. S.), 576 : 4 L. T., 513.)

1886.   [1720]
Reg. v. *Wells Water Co.* " Waterworks Clauses Act, 1847 "—A water company is not bound under § 38 to provide a main sufficient for a fire-plug, even though Justices decide that there ought to be a fire-plug at the *locus in quo*. (55 L. T., 188 : [*W.* v. *W.*] 51 J. P., 135.)

1886.   [1721]
Reg. v. *Wexford, Mayor.* " Public Health (Ireland) Act, 1878," §. 227 [= § 277 of English Act of 1875]—This section held to remove the limit fixed by a Provisional Order of prior date for a Rate to pay off instalments of borrowed money—The term for repayment being still current, such a Rate is not retrospective. (18 L. R., Ir., 119.)

1885.   [1722]
Richards v. *West Middlesex Water Co.* Special Acts—Power to distrain for non-payment of Water Rate held not taken away. (54 L. J., Q. B., 551 : L. R., 15 Q. B. D., 660 : 49 J. P., 631.)

1876.   [1723]
Richmond Water Co. & Southwark Water Co. v. *Richmond Vestry.* " Public Health Act, 1875," § 52—Failure of the Water Company of the district and transfer to an outside Company —Held that the first Company being unable, and the second Company not having Parliamentary authority to supply water, neither was entitled to the privilege accorded by § 52. (45 L. J., Ch. 441 : L. R., 3 Ch. D., 82 : 34 L. T., 480)

1888.   [1724]
Ridge v. *Midland R. Co.* It is not every disagreeable smell that gives rise to an Action of wrong and its consequences—The determining question is : Will the supposed wrongful proceeding abridge and diminish seriously the ordinary comfort of existence to the occupiers whatever their rank or state of health ?—When a person empties foul water into a stream reference will be had in an Action against him, to the proportion and effect of such discharge. (53 J. P., 55.)

1880.   [1725]
Sheffield Water Co. v. *Bingham.* (1). " Sheffield Waterworks Act, 1853," §§ 79, 81.—Special provisions as to Water used for baths—The expression " Domestic purposes " held under the circumstances not to include baths. (L. R., 25 Ch. D., 446, n.)

1883.   [1726]
Sheffield Water Co. v. *Bingham* (2). " Waterworks Clauses Act, 1863," § 14—Company bound to supply by measure—Some automatic and self-registering meter or other instrument

must be used, provided by consumer at his own expense—A mere expedient for guessing a quantity of water, such as painting a line round a bath, held not sufficient—*Sheffield* v. *Carter* distinguished. (52 L. J., Ch. D., 624 : L. R., 25 Ch. D., 413 : 48 L. T., 604.)

1882. [1727]
Sheffield Water Co. v. *Carter.* Powers of Company as to cutting off supply—Failure of occupier to pay or tender Rate in advance. (51 L. J., M. C., 97 : L. R., 8 Q. B. D., 632 : 46 J. P., 548.)

1879. [1728]
Sheffield Water-works Proprietors v. *Wilkinson.* "Waterworks Clauses Act, 1847," § 74—Water cut off because late tenant in arrear—Proceedings by new tenant to compel the Company to make a new connection and resume supply — Judgment for Company, there being no such obligation on Company as the plaintiff contended—Held that Company had no right to refuse to allow the restoration of the connecting pipe and the supply of water till the bygone Rates were paid. (48 L. J., C. P., 145 : L. R., 4 C. P. D., 410 : 41 L. T., 251 : 43 J. P., 703.)

1888. [1729]
Slater v. *Burnley, Mayor.* "Waterworks Clauses Act, 1847": Local Act—"Annual value" Principle of assessment—Water rent voluntarily (but ignorantly) paid on a wrong basis, and therefore overpaid—Held that the Consumer could recover back the amount so overpaid. (59 L. T., 636 : 53 J. P., 70 : and see p. 535 of same vol.)

1883. [1730]
Smith v. *Birmingham Mayor.* Special Act—Water Rates to be calculated on "annual rent"—This held to mean "gross estimated rental" — Deductions for compounded Rates. (52 L. J., M. C., 81 : L. R., 11 Q. B. D., 195 : 49 L. T., 25 : 47 J. P., 615.) [But see *Dobbs* v. *Grand Junction Co.*]

1886. [1731]
South Staffordshire Waterworks Co. v. *Mason.* "Waterworks Clauses Act, 1847"—Deposit of plans pursuant to §§ 19-20 a condition precedent to a right to support under § 28—Where this not done no right to recover for injury done to Water mains by working of Minerals. (56 L. J., Q. B., 255 : 57 L. T., 116.)

1884. [1732]
Southend Water Co. v. *Howard.* "Public Health Act, 1875, § 62—Non-compliance of house-owner with notice from Local Authority to obtain a supply of water—Owner held liable, and that it was not a condition precedent that the works necessary to take water into the house should have been executed by plaintiff. (53 L. J., Q. B. D., 354 : L. R., 13 Q. B. D., 215 : 48 J. P., 469.)

1889. [1733]
Southwark & Vauxhall Water Co. v. *Dickenson.* "Southwark, &c., Water Act, 1852," §§ 53, 56, 57—There is nothing herein to preclude a Water Company from entering into a contract for the supply of Water for domestic purposes. (5 *Times* L. R., 251.)

1888. [1734]
Stevens v. *Barnet Gas & Water Co.* "Waterworks Clauses Act, 1847," § 68 : Special Act—"Annual value" held equivalent to "annual rack-rent," and owner occupying his own house held liable to pay Water Rates on its "gross estimated rental." (57 L. J., M. C., 82 : 36 W. R., 924.) [Cf. *Warrington* v. *Longshaw.*]

1888. [1735]
Styles v. *East London Waterworks Co.* Negligence—Liability—Defective state of Water-plug. (4 *Times* L. R., 190.)

1879. [1736]
Tatton v. *Staffordshire Potteries Waterworks Co.* "Waterworks Clauses Act, 1847," § 6—Stream fouled by Water Co.—Business of plaintiff, an owner of Dye-works, injured, whereby the saleable value thereof was depreciated—Plaintiff held entitled to recover damages for weekly loss of profits, but not for amount of depreciation as shewn by result of sale. (44 J. P., 106.)

1890. [1737]
Ward v. *Folkestone Water Co.* Local Act—A "screw-down" valve is not an apparatus for regulating the supply of water to a house the non-provision of which justifies a Water Company in cutting off the supply. (59 L. J., M. C., 65 : L. R., 24 Q. B. D., 334 : 62 L. T., 321 : 54 J. P., 628.)

1882. [1738]
Warrington Water Co. v. *Longshaw.* "Waterworks Clauses Act, 1847," § 68 : Special Act—Water Rates are payable on the "Rateable Value" of the premises, and not on the "Gross Estimated Rental." (51 L. J., Q. B., 498 : L. R., 9 Q. B. D., 145 : 46 L. T., 815 : 46 J. P., 773.)

1883. [1739]
Wearer v. *Cardiff Corporation.* Local Act — Bath in private house held used for a "Domestic" purpose, and therefore not subject to a special charge leviable on "baths, wash-houses, or public purposes." (48 L. T., 906 : 47 J. P., 599.)

1885. [1740]
West Middlesex Water Co. v. *Coleman.* Premium paid for lease may be taken into account in fixing annual value of premises. (54 L. J., M. C., 70 : L. R., 14 Q. B. D., 529 : 52 L. T., 578 : 49 J. P., 341.)

1889. [1741]
West Middlesex Water Co. v. *Tappenden.* Special Acts—Held that under the circumstances the Company was not bound to provide a constant supply. (*Times*, May 18, 1889.)

1884. [1742]
Whitehaven Union v. *Cockermouth & Workington Joint Water Committee.* Contract to "supply" water by meter—Maximum quantity specified—Held that no particular pressure was to be understood. (*Times*, April 25, 1884.)

1884. [1743]
Whiting v. *East London Water Co.* "Waterworks Clauses Act, 1847," § 68—Dispute as to Rate — Justices must define "annual

value" before occupier can sue for cutting off and overcharge. (1 Cab. & Ellis, 331.)

1890.   **[1744]**
Wolverhampton Corporation v. Bilston Commissioners. "Public Health Act, 1875," § 52— Corporation held to be undertakers supplying water for their own profit—Injunction granted against defendants seeking to set up a competitive supply. (L. R., 1 Ch., 315.)

1888.   **[1745]**
Yeadon L. B. and Yeadon Water Co. Arbitration, In re. "Public Health Act, 1875" § 52— Deficient supply of water—Notice of Arbitration—Umpire's award—Award held duly made although larger in scope than Water Company intended. (58 L. J., Ch. 563 : L. R., 41 Ch. D., 52 : 60 L. T., 550.)

80. WATER, POLLUTION OF.

(i.) BY GAS.

1860.   **[1746]**
Hipkins v. Birmingham & Staffordshire Gas-light Co. Special Act—"Suffer to flow"—Pollution of well by percolation of Gas washings —Company held liable, though such percolation was due to the working of a mine by strangers. (30 L. J., Ex., 60 : 6 H. & N., 250 : * 1 L. T., 303.)

1874.   **[1747]**
Millington v. Griffiths. Pollution of well by Gas Company—Where noxious matter percolates through soil from Gas-works, such percolation renders Gas Owners liable to penalty prescribed by "Lighting Act, 1833," § 50—A well does not cease to be entitled to protection merely because out of use—Judgment for plaintiff. (30 L. T., 65.)

1863.   **[1748]**
Parry v. Croydon Commercial Gas & Coke Co. "Gas-works Clauses Act, 1847," § 21. (15 C. B., (N. S.), 568.) [Part of decision rendered nugatory by "Public Health Act, 1875," § 310.]

1834.   **[1749]**
Rex v. Medley. Pollution of River by Gas-washings—Indictment against the chairman and officers of a Company—Verdict of "Guilty" against several of the defendants. (6 C. & P., 292.)

1880.   **[1750]**
Stansfield v. Yeadon Gas Co. "Public Health Act, 1875," § 68—The object of this section is to protect any water from being fouled, whether running or not—The "stream" need not be vested in one person—Any one of several riparian owners may sue for the penalty, but the penalty can only be recovered once, and that by the person who first obtains judgment. (2 *Municip. Corp. Assoc. Month. Circular,* 289.)

(ii.) BY SEWAGE.

1872.   **[1751]**
Askew v. Ulverstone L. B. Pollution of Stream by Sewage—Complaint not supported by the evidence—Injunction refused, without costs. (W. N., 1872, p. 81.)

1873.   **[1752]**
A.-G. v. Aylesbury L. B. H. Pollution of Stream by Sewage—Injunction granted and temporarily suspended. (*Times*, Dec. 18, 1873.)

1874.   **[1753]**
A.-G. v. Barnsley, Mayor. Pollution of River by Sewage—Offensive smells in hot weather —Case fully established—Injunction granted —*Per* James, L.J.: "There could be no prescriptive right to justify a public nuisance." (W. N., 1874, p. 37.)

1876.   **[1754]**
A.-G. v. Basingstoke, Mayor. Pollution of disused canal by Corporation sewage—Injunction granted, though Corporation derived no advantage from the practice which caused the nuisance. (45 L. J., Ch., 726 : 24 W. R., 817.)

1871.   **[1755]**
A.-G. v. Birmingham Council (2). Nuisance— Sewage—Injunction granted, and considerable suspension of it refused because Council had been remiss in adopting remedial expedients. (4 K. & J., 528 : 24 L. T., 224 : 19 W. R., 561.)

1881.   **[1756]**
A.-G. v. Birmingham, Mayor. Decree made restraining the pollution of a stream by sewage, but its operation suspended for 5 years to permit remedial works—On a different Authority being created, with a different area, but clothed with the powers, &c., of the Authority against which the Decree had been originally made, held, that the Bill could not be amended after final Decree by adding the new Authority as parties, and that the Decree could only be enforced by an Action brought for the purpose. (L. R., 15 Ch. D., 423 : 43 L. T., 77.) A fresh Action having been brought (*nom. A.-G. v. Birmingham, Tame, & Rea Drainage Board*) a demurrer was allowed, the proper remedy being an entirely fresh Action on fresh proof of nuisance— § 275 of the "Public Health Act, 1875," only relates to obligations under the Act, and does not extend to independent proceedings or Decrees or Orders made thereunder—The Injunction granted in the original suit would not run with the land so as to affect a transferee or purchaser. (50 L. J., Ch., 786 : L. R., 17 Ch. D., 685 : 44 L. T., 906 : 46 J. P., 36.)

1884.   **[1757]**
A.-G. v. Burslem L. B. Pollution of stream by sewage—Injunction followed by Order for sequestration—Latter Order not to be enforced for 6 months—Orders so conditioned disapproved of by the Court. (*Times*, Feb. 16, 1884.)

1872.   **[1758]**
A.-G. v. Castleford L. B. Suit to restrain pollution of River—Proof of plaintiff's title— Practice—Affidavits as to documents. (27 L. T., 644 : 21 W. R., 117.)

1874.   **[1759]**
A.-G. v. Cockermouth L. B. Information by the Attorney-General and Bill by one Local

Board against another—Pollution of river by sewage—Bill dismissed, the evidence of nuisance being insufficient, but Injunction granted on the information, on ground of infringement of 24 & 25 Vict , c. 61 [="Public Health Act, 1875," §§ 16-17]. (44 L. J., Ch. 118: L. R., 18 Eq., 172: 30 L. T., 590: 38 J. P., 660.)

1868.   [1760]
A.-G. v. Colney Hatch Lunatic Asylum. Nuisance from overflow of sewage—Principles on which the Court will proceed when applied to for an Injunction—If a public Body with Statutory Powers for a particular obj. ct exercises its Powers so as to injure property it is responsible for the injury unless the act done was absolutely necessary to carry out the Statutory duty. (38 L. J., Ch., 265 : L. R., 4 Ch. App., 146 : 19 L. T., 708.)

1875.   [1761]
A.-G. v. Darlington, Mayor. Pollution of river by refuse from sewage deodorisation works—Injunction granted. (*Times,* March 24, 1875.) Extension of time allowed. (*Times,* Nov. 26, 1875.) Further extension allowed. (*Times,* May 26, 1876.)

1881.   [1762]
A.-G. v. Dorking Union. Pollution of Watercourse by town Sewage flowing through certain Sewers made by a Highway Board—Neglect of Sanitary Authority to provide drainage not a ground of Action by an individual for damages or an Injunction—*Remedy—Mandamus—Glossop v. Heston L. B.* followed. (*Times,* Jan. 25, 1881.) Subsequently, on a Local Board being established for the District, and an Appeal against the above decision being lodged, an application was made to the Court that the Local Board should be added as defendants—Application refused—New proceedings must be taken if desired—*A.-G. v. Birmingham, Mayor,* followed. (*Times,* May 26, 1881.)

1882.   [1763]
A.-G. v. Dorking Guardians. Action by Landowner to restrain pollution of stream by sewage where defendants neglected to take any remedial measures—Judgment for defendants—*Glossop v. Heston* followed. (51 L. J., Ch., 585 : L. R., 20 Ch. D., 595 : 46 L. T., 573.)

1870.   [1764]
A.-G. v. Gee. Nuisance—Pollution of Stream by Sewage—Injury trifling—Injunction refused—Consideration of circumstances under which the Court will interfere. (L. R., 10 Eq., 131 : 23 L. T., 299 : 34 J. P., 596.)

1875.   [1765]
A.-G. v. Hackney B. W. Pollution of watercourse by sewage—Defence that the watercourse was a sewer held bad—Injunction. (44 L. J., Ch., 545 : L. R., 20 Eq., 626 : 33 L. T., 245.)

1869.   [1766]
A.-G. v. Halifax Corporation. Nuisance—Pollution of stream—Injunction granted. (39 L. J., Ch., 129 : 21 L. T., 52 : [Costs] L. R., 12 Eq., 262.) [It was intimated by the

Court in *North Staffordshire Railway* v. *Tunstall* that the Order here made would be treated as a "Model Order."]

1865.   [1767]
A.-G. v. Kingston-on-Thames, Mayor. Nuisance by discharge of Sewage into a river—Information dismissed without prejudice to a future application. (34 L. J., Ch., 481 (*bis*): 12 L. T., 665 : 29 J. P., 515.)

1870.   [1768]
A.-G. v. Leeds, Mayor. Local Act—Pollution of river by sewage—If a nuisance is proved the relators must be protected whatever may be the consequences—Injunction granted. (39 L. J., Ch., 254 : L. R., 5 Ch. App., 583 : 22 L. T., 330.)

1856.   [1769]
A.-G. v. Luton L. B. H. Pollution of River—Increase of population no answer—Injunction granted. (27 L. T., (o. s.), 212 : 20 J. P., 163.)

1863.   [1770]
A.-G. v. Metropolitan B. W. Pollution of River—Statutory powers — Modified Injunction granted—General remarks on the dealings of public Bodies with individuals affected, as regards courtesy in correspondence, &c. (1 H. & M., 298 : 9 L. T., 139.)

1875.   [1771]
A.-G. v. Newcastle-under-Lyne Corporation. Non-compliance with an Injunction issued 16 years previously to stop flow of sewage—Sequestration issued. (*Times,* Dec. 10, 1875.)

1866.   [1772]
A.-G. v. Richmond. "Nuisances Removal Acts" [Repealed]—Highway Board the Local Authority—Pollution of a brook—Injunction granted. (35 L. J., Ch., 597 : L. R., 2 Eq., 306 : 14 L. T., 398 : 30 J. P., 708.)

1875.   [1773]
A.-G. v. Tunstall L. B. H. Pollution of river by sewage outfall works—Injunction. (W. N., 1875, p. 66.)

1878.   [1774]
A.-G. v. Walthamstow L. B. Information filed at the relation of an adjacent Local Authority to restrain the pollution of a brook—Injunction granted—On further default after 3 years in remedying nuisance Sequestration applied for. (W. N., 1878, p. 90.)

1885.   [1775]
Ballard v. Tomlinson. Water in well polluted by sewage sent into another well 99 yards distant—Held that though the pollution resulted from underground percolation there was a remedy at Law. (54 L. J., Ch., 454 : L. R., 29 Ch. D., 115 : 52 L. T., 942: 49 J. P., 692.)

1862.   [1776]
Bidder v. Croydon L. B. Pollution of river by sewage imperfectly deodorised—Fish killed—Injunction granted. (6 L. T., 778.)

1871.   [1777]
Birt v. Monmouthshire Sewers Commissioners Pollution of stream by refuse—Claim of user for 60 years—Conviction quashed, it not being clear that there was a public nuisance. (35 J. P., 372.)

1873.   [1778]
Broughton v. *Crewe L. B.* Pollution of Stream—
Injunction granted, but time allowed and
then extended. (*Times*, Nov. 26, 1873.)

1864.   [1779]
Cator v. *Lewisham B. W.* Pollution of Stream
by new system of Sewers—Action for Nuis-
sance held maintainable — No remedy by
compensation. (34 L. J., Q. B., 74 : 5 B. & S.,
115 : 13 L. T., 212.)

1889.   [1780]
Chapman v. *Auckland Union.* A Sanitary Authority polluted a stream with sewage causing a
nuisance to a Riparian owner—On an Action
for an Injunction the Judge, thinking the
nuisance to be one not likely to recur except
in very dry seasons, awarded damages in lieu
of an Injunction—Held that this was legal
though no notice of action had been given
pursuant to the "Public Health Act, 1875,"
§ 264. (58 L. J., Q. B., 504 : L. R., 23
Q. B. D., 294 : 61 L. T., 446 : 53 J. P., 820.)

1883.   [1781]
Charles v. *Finchley L. B.* Action against Board
for not prosecuting a third party polluting a
stream held maintainable, the third party
being under contract with the Board, and
having failed to comply with the conditions
of his contract—*Glossop* v. *Heston* and other
analogous cases distinguished. (52 L. J.,
Ch., 554 : L. R., 23 Ch. D., 767 : 48 L. T.,
569 : 47 J. P., 791.)

1888.   [1782]
Clarke v. *Somerset Drainage Commissioners.* A
prescriptive right to pollute a stream with
refuse of one sort does not render lawful another sort of pollution caused by a different
method of carrying on an offensive trade—
Conviction affirmed. (52 J. P., 308.)

1867.   [1783]
Crossley v. *Lightowler.* Nuisance—Prescriptive
right to pollute a Stream—Rights of Riparian
Proprietors generally—Injunction granted—
A nuisance cannot be justified by the existence of other nuisances of a similar character.
(36 L. J., Ch., 584 : L. R., 2 Ch. App., 478 :
16 L. T., 438.)

1888.   [1784]
Downing v. *Falmouth Sewage Board.* Pollution
of water by sewage—Practice—Affidavits as
to documents. (58 L. T., 296.)

1866.   [1785]
Feilden v. *Blackburn Corporation.* Pollution of
river by sewage — Injunction granted.
(W. N., 1866, p. 256.)

1884.   [1786]
Fletcher v. *Bealey.* Apprehended pollution of
stream by Alkali Works—In order to maintain a *Quia timet* Action to restrain an apprehended injury plaintiff must prove imminent
danger of a substantial kind, or that the
apprehended injury, if it does come, will be
irreparable. (54 L. J., Ch., 424 : L. R., 28
Ch. D., 688 : 52 L. T., 541.)

1890.   [1787]
Giffard v. *Wolverhampton Corporation.* Sewage
farm — Effluent water impure and trout

stream polluted—Prolonged correspondence
and legal proceedings—Sequestration granted
but suspended for 6 months. (*Times*, May
2, 1890.)

1879.   [1788]
Glossop v. *Heston and Isleworth L. B.* Pollution of
stream by sewage, numerous houses having
been built for the sewage of which no provision had been made by the Local Authority—
Action held not maintainable—Remedy, Pre-
rogative *Mandamus*—Neglect by a Board to
perform a public Statutory duty does not
entitle every individual damnified thereby to
bring an Action for damages or to obtain a
mandatory injunction—But where Board has
done acts to create or increase a nuisance the
Board is liable at Common Law. (49 L. J.,
Ch., 89 : L. R., 12 Ch. D., 102 : 40 L. T., 736 :
44 J. P., 36.)

1866.   [1789]
Goldsmid v. *Tunbridge Wells Improvement Commissioners.* Nuisance—Sewage—A prospective nuisance is not in itself a ground for
interference, but if some present nuisance
exists the Court will consider its probable
increase ; a prospective right to pollute a
stream can only be acquired by the continuance of a perceptible amount of injury for
20 years—*Per* Turner, L.J. : "It is not in
every case of Nuisance that the Court will
interfere. I think that it ought not to do so
where the injury is merely temporary and
trifling." (35 L. J., Ch., 382 : L. R., 1 Ch.
App., 349 : 14 L. T., 154 : 30 J. P., 419.)

1858.   [1790]
Higgs v. *Godwin.* Patent for Utilization of Sewage—Where a Local Board uses a patent
process not for commercial profit, but merely
for the purification of sewage water, it is not
necessarily guilty of an infringement of the
patent. (27 L. J., Q. B., 421 : E. B. & E.,
529 : 31 L. T., (o. s.), 196.)

1873.   [1791]
Isle of Wight Oyster Fishery Co. v. *Newport, Mayor.*
Sewage Outfall—Alleged injury to oyster
beds—Injunction refused. (*Times*, Nov. 21,
1873.)

1885.   [1792]
Jersey (Earl of) v. *Woodward.* Stream polluted
by sewage—Injunction granted to restrain
any more sewer connections being made
whereby the pollution would be increased.
(*Times*, Jan. 27, 1885.)

1892.   [1793]
Kirkheaton L. B. v. *Ainley* (2). "Public Health
Act, 1875," § 21 : "Rivers Pollution Act,
1876," § 3 : "County Courts Act, 1888," §§
120, 124—A person who permits sewage from
his premises to drain into a natural watercourse which has become a sewer under the
"Public Health Act" and which sewer pol-
lutes a stream is not to be deemed a person
polluting the stream within the "Rivers
Pollution Act." (L. R., 2 Q. B., 274 : 66 L. T.,
340 : 56 J. P., 374.)

1884.   [1794]
Lea Conservancy Board v. *Hertford, Mayor.* Se-

wage disposed of in a way and under conditions prescribed by Parliament—The Parliamentary conditions having been complied with, Action held not maintainable, although some evidence of nuisance was forthcoming. (1 Cab. & Ellis, 290: 48 J. P., 628.)

1867.   [1795]
Lillywhite v. *Trimmer.* Nuisance—Pollution of Stream by Sewage—Injunction refused, the plaintiff not having sustained material injury —Consideration of the circumstances under which the Court will interfere. (36 L. J., Ch., 525: 16 L. T., 318.)

1877.   [1796]
Londonderry (Marquis of) v. *Rhoseydol Lead Mining Co.* Fish poisoned by refuse from Lead Works—Injunction granted. (*Times,* Aug. 3, 1877.)

1857.   [1797]
Manchester, Sheffield, & Lincolnshire Railway Co. v. *Worksop B. H.* Pollution of Canal by sewage—Injunction granted—Claim under Statute to exclusive rights of water. (26 L. J., Ch., 345: 23 Bea., 198: 29 L. T., (o. s.), 6.)

1884.   [1798]
Marsh v. *Sheffield Guardians.* Injunction to stop flow of sewage having been disregarded—Sequestration ordered—The Court will be lenient in stopping the misuse of old sewers, but peremptory in dealing with nuisances from newly constructed sewers. (*Times,* Aug. 9, 1884.)

1870.   [1799]
North Staffordshire Railway Co. v. *Tunstall L. B. H.* Pollution of River by sewage—Injunction. (39 L. J., Ch., 131.)

1891.   [1800]
Ogilvie v. *Blything Union.* "Public Health Act, 1875," § 13, &c.—Nuisance from sewage—§ 13 only confers on a Local Authority restricted rights of ownership—Held under the circumstances that the Local Authority had done its best, and that the Action could not be maintained—*A.-G.* v. *Dorking* [No. 1763, *ante*] followed. (67 L. T., 18.)

1855.   [1801]
Oldaker v. *Hunt.* "Public Health Act, 1848," §§ 45 and 46 [= "Public Health Act, 1875," §§ 15-16, 18-19, &c.]—Pollution of River by Sewage—Interference with watering-place for cattle—Right of fishery—Injunction granted. (19 Bea., 485 : affirmed on appeal; 6 De G. M. & G., 376 : 1 Jur., (N. s.), 785.)

1875.   [1802]
Richmond Vestry v. *Thames Conservators.* Local Act—"Continuing offence"—Conviction for sending sewage into the Thames held good. (*Times,* April 26, 1875.)

1885.   [1803]
Selous v. *Croydon R. S. A.* Pollution of stream by sewage—Sequestration—Costs—Practice. (53 L. T., 209.)

1884.   [1804]
Snow v. *Whitehead.* Escape of water from cellar of one house to cellar of adjoining house—Owner of former house held liable for damage

done. (53 L. J., Ch. D., 885; L. R., 27 Ch. D., 588; 51 L. T., 253.)

1865.   [1805]
Spokes v. *Banbury L. B.* Pollution of River by Sewage —Injunction — Breach —Sequestration issued for contempt in disobeying Order by alleging that compliance was practically impossible. (35 L. J., Ch., 105 : L. R., 1 Eq., 42 : 13 L. T., 428 and 453.)

1877.   [1806]
Sutton v. *Barnet L. B.* Undertaking on part of a Board to discontinue sending sewage into a stream—Breach—Application that a sequestration should issue and certain members of the Board be committed to prison—Sequestration granted with costs against the Board, but committal refused, with costs against the plaintiff. (W. N., 1877, p. 167.)

1884.   [1807]
Taylor v. *Barnet Union.* Pollution of watercourse by sewage flowing from Sewage Works and tanks—No real effort having been made to mitigate the nuisance, Injunction granted, framed to extend not only to defendants' own acts but to acts permitted by them. (*Times,* Feb. 16, 1884.)

1885.   [1808]
Taylor v. *Friern Barnet L. B.* Rural Sanitary Authority replaced by Local Board—Injunction granted promptly against new Body to restrain pollution of stream by sewage although the old Body had commenced the mischief. (*Times,* Jan. 13, 1885.)

1885.   [1809]
Thames Conservators v. *Chertsey R. S. A.*   29 & 30 Vict. c. 89, § 65—Pollution of river by Sewage—A Notice of complaint should specify the particular drain complained of—Conviction quashed. (49 J. P., 404.)

1890.   [1810]
Warwick and Birmingham Canal v. *Burman.* Pollution of stream by sewage of Local Board —Mandamus or Injunction—Damages held recoverable. (63 L. T., 670.)

1867.   [1811]
Womersley v. *Church.* Nuisance—Pollution of Well by percolation from Cesspool—Injunction granted—Though owner not entitled to water till he gets it, yet having got it he is entitled to have it protected. (17 L. T., 190.)

1875.   [1812]
Wood v. *Harrogate Commissioners.* Pollution of Stream by Sewage—Agreement for compromise of a former suit—Breach thereof—Injunction granted—Non-compliance therewith—Sequestration issued. (W. N., 1874, p. 225 : *Times,* Dec. 10, 1875.)

(iii.) VARIOUS.

1880.   [1813]
Aspinall v. *Mitchell.* Pollution of a stream by refuse from a Paper Mill—Injunction granted. (*Times,* July 28, 1880.)

1887.   [1814]
Blair v. *Deakin.* Stream polluted by several manufacturers—On action by riparian owner

against one manufacturer—Defence set up that his share was infinitesimal—Held, no defence, for owner had tho right to take the manufacturers in detail and prevent each from sending into the stream his contribution. (57 L. T., 522 : 52 J. P., 327.)

1884.   [1815]
Bristol, Mayor v. *Gee.* Pollution of stream by washings from Glue-works—Application to commit defendants to prison for breach of an Injunction, adjourned for one month. (*Times*, Jan. 16, 1884.)

1872.   [1816]
Clowes v. *Staffordshire Potteries Waterworks Co.* Fouling a river by mud—Water unfit for Silk Dyeing—Injunction granted. (42 L. J., Ch., 107 : L. R., 8 Ch., 115 : 27 L. T., 521 : 36 J. P., 760.)

1849.   [1817]
Elmhurst v. *Spencer.* Water diverted from a stream, polluted, and then restored to tho stream fairly innocuous—Injunction dissolved, no sufficient injury being shewn, and no proceedings at Law having been taken. (2 M. & Gord., 45.)

1863.   [1818]
Hodgkinson v. *Ennor.* Pollution of water flowing along an underground channel—Judgment for the plaintiff's—Owner one higher ground bound to see that his refuse water does no injury to his neighbour. (32 L. J., Q. B., 231 : 4 B. & S., 229 : 8 L. T., 451.)

1877.   [1819]
Pennington v. *Brinsop Hall Coal Co.* Pollution of stream by acidulated water which damaged the machinery of the plaintiff—Injunction granted, and damages to be a matter of inquiry in addition—Illustration of the difference between " injury " and " damage." (46 L. J., Ch., 773 : L. R., 5 Ch. D., 769: 37 L. T., 149 : [*Fennington* v. *B.*] 41 J. P., 758.)

1865.   [1820]
Reg. v. *Bradford Navigation.* Canal in a foul state—Owners held indictable. (34 L. J., Q. B., 191 : 6 B. & S., 631.) [See also *A.-G.* v. *Bradford Canal.*]

1866.   [1821]
Reg. v. *Stephens.* Obstruction of a river by deposit of refuse—Master held liable for the acts of his servants. (35 L. J., M. C., 251 : L. R., 1 Q. B., 702 : 7 B. & S., 710 : 14 L. T., 593.)

1876.   [1822]
Smith v. *Barnham.* Local Navigation Act—Refuse from Tannery—Definition of " Watercourse "—Held that the plaintiff ought not to have been convicted as he had acted beyond the Navigation limits. (L. R., 1 Ex D., 419 : 34 L. T., 774 : 40 J. P., 710.)

1875.   [1823]
Stansfield v. *Peate.* Pollution of stream by Mill refuse—Long-standing Agreement to purify the waste-water before letting it enter the stream—Decree for Specific Performance. (*Times*, March 23, 1875.)

1861.   [1824]
Stockport Waterworks Co. v. *Potter* (1). Fouling

of brook—Calico Works—A lawful trade but evidence wanting that it was carried on in a reasonable manner. (31 L. J., Ex., 9 : 7 H. & N., 160.)

1858.   [1825]
Whaley v. *Laing.* Water rights — Fouling of water used permissively not of right—Held there was no Right of Action. (27 L. J, Ex., 422 : 2 H. & N., 476 : 3 H. & N., 675 and 901 : 31 L. T., (o. s.), 368.)

81. WATER, RIGHTS AS TO.

1843.   [1826]
Acton v. *Blundell.* Interference with water by subterranean works. (13 L. J., Ex., 289 : 12 M. & W., 324.)

1881.   [1827]
Appleton v. *Bolton Corporation.* Statutory agreement to supply Millowners with water for trade purposes—Water often muddy—Held that the contract implied the delivery of water in a condition fit for immediate use, and that there had been a breach. (*Times*, May 6, 1881.)

1866.   [1828]
Bickett v. *Morris.* Though a riparian owner is the owner in severalty of half the *alveus* of a stream he has no right to build upon such *alveus*, even though no damage is occasioned thereby. (L. R., 1 H. L., Sc. App. 47 : 14 L. T., 835.)

1860.   [1829]
Briscoe v. *Drought.* Definition of " watercourse "—To constitute a watercourse in which rights may be acquired by user the flow of water must possess that unity of character by which the flow on one person's land can be identified with that on his neighbour's land—Water which squanders itself over an indefinite surface is not a proper subject-matter for the acquisition of a right by user. (11 Ir., C. L. R., 250.)

1856.   [1830]
Broadbent v. *Ramsbotham.* There is an absolute right of the Owner of the Soil to Water before it reaches a definite natural watercourse. (25 L. J., Ex., 115 : 11 Ex., 602.)

1859.   [1831]
Chasemore v. *Richards.* Underground Water—Owner of ancient Mill held to have no right of Action against a Local Board which by digging a Well deprived the Mill of Water. (29 L. J., Ex. 81 : 7 H. L. C., 349 : 33 L. T., (o. s.), 350.) [This is a " Leading Case," and the opinion of the Judges consulted by the House of Lords is both clear and exhaustive.]

1852.   [1832]
Dickinson v. *Grand Junction Canal Co.* Local Act—Subterraneous Water—Abstraction of Water which both had formed part of a Stream, and which would have done so but for the defendants' Well-sinking operations—Action maintainable. (21 L. J., Ex., 241 : 7 Ex., 282 : 18 L. T., (o. s.), 258.) [Questioned in *Chasemore* v. *Richards.*]

I

1868.   [1833]
Edleston v. *Crossley*. Running Stream—Obstruction to the flow thereof—Where extent of injury is uncertain the person aggrieved should proceed by Action and not by application for Mandatory Injunction. (18 L. T., 15.)

1877.   [1834]
Edwards v. *Jolliffe*. "Public Health Act, 1875," § 64—Failure of water in wells vested in Local Authority owing to lawful excavations carried on by plaintiff—Whereupon other excavations by defendant as Surveyor of Local Authority—Injunction granted to restrain such works—§ 64 does not authorise a Local Authority to enter upon land and help themselves to water. (W. N., 1877, p. 120.)

1851.   [1835]
Embrey v. *Owen*. Watercourse—Rights of adjacent proprietors—An action will lie for the unreasonable and unauthorised use of water —Right as to water analogous to right in respect of air and light. (20 L. J., Ex., 212 : 6 Ex., 353 : 17 L. T., (o. s.), 79.) [This case is thus alluded to in *Chasemore* v. *Richards* : —" The Law respecting the right to Water flowing in definite, visible channels . . . is very clearly enunciated in *Embrey* v. *Owen*."]

1865.   [1836]
Gaved v. *Martyn*. Diversion of Watercourse— Prescriptive right—Cornish Mine Law. (34 L. J., C. P., 353 : 19 C. B., (N. S.), 732 : 13 L. T., 74.)

1871.   [1837]
Grand Junction Canal Co. v. *Shugar*. Surface and subterraneous Water—A Local Board will be restrained from interfering with a watercourse in a way not authorised by Parliament —The aggrieved person will not be left to seek remedy by compensation under the "Public Health Act." (L. R., 6 Ch. App., 483 : 24 L. T., 402.)

1874.   [1838]
Halifax Corporation v. *Soothill, Upper, L. B.* A Local Board entitled by special Act to buy Water of a Corporation held justified in re-selling its surplus, inasmuch as it was compelled to pay for a minimum quantity which was in excess of its own requirements. (31 L. T., 6.)

1868.   [1839]
Harrop v. *Hirst*. Diversion of Water—Custom— Action held maintainable. (38 L. J., Ex., 1 : L. R., 4 Ex., 43 : 19 L. T., 426.)

1875.   [1840]
Holker v. *Porritt*. Diversion of Stream—Riparian rights of owner below against owner above. (44 L. J., Ex., 52 : L. R., 10 Ex., 59 : 33 L. T., 125 : 39 J. P., 196.)

1881.   [1841]
Leadgate L. B. v. *Bland*. Public pond, naturally formed, used from time immemorial for watering cattle by anybody who liked to use it— Wall erected by Board to protect one side of pond—Wall partly pulled down by adjacent landowner to give him access to pond on that side—Action for damages for the Trespass—

Held that the pond was vested in the Board under the "Public Health Act, 1875," § 64 —*Per* Kay, J.:—" The purpose of the Act was undoubtedly to enable the Local Board to take the management and control of the water supply of the village or district, and to improve it; to make it pure if impure, and to maintain it and prevent it being made impure. That being the purpose of the Section, he thought it wrong to say that it should only apply to artificial reservoirs. He therefore held that a natural reservoir if used from time immemorial for public purposes, came within the section." Verdict for plaintiffs for 40s., with Injunction to restrain defendant from interfering with any part of the wall. (At *Nisi Prius*: Durham Assizes, July, 1881.) (45 J. P., 526.)

1875.   [1842]
Lyon v. *Fishmongers' Co.* A riparian owner on a navigable tidal river may possess private rights over the foreshore; his right to use the stream does not depend on the ownership of the soil of the stream. (46 L. J., Ch., 68 : L. R., 1 App. Cas., 622 : 35 L. T., 569 : 42 J. P., 163.)

1840.   [1843]
Magor v. *Chadwick*. A right to the use of an artificial watercourse may be acquired so as to sustain an Action for fouling it. (9 L. J., Q. B., 159 : 11 A. & E., 571 : 3 P. & D., 367.)

1833.   [1844]
Mason v. *Hill*. Diversion of Water-course— Water rights of Riparian proprietors—Mill-dam. (5 B. & Ad., 1 : 2 N. & M., 747.)

1861.   [1845]
Medway Navigation Co. v. *Romney* (*Earl of*). Company held entitled to sue persons, who, not being Riparian proprietors, abstracted water which the special Act vested in the Company. (30 L. J., C. P., 236 : 9 C. B., (N. S.), 575 : 4 L. T., 87.)

1858.   [1846]
Minor v. *Gilmore*. A Riparian owner has a right to use water, provided he does not interfere with the rights of other proprietors; but he must not interrupt the regular flow to the injury of other proprietors. (12 Moo., P. C. C., 131 and 156.) [See observations on this case in *Norbury* v. *Kitchin* (2), 7 L. T., 685.]

1859.   [1847]
National Manure Co. v. *Donald*. A Company with Parliamentary Powers to take Water for a specific purpose cannot by user acquire under the "Prescription Act," 2 & 3 Will. IV., c. 71, § 2, a prescriptive Right to take the Water for any other purpose—An easement to take water to fill a canal ceases when the canal ceases to exist. (28 L. J., Ex., 185 : 4 H. & N., 8.)

1860.   [1848]
New River Co. v. *Johnson*. "Waterworks Clauses Act, 1847," § 12—Abstraction of water— Compensation cannot be recovered under this Statute for an injury for which no Action

would have been, but for the Statute, maintainable. (29 L. J., M. C., 93: 2 E. & E., 435: 1 L. T., 295: 24 J. P., 244.)

1862.   [1849]
Norbury (Earl of) v. *Kitchin* (1). Diversion of Water—Verdict for the plaintiff—Nominal Damages. (3 F. & F., 292.)

1863.   [1850]
Norbury (Earl of) v. *Kitchin* (2). Diversion of Water—Riparian proprietor may abstract a reasonable quantity of water with reference to the rights of other proprietors. (7 L. T., 685: 9 Jur. (N. S.), 132.)

1867.   [1851]
Norbury (Earl of) v. *Kitchin* (3). An obstruction to a Stream will be enjoined against at the suit of a Riparian owner irrespective of actual damage. (15 L. T., 501.)

1866.   [1852]
Nuttall v. *Bracewell.* Watercourse—Abstraction of Water—General principles—Action held maintainable. (36 L. J., Ex., 1: L. R., 2 Ex., 2: 4 H. & C., 714: 15 L. T., 313: 31 J. P., 8.)

1874.   [1853]
Owen v. *Davies.* Water Rights—Diversion of Stream by a Local Board in order to obtain a supply of Water—Injunction against the Board granted—"The Board had only the ordinary rights of a Riparian owner." (W. N., 1874, p. 175.)

1855.   [1854]
Rawstron v. *Taylor.* Right to Surface Water—Diversion—A landowner has an unqualified right to drain his own land, even to the detriment of a neighbour who otherwise would have derived benefit from the water finding its own course. (25 L. J., Ex., 33: 11 Ex., 369.)

1875.   [1855]
Reg. v. *Kettering Union.* Filling up a well, overflow from which had been used by a tanner—Held that compensation was payable—*Mandamus* granted. (*Times,* Dec. 17, 1875.)

1863.   [1856]
Reg. v. *Metropolitan Board of Works* (1). Construction of Sewer resulting in the abstraction of underground water from plaintiff's ponds—No right to compensation, the damage occurring underground. (32 L. J., Q. B., 105: 3 B. & S., 710: 8 L. T., 234.)

1865.   [1857]
Roberts v. *Rose.* Obstruction of Watercourse—A person in abating a nuisance to his property may justify an interference with the property of the wrong-doer, but only so far as is necessary to abate the nuisance—He must execute his works of abatement in the least injurious way possible, taking peculiar care not to injure an innocent third person—Pleading. (35 L. J., Ex., 62: L. R., 1 Ex., 82: 13 L. T., 471: 4 H. & C., 103.)

1880.   [1858]
Smith v. *Archibald.* "Public Health (Scotland) Act, 1867," § 89 (4)—Right of Local Authority as representing the inhabitants to repair a public well situated on private

ground, and to erect a pump, held established. (L. R., 5 App. Cas., 489: 28 W. R. Dig., col. 136.)

1862.   [1859]
Stockport Waterworks Co. v. *Manchester, Mayor.* Rival Water Companies—A suit by one rival Company against another alleging proceedings *ultra vires* will not be entertained if the plaintiffs shew no private injury. (7 L. T., 545: 9 Jur., (N. S.), 266.)

1864.   [1860]
Stockport Waterworks Co. v. *Potter* (2). Fouling of Water—Grant of a portion of a Riparian Proprietor's back land—Water rights of the Grantee. (3 H. & C., 300: 10 L. T., 748.)

1863.   [1861]
Sutclife v. *Booth.* Water Rights—An artificial watercourse may possess or acquire the qualities of a natural stream. (32 L. J., Q. B., 136: 9 Jur., (N. S.), 1037.)

1877.   [1862]
Taylor v. *St. Helens Corporation.* Grant of a "Watercourse" held not to carry a right to enlarge the watercourse: the grant was of a certain watercourse not of all the water which could be made to reach the watercourse if it were altered. (46 L. J., Ch., 857: L. R., 6 Ch. D., 264: 37 L. T., 253.)

1861.   [1863]
Waller v. *Manchester, Mayor.* Water Rights—Diversion of Water—Mill—For geological reasons statutory guaranteed quantity not able to be given—Action maintainable for the original diversion, but not for failure to comply with Statute. (30 L. J., Ex., 293: 6 H. & N., 667.)

1860.   [1864]
Wardle v. *Brocklehurst.* Water Rights—Effect of Conveyance—The owner of land through which subterraneous water flows cannot maintain an Action for Diversion. (29 L. J., Q. B., 145: 1 E. & E., 1065: 1 L. T., 519.)

1859.   [1865]
William v. *Heath.* Water Rights—Abstraction of water from Watercourse—Injunction refused—A Defendant held entitled to require that Action at Law be brought to establish the alleged Rights of the plaintiff. (1 L. T., 267.)

1876.   [1866]
Wilts & Berks Canal Co. v. *Swindon Waterworks Co.* Special Acts—A riparian proprietor's rights as to water do not include a right to sell it to the inhabitants of a neighbouring town needing water. (45 L. J., Ch., 638: L. R., 7 H. L., 697: 33 L. T., 513: 40 J. P., 804.)

1851.   [1867]
Wood v. *Satcliffe.* Water polluted by increase of population and by certain Dye-works of defendants — Injunction against discharging polluted water refused on the ground that it would seriously injure defendants and do no real good to plaintiffs. (21 L. J., Ch., 253: 2 Sim. (N. S.), 163.)

1849.   [1868]
Wood v. *Waud.* Riparian rights of upper and

I 2

lower proprietors as to pollution and diversion of water under special circumstances. (18 L. J., Ex., 305 : 3 Ex., 748.)

82. WORKS.

1880.   [1869]
Bolton, Mayor v. Bolton Guardians. Action to restrain defendants from constructing sewerage works outside their own district, and within the district of the plaintiffs, without, it was alleged, having given the requisite notices to the occupiers, and without the consent of the Local Government Board—Compromise suggested by the V. C. and agreed to. (*Times*, January 23, 1880.)

1887.   [1870]
Butcher v. Ruth. "Public Health (Ireland) Act, 1878," §§ 110, 120 [="Public Health Act, 1875," §§ 94, 104]—Notice not served on Lessor of house—A Lessee cannot set off expenses incurred by him in abating a nuisance (assuming it to arise from defective condition of a structural convenience) against the rent due from him to Lessor. (22 L. R., Ir., 380.)

1886.   [1871]
Parker v. Inge. "Public Health Act, 1875," § 96—Where a notice to abate a nuisance served on an owner cannot be complied with by him because of the premises being let to a tenant, the Local Authority may step in and execute the works, on the ground that the owner is in default. (55 L. J., M. C., 149 : L. R., 17 Q. B. D., 584 : 55 L. T., 300 : 51 J. P., 20.)

1885.   [1872]
Reg. v. Kent JJ. "Public Health Act, 1875," § 96—Order to abate a nuisance by applying a specific remedy held good — *Whitchurch, Ex parte* not followed. (55 L. J., M. C., 9 n. : 49 J. P., 404.)

1884.   [1873]
Reg. v. Llewellyn. "Public Health Act, 1875," §§ 94–6—Notice to defendant to do various specified works in and about privy—Order of Justices to enforce notice, upheld—*Saunders, Ex parte* followed : *Whitchurch, Ex parte* distinguished or dissented from. (55 L. J., M. C., 9 n. : L. R., 13 Q. B. D., 681 : 49 J. P., 101.)

1880.   [1874]
Reg. v. Sherborne L. B. Water-closets found defective for want of proper flushing apparatus—Order of Board that owner should supply such—On default work done by Board—On Application to Justices they made an Order on owner to re-imburse Board —On Motion to remove the Order into the Q. B. D. with a view to its being quashed the Court declined to review the decision of the Board which had exercised its discretion in the matter under the advice of its Surveyor. (In the Q. B. D., May 1880, MS.) [But see *Whitchurch, Ex parte.*]

1885.   [1875]
Reg. v. Wheatley. "Public Health Act, 1875,"

§ 96—Order to abate a nuisance held bad because it did not specify what works and things were to be done. (55 L. J., M. C., 11 : L. R., 16 Q. B. D., 34 : 54 L. T., 680 : 50 J. P., 424.)

1882.   [1876]
Saunders v. Barstow. "Metropolis Management Acts"—Neglect to provide sufficient water-closets—Penalties inflicted in case of 11 houses—Wrong penalties having been inflicted the Quarter Sessions revised the amounts, but confirmed the convictions generally. (46 J. P., 361.)

1883.   [1877]
Saunders, Ex parte. "Public Health Act, 1875," §§ 94–6—On default of owner to move a water-closet which was a nuisance to another and specified situation, Justices issued an Order under § 96—Order held good—*Whitchurch, Ex parte* distinguished. (52 L. J., M. C., 89 : L. R., 11 Q. B. D., 191 : 47 J. P., 584.)

1890.   [1878]
St. James, Clerkenwell, Vestry v. Feary. "Metropolis Management Act, 1855," § 81: "Amendment Act, 1862," § 64—A Vestry ordered an owner to furnish a Water-closet with a sufficient door—On his default they summoned him, but the Magistrate being of opinion that there already was a sufficient door and that the Vestry had no right to interfere, dismissed the summons—Held that the Vestry had jurisdiction to make the Order and that the Magistrate only had jurisdiction to inquire whether the Vestry's Order had or had not been obeyed. (59 L. J., M. C., 82 : L. R., 24 Q. B. D., 703 : 62 L. T., 697 : 54 J. P., 676.)

1862.   [1879]
St. Luke's, Middlesex, Vestry v. Lewis. "Metropolis Management Act, 1855," § 226—Non-compliance with requisition to substitute Water-closet for privy—Whereupon Works carried out by Vestry—Vestry held entitled to recover. (31 L. J., M. C., 73 : 1 B. & S., 865 : 5 L. T., 608.)

1858.   [1880]
Sutton v. Norwich, Mayor. "Public Health Act, 1848," §§ 43–6 [="Public Health Act, 1875," §§ 13–19, &c.]—A Local Board has no power to enter upon land in order to make a sewage tank without the consent of the owner—Injunction granted—Definition of "Sewer." (27 L. J., Ch., 739 : 31 L. T., (n. s.), 389.)

1858.   [1881]
Tinkler v. Wandsworth B. W. "Nuisances Removal Act, 1855," § 11 [= "Public Health Act, 1875," § 102]—Erection of Water-closets—Not until the Justices have made an Order which has not been obeyed can a Board enter and execute structural works— A Board must determine every case as to alterations on its own merits, and not lay down a general rule. (27 L. J., Ch., 342 : 2 De G. & J., 261 : 30 L. T., (o. s.), 146 : 22 J. P., 223.)

1885.   [1882]
Whitaker v. *Derby U. S. A.* "Public Health
Act, 1873," §§ 94, 96—Order under § 94 to
abate nuisance not complied with—Order by
Justices under § 96, specifying the works to
be done, held good. (55 L. J., M. C., 8 : 50
J. P., 359.)

1881.   [1883]
Whitchurch, Ex parte. "Public Health Act
1875"—Nuisance—Order under § 94 by
Local Authority that a privy and ashpit
should be replaced by a closet—Default by
Owner—Whereupon Order to same effect
under § 96 by Justices—Order of Justices
held *ultra vires*—The Section quoted requires
simply the abatement of the nuisance but
confers no powers on Local Authority to
insist on a particular *modus operandi*. (50
L. J., M. C., 99 : L. R., 6 Q. B. D., 545 : 45
J. P., 617.) [Subsequent Appeal dismissed
for want of Jurisdiction, the Court being of
opinion that the subject was a criminal
matter within the "Judicature Act, 1873,"
§ 47, and that therefore no appeal lay.]
(*Reg.* v. *Whitchurch.* L. R., 7 Q. B. D., 534 :
[*W. Ex p.*] 45 L. T., 379 : 46 J. P., 134.)

1886.   [1884]
Wimbledon L. B. v. *Croydon R. S. A.* "Public
Health Act, 1875," § 32—The cleaning,
levelling, and cementing of a pool into which
effluent water from sewage works flows is a
work for sewage purposes. (56 L. J., Ch.,
159 : L. R., 32 Ch. D., 421 : 55 L. T., 106.)

PART II.—HIGHWAYS.

1865	1894

1865

1. AUTHORITIES MANAGING HIGHWAYS.

(1.) HIGHWAY BOARDS.

1883.   [1885]
Billericay H. B., In re. Although a Highway Board becomes dissolved *pendente lite*, it is nevertheless entitled to recover the unpaid costs of an Appeal. (52 L. J., M. C., 124.)

1865.   [1886]
Giles v. Glubb. "Highway Act, 1862," §§ 2 and 5—Ancient Borough having Charters with non-intromittent clauses, and being entirely within the limits of its County, held, notwithstanding § 2, to be properly included within a Highway District by the County Justices. (12 Jur., (N. S.), 389 : 13 L. T., 526.)

1885.   [1887]
Phelps v. Upton Snodsbury H. B. Plaintiffs, solicitors, employed to petition against Railway Bill calculated to injure Board's roads—Retainer held not to be for a purpose incidental to Highway Board business, and not being under seal Plaintiffs held not entitled to recover their costs, or even moneys actually paid. (1 Cab. & Ellis, 524 : 49 J. P., 408.)

1839.   [1888]
Reg. v. Bush. "Highway Act, 1835," § 18—Parish comprising several Tithings, each of which had always repaired its own highways — Surveyors appointed by the different Tithings sitting together as a Board and making a separate Rate for each Tithing—Such Rates held bad because made by the so-called Board, and not by the respective Surveyors. (8 L. J., M. C., 39 : 9 A. & E., 820 : 1 P. & D., 586.)

1878.   [1889]
Reg. v. Cumberland JJ. "Highway Act, 1862," § 6 : "Highway Act, 1864," § 46—Provisional Order to withdraw certain Townships from a Highway District quashed by Quarter Sessions—Held, that these proceedings were void, the Court being improperly constituted, one of the Justices present being a member of the Highway Board concerned, and having himself appeared by Counsel against the Confirmation of the Order which had been quashed—*Quære,* Whether the mere giving of evidence simply, in such a matter, would have disentitled him to vote? (42 J. P., 361.)

1894

1865.   [1890]
Reg. v. Gascoigne. "Highway Act, 1864," § 5—Highway District—Each parish to elect one Waywarden—Town of M. formed part of but was not co-extensive with Parish of M.—Town highways repaired under Local Act—Suburban part of M. held a place separately maintaining its own highways, and that suburban Ratepayers only could vote for Waywarden. (29 J. P., 389.)

1865.   [1891]
Reg. v. Heath. "Highway Act, 1862," § 20—Indictment by Highway Board against an individual for an encroachment and obstruction —Conviction—Taxed Costs held an "expense in relation to a Highway" which was payable out of the Rates. (12 L. T., 492 : [*Heath v. West Eddisbury H. B.*] 13 W. R., 805.)

1863.   [1892]
Reg. v. How. "Highway Act, 1835," § 18—The Common Law right to demand a poll is not affected by a statutory enactment giving power to a majority of Vestrymen present at a meeting to form a Highway Board. (33 L. J., M. C., 53 : 9 L. T., 385 : 27 J. P., 1773.)

1868.   [1893]
Reg. v. Kingsbridge H. B. "Highway Act, 1864," § 32—A Highway Board having incurred expenses in opposing a Bill in Parliament held to have no power to charge them on the Parishes, even though the Bill affected such Parishes and the opposition was *bona fide* and likely to be beneficial—The expenses could not be said to be incurred for the common use or benefit of the whole District—*Quære,* Whether the sanction of the various Vestries would have justified the Board in taking proceedings ? (18 L. T., 554 : 16 W. R., 1115.)

1865.   [1894]
Reg. v. Lindsey JJ. "Highway Act, 1862," §§ 8, 10 : "Highway Act, 1864," § 12—An Order for the formation of a Highway Board fixing the first meeting for the Thursday after March 25, held valid, the Quarter Sessions not being bound to appoint a day which would be after the expiration of the time limited by law for the election of Waywardens, viz., within 14 days after March 25 —As a matter of practice it is better to postpone the day to one of the 7 days after such limited time—When a Rule *nisi* for a *Certiorari* to remove an Order with the view to quashing it is obtained within 3 months the case is taken out of the operation of § 8,

though the Rule may not be returnable till after the 3 months. (35 L. J., M. C., 90 : L. R., 1 Q. B., 68 : 6 B. & S., 892 : 13 L. T., 524.)

1864.   [1895]
Reg. v. *Sussex.* "Highway Act, 1862," § 5— When Justices propose to form a Highway District it is a condition precedent that notice be first sent to all the Parishes proposed to be included, and the Order is bad if any Parish has not had notice. (28 J. P., 469.)

1865.   [1896]
Reg. v. *Yorkshire, W. R., JJ.*(3). "Highway Act, 1862," § 6—Highway District—Three hamlets in one township, each hamlet maintaining its own highways — Provisional Order appointing one Waywarden for the entire township—Order silent as to combining the three hamlets under § 7—Order held bad. (34 L. J., M. C., 227 : 12 L. T., 580.)

(2.) SURVEYORS OF HIGHWAYS.

1874.   [1897]
Barton v. *Piggott.* "Highway Act, 1835," § 46— Surveyor of Highways charging in his accounts for work done by his own horses without previous written Order of Justices—Held, that such charges ought to have been disallowed by the Justices. (44 L. J., M. C., 5 : 31 L. T., 404 : 39 J. P., 454.)

1888.   [1898]
Croft v. *Rickmansworth H. B.* "Highway Act, 1835," § 67—A shaft to facilitate the percolation away of surface water is not "a drain or watercourse" within this section which a Highway Authority may conduct or maintain on private land. (58 L. J., Ch., 14 : L. R., 39 Ch. D., 272 : 60 L. T., 34.)

1876.   [1899]
Denny v. *Thwaites.* "Highway Act, 1835," § 67 —Covered brick drain laid down by owner of a house at the point where his carriage drive opened on the highway—Held, that interference on the part of a Highway Surveyor with such drain was not a "wilful or malicious injury to property" within 24 & 25 Vict., c. 97, §52—Consideration of the circumstances under which an interference with private property is justifiable on the part of a Highway Surveyor. (46 L. J., M. C., 141 : L. R., 2 Ex. D., 21 : 41 J. P., 164.)

1871.   [1900]
Driver v. *Kingston H. B.* Adoption by a Parish of "Local Government Act, 1858 "—Repair of highways—Outstanding contract with the Highway Board which formerly comprised such Parish—The Board continued to repair with materials supplied by the Plaintiff for 4 months after the resolution adopting the Act—Held, that the Plaintiff was on the facts entitled to recover as for goods sold and delivered, and that the answer that the proceedings were *ultra vires* on the part of the Board could not prevail. (24 L. T., 480 : 20 W. R., 20.)

1860,   [1901]
Ellis v. *Woodbridge.* "Highway Act, 1835," § 24—Bridle-way—A Highway Surveyor is not bound to bar the entrance to a bridle-way against vehicles—§ 24 refers only to causeways by the side of carriage-ways. (29 L. J., M. C., 183 : 2 L. T., 237.)

1841.   [1902]
Growsmith, Ex parte. "Highway Act, 1835," § 6 —Election of Surveyor—Two candidates— Show of hands—Poll demanded but refused —Refusal of Justices to put in force § 11 of the Act which permits Justices in certain cases to appoint a Surveyor, they being of opinion that as a poll had been refused by the Chairman of the Vestry the candidate who had a majority on the show of hands was not duly elected—Rule *nisi* for a *Mandamus* to inhabitants to meet in Vestry for a poll. (10 L. J., Q. B., 359 : 5 Jur., 551.)

1825.   [1903]
Lowen v. *Kay.* "Highway Act, 1773," §§ 6 and 64 [Repealed]—Road less than 30 ft. wide —Held that the Surveyor was not entitled to remove a fence in front of a house in order to widen a highway unless the fence supposed to be an encroachment was actually on the highway. (3 L. J., (o. s.), K. B., 123 : 4 B. & C., 3 : 6 D. & R., 20.)

1864.   [1904]
Marlborough (Duke of) v. *Osborn.* An obligation to furnish "team-work" with 2 horses and 1 driver does not imply that the owner of the team is to furnish a cart also. (5 B. & S., 67 : 10 L. T., 28.)

1844.   [1905]
Peters v. *Clarson.* "Highway Act," 1835," §§ 54, 67-8—Trespass does not lie against a Surveyor for entering lands and making a drain without tendering amends, the ascertainment of the damage and the payment of the amount not being a condition precedent to the authority to enter — Justices in such case to ascertain the damages payable. (13 L. J., M. C., 153 : 7 M. & G., 548 : 8 Scott, N. R., 381 : 1 New Sess. Cas., 510.)

1847.   [1906]
Reg. v. *Best.* "Highway Act, 1835," § 11—Appointment of Surveyor by Justices on neglect of Parish to appoint held bad because made at same Sessions at which such neglect was notified — A Vestry for purposes of the "Highway Act" must be duly convened under the "Vestries Act, 1818 "—Where two Rates are co-existent it will not be presumed that they are concurrent and therefore invalid. (16 L. J., M. C.; 102: 5 Dowl. & L., 40 : 2 New Sess. Cas., 655.)

1864.   [1907]
Reg. v. *Bluffield.* "Highway Act, 1862," § 43— When a Parish becomes incorporated into a Highway District, it is the duty of the Surveyors about to be superseded to collect an outstanding Rate — The words "and then remaining unpaid" in § 43 mean remaining unpaid at the end of 7 days from the appoint-

ment of the District Surveyor. (11 L. T., 337.)

1872.   [1908]
Reg. v. *Cooper.* *Quo Warranto*—Election of a Waywarden—Poll demanded but not taken because of alleged retirement of candidate who obtained a majority of votes on the show of hands—Held that as there was no Poll taken a certificate that such candidate had been elected was invalid. (39 L. J., Q. B., 273 : L. R., 5 Q. B., 457.)

1866.   [1909]
Reg. v. *Dix.* "Highway Act, 1835," § 7—*Quo Warranto* lies for usurping the office of Surveyor of Highways. (30 J. P., 390.)

1876.   [1910]
Reg. v. *Drayton H. B.* "Highway Act, 1835," § 48—Competitive offers are not to affect the "fair and reasonable" price at which a person entitled to a right of pre-emption is to be allowed to purchase surplus land. (L. R., 1 Q. B. D., 608.)

1852.   [1911]
Reg. v. *Hillingdon, Vicar.* "Highway Act, 1835," § 6—Meeting to appoint Surveyors—Show of hands—Agreement to abide by decision of a Poll then and there taken and in accordance with the "Vestries Act, 1818"—Held that the Meeting having unanimously agreed to a Poll, limited as above, no one was entitled to demand afterwards a general Poll of the whole Parish—Election held good. (18 Q. B., 718 : 19 L. T., (o. s.), 184.)

1856.   [1912]
Reg. v. *Kershaw.* "Highway Act, 1835," § 6—Election of Surveyor—Held that a person rateable, though not rated, is entitled to vote. (26 L. J., M. C., 19 : 6 E. & B., 999 : 28 L. T., (o. s.), 101.)

1849.   [1913]
Reg. v. *Paynter.* "Highway Act, 1835," §§ 27 and 113—§ 113 does not exempt from the ordinary Highway Rate a bridge paved, &c., under a Local Rate—Such exemption applies only to the interference of Highway Surveyors with such a bridge. (18 L. J., M. C., 169 : 13 Q. B., 399 : 12 L. T., (o. s.), 450.)

1859.   [1914]
Reg. v. *Richardson.* Surveyor of Highways having authority to order gravel for roads doing so and applying it to his own use held not liable on a charge of obtaining it by false pretences—Nor for larceny unless it appeared that he did not mean to pay for it. (1 F. & F., 488.)

1844.   [1915]
Reg. v. *Rose.* "Highway Act, 1835," § 27—"Usually rated" refers to a matter of fact as to the practice of rating in the particular parish. (13 L. J., M. C., 155 : 6 Q. B., 153 : 1 Dav. & M., 300 : 1 New Sess. Cas., 272.)

1855.   [1916]
Reg. v. *Saunders.* "Highway Act, 1835," § 27—"Usually rated" applies not only to Mines actually rated previously, but also to Mines

. of the same description opened subsequently. (24 L. J., M. C., 57 : 24 L. T., (o. s.), 235 : [*Reg.* v. *Randall*] 4 E. & B, 564.)

1855.   [1917]
Reg. v. *Uttermere.* "Highway Act, 1835," §§ 29 and 111—*Semble* the limitation of Rate in § 29 does not apply when funds have to be raised by an "additional Rate," under § 111 for legal proceedings to defend an Indictment for non-repair—The words "in the same manner," in § 111 apply only to the method of making and collecting the Rate. (26 L. T., (o. s.), 94 : 29 J. P., 36.)

1797.   [1918]
Rex v. *Baldwin.* If there be an objection to the appointment of Surveyors the party objecting should first remove the appointments by *Certiorari*, and then move to quash them—An objection to the appointment of 3 Surveyors, each for a particular division of a Parish, overruled, it appearing that such a mode of appointment had prevailed for several years. (7 T. R., 169.)

1803.   [1919]
Rex v. *Denbyshire.* "Highway Act, 1773," § 1 [Repealed]—This is only directory to the Justices to make the appointment at the time mentioned; but there are no negative words to prevent them from doing so at any subsequent Special Sessions if it shall be necessary ; and common sense requires that if the appointment be not made at the first Special Sessions, it should be made afterwards. (4 East, 142.)

1831.   [1920]
Rex v. *King's Newton Inhabitants.* The appointment of separate Surveyors for separate Townships of a Parish may be good by usage or custom—Parish comprising 2 Townships—Surveyor chosen for each—Subsequently, to save expense, 2 were appointed at one general Vestry, one for each Township—Separate Rates, expenditure, and accounts, but one allowance by Vestry—Occupiers rated in each Township for the roads thereof only—Held sufficient evidence that each Township was immemorially bound to repair its own roads, and therefore that there might be separate appointments of Surveyors. (9 L. J., (o. s.), M. C., 54 : 1 B. & Ad., 826.)

1835.   [1921]
Rex v. *Round.* *Mandamus* to Surveyor of Highways after expiration of his term of office to deliver up books—Return that neither on the day of the *Teste*, nor since, nor now, nor when applied to on behalf of the Churchwardens had he any such books ; not stating whether he had had them between the Requisition and the *Teste*, nor what he had done with them—Return held good but costs refused; the return ought to have been fuller. (4 A. & E., 139 : 5 N. & M., 427.)

1825.   [1922]
Rex v. *St. Albans JJ.* "Highway Act, 1773," § 81 [Repealed]—An appointment of Surveyors cannot be removed into the Queen's Bench by *Certiorari*—The remedy for a bad

appointment is appeal to the Sessions, a bad appointment being a thing done in pursuance of the Act and every inhabitant being thereby "aggrieved." (3 B. & C., 698: 5 D. & R., 538.)

1859.   [1923]
Sutcliffe v. *Sowerby Highway Surveyors.* Foot-way across a Brook formed of Stepping-stones —Stones reduced in number by the Sur-veyors and the foot-way made continuous by means of flag-stones—Held that the Sur-veyors had been guilty of a trespass, and that the adjacent Landowner was justified in removing the flag-stones, and ought not to have been convicted under the " Highway Act, 1835," § 72. (1 L. T., 7: 8 W. R., 40.)

1865.   [1924]
Wakefield v. *Seneschall.* "Highway Act, 1835," § 46—A Surveyor who does repairs without the consent of the Vestry, doing the work himself without the necessary Certificate from 2 Justices, is not entitled to be repaid the cost of materials or labour supplied by him. (29 J. P., 375.)

1859.   [1925]
Whitaker, Ex parte. "Highway Act, 1835," § 72 —Surveyor convicted for removing Stepping-stones over a Brook, and substituting a Bridge—Conviction held bad—Such an act is within his powers. (23 J. P., 84.) [See *Sutcliffe* v. *Sowerby.*]

1880.   [1926]
Williams v. *Ellis.* Highway—Turnpike—Special Act, 3 Will. IV., c. lv.—Bicycle held not to be a "carriage." (49 L. J., Q. B., 47: L. R., 5 Q. B. D., 175: 42 L. T., 249: 44 J. P., 394.)

1865.   [1927]
Wrexham H. B. v. *Hardcastle.* "Highway Act, 1835," § 42: "Highway Act, 1862," §§ 11 and 43—A, a Surveyor, went out of office on March 25, and B was appointed his suc-cessor—B never acted, for within a few days a Highway Board was formed—Held that A was the "out-going" Surveyor, with duties and privileges accordingly. (19 C. B., (N. s.), 177.)

(3.) VARIOUS SPECIAL POWERS UNDER THE "HIGH-WAYS ACT, 1878," (41 & 42 VICT., C. 77).

1890.   [1928]
Burnley, Mayor v. *Lancaster County Council.* "Highways Act, 1878," §§ 13, 14, 18: "Local Government Act, 1888"—Expenses of Sca-venging held an item which might be in-cluded in the cost of maintenance of Main road. (54 J. P., 279.)

1886.   [1929]
Lancaster JJ. v. *Newton-in-Makerfield Commis-sioners.* Turnpike Road ceasing to be such and becoming a main Road—*Yorkshire W. R., JJ.* v. *The Queen,* followed. (56 L. J., M. C., 17: L. R., 11 App. Cas., 416: 55 L. T., 615: 51 J. P., 68.)

1881.   [1930]
Lancashire JJ. v. *Rochdale, Mayor.* Certain roads which had been turnpike roads held not to have become chargeable in part to the county (under the "Highways Act, 1878," § 13), when by reason of an enlargement of the borough boundaries such roads ceased to be turnpike property. (53 L. J., M. C., 5: L. R., 8 App. Cas., 494: 49 L. T., 368: 48 J. P., 5.)

1888.   [1931]
Leek Commissioners v. *Staffordshire JJ.* "High-ways Act, 1878," § 13—Converting a mac-adamised road into a paved road does not come within the term "maintenance," and a Highway Authority cannot recover half the expenses from the County Authority. (57 L. J., M. C., 102: L. R., 20 Q. B. D., 794.)

1883.   [1932]
Middlesborough Overseers v. *Yorkshire, N. R., JJ.* "Highways Act, 1878," § 13: Local Act—Local Act held not available to exempt in-habitants of an extended Borough area from payment of County Rates in respect of Main Roads outside extended limits. (L. R., 12 Q. B. D., 239: 32 W. R., 671.)

1884.   [1933]
Over Darwen, Mayor v. *Lancaster JJ.* "High-way Act, 1862," § 2: "Highways Act, 1878," §§ 13, 38—"County Authority" held liable in respect of a disturnpiked Road within the limits of a newly incorporated Borough. (54 L. J., M. C., 51: L. R., 15 Q. B. D. 20: 51 L. T., 739 · 48 J. P., 437.)

1881.   [1934]
Pearce v. *East Ashford Union.* "Highways Act, 1878"—A Rural Sanitary Authority exer-cising the powers of a Highway Board is not a Highway Authority within § 10, as inter-preted by § 38. (At Q. Sess.) (45 J. P. 457.)

1884.   [1935]
Reg. v. *Dover Recorder.* "Highways Act, 1878," § 15—A Borough Recorder may be a "County Authority" within this enactment. (49 J. P., 86: see also 49 J. P., 456.)

1885.   [1936]
Reg. v. *Local Government Board* (3). "Highways Act, 1878," § 16—The Local Government Board may make a Provisional order on an application made later than Feb. 1, 1879. (54 L. J., M. C., 104: L. R., 15 Q. B. D., 70: 53 L. T., 194: 49 J. P., 580.)

1883.   [1937]
Yorkshire, W. R., JJ. v. *The Queen.* "Highways Act, 1878," § 13—A Turnpike road does not cease to be a Turnpike road within this section merely because by an arrangement with an Urban Authority it becomes an Urban Street—Nor does so cease on the removal, by arrangement, of certain Toll-gates. (53 L. J., M. C., 41: L. R., 8 App. Cas., 781: 49 L. T., 786: [Y. v. *Sheffield*] 48 J. P., 228.)

2. LEGAL PROCEEDINGS BY AND AGAINST AUTHORITIES MANAGING HIGHWAYS.

** See also "Liability for Accidents" (Part I., § 47, ante).

1832.   [1938]
Alston v. Scales. A Surveyor is liable to a reversioner for cutting away a portion of a bank by the side of a road though the property is improved thereby—Removal of the smallest portion of soil must in general be esteemed an injury to land, as tending to alter the evidence of title. (1 L. J., M. C., 95 : 9 Bing., 3 : 2 M. & Scott, 5.)

1845.   [1939]
Barber, In re. "Attorneys and Solicitors Act, 1843," 6 & 7 Vict., c. 73, § 37—Attorney employed by Highway Surveyor to conduct an Indictment for an obstruction and for other business—Whole Bill of Costs paid out of Highway Rate—Held that Ratepayers were not persons "liable to pay" within the above enactment, and could not therefore apply to have the bill taxed. (15 L. J., Ex., 9 : 14 M. & W., 720 : 3 Dowl. & L., 244.)

1811.   [1940]
Boyfield v. Porter. "Highway Act, 1773," §§ 27 and 29 [Repealed but re-enacted in nearly the same terms in the "Highway Act, 1835," §§ 51 and 54]—Surveyors having broken a new way over the Plaintiff's Land in order to move materials to be used for repairs although an old but circuitous road existed; and having after the damage done, and after an Action of Trespass brought against them, paid money into Court by way of amends—Held that the sufficiency of such amends could not be questioned at *Nisi Prius,* the Statute having referred the *quantum* of amends, if not agreed upon, to Justices—But it is competent to the Plaintiff in such Action to show that the making of such new road over his land was maliciously or wantonly done by the Surveyors, and not for the necessary or convenient conveyance of the materials over the land for the purposes of the Act; and in such case he would not be concluded by the amends tendered or paid into Court. (13 East, 200.)

1883.   [1941]
Carter v. St. Giles's B. W. Application for Injunction to restrain the narrowing of a cartway by abstracting space for formation of a footway—Application refused, it being shown that a footway was desirable, and that defendants had not exceeded their powers. (*Times,* June 23, 1883.)

1892.   [1942]
Cowley v. Newmarket L. B. Action for personal injuries caused by stepping off a pathway unprotected by a dwarf wall—Held that no duty lay on the Board to guard the wall—*Russell v. Men of Devon,* and *Mackinnon v. Penson* followed : *Hartnall v. Ryde* distinguished. (L. R., A. C., 345.)

1879.   [1943]
Danby v. Hunter. "Highway Act, 1835," § 76—"Waggon"—Cart without name on it—The section applies to a cart or carriage, *ejusdem generis,* with a waggon, and not to a light spring cart much used for carrying persons and paying duty under 32 & 33 Vict., c. 14, § 18. (49 L. J., M. C., 15 : L. R., 5 Q. B. D., 20 : 41 L. T., 622 : 43 J. P., 781.)

1845.   [1944]
Davis v. Curling. "Highway Act, 1835," § 109—Alleged neglect of Surveyor to remove or protect a heap of gravel—Held that the defendant was entitled to Notice of Action. (15 L. J., Q. B., 56 : 8 Q. B., 286.)

1839.   [1945]
Duncan v. Findlater. The Trustees under a Public Road Act held not responsible for an injury occasioned by the negligence of the men employed in making or repairing their road—The funds raised under such Act cannot be charged with compensation for such an injury ; the persons employed on the road not being in the situation of servants to the Trustees. (6 Cl. & Fin., 894.) [A Scotch case which contains a summary of previous English decisions.]

1861.   [1946]
Hardwick v. Moss. "Highway Act, 1835," § 109—Erection of Weighing-machine—Excavation made in highway for the purpose of placing the machine, and materials excavated left in a heap and unlighted—Accident to Vehicle—A Surveyor who has reasonable ground for believing that he is acting "under the authority of the Act" is entitled to Notice of Action. (31 L. J., Ex., 205 : 7 H. & N., 136 : 4 L. T., 802.)

1876.   [1947]
Holland v. Northwich H. B. "Highway Act, 1835," § 109—Neglect to repair a handrail on a bridge—Injury to traveller—Such an act of omission to repair held to come within the definition of "something done under the Statute," and Notice of Action necessary. (34 L. T., 137 : 40 J. P., 317.)

1846.   [1948]
Huggins v. Waydey. "Highway Act, 1835," § 109—Tree cut down by Surveyor informally appointed but *bonâ fide* believing the contrary and acting in pursuance of the Act—Action for Trespass—Held, that the Surveyor was entitled to Notice of Action. (16 L. J., Ex., 136 : 15 M. & W., 357.)

1886.   [1949]
Loughborough H. B. v. Curzon. Proceedings before Justices for non-repair—A *bonâ fide* admission by a Waywarden that a road is a highway repairable, &c., is binding on the Highway Board and cannot afterwards be repudiated. (55 L. J., M. C., 122 : L. R., 17 Q. B. D., 344 : 55 L. T., 50 : 50 J. P., 788.)

1864.   [1950]
Ohrby v. Ryde Commissioners. "Towns Improvement Clauses Act, 1847," § 52—Neglect to

fence a dangerous footpath—Defendants held liable—Commissioners acting gratuitously in the discharge of a public duty are liable for an injury caused by a breach of duty on their part, without proving that they possess funds, or means of raising funds. (33 L. J., Q. B., 296 : 5 B. & S., 743.)

1867. [1951]
Parsons v. *St. Matthew's, Bethnal Green, Vestry.* The Common Law liability being on the Parish, an action for non-repair of a highway will not lie against a Vestry under the "Metropolis Local Management Act, 1855." (37 L. J., C. P., 62 : L. R., 3 C. P., 56 : 17 L. T., 211.)

1857. [1952]
Reg. v. *Arnould.* "Highway Act, 1835," § 94—On a summons against a Surveyor or other person for non-repair, if the obligation to repair is denied, the Justices have no jurisdiction to make an Order; but are bound under § 95 to direct that an Indictment be preferred. (27 L. J., M. C., 92 : 8 E. & B., 550 : [*Reg.* v. *Berkshire JJ.*] 30 L. T., (o. s.), 149.)

1839. [1953]
Reg. v. *Bedfordshire JJ.* Highway Act, 1835," § 105—Notice of appeal against a conviction by 2 Justices—Notice served on Surveyors and on only one Justice, though addressed to both, held bad. (9 L. J., M. C., 8 ; 11 A. & E., 134 : 3 P. & D., 21.)

1867. [1954]
Reg. v. *Burrell.* Trifling encroachment on a highway sanctioned verbally by the Officers of the Trustees, and afterwards approved by the Trustees, but such approval not entered in the Minute Book.—Held that the Defendant was, under the circumstances, improperly convicted of an encroachment. (16 L. T., 572 : 10 Cox, C. C., 462.)

1863. [1955]
Reg. v. *Dukinfield Township.* "Highway Act, 1835," § 23 : "Public Health Act, 1848," §§ 69-70—Highway—Dedication—In places where a Local Board are Surveyors, the "Highway Act, 1835," is constructively superseded so far as regards the steps to be taken to secure the "adoption" of a road, and therefore the road must be made to the satisfaction of the Board. (32 L. J., M. C., 230 : 4 B. & S., 158.)

1888. [1956]
Reg. v. *London & North Western Railway Co.* Indictment for flooding a highway—Application that the fine imposed shall be large enough to cover all the Costs incurred by Prosecutors, refused—The Court will impose a proper fine but will not do indirectly that which it could not do directly, i.e., make the unsuccessful defendant pay all the costs of the prosecution. (52 J. P., 821.)

1880. [1957]
Reg. v. *Platts.* A Local Board has no power *mero motu* to authorise encroachments on a highway by a landowner, even to a very small

extent, and with a view of improving the line of the road—Such powers can only be had by resort to the formalities of the "Highway Acts"—Indictment by a neighbour, who conceived himself prejudiced by Board's action—Verdict of guilty against encroaching landowner held good. (49 L. J., Q. B., 849 : 43 L. T., 159 : 44 J. P., 765.)

1864. [1958]
Reg. v. *Wadhurst.* Semble that an Indictment for non-repair though in form a criminal proceeding is in substance and truth a civil proceeding, and therefore may be referred. (At *Nisi Prius.*) (*Times*, March, 24, 1864.)

1797. [1959]
Rex v. *Bagshaw.* "Highway Act, 1773," § 82 [Repealed]—Inquisition by Jury to assess compensation—It must appear on the face of the proceedings that notice has been given to the owners of the land. (7 T. R., 363.)

1836. [1960]
Rex v. *Norwich & Watton Road Trustees.* "Turnpike Act, 1822," § 85—Compensation for taking land—Where there are several parties with separate interests in the same premises, the Inquisition must specify the compensation to be given to each—An Inquisition awarding a lump sum to the whole of the parties, quashed. (6 L. J., K. B., 41 : 5 A. & E., 563 : 1 N. & P., 32 : 2 H. & W., 385.)

1840. [1961]
Rix v. *Borton.* "Highway Act, 1835," § 109—The enactment that 21 days' Notice of Action is to be given to Justices, &c., does not by implication repeal the privilege of a Justice to have, under 24 Geo. II., c. 44, § 1, a month's notice. (9 L. J., M. C., 93 : 12 A. & E., 470 : 4 P. & D., 182.)

1812. [1962]
Roberts v. *Read.* "Highway Act, 1773," § 81 [Repealed] — Wall adjoining a highway undermined by Surveyors—Eventual fall thereof—The limitation of time for bringing an Action held to run not from the date of the undermining, but from the date of the accident. (16 East, 215.)

1878. [1963]
Robinson v. *Stevenitt.* "Highway Act, 1835"—Summons under § 20 against a Surveyor for neglecting to repair a road—No proceedings under § 94—Held that the procedure pointed out in § 94 must be followed, and that the Surveyor could not be convicted summarily under § 20. (38 L. T., 611 : 42 J. P., 356.)

1847. [1964]
Smith v. *Hopper.* "Highway Act, 1835," § 109 —Surveyor ordered by Highway Board to remove a gate which obstructed a supposed ancient foot-way without first applying to Justices—Action for Trespass against various members of the Board and the Surveyor—Held that Notice of Action was necessary, the act being done *bonâ fide*, and not being utterly unreasonable. (16 L. J., Q. B., 93 : 9 Q. B., 1005 : 8 L. T., (o. s.), 409.)

1877. [1965]

Taylor v. Meltham L. B. H. "Highway Act, 1835," § 109: "Public Health Act, 1848," §§ 117 and 139 [Repealed]—Held that an Action of Trespass commenced after the expiration of the 3 months mentioned in the former Act, but before the expiration of the 6 months mentioned in the latter Act, was commenced in time, the later Act operating to extend the earlier one. (47 L. J., C. P., 12.)

1864. [1966]

Thomas v. Marshall. Obstruction of highway by stones placed there—Conviction of a Surveyor of Highways set aside because there was no evidence that he caused the obstruction, or was the Surveyor. (29 J. P., 23.)

1854. [1967]

Tryddyn Surveyors, In re; Harrison, Ex parte. "Highway Act, 1835," §§ 95, 103—Indictment for non-repair—Costs payable under § 95 are not recoverable by Distress against the Surveyor, but are to be paid out of a Rate —If needs be, a Rate must be levied. (23 L.J., M. C., 45 ; [*Reg. v. Eyton*] 3 E. & B., 390; [*Reg. v. Flintshire JJ.*] 22 L. T., (o. s.), 281.)

1825. [1968]

Underhill v. Ellicombe. "Highway Act, 1773," § 34 [Repealed]—Held that Surveyors could not maintain an Action for debt to recover composition money, duly assessed in lieu of Statute Duty, a specific remedy by Distress having been prescribed—When a Statute prescribes a particular remedy, that remedy must be taken, and no other. (M'Cleland & Y., 450.)

1832. [1969]

Witham Navigation Co. v. Padley. "Highway Act, 1773," §§ 12 and 82 [Repealed]—Action for Trespass against Surveyors for removing a watch-house—Power to Surveyors to remove Nuisances on Highways held not to authorise them to pull down a building—They should have resorted to their remedy at Common Law. (2 L. J., M. C., 29 : 4 B. & Ad., 69.)

1863. [1970]

Young v. Davis. "Highway Act, 1835," § 109— No Action lies against a Surveyor for damage resulting from neglect to repair a highway— The proper remedy would be by Indictment against the Parish. (2 H. & C., 197 : 9 L. T., 145.)

3. HIGHWAY ACCOUNTS (a).

1858. [1971]

Adams v. Lakeman. "Highway Act, 1835," § 44, imposing penalty on Surveyor for not accounting, only applies to an ordinary Surveyor ; not to the Assistant Surveyor of a Board formed under § 18 of that Act. (27 L. J., M. C., 307 : E. B. & E., 615 : 31 L. T., (o. s.), 199.)

(a) For other cases connected with this subject, see Chambers's *Local Rates*, 2nd ed., 8vo. London, 1889.

1836. [1972]

Addison v. Round. Highway Act, 1773," § 48 [Repealed]—Held that Churchwardens and Overseers, as representing the Parish, had not such a property in the books of an outgoing Surveyor as to entitle them to maintain Trover—The only remedy was that provided by the Statute, viz., a penalty for non-compliance with the directions of the Statute as to the delivery of the books. (5 L. J., K. B., 152 : 4 A. & E., 799 : 6 N. & M., 422.)

1877. [1973]

Ashworth v. Hebden Bridge L. B. Motion to restrain a Local Board from levying a Rate to repair a road until the Queen's Bench Division had disposed of a special case stated to ascertain whether the road was a highway or not—Injunction granted till the question had been decided, but plaintiff meanwhile to pay into Court the amount in dispute. (47 L. J., Ch., 195 : W. N., 1877, p. 247 : 37 L. T., 496.)

1862. [1974]

Cave v. Mills. A Turnpike Surveyor for several years knowingly omitted in his accounts liabilities duly incurred by him—The Trustees settled each year the accounts of that year, except the last—Held that the Surveyor could not recover any omitted sums except those which belonged to the last year. (31 L. J., Ex., 265 : 7 H. & N., 913: 6 L. T., 650.)

1861. [1975]

Champ v. Stokes. Attorney's Bill of Costs against a Highway Surveyor in respect of certain Highway business—Held that the Heading "To the Surveyor," &c., was a sufficient delivery of the Bill within the "Attorneys and Solicitors Act, 1843," § 37. (30 L. J., Ex., 242 : 6 H. & N., 683 : 4 L. T., 334.)

1830. [1976]

Heudebourck v. Langton. "Highway Act, 1773," § 48 [Repealed]—Held that an incoming Surveyor could not maintain an Action against his predecessor for balance in hand, until the accounts had been allowed or disallowed in manner directed by the Act. (8 L. J., (o. s.), M. C., 134 : 10 B. & C., 546.) (S. C. at *Nisi Prius* : 3 C. & P., 566 : 1 Mood. & Mal., 402, n.)

1851. [1977]

Kilham v. Collier. "Highway Act, 1835," § 103 —Law Expenses incurred by Surveyor without sanction of Vestry—Consequent refusal of Vestry to pass his accounts—Offer by him to hand over to new Surveyor a sum of money if opposition were withdrawn—Agreement to this effect endorsed on the accounts, and opposition accordingly withdrawn—The money remaining unpaid, Action in County Court by the new Surveyor, who was one of those who signed the agreement—Held that there was no contract with the plaintiff in particular, and that the other Vestrymen should have been joined as co-plaintiffs, and that if the money was to be treated as a balance due from one Surveyor to another, the procedure prescribed in "Highway Act, 1835," § 103, namely, Summary process, should have been resorted to—*Semble*, that the arrangement with the Vestry was illegal as against public policy. (21 L. J., Q. B., 65 : [*Collier* v. *Killham*] 15 Jur., 1175 : 18 L. T., (o. s.), 121.)

1835.   [1978]
Liddard v. *Holmes.* Agreement by A, one of 2 Surveyors, to hand over to B, the other, the Rate-Book on promise that A should be reimbursed out of the next Rate money advanced by him for Highway purposes—Money was afterwards collected by B, but B spent it all in repair of roads and refused to repay A—Held that A was entitled to sue B for the amount due as on an account stated. (2 C. M. & R., 586 ; 1 Tyr. & G., 9.)

1857.   [1979]
Reg. v. *Leicestershire JJ.* "Highway Act, 1835," § 44—Accounts of Surveyor allowed in part, disallowed as to the remainder, by the Justices at Special Sessions—Held that no appeal either by Parishioners or by Surveyor lay to the Quarter Sessions. (8 E. & B., 557 : 21 J. P., 772.)

1858.   [1980]
Reg. v. *Padwick.* "Highway Act, 1835," § 105 : 12 & 13 Vict., c. 45, §§ 5-6—Appeal to Special Sessions against an allowance of accounts of Surveyors—Appeal dismissed—Thereupon an Appeal to Quarter Sessions—That Appeal also dismissed for want of jurisdiction—Order of Quarter Sessions that Appellant should pay costs held good under 12 & 13 Vict., c. 45. (27 L. J., M. C., 113 : 8 E. & B., 704 : [*R.* v. *Packwick*] 30 L. T., (o. s.), 255.)

1841.   [1981]
Reg. v. *Yorkshire, W. R., JJ.* (1). "Highway Act, 1835," § 44—No Appeal lies to Quarter Sessions against the allowance of Surveyor's accounts at Special Sessions—Nor will the Court grant a *Mandamus* to Petty Sessions to re-examine accounts once passed, although improper items have been passed, and the accounts were not fully investigated because it was supposed that an appeal lay to Quarter Sessions and that the case involved important questions of Law. (10 L. J., M. C., 137 : 1 Q. B., 624 : 1 G. & D., 198.)

1834.   [1982]
Rex v. *Fowler.* "Highway Act, 1773," [Repealed] —Law Expenses *bonâ fide* incurred by Surveyors and allowed by Justices, notwithstanding opposition of inhabitants although not agreed to or allowed before charged—Such allowances held good. (1 A. & E., 836 ; 3 N. & M., 826.)

1833.   [1983]
Rex v. *Lewis.* Where a Surveyor had improperly allowed the time for producing his accounts and getting them passed, to elapse, a *Mandamus* was granted to compel their production. (1 Dowl., P. C., 530.)

1886.   [1984]
Sheppey San. A. v. *Elmley Overseers.* Rural Sanitary District and Highway Board District formerly conterminous but one Parish taken out of Highway District by vote of Quarter Sessions—Such Parish held exempt from continuing to contribute to general Highway Rate—A Rural Sanitary Authority acting as a Highway Board under the "Highways Act, 1878," § 4; has no power to tax a parish withdrawn. (55 L. J., M. C., 176 : L. R., 17 Q. B. D., 364 : 50 J. P., 343.) Parish restored (51 J. P., 261.)

1862.   [1985]
Taylor v. *Stansfield.* Highway accounts—Balance due to Surveyors on an old account required out of the Rates after the lapse of 4 years—Held that the payment ought to be disallowed. (6 L. T., 26.)

1884.   [1986]
United Land Co. v. *Tottenham L. B.* "Highway Act, 1835,"—Costs of solicitor employed by Local Board to take steps to obtain diversion at request of private person are not "expenses" within § 84, which Board can recover summarily under § 101, though perhaps they might be recoverable by Action. (53 L. J., M. C., 136 : 51 L. T., 364 : 48 J. P., 727.)

1885.   [1987]
Worthington v. *Gill.* "Highway Act, 1864," § 33 —Allowance of Highway Rate by Justices is not necessary. (49 J. P., 629.)

4. CREATION OF HIGHWAYS.

(1.) PROOFS GENERALLY OF A WAY BEING A HIGHWAY.

1678.   [1988]
Absor v. *French.* If a highway be founderous a passenger may go over the next adjoining land without being guilty of a trespass. (2 Shower, 28.)

1876.   [1989]
Bailey v. *Jamieson.* A Way ceases to be a "Public Highway" where access to it at both ends becomes impossible by reason of Ways leading to it having been legally stopped up. (L. R., 1 C. P. D., 329 : 34 L. T., 62.)

1852.   [1990]
Bateman v. *Bluck.* A *cul-de-sac* may be a public highway. (21 L. J., Q. B., 406 : 18 Q. B., 870 : 19 L. T., (o. s.), 95.)

1889.   [1991]
Bourke v. *Davis.* The River Mole, a non-tidal tributary of the Thames, held on the evidence not a public highway over which there existed unrestricted rights of user by the public—*Marshall* v. *Ullswater Steam Navigation Co.*, considered. (L. R., 44 Ch. D., 110.)

1815.   [1992]
Bullard v. *Harrison.* Though a man may deviate on to adjoining land if a public highway is impassable, yet this rule does not apply to

the case of a private way which becomes impassable—In this case, therefore, the person who deviates becomes a trespasser. (4 Maule & S., 387.)

1853. [1993]
Campbell v. *Lang.* A public right of way means a right to the public to pass from one public place to another public place—*Semble* that the *terminus* of a public way need not itself be a public place, if it *lead* to a public place. (1 Macq., H. L. C., 451.)

1851. [1994]
Campbell v. *Race.* Way blocked by snow—A traveller on a highway rendered impassable by a sudden and recent obstruction may pass over adjoining fields so far as is necessary to avoid the obstruction, doing no unnecessary damage, without being guilty of a Trespass. (7 Cushing, (U.S.) R., 408.)

1868. [1995]
Cook v. *Bath, Mayor.* Right of way to back of house—Non-user for many years followed by a resumption of user—Proposal of Corporation to build so as to obstruct the way—Conflicting evidence as to way being public or private—Where a plaintiff suffers a particular injury from the obstruction of a public way an Injunction will lie, and the Attorney-General need not be a party—Circumstances which will amount to an abandonment of an easement, considered. (L. R., 6 Eq., 177 : 18 L. T., 123.)

1839. [1996]
Cotterill v. *Starkey.* A foot passenger has a right to cross a road, and the driver of a carriage is liable to an Action if he does not take care to avoid driving against him—It is no defence that such driver cannot pull up in time because his reins break, for he is bound to have proper tackle—The rule as to a carriage being on its proper side of the road does not apply where a carriage and a foot passenger are concerned ; for as regards foot passengers a carriage may go on either side of the road—In an Action of Trespass for driving a carriage against the plaintiff, the defence of inevitable accident must be specially pleaded. (8 C. & P., 691.)

1863. [1997]
Coventry (Earl of) v. *Willes.* Declaration in Trespass for entering certain lands—Plea, public highway available during horse races, with an allegation of common right to go and witness the races—Other similar pleas—Pleas held bad—A customary right can only be applicable to certain inhabitants of the district where the custom is alleged to exist, and cannot be claimed for the public at large—*Fitch* v. *Rawling* followed. (9 L. T., 384 : 12 W. R., 127.)

1873. [1998]
Cubitt v. *Maxse.* Land set out under an Inclosure Act for a highway—Proposed line of way fenced but no way ever formed—Held that the mere allotment of a piece of land for a highway did not make it such, when no steps had been taken to comply with the formali-

ties prescribed by Parliament—There being no evidence of user, the adjacent owner, holding by adverse possession for more than 20 years, held entitled to the land. (42 L. J., C. P., 278 : L. R., 8 C. P., 704 : 29 L. T., 244.)

1870. [1999]
Greenwich B. W. v. *Maudsley.* Right of way along a Sea Wall—Dedication may be pro-sumed so far as it is not inconsistent with the purpose of the Wall. (39 L. J., Q. B., 205 : L. R., 5 Q. B., 397 : 23 L. T., 121 : 35 J. P., 8.)

1859. [2000]
Harper v. *Forbes.* The widening of a road by adding to it a strip of consecrated ground cut off from a Churchyard held *ultra vires*—No Ecclesiastical Court can authorise any portion of ground that has been once consecrated to be devoted to secular uses. (5 Jur., (N. S.), 275.)

1860. [2001]
Hutton v. *Hamboro.* Per Cockburn, J. : A public right of way over waste land, or between two points, extends to every part of the land, access to, or along which there is the right of way—A private right is not necessarily so extensive, but may be confined within certain limits. (2 F. & F., 218.) [The meaning of this decision seems to be that in the case of a public right of way the right extends over all the land, so that, for instance, if one path becomes impassable the public may make another, but that such an exte ded power does not of necessity inhere where there is only a private right of way.]

1856. [2002]
Petrie v. *Nuttall.* A verdict of "Guilty," and Judgment thereon, in an Indictment for obstructing a highway cannot be pleaded as an estoppel in an Action brought by the party convicted against a third person for using the way—An estoppel must be mutual, and a verdict between two parties can be no estoppel as against other persons. (25 L. J., Ex., 200 : 11 Ex., 569.)

1858. [2003]
Pipe v. *Fulcher.* Action of Trespass—Old map, which had been used by deceased and present Stewards for defining copyholds, put in by defendant to prove a highway held not admissible evidence as amounting to a declaration by a deceased person as to a public right, inasmuch as it had been used only for another purpose, and did not describe the way as a highway. (28 L. J., Q. B., 12 : 1 F. & F., 111 : 32 L. T., (O. S.), 105.)

1861. [2004]
Reed v. *Jackson.* Action for Trespass—Record of Verdict negativing claim of public right of way held admissible evidence in Trespass against another defendant who sought to justify under the same right—Reputation would be evidence as to a public right, *à fortiori* a verdict would be evidence—Reputation is evidence in a claim of public but not of private right. (1 East, 355.)

1853. [2005]
Reg. v. *Aldborough.* Though "Public Highway" *primâ facie* imports a road for carriages as well as for other purposes, it may mean simply a "Public Bridleway"—User for 39 years as a bridleway held decisive evidence that it was no more than such. (17 J. P., 648.)

1837. [2006]
Reg. v. *Bliss.* Evidence of Highway – Road, public or private?—Evidence that a deceased person had planted a willow adjoining the road, saying that it would mark the boundary, held not admissible evidence either to show reputation of the road being public, or as a statement accompanying an act, or as the admission of an occupier against his own interest since he could not bind the interest of his landlord—Hearsay evidence must only be received as showing general reputation and must not touch particular facts. (7 L. J., Q. B., 4 : 7 A. & E., 550 : 2 N. & P., 464.)

1875. [2007]
Reg. v. *Burney.* A public footpath having been blocked up at one end by works executed under the authority of Parliament had ceased to be of public utility—Indictment for misdemeanour in obstructing it—Conviction—That the way had become of little utility might be a reason for mitigating the punishment inflicted on the guilty party, but it was no justification for the act of obstruction—A *cul-de-sac* may be a public highway. (31 L. T., 828.)

1850. [2008]
Reg. v. *Lordsmere Inhabitants* (1). Turnpike road partly formed by turning to account an existing road—Portion of road out of repair during continuance of Turnpike Act—Indictment of Parish for non-repair—Held that the road was a common highway in spite of its temporary Turnpike character, and that the Parish was liable. (19 L. J., M. C., 215 : 15 Q. B., 689 : 4 New Sess. Cas., 205.)

1879. [2009]
Reg. v. *Ward* (2). Indictment for obstructing an alleged Right of Way over a causeway leading to sea-shore—Powers of Local Board —Question of evidence of dedication—New trial granted on the ground that the verdict for the Crown was against the evidence. (*Times,* June 28, 1879.)

1825. [2010]
Rex v. *Lyon.* Arched carriage-way—A way is none the less a public carriage-way because only vehicles of limited dimensions can traverse it—Where a way has been recognised in a Statute as public it is not necessary that a Parish should adopt it, in order to make it a public way. (5 D. & R., 497 : Ryan & M., 151.)

(?) [2011]
Rex v. *St. James, Taunton, Inhabitants.* Where there once has been a public highway no length of time during which it may not have

been used will prevent the public resuming the right, if they think proper [unless it has been formally stopped]. (2 Selw., N. P., 13th Ed., 1264.)

1819. [2012]
Rex v. *Severn & Wye Railway Co.* Railway or Tramroad made under a Statute whereby it was provided that it should be available to public generally, held to be a highway—On its being pulled up, *Mandamus* granted for its restoration. (2 B. & Ald., 646.)

1670. [2013]
Rex v. *Stoughton.* If one inclose land on one side, which hath been anciently inclosed of the other side, he ought to repair all the way, but if there be not such an ancient inclosure of the other side, he ought to repair but half that way. (1 Hawk., P. C., c. 32, § 7 : 2 Keble, 665 : 2 Saunders, 157.)

1852. [2014]
St. John, Walbrook, Rector v. *Parishioners.* No Judge has power by the general law to grant a Faculty for the surrender of part of a Churchyard for widening a highway even though consent be given by all parties interested [the reason apparently being that a sentence of consecration is definite]. (2 Robertson, Eccl., 515.)

1878. [2015]
St. Mary, Whitechapel, In re. Application for faculty to authorise part of a Churchyard to be given up to widen a highway—Application granted on condition that tombstones and human remains were carefully removed ; ground taken to revert to Churchyard if hereafter not wanted for the highway. (*Times,* July 30, 1878.)

1820. [2016]
Sutcliffe v. *Greenwood.* A highway may be created by Act of Parliament, and therefore a plea of a right to pass at pleasure along a public highway "paying a certain toll" is not inconsistent or contradictory. (8 Price, 535.)

1781. [2017]
Taylor v. *Whitehead.* The general right to pass across adjoining land wh n a way is found. crous only applies in the case of public highways—Therefore where a way over which there existed a private right to pass became impassable owing to a flood the defendant was held liable to an action for Trespass for going over private lands adjoining. (2 Dougl., 745.)

1857. [2018]
Thompson v. *West Somerset Mineral Railway Co.* A highway is strictly speaking a road leading from one place to another with a foot and carriage way, and the public are entitled to have it kept free from impediments—A pier is not a highway, least of all a pier across which ropes and chains are placed as of right for the mooring of vessels. (29 L. T., (o. s.), 7 ; 21 J. P., 278.)

1836. [2019]
Walter v. *Montague.* Public footway through a Churchyard—*Per* Dr. Lushington :—" I ap-

prehend that neither the Rector nor the Churchwardens can make a new path without a Faculty from this [Consistory] Court. In strictness that is by Law required." (1 Curt., 253, at p. 260.)

1838.   [2020]
Williams v. *Wilcox*. *Per* Lord Denman, C.J.:— "It cannot be disputed that the channel of a public navigable river is a King's Highway, and is properly so described. The absence of any right to go *extra viam* if the channel is choked, and the want of a definite obligation on anyone to repair, render it more important, in order to make the highway effectual, that the right of passage should extend to all parts of the channel." (8 A. & E., 314 at p. 329.)

1875.   [2021]
Wimbledon & Putney Commons Conservators v. *Dixon*. There may be a right of way across a Common without any one track in particular being adhered to, provided that the *terminus a quo* and the *terminus ad quem* are known. (45 L. J., Ch., 353: L. R., 1 Ch. D., 362: 33 L. T., 679: 40 J. P., 102.)

1845.   [2022]
Wood v. *Wedgewood*. A declaration in Trespass contained a Count for trespass in two closes and a Count for trespass "in other parts" of the same closes—Plea of Justification under one public Right of Way over the two Closes held good in answer to both Counts. (14 L. J., C. P., 132: 1 C. B., 273.)

(2.) DEDICATION OF HIGHWAYS.

(i.) *Generally*.

1806.   [2023]
Allen v. *Ormond*. Proof of a *terminus ad quem* being a public highway is afforded by proving a public footway. (8 East, 4.)

1789.   [2024]
Aspindall v. *Brown*. In pleading "public highway" it is sufficient to allege the fact, without showing how it became so, or that it has been so from time immemorial. (3 T. R., 265.)

1875.   [2025]
Bagshaw v. *Buxton L. B.* Strip of highway wrongfully enclosed—Lapse of many years—Held that the Board was entitled to require the surrender of the land—No lapse of time, in fact nothing but legal process, can bar the public right as to what can clearly be proved to have been once a highway. (45 L. J., Ch., 260: L. R., 1 Ch. D., 220: 34 L. T., 112: 40 J. P., 197.)

1808.   [2026]
Ballard v. *Dyson*. Evidence of a prescriptive right of way for all manner of carriages does not necessarily prove a right of way for all manner of cattle—But it is some evidence of a drift-way—A carriage-way will comprehend a horse-way, but not necessarily a drift-way—The extent of usage is evidence of a right only commensurate with the user. (1 Taunt., 279.)

1838.   [2027]
Barraclough v. *Johnson*. In determining whether a way has or has not been dedicated to the public the proprietor's intention must be considered—If it appear only that he has suffered a continual user that fact may prove a dedication; but such proof may be rebutted by evidence of acts showing that he contemplated only a licence revocable in a particular event—Documentary evidence as to reputation admitted. (7 L. J., Q. B., 172: 8 A. & E., 99: 3 N. & P., 233.)

1833.   [2028]
British Museum Trustees v. *Finnis*. If a person allows the public to pass over his land continuously, user for a very few years would establish a right of way; if it is not his intention to dedicate he must do some act, such as, for instance, shut it up one day in a year, to show that he intends to give a licence only —If there is an old way near a person's land, and by reason of the decay of fences the public come on the land, no dedication is to be presumed. (5 C. & P., 460.)

1862.   [2029]
Chapman v. *Cripps*. The mere use by people of tracks through a wood where they are free to wander as they please is not enough to show dedication of such tracks as public foot-ways. (2 F. & F., 864.)

1892.   [2030]
Eyre v. *New Forest H. B.* A tenant for life cannot dedicate a way as a highway against the remainderman—It is by the continual passage of people who wish to go along a particular way that evidence of there being a highway is established. (56 J. P., 517.)

1888.   [2031]
Grand Junction Canal Co. v. *Petty*. Land acquired for a Statutory purpose may be dedicated as a public highway subject to its use for the Statutory purpose—Held that a Canal Towing-path might be dedicated as a public footpath. (57 L. J., Q. B., 572: L. R., 21 Q. B. D., 273: 59 L. T., 464: 52 J. P., 692.)

1825.   [2032]
Harper v. *Charlesworth*. Public footway over Crown land extinguished by an Inclosure Act nevertheless used by the public for 20 years afterwards—Held no evidence of dedication, as there was no proof that the user was with the knowledge or consent of the Crown. (3 L. J., (o. s.), K. B., 265: 4 B. & C., 574: 6 D. & R., 572.)

1735.   [2033]
Lade v. *Shepherd*. In dedicating land for a highway the landowner only gives a right of passage—There is no transfer of the property of the soil. (2 Str., 1004.)

1862.   [2034]
Mildred v. *Weaver*. A right of way may be obtained by user for pleasure purposes only —Non-repair by Parish is cogent but not conclusive evidence against way over private property being a Highway—Proof of general user is strong evidence of dedication, but it is to be considered with reference to gates,

repairs, permission, and the like—Payment
for user is cogent but not conclusive evidence
against the right. (3 F. & F., 30: 6 L. T.,
225.)

1821.   [2035]
Moore v. *Rawson*. A way over the lands of
another can only be lawfully used, in the
first instance with his consent, expressed or
implied—A party using the way without
such consent would be a wrong-doer—But
when such a user, without interruption, has
continued for 20 years, the owner's consent
is not only implied during that period, but a
grant of the easement is presumed to have
taken place before the user commenced. (3
B. & C., 332, at p. 339: 5 D. & R., 234, at
p. 239.)

1848.   [2036]
Reg. v. *East Mark Tything*. Waste land of a
manor set out as a private road but used by
the public—If a road has been used by the
public for many years dedication by the
owner may be presumed; it is not material
to inquire who was the owner or whether he
intended to dedicate—The Crown equally
with a private owner may be presumed to
dedicate. (17 L. J., Q. B., 177: 11 Q. B.,
877: 3 Cox, C. C., 60: 11 L. T., (o. s.), 63.)

1862.   [2037]
Reg. v. *Hawkhurst Parish* (1). Dedication for a
limited purpose—Road leading to a Private
Park—Though the road had been repaired
by the Parish from time immemorial, held
that the evidence of dedication and user
was insufficient, and that the Parish was not
bound to repair the road. (7 L. T., 268: 11
W. R., 9.)

1863.   [2038]
Reg. v. *Horley Inhabitants*. Occupation road set
out under an Inclosure Act—Road a soft
road but entirely free to the Public, and
repaired on 2 occasions by Public Subscription—Held that there had been sufficient
dedication to render the Parish liable to
repair it, although there never had been any
formal adoption. (8 L. T., 382: 11 W. R.,
433.)

1821.   [2039]
Rex v. *St. Benedict Inhabitants*. Road set out
under a Local Act for use of certain persons
only, used by the Public for many years.—
Held that there was no sufficient dedication.
(4 B. & Ald., 447.) [This case was also an
authority for the necessity of acquiescence
in dedication on the part of a Parish, in
order that it might be liable to repair, but
as regards this point the case has been overruled.]

1790.   [2040]
Rouse v. *Bardin*. In pleading "Public highway," it is not necessary to specify any termini; but if stated they must be proved.
(1 H. Bl., 351.)

1862.   [2041]
Schwinge v. *Dowell*. Evidence that in a place of
resort for pleasure, such as a wood, people
have moved about whither they pleased,

there being no definite trackway in any particular direction, but merely temporary tracks
not passable in wet weather and varying in
every season and never shown to be repaired,
is not evidence of a public highway or of a
public right of resort for air, or of a prescriptive right of way. (2 F. & F., 845.)

1888.   [2042]
Spedding v. *Fitzpatrick*. Dedication may be
proved not only by evidence of public user
(which is in general sufficient) but by acts
and declarations of owner—Where in an
Action to restrain trespass to roads defendants allege that the roads are highways,
they ought if they rely on anything but user
to inform the plaintiff before the trial what
is the nature of the acts and declarations
on which they rely,' setting forth dates and
the names of the persons by whom the same
were done or made. (L. R., 38 Ch. D., 410.)

188–.   [2043]
West v. *Derby Corporation*. "Public Health Act,
1875," § 150—Land laid out for new street
and built upon throughout its entire length
barring the last 20 ft., which portion was
blocked by transverse fence—Fence broken
down and so whole of street used by foot
passengers as a thoroughfare but only as a
cul-de-sac by carriages—Water main and
sewer laid opposite houses only—Held nevertheless that there was evidence of complete
dedication of the entire street, and that the
restoration and maintenance of a fence cutting off the 20 ft. at the end was a nuisance
which the Local Authority was justified in
pulling down. (*Municip. Corp. Assoc. Digest*,
col. 101.)

1822.   [2044]
Wood v. *Veal*. Land leased for 99 years—User
of a way over it by the Public for most of
this time—Lighted and paved under authority of an Act which mentioned it as a
"street"—Subsequent inclosure by owner—
Held that the Jury was justified in finding
no right of way—There can be no dedication
by tenants for a term, or by anyone, except
the owner in fee. (5 B. & Ald., 454: 1
D. & R., 20.)

1854.   [2045]
Young v. *Cuthbertson*. Although a public way
may pass through private property, it must
have at each end a public *terminus*, which
may, however, be a *cul-de-sac*—A mere private place, not admitting of a passage
through or beyond it, cannot form the terminus of a public way—Non-user of a right
of way may be evidence against the existence
of such right, but *quære* whether it can be
evidence to show that the right has been lost.
(1 Macq., H. L. C., 455.)

(ii.) *Acquiescence in, and Presumptions as to,
Dedication.*

1832.   [2046]
Baxter v. *Taylor*. Land under lease—Way
claimed as of right—Action by reversioner
against a trespasser held not maintainable,
there being no necessary injury to the re-

K

version—Acquiescence in acts of Trespass would not, under the circumstance of there being a lease, be evidence against the reversioner of dedication. (2 L. J., K. B., 65: 4 B. & Ad., 72: 1 N. & M., 11.)

1865.   [2047]
Bermondsey Vestry v. *Brown*. Dedication to a particular *Parish* cannot be presumed; dedication from uninterrupted use can only be presumed in favour of the Public generally—During the continuance of a lease no intention to dedicate on the part of the reversioner in fee is to be presumed. (L. R., 1 Eq., 204: 35 Bea., 226: 13 L. T., 574.)

1836.   [2048]
Davies v. *Stephens*. The user of a way during occupation by tenants does not bind the landlord, unless he was aware of it, but if the user extends over a long period of time it may be presumed that the landlord was aware of it—A plea of a "foot-way" is supported by proof of a carriage-way, as "a carriage-way always includes a foot-way"—A gate being kept across a way is not conclusive that it is not a public way, for the way may have been dedicated with a reservation of a right to keep a gate across it, in order to prevent cattle from straying. (7 C. & P., 570.)

1873.   [2049]
Hamilton v. *St. George's, Hanover Square, Vestry*. The owner of a cellar over which there exists a paved public foot-way is not bound to keep the foot-way in repair if the cellar existed before the foot-way was dedicated. (Metropolis.) (43 L. J., M. C., 41; L. R., 9 Q. B., 42: 29 L. T., 428: 38 J. P., 405.)

1859.   [2050]
Holden v. *Tilley*. Action for Trespass—Pleas, immemorial right of way, and user for 40 and 20 years respectively—About 19 years previously to Action a Statute had extinguished all ways not set out in an Inclosure Award—Way in question not so set out—Held that it could not be presumed from the user that the Award was otherwise than properly made, and less than 20 years having elapsed since the Award, no right had been gained under the "Prescription Act, 1832," 2 & 3 Will. IV., c. 71, § 2. (1 F. & F., 650.)

1826.   [2051]
Jarvis v. *Dean*. Persons had been for some years in the habit of passing along a new unpaved, unfinished street, terminating in fields where other houses were built—A Jury having found a dedication of it, the Court refused a new trial, which was moved for on the grounds that the evidence did not disclose adequate proof of dedication. (3 Bing., 447: 11 Moore, 354.)

1880.   [2052]
Powers v. *Bathurst*. Dedication—Presumption—Long user by the Public of a way across Copyhold land is evidence of a dedication by both Lord and Copyholder—*Reg.* v. *Petrie* followed. (49 L. J., Ch., 294: 42 L. T., 123.)

1872.   [2053]
Pryor v. *Pryor*. Land let on building leases for 60 years—Street thereon used by the Public by consent for more than 20 years—Held that an intention to dedicate must be inferred from the facts. (26 L. T., 758.)

1857.   [2054]
Race v. *Ward*. "Inclosure Act, 1801," §§ 11 and 14—Custom to take water from a well—Highway to well—Award inclosing land where well was situated and extinguishing ways, held not to operate as an extinction of the right to use the well—The Public having since the Inclosure been in the habit of crossing the plaintiff's close to get the water, *Semble*, that the ancient right of access was not extinguished. (26 L. J., Q. B., 133; 7 E. & B., 384; 28 L. T., (o. s.), 288.)

1860.   [2055]
Reg. v. *Brailsford Inhabitants*. Indictment for non-repair—Misdirection—New trial—The fact that a road is impassable in winter, is no presumption against its dedication to the Public. (2 L. T., 508.)

1859.   [2056]
Reg. v. *Broke*. In an Indictment for stopping up a highway, removed by *Certiorari*, and tried at the Assizes, Counsel for the defendant may sum up his evidence at the close of his case as in a civil Action—If a particular class of persons use a way, and the owner of the land does not communicate to them his reasons for letting them pass to the exclusion of all others, they must be deemed to pass as by right, and their user for 20 years will suffice to establish a right for the public generally. (1 F. & F., 314.)

1848.   [2057]
Reg. v. *Chorley*. Indictment for obstruction of footway by driving a carriage along it—Claim of private right of carriage-way—Alleged Waiver—Proof that before the public footway existed the Defendant's predecessors in title were entitled to a carriage-way over the *locus in quo*—Contention on the part of the Crown that public user inconsistent with the assertion of the private easement had determined it—Direction by the Judge that no interruption for less than 20 years would destroy the private right held a mis-direction—The period is only one element from which the grantee's intention to retain or abandon his right may be inferred, and the sufficiency or otherwise of the period in any particular case must depend on all the accompanying circumstances, including the adverse acts acquiesced in by him. (12 Q. B., 515: 3 Cox, C. C., 262.)

1855.   [2058]
Reg. v. *Petrie*. Highway—User by the Public for some time is *primâ facie* evidence of dedication: it is not necessary to inquire from whom the dedication first proceeded. (24 L. J., Q. B., 167: 4 E. & B., 737: 24 L. T., (o. s.), 271.)

1814.   [2059]
Rex v. *Barr.* Where a way is used for a great number of years over a close in the possession of a succession of tenants, the privity of the landlord and dedication by him is to be presumed, although he was never in actual possession or personally near the spot—Knowledge of the user and acquiescence by the steward is knowledge and acquiescence by the landlord. (4 Camp., 16.)

1808.   [2060]
Rex v. *Lloyd* (2). If the owner of the soil throws open a passage and neither marks by any visible distinction that he means to preserve his rights, nor excludes by positive prohibition persons from passing, intention to dedicate is to be presumed—Although the passage may have been originally intended only for the private convenience of particular houses, the Public are not to be excluded after long and uninterrupted user—A way may be a highway although very circuitous. (1 Camp., 260.)

1790.   [2061]
Rugby Charity Trustees v. *Merryweather.* Dedication may be presumed from user for a shorter time than is necessary to establish a right of possession to the land—User by the Public for 8 years and 6 years respectively held to justify a presumption of dedication. (11 East, 375, n.)

1855.   [2062]
Stone v. *Jackson.* Action for negligence in leaving a cellar unfenced close to a public footway—Evidence that many persons were in the habit of crossing near the spot, as a short cut to another road, but that persons were often turned back by the owner—Held that there was no proof of the way being public. (16 C. B., 199.)

1860.   [2063]
Thomas v. *Williams.* Highway—User—Evidence that a Local Board had repaired the street, and had put up notices under the "Public Health Act, 1848," § 70, for its adoption, held evidence of dedication sufficient to sustain a conviction for injuring the street. (24 J. P., 821.)

(iii.) *Limited Dedication: Bars and Gates.*

1871.   [2064]
Arnold v. *Blaker.* Highway—Footpath across an arable field—Held on the evidence that the Surveyors were not entitled so to repair the footpath that it could not be ploughed up, there appearing to have been only a limited dedication, subject to a right to plough. (40 L. J., Q. B., 185: L. R., 6 Q. B., 433.)

1873.   [2065]
Arnold v. *Holbrook.* Highway—Footpath across an arable field—Held that when a footpath was lawfully ploughed up and trespassing took place, to prevent which the occupier puts up hurdles, the Public must neither go off the line nor pull down the hurdles—The fact that the path became impassable after being lawfully ploughed conferred no right

on the Public, in the absence of prescriptive right, to deviate. (42 L. J., Q. B., 80: L. R., 8 Q. B., 96: 28 L. T., 23: 37 J. P., 229.)

1878.   [2066]
A.-G. v. *Bi-phosphated Guano Co.* Footway diverted, subject to an agreement between the Local Authority and an intending lessee that the latter should form a new road in substitution—Lease granted for 80 years, the demise being "subject to existing rights of way"—The new road shown on plan annexed, but marked "private road"—Subsequent assignments of the lease, of which the present defendants eventually became sub-lessees and they obstructed the way—Held that there had been no sufficient dedication to bind purchasers for value without notice. (W. N., 1878, p. 50.)

1845.   [2067]
Bateman v. *Burge.* If there be a public footway with a stile across it of a certain height no one has a right to replace the stile by a gate of greater height, and the former existence of gates in other parts of the same way will be no defence—If there be an obstruction of a public way, and any person receives a special injury from it, he may maintain an Action. (6 C. & P., 391.)

1869.   [2068]
Brackenborough v. *Thoresby.* "Highway Act, 1835," § 72—A footway across a field may be a "Highway," and a conviction will lie for injuring (in this case, ploughing up) the same. (19 L. T., 692.)

1840.   [2069]
Brownlow v. *Tomlinson.* Per Lord Denman, C.J.: —A road may be an occupation way at the same time that it is a highway; by the owner of the soil making it the latter it does not cease to be the former so as to deprive of his rights the party entitled to the private way. (1 M. & G., 484, at p. 487: also reported generally, 1 Scott, N. R., 426.)

1879.   [2070]
Chelsea Vestry v. *Stoddard.* Carriages standing in front of stables—Claim of right to use the highway whilst the carriages were being cleaned—Claim held valid, the highway having been dedicated subject to the right to obstruct it occasionally for the purpose in question. (43 J. P., 782.)

1862.   [2071]
Cooper v. *Walker.* Obstruction of Highway—Projecting stone steps—Held that though in fact an obstruction, they were no obstruction in Law, it being a fair presumption that the street was dedicated subject to the right to continue the inconvenience. (31 L. J., Q. B., 212 : 2 B. & S., 770 : 6 L. T., 711.)

1855.   [2072]
Cornwell v. *Metropolitan Commissioners of Sewers.* Ancient tidal sewer running along a highway—Held that the right to the highway was subject to the sewer, and that the owner of the sewer was not bound to fence. (10 Ex., 771 : 3 C. L. R., 417 : 19 J. P., 313.)

K 2

1861. [2073]
Dawes v. *Hawkins.* Ancient highway illegally obstructed and new road substituted—The new road having been used for more than 20 years the old road was restored and the new one closed by the landowner—Held that he was justified in stopping it up, there being no evidence of dedication—There can be no dedication of a way for a limited time, certain or uncertain; if dedicated at all it must be in perpetuity—Nor can the Public by nonuser release their rights. (29 L. J., C. P., 343 : 8 C. B., (N. S.), 848 : 4 L. T., 288.)

1845. [2074]
Ferrand v. *Milligan.* Action of Trespass for breaking open gates, &c.—Plea, public highway—Proof of the same, that the Township Surveyor had repaired the road—Replication, that this officer had executed some repairs by agreement with the landowner's steward and on promise of repayment—Held that the agreement was rightly admitted as evidence to explain why the Surveyor had interfered with a road if it was not a public highway. (15 L. J., Q. B., 103 ; 7 Q. B., 730.)

1862. [2075]
Fisher v. *Prowse.* Obstruction of highway—Projecting Cellar flap—If land with an obstruction on it is dedicated to the Public, such dedication is subject to the risk arising from such obstruction. (31 L. J., Q. B., 212 : 2 B. & S., 770 : 6 L. T., 711.)

1828. [2076]
Fitzpatrick v. *Robinson.* A user by the Public of an open strand or waste does not necessarily imply that the owner of the soil has abandoned his rights and given it to the Public—Although dedication may be partial or limited as to the sort of way (as to a horseway, &c.), yet there cannot be a qualified dedication subject to a power of resumption ; for that would be the reservation of a right inconsistent with dedication to the public. (1 Hudson & Brook, 585.)

1888. [2077]
Leicester Urban S. A. v. *Holland.* "Towns Police Clauses Act, 1847," § 28—Claims of right to occupy part of pavement with goods—Whereupon Justices dismissed summons—Held that they were wrong: they ought to have inquired and decided whether the footway had been dedicated subject to the encroachment as alleged. (57 L. J., M. C., 75 : 52 J. P., 788.)

1808. [2078]
Lethbridge v. *Winter.* Footpath stopped by a gate—Gate removed for 12 years and access of the Public permitted—New gate then erected—Held that the owner had not lost his right to stop the path by means of a gate, and that there was no sufficient proof of dedication. (1 Camp., N. P., 262, n.)

1880. [2079]
London Corporation v. *Riggs.* A "way of necessity" is not a general right of way for all purposes to or from the inclosed lands, but only a right of way so far as might be necessary for the enjoyment of the inclosed land in the state in which it happened to be when the right arose—Owner of a limited right of access to agricultural land not entitled to access to the same land in order to use it as building land. (49 L. J., Ch., 297 : L. R., 13 Ch. D., 798 : 42 L. T., 580 : 44 J. P., 345.)

1869. [2080]
Mercer v. *Woodgate.* Highway—Footpath through a ploughed field—Whether or not it is lawful to plough up a highway depends on the facts of the case—There may be a dedication of a right of way subject to a right to plough. (39 L. J., M. C., 21 : L. R., 5 Q. B., 26 : 10 B. & S., 833 : 21 L. T., 458.)

1889. [2081]
Mitchell v. *Haswell Co-operative Society.* Plaintiff a grantee of a right of way—Arch erected by defendants giving a headway of 14 ft.——Held that such an arch would not interfere with the ordinary user of the right of way, it not being shown that the ordinary vehicles of the district were ever higher or loaded higher than 14 ft.—*Semble* that even if it had been shown that the *locus in quo* was a public highway the same argument would have been applicable. (Durham Chancery Court.) (24 L. J. Newspaper, 226.)

1861. [2082]
Morant v. *Chamberlain.* A highway may be dedicated subject to a pre-existing right of user by adjoining occupiers for the deposit of goods on parts thereof. (30 L. J., Ex., 299 : 6 H. & N., 541.)

1843. [2083]
Poole v. *Huskinson.* A way may be dedicated for a *limited purpose, e.g.,* as a foot-way only, but there cannot be a dedication to a *limited portion of the Public, e.g.,* the inhabitants of one Parish in particular—Such a partial dedication is of no effect as a dedication—To constitute dedication there must be an intention to dedicate ; of this, user is evidence, but such evidence may be rebutted by contrary evidence of interruption by owner—Notwithstanding an Award by Inclosure Commissioners of land for a public bridle-way and drift-way and private carriage-way the ownership of the soil still remains in the Lord of the Manor. (11 M. & W., 827.)

1851. [2084]
Reg. v. *Charlesworth.* Turnpike road crossed at various places by Colliery Tramways—Held that the tramways were indictable as obstructions to the highway, notwithstanding that the Turnpike Trustees had power to grant licences for these tramways, which, however, they had not done in the present case—Though a landowner may dedicate a road with a reservation, a claim to cross it anywhere with tramrails is too large a reservation to be sanctioned without some express agreement. (20 L. J., M. C., 181 : 16 Q. B., 1012 : 5 Cox, C. C., 174 : 17 L. T., (O. S.), 91.)

1731.   [2085]
Rex v. *Hudson.* Common foot-way prescribed for the duration of a lease of 56 years—Defendant stopping it up within 4 years of the expiration of the lease held not guilty of stopping up a public way—Where the origin of a way is accounted for, the prescription is destroyed. (2 Str., 909.)

1863.   [2086]
Robbins v. *Jones.* Defective flagging and grating—Dedication to the public of a highway with a feature which afterwards became a dangerous nuisance—No action will thereafter lie against the dedicator for an injury caused by such nuisance—The dedication must be treated as accepted by the Public, subject to the inconvenience or risk, if any. (33 L. J., C. P., 1 : 15 C. B., (N. S.), 221 : 9 L. T., 523.)

1803.   [2087]
Roberts v. *Karr.* The erection of a bar, although it may have been afterwards knocked down, rebuts the presumption of a dedication to the Public. (1 Camp., 262, n.)

1862.   [2088]
Selby v. *Crystal Palace Gas Co.* Private road through an estate cut up into building-plots—Covenant by Freeholder that the occupiers might use the road as if it were public—Road broken up by Gas Company at the invitation of some of the occupiers, but without the consent of the Freeholder—Bill filed by him against the Company for an Injunction—Bill dismissed—Occupation roads through an estate formed for the convenience of the tenants do not thereby become dedicated to the public as of course. (31 L. J., Ch., 595 : 4 De G. F. & J., 246 : 30 Bea., 606 : 6 L. T., 790.)

1827.   [2089]
Stafford (Marquis of) v. *Coyney.* Road through a private estate permitted to be used by the Public for all purposes save the carriage of coals—Held that this was either a limited dedication or no dedication at all, but only a revocable licence, and that a person carrying coals along the road after notice not to do so was a trespasser—There may be a limited dedication. (5 L. J., K. B., 285 : 7 B. & C., 257.)

1813.   [2090]
Woodyer v. *Hadden.* *Per* Heath, J. :—"Until the owner has shown some intention of dedicating the soil to the Public his right continues of putting up a bar and excluding them, otherwise the building of every house and laying out a way to it would establish a public way." (5 Taunt., 125.)

(iv.) *In accordance with the "Highway Acts."*

1874.   [2091]
Reg. v. *Bagge.* "Highway Act, 1835," § 23—Proposal by landowner to dedicate new road—Acceptance by the Parish as a condition precedent to dedication—A meeting informally convened refused to accept the road—*Mandamus* to compel Justices to certify under

§ 23 refused—*Semble*, that a *Mandamus* would lie to compel the Surveyors to summon a proper meeting, even after the 3 months mentioned in the notice has expired. (44 L. J., M. C., 45 : [*Reg.* v. *Norfolk JJ.*] 31 L. T., 585.)

1858.   [2092]
Reg. v. *Derbyshire JJ.* "Highway Act, 1835," § 23—Decision of Vestry that a way proposed to be dedicated was not of sufficient utility to justify its repair by the Parish—Order by Justices in Special Sessions to the like effect—Appeal by landowners to Quarter Sessions—Decision of Quarter Sessions that they had no jurisdiction—*Mandamus* granted to hear the appeal. (27 L. J., M. C., 189 : E. B. & E., 69 : 31 L. T., (o. s.) 80.)

1861.   [2093]
Reg. v. *Surrey JJ.* (2). "Highway Act, 1835," § 23 Refusal of Justices to grant a Certificate on the ground that a road, part of which passing through a tunnel under a railway, was not of the required width, was to be treated as one road; and a part was not of the requisite width—Held that the Justices were right in their decision. (3 L. T., 808.)

1857.   [2094]
Reg. v. *Thomas.* "Highway Act, 1835," § 23—Road made by Turnpike Trustees under a Temporary Act—Part of the line of road never completed—Road used by the Public and repaired by the Parish both before and after the expiration of the Act—Held that there was evidence of dedication and adoption, and that though the fact that the road was originally made under a Turnpike Act might explain away such evidence in fact, it did not conclusively in Law rebut it—§ 23 does not apply to a road made by Turnpike Trustees, and therefore the absence of a Certificate by 2 Justices, &c., did not prevent the road from becoming compulsorily repairable by the Parish, on a dedication by the owners of the soil at the expiration of the Turnpike Act. (7 E. & B., 399 : 28 L. T., (o. s.), 303 : 5 W. R., 321.)

1850.   [2095]
Roberts v. *Hunt.* "Highway Act, 1835," § 23—A road intended to be dedicated, and actually used, but as to which the requisite formalities for dedication under § 23 have not been taken, may nevertheless be a highway in other respects—Action for obstructing such a road, whereby an accident happened to the plaintiff, held maintainable. (15 Q. B., 17 : 15 L. T., (o. s.), 66.)

1840.   [2096]
Reg. v. *Westmark Tithing.* "Highway Act, 1835," § 23—This section is not retrospective : it applies to roads made but not completely dedicated by user or otherwise at the passing of the Act—An Indictment for non-repair is not supported by proof of a highway having been extinguished as such, 60 years previously, by an Inclosure Act, but since used by the Public, and repaired by the district sought to be charged. (2 Moo. & Rob., 305.)

1889.   [2097]
Warner v. *Wandsworth B. W.* When a highway
is dedicated with a dangerous obstruction
the public use it subject to the obstruction
and no action lies against the Highway
Authority—*Fisher* v. *Prowse* followed. (53
J. P., 471.)

(3.) RIGHTS AS TO SOIL ADJACENT TO HIGHWAYS.

1768.   [2098]
Anon. (Lofft, 358.) The presumption that waste
land adjoining a road belongs to the adjacent
owners and not to the Lord of the Manor
may be rebutted by evidence of acts of
ownership on the part of the Lord. (Lofft,
358.)

1861.   [2099]
Berridge v. *Ward.* Where a piece of land adjoining a highway is conveyed by general
words the presumption of Law is that the
soil *usque ad medium filum viæ* passes by the
conveyance, even though reference is made
to a plan annexed, the measurement and
colouring of which would exclude it. (30
L. J., C. P., 218: 10 C. B., (N. S.), 400: S. C.
at *Nisi Prius*, 2 F. & F., 208.)

1823.   [2100]
Cooke v. *Green.* Ownership of land adjoining
either side of a road is *primâ facie* evidence
of a right to the soil extending to the centre
of the road—A recent right founded on an
Inclosure under an Act makes no distinction
as to the general Law. (11 Price, 736.)

1878.   [2101]
Coverdale v. *Charlton.* "Public Health Act,
1875," § 149—Herbage alongside a public
highway held to be vested in a Local
Board (as Surveyors of Highways), so that
the Board could let the same, and Board's
tenant maintain an Action against a Trespasser thereon — *Per* Cockburn, C.J.:—"It
may be that this interpretation which we are
giving to the Statute presses hardly on the
owners of the soil on each side of the road,
reversing as it does the maxim *usque ad
medium filum.* But the Legislature is
omnipotent." (47 L. J., Q. B., 446: L. R.,
3 Q. B. D., 376: 38 L. T., 687: 42 J. P.,
517.) [Effect of decision set aside in part by
the "Highway Act, 1878."]

1835.   [2102]
Doe dem. Barrett v. *Kemp.* Where it was questioned whether a strip of land between old
inclosed lands and a highway belonged to
the Lord of the Manor or the adjacent
owner, it was held that in order to rebut the
presumption of Law evidence might be received of acts of ownership by the Lord on
similar strips bordering another part of the
same road and not adjoining his freeholds.
(2 Scott, 9: 2 Bing., N. C., 102: 1 Hodges,
231.)

1847.   [2103]
Doe dem. Harrison v. *Hampson.* The presumption of Law that slips of waste land adjoining
a highway belong to the owner of the adjacent inclosed land may be rebutted by

evidence tending to raise a contrary presumption. (17 L. J., C. P., 225: 4 C. B.,
267.)

1824.   [2104]
Doe dem. Jackson v. *Wilkinson.* Defendant inclosed a piece of waste land adjoining a
highway and occupied it for 30 years without
paying rent; then the adjacent owner demanded a rent of 6d. which was paid 3
times—Held that in the absence of other
evidence this was conclusive to show that
the occupation began with the owner's permission—Verdict for the plaintiff as owner
held good. (3 B. & C., 413.)

1827.   [2105]
Doe dem. Pring v. *Pearsey.* It is a presumption
of Law that waste land adjoining a road
belongs to the owner of the adjoining
inclosed land, whether freeholder, leaseholder, or copyholder, and not to the Lord
of the Manor. (5 L. J., (O. S.), K. B., 310:
7 B. & C., 304: 9 D. & R., 908.)

1757.   [2106]
Goodtitle v. *Alker.* An Action of Ejectment lies
by the owner of the soil for land over which
a highway runs, notwithstanding the right
of way. (1 Burr., 133.)

1816.   [2107]
Grose v. *West.* Though the presumption is that
waste land adjoining a road belongs to the
adjacent owners, yet if the waste strips communicate with open commons or other larger
portions of land the presumption is either
done away with, or considerably narrowed,
for evidence of ownership of the larger portions applies also to the strips of land which
are in communication with them. (7 Taunt.,
39.)

1865.   [2108]
Harris v. *Hoskins.* Waste land by the side of a
highway held to be part of the highway, and
not "open land," within the "Night Poaching
Act," 9 Geo. IV., c. 49, § 1. (34 L. J., M. C.,
145: [*Reg.* v. *Harris*] 12 L. T., 303: 13
W. R., 652.)

1816.   [2109]
Headlam v. *Headley.* It is only a presumption
of Law (in the absence of positive evidence)
that the right of the soil in a public highway
belongs (when no other proprietor appears)
to the owner of the adjoining closes *usque ad
medium filum viæ*—If there are circumstances
which throw doubt upon this presumption, a
plaintiff who claims the road in an Action of
Trespass must bring some direct evidence of
his title. (Holt, N. P., 463.)

1859.   [2110]
Holmes v. *Bellingham.* The presumption which,
in the absence of evidence, prevails in the
case of a public highway, that the soil *usque
ad medium filum viæ* belongs to the adjacent
owners applies also to the case of a private
way. (29 L. J., C. P., 132: 7 C. B., (N. S.),
329: 33 L. T., (O. S.), 239.)

1840.   [2111]
Holmes v. *Upton.* Encroachment on private lands
by Turnpike Trustees erecting buttresses

to sustain an embankment, such buttresses being erected in defiance of the protest of the owner—Mandatory Injunction to remove them granted. (L. R., 9 Ch. App., 214, n.)

1878.   [2112]
Lang v. Kerr, Anderson, & Co. Local Act—Requisition at the instance of a Local Authority on a landowner to fence a public footpath running alongside the river Clyde and over landowner's property—Held that the Local Act contained no provision justifying the requisition of the Local Authority. (W. N., 1878, p. 54.)

1885.   [2113]
Langley v. Churton. "Highway Act," 28 & 29 Vict., c. 107, § 2—Wrongful inclosure of strip of land alongside of highway—Conviction affirmed—Jurisdiction of Justices is not necessarily ousted by a bare assertion that the title to land is in question—Unmetalled sides of a road may be as much "highway" as the metalled centre. (*Times,* July 3, 1885.)

1831.   [2114]
Loveridge v. Hodsell. Per Taunton J.:—"A footpath by the road-side, included within the hedge or fence of the road, is as much part of a public highway as that which is travelled over by carriages." (2 B. & Ad., 602, at p. 610.)

1883.   [2115]
Nichol v. Beaumont. The cutting of trenches through the unmetalled sides of a road in order to hinder traffic passing over the grass, held, under the circumstances, illegal, because the grant was of a right of way as "fully as if the same were a public highway"—*Turner v. Ringwood H. B.* followed as regards public rights of highway not being limited to the *via trita.* (53 L. J., Ch., 853 : 50 L. T., 112.)

1859.   [2116]
Potter v. Perry. There is no general law imposing on the owner of lands adjoining a public road, the obligation to maintain fences. (23 J. P., 644.)

1859.   [2117]
Reg. v. Johnson (1). The common notion that owners of land on the sides of a highway, may encroach up to within 15 ft. of the centre is (*Per* Erle, C.J.,) erroneous; the question will always be whether the parts inclosed have or have not been used as part of the highway. (1 F. & F., 657.)

1862.   [2118]
Reg. v. U. K. Electric Telegraph Co. Indictment for obstructing highways by Telegraph posts —In an ordinary highway, unless there is evidence to the contrary, the rights of the Public extend to the whole space within the fences, whether metalled or not—If the obstruction is permanent, and interferes with the free use of the way by foot passengers, it does not avail as a defence that the posts are placed off the carriage-way and ordinary foot-way. (31 L. J., M. C., 166 : 2 B. & S., 647, n. : 6 L. T., 378.)

1788.   [2119]
Rex v. Llandilo Roads Commissioners. Road Trustees diverting a road and carrying it through inclosed lands, erecting fences and repairing such fences for a time, cannot be held perpetually liable for the maintenance of such fences unless the duty is cast on them by Statute—A "road" is to be taken to mean only the surface, over which the Public have a right of passage. (2 T. R., 232.)

1880.   [2120]
Rolls v. St. George's, Southwark, Vestry. "Metropolis Management Act, 1855," § 96—Meaning of the word "vest" as applied to the interest of Vestries in the soil of highways —A street on becoming stopped up and disused held to revert to the owner of the land on whose property it had been made—*Coverdale v. Charlton* explained. (49 L. J., Ch., 691 : L. R., 14 Ch. D, 785 : 43 L. T., 110 : 44 J. P., 680.)

1858.   [2121]
Salisbury (Marquis of) v. Great Northern Railway Co. Land purchased under Turnpike Acts— Held that the presumption that the soil of a road was vested in the plaintiff as owner of the adjacent land, was not rebutted by the Turnpike Acts, so as to cast upon him the onus of showing that the soil of the road had not been purchased by the Turnpike Trustees. (28 L. J., C. P., 40 : 5 C. B., (N. S.), 174 : 32 L. T., (o. s.), 175.)

1828.   [2122]
Scales v. Pickering. Special Act authorising the breaking up of highways, footways, and streets, by a Water Company—Proviso; not to enter private lands without owner's consent—Held that the Company had no authority to enter a private field merely because there was a public footpath across it—"Footways" must in such an instance be limited to paved ways running by adjacent buildings, and cannot extend to a path over a private ground. (6 L. J., (o. s.), C. P., 53 : 4 Bing., 448 : 1 Moo. & P., 195.)

1860.   [2123]
Scannell v. French. The owner of land contiguous to a public road stopped up a gap in a ditch which separated his land from the road, through which gap water off the road had been accustomed to flow—Held that he had not been guilty of an obstruction. (11 Ir. C. L. R., 275 : 2 L. T., 94.)

1839.   [2124]
Seoones v. Morrell. Where strips of land lie between a highway and an adjacent inclosure the legal presumption is that the soil belongs to the owner of the adjoining inclosure. (1 Bea., 251.)

1860.   [2125]
Simpson v. Dendy. Waste land adjoining a highway—The ordinary presumption of ownership in favour of the owner of adjacent inclosed land is strongly confirmed by proof of distinct acts of ownership on his part

extending over many years, and never questioned. (8 C. B., (N. s.), 433: 6 Jur., (N. s.), 1197.)

1809. [2126]
Smith v. *Mackie.* "Turnpike Act, 1822," § 118—Conviction for breaking up soil of land, to wit, a bank formed of road scrapings which had become turfed over—Conviction affirmed. (21 L. T., 392.)

1819. [2127]
Steel v. *Prickett.* The presumption is that waste land adjoining a road belongs to the adjacent owner and not to the Lord of the Manor; but reputation is admissible to rebut this presumption, and to prove the existence of a manor, even where no manorial rights can be proved to have been actually exercised. (2 Stark., N. P. C., 463.)

1809. [2128]
Stevens v. *Whistler.* An owner of land abutting on one side of a public highway is *primâ facie* owner of the soil of one half of the highway in width, and a defendant in Trespass must plead soil and freehold in another, in order to compel the plaintiff to new assign so as to confine the trespass to the part of the highway which was his property. (11 East, 51.)

1844. [2129]
White v. *Hill.* Presumptions as to ownership of soil by the side of a highway—The ordinary presumption is that as against the Lord, an adjoining owner is owner of all land *ad medium filum viæ*—This presumption does not apply to cases between freeholders, both claiming under the same title, and it may be rebutted. (14 L. J., Q. B., 79: 6 Q. B., 487.)

1883. [2130]
Wilkins v. *Day.* Owner of lands on each side of a highway held liable for injury occasioned by his leaving an agricultural roller upon a green strip between the hedge and the metalled part of the highway. (L. R., 12 Q. B. D., 110: 49 L. T., 399: 32 W. R., 123.)

5. STOPPAGE, DIVERSION, AND WIDENING OF HIGHWAYS.

(1.) NOTICES, AS TO.

1818. [2131]
Reg. v. *Arkwright.* 59 Geo. III., c. 134, § 39, enables the Church Commissioners to stop up paths and entrances to Churchyards with the consent of Justices, and on notice being given in the manner and form prescribed by the "Highway Act, 1815" [Repealed]—Held that the notice required must, under the circumstances, be given *before* the making of the Order of the Commissioners—The words "on notice being given" must in this case be read as "after notice given." (18 L. J., Q. B., 26: 12 Q. B., 960: 12 L. T., (o. s.), 271.)

1865. [2132]
Reg. v. *Huntingdonshire JJ.* 8 & 9 Vict., c. 118, §§ 62-3—A notice of appeal to Quarter Sessions against stopping up a road cannot be objected to on the ground that it comprises part of the road only—An increase in an appellant's liability as a Ratepayer is not to be reckoned in considering whether he is aggrieved—*Quære,* whether the legal effect of the appeal, if successful, would be to leave the whole road open? (L. R., 1 Q. B., 36: 13 L. T., 443.)

1873. [2133]
Reg. v. *Powell* (1). 59 Geo. III., c. 69, § 1 : "Highway Act, 1835," § 84 — Legal proceedings pending against a Surveyor for not repairing a certain highway—A notice calling a Vestry Meeting for taking into consideration such proceedings and for "other purposes connected with the highways" of a certain hamlet held sufficient to cover a proposal for stopping up the highway alluded to. (42 L. J., M. C., 129: L. R., 8 Q. B., 403: 28 L. T., 697.)

1838. [2134]
Reg. v. *Stock.* 59 Geo. III., c. 134, § 39—Churchyard Paths—There is no appeal against an order of the Church Commissioners stopping up, under this section, a useless footway through a Churchyard—Though the section incorporates the form of notice annexed to the "Highway Act, 1815" [Repealed], it gives thereby no right of appeal, for no such right can be given by implication only; had such right been given by reference the repeal of the Statute to which reference is made would not have taken it away. (7 L. J., M. C., 93 : 8 A. & E., 405.)

1870. [2135]
Reg. v. *Surrey JJ.* (4). "Highway Act, 1835," § 85 : "Highway Act, 1864," § 21—Notices for stopping up a highway—*Certiorari*—A person residing near a highway to be affected, is to be regarded as a person aggrieved—The publication of notices at each end of the highway to be stopped up is a condition precedent, and where roads form one system, if each has been treated as a separate road, notices must be posted at each end of each road. (39 L. J., M. C., 145; L. R., 5 Q. B., 466.)

1892. [2136]
Reg. v. *Surrey JJ.* (6). "Highway Act, 1835," § 85—Notices to be affixed at "end of highway"—Condition complied with if notices affixed at end of intermediate portion of highway, which portion alone is intended to be diverted. (61 L. J., M. C., 153: L. R., 1 Q. B., 867: 66 L. T., 578: 56 J. P., 695.)

1883. [2137]
Reg. v. *Yeadon.* Proposed stopping up of a highway—A notice of objection stating that the proposal would be an "inconvenience" held sufficiently explicit, and that the appeal might be heard on such notice. (47 J. P., 260.)

1831.   [2138]
Rex v. *Horner.* "Highway Act, 1815" [Repealed]—An Order for diversion, &c., described a highway by its *termini* and by reference to marks on a plan annexed—Notice published of Order but no plan annexed to notice, and only a description given of *termini* and length in yards—Order held to be explained by plan, and good; but notice, insufficient. (2 B. & Ad., 150.)

1822.   [2139]
Rex v. *Townsend.* Local Inclosure Act—Commissioner empowered to stop up any way under an order of 2 Justices, subject to appeal as though the Order had been originally made by Justices—Further, liberty to a party aggrieved to appeal within 6 months—Road stopped up with consent of Justices but without the notices required by the "Highway Act, 1815," § 2 [Repealed] having been given—Held that under these circumstances an appeal within 6 months was good, notwithstanding the want of notices. (5 B. & Ald., 420.)

(2.) ORDERS FOR STOPPING UP, &c.

1838.   [2140]
Allen v. *Hatfield Chase Warping Co.* Special Act for the Improvement of certain land and authorising the stopping up of roads on the substitution of others equally convenient—Road stopped and another substituted which was not equally convenient to plaintiff—Injunction refused: plaintiff's remedy was by Action for damages. (32 *Sol. Journ.*, 542.)

1800.   [2141]
Davison v. *Gill.* "Highway Act, 1773," § 19 [Repealed and re-enacted by the "Highway Act, 1835," § 118]—The enactment that the forms set forth in the Schedule "shall be used on all occasions with such additions and variations only as may be necessary," is to be construed literally; a material variation from the form prescribed for stopping up held fatal and liable to be taken advantage of in a collateral proceeding. (1 East, 64.) [Statute held in *Rex* v. *Casson* (3 D. & R., at p. 40) to be directory only, so far as concerns recital of names of proprietors along new road.]

1814.   [2142]
De Ponthieu v. *Pennyfeather.* "Highway Act, 1773," § 19 [Repealed]—An Order of Justices which recited that they had viewed a new road and found it in good condition and repair held a sufficient Certificate—If the Certificate be deposited with the Clerk of the Peace the Statute is satisfied, enrolment being only directory—Where a road is stopped by Order of Justices and a new one substituted, partly over the ground of a stranger and partly over an accustomed road, that is a sufficient compliance with the Statute, provided the new road conveys the Public to the same place as the old one did. (1 Marsh., 261; 5 Taunt, 634.)

1821.   [2143]
Harber v. *Rand.* "Inclosure Act, 1801," § 8: Local Act—Old footway omitted from new map because intended to be stopped up—Map duly signed by Commissioners and by 2 Justices—Held that such omission, even with such signatures, did not satisfy the Statute, and that an Order made in form of Law and subject to appeal was necessary. (9 Price, 58.)

1835.   [2144]
Hurst v. *Taylor.* Precautions to be observed for fencing a highway lawfully diverted. (54 L. J., Q. B., 310: L. R., 14 Q. B. D., 918: 49 J. P., 359.)

1826.   [2145]
Logan v. *Burton.* "Inclosure Act, 1801," § 8, authorising Commissioners to appoint public carriage roads and highways, and to stop up any roads or tracks; with proviso for consent of 2 Justices: Local Act authorising Commissioners with such consent to stop up old roads besides those over the lands to be inclosed—Held that the enactment in the General Act included footways, and that such footways were subject to the proviso—Therefore the said consent was requisite in order to stop up a footway passing partly over land to be enclosed and partly over an old inclosure. (4 L. J., (o. s.), K. B., 217: 5 B. & C., 513: 8 D. & R., 299.)

1890.   [2146]
Reg. v. *Cloete.* 57 Geo. III., c. 27, § 79—Proposed stopping up of a passage as likely to become a receptacle for filth—Held that the Justices had jurisdiction if they thought fit to exercise it. (54 J. P., 740.)

1874.   [2147]
Reg. v. *Harvey.* "Highway Act, 1835," § 85—A Certificate under the hands of 2 Justices is sufficient if it states the existence of the circumstances required by § 85—It is unnecessary that it should recite that the preliminaries required by § 84 have been complied with—Dictum in *Reg.* v. *Worcestershire* (23 L. J., M. C., 113) countenancing an objection on the ground of such omission, not followed. (44 L. J., M. C., 1: L. R., 10 Q. B., 46: 31 L. T., 505: [*Harvey* v. *Bethnal Green Vestry*] 39 J. P., 272.)

1840.   [2148]
Reg. v. *Jones* (1). "Highway Act, 1815," § 2—Order for stopping up a highway—"We," &c., "*having viewed,*" &c., "*and it appearing to us* that such highway is unnecessary," &c., held bad—The words do not necessarily imply that the Order was made "upon the view" "of the said Justices" according to the Act—They may imply that it appeared by evidence which was independent of the view. (10 L. J., M. C., 5: 12 A. & E., 684: 4 P. & D., 520: 1 Arn. & H., 113.)

1871.   [2149]
Reg. v. *Maule.* "Highway Act, 1835," §§ 84 and 88—Proceedings taken by a private individual to divert a highway accepted by Vestry but no order in writing given by Chairman of Vestry to Surveyor to apply to Justices—The Quarter Sessions held that a

10 days' notice of appeal was sufficient, but that the Certificate was bad for not alleging a Chairman's order in writing—Held by Superior Court that the Quarter Sessions were wrong on both points. (41 L. J., M. C., 47: 23 L. T., 859.)

1866.   [2150]
Reg. v. *Phillips.*   "Highway Act, 1835," § 85—Certificate of Justices showing that a way proposed to be substituted was not entirely new, but comprised two existing ways which would be widened and enlarged so as to make them more commodious and convenient—Held (*Welch* v. *Nash,* 8 East, 324, dissented from) that it was not necessary that the substituted highway should be entirely new—" nearer or more commodious "—It is sufficient that the Certificate alleges one alternative (*Reg.* v. *Shiles,* 1 Q. B., 919, dissented from)—It is not necessary that the proposed new highway should be completed before the Certificate is obtained, and therefore the Certificate may allege that the old highway *will be* unnecessary when the proposed alterations are completed. (35 L. J., M. C., 217 : L. R., 1 Q. B., 618 : 7 B. & S., 593.)

1872.   [2151]
Reg. v. *Surrey JJ.* (5). "Highway Act, 1835," § 84—Diversion—Certificate by Justices that new path would be more commodious but no mention made of owner's consent—Written consent of owner enrolled with Certificate and Plan—Held that the requirements of the Act had been in substance complied with—*Certiorari* refused. (26 L. T., 22.)

1879.   [2152]
Reg. v. *Wallace* (2). "Highway Act, 1835," §§ 85, 91—Where Justices certify that a new road will be more commodious than the one for which it is proposed to be substituted, it must unequivocally appear on the face of their certificate that they have arrived at that conclusion from personal inspection, and not from statements made to them—A certificate for a diversion need not specifically state that the old road would become unnecessary. (L. R., 4 Q. B. D., 641 : 40 L. T., 518 : 43 J. P., 493.)

1875.   [2153]
Reg. v. *Waller.* "Highway Act, 1773," § 17 [Repealed]—Old highway stopped up and sold subject to a right of way in order to give access to a certain footpath—Held that another footpath which had communicated with the disused highway, having by virtue of the order of the Justices become a *cul-de-sac,* the adjacent landowner was justified in obstructing the way at the point of communication. (31 L. T., 777.)

1854.   [2154]
Reg. v. *Worcestershire JJ.* Appeal against Order for stopping a highway—The Sessions have jurisdiction to consider any substantial defect which appears on the face of a Certificate and are not limited to trying by a Jury the three questions specified in the "Highway Act, 1835," § 89—Where there is no appeal it is

the duty of the Sessions to be satisfied that the Certificate is correct on its face, and accompanied by plan and proof such as the Statute requires. (23 L. J., M. C., 113 : 3 E. & B., 477 : 2 C. L. R., 1333 : 22 L. T. (o. s.), 332.) [See *Reg.* v. *Harvey.*]

1777.   [2155]
Rex v. *Balme.* "Highway Act, 1773," § 16 [Repealed]—The power herein conferred on Justices to order any highway to be widened extends to roads repairable *ratione tenuræ*—On disobedience to such an Order the party may be proceeded against, either summarily under the Statute, or by Indictment. (2 Cowp., 648.)

1835.   [2156]
Rex v. *Cambridgeshire JJ.* "Highway Act, 1815," § 2 [Repealed]—An Order of Justices for stopping up a highway must show that the Justices viewed the highway together, and that the finding it unnecessary was the result of that view. (5 L. J., M. C., 6 : 4 A. & E., 111 : 5 N. & M., 410 : 1 H. & W., 600.)

1836.   [2157]
Rex v. *Downshire (Marquis of).* "Highway Act, 1815," § 2 [Repealed]—Order of Justices recited that " having particularly viewed the public roads " within the parish ; then other words ; and then the words " and being satisfied," &c., held bad, because the latter words were separated in a marked manner from the former words : the decision might have been based on reasons, stated or otherwise, other than the simple " view." *Per* Lord Denman, C.J. :—" If so, the Justices never obtained jurisdiction over the subject "—Justices in Special Sessions having made an Order to stop a highway and the time for appeal having elapsed, it cannot be contended, on a prosecution for obstructing such way, that the Order was bad because the Justices were not properly summoned to the Sessions—*Quære,* If a road long used as a public thoroughfare be lawfully stopped up at one end the right of way over the remainder is gone? *Per* Patteson, J. : It is not. (5 L. J., M. C., 72 : 4 A. & E., 698 : 6 N. & M., 92.)

1815.   [2158]
Rex v. *Hertfordshire JJ.* "Highway Act, 1773," § 19 [Repealed]—If Justices make an Order to divert a highway, and afterwards an Order to stop up the old way, a party aggrieved may appeal against the last Order though too late to appeal against the first. (3 Maule & S., 459.)

1810.   [2159]
Rex v. *Incledon.* If the Court are satisfied that a nuisance indicted is already effectually abated before Judgment is prayed upon the Indictment they will not in their discretion give Judgment to abate it—And they refused to give such Judgment upon an Indictment for obstructing a highway where the highway was, after the conviction, duly diverted and stopped up, there being the requisite Certificate that the new way was open for traffic

and so much of the old way as was retained had been freed from obstructions. (13 East, 164.)

1823.   [2160]
Rex v. Kent JJ. "Highway Act, 1815," § 2 [Repealed]—Order for diversion of footway based *inter alia* on the consent of an attorney for a landowner acting under a power of attorney, but the power did not appear on the face of the Order—Order held bad. (1 B. & C., 622 : [*Rex v. Crewe*] 3 D. & R., 6.)

1830.   [2161]
Rex v. Kent JJ. Order of Justices diverting a highway and substituting a new one, containing also an Order for stopping up the old highway held bad—Justices have no power to stop up an old road until the new one is made. (8 L. J., (o. s.), M. C., 73 : 10 B. & C., 477.) [See *Reg. v. Phillips*, on the last point.]

1827.   [2162]
Rex v. Kenyon. "Highway Act, 1815," § 2 [Repealed]—An Order of Justices for stopping up a footway must distinctly state in what Parish the footway is situated, and must describe its length and breadth—*Semble*, that the Order must be for sale as well as for stopping up. (6 B. & C., 640 : 9 D. & R., 694.)

1822.   [2163]
Rex v. Kirk. "Highway Act, 1815," § 2 [Repealed]—Order for the diversion of a highway reciting the consent of a former owner who was dead when the order was actually made, held bad—An Order must show the consent in writing under seal of the actual owner for the time being of the land through which the proposed new highway is to run. (1 B. & C., 21 : [*Rex v. Denbighshire JJ.*] 2 D. & R., 52.)

1836.   [2164]
Rex v. Middlesex JJ. "Highway Act, 1815" [Repealed]—Held that Justices in Special Sessions could not by one and the same Order direct that a highway should be diverted, a new one being substituted, and that the old way should be stopped—There must be two Orders, one for diverting and substituting; the other for stopping up; and the former must precede the latter. (6 L. J., M. C., 10 : 5 A. & E., 626 : 1 N. & P., 92 : 2 H. & W., 407.)

1836.   [2165]
Rex v. Milverton Inhabitants. "Highway Act, 1815," § 2 [Repealed]—An Order for stopping up a highway containing the expression "having upon view found and it appearing to us" that a certain highway, &c., is unnecessary, would be good; such recital does not imply that the Justices acted upon other information than their own view—An Order is bad if it stop up half the breadth of a highway leaving the rest open; even though the other half is not within the division of the Justices making the Order; Justices have no authority to narrow a highway, or in the same Order to stop more than one highway—*Quære,*

Whether the Justices of two divisions within which opposite halves of the road lay could, by orders made concurrently, stop both sides? (6 L. J., M. C., 73 : 5 A. & E., 841 : 1 N. & P., 179 : 2 H. & W., 434.)

1828.   [2166]
Rex v. Rogers. "Highway Act, 1815," § 2 [Repealed]—An Order for stopping up a highway must clearly recite that it appeared to the Justices, *on view*, that the highway was unnecessary — An Order stating that they "had, on view, found *or* that it appeared" to them, &c., held bad. (6 L. J., (o. s.), M. C., 106 : 2 M. & R., 289 : [*Rex v. Worcestershire*] 8 B. & C., 254.)

1826.   [2167]
Rex v. Somersetshire JJ. "Highway Act, 1773," § 48 [Repealed]—Where Justices act wholly without jurisdiction *Certiorari* remains available notwithstanding that the Statute under which they professed to act takes away the right to a *Certiorari*—In such a case the proceeding is *coram non judice* and their "Order" is not an Order in pursuance of the Statute relied on. (5 B. & C., 816 : 6 D. & R., 409.)

1828.   [2168]
Rex v. Winter. An Order for diverting and stopping up a highway and substituting a road is bad, unless it appears that the Public acquire as permanent a right in the latter as they had in the former—*Semble*, that when a highway is diverted, the old road cannot be continued for foot-passengers only. (7 L. J., (o. s.), M. C., 15 : 3 M. & R., 433 : 8 B. & C., 785.)

1879.   [2169]
Turner v. Crush. "Inclosure Act, 1845," 8 & 9 Vict., c. 118, § 68—Proceedings for the inclosure of waste lands in a parish—Certain ways held duly extinguished under an Inclosure Award, and Action of Trespass held maintainable against a person entering the lands where the ways had once existed. (48 L. J., Ex., 481 : L. R., 4 App. Cas., 221 : 40 L. T., 661.)

1807.   [2170]
Welch v. Nash. "Highway Act, 1773, § 19—A new highway must be set out before the old one is stopped up : it is not sufficient that another old highway is widened in parts to answer the purpose of a new road—The power of Justices being confined to diverting an old road and substituting a new one, they acquire no right to abolish a road merely by improving another which exists at the time—If a new highway be not set out before the old one is stopped up, the legality of the Orders of Justices for diverting the old road and stopping it may be questioned in an Action of Trespass, notwithstanding that such Orders were confirmed by the Sessions on Appeal, stating the fact of a new road being set out in lieu of the old one. (8 East, 394.)

1859.   [2171]
Williams v. Eyton. Inclosure Award directing the stopping up of a road subject to the sanction of Justices—Road stopped by a gate and disused for 28 years, except as to some slight

user by foot passengers—No direct evidence that Justices had issued an Order, though a Certificate that the new roads had been formed was produced—Held nevertheless that a Jury might from so long a disuse of the road infer that there had been the proper Order. (28 L. J., Ex., 146: 4 H. & N., 357: 32 L. T., (o. s.), 336.)

1863. [2172]

Wright v. *Frant Overseers.* "Highway Act, 1835," §§ 85 and 113—Proposed diversion—Certificate under § 85, by Justices after a meeting of inhabitants of Parish within which the footway was situated—But inasmuch as that part of the Parish had been annexed to an Improvement Act District, held that the meeting ought to have been of the Ratepayers of such District—"Highway Act, 1835," did not apply—*Semble*, that a certificate need not state that a proposed new highway is nearer and more commodious to the public; *Reg.* v. *Shiles* disapproved of. (32 L. J., M. C., 204: 4 B. & S., 118: [*Reg.* v. *Wright*] 8 L. T., 455.)

(3.) APPEALS AGAINST ORDERS.

1841. [2173]

Lock v. *Sellwood.* "Highway Act, 1835," § 88—Distress Warrant issued to levy the Costs incurred by a party in prosecuting an Appeal under this section which Warrant did not recite any Order of Quarter Sessions for the payment of such costs, but was founded on a subsequent conviction by 2 Justices out of Sessions for non-payment of such Costs—Warrant held illegal, and no property passed to the purchaser of goods seized and sold under it. (1 Q. B., 736.)

1854. [2174]

Reg. v. *Finchley Surveyors: Pouncey, Ex parte.* The Quarter Sessions have no discretion as to the award of Costs under the "Highway Act, 1835," § 90—It is imperative on the Court to award Costs. (2 C. L. R., 1593.)

1857. [2175]

Reg. v. *Lancashire JJ.* (1). "Highway Act, 1835," § 88—Where the General Quarter Sessions commences on a certain day, and is afterwards adjourned and held on another day at another place in order to decide matters arising in the vicinity of the latter place, the requisite notice of appeal under the "Highway Act, 1835," § 88, must be given 10 days before the day first mentioned, though the highway be in the vicinity of the latter place. (27 L. J., M. C., 161: 8 E. & B., 563: 30 L. T., (o. s.), 149.) [See *Reg.* v. *Sussex,* 34 L. J., M. C., 69.]

1864. [2176]

Reg. v. *Midgley L. B.* "Highway Act, 1835," §§ 84-9—Stopping up and diversion of a highway—Certificate of Justices—Jurisdiction of Sessions—Justices have no power to stop up a highway because at some future time a road not yet made will when completed be more commodious—On an appeal against an Order to divert some roads and

stop up others, the Quarter Sessions may, under § 87, confirm the Order as to the stopping up, and quash it as to the diverting. (33 L. J., M. C., 188 : 5 B. & S., 621.)

1869. [2177]

Reg. v. *Surrey JJ.* (3). "Highway Act, 1835," §§ 85 and 88: "Highway Act, 1864," § 21—Order of Special Sessions for discontinuance of highway—Held that under the later Act an Appeal lay to the Quarter Sessions, for the words "like proceedings" must be taken to include all proceedings in reference to an Appeal given by § 88 of the earlier Act, as well as all proceedings directed by § 85, for the purpose of procuring the discontinuance of a highway. (39 L. J., M. C., 49 : L. R., 5 Q. B., 87 : 18 W. R., 166.)

1845. [2178]

Reg. v. *Yorkshire, N. R., JJ.* "Highway Act, 1835," § 105—Notice to a Justice of intended Appeal need not be served on the Justice personally—Leaving the notice at his dwelling-house suffices. (14 L. J., M. C., 91 : 7 Q. B., 154 : 1 New Sess. Cas., 574.)

1862. [2179]

Reg. v. *Yorkshire, W. R., JJ.* (2). "Highway Act, 1835," § 90—Notice of Appeal against Order of Justices for a diversion of a highway—Notice by the person who had obtained the Order of his intention to abandon it—Appeal entered at Sessions—Held that the person who intended to appeal was entitled to his Costs notwithstanding the abandonment—He might apply at any time during the day of Sessions. (31 L. J., M. C., 271 : 2 B. & S., 811 : 6 L. T., 494.)

1835. [2180]

Rex v. *Adey.* "Highway Act, 1815," § 3 [Repealed]—Order to stop up—A notice of Appeal is sufficient which states that the appellants are aggrieved by being compelled to travel a greater distance to their market town from their respective residences, than they would have had to have travelled if the road intended to be stopped up were kept in a proper state of repair—The notice need not state that they were aggrieved *by the Order.* (4 L. J., M. C., 76 : 4 N. & M., 365 : 1 H. & W., 42.)

1826. [2181]

Rex. v. *Essex JJ.* "Highway Act, 1815," § 2 [Repealed]—An Appeal against an Order stopping up a highway must emanate from some person "injured or aggrieved" (pursuing the language of the Appeal clause) [now "Highway Act, 1835," § 88], or the appellant will have no *locus standi*—The Act does not give an appeal to all persons promiscuously—The words "injured or aggrieved," refer to special interests arising out of nearness of habitation or frequent occasion for user. (5 L. J., (o. s.), M. C., 65 : 7 D. & R., 658 : 5 B. & C., 431.)

1802. [2182]

Rex v. *Staffordshire JJ.* "Highway Act, 1773," § 19 [Repealed]—Order for stopping highway—Held that the Appeal must in literal compliance with the Statute be to the next Quarter Sessions after the Order made, without reference to any notice received by the appellant of such Order. (3 East, 151.)

1828.   [2183]
Rex v. *Yorkshire, W. R., JJ.* (2). Local Act—Right to appeal against Order to stop old highway—Held that in the notice of Appeal it was necessary to aver that the party intending to appeal was aggrieved by the Order. (6 L. J., (o. s.), M. C., 59; 7 B. & C., 678 : 1 M. & R., 547.)

1835.   [2184]
Rex v. *Yorkshire, W. R., JJ.* (3). 58 Geo. III., c. 68, § 3—Order to stop a highway—Appeal —It sufficiently appears that an appellant is a party "aggrieved" if the notice states that he and his tenants, occupiers of lands near the highway, and who have hitherto rightfully used it, and also the Public, will be put to great inconvenience by being obliged henceforth to use a more circuitous road— A Statute required "ten days' notice" of an Appeal—Held, notwithstanding a rule of Sessions, that this must be taken to mean that one day was to be reckoned inclusively, and one, exclusively : If both days were to have been excluded from the computation the Legislature would probably have said "ten *clear* days' notice"—An appellant appealed against 3 Orders, but paid the fee as upon one Appeal: at Sessions his counsel, called upon to make an election, elected to proceed on one which was dismissed because of a supposed informality; nothing was said about the other 2 Orders—The Superior Court, holding that the decision of the Sessions was erroneous on the supposed informality (which was common to all 3 Orders), granted a *Mandamus* to hear Appeals against all 3 Orders. (2 L. J., M. C., 93 : 4 B. & Ad., 685 : 1 N. & M., 426.)

1841.   [2185]
Sellwood v. *Mount.* "Highway Act, 1835," § 90 —Costs cannot be awarded generally; a specific amount must be named, and an Order which fails to do this cannot be enforced— The non-payment of Costs awarded under § 90 is not an "offence" for which the party in default can be convicted under § 101—A Warrant of Distress under § 103, and founded, not on the Order of Sessions itself, but on a subsequent conviction for non-payment, is void, and no defence in an Action of Trespass against the convicting Justices who issue it. (10 L. J., M. C., 121 : 1 Q. B., 726 : 1 G. & D., 358.)

1873.   [2186]
Swift v. *Lancashire JJ.* "Highway Act, 1835," § 88—Order to stop up highway—Notice of Appeal must be given 10 days before original Quarter Sessions, not 10 days before the adjourned Sessions of the district in which the highway is situated—*Reg.* v. *Sussex* (34 L. J., M. C., 69) distinguished. (22 W. R., 76.)

(4.) POWERS AND DUTIES OF RAILWAY COMPANIES.

1887.   [2187]
A.-G. v. *Barry Docks Co.* Diversion of road under statutory powers—Proceedings at instance of Highway Board to restrain disuse of old road till new one was fit and safe for traffic. (56 L. J., Ch., 1018 : L. R., 35 Ch. D., 573 : 56 L. T., 559 : 51 J. P., 644.)

1860.   [2188]
A.-G. v. *Dorset Railway Co.* "Railways Clauses Act, 1845," § 53—Plans and sections showing that a highway would be crossed by a skew-bridge—Variation from plan, and road wrongfully diverted and 2 abrupt turns made in it so as to enable the railway to cross the road at a right angle—Injunction granted at the suit of the Road Authority to restrain the prosecution of the proposed diversion. (3 L. T., 608 : 9 W. R., 189.)

1842.   [2189]
A.-G. v. *Eastern Counties Railway Co.* Statutory powers of a Railway Company to arch over public thoroughfares for the construction of its Railway held to include the right to do the same thing for the erection of a station. (12 L. J., Ex., 106 ; 10 M. & W. 263 : 2 Rail. Cas., 823.)

1869.   [2190]
A.-G. v. *Ely, Haddenham, & Sutton Railway Co.* "Railways Clauses Act," 1845," §§ 16, 46, 53, and 56—If a Railway crosses a highway without diverting it, a bridge must be made according to § 46, but the highway may be diverted to a place where there is a level crossing, if the road so diverted will be more convenient than a bridge. (38 L. J., Ch., 258 : L. R., 4 Ch. App., 194 : 20 L. T., 1.)

1878.   [2191]
A.-G. v. *Furness Railway Co.* "Railways Clauses Act, 1845," § 49 : Special Act—Bridge over road to be 16 ft. 3 in. high, but nothing said about height of headway—Bridge made of proper height but with only a 14 ft. headway —Road flooded at times owing to its having been sunk 2 ft.—Evidence that if road were raised 2 ft. liability to flooding would cease, and that a headway of 12 ft. would suffice for the usual traffic—Injunction granted restraining the Company from maintaining the bridge with less headway than 15 ft , or any bridge with such a road under as might be likely to cause flooding. (47 L. J., Ch., 776 : 38 L. T., 555 : 26 W. R., 650.)

1873.   [2192]
A.-G. v. *Great Eastern Railway Co.* Special Act, incorporating "Lands Clauses Act, 1845," and giving power to stop up streets within a given area—S. Street within the area, but shown on the deposited plans as crossed by an arch, and mentioned in a subsequent Act as crossed by a tunnel—Held that the Company might stop up the street, the power to cross by an arch or tunnel not limiting their full rights within the prescribed area. (41 L. J., Ch., 505 : L. R., 6 H. L., 367 : 26 L. T., 749.)

1850.   [2193]
A.-G. v. *Great Northern Railway Co.* "Railways Clauses Act, 1845," § 56—Two Roads—One stopped up by Company who contended that the use of the other road was a sufficient substitution, such other road being as convenient as any entirely new road could be—Held that the requirement of the Statute would not be satisfied without the formation of a new road to take the place of the one stopped—An application for an Injunction deferred until the road was made entirely impassable, held not made too late. (4 De G. & S., 75 : 14 Jur., 684.)

1849.   [2194]
A.-G. v. *London & South Western Railway Co.* "Railways Clauses Act, 1845," § 56—Proposed interference with a road by a Railway Company diverting the line of the road in order to save the expense of raising part of it—Effect of the diversion that a sharp turn would be introduced into a road previously straight—Injunction granted, it being shown that the Company was not doing the minimum of damage, and might effect the crossing without such material inconvenience to the Public by works somewhat more expensive to itself. (3 De G. & S., 439 : 13 Jur., 467.)

1837.   [2195]
A.-G. v. *London & Southampton Railway Co.* Special Act wherein was prescribed the future minimum width of the roadways of roads which were to be crossed by Railway arches—Held that a portion of an existing road might be occupied by necessary piers, provided that a roadway of the prescribed minimum width was in all cases secured. (7 L. J., Ch., 15: 9 Sim., 78 : 1 Rail. Cas., 302.)

1867.   [2196]
A.-G. v. *Mid Kent Railway Co.* A Local Board withdrew its opposition to a Railway Bill on the insertion of a clause that all bridges carrying roads over the Railway were to be approached by gradients not exceeding 1 in 30—In a certain case to make a road rise 1 in 30 an encroachment on private land would be necessary; the owner obtained an Injunction to prevent such encroachment—Whereupon the Company formed the road with a gradient of 1 in 20—Held that there must be no bridge with a steeper gradient than 1 in 30, and it was no answer to say that this requirement could not be complied with without stopping the Railway. (L. R., 3 Ch. App., 100: 16 W. R., 258.)

1863.   [2197]
A.-G. v. *Tewkesbury & Great Malvern Railway Co.* Where the deposited plans and sections specify the space and height of a bridge by which a railway is to be carried over a road the Company will not be allowed to depart from its plans and sections, notwithstanding that § 49 of the "Railways Clauses Act, 1845," if it stood alone, would permit a less space—That Section only imposes restrictions where the mode of building bridges is not defined

by any special directions. (32 L. J., Ch., 482 : 1 De G. J. & S., 423 : 8 L. T., 682.)

1874.   [2198]
A.-G. v. *Widnes Railway Co.* "Railways Clauses Act, 1845," § 53—Obstruction of public highway by laying down rails pending the construction, in due course, of a new highway to take the place of the one prematurely interfered with—Injunction granted at the suit of the Local Board, on ground that the highway had been rendered "dangerous and extraordinarily inconvenient," though there was no evidence that the Public had been greatly inconvenienced. (30 L. T., 449 : 22 W. R., 607.)

1858.   [2199]
Barrett v. *Midland Railway Co.* Where persons are in the habit of crossing a Railway at a particular place, though no right of way there, it throws on the Company the responsibility of taking reasonable precautions as to the user of their line there. (1 F. & F., 361.)

1849.   [2200]
Beardmer v. *London & North Western Railway Co.* "Railways Clauses Act, 1845," §§ 14 and 16 —Where in consequence of a railway being raised in level, but within the lawful limits of vertical deviation, it became necessary to raise the height of a bridge over which a road was to be carried, it was held that there was no restriction as to the powers of the Company to alter the levels of the approaches to the bridge, provided the land to be affected was included within the deposited plans and sections, or mentioned in the book of reference; and that full satisfaction was made for damage done. (18 L. J., Ch., 432 : 1 Mac. & G., 112 : 1 Hall & T., 161.)

1865.   [2201]
Bilbee v. *London, Brighton, & South Coast Railway.* Level crossing on a highway—Swinggates for foot-passengers—Many trains and an obstruction to view—No Gate-keeper—Accident—Held that there was evidence of negligence on the part of the Company. (34 L. J., C. P., 182 : 18 C. B., (N. S.), 584.)

1846.   [2202]
Braynton v. *London & North Western Railway Co.* "Railways Clauses Act, 1845," § 16—Statutory power to alter the level of a highway— Allegation that an agreement with an adjacent owner precluded any interference with the said level—Held that as the exercise of the option conferred by the Act would be beneficial to the Public, whereas the execution of the agreement would be prejudicial, the Act must prevail—*Semble,* that a Public Company cannot contract itself out of powers given to it for the public benefit or protection. (4 Rail. Cas., 553 : [*Braynton* v. &c.,] 10 Bea., 238.)

1862.   [2203]
Bristol & Exeter Railway Co. v. *Tucker.* Special Act incorporating so much of the "Railways Clauses Act, 1845," as relates to the mode of crossing roads and the construction of bridges

—Held that not only were the sections directly named incorporated, but that others not mentioned (§§ 65 and 145 and subsequent sections) prescribing the necessary machinery for enforcing penalties, were also to be deemed incorporated. (13 C. B., (N. S.), 207 : 7 L. T., 464.)

1858. [2204]
Burgess v. *Great Western Railway Co.* A Railway Company is bound so to fence a station that the Public may not be misled, by seeing a place unfenced, into passing that way, being the shortest, to a station, and incurring risk in consequence. (32 L. T., (O. S.), 76.)

1888. [2205]
Charman v. *South Eastern Railway Co.* "Railways Clauses Act, 1845," § 47—Cattle straying—Accident—Held there was evidence of negligence—A Railway Company must not only guard the exact width of a road, but must provide such continuation fences as will prevent animals using the road in the ordinary way from entering on the Railway—Swing gate and fence out of repair. (57 L. J., Q. B., 597 :· L. R., 21 Q. B. D., 524 : 53 J. P., 86.)

1889. [2206]
Cole v. *Miles.* A Right of Way is not necessarily extinguished by a railway intersecting it unless some special provision for a means of crossing is made by the Railway Company. (57 L. J., M. C., 132 : 60 L. T., 145 : 53 J. P., 228.)

1861. [2207]
Dover Harbour Warden v. *London Chatham & Dover Railway Co.* "Railways Clauses Act, 1845," §§ 45-6—Enactment in Special Act that it should be lawful for the Railway to cross a public road on a level provided a footbridge were erected, held permissive and not mandatory—And that if the Company preferred to raise the road and take the railway under the road so raised they were at liberty to do so, according to the provisions of the General Act. (30 L. J., Ch. 474 : 3 De G. F. & J., 559 : 4 L. T., 387.)

1857. [2208]
Ellis v. *London & South Western Railway Co.* "Railways Clauses Act, 1845," §§ 46, 61, 68 —Occupation road with a public footpath along it crossed on a level by a Railway—Footpath ignored and locked gates erected —Key lost; gates left insecure; cattle straying; accident to such cattle—Held that it was a question for the Jury whether the plaintiff as owner of the cattle was guilty of contributory negligence—If a Railway Company blocks up a public way it is the duty of the Public to invoke the assistance of the law and not to take the law into its own hands and break down the obstruction. (26 L. J., Ex., 349 : 2 H. & N., 424 : 29 L. T., (O. S.), 389.)

1852. [2209]
Exeter Road Trustees, Ex parte. "Railways Clauses Act, 1845," § 58—County bridge pulled down by Company and another bridge erected under agreement with the Road Trustees—The Company to repair such portions of the approaches to the bridge as had been previously repaired by the County— Held that the Company had not so interfered with the road as to bring the case within § 58—The liability of the County as to the approaches had ceased, as the bridge was gone; the repair of the road, therefore, fell on the persons who would have been liable if the bridge had never existed, *i.e.*, the Trustees, who would have a remedy on the agreement against the Company—*Mandamus* to the Company to repair therefore refused. (16 Jur., 669 : 19 L. T., (O. S.), 190.)

1851. [2210]
Fawcett v. *York & North Midland Railway Co.* "Regulation of Railways Act, 1842," 5 & 6 Vict., c. 55, § 9—Railway crossing a highway on a level—Accident to horses which had strayed from a field on to the highway, and thence on to a Railway, the gates of the crossing having been left open, contrary to the Statute—Held that the road having been generally used was a highway though never taken over by the Parish ; and that, as against the Company, the horses were lawfully on the highway, and therefore that the Company was liable for the neglect of its servants to keep the gates of the crossing closed. (20 L. J., Q. B., 222 : 16 Q. B., 610.)

1865. [2211]
Freeman v. *Tottenham & Hampstead Railway Co.* "Railways Clauses Act, 1845," §§ 53-5— Restrictions as to Company stopping up a highway held not to apply to a way the rights over which had been lost by the Public— Motion for an Injunction at the suit of an adjacent owner privately prejudiced by the stoppage, refused, and the owner referred to his rights under § 55. (11 L. T., 702 : 11 Jur., (N. S.), 107 : 13 W. R., 335.)

1890. [2212]
Great Western Railway Co. v. *Phillips.* Road along a foreshore on which the public had long been accustomed to land and, using the road, so by footways, reach other inland roads —Footways absorbed in railway and no other footways provided in substitution—Held that the public rights of passage from the landing-place to the inland road had not been taken away by the Act authorising the construction of the railway and that the Railway Company must re-open the communication. (*Times*, April 3, 1890.)

1860. [2213]
Leech v. *North Staffordshire Railway Co.* "Railways Clauses Act, 1845," § 46—Special Act incorporating General Act but varying it as to the dimensions applicable to a particular bridge, and providing by special words for repairs thereof for 12 months—Held that this did not operate so as to relieve the Company of its perpetual obligation to repair under the General Act. (29 L. J., M. C., 150 : 1 L. T., 332 : [*Newcastle-under-Lyne* v. *N. S. R.*] 5 H. & N., 160.)

1864.   [2214]
London & North Western Railway Co. v. *Skerton Highway Surveyors.* "Railways Clauses Act"—Highway lowered to accommodate it to the levels—Held that the road thus lowered was not an "immediate approach" or "necessary work" which the Company was bound to keep in repair. (33 L. J., M. C., 158 : 5 B. & S., 559 : 10 L. T., 618.)

1851.   ·   [2215]
London & North Western Railway Co. v. *Wetherall.* "Railways Clauses Act, 1845," § 58—An Order of Justices directing a Railway Company to repair damage done by them to a road need not specify particulars of the damage or of the repairs intended to be ordered : it suffices if it states the length of road injured and directs the damage done to be made good—One such Order and one Conviction for default may include several roads in the same parish. (20 L. J., Q. B., 337 : 16 L. T., (o. s.), 438.)

1842.   [2216]
Manchester & Leeds Railway Co. v. *Rey.* Railway Company empowered to cross roads but to give a headway of 18 ft., and empowered to lower roads—Held that the Company was not bound to lower the footpath as well as the carriage-way so as to give such headway over footpath. (3 Rail. Cas., 633 : 3 G. & D., 269 : [*Reg.* v. *M. & L.*] 3 Q. B., 528, at p. 538.)

1854.   [2217]
Manchester, Sheffield, & Lincolnshire Railway Co. v. *Wallis.* "Railways Clauses Act, 1845," § 68—This section, which imposes on a Railway Company the duty of making a fence between Railway land and a public highway running alongside, imposes only a duty co-extensive with the Common Law prescriptive obligation to repair fences—A person using the highway must be doing so in a lawful manner or he will have no right of Action in consequence of the fence being out of repair—For horses trespassing on the highway and meeting with an accident on the adjoining railway because of the fence being insufficient or a gate open the owner has no remedy against the Company. (23 L. J., C. P., 85 : 14 C. B., 213 : [*Wallis* v. *Manchester, &c.*] 22 L. T., (o. s.), 286.)

1863.   [2218]
Manchester, S. Junction, & Altrincham Railway Co. v. *Fullarton.* Where a railway crosses a highway on a level at a place where there is a considerable traffic the fact that an engine-driver blow off steam and frightened horses waiting to cross is evidence of actionable negligence — A Railway Company must exercise its powers with due regard to the rights and safety of the Queen's subjects. (14 C. B., (N. S.), 54.)

1878.   [2219]
Matson v. *Baird.* "Highway Act, 1835," § 71—Horse straying without negligence on to a private branch railway at a level crossing, the gates of which had been left open, and thence

on to a public main line—Horse killed—Held that the owners of the private branch were not liable, as they had no statutory right to cross the high road, and only did so by the sufferance of the Road Trustees. (W. N., 1878, p. 167.)

1871.   [2220]
North of England Railway Co. v. *Langbaurgh.* "Railways Clauses Act, 1845," § 20—A Railway Company having carried a road over its railway by means of a bridge must repair the bridge, the road, and the approaches; and the repair must include both the structure of the bridge and approaches and the metalling on both. (24 L. T., 544.)

1858.   [2221]
North Staffordshire Railway Co. v. *Dale.* "Railways Clauses Act, 1845," § 46—Where a Railway Company carries a road over its railway by means of a bridge it is bound to repair not only the bridge and the roadway of the bridge, but the approaches thereto, and the metalling of the bridge and of the approaches. (27 L. J., M. C., 147 : 8 E. & B., 836.)

1862.   [2222]
Phillips v. *London, Brighton & South Coast Railway Co.* "Railways Clauses Act, 1845," § 16—This section authorises the permanent diversion of roads, and not only a merely temporary diversion during the construction of a railway. (4 Giff, 46 : 7 L. T., 663.)

1841.   [2223]
Reg. v. *Birmingham & Gloucester Railway Co.* Railway Company empowered to raise roads to cross its line, the necessary bridges to be at least 15 ft. wide in the clear, but the roads to be continued as convenient as the roads raised—Held that to construct a bridge 15 ft. wide with approaches 30 ft. wide, the previous width of the road having been 40 ft., was not as regards the approaches a compliance with the Special Act, the power to narrow any part of the road being confined to the actual bridge itself. (10 L. J., Q. B., 322 : 1 G. & D., 324 : 2 Q. B., 47 : 2 Rail. Cas., 694.)

1853.   [2224]
Reg. v. *East & West India Docks & Birmingham Junction Railway Co.* "Railways Clauses Act, 1845," §§ 16 and 50—Writ suggesting that a Turnpike road had been raised to cross a railway and with an ascent greater than 1 in 30 : and that the formation level of the railway had been made 2 ft. higher than was authorised—On trial of the issues raised it was found (1) that the way was not a Turnpike road but only a highway; and (2) that the allegation of the level being altered was true—*Mandamus* (1) to alter the gradient, and (2) to make the level conform to the Statute—*Mandamus* held bad as to (1) the gradient being such as was proper for a road of the class in question, and therefore as it was bad in part it was bad altogether—A carriage road is not a Turnpike road unless it is repaired by Trustees out of tolls payable by passengers — The proviso in

§ 16 that the Company shall do as little damage as can be, relates to the mode of doing works, and does not regulate what the works are to be. (22 L. J., Q. B., 380: 2 E. & B., 466: 21 L. T., (o. s.), 180.)

1842.   [2225]
Reg. v. *Eastern Counties Railway Co.* Special Railway Act requiring a headway of 16 ft. for a bridge over a public carriage road and giving power to raise and lower roads — General Proviso in Act that the rights of Parishes under Local Acts were not to be prejudiced — Local Paving Act forbidding interference with pavements, &c.—Held that under the Special Railway Act, which was subsequent to the Local Act, the Railway Company was justified in lowering the carriage road if necessary to obtain the 16 ft. headway. (11 L. J., Q. B., 178: 2 Q. B., 569: 3 Rail. Cas., 22: 2 G. & D., 1.)

1846.   [2226]
Reg. v. *Great North of England Railway Co.* Indictment for obstructing a highway by cutting through it and executing works not within the Parliamentary Powers of the Company— A Corporation aggregate may be indicted for a misfeasance. (16 L. J., M. C., 16 : 9 Q. B., 315.)

1839.   [2227]
Reg. v. *London & Birmingham Railway Co.* Special Act requiring that when any public carriage-road was interfered with and carried over the railway by a bridge the minimum width should be 15 ft., and that any new road generally should be as convenient for passengers and carriages as the old road for which it was a substitute—Held that the Company was only authorised to contract so much of the road as was over the bridge, and that having contracted the approaches to the bridge and made the road there narrower than the old road there must be a verdict of " Guilty " — The expression " convenient " means convenient for a drift-way as well as for passengers and carriages. (1 Rail. Cas., 317.)

1838.   [2228]
Reg. v. *London & Southampton Railway Co.* Mere expense is no sufficient reason for a Railway Company not making a substituted road as convenient as the original road. (3 Rail. Cas., 34, n.)

1850.   [2229]
Reg. v. *Newmarket Railway Co.* " Highway Act, 1835," § 82—Order for diversion—Directions, *inter alia,* that no building or yard was to be interfered with—Line of new highway being found to pass over a building and yard the Surveyors shifted the line just enough to avoid the obstacle—Held that either the Order was bad as delegating to the Surveyors a discretion as to the new line; or, if words to this purport were rejected, it did not appear that the Order had been obeyed : and that therefore the old highway was not shown to have been legally disused and capable of being stopped. (19 L. J., M.C., 24 : 15 Q. B., 702 ; 4 New Sess. Cas., 241.)

1865.   [2230]
Reg. v. *Rawson.* " Railways Clauses Act, 1845," § 58—The Justices who make an order for repairs, and none others, are the proper persons to impose the penalty for default in carrying the Order into effect. (15 L. T., 179.)

1850.   [2231]
Reg. v. *Rigby.* " Railways Clauses Act, 1845," §§ 49 and 51—The effect of those Sections is that if the available width of a road for carriages is more than 35 ft., the road may be narrowed to 35 ft. under an arch ; where it is less, the arch may be made of the same width as the road, so that it be not less than 20 ft.: if the road is afterwards widened the arch must be widened in proportion up to, but not beyond 35 ft.—Footpaths are not to be taken as part of the road. (19 L. J., Q. B., 153: 14 Q. B., 687: 6 Rail. Cas., 479.)

1842.   [2232]
Reg. v. *Scott.* Special Act authorising the obstruction of roads on condition that other roads as convenient or as nearly so as might be, should be substituted—The Company having obstructed a road and replaced it by one not so convenient, held, that they were indictable at Common Law for a nuisance to the old highway. (11 L J., Q. B., 254 : 3 Q. B., 543: 2 G. & D., 729 : 3 Rail. Cas., 187.)

1840.   [2233]
Reg. v. *Sharpe.* Special Act authorising Company to alter roads " in order the more conveniently to carry them under or over " the line—Road carried under a Railway by a skew-bridge, angle 45°, the former angle of the road having been 34°—Indictment—Direction of the Judge that if the work was done as an experienced engineer would do it, having reasonable regard to the interests both of the Company and of the Public, the Company had a right to make the diversion —The jury having found for the Company, new Trial refused—*Semble,* " conveniently " refers to the Company as well as to the Public. (3 Rail. Cas., 33.)

1853.   [2234]
Reg. v. *South Eastern Railway Co.* (1). " Railways Clauses Act, 1845," § 46—Option conferred on a Railway Company to cross over or under a highway—A *Mandamus* to Company to do one of these two things is defective unless it shows on the face of it circumstances which establish the original impossibility or the original or subsequent impracticability of the Company exercising this option. (17 Q. B., 485 : Aff. on App., 4 H. L. C., 471 : 21 L. T., (o. s.), 282.)

1852.   [2235]
Reg. v. *Wilson.* " Railways Clauses Act, 1845," §§ 56-7—Road dedicated to the Public but certain of the formalities required by the " Highway Act, 1835," not complied with— Road improperly cut across by a Railway— Held that though the original owner has exercised control over the road in various

L

ways and executed repairs down to a recent period he is nevertheless not the person "having the management" of such road within § 57 of the above Act, and entitled to recover penalties accordingly—To be a person "managing" he must be clothed with some duty in respect of the public *ejusdem generis* with that of "Trustees. Commissioners, or Surveyor"—*Quære*, whether the Company could be indicted for obstruction by severing and not restoring the road. (21 L. J., Q. B., 281 : 18 Q. B., 348: 19 L. T., (O. S.), 86.)

1849.   [2236]
Reg. v. *Wood Ditton Surveyors.* Rule *absolute* for *Mandamus* to Surveyors of Highways to make a road in accordance with a plan annexed to an Order made by Quarter Sessions —Surveyors under the influence of a Railway Company whose interest it was that the Order of Sessions should not be complied with—The general rule that Indictment and not *Mandamus* is the proper mode of enforcing obedience by a ministerial officer to an Order of Sessions does not prevail where the Court sees that the officer is put forward merely as a nominal party, and that performance of the duty really falls to other parties. (18 L. J., M. C., 218.)

1867.   [2237]
Reg. v. *Wycombe Railway Co.* "Railways Clauses Act, 1845," § 16—The powers herein must be understood to be restricted to acts *necessary* to the construction of the Railway and do not extend to acts done merely to save expense or inconvenience to the Company— *Mandamus* granted to restore the continuity of a highway unnecessarily diverted—Deposited plans do not authorise needless diversion of a highway unless special power is given by the Special Act. (36 L. J., Q. B., 121 : L. R., 2 Q. B., 310: 8 B. & S., 259 : 15 L. T., 610.)

1832.   [2238]
Rex v. *Pease.* A Railway duly constructed under Parliamentary powers is not in Law a nuisance to a highway—Interference with the rights and comfort of the Public must be deemed to have been a matter contemplated and sanctioned by the Legislature. (2 L. J., M. C., 26 : 4 B. & Ad., 30.)

1888.   [2239]
Simkin v. *London & North Western Railway Co.* Accident to carriage through horse being frightened by engine blowing off steam at station—Railway not screened—Held that there was no sufficient evidence of negligence in not properly screening the railway, and that even if there had been such negligence there was no evidence to justify the Jury in finding that such negligence caused the accident. (L. R., 21 Q. B. D., 453: 59 L. T., 797 : 53 J. P., 85.)

1868.   [2240]
Taff Vale Railway Co. v. *Davies.* Railway Act antecedent to "Lands Clauses Act, 1845"— Non-repair of approaches to a bridge carry-

ing a turnpike road over a Railway—Held that the Special Act did not impose any liability, and that as the "Lands Clauses Act, 1845," § 130, had no retrospective operation, the Company could not be compelled to repair. (19 L. T., 278.)

1855.   [2241]
Tanner v. *South Wales Railway Co.* "Railways Clauses Act, 1845," §§ 53 and 55—§ 53 only applies to a temporary interference with a highway and not where the object of the Special Act is to change the nature of the road—Therefore when a Special Act authorised the conversion of a public Tramway into a Railway the promoters were held not bound to provide an equally convenient Tramway in substitution—The enactment that if any road be altered another shall be substituted must be read as if it had said "any road other than that which the Special Act directs to be altered." (25 L. J., Q. B., 7 : 5 E. & B., 618 : 26 L. T., (O. S.), 88.)

1865.   [2242]
Wakefield L. B. H. v. *West Riding & Grimsby Railway Co.* "Railways Clauses Act, 1845." § 58—A Justice though interested is not incompetent to act if the objection against him is raised at the time of his making the Order, and waived by the parties—In such a case the objection of want of jurisdiction cannot afterwards be raised. (35 L. J., M. C., 69 : L. R., 1 Q. B., 84: 6 B. & S., 794 : 10 Cox, C. C., 162 : 13 L. T., 590.)

1862.   [2243]
Wandsworth B. W. v. *London & South Western Railway Co.* Road crossed by a Railway Bridge—Necessity for widening the Railway —Company owners of land on either side of the road but road vested in plaintiffs as Surveyors of Highways by Act subsequent to Railway Act—Held that the soil of the road was only vested in the Board upon a dry legal title, and to promote the public convenience—That the public convenience required the lateral enlargement of the Railway, and as the only obstruction would occur whilst the works were in progress, and the road would not ultimately be narrowed in its width, the case was not one for the extraordinary interference of the Court—Injunction refused with costs. (31 L. J., Ch., 854 : 10 W. R., 814.)

1864.   [2244]
West Riding & Grimsby Railway Co. v. *Wakefield L. B. H.* "Railways Clauses Act, 1845," § 58—Damage to roads by the carts of a Railway Contractor—Held that the Justices had power to make an Order on the Company which employed the Contractor. (33 L. J., M. C., 174 : 5 B. & S., 478.)

1864.   [2245]
Wood v. *Stourbridge Railway Co.* If inconvenience or annoyance suffered by a private person is such as is common to all the Queen's subjects no private right of Action would lie, and therefore no right of compensation under the "Lands Clauses Act, 1845"

—Therefore no compensation can be claimed under the Act for inconvenience sustained from the authorised crossing on a level of a public road by a Railway. (16 C. B., (N. S.), 222.) [See also *Caledonian Railway* v. *Ogilvy*, 2 Macq., II. L. C., 229.]

1865.   [2246]
Wyatt v. *Great Western Railway Co.* "Railways Clauses Act, 1845," § 47—Level crossing—No Railway servant in attendance to open the gates—Gates opened by plaintiff, who thereupon received an injury—Held that all such gates are under the exclusive control of the Railway Company, and that no member of the Public, even if hindered from passing, is entitled to open them for himself—If hindered owing to the Company neglecting a statutory duty he would have a remedy against the Company — Plaintiff, having therefore committed an illegal act, held not entitled to recover damages for the injury. (6 B. & S., 709 : 12 L. T., 568 : 13 W. R., 837.)

1878.   [2247]
Yarmouth Corporation v. *Simmons.* "General Pier and Harbour Act, 1861," 24 & 25 Vict., c. 45, § 11 — Pier erected under a Provisional Order, duly confirmed—Alleged public right of way obstructed—Held that as the statutory powers authorised the erection of the pier so as to render the existence of the way inconsistent with that of the pier, the right of way must be deemed abolished by Statute. (L. R., 10 Ch. D., 518: 38 L. T., 881 : 26 W. R., 802.)

6. OBSTRUCTION OF, AND NUISANCES ON HIGHWAYS.

(1.) WHAT AMOUNTS TO.

1887.   [2248]
Back v. *Holmes.* Obstruction of street by a preacher—Collecting a crowd—The "Highway Act, 1835," § 72, applies to the Metropolitan area. (56 L. T., 713 : 51 J. P., 276.)

1881.   [2249]
Baker v. *Wood.* Obstruction of a public way by a newly-erected building — Defendant ordered to remove the building and restore the passage to its former state. (W. N., 1881, p. 7.)

1884.   [2250]
Beaty v. *Glenister.* Local Act prohibiting disturbance of the Public Peace — Salvation Army procession — Salvationists held improperly convicted of disturbing the Peace. (51 L. T., 304.)

1858.   [2251]
Chapman v. *Robinson.* "Highway Act, 1835," § 69—The erection of a building within 15 ft. of the centre of a carriage-way repaired by the Surveyor within 6 months preceding, but on a part not actually repaired or used for many years, held not to be an encroachment which Justices could deal with summarily under this Section. (28 L. J., M. C., 30 : 1 E. & E., 25 : 32 L. T., (O. S.), 89.)

1882.   [2252]
Deakin v. *Milne.* "Unlawful Conventions Act, 1606": (Jac. VI. Scot., cap. 17)—Salvation Army Procession on a Sunday prohibited as likely to lead to a breach of the Peace—Proclamation of Magistrates disregarded—Conviction of Salvationists affirmed. (5 Ct. of Justiciary Cases, 4th Ser., 22.) [See now the "Burgh Police (Scotland) Act, 1892."]

1847.   [2253]
Dobson v. *Blackmore.* Obstruction of access by means of a public navigable river to premises let on lease—Action by reversioner—Judgment for the plaintiff, the reversioner, arrested on the ground that the obstruction being caused by barges and planks, no permanent injury to the reversioner was shown. (16 L. J., Q. B., 233; 9 Q. B., 991.)

1795.   [2254]
Dovaston v. *Payne.* The Public have no general right to the use of a public highway except for the purpose of passing along it. [*See* Judgment of Buller, J.] (2 H. Bl., 527.)

1871.   [2255]
Easton v. *Richmond H. B.* "Highway Act, 1864," § 51—Conviction for encroaching on a highway by building a wall within 15 ft. of its centre but on land which had never been dedicated—Held that the Section only referred to land forming part of the highway, whether metalled or not, and that the Conviction was bad. (41 L. J., M. C., 25 : L. R., 7 Q. B., 69 : 25 L. T., 586.)

1874.   [2256]
Edgware H. B. v. *Harrow Gas Co.* Agreement for permission to the defendants to open a road, they to make good the same and pay money — Action for breach—Defence that the agreement was invalid on the ground of want of consideration and as authorising a nuisance — Judgment for the plaintiffs. (44 L. J., Q. B., 1; L. R., 10 Q. B., 92 : 31 L. T., 402.)

1843.   [2257]
Evans v. *Oakley.* "Highway Act, 1835," § 69— To justify a Surveyor in taking down a fence two things must concur : (1.) The fence must be within 15 ft. of the centre of the road ; (2.) It must be *on* the road. (1 C. & K., 125.)

1869.   [2258]
Field v. *Thorne.* "Highway Act, 1864," § 51— Fence erected on site of a private ditch so as to be less than 15 ft. from centre of roadway—Held no encroachment ; the owner had not exceeded his rights. (20 L. T., 563 : [*T.* v. *F.*] 33 J. P., 727.)

1886.   [2259]
Horner v. *Cadman.* Salvation Army preacher—Obstruction of part only of highway—Conviction Held good. (55 L. J., M. C., 110 : [*Homer* v. *C.*] 54 L. T., 421 : 50 J. P., 454.)

1630.   [2260]
James v. *Hayward.* If a *new* gate be erected across a highway it is a common nuisance although not fastened, and any of the King's subjects passing that way may cut it down

and destroy it. (Croke, Car., 184: Sir W. Jones, 221.)

1853.   [2261]

Keane v. *Reynolds.* " Highway Act, 1835," § 69 —Plaintiff convicted of an encroachment, whereupon the defendant, the Surveyor, pulled down the encroachment which was a cottage—Action for Trespass—Held that the Conviction, even if erroneous, was a defence to this Action, as the present defendant was a person bound to execute and was executing the judgment of a Court of competent jurisdiction. (2 C. L. R., 245 ; 2 E. & B., 748.)

1869.   [2262]

Rankin v. *Forbes.* " Highway Act, 1864 "—Encroachment on highway by erection of fence within 15 ft. of centre—Proceedings for penalty must be within 6 months of erection —Offence not a continuing one. (34 J. P., 486.)

1885.   [2263]

Reg. v. *Chittenden.* Persons using a traction engine and trucks may be indicted for obstructing a highway if they occasion substantial delay and inconvenience to the public. (At *Nisi Prius.*) (49 J. P., 503.)

1881.   [2264]

Reg. v. *Duncan.* Indictment for Obstruction— Special finding that there was once a road but that the improvements which defendant had made were not of material damage to the public—Whereupon the Judge directed a verdict of "Not Guilty"—Practice—New Trial refused when a defendant has been in peril of imprisonment. (50 L. J., M. C., 95: L. R., 7 Q. B. D., 198: 44 L. T., 521: 45 J. P., 456.)

1866.   [2265]

Reg. v. *Lepine.* Indictment for obstruction by encroachment—Verdict that the obstruction was " inappreciable" held equivalent to "Not Guilty." (15 L. T., 168: [*Reg.* v. *Lepille*] 15 W. R., 45.)

1857.   [2266]

Reg. v. *Lister.* It is an indictable offence to keep dangerously inflammable materials near a common highway—On the trial of an Indictment for this offence it is a question of fact for the Jury whether the keeping and depositing, or the manufacturing, of such substances does really create danger to life and property as alleged. (26 L. J., M. C., 196: 1 Dears. & B., C. C. R., 209.)

1861.   [2267]

Reg. v. *Mathias.* One of the Public has a right to remove from off a highway anything that is a nuisance and interferes with the convenient use of the way by passengers—The owner of the soil of a highway has, moreover, the right to remove anything encumbering the way, even if not actually a nuisance—But anything which is the usual accompaniment of a large class of foot-passengers and is so small and light as to be neither a nuisance nor injurious to the soil cannot be interfered with — *Quære*, whether a perambulator comes within this definition ? (2 F. & F., 570.)

1864.   [2268]

Reg. v. *Mutters.* Negligently to perform blasting operations in a stone quarry whereby fragments fall on a highway and so endanger the traffic is a misdemeanour indictable at Common Law—Prosecution at the instance of the Local Board—Conviction affirmed. (34 L. J., M. C., 22: 10 Cox, C. C., 6: Leigh & C., C. C., 491: 11 L. T., 386.)

1862.   [2269]

Reg. v. *Train.* Tramway laid down without the authority of Parliament, but with the consent of the Local Authority (a Metropolitan Vestry)—Indictment for Nuisance—Verdict of " Guilty "—To withdraw part of a public highway from the use of the public is a general nuisance, and a street Tramway is such withdrawal and therefore such nuisance —It is no answer that the consent of the Local Highway Authority has been duly given, for such consent is *ultra vires*. (31 L. J., M. C., 169: 9 Cox, C. C., 180 : 2 B. & S., 640: 6 L. T., 380: S. C., at *Nisi Prius*, 3 F. & F., 22.)

1834.   [2270]

Rex v. *Carlile.* If a person having a house in a street exhibits effigies at the windows and thereby attracts a crowd which causes the footway to be obstructed so that the Public cannot pass as they ought to do, this is an indictable nuisance—It is not necessary to show that the effigies are libellous or that the crowd consisted of idle, disorderly, and dissolute persons. (6 C. & P., 636.) [See No. 2320.]

1812.   [2271]

Rex v. *Dewsnap.* Per Lord Ellenborough, C.J.: —" In the case of stopping a common highway which may affect all the subjects, yet if a particular person sustains a special injury from it, he has an Action." (16 East, 194.)

1812.   [2272]

Rex v. *Jones.* Obstruction of street—A tradesman unloading goods must not occupy the public highway for an unreasonable time— " He is not to eke out the inconvenience of his own premises by taking in the public highway into his yard. . . he must remove to a more convenient situation." (3 Camp., 229.)

1830.   [2273]

Rex v. *Morris.* Tramway laid along a highway by a private individual, who allowed the public to use it on paying toll—Held that the facts proved an obstruction of the highway, and that the plea of public convenience was no justification. (9 L. T., (o. s.), K. B., 55: 1 B. & Ad., 441.)

1805.   [2274]

Rex v. *Russell.* Indictment for obstructing a highway, being a street in a town, by keeping waggons a long and unreasonable time loading and unloading, though there was room for two carriages to pass on opposite sides— Per *Curiam:* —" The primary object of the street was for the free passage of the Public, and anything which impeded that free passage, without necessity, was a nuisance. If the nature of the defendant's business were such as to require the loading and unloading of so many more of his waggons than could conveniently be contained within his own private premises, he must either enlarge his premises or remove his business to some more convenient spot. But the Court could not be parties to any compromise for his using the street as his own for any part of his business." (6 East, 427 : 2 Smith, 424.)

1758.   [2275]
Rex v. *Sarmon*. Indictment for setting a person on a footway to distribute handbills, whereby footpath was impeded and obstructed—Held to be not an indictable offence. (1 Burr., 516.)

1802.   [2276]
Rex v. *Smith*. An Indictment will not lie for obstructing a highway by holding a fair or market, if there has been an uninterrupted custom for 20 years. (4 Esp., 111.)

1836.   [2277]
Rex v. *Ward*. In an Indictment for a nuisance on a highway it will be no answer that though the work be in some degree a hindrance or nuisance yet the inconvenience is more than counterbalanced by some public benefit in another way. (L. J., 5 K. B., 221 : 4 A. & E., 384 : 6 N. & M., 38.)

1872.   [2278]
Simpson v. *Wells*. "Highway Act, 1835," § 72 —Obstruction of highway—Statute Sessions for hiring servants — Distinguished from markets and fairs—There is no good custom to set up refreshment stalls at such Sessions notwithstanding a user of more than 50 years, and that the Sessions had been held before 5 Eliz., c. 4—Nor is there sufficient appearance of *bona fide* claim of right by custom so as to oust the jurisdiction of Justices in case of obstruction. (41 L. J., M. C., 105 : L. R., 7 Q. B., 214 : 26 L. T., 163.)

1875.   [2279]
Spice v. *Peacock*. Obstruction of a partly paved footway by goods exhibited for sale—Held that the appellant was rightly convicted. (39 J. P., 581.)

1835.   [2280]
Wilkes v. *Hungerford Market Co*. Where a highway is obstructed for an unreasonable time by an obstruction lawful in itself for a temporary purpose (*e.g.*, a hoarding round new buildings in a street), a private right of Action accrues to a person who can show that the obstruction has inflicted damage on him in his trade. (2 Bing., N. C., 281.)

(2.) BY RUBBISH AND MATERIALS, INCLUDING EXCAVATIONS AND UNFENCED HOLES.

1862.   [2281]
Binks v. *South Yorkshire Railway Co*. The owner of land adjoining a public road is under no obligations to fence excavations in his land unless they are so near the road as to be dangerous to persons lawfully using it — Where the Public have a mere permission to pass over the intermediate space, they take

that permission subject to the chance of accident. (32 L. J., Q. B., 26 : 3 B. & S., 244 : 7 L. T., 350.)

1878.   [2282]
Blakeley v. *Baker*. "Highway Act, 1835," § 70 —Excavation made within 5 yards of a highway, but duly fenced—Fence run against by plaintiff's horse and cart, the latter loaded with a weight of one ton—Fence broken down, and horse precipitated into hole, and horse killed—Held that the fence was sufficient to comply with the Statute, and that there was no legal duty on the defendant to provide a fence strong enough to withstand such a shock as the one in question. (39 L. T., 259.)

1878.   [2283]
Clark v. *Chambers*. A person placing a dangerous obstruction in a highway, or in a private road over which there is a right of way, is bound to take all necessary precautions to protect persons exercising their right of way—On neglect to do so he is liable for the consequences. (47 L. J., Q. B., 427 : L. R., 3 Q. B. D., 327 : 38 L. T., 454 : 42 J. P., 438.)

1858.   [2284]
Corby v. *Hill*. Building Materials unlighted by night, negligently placed by a builder in a private road by permission of the Freeholder —On an accident happening to a third party lawfully using the road, held that the builder was liable to him. (27 L. J., C. P., 318 : 4 C. B., (N. S.), 556 : 31 L. T., (O S.), 181.)

1813.   [2285]
Coupland v. *Hardingham*. Unfenced area—Accident—Action—It is universally the duty of the occupier of a house having an area adjoining a public street so to fence it as to make it safe for passengers—It is no answer to an Action to plead that the area has been unfenced as long back as could be remembered. (3 Camp., 398.)

1879.   [2286]
Fearnley v. *Ormsby*. "Highway Act, 1835," § 72 —Stones placed on a road by a Surveyor allowed to remain at night insufficiently fenced and lighted—Held that the Surveyor was properly convicted under § 72, although he might also have been guilty of an offence under § 56. (L. R., 4 C. P. D., 136 : 43 J. P., 384.)

1880.   [2287]
Fritz v. *Hobson*. Public nuisance by obstruction of highway by building materials—Interference with access to house—Loss of custom in trade—Held that on proof of the fact of excessive obstruction, plaintiff was entitled to damages in respect of the time during which the wrong continued. (49 L. J., Ch., 735 : L. R., 14 Ch., 542 : 42 L. T., 225.)

1883.   [2287a]
Gully v. *Smith*. "Highway Act, 1835," § 72— Landslip on Highway—Owner of soil which had slipped, Held guilty of obstructing highway, he not having removed same after

notice. (53 L. J., M. C., 35: L. R., 12 Q. B. D., 121: 48 J. P., 309.)

1865. [2288]

Hadley v. *Taylor.* Unfenced hoist-hole within 14 inches of a public way—Defendant occupier on sufferance, during the preparation of a lease—Held that the Action was rightly brought against him and that the hole was near enough to the highway to be a "nuisance." (L. R., 1 C. P., 53: 13 L. T., 368.)

1859. [2289]

Hardcastle v. *South Yorkshire Railway, &c., Co.* No obligation to fence an excavation is cast upon an owner unless such excavation substantially adjoins a highway. (28 L. J., Ex., 139: 4 H. & N., 76: 32 L. T., (o. s.), 297.)

1860. [2290]

Hounsell v. *Smyth.* A landowner cannot be compelled to fence an excavation, unless it is adjacent to a highway, so as to constitute a public nuisance—The fact that the excavation is made in open waste does not impose any liability upon the owner, unless he holds out any inducement to persons to come upon the land. (29 L. J., C. P., 203: 7 C. B., (N. s.), 731: 1 L. T., 440.)

1863. [2291]

Hughes v. *Macfie.* Cellar-flap lawfully maintained in a street that was a public highway —Flap properly left open, and accident to passenger unlawfully meddling with it— Held that no Action lay at the suit of the person meddling—*Sed aliter* at the suit of a third person innocently suffering. (32 L. J., Ex., 177: 2 H. & C., 744: 12 W. R., 315.)

1885. [2292]

Jones v. *Matthews.* "Highway Act, 1835," § 72: "Towns Police Clauses Act, 1847," § 28— Wooden boxes, with rolls of flannel on them, frequently during 40 years, placed by a draper on a footway fronting his premises— No evidence as to how much of the footway had been dedicated, or that the appellant's acts amounted to a nuisance.— Conviction quashed. (*Times*, May 12, 1885.)

1871. [2293]

Kearney v. *London, Brighton, & South Coast Railway Co.* Bridge over highway—Fall of an insecure brick and injury to plaintiff—Held that the Company was bound to keep the brickwork in proper repair, and that there was evidence from which the Jury might infer negligence. (40 L. J., Q. B., 285 : L. R., 6 Q. B., 759: 24 L. T., 913.)

1840. [2294]

Marriott v. *Stanley.* Action for compensation for injury occasioned by an obstruction in a highway—Left to the Jury to say whether the plaintiff was guilty of contributory negligence; whether he had acted with such a want of reasonable and ordinary care as to disentitle him to recover—Held that such a direction was proper. (1 Scott, N. R., 392:

4 Jur., 320 : S. C. as to Costs, 10 L. J., C. P., 50.)

1842. [2295]

Morgan v. *Leach.* "Highway Act, 1835," §§ 20 and 73—Held that no duty is imposed by the Act on a Surveyor to fence a dangerous pit—Conviction quashed. (12 L. J., M. C., 4 : 10 M. & W., 558.)

1844. [2296]

Mould v. *Williams.* "Highway Act, 1835," § 73 —A Justice's Order reciting that timber has been laid on a highway, and directing its removal is conclusive to show that the *locus in quo* is a highway, and the owner cannot in an Action of Trespass against the Justice dispute his jurisdiction on the ground that the *locus* was not a highway; he ought to have raised the objection at the hearing before the Justices. (5 Q. B., 469: Dav. & Mer., 631.)

1878. [2297]

Plant v. *Pease.* Bank on Private Land by side of Road—Footpath along bank used by the Public on sufferance — Boundary Wall of bank Dilapidated—Injury to foot passenger —Held that no right of Action was disclosed, there being no duty on the landowner to keep up the wall. (*Times*, Nov. 13, 1878.)

1837. [2298]

Reg. v. *Dunraven (Earl of).* Indictment for obstructing a highway by erecting a building— No real inconvenience experienced by the Public, the chief sufferer being a private individual who was debarred from access to his premises, and who, it was admitted, had his private remedy—In such a case the Court will discharge an Indictment on a merely nominal fine when the nuisance has ceased ; for instance, by the opening of a substituted road—But such a Rule will not be made *Absolute* in the first instance. (W. W. & D., 577.)

1867. [2299]

Rhodes v. *Thomas.* "General Turnpike Act, 1822," § 118—Orchard abutting on road; access to it obtained by the construction of a roadway over an intervening ditch, pipes being put in the ditch—Flow of water partially obstructed, notwithstanding the pipes —Held that the occupier was rightly convicted of obstructing the ditch. (31 J. P., 117.)

1884. [2300]

Rotherham, Mayor, v. *Fullerton.* Local Act— Special powers as to fencing of dangerous excavations by the sides of streets—Act held not to apply to fences on a highway, but only to fences put upon landowner's own soil—Moreover, not to apply to ancient streets, but only to new streets where there were no fences, and the Corporation thought there ought to be fences. (50 L. T., 364.)

1882. [2301]

Stockport H. B. v. *Grant.* Defendant's wall having fallen down was rebuilt by plaintiffs because their highway was endangered—

Held that they could not recover the cost of this rebuilding, there being no duty on the owner of the wall to keep it in repair in the absence of express covenant to do so. (51 L. J., Q. B., 357: 46 L. T., 388: 46 J. P., 437.)

1885.   [2302]
Watson v. *Ellis.* Obstruction of highway by carpet negligently laid across from front door for carriage passengers to alight on—Accident to plaintiff—Jury having found for plaintiff the Court refused to set aside the verdict. (49 J. P., 148.)

1864.   [2303]
Wettor v. *Dunk.* If an excavation has been made so near a highway since its adoption as to create or increase danger to the Public, and an accident happens thereby, the person making the excavation is not absolved from liability by reason that a statutory obligation to fence the highway is imposed upon other parties who have neglected to do so. (4 F. & F. 298.)

1862.   [2304]
Williams v. *Adams.* "Highway Act, 1835," § 78—Placing rubbish on a road by an adjacent owner—Defence that as he claimed the road, subject only to private rights of way, the Justices had no jurisdiction on the ground that a question of title to land was involved—Held that the Justices had jurisdiction to try whether the road was a highway, or only an occupation road. (31 L. J., M. C., 109: 2 B. & S., 312: 5 L. T., 790.)

1890.   [2305]
Windhill L. B. v. *Vint.* Highway obstructed by quarry refuse—Indictment—Agreement that if highway were reinstated the plaintiff Board would consent to a verdict of "Not Guilty"—Highway not restored—Whereupon Action for specific performance of agreement —Held that the agreement was founded on an illegal consideration and could not be enforced—An agreement to compromise an Indictment for a nuisance is not less illegal than an agreement to compromise a prosecution for any other criminal off. nec. (59 L. J., Ch., 608: L. R., 45 Ch. D., 351: 63 L. J., 366.)

(3.) BY CATTLE AND ANIMALS, INCLUDING VEHICLES, RIDING, AND DRIVING.

1832.   [2306]
Boss v. *Litton.* A foot-passenger, though infirm, has a right to walk in a carriage-way if he pleases—It is a way for foot-passengers as well as for carriages—A foot-passenger is entitled to the exercise of reasonable care on the part of drivers using the road—Damages awarded for personal injury. (5 C. & P., 407.)

1871.   [2307]
Rothamley v. *Danby.* "Highway Act, 1864," § 25—Sheep depastured by right on a fen barrier bank along the top of which there was a public highway—Such bank held not to be uninclosed land within the Section, and

therefore a Conviction for allowing the sheep to stray on the metalled part of the highway was good. (24 L. T., 656.)

1809.   [2308]
Butterfield v. *Forrester.* A person who is injured by falling against an obstruction in a highway cannot maintain an Action if it appears that he was riding with great violence and want of ord nary care, but for which he might have seen and avoided the obstruction. (11 East, 60.)

1866.   [2309]
Cotton v. *Wood.* Accident to Foot-passenger—Action under "Lord Campbell's Act," 9 & 10 Vict. c. 93—Foot-passengers crossing a highway are bound to take care to avoid vehicles; and the drivers of vehicles are bound to take case to avoid foot-passengers—To enable a plaintiff to recover there must be proof of well-defined negligence, not merely some proof of negligence—Where the evidence is equally consistent with either negligence or no negligence it is not competent for the Judge to leave it to the Jury to find either alternative, but it must be taken to be no proof. (29 L. J., C. P., 333.)

1869.   [2310]
Freestone v. *Casswell.* "Highway Act, 1864," § 25—A highway with mere strips of greensward along its sides on which there exists a right of depasturing cattle is not a highway passing over "any common, or waste, or uninclosed, land"—As to liability for straying cattle, *Golding* v. *Stocking* followed. (L. R., 4 Q. B., 519: 10 B. & S., 351: 20 L. T., 918.)

1864.   [2311]
Gerring v. *Barfield.* "Highway Act, 1835," § 72 —Use by an Innkeeper for 20 years of a strip of highway as a stand for the vehicles of his customers on market-days—Such user held no defence to a charge of obstructing the highway. (16 C. B., (N. s.), 597: 11 L. T., 270.)

1869.   [2312]
Golding v. *Stocking.* "Highway Act, 1864," § 25 —Though a man possess a right of pasturage on the sides of a highway, he will nevertheless become liable to a penalty under the Section if his cattle stray on to the metalled part. (38 L. J., M. C., 122: L. R., 4 Q. B., 516: 10 B. & S., 348: 20 L. T., 479.)

1859.   [2313]
Goodwyn v. *Cheveley.* Where cattle passing along a public highway stray into an adjoining field the owner must remove them within a reasonable time; and what is a "reasonable time" is not a question of law for the Judge, but a question of fact for the Jury. (28 L. J., Ex., 298: 4 H. & N., 631: 33 L. T., (o. s.), 284.)

1878.   [2314]
Harris v. *Mobbs.* Accident to horse and cart, horse being frightened by traction engine and van drawn up for the night by the side of a highway but 4 ft. or 5 ft. from the metalled part—Action under "Lord Camp-

bell's Act"—Verdict for the plaintiff, the Jury finding that the engine was left unreasonably and negligently, and was a source of appreciable danger. (L. R., 3 Ex. D., 268 : 39 L. T., 164.)

1823.   [2315]
Jones v. *Owen.* "Highway Act, 1773," § 60— [Repealed]—Offence committed in view of a Justice—Owner's name concealed by driver sitting in front of board—Forcible removal of driver from his seat by Justice held a trespass giving driver a right of Action against the Justice. (1 L. J., (o. s.), K. B., 133 : 2 D. & R., 600.)

1868.   [2316]
Lawrence v. *King.* "Highway Act, 1864," § 25 —Cattle, &c., lying about a highway are within the prohibition even if in charge of a keeper—The Legislature in replacing § 74 of the "Highway Act, 1835," by a new enactment from which the words "without a keeper" have disappeared must be taken as having intended to prohibit cattle, &c., from lying about a highway at all. (37 L. J., M. C., 78 : L. R., 3 Q. B., 345 : 18 L. T., 356.)

1859.   [2317]
Lloyd v. *Ogleby.* The mere fact of a man's driving on the wrong side of a road is no evidence of negligence, in an Action brought against him for running over a foot-passenger who was crossing the road. (5 C. B., (N. S.), 667.)

1866.   [2318]
Morris v. *Jeffries.* "Turnpike Amendment Act, 1823," 4 Geo. IV., c. 95, § 75 —Animals grazing on the side of a Turnpike road in charge of, and actually under the control of, a keeper are not liable to be impounded as "wandering, straying, or lying"—The presence of a keeper is not, however, conclusive— The matter is one for Justices on the evidence. (35 L. J., M. C., 143 : L. R., 1 Q. B., 261 : [*Norris* v. *J.*] 13 L. T., 629.)

1881.   [2319]
Parkyns v. *Priest.* "Locomotive Acts," 1861, §§ 8, 12 : 1865, §§ 3, 4. 7 : "Highways Act, 1878," §§ 28–9, 38—Tricycle propelled by steam generated invisibly by means of a spirit-lamp, held within the Acts—Conviction affirmed. (50 L. J., M. C., 148 : L. R., 7 Q. B. D., 313 : 45 J. P., 751.)

1881.   [2320]
Reg. v. *Lewis.* Street obstructed by crowd gathering round a shop filled with pictures—Shopkeeper indicted for nuisance, convicted, fined, and required besides to enter into recognizances of 500*l.* for each partner not to repeat the offence. (*Times,* Nov. 19, 1881.)

1867.   [2321]
Reg. v. *Pratt.* "Highway Act, 1835," § 72— This prohibition as to riding on footways applies only to such footways as are by the side of a road and not to footways in general. (37 L. J., M. C., 23 : L. R., 3 Q. B., 64 : 32 J. P., 256.)

184–.   [2322]
Reg. v. *Smith.* "Highway Act, 1835," § 78—*Per* Lord Denman, C.J.:—"A driver seen riding upon his waggon is *primâ facie* a fit subject for punishment; but if he shewed that he was compelled to do so from a sudden fit of illness, or from some accident which prevented him from walking he would avoid the penalty." (Glen, *Highways*, p. 360.) [The reference to L. J., given by Glen is wrong.]

1665?   [2323]
Rex v. *Egerly.* It is an indictable nuisance to traverse a highway with waggon carrying an excessive weight drawn by an unusual number of horses whereby the highway is damaged. (3 Salk., 183.)

1858.   [2324]
Robertson v. *Birkett.* "Highway Act, 1835," § 77 —A was driving two carts and the horse of the hinder cart was attached by a rope from its head, which, after being passed over the back of the first cart was fastened to the body of the first cart about the centre and the horse's head was drawn close up to the back of the first cart—Held that the Statute had not been infringed. (7 W. R., 50 : 32 L. T., (o. s.), 105.)

1863.   [2325]
Sherborn v. *Wells.* 2 & 3 Vict. c. 47, § 54—Cattle grazing by the side of a highway are not necessarily "turned loose" because not held by halters, provided there be someone in charge of them. (Metrop.) (32 L. J., M. C., 179 : 3 B. & S., 784 : 8 L. T., 274.)

1863.   [2326]
Sowerby v. *Wadsworth.* A right of highway does not include a right to race—A person who had been a party to a "hurdle-race" held jointly liable for trespass for fixing hurdles on some ground, although he did not take part in that particular act. (3 F. & F., 731.)

1879.   [2327]
Taylor v. *Goodwin.* "Highway Act, 1835," § 78— A bicycle is a "carriage" within this enactment, and the rider may be convicted of "furious driving"—Conviction affirmed. (48 L. J., M. C., 104 : L. R., 4 Q. B. D., 228 : 40 L. T., 458 : 43 J. P., 653.)

1885.   [2328]
Weedon v. *Gas-light & Coke Co.* Accident to cab running against a heap of stones in a private road—Verdict of Jury for defendants —Application for new trial refused—*Per* Pollock, B. :—"I shall not lay it down as Law that the driver of a vehicle is always bound to carry lights—The object of lights is ordinarily rather that others may see the vehicle than that the driver should see his way." (*Times,* Nov. 27, 1885.)

1885.   [2329]
Welland v. *Southern.* Collision between two vehicles—Accident to pedestrian—Drivers of vehicles have no paramount right to the use of a roadway; a pedestrian has an equal right; and a driver must use reasonable care to avoid running down people. (*Times,* Dec. 9, 1885.)

1875.   [2330]
Wemyss v. *Hopkins*. A conviction under the
"Highway Act, 1835," § 78, at the instance
of the Police is a bar to proceedings under
24 & 25 Vict. c. 100, § 42, at the instance of
the person injured. (44 L. J., M. C., 101:
L. R., 10 Q. B., 378 : 33 L. T., 9.)

1876.   [2331]
Williams v. *Evans*. "Highway Act, 1835," § 78
—Conviction for furious driving—Held that
though the word "rider" is not mentioned
in the penal clause of the Section, it must,
nevertheless, be held to be included in the
word "driver"—Conviction affirmed. (L. R.,
1 Ex. D., 277 : 55 L. T., 864 : 41 J. P., 151.)

1852.   [2332]
Williams v. *Richards*. To sustain an Action for
an injury caused by negligent driving the
injury must be caused by the negligence of
the defendant only, without any contributory
negligence on the part of the plaintiff—A
person driving over a foot-crossing at the
mouth of a street must drive slowly, cau-
tiously, and carefully ; but a foot-passenger
must also use due care and caution in going
upon such crossing, so as not to get amongst
carriages and thus receive injury. (3 C. &
K., 81.)

(4.) BY FIRES AND SMOKE, INCLUDING FIREARMS,
STEAM ENGINES AND GAMES.

1891.   [2333]
Allman v. *Grist*. "Highways Act, 1878," § 32—
Steam roller held a "locomotive," and licence
necessary. (55 J. P., 724.)

1877.   [2334]
A.-G. v. *Mouse*. Information by County Surveyor to restrain builders from taking traction engines over a bridge not capable of
bearing great weights—Injunction granted.
(*Times*, July 17, 1877.)

1887.   [2335]
Birkenhead Corporation, In re. "Highways Act,
1878," § 28—This section is permissive and
not compulsory, and confers on Local Authorities a discretion as to whether they shall
allow Locomotives beyond a certain weight,
&c., to use the highways within their District. (*Times*, April 28, 1887.)

1878.   [2336]
Body v. *Jeffery*. "Locomotives Act, 1861," § 3
—Wheels with 18-inch tires fitted with
shoes 9¾ inches wide and 3 inches broad
arranged alternately on each edge of the tire
and overlapping in the centre held not to be
in conformity with the Act, though there
was always a bearing surface of 9 inches on
the road—To comply with the Act there
must be one uninterrupted pressure of 9
inches from side to side of the wheel and
that pressure must be in one continuous band
throughout the whole circumference of the
wheel except so far as the necessary joints
in the material might render absolute continuity impossible. (47 L. J., M. C., 69 :
L. R., 3 Ex. D., 95 ; 38 L. T., 68 : 42 J. P.,
121.)

1879.   [2337]
Davis v. *Browne*. "Locomotive Act, 1865 : "
"Highways Act, 1878," § 29—Traction engine—Third man in front with flag exhibited
on a pony cart, he himself being in charge
of the cart—Justices considered that a man
so occupied was not free to give help to the
engine if required, and convicted the engine-
driver of travelling without his proper com-
plement of helpers; but the Superior Court
quashed the conviction. (48 L. J., M. C.,
92 : 40 L. T., 557 : 43 J. P., 416.)

1883.   [2338]
Dawson v. *Cruit*. An engine stationary in a
road drew waggons over a bridge by means
of a rope—Held that this was not using the
engine *on* the bridge. (48 J. P., 149.)

1878.   [2339]
Edmunds v. *Savin*. "Locomotives Act, 1861,"
§ 3—Whether the wheels of a traction engine
are fitted with "shoes" within the meaning
of the Statute is a question of fact for the
Justices to determine—Cases remitted to be
re-stated. (In the Q. B., May, 1878, MS.)

1880.   [2340]
Ellis v. *Hulse*. "Highways Act, 1878," § 32—
Locomotive used solely for agriculture held
exempt even though owner was not an agri-
culturalist, but only an engine-owner letting
for hire. (58 L. J., M. C., 91 : L. R., 23
Q. B. D., 24 : 60 L. T., 836 : 53 J. P., 598.)

1889.   [2341]
Galer v. *Rawson*. Traction Engine—Accident to
Horse—*Per* Lord Esher, M.R. :—"The law
is clear that if an engine of this kind on a
highway is calculated to frighten horses of
ordinary nerve and courage, it is a nuisance,
and notwithstanding that all the requirements of the 'Locomotive Acts' had been
complied with, the owner of the engine
would be liable in damages for any injury
resulting from it. But the fact that the
engine was a nuisance must be proved by
evidence, which has not been done." (W. N.,
1889, p. 180 : 88 *Law Times* Newspaper,
22.)

1862.   [2342]
Harrison v. *Leaper*. "Highway Act, 1835," § 70
—Steam thrashing-machine, lent for hire to
a farmer under the superintendence of the
owner's man, erected within 25 yards of a
highway, contrary to the Statute—Conviction of owner held bad, there being nothing
to shew that the machine was placed in its
illegal position by the owner's direction.
(5 L. T., 640.)

1885.   [2343]
Hartley v. *Wilkinson*. Steam emitted by Tramway Engine so as to be a nuisance—Appellant, the driver, held rightly convicted. (49
J. P., 726.)

1887.   [2344]
Hill v. *Somerset*. "Highway Act, 1835," § 72—
Conviction for rolling a lighted tar barrel
along a street held bad, it being shewn that
no injury to the highway or to a person had
occurred. (51 J. P., 356.)

1881. [2345]
London & South Western Railway Co. v. *Myers.*
Tramway along street—Held that to use a locomotive on the same was a breach of the "Locomotive Acts," notwithstanding that the tramway itself had been constructed under Parliamentary Powers. (45 J. P., 452.)

1863. [2346]
Mayhew v. *Wardley.* A person enjoys an easement in the soil of a highway for lawful purposes only, and when he uses it for unlawful purposes (*e. g.*, for taking game) he becomes a mere trespasser—Firing at game from a highway is a trespass in pursuit of game within 1 & 2 Will. IV., c. 32. (14 C. B., (N. s.), 550 : 2 N. & R., 325 : 8 L. T., 504.)

1891. [2347]
Murch v. *Baker.* "Highways Act, 1878," § 32—A traction engine drawing a threshing machine from one farm to another for use there is being employed "solely for agricultural purposes," and is exempt from licence duty. (55 J. P., 583.)

1879. [2348]
New River Co. v. *Kitchener.* "Locomotives Act, 1861"—Bridge over river broken down by locomotive—Damage to bridge and damage to locomotive—Cross Actions between the owners of the bridge and of the locomotive—Held that the owners of the bridge were entitled to recover for the damage done to the bridge, but were not liable for the damage done to the locomotive. (*Times,* June 25, 1879.)

1863. [2349]
Pappin v. *Maynard.* "Highway Act, 1835," § 72—A game which consisted of one man representing a stag being pursued by others, held within the prohibition of the Act. (9 L. T., 327.)

1875. [2350]
Pease v. *Paver.* "Highway Act, 1835," § 72—Damage to highway by mining operations—Defence that the lessees were legally entitled to carry on their mining operations irrespective of the effect thereof on the highway—Conviction of lessees quashed. (39 J. P., 407.)

1891. [2351]
Pitt-Rivers v. *Glasse.* "Highways Act, 1878," § 30—In a prosecution for engine not consuming its own smoke the burden of proof that it does so lies with defendant. (55 J. P., 663.)

1880. [2352]
Powell v. *Fall.* "Locomotives Act, 1865," § 12—Rick set on fire by traction engine passing along road—Held that owner was liable at Common Law for damage done. (49 L. J., Q. B., 428 : L. R., 5 Q. B. D., 597 : 43 L. T., 562 : 45 J. P. 156.)

1873. [2353]
Reg. v. *Kitchener.* "Locomotives Act, 1861"—Engine breaking down a bridge—Neglect of owner of engine to repair—Held that § 7 does not apply to a County bridge—Owner held not liable—The protection of County

bridges is provided for by §§ 6 and 13. (43 L. J., M. C., 9 : L. R., 2 C. C. R., 88 : 29 L. T., 697.)

1871. [2354]
St. Mary's, Newington, Vestry v. *Jacobs.* "Highway Act, 1835," § 72—Premises used by owner for the storage of heavy machinery, the removal of which to and from the premises was attended with injury to the footway—Summons under § 72 dismissed—Held that the Magistrate was justified in dismissing the summons if of opinion that the defendant, as successor in title of the original owner, was not exceeding his reasonable rights of ownership, for an owner of land who dedicates part thereof as a public way parts with no other right than a right of passage to the Public, and he may enjoy all rights not inconsistent with dedication. (41 L. J., M. C., 72 : L. R., 7 Q. B., 47 : 25 L. T., 800.)

1863. [2355]
Smith v. *Stokes.* "Highway Act, 1835," § 70—A portable steam-engine is within the Act—"Erection" need not be of a permanent character, and the engine need not be in any way fixed in the soil. (32 L. J., M. C., 199 : 4 B. & S., 84 : 8 L. T., 425.)

1866. [2356]
Stinson v. *Browning.* "Highway Act, 1835," § 72—To constitute the making of a fire within 50 ft., &c., an offence within § 72, it must be shown that the act is to the injury of the highway or to the injury, interruption, or danger of persons travelling thereon—The whole passage in the Section must be read together. (35 L. J., M. C., 152 : L. R., 1 C. P., 321 : 1 H. & R., 263 : 13 L. T., 799.)

1877. [2357]
Stringer v. *Sykes.* "Locomotives Act, 1861"—Engine fitted with shoes on its wheels laid obliquely—Held that the bearing surface not being continuous the Statute was not complied with—Conviction affirmed. (46 L. J., M. C., 139 : L. R., 2 Ex. D., 240 : 36 L. T., 152 : 41 J. P., 296.)

1861. [2358]
Watkins v. *Reddin.* "Locomotives Act, 1861"—Accident to a coachman—Action against owner of a traction engine held maintainable—Such an engine is calculated by its noise and appearance to frighten horses—*Semble,* that *scienter* on the part of owner is immaterial. (2 F. & F., 629.)

1860. [2359]
Wooley v. *Corbishley.* "Highway Act, 1835," § 72—Game of football in a public highway—Evidence of a constable that he saw the game and saw 2 horses frightened held sufficient to sustain a conviction. (24 J. P., 773.)

(5.) BY TREES AND WATER.

1890. [2360]
Clarson v. *Arnold.* Wire fence erected 8 ft. from centre of highway as a temporary protection to a permanent quickset hedge at the proper distance, held an offence against the "Highway Act, 1864," § 51. (54 J. P., 630.)

1862.   [2361]
Croasdill v. *Ratcliffe.* "Highway Act, 1835,"
§ 72—Interference with footway by dripping
of rain-water from eaves of buildings—Occupier held not guilty of an "obstruction." (5
L. T., 834.)

1838.   [2362]
Frompton v. *Tallin.* "Highway Act, 1835," § 65
—Refusal to obey an Order of Justices to lop
trees which were ornamental—Injunction
granted to restrain Surveyors from interfering
with the trees pending an appeal to Justices
at Quarter Sessions under § 105—Justices
have no summary power to cut down or lop
trees planted for ornament or shelter. (2 Jur.,
986.)

1844.   [2363]
Jenney v. *Brook.* "Highway Act, 1835," § 65—
Action of trespass against a Surveyor—Order
of Justices on an owner to cut, prune, and
plash certain hedges and trees which excluded sun and wind from a highway and
caused an obstruction held void for uncertainty as regards the cutting (because it did
not specify in what manner or to what extent), but good as to the removal of an obstruction—On default by owner Surveyor
executed the work—Held that the Order so
far as it was good protected the Surveyor;
as to the trees it was bad because it did not
negative that they were planted for ornament, or for shelter to a hop-ground, which
trees are excepted by § 65—A statement that
the hedges, &c., were growing on the plaintiff's farm and on the side of the carriage-way
was equivalent to a statement that he was
the owner of the land adjoining the carriage-
way, and a sufficient averment—*Venire de
novo* awarded. (13 L. J., Q. B., 376 : 6 Q. B.,
323 : 1 New Sess. Cas., 323.)

1888.   [2364]
London & North Western Railway, In re. Highway flooded by reason of negligence on part
of the Company—Indictment—Fine of £300
inflicted. (*Times*, June 13, 1888.)

1886.   [2365]
Reg. v. *Lewes Corporation.* Indictment for obstructing highway by planting ornamental
trees—Conviction—Nominal fine—No order
as to Costs—Prosecutor left to pay his own
Costs the Court apparently thinking his
conduct unreasonable. (*Times*, March 9,
1886.) [See now "Public Health Amendment Act, 1890," § 43.]

1888.   [2366]
Surbiton Commissioners v. *Metcalfe.* Tree in
street alleged by defendant to be an obstruction to his use of his premises—Plaintiff indicted for nuisance in respect of the tree, but
Bill thrown out by the Grand Jury—Whereupon defendant threatened to cut down the
tree—Perpetual Injunction against his doing
so, granted. (*Times*, Nov. 15, 1888.)

1870.   [2367]
Turner v. *Ringwood H. B.* "Highway Act,
1862," § 17—Road set out 50 ft. wide under
an Inclosure Allotment—Width of only 25 ft.
actually used as road—Trees growing for

25 years alongside the hard road, within the
50 ft. limits—Held that the public were entitled to the whole 50 ft. and not merely to
the *via trita*; also that the adjacent owner
had no rights over the soil to entitle him to
an Injunction to restrain the cutting of the
trees; but, *semble*, that though the Highway
Board was entitled to remove the trees as obstructions to road, it had no power as against
owner of soil to sell the timber. (L. R., 9 Eq.,
418 : 21 L. T., 745.)

1891.   [2368]
Unwin v. *Hanson.* "Highway Act, 1835," § 65
—"Lop" means to cut laterally and does not
authorise the "topping" of a tree. (L. R.,
2 Q. B., 115 : 65 L. T., 511 : 55 J. P., 662.)

1875.   [2369]
Walker v. *Horner.* Free passage of a bridle-way
obstructed by reason of landowner allowing
trees to grow over it—Such an obstruction
held not to be "wilful," so as to be within
the "Highway Act, 1835," § 72. (L. R., 1
Q. B. D., 4 : 33 L. T., 601.)

1840.   [2370]
Whitmarsh, Ex parte. "Highway Act, 1835,"
§ 65—Application for *Mandamus* to Justices
to issue Warrant for levy of expenses of
cutting a hedge—Such an application will
not be granted unless a demand of the expenses has been made of the person sought
to be charged, and the Justices were informed
of such demand. (8 Dowl., P. C., 431 : 4
Jur., 823.)

1879.   [2371]
Woodard v. *Billericay L. B.* "Highway Act,
1835," § 65—Duty as to keeping trees lopped
—The word "owner" in this Section is to
be deemed to mean the actual occupier,
whether "owner" properly so called, or a
mere tenant—Service of notice on the occupier therefore suffices, and the owner of trees
is not entitled to any notice. (48 L. J., Ch.,
535 : L. R., 11 Ch. D., 214 : 43 J. P., 224.)

(G.) LEGAL PROCEEDINGS AS TO OBSTRUC-
TIONS, &c.

*** See also "Legal Proceedings by Authorities
Managing Highways" (§ 2, *ante*).

1882.   [2372]
A.-G. v. *Shrewsbury (Kingsland) Bridge Co.*
When an illegal act is being committed
(such as an interference with a highway or
navigable stream) the Attorney-General can
maintain an Action, and an Injunction will be
granted, even although no evidence of actual
injury is given. (L. R., 21 Ch. D., 752.)

1606.   . [2373]
Baker v. *Moore.* Loss of Tenants is a sufficient
special damage to support an Action for a
public nuisance, in this case the obstruction
of a highway. (Cited 1 Ld. Raym., 491.)

1856.   [2374]
Blagrave v. *Bristol Waterworks Co.* Obstruction
of public footway whereby plaintiff was deprived of the use of it for passing from one
part of his property to another, and the time
of his servants was wasted in going by a

longer route to and from their work—Held that this was a good cause of Action to which it was no answer that the defendants did the acts complained of under the authority of their Act—But that it is no ground of Action that a person, by stopping up on his own land the continuation of a public footway over his neighbour's land, causes the public to trespass on other parts of his neighbour's land to the damage thereof. (26 L. J., Ex., 57 : 1 H. & N., 369.)

1862.   [2375]
Bolch v. *Smith.* A workman lawfully passing along a certain private path in a Royal dockyard accidentally fell and injured his arm owing to a shaft put up by a contractor by permission of the Government being insufficiently fenced—Held that the contractor was not liable, as the plaintiff had merely *permission* to use the path ; no *right* to do so, and no obligation, for there was an alternative route—But, *aliter*, if the machinery had been in any way concealed from view, or in the nature of a trap. (31 L. J., Ex., 201 : 7 H. & N., 736 : [*Bolett* v. *S.*] 6 L. T., 158.)

1738.   [2376]
Chichester v. *Lethbridge.* An Action will not lie by an individual for the obstruction of a highway unless he sustain a particular damage which must appear on the Record—But if the plaintiff aver that he was obstructed by a ditch and gate across a road which compelled him to go a longer way round, and that the defendant opposed him in attempting to remove the nuisance this is sufficient damage to support the Action—A general and a private way by prescription are inconsistent and cannot be claimed together. (Willes, 71.)

1842.   [2377]
Davis v. *Mann.* Ass tethered on highway killed by defendant's waggon—Held that though the ass might have been improperly placed where it was, the plaintiff as owner was entitled to recover, as the waggoner might by ordinary care have avoided the ass—In order to preclude a plaintiff from recovering in such a case it must be proved that he might with reasonable exertion and ordinary care have avoided the consequences of defendant's negligence. (12 L. J., Ex., 10 : 10 M. & W., 546.)

1850.   [2378]
Dimes v. *Petley.* A private individual cannot justify damaging the property of another on the ground that it is a nuisance to a public right, unless it does him a special injury. (19 L. J., Q. B., 449 : 15 Q. B., 276.)

1810.   [2379]
Flower v. *Adam.* If the proximate cause of damage be the plaintiff's unskilfulness though the primary cause be the misfeasance of the defendant he cannot recover ; at least if the mischief be in part occasioned by the misfeasance of a third person, not sued—A. placed lime on a highway ; dust from it frightened B.'s horse and he was nearly car-

ried into contact with a passing waggon, to avoid which he turned the other way, and was upset and hurt by other rubbish placed on the road by C.—Held that B. could not recover against A. (2 Taunt., 314.)

1824.   [2380]
Greasley v. *Codling.* Obstruction of a highway whereby plaintiff was forced to travel by a more circuitous route and could not perform so many journeys in a day as he could otherwise have done—Held that the mere fact of the delay was to him an injury sufficient to give a right of Action. (3 L. J., (o. s.), C. P., 262 : 2 Bing., 263 : 9 Moore, C. P., 489.)

1794.   [2381]
Hubert v. *Groves.* Any obstruction to a highway is a nuisance, and the only remedy is an Indictment — A party obstructed cannot maintain an Action unless he experiences private and particular damage. (1 Esp., 148.)

1884.   [2382]
Hyde v. *Entwistle.* 9 Geo. IV., c. 77, § 18—Time begins to run from period when a substantial encroachment is caused ; not from the moment when the building or other encroachment is finally completed—In dealing with such an encroachment as a porch Justices must consider whether enough of the porch to constitute an encroachment had been erected more than 6 months before the Information was laid ; if so they must dismiss the . Information—A substantial addition within 6 months to an encroachment would constitute a fresh offence. (52 L. T., 760 : 49 J. P., 517.)

1699.   [2383]
Iveson v. *Moore.* No Action lies for a public nuisance except on account of special damage to the plaintiff. (1 Ld. Raym., 486.)

1697.   [2384]
Lodie v. *Arnold.* A person who has a right to abate a public nuisance is not bound to do it orderly and with as little hurt as can be. (2 Salk., 458.)

1665.   [2385]
Maynell v. *Saltmarsh.* Action for obstructing a highway, whereby the plaintiff was prevented from moving his corn, which was consequently spoilt—Held, a sufficient special damage to entitle him to a verdict. (1 Keble, 847.)

1691.   [2386]
Pain v. *Patrick.* An action on the Case will not lie for hindering a passage in a common highway unless some special damage ensue—The proper remedy is by Indictment. (3 Mod., 289.)

1892.   [2387]
Ramuz v. *Southend L. B.* Landowner whose land adjoined a public promenade which had been used for many years as a highway for foot-passengers deprived of his access to the promenade by a fence erected by the Board in whom the promenade had been vested—Mandatory Injunction issued to compel removal of fence and an inquiry as to damages

directed—A landowner whose land runs right up to a public highway is entitled to access to that highway from his land. (67 L. T., 169.)

1861. [2388]
Reg. v. *Bowles.* Indictment for obstructing a highway—The trial of such an Indictment will not be postponed at the instance of the defendant until after the trial of an Action against him by the prosecutor for injury arising out of the same act of obstruction. (2 F. & F., 371.)

1861. [2389]
Reg. v. *Field.* Trial of an Indictment for obstructing a highway—At the close of the examination of the defendant's witnesses his Counsel claimed the right to sum up his evidence—Held that no such right existed. (2 F. & F., 498.) [See now 28 Vict., c. 18, § 2.]

1838. [2390]
Reg. v. *Fisher.* Obstruction of a highway in a town—Road stated in Indictment to run *from* the town *to* H.—Therefore the town must be excluded, and the nuisance being within the town there was a variance between the Indictment and the proof, and defendant was acquitted (8 C. & P., 612.)

1892. [2391]
Reg. v. *Heal.* Indictment for obstruction of highway by inclosing certain strips of turf on the sides of a road—True bill found, but before the trial an arrangement made between Counsel on both sides at the invitation of the Chairman of the Sessions—Terms did not involve the taking of a verdict but left the Indictment to stand without trial—Arrangement disapproved of by prosecutors who applied for *Certiorari* to remove the case to the High Court—*Certiorari* refused; no reason why the case should not be tried at the Sessions. (*Times*, Feb. 12, 1892.)

1860. [2392]
Reg. v. *Johnson* (2). Obstruction of highway—Indictment for a nuisance—Verdict "Not Guilty"—After such a verdict a new trial will not be granted on the ground that the verdict is against the evidence, even though the Judge states that he is dissatisfied. (29 L. J., M. C., 133 : 2 E. & E., 613 : 1 L. T., 513.)

1878. [2393]
Reg. v. *Lancashire JJ.* (2). "Highway Act, 1835," §§ 72 and 105—Alleged obstruction of highway—Refusal of Justices to convict—Refusal of Quarter Sessions to hear an appeal against the dismissal of the complaint on the ground that the informer was not a party aggrieved—*Mandamus* to Sessions to hear the appeal refused. (*Times*, July 2, 1878.)

1890. [2394]
Reg. v. *London, County of, JJ.* "Highway Act, 1835," §§ 72, 105—Where a summons for obstructing a highway under § 72 is dismissed the Informant has no right of appeal against the acquittal of the accused. (59 L. J., M. C., 146 : L. R., 25 Q. B. D., 357 : 63 L. T., 243 : 55 J. P., 56.)

1864. [2395]
Reg. v. *Maybury.* Indictment for continuing an obstruction on a highway—Trial thereof removed by *Certiorari* and sent to the Assizes—A plea of *autrefois convict* on a former Indictment for the same nuisance not allowed to be added even by consent, the Judge having no jurisdiction to receive it—The nuisance (a wall) proved to be still standing —Held that the Judgment on the previous Indictment was conclusive, and that there must be again a verdict of "Guilty." (4 F. & F., 90.)

1862. [2396]
Reg. v. *Paget.* Indictment for obstructing a highway—Removal of obstruction before trial— *Per* Wightman, J. :—In such a case " there is nothing to try "—Verdict of ." Not Guilty " by consent, the defendant undertaking not to renew the obstruction. (3 F. & F., 29.)

1884. [2397]
Reg. v. *Phillimore.* "Highway Act, 1864," § 51 Alleged encroachment—Claim of right— Whereupon Justices refused to adjudicate— Held that they were wrong—*Mandamus* granted. (51 L. T., 205 : 48 J. P., 774.)

1854. [2398]
Reg. v. *Russell.* Indictment for obstructing a navigable strait—Held that no new trial could be granted in such a case—Where a proceeding, though criminal in form, is really for the trial of a civil right a new trial after acquittal will be granted if the Jury have been clearly misdirected or have returned a previous verdict—But the Court will not interfere if a real offence is charged, or merely because the Judge happened to use an inaccurate expression, if the Jury have not been misled. (23 L. J., M. C., 173: 3 E. & B., 942.)

1854. [2399]
Reg. v. *Sturge.* Indictment for obstructing a footway from A. to C.—Evidence that there was a way from A. to C. but that it passed through an intermediate point B.; was a carriage-way from A. to B., and a footway from B. to C. only.—The obstruction was between B. and C.—Held that assuming this to be a misdescription the Indictment might, under 14 & 15 Vict. c. 100, § 1, be amended at the trial by substituting a description of the way as a footway leading from B. to C. (23 L. J., M. C., 172: 3 E. & B., 734.

1883. [2400]
Reg. v. *Young.* Local Act—Alleged obstruction of a street—Claim of right to use the ground as not being part of a public way—Held that the jurisdiction of the Justices was not ousted, but that they might determine whether the *locus in quo* was public or private. (52 L. J., M. C., 55 : 47 J. P., 519.)

1717. [2401]
Rex v. *Hamond.* In Indictments for nuisances on highways it is not necessary to specify the *termini*—A navigable river is esteemed a highway. (Strange, 44 : 10 Mod., 382.)

1836. [2402]
Rex v. Joule. Indictment for obstructing a highway—A defendant applying to remove an In lictment from the Sessions by *Certiorari* on the plea that difficult points of law will arise must specify in his Affidavit grounds of such difficulties—A statement that the obstruction consists of valuable buildings of old date is insufficient. (5 A. & E., 539 : 1 N. & P., 28 : 5 Dowl., P. C., 435.)

1796. [2403]
Rex v. Williamson. 5 Will. & M., c. 11, § 3—A person who has used a common footway for some years before it was stopped up, and who prosecutes an Indictment, is a party grieved within the above Statute so as to be entitled to have Costs awarded to him. (7 T. R., 32.)

1798. [2404]
Rex v. Yorkshire, W.R., JJ. (1). On an Indictment for a nuisance in *continuing* a wall across a road (not for *continuing* the nuisance) it is no objection to the sufficiency of the Judgment that it does not adjudge that the nuisance be abated. (7 T. R., 467.)—*Secus* where it is stated in the Indictment that the nuisance is an existing one. (S. C., *nom. Rex v. Stead* : 8 T. R., 142.)

1800. [2405]
Usher v. Luxmore. Lane 4 ft. 6 in. wide—2 Posts erected in it to prevent cattle straying when driven across the lane from one field to another, both fields and the soil of the lane belonging to one and the same landowner—Persons convicted of pulling up one of the posts held wrongfully convicted, they having put in a fair claim of right to the user of the whole width of the highway, and being therefore protected by the proviso to § 52 of the "Malicious Injuries to Property Act." (54 J. P., 405.)

1867. [2406]
Winterbottom v. Derby (Earl of) In an Action for obstructing a highway the plaintiff must show substantial damage peculiar to himself —The mere fact that he was forced to turn back and proceed by a less direct route, or to remove the obstruction, and that he was delayed and put to expense in doing so, is not sufficient—From evidence of user extending back during living memory, during which time the land was under lease, a Jury may presume dedication anterior to the lease. (36 L. J., Ex., 194 : L. R., 2 Ex., 316 : 16 L. T., 771.)

1830. [2407]
Wordsworth v. Harley. "Highway Act, 1773," § 81 [Repealed]—Action of Trespass against Surveyor for severing land from a close and erecting a dwarf boundary wall and raising severed portion to public road—Wall subsequently raised by Surveyor—Held that the offence was complete by the erection of the wall in its original state, and that the limitation of time for bringing an Action run from the date when the severance was first completely effected. (9 L. J., (o. s.), 50 : 1 B. & Ad., 391.)

7. REPAIR OF HIGHWAYS.

(1.) LIABILITY TO REPAIR.

i. *In Parishes and Townships.*

1698. [2408]
Anon. (1 Ld. Raym., 725.) The inhabitants of every parish ought to repair the highways —And therefore if by Statute particular persons are chargeable and they become insolvent, the Justices may put the charge on the rest of the inhabitants. (1 Ld. Raym., 795.)

1671. [2409]
Austin's Case. Per Hale, J. :—"If there be a public way of common right the Parish is to repair it, unless a particular person be obliged by prescription or custom." (1 Ventr., 189.)

1860. [2410]
Bartlett, Ex parte. To give Justices jurisdiction to make an Order to repair a highway or to indict the Parish where the liability to repair is denied, two facts must be proved : the road must be a highway, and it must be out of repair—Where the liability is denied and an Indictment is preferred under §§ 94-5, and a verdict of "Not Guilty" found, the Justices are not bound to direct a second Indictment on a fresh Information. (30 L. J., M. C., 64 : 3 E. & E., 253 : [*Reg. v. Somersetshire, JJ.*] 3 L. T., 316.)

1843. [2411]
Little Bolton Inhabitants v. Reg. Local Paving Act exonerating Turnpike Trustees from repairing roads, and making new provision for such repairs, and also exonerating from contribution to repairs of highways all persons rated under the Act—Unfinished street forming part of an old road, as to which the liability of repairs under the Act did not as yet attach—Held that the inhabitants were liable notwithstanding their exoneration, and that they might be indicted for non-repair. (12 L. J., M. C., 104.)

1878. [2412]
Reg. v. Ardsley Inhabitants. Parish divided into Townships—Each Township liable by immemorial custom for its own roads except that the road indicted had for some time been repaired by an adjoining Township— Held that this system must cease, for that it must be presumed that it had existed under some arrangement between the two townships, and that no such arrangement could be binding unless there was evidence of some adequate consideration. (47 L. J., M. C., 65 : L. R., 3 Q. B. D., 255 : 38 L. T., 71 : 42 J. P., 262.)

1865. [2413]
Reg. v. Ashby Folville Inhabitants. Indictment against Parish A. for non-repair—Plea that Parish G. from time immemorial and in consideration of levying certain Rates on lands in A. adjacent to the highway had repaired and ought to repair such highway—Replication, that the agreement between the two parishes purported to have been determined by notice—Held that the consideration was

insufficient to support the alleged liability of G., as neither could the consideration be enforced, nor could it be immemorial, for it must have arisen since the Statutes creating the power to levy Rates—That the alleged liability amounted, therefore, to no more than an arrangement between the two parishes which could be terminated at any time—*Semble*, that a parish cannot be bound by prescription to repair highways in another parish. (35 L. J., M. C., 154 : L. R., 1 Q. B., 213 : 7 B. & S., 277.)

1843.   [2414]
Reg. v. *Barnoldswick Inhabitants.* On an Indictment against a Parish for non-repair of a highway it is not essential, in support of a plea that the several Townships in it have been accustomed from time immemorial to repair their own highways, to show by direct affirmative evidence that there have been ancient highways in each of the Townships —The existence and several repair of ancient highways in one Township may be inferred from their existence and several repair in the other Townships. (12 L. J., M. C., 44 : 3 G. & D, 545 : 4 Q. B., 490.)

1877.   [2415]
Reg. v. *Central Wingland Inhabitants.* "Highway Act, 1862," § 32—Indictment for non-repair of a highway in an Extra-parochial place—Held that § 32 only made the place a Highway Parish liable to be included in a Highway District, and did not impose on it all the Common Law liabilities of a Parish in respect of highways, and therefore that it could not be indicted. (46 L. J., M. C., 282 : L. R., 2 Q. B. D., 349 : 36 L. T., 798 : 41 J. P., 711.)

1883.   [2416]
Reg. v. *Cheshire JJ.* Road out of repair—Dispute as to way being public or private—Quarter Sessions held bound to order an Indictment notwithstanding *Reg.* v. *Farrar.* (50 L. T., 483 : 48 J. P., 262.)

1866.   [2417]
Reg. v. *Farrer.* "Highway Act, 1862," §§ 18-19 —Summons for non-repair—Justices have no jurisdiction to order an Indictment where it is *bona fide* denied that the road is a highway, and the liability to repair the road if it is proved to be a highway is not denied. (35 L. J., M. C., 210 : L. R., 1 Q. B., 558 : 7 B. & S., 554 : 14 L. T., 515.)

1841.   [2418]
Reg. v. *Heage Inhabitants.* Indictment charging a Township with a customary liability to repair *all* public roads within its limits not adding such words as "which but for such custom would be repairable by the Parish at large"—Indictment held good on the ground that there might be such a custom as alleged, and that if there was any roads repairable *Ratione tenuræ* or otherwise it was for the defendants to show it as a matter of evidence. (10 L. J., M. C., 145 : 1 G. & D., 548 : 2 Q. B., 128.) [But see *Reg.* v. *Colling.*]

1859.   [2419]
Reg. v. *High Halden Inhabitants.* A Parish bound to repair a road must make it reasonably passable for the ordinary traffic of the neighbourhood at all times of the year, but is not necessarily bound to make it hard. (1 F. & F., 678.)

1843.   [2420]
Reg. v. *Midville Inhabitants.* The *primâ facie* liability to repair roads attaches only to a *Parish* and not to any Township or other sort of district, even though it be no part of any Parish—Roads set out in a tract of Extra-parochial and uncultivated land, part of a fen, under Local Acts, held not repairable under the circumstances by the Township, the Local Acts which instituted a *quasi* parochial machinery not mentioning the subject of highways. (3 G. & D , 522 : 4 Q. B., 240.)

1869.   [2421]
Reg. v. *Odell Inhabitants.* "Highway Act, 1862," § 18—Justices have no jurisdiction to order a Board to repair a highway if the Waywarden deny that the road is such—Though the denial if not made *bonâ fide* will not oust the jurisdiction of the Justices if they are satisfied that the road is a highway, yet their decision that the denial is not made *bonâ fide* is not conclusive and may be reviewed by the Superior Court. (21 L. T., 556.)

1840.   [2422]
Reg. v. *Oxford & Witney Turnpike Trustees.* To apply for a *Mandamus* to repair a road is not a proper proceeding; the Parish should be indicted, and it can then have its remedy under the "Turnpike Act, 1822," § 110—It was so held in a case where the question was which of two parties were liable to the repair under Local Acts. (12 A. & E., 427 ; 4 P. & D., 154.)

1875.   [2423]
Reg. v. *Rollett.* Hamlet which had never in the memory of man been liable to Highway Rates, &c.—No public roads in the hamlet— Held that these circumstances were not sufficient to establish a custom exempting the occupiers of the hamlet from contributing to the repairs of highways outside its limits but within the Township of which it formed part. (L. R., 10 Q. B., 469 : [*Rollett* v. *Corringham*] 32 L. T., 769.)

1863.   [2424]
Rex v. *Edge Lane Inhabitants.* Trustees empowered to make a road which, when made, was to be repairable by the Public—Portion of the road ending at a highway made and used for 26 years—Remainder unfinished— Held that no duty to repair lay upon the inhabitants — *Rex* v. *Cumberworth* followed. (5 L. J., M. C., 91 : 4 A. & E., 723 : 6 N. & M., 81.)

1831.   [2425]
Rex v. *Edmonton Inhabitants.* A Parish is not bound to repair a way used by the Public and repaired by the Parish for more than 20 years if there be no power who could dedicate it, and the repairs be shown to have

been begun and continued under a mistaken notion as to the liability of the inhabitants to repair—But the inhabitants are bound by such repairs if made with a full knowledge of the facts and with the intention of taking upon themselves the public duty—*Semble*, that roads set out under Inclosure Acts do not by presumption of law belong to the adjacent owners. (1 Mood. & Rob., 24.)

1771. [2426]
Rex v. *Great Broughton Inhabitants.* By Common Law and of common right the inhabitants of the Parish at large are bound to repair the highways, and an Indictment against a Division of a Parish for non-repair must prove liability. (5 Burr., 2700.)

1814. [2427]
Rex v. *Haslingfield Inhabitants.* Indictment for non-repair—Plea that though as a matter of fact the Parish had repaired both before and since a certain Inclosure Award yet by virtue of that Award the road was really in the adjoining Parish—Held that the Award was not available as evidence of the fact stated, in the absence of proof that certain formalities in the way of notices had been duly complied with before the Award was made. (2 Maule & S., 558.)

1820. [2428]
Rex v. *Hatfield Inhabitants* (1). Where, in an Indictment for the non-repair of a road, the prescription proved was that its inhabitants had been immemorially used to repair all roads within it which but for such usage would have been repairable by the inhabitants at large—Held that this placed the Township in the position of a Parish, and that it was necessary for the defendants to prove with certainty that some other persons were liable, in order to exonerate themselves from their liability. (4 B. & Ald., 75.)

1823. [2429]
Rex v. *Kingsmoor.* A Parish is liable as of common right to repair all highways therein, but an Indictment will not lie against a district called an Extra-parochial hamlet, for non-repair of a highway therein, unless some special ground of liability to repair is alleged. (2 B. & C., 190: 3 D. & R., 398.)

1834. [2430]
Rex v. *Landulph Inhabitants. Semble*, that where a public way crosses the bed of a river, which washes over it at every tide leaving a deposit of mud, the Parish is not bound to make it good—Where a stream separates two parishes, the *medium filum* is presumptively the boundary. (1 Mood. & Rob., 393.)

1833. [2431]
Rex v. *Leake Inhabitants.* A Parish is bound to repair all roads within it, dedicated to, and used by, the public, although there is no formal adoption of such roads—Where land is vested in Trustees for certain public purposes they may dedicate the surface as a highway provided such use be not inconsistent with the purposes for which the land is vested in them—Material excavated in

cutting a drain formed into an embankment on a strip of land primarily purchased for drain purposes—Held that it was competent for the Trustees to dedicate the surface of such bank as a public Highway.—*Quære*, could one act of repair by Parish be construed as evidence of adoption? (5 B. & Ad., 469: 2 N. & M., 583.)

1818. [2432]
Rex v. *Netherthong Inhabitants.* Where a highway is formed under a Local Act and passes through a township whereof the inhabitants are by prescription bound to repair all roads within it, and the road is placed under the management of Trustees, with a power to collect tolls to be applied to the repairs, if the way be out of repair the Parish (or Township) are the only persons liable to be indicted, but they may after conviction seek for relief against the Trustees under 13 Geo. III. c. 84, § 33. [Repealed.] (2 B. & Ald., 179.)

1788. [2433]
Rex v. *Penderryn Inhabitants.* None but the parish at large being liable of common right to repair highways, an Indictment for non-repair against part of a Parish is bad unless it show expressly how such part became liable. (2 T. R., 513.)

1837. [2434]
Rex v. *Scarisbrick Inhabitants.* Township A., in a Parish all the Townships in which were liable by custom to repair their own highways, indicted for non-repair—Defence that Township B. was liable—In proof of this plea an agreement produced dated 1591 and made between the owners of the soil of the two Townships, by which the owner of B. agreed to repair that part of the road in A. which was the subject of the Indictment, and a lawyer was to be chosen to make further assurance for the performance of the agreement—Proof also that the road had been repaired in conformity with the agreement until within a short time of the trial—This evidence held not sufficient for a Jury to infer the existence of an Instrument to bind the owner of B., and persons claiming through him, to repair, assuming that such an instrument could have been made so as to exonerate the inhabitants of A. (6 L. J., M. C., 103: 6 A. & E., 509: 1 N. & P., 582: W. W. & D., 246.)

1787. [2435]
Rex v. *Sheffield Inhabitants.* If the inhabitants of a Township bound by prescription to repair the roads within the Township be expressly exempted by the provisions of a Road Act from the charge of repairing new roads to be made within the township, that charge must necessarily fall on the rest of the Parish—By the general law of the land the Parish at large is *primâ facie* bound to repair all highways lying within it unless by prescription they can throw the *onus* on particular persons by reason of their tenure. (2 T. R., 106.)

1837.   [2436]
Rex v. *Whitney Inhabitants.* Inhabitants will not be discharged from an Indictment for non-repair until it is ascertained whether the repairs effected will stand a winter's wear, notwithstanding a favourable Certificate from Justices. (5 Dowl., P. C., 728: W. W. & D, 381.)

1754.   [2437]
Vennor, Ex parte. Where a new road is made by competent authority, *e.g.* by Statute, or by a Writ of *ad quod damnum*, and the Parish is to be at no further expense with regard to the old one, the Parish and not the owner of the land must repair the new road, unless the Jury under the Writ impose the duty on the owner suing for the Writ; or the new road lies in another Parish. (3 Atkyns, 766.)

(ii.) *Liability Ratione Tenuræ.*

1843.   [2438]
Reg. v. *Bamber.* Indictment for non-repair of a highway, alleging liability *Ratione tenuræ*—Special verdict finding that the defendant's land adjoined the sea; that anciently a highway existed over this land, and had been repaired by defendant's predecessors; that within living memory the sea had encroached and covered the highway; that defendant's predecessors had gradually shifted the line of the highway and had appropriated other land, and that they had always repaired such new highway; that the highway mentioned in the Indictment was part of the new highway which passed over land totally distinct from that occupied by any part of the ancient way; that the sea had recently washed away part of the highway alleged to be out of repair, and that what remained of the more modern road was too narrow for a passage and was bounded by a precipitous bank—Held that the defendant's liability *Ratione tenuræ* must be deemed discharged. (13 L. J., M. C., 13: Davis. & Mer., 367: 5 Q. B., 279.)

1890.   [2439]
Reg. v. *Barker.* An owner of lands who is not the occupier cannot be charged *ratione tenuræ* with the repair of a common highway—Where a highway so repairable is, under Statutory powers, so altered in its nature and course as practically to be destroyed, the liability to repair, *ratione tenuræ*, ceases. (59 L. J., M. C., 105: L. R., 25 Q. B. D., 213: 54 J. P., 615.)

1839.   [2440]
Reg. v. *Beeby.* Indictment for non-repair, *ratione tenuræ*—Ancient Deed put in by defendant, being an agreement between certain inhabitants of the Parish and a former owner of defendant's land whereby the said inhabitants gave to the said owner the land in consideration of his repairing an existing highway: the grantee covenanted to repair it, and it was stipulated that if through his neglect the Parish were indicted, there should

be a right of re-entry, and the agreement should be void—Held that this deed did not constitute a liability *Ratione tenuræ*—*Quære*, whether a liability to repair, *Ratione tenuræ*, must be immemorial?—*Per* Denman, C.J.:— "Such a liability might under some circumstances be newly created." (8 L. J., M. C, 38.)

1874.   [2441]
Reg. v. *Bradfield Inhabitants.* Land set out under an Inclosure Act for a private road to be repaired by the adjoining landowners—User by the Public—Indictment against Parish for non-repair—Defence, repairable *Ratione tenuræ*—Held that this plea might be rebutted by evidence of public user sufficient to support a presumption of dedication in the ordinary way. (43 L. J., M. C., 155: L. R., 9 Q. B., 552: 30 L. T., 700.)

1841.   [2442]
Reg. v. *Mizen.* An Indictment for non-repair of a highway in Parish A., alleging the liability by reason of the tenure of certain lands in such Parish is not supported by proof of liability to repair a way extending through A. and other parishes by reason of the tenure of a farm made up of lands in A. and in such other parishes. (2 Mood. & Rob., 382.)

1849.   [2443]
Reg. v. *Perkins.* "Highway Act, 1835," § 58—The proviso only applies to cases where a boundary runs along a highway, and where the liability to repair is not at Common Law, but *Ratione tenuræ* or *clausuræ*. (19 L. J., M. C., 105: 14 Q. B., 229: 14 L. T., (o. s.), 250.)

1877.   [2444]
Reg. v. *Pickering Township.* Narrow highway repairable *Ratione tenuræ* converted into a Turnpike road and much widened—Expiration of Turnpike Trust—Held that the original private liability had been destroyed, and that the Parish was now liable. (41 J. P., 564.)

1858.   [2445]
Reg. v. *Ramsden.* The liability to repair a highway *Ratione clausuræ* is in the occupier of the lands inclosed; not in the owner *quâ* owner—The liability does not attach where the way is not immemorial, or where the land inclosed has not been used for passage before the inclosure. (27 L. J., M. C., 296: E. B. & E., 949: 21 L. T., (o. s.), 327.)

1849.   [2446]
Reg. v. *Sheffield Canal Co.* Local Act requiring a Navigation Company to make and maintain a certain road at least 7 yards wide on pain of liability to be indicted for neglect; tonnage dues leviable, and to be applied in making, &c., the road—Subsequent Act empowering the defendants (a different company) to purchase the rights of the first-named company and assume its liabilities—The road was kept in repair to a width of 12 yards by the first-named company up to the time of transfer in 1817 and by the defendants till 1846, when they reduced the

M

width to 7 yards—Hold that they were liable for the full width of 12 yards, and this notwithstanding that the dues which they were empowered to levy were insufficient to repair the road—A count alleging liability to repair *Ratione tenuræ* held not maintainable—*Quære*, whether there may be a liability, not immemorial, to repair *Ratione tenuræ?* (19 L. J., M. C., 44 : 13 Q. B., 913 : 4 New Sess. Cas., 25.)

1841.   [2447]
Reg. v. *Watertree Inhabitants.* Evidence of reputation is not admissible to show a liability in the occupiers of land to repair a road, *Ratione tenuræ*, that liability being a matter of a private nature. (2 Mood. & Rob., 353.)

1813.   [2448]
Rex v. *Cotton.* Indictment for non-repair—Allegation of liability *Ratione tenuræ*—An Award under a submission by a former tenant of the premises adduced in support can neither be received as an adjudication, the tenant having no authority to bind his landlord, nor as evidence of reputation, being *post litem motam.* (3 Camp., 444.) [See 2 Mood. & Rob., 353, n., where this case is discussed.]

1820.   [2449]
Rex v. *Hayman.* An Indictment for non-repair of a road or bridge, on a liability *Ratione tenuræ*, cannot be sustained where it appears that the tenement on which the liability is charged originated within time of legal memory. (Mood. & Mal., 401.)

1674.   [2450]
Rex v. *St. Andrew's, Holborn.* On an Indictment for non-repair a plea of "Not Guilty" merely traverses the facts as to the state of the road—If the defence is that by prescription or *Ratione tenuræ* someone else is liable such defence must be specially pleaded. (1 Mod., 112 : 3 Keble, 301 : 3 Salk., 183 : 1 Ventr., 256.)

1776.   [2451]
Rex v. *Wingfield.* Indictment for non-repair of a highway *Ratione tenuræ*—Fine held payable to the Surveyor, and prosecutor's costs to be paid by the person indicted. (1 W. Bl., 602.)

(iii.) *By Statute, including Contributions for Turnpike Roads.*

1774.   [2452]
Anon. (Lofft, 465.) A power contained in an Act to continue private ways does not alter the liability of parties to repair them—Those who were liable to repair previously shall be bound still to repair. (Lofft, 465.)

1870.   [2453]
Brighton, &c., Turnpike Trustees v. *Preston Highway Surveyors.* Local Act—Insufficiency of Funds—Contribution from Rates—Mode of calculation to be according to the requirements of each Parish and not by mileage. (39 L. J., M. C., 83 : L. R., 5 Q. B., 146 : 22 L. T., 92.)

1865.   [2454]
Brown v. *Evans.* 4 & 5 Vict., c. 59—Justices cannot make an Order towards payment of repairs already done—The Justices, in the absence of proof to the contrary, need not, when making an Order under the above Act, inquire whether the Trust funds have been properly applied. (34 L. J., M. C., 101 : 13 W. R., 680 : 29 J. P., 311.)

1870.   [2455]
Bruton Turnpike Trustees v. *Wincanton H. B.* Right to claim a Contribution from the Rates—Local Act providing that tolls should be applied, first to payment of costs, then of interest on mortgages, then in repairs, and lastly in payment of principal and of debts—Insufficiency of funds—Held that the Trustees might apply tolls to payment of arrears of interest in priority to repairs; and as the funds were not sufficient for both, the Justices could not order them to contribute under the "Highway Act, 1835," § 94. (39 L. J., M. C., 155 : L. R., 5 Q. B., 437 : 22 L. T., 605.)

1843.   [2456]
George v. *Chambers.* "Highway Act, 1835," § 91—A single Justice has no authority to summon the Surveyor of a Turnpike road—Even if properly summoned, Justices cannot inflict Costs upon him under 18 Geo. III., c. 19, § 1 [repealed], unless they find that he is bound to repair the road on the ground that he has funds in hand for the purpose, and they must give him an opportunity of showing that he has no such funds—Nor can they order him to repair and at the same time order him to pay Costs, for in such case he has obeyed no Order—Replevin will lie for a Distress levied under a Warrant of Justices. (12 L. J., M. C., 94 : 11 M. & W., 149 : 2 Dowl., (N. S.), 783.)

1886.   [2457]
Hooper v. *Hawkins.* "Highway Act, 1835," §§ 53–4—An Order to take materials for repairs must specify with some exactness the place at which the materials must be dug. (51 J. P., 246.)

1873.   [2458]
Market Harborough Turnpike Trustees v. *Kettering H. B.* Local Act—Arrears of Interest to Mortgagees—Enactment that the tolls should be applied first to pay "interest from time to time owing in respect of money borrowed," then in repairs, and lastly in paying principal—Proposed Contribution—Held that the arrears ought not to be paid, and therefore that a contribution was not payable. (42 L. J., M. C., 137 : L. R., 8 Q. B., 308 : 28 L. T., 446 : 37 J. P., 551.)

1873.   [2459]
Market Harborough Turnpike Trustees v. *Market Harborough H. B.* Tolls on condition of repair of that part of road which was in a particular Parish—Tolls taken were adequate for repair of such part, but not for all the roads of the Trust—Held that a Contribution was not payable by the said Parish. (42

L. J., M. C., 139: L. R., 8 Q. B., 327: 28
L. T., 660: 37 J. P., 614.)

1864. [2460]
Mawby v. Hopkinson. Local Turnpike Act—
Available Funds insufficient—Held that notwithstanding that a limit was specified in the
Local Act as to the amount to be spent in
repairs, the approved deficiency might be
made good from the Highway Rate under 4
& 5 Vict., c. 59. (10 L. T., 27.)

1887. [2461]
Over Darwen, Mayor v. Lancashire JJ. (2). Disturnpiked main Road upon which a Steam
Tramway had been constructed—County An-
thority held liable to contribute. (58 L. T.,
51.)

1840. [2462]
Reg. v. Berks JJ. 2 & 3 Vict., c. 81, § 1 [Re-
pealed]—A Special Sessions may make an
Order on a Highway Surveyor to pay a
specific sum to Turnpike Trustees, though
the Turnpike funds be not altogether exhausted. (8 Dowl., P. C., 726.)

1701. [2463]
Reg. v. Cluworth Inhabitants. A Parish is not
bound to repair a road so as to make it better
than it has ever been time out of mind, but
as it has been usually at the best. (1 Salk.,
359.)

1879. [2464]
Reg. v. French. 4 & 5 Vict., c. 59, § 1—Statute
authorising the construction of various roads
and empowering the Trustees to take tolls
for the maintenance thereof—All the roads
except one duly made—Held that the Trust
was a Turnpike Trust, and that the construction of all the roads was not a condition
precedent to the Trust becoming entitled to
claim a contribution from the Rates—*Reg. v.
York & North Midland Railway* followed.
(48 L. J., M. C., 175 : L. R., 4 Q. B. D., 507 :
41 L. T., 63 : 43 J. P., 699.)

1845. [2465]
Reg. v. Hertfordshire JJ. 4 & 5 Vict., c. 59, § 1
—Order of Quarter Sessions confirming an
Order of Special Sessions directing a Parish
Surveyor to pay a Contribution—A Justice
who was a creditor of the Turnpike Trust,
and another Justice who was a party to the
original Order and a respondent in the
Appeal, held to be interested parties and
disqualified — Order of Quarter Sessions
quashed. (14 L. J., M. C., 73 : 6 Q. B., 753 :
1 New Sess. Cas., 470.)

1851. [2466]
Reg. v. Hutchinson. "Highway Act, 1835," § 94
—Turnpike road out of repair—Order of
Sessions on Trustees to pay Surveyors a sum
for repairs held good—Trustees directed to
apply their tolls in "keeping down" the
interest of borrowed money, and then towards
repairs, held not justified at a time when
repairs were necessary in paying off old
arrears of interest before defraying the repairs; but only the interest periodically
falling due—Before Justices issue an Order
under § 94 they must investigate the Turn-

pike accounts and ascertain that there is
money at command to satisfy any Order
which they may make. (24 L. J., M. C., 25 :
4 E. & B., 200 : 3 C. L. R., 104 : 24 L. T.,
(o. s.), 141.)

1860. [2467]
Reg. v. Manchester, Mayor (2). Part of a footway
adjoining a Turnpike road gravelled, and
part paved sufficiently for practical purposes
—Held that it was a question of fact whether
this was a pavement or paved footway within
the "Turnpike Act, 1822," § 112, and it being
left to the Court to decide the point, the
Court decided that it was, and that therefore
the Trustees were exempt from liability to
repair under § 112. (2 L. T., 280.)

1845. [2468]
Reg. v. Morice. 4 & 5 Vict., c. 59, § 1—An Order
under this Section must show that the road
which is in question is within the Division
of the County for which the Special Sessions
is held—It need not show in what proportion
of the Rate the sum to be paid stands—Nor
out of which of the three Rates permitted by
the "Highway Act, 1835," the sum is to be
taken—The 6 months within which a *Certiorari* can be had run from the date of confirmation by the Quarter Sessions, and not
from the date of the original Order of the
Special Sessions—The "Special Sessions"
mentioned in the Section cited means such
Special Sessions as are held by annual
appointment under the "Highway Act,
1835," § 45. (14 L. J., M. C., 75 : 1 New
Sess. Cas., 585 : 2 Dowl. & L., 952.)

1847. [2469]
Reg. v. Patty. 4 & 5 Vict., c. 59—A Summons to
a Surveyor that a contribution will be applied
for need not be very precise, if it give a
general but clear intimation of the matters
which the parties are called upon to answer.
(11 Jur., 288 : 8 L. T., (o. s.), 370.)

1838. [2470]
Reg. v. Preston Inhabitants (1). If a Turnpike road
be out of repair the Inhabitants are liable to
be indicted, notwithstanding that the tolls
are appropriated by Statute to the repairs—
In such case the Inhabitants must seek relief
from the Turnpike Trustees, under the provisions of "Turnpike Act, 1822," in that
behalf. (2 Lewin, C. C., 193.)

1848. [2471]
Reg. v. Preston (3). 4 & 5 Vict., c. 59, § 1—The
notice of an intended Information before a
Special Sessions with the view of obtaining a
contribution from the Highway Rate need
not state what part of the Turnpike road is
out of repair, or to what particular purpose
the money is to be applied, or that the road
is within the Petty Sessional Division in
which the application will be made—The
Order made will be sufficient if it shows that
an Information has been exhibited, and acted
upon by the Justices—The object of the
Statute is to ascertain the amount requisite
for the repair of so much of the road as is
within the Parish. (18 L. J., M. C., 4 : 12
Q. B., 816 : 3 New Sess. Cas., 333.)

1853. [2472]
Reg. v. *St. Alban's JJ.* If a Turnpike road be out of repair a single Justice has no power under the "Highway Act, 1835," § 94, to summon a Turnpike officer before him at Special Sessions—Order to be quashed as *ultra vires*—Justices are not justified in making any Order for payment of moneys necessary for repairs without inquiring into the sufficiency of the funds—*George* v. *Chambers* followed. (23 L. J., M. C., 142: 17 Jur., 531.)

1854. [2473]
Reg. v. *South Shields Turnpike Trustees.* 4 & 5 Vict., c. 59—Local Turnpike Act providing that fundsshould be applied first to repair the roads, and afterwards to pay interest on borrowed money—Trustees applied funds to pay arrears of interest, and the balance being insufficient for repairs, Justices made an Order for contribution—Order quashed at Quarter Sessions —Held that the order of appropriation in Local Act was not altered by 4 & 5 Vict., c. 59, and that the payment by the Trustees was improper—That nevertheless the Justices had power to make an Order, if expedient, although the deficiency was caused by misappropriation, but that the Quarter Sessions had exercised a sound discretion in reviewing their decision. (23 L. J., M. C., 134: 3 E. & B., 599: 2 C. L. R., 1506: 24 L. T., (o. s.), 143.)

1856. [2474]
Reg. v. *Trafford.* "Highway Act, 1835," § 94— Summons against Surveyors for non-repair —Road ascertained to be Turnpike—Complainant offered to show that Trust had no funds, he appearing on behalf of the Trust— Complaint dismissed by Justices on the ground that proceedings under § 94 were improper—Held that the Justices were right; otherwise they would have convicted the wrong parties, the liability resting in the first instance on the Turnpike Officers. (5 E. & B., 967.)

1843. [2475]
Reg. v. *White* (1). 2 & 3 Vict., c. 81 [Repealed.] Turnpike Act directing Tolls to be devoted first to repairs and then to payment of interest —Income sufficient for repairs—But not for repairs and interest in addition—Held that the Justices had a discretion to make an Order for a contribution out of the Highway Rate, the Tolls being insufficient for both the purposes. (12 J., J., M. C., 31 : 4 Q. B., 101.)

1840. [2476]
Reg. v. *Wilts JJ.* Highway out of repair—Appointment by Justices of a viewer—Justices are not bound by his report but may exercise their own discretion whether they will convict the Surveyor or not—*Mandamus* to Justices to convict and fine a Surveyor, refused —If certain Justices attending at Special Sessions do not take part in a decision of the Sessions they ought not to be brought before the Queen's Bench on an application for a *Mandamus* in respect of that decision—*Per* Coleridge, J. :—"It is said that this penalty

if inflicted would come out of the Highway Rate, but I do not think that § 96 bears out that construction." (8 Dowl., P. C., 717 : [*Reg.* v. *Bouverie*] 4 Jur., 460.)

1854. [2477]
Reg. v. *Worthing Roads Trustees.* Local Acts— Turnpike Road—Part of a parish formed into a Local Government District—4 & 5 Vict., c. 59, held applicable, and contribution payable to the Turnpike out of the Highway Rate, but that the two parts of the Parish became distinct for the purpose of repairs both of highways and turnpike roads, and that only the Urban Highway Rate was to contribute to the Urban portion of the Turnpike and Rural to Rural. (23 L. J., M. C., 187 : 3 E. & B., 989 : 2 C. L. R., 1678 : 23 L. T., (o. s.), 169.)

1832. [2478–79]
Rex v. *Cumberworth Inhabitants.* (1). Where Trustees are authorised by Statute to make a road the making of the whole of it is a condition precedent to any part becoming a public highway—Therefore, where 12 miles of road were to have been made, and 11½ miles (ending at a highway) only were made, no duty to repair was cast upon the Township. (1 L. J., M. C., 86 : 3 B. & Ad., 108.) (2) In 1836 there was a second case of *Rex* v. *Cumberworth Inhabitants.* The trunk road mentioned above had been completed, but not a branch road, and the Court adhering to its former view, held (*Per* Patteson, J.), that "there is a bargain with the public, and . . . unless the Trustees make all the roads they do not complete their bargain"—Rule *absolute* for a Verdict of "Not Guilty." (6 L. J., M. C., 21 : 4 A. & E., 731 : 1 N. & P., 197.) [See *Roberts* v. *Roberts.*]

1812. [2480]
Rex v. *St. George, Hanover Square, Inhabitants.* Where the duty to repair a highway is transferred by Statute from a Parish to other persons, if the Parish be indicted for non-repair a special plea stating who is bound to repair is not requisite, but the exemption may be taken advantage of under the general issue of "Not Guilty"—Although a Statute enact that the paving of a particular street shall be done by certain Commissioners and provides the requisite funds, and another Act for paving the streets in the Parish contains a clause that it shall not extend to the particular street, the Inhabitants are not exempted from their Common Law liability to keep that street in repair. (3 Camp., 222.)

1835. [2481]
Rex v. *Siviter.* Charter granted by Elizabeth and confirmed by Charles I. exempting the tenants of certain ancient demesne lands from payment of Road Money (*Chimagium*) held not to exempt them from Statute Duty under the "Highway Acts"—These Statutes taken to repeal, *pro tanto*, the Charters. (4 L. J., M. C., 108 : 5 N. & M., 125.)

1862. [2482]
Roberts v. *Roberts.* Act for construction of a Turnpike Road—Part only of the road made

—Held that Justices could make an Order under 4 & 5 Vict., c. 59, for the repair of the part which had been completed and opened to the public. (3 B. & S., 183 : 7 L. T., 320.)

1861.   [2483]
Sunk Island Turnpike Trustees v. *Patrington Highway Surveyors.* 4 & 5 Vict., c. 59, § 1 —This Statute applies to Turnpike Roads not in existence when it was passed—A Trust is none the less a Trust within the Act because its funds are derived from other sources than Tolls taken on the road. (31 L. J., M. C., 18 : 1 B. & S., 747.)

1866.   [2484]
Weardale H. B. v. *Alston Turnpike Trustees.* Local Act—Revenue more than sufficient to defray lawful expenditure and a small surplus available for paying off debts—Held that under these circumstances no contribution from the Highway Rates could be claimed, and that the Trustees were-bound to apply their funds in the order and to the extent provided by their Act; and that 4 & 5 Vict., c. 59, could not override the subsequent Local Act—Justices' Order for a payment for this purpose held bad—*Reg.* v. *White* (1) distinguished. (35 L. J., M. C., 173 : 14 L. T., 546: [*W.* v. *Bainbridge*] L. R., 1 Q. B., 396.)

1797.   [2485]
Wilkinson v. *Bagshaw.* Local Turnpike Act—New road made under a Statute which likewise authorised the sale of the land which formed the old road unless it led to some place to which the new road did not lead—Held that the Trustees could not make a partial destruction of the road ; but that if it led to any place, even a single house, not served by the new road the old road must remain open. (Peake, Add. Cas., 165.)

(iv.) In respect of " Extraordinary Traffic " under the " Highways Act, 1878," § 23.

1883.   [2486]
Amesbury Guardians. v. *Wills JJ.* "Highways Act, 1878," § 13—Expenses of removal of snow from main road held expenses, half of which could be recovered from County Authority. (52 L. J , M. C., 64 : L. R., 10 Q. B. D., 480 : 47 J. P., 184.)

1879.   [2487]
Aveland (Lord) v. *Lucas.* "Highway Act, 1878," § 23—Damage to road by traction-engine drawing heavy materials—Engine within the statutory weight, and the materials ordinary materials— Held, nevertheless, that the owner was liable — What is " excessive weight " and extraordinary traffic must be determined in each case, with reference to the ordinary traffic of the road affected. (49 L. J., C. P., 643: L. R., 5, C. P. D., 351 : 42 L. T., 788 : 44 J. P., 360.)

1882.   [2488]
Barnett v. *Hoo H. B.* " Extraordinary traffic " caused by contractor carting bricks—Held that the " Railway Clauses Act, 1845 " § 58,

dealing with liabilities of Railway Companies as to highways did not operate to relieve the contractor of his obligations under the "Highway Act, 1878," § 23. (46 J. P., 805.)

1881.   [2489]
Exford Iron Co. v. *Dulverton H. B.* "Highway Act, 1878." §§ 23, 36 — "Extraordinary traffic "—What evidence is necessary to support a demand for a special contribution— Company held liable for serious damage done by carting immediately after a thaw. (At Q. Sess.) (45 J. P., 80.)

1888.   [2490]
Lancaster v. *Harlech H. B.* "Highways Act, 1871," § 23—Surveyor's certificate upheld ; though he had never been appointed under seal he was *de facto* surveyor, and so qualified to certify. (52 J. P., 805.)

1885.   [2491]
Lapthorne v. *Harvey.* "Highway Act, 1878," § 23.—Cartage of stone required by a Government contractor — Sub-contract — Held that the sub-contractor who actually moved the stone was the party to be proceeded against. (49 J. P., 709.)

1880.   [2492]
Northumberland Whinstone Co. v. *Alnwick H. B.* "Highways Act, 1878," § 23 — "Extraordinary traffic "—*Williams* v. *Davies* followed. (44 J. P., 360.)

1881.   [2493]
Pickering H. B. v. *Barry.* "Highway Act, 1878," § 23. Heavy traffic in bricks carted for building a house—Such traffic held not " extraordinary "—*Per* Lopes, J. :—" (Excessive weight) was something unusual in weight: (extraordinary traffic) was something unusual in the kind of traffic. I think that the legislature intended something unusual in weight or extraordinary in kind of traffic, either as compared with what is usually carried over roads of the same nature in the neighbourhood, or as compared with what the road in its ordinary and fair use might be reasonably subjected to. It would not be sufficient to compare the weight and traffic complained of with traffic usually carried on the particular road. It might be traffic was usually of the lightest kind, but surely the legislature never intended that a man was not to use the road for carrying materials for building a dwelling-house, a farm-house, or a barn, provided he used it in a reasonable way for those purposes." (51 L. J., M. C., 17 : L. R., 8 Q. B. D., 59: 45 L. T., 655 : 46 J. P., 215 : *Times*, Dec. 2, 1881.)

1882.   [2494]
Pool and Forden H. B. v. *Gunning.* "Highway Act, 1878," §§ 23 and 36—The 6 months within which summary proceedings to recover expenses must be taken run from date of Surveyor's certificate, and not from date of demand. (51 L. J., M. C., 49 : 46 L. T., 163 : 46 J. P., 708.)

1881. [2495]
Raglan H. B. v. *Monmouth Steam Mills Co.*
"Highway Act," 1878, § 23—"Extraordinary Traffic"—Haulage of timber in a district where timber had long been a common article of trade held not to be " extraordinary traffic," although it was only at intervals of some years that particular coppices being cut unusual traffic occurred. (46 J. P., 598.)

1882. [2496]
Reg. v. *Ellis* (1). "Highway Act, 1878," § 23—The conveyance of manure by truck drawn by traction engine along a road not ordinarily traversed by such engines, and unfit to bear their weight, held "extraordinary traffic." (L. R., 8 Q. B. D., 466 : 30 W. R., 613 : [*Ellis* v. *Maidstone*] 46 J. P., 293.)

1881. [2497]
Reg. v. *Williamson.* "Extraordinary expenses"—Defendant the only mineral owner using a road, all other owners sending their stone by railway—Defendant's traffic held not "extraordinary" merely because he made frequent use of the road whilst others preferred another mode of conveyance. (45 J. P., 505.)

1880. [2498]
Savin v. *Oswestry H. B.* "Highway Act, 1878," § 23—"Extraordinary traffic"—Highways so seriously damaged so as to need entire reconstruction—Held that as the expenses of reconstruction could not be separated from the expenses of repairs the defendant was properly adjudged to pay the large sum of £500, and this notwithstanding that the road had not been originally well formed—Where the Q.B.D. exercises its Common Law Jurisdiction there may be appeal to Court of Appeal though leave refused. (L. R., 6 Q. B. D., 309 : 44 J. P., 766.)

1884. [2499]
Tunbridge H. B. v. *Sevenoaks H. B.* "Highway Act, 1878," § 23—Cartage of stone along an agricultural road never before used for such a purpose held to be " extraordinary traffic." (49 J. P., 310 : 33 W. R., 306.)

1881. [2500]
Wallington v. *Hoskins.* "Highway Act, 1878," § 23—Carriage of stone—A waggon may be loaded with a weight which absolutely may be very heavy, and yet the weight may not be extraordinary within the statute if such weights are usual in the locality' and necessary. (50 L. J., M. C., 19 : L. R., 6 Q. B. D., 206 : 43 L. T., 597 : 45 J. P., 173.)

*1881. [2500a]
White v. *Colson.* "Highway Act, 1878," § 23. (46 J. P., 565.) [See *Pool & Forden* v. *Gunning.*]

1891. [2501]
Whitehead v. *Sevenoaks H. B.* "Highways Act, 1878," § 23—Light country road injured during 7 years by cartage of stone from a quarry—Appellant held chargeable with the payment of " extraordinary expenses "; the length of time which had elapsed before proceedings were commenced did not diminish his liability. (61 L. J., M. C., 59 : [*Whit-*

bread v. &c.] L. R., 1 Q. B., 8 : 65 L. T., 855 : 56 J. P., 214.)

1880. [2502]
Williams v. *Davies.* "Highways Act, 1878," § 23.—The question of what is "extraordinary" traffic is a question of fact—The decision of Justices that the cartage of an unusual quantity of heavy timber was "extraordinary traffic" for which the owner was liable, held good. (44 J. P., 317.)

(v.) *Arising out of Inclosures.*

1877. [2503]
Benfieldside L. B. v. *Consett Iron Co.* Company lessees from Lord of Manor of lands inclosed under an Inclosure Act which provided for the setting out of roads as public highways, and reserved to the Lord all manorial rights and mines with power to do all acts for working the mines as freely as though the Act had not been passed, without paying any damages for so doing—Held that the Lord's assignees were not entitled so to work the mines as to damage the roads, and that the reservation to the Lord was subject to the public right created by the Act and did not protect the defendants from liability. (47 L. J., Ex., 491 : L. R., 3 Ex. D., 54 : 38 L. T., 530.)

1635. [2504]
Duncomb's Case. The owner of the land over which there is an open road may inclose the land, but he must leave a sufficient way, and repair it at his own charge. (Croke, Car. I., 366.)

1632. [2505]
Henn's Case. "In case where a man incloseth, and doth not make a good way, it is lawful for passengers to make gaps in his hedges, to avoid the ill way, so that they do not ride further into his enclosed grounds than is needful for avoiding the bad way.' (Sir W. Jones, 296.)

1888. [2506]
Hornby v. *Silvester.* "Inclosure Act, 1845," § 62. The power of stopping up roads under this Act is not confined to roads passing through old inclosures or intakes from the waste or common, the subject of inclosure, but extends to the roads passing through any old inclosures in the parish. (57 L. J., Q. B., 558 : L. R., 20 Q. B. D., 797 : 59 L. T., 666 : 52 J. P., 468.)

1843. [2507]
Manning v. *Eastern Counties Railway Co.* An Inclosure Act authorised certain Commissioners to stop up any old road, subject to the concurrence and Order of 2 Justices—The Commissioners by their Award stopped up certain footpaths and the Award recited the concurrence, &c.—No Order of Justices could be found in the place of deposit mentioned in the Act for the Award and documents relating thereto—Held that the Award with the recital therein was *primâ facie* evidence that the paths had been lawfully stopped up, the subsequent enjoyment not being shown to be inconsistent with the Award. (13 L. J., Ex., 265 : 12 M. & W., 237.)

1830. [2508]
Reg. v. Cricklade, St. Sampson, Inhabitants. Public bridleway across a Common but with no definite track—Common inclosed by Commissioners who set out a road 30 feet wide with the same *termini* and line of direction as the old bridleway—Award that this way should be both a public bridleway and a private carriage road for certain persons who were to repair—Indictment against Parish for non-repair—No Order or Certificate of Justices proved—Held that the old bridleway was never effectually stopped; that the road set out was in effect the same way; and that the Parish was still liable to repair it as a bridle-road, although it had also been set out as a private carriage road. (19 L. J., M. C., 109 : 14 Q. B., 735 : 15 L. T., (o. s.), 296.)

1839. [2509]
Reg. v. East Hagbourne Inhabitants. Ancient highway altered by Award of Inclosure Commissioners under 6 & 7 Will. IV., c. 115—Original road entirely comprehended within the new road—Road repaired by Parish both before and since the Award—No declaration by Justices that the road had been fully completed and repaired, or proceedings under the "Highway Act, 1835," § 23—Held that the Parish was not liable to repair. (28 L. J., M. C., 71: Bell, C. C. R., 135 : 32 L. T., (o. s.), 339.)

1856. [2510]
Reg. v. Gate Fulford Inhabitants. Parish comprising two Townships, G. Fulford and W. Fulford—Inclosure Act directing that roads should be set out and should be repaired by G. Fulford—Roads all in that Township at the time of making the Award—Award directing that the roads should be repaired by "Fulford"—Held that G. Fulford was liable to repair, though the road ran through what at time of the trial was understood to be part of W. Fulford. (Dears & B., C. C., 74.)

1854. [2511]
Reg. v. Nether Hallam Inhabitants. Commissioners under an Inclosure Act for Township A. set out an old road belonging to township B. of an increased width, and directed it to be repaired in future by A., though there was no dispute as to boundary so as to give them jurisdiction to alter or settle it—Held that the Award was of no avail to shift the liability from B. to A. (3 C. L. R., 94: 6 Cox, C. C., 435.)

1758. [2512]
Rex v. Flecknow Inhabitants. An owner of land over which there is a highway may exercise his rights to inclose the land under an Inclosure Act without taking upon himself any obligation to repair the road the duty as to which continues with the Parish. (2 Ld. Keny., 261 : 1 Burr., 461.) [As to the value of this decision see the foot-note on p. 465 of Burrow's Report.]

1835. [2513]
Rex v. Hatfield Inhabitants (2). "Inclosure Act, 1801," § 9—A road continued, as well as a road newly made, under the Award of Commissioners of Inclosure, must be declared by Justices in Special Sessions to be fully completed and repaired before the Inhabitants can be indicted for neglect to repair—Where the herbage of a road becomes vested by § 11 in the owners of allotments on each side, no presumption arises that the soil itself belongs to such owners. (4 A. & E., 156.)

1800. [2514]
Rex v. Richards. An Award under an Inclosure Act set out a road for the use of the Inhabitants of 9 Parishes directing 6 of those Parishes to repair it—Held that no Indictment could be supported against the latter for non-repair, the road being in effect only a private road. (8 T. R., 634.)

1832. [2515]
Rex v. Wright. Where Commissioners, empowered under an Inclosure Act to set out public and private roads, the former to be repaired by the Township and the latter by such persons as they should direct, exceeded their authority in awarding that private roads should be repaired by the Township, it was held, upon the whole evidence, to be a proper question for a Jury whether or not one of such private roads which had been repaired by the Township, though originally intended to be private had not been dedicated to, and adopted by the public—*Per* Lord Tenterden, C. J.:—"I am strongly of opinion when I see a space of 50 or 60 ft. through which a road passes, between enclosures set out under Act of Parliament, that, unless the contrary be shown, the Public are entitled to the whole of that space, although perhaps from economy the whole may not have been kept in repair. If it were once held that only the middle part, which carriages ordinarily run upon, was the road, you might by degrees inclose up to it so that there would not be room left for 2 carriages to pass. The space at the sides is also necessary to afford the benefit of air and sun. If trees and hedges might be brought up close to the part actually used as the road, it could not be kept sound." (1 L. J., M. C., 74 : 3 B. & Ad., 681.)

1832. [2516]
Thackrah v. Seymour. "Inclosure Act, 1801," §§ 8 and 11—Award under a Local Act, omitting mention of an ancient footway, and setting out no new footway—Held that the allotment did not operate to extinguish the old way. (2 L. J. Ex., 10 : 1 Cr. & Mee., 18 : 3 Tyr., 87.)

(2.) HIGHWAYS IN DIFFERENT PARISHES.

1856. [2517]
Gwyn v. Hardwicke. Footway in 2 Parishes—Power under an Inclosure Act to stop up (subject to appeal to Sessions) so much of it as lay in one Parish duly exercised, whereby the residue of the way became a *cul-de-sac*—Held that there having been no appeal the

way was duly stopped in one Parish notwithstanding that the unstopped residue in the other Parish became useless as a thoroughfare—*Semble*, the latter part remained a public way. (25 L. J., M. C., 97 : 1 H. & N., 49 : 27 L. T., (o. s.), 72.)

1805. [2518]
Nicholls v. *Parker*. Traditionary reputation is evidence of boundary between 2 Parishes and manors—Evidence was admitted of what old persons, dead before the trial, had said concerning the boundaries, although they claimed rights of Common on the respective Wastes, which might be enlarged by such evidence ; their evidence was admissible because there was no litigation pending, or in contemplation, at the time to give a reason for suspecting the motives of their testimony. (14 East, 331, n.)

1845. [2519]
Reg. v. *Hichling Inhabitants*(1). 34 Geo. III., c. 64, § 2 [Repealed]: "Highway Act, 1835," §§ 58-9—An Order of Justices dividing for purposes of repair a road lying in 2 Parishes and following the form prescribed by the Statute is conclusive as to the liability of each Parish—It is not open to either Parish on an Indictment for non-repair of the portion so allotted to impeach the jurisdiction of the Justices by producing evidence to prove that no part of the road ever was within such Parish—The Order of the Justices must show on its face that it was made at a Special Sessions for highways. (14 L. J., M. C., 177 : 7 Q. B., 880 : 2 New Sess. Cas., 117.)

1864. [2520]
Reg. v. *Strand B. W.* Where a highway is employed to define the boundary of a district the *medium filum viæ* must (in the absence of contrary evidence) be deemed the actual boundary. (Metropolis.) (33 L. J., Q. B., 299 : 4 B. & S., 551 : 11 L. T., 183.)

1780. [2521]
Rex v. *Townshend*. "Highway Act, 1773," § 47 [Repealed]—If a Parish consisting of 2 districts, each bound to repair separately, be convicted and fined for the non-repair of a road in one district, the other having no notice of the Indictment, the Court will consider it as being substantially the conviction of the one district, and if the fine be levied on an inhabitant of the other, will grant a special *Mandamus* for a Rate to be levied on the district bound to repair the indicted part of the Road. (2 Doug., 420.)

(3.) OBTAINING MATERIALS FOR REPAIRS.

1881. [2522]
Alresford Rural Authority v. *Scott.* "Highway Act, 1835," § 51—A Surveyor may obtain a license from Justices (if they think fit to grant one) to "gather" stones lying upon any enclosed lands in the parish without making any satisfaction to the owner for the stones taken. (50 L. J., M. C., 103 : L. R., 7 Q. B. D., 210 : 45 L. T., 73 : 45 J. P., 619.)

1851. [2523]
Clowes v. *Beck.* Injunction granted against Surveyors of Highways to restrain them from removing beach and sand from a sea-shore for road repairs notwithstanding that plaintiff's title was doubtful and that he ought to proceed at Law to establish it—The Court so decided on the ground that the balance of probable injury was with the plaintiff rather than with the Surveyors, it appearing that the continued removal of the beach was doing irreparable injury by causing the sea steadily to encroach on the land of the plaintiff. (20 L. J., Ch., 505 : 13 Bea., 347 : S. C. on appeal, 2 De G. M. & G., 731.)

1863. [2524]
Constable v. *Nicholson.* The alleged right for the inhabitants of a Township to take stones from the land of another person for the purpose of repairing highways is a claim to a profit *à prendre*, and cannot therefore be claimed by custom—Neither can it be claimed by prescription or grant, as inhabitants are incapable by that description of taking such an easement, unless they can prove incorporation. (32 L. J., C. P., 240 : 14 C. B., (N. s.), 230.)

1876. [2525]
Ellis v. *Bromley L. B.* A right given by Statute to Highway Surveyors to dig gravel from an existing pit held to authorise a lateral as well as a vertical extension of a pit. (45 L. J., Ch., 763 : 35 L. T., 182.)

1849. [2526]
Huntley v. *Russell.* Gravel-pit on the soil of a Rectory opened and kept open by orders of Justices under the "Highway Act, 1773," § 29 [repealed], and the "Highway Act, 1835," § 54—Soil not sloped down or filled up according to § 31 of former Act or § 55 of latter Act—No step taken during the Incumbency to enforce this duty on Surveyors—While pit was open some gravel was sold by Rector's lessee to private purchasers without sloping, &c.—Action against Rector's Executors for dilapidations—Held that the excavations for the highways were not chargeable as acts of Waste on the part of the Rector, being done under the Statute, but that the digging and sale of gravel to private purchasers was Waste for which the Executors were liable—*Quære*, whether the Executors could be charged in any form for the Rector's omission to slope or fill up the excavations or oblige the Surveyors to do so? (18 L. J., Q. B., 239 : 13 Q. B., 572 : 13 L. T., (o. s.), 526.)

1878. [2527]
Manners (Earl) v. *Bartholomew.* "Highway Act, 1835," §§ 53-4—A licence to get materials for repairs of highways applies only to the necessities of the particular occasion in respect of which it is granted, and is not of indefinite duration. (48 L. J., M. C., 3 : L. R., 4 Q. B. D., 5 : 39 L. T., 327 : 42 J. P., 740.)

1852. [2528]
Padwick v. *Knight.* A Highway Surveyor cannot

justify a trespass under a prescriptive right, or a custom, to take stones from the Waste, whether adjoining the sea-shore between high- and low-water mark, or otherwise, for the purpose of repairing the highways of a Parish—*Semble*, that it would be a good justification to plead a prescriptive right of the inhabitants alleging the Surveyor to be an inhabitant. (22 L. J., Ex., 198 : 7 Ex., 854 : 19 L. T., (o. s.), 206.)

1871. **[2529]**

Pitts v. *Kingsbridge H. B.* "Highway Act, 1835," §§ 51-2—A Highway Board must not take shingle from a beach below high-water-mark so as to cause an increased risk of encroachment by the sea—A special custom to take shingle from a beach above high-water-mark for repair of highways is bad as to such part of the beach as is private property—A contractor's employers are liable for injurious acts properly arising out of the contract, but the contractor is personally liable for such acts if foreign to the contract. (25 L. T., 195 : 19 W. R., 884.)

1881. **[2530]**

Ramsden v. *Yeates.* "Highway Act, 1835," §§ 53-4—Available materials in a field not accessible otherwise than by a road through private avenue—Held, nevertheless, that the material might be got, and if damage were done to the avenue, further compensation would be payable. (50 L. J., M. C., 135 : L. R., 6 Q. B. D., 583 : 44 L. T., 612 : 45 J. P., 538.)

1757. **[2531]**

Rex v. *Manning.* Local Turnpike Act—An Order of Sessions for entering land to obtain materials should show notice to the occupier, the necessity for the Order, the kind of provision wanted, and the fields which it was intended to search ; and should award satisfaction to the owner and occupier—Order defective on these points, quashed—"All special authorities must be strictly pursued." (1 Burr., 377 : 2 Keny., 561.)

1845. **[2532]**

Rylatt v. *Marfleet.* Inclosure Act, allotting land to be reserved for supplying stones, &c., to repair roads—Held that the parishioners were not entitled to get stones for any other purposes. (14 L. J., Ex., 305 : 14 M. & W., 233.)

1869. **[2533]**

Smith v. *Stocks.* Gravel-pit allotted by Inclosure Commissioners to Surveyors of Highways for getting road materials—Rights not claimed for 26 years—Pit and road thereto ploughed up and cultivated—Held that the rights of the Surveyors were extinguished by the Statute of Limitations—Nor did the fact that the tenant of the land had, after possession taken, been himself a Surveyor of Highways make any difference. (38 L. J., Q. B., 306 : 10 B. & S., 701 : 20 L. T., 740.)

1841. **[2534]**

Tapsell v. *Crosskey.* "Turnpike Act, 1822," §§ 97-8—The words "inclosed lands" are used in their popular sense as denoting lands actually inclosed within fences—A Surveyor may take materials from private lands ("Downs") not inclosed or fenced off without any Order of Justices under § 98—Land surrounded by a fence out of repair and therefore in one sense "open" is to be deemed "inclosed" and protected by § 98. (10 L. J., Ex., 188 : 7 M. & W., 441.) [Effect of decision modified by 4 & 5 Vict., c. 51, § 1.]

1862. **[2535]**

Thew v. *Wingate.* Adverse possession for 20 years against Highway Surveyors bars their claims in respect of land allotted to them by the Inclosure Commissioners for the purpose of providing road materials. (10 B. & S., 714, n.)

(4.) INDICTMENT FOR NON-REPAIR.

*** The Practice mentioned in some of the Cases which follow under this head must now be deemed obsolete.

1883. **[2536]**

Illingworth v. *Bulmer East H. B.* "Highway Act, 1862," § 18—Neglect to repair highway —Grounds on which an appeal to sessions might be had against an Order of Justices. (53 L. J., M. C., 60 : 48 J. P., 37.)

1587. **[2537]**

Maddox's Case. Indictment for a nuisance to a "horseway," quashed—It should have been to the "Queen's Highway," or "the Highway." (Croke, Eliz., 63.)

1841. **[2538]**

Reg. v. *Barnard Castle Inhabitants.* Indictment for non-repair—The fine imposable under § 96 can only be applied towards the repair of the highway indicted—If therefore after conviction and Order and before payment of the fine the defendants effectually repair the way they are entitled to have the proceedings stayed—And the prosecutors cannot claim the fine on behalf of third parties for repairs done previously to the conviction—Where defendants remove an Indictment by *Certiorari*, a merely nominal prosecutor is not entitled to costs under 5 W. & M., c. 11, § 3, as being a party "grieved or injured." (10 L. J., M. C., 53 : 5 Jur., 799.)

1841. **[2539]**

Reg. v. *Botfield.* Per Coleridge, J.:—"In an Indictment for a nuisance by not repairing a road, the words 'from' and 'to' exclude the *termini*"—So in an Indictment for obstructing a highway leading *from A. to B.* by placing a gate across it A. and B. are excluded, and therefore if the gate is put up in one of the terminal Townships the defendant must be acquitted. (Carr. & M., 151.)

1849. **[2540]**

Reg. v. *Brightside Bierlow Inhabitants.* Navigation Act requiring the proprietors to keep in repair an ancient highway subject to liability to Indictment for default—Proviso to Act that the inhabitants of the Townships through which the highway ran were not to be excused from contributing to the repairs—

Held that the Township was not exempt from its Common Law liability to repair—In an Indictment for non-repair it is admissible evidence, in order to prove a highway, to prove that an Indictment against an adjoining Parish in respect of a highway which is a continuation of the one in dispute was either submitted to, or prosecuted to a conviction. (19 L. J., M. C., 50 : 13 Q. B., 933 : 4 New Sess. Cas., 47.)

1865.   [2541]
Reg. v. *Buckland Inhabitants.* "Highway Act, 1862," § 19—Indictment for non-repair—"Not Guilty" on the ground that the road was a private road and not a highway—In such a case the Court has no jurisdiction to award Costs : under the Act of 1862 the law is the same as it was under the Act of 1835 (§ 95). (31 L. J., M. C., 178 : 6 B. & S., 397 : 42 L. T., 380.)

1841.   [2542]
Reg. v. *Challicombe Inhabitants.* Indictment for non-repair—Verdict for defendants—In such a case the Court will not grant a New Trial on the ground of misdirection, but will in its discretion suspend the Judgment in order that a new Indictment may be preferred. (6 Jur., 481 : 2 Mood. & R., 311.)

1844.   [2543]
Reg. v. *Clark.* Where Justices have directed an Indictment for non-repair and the Judge of Assize orders payment of the Costs out of the Highway Rate, he must ascertain the amount and order payment of the sum so ascertained—A Judge's Order to pay Costs generally, cannot be enforced by *Mandamus* —*Quære*, whether the amount can be ascertained after the commission of the Judge of Assize has expired? (13 L. J., M. C., 91 : 5 Q. B., 887 : 1 New Sess. Cas., 143 : Dav. & Mer., 687.)

1855.   [2544]
Reg. v. *Claxby Inhabitants.* Indictment for non-repair—Verdict "Guilty"—A Parish is not to be excused from putting a road into good repair by the fact that the road is little used, has never been repaired with hard materials, is formed of various tracks and passes over ascents and descents, and terminates in another Parish which denies it to be a highway, and even if repaired would be useless unless the portion in the adjoining Parish were also repaired—The Court will not prescribe the particular mode of repair, but when it appears that a certain amount is necessary to put the highway into substantial repair a fine to the requisite amount will be imposed. (24 L. J., Q. B., 223 : 3 C. L. R., 986.)

1864.   [2545]
Reg. v. *Cleckheaton Inhabitants.* "Highway Act, 1835," §§ 94-5—Indictment for non-repair of a Highway—Counts for a cart and carriage-way and also for a pack and prime-way—Verdict of the Jury that the way was not a cart, &c., way, and that as a pack, &c., way it was not out of repair—Verdict entered for defendants, and prosecutor held not entitled to Costs. (11 L. T., 305.)

1847.   [2546]
Reg. v. *Colling.* An Indictment against a Township for the non-repair of a highway must aver that the road in question was not a road which, but for the custom, would have been repairable by the Parish. (2 Cox, C. C., 184.)

1852.   [2547]
Reg. v. *Denton Inhabitants* (1). Where between the finding of an Indictment for non-repair of a road and plea pleaded the Statute on which alone the Indictment could be supported was repealed without any reference to pending prosecutions, and afterwards a conviction was obtained nevertheless, the Court arrested the Judgment—*Quære*, is it necessary, in Indictment against inhabitants of district charging liability to repair highway, to prove consideration for such liability, or is it to be inferred from the fact of repair? (21 L. J., M. C., 207 : 18 Q. B., 761 : 1 Dears. & P., C. C., 3.)

1854.   [2548]
Reg. v. *Denton Inhabitants* (2). "Highway Act, 1835," § 98—Indictment for non-repair—A mere plea of "Guilty" is not a frivolous or vexatious "defence :" in point of fact it is no defence at all and therefore costs cannot be awarded. (34 L. J., M. C., 15 : 5 B. & S., 821 : 11 L. T., 371.)

1845.   [2549]
Reg. v. *Down Holland Township.* "Highway Act, 1835," § 95—A certificate for Costs can only be granted when the road indicted is proved affirmatively to be a highway—The Court will not go into the question on affidavits. (15 L. J., M. C., 25 : 2 New Sess. Cas., 177.)

1865.   [2550]
Reg. v. *East Stoke Inhabitants.* A prosecutor removing by *Certiorari* an Indictment for non-repair is only liable for Costs by virtue of the recognizance required by 16 & 17 Vict. c. 30, § 5, and if he has not entered into such a recognizance Costs cannot be recovered against him—The proper remedy for such a default is given by § 7 which provides that in that case the *Certiorari* may be disregarded. (6 B. & S., 536 : 13 W. R., 737.)

1848.   [2551]
Reg. v. *Fifehead Inhabitants.* If at the trial of an Indictment for non-repair it appears that the road actually indicted is not the road set out in the Order of Justices under the "Highway Act, 1835," § 94, and the prosecution fails in consequence the Judge cannot certify for Costs under § 95. (3 Cox, C. C., 59.)

1843.   [2552]
Reg. v. *Great Broughton Inhabitants.* "Highway Act, 1835," § 95—A Judge at *Nisi Prius* may order payment of prosecutor's Costs though the Indictment had been removed

from Sessions by *Certiorari*. (2 Mood. & R., 444.)

1883.   [2553]
Reg. v. *Halliday*. Part of a road wholly destroyed by landslip — Nevertheless, *Mandamus* to repair, issued, on its being shown that £200 would reinstate the part destroyed—*Worthing* v. *Lancing* not followed. (*Times*, July 31, 1883.)

1862.   [2554]
Reg. v. *Haslemere Inhabitants*. "Highway Act, 1835," § 95—Indictment for non-repair of highway—Plea of "Guilty" and no actual trial, notice having been given of intention so to plead—Held nevertheless that a Judge of Assize has power to award Costs against the Parish. (32 L. J., M. C., 80: 3 B. & S., 313 : 7 L. T., 382.)

1853.   [2555]
Reg. v. *Haughton Inhabitants*. Upon the trial of an Indictment against the inhabitants of Township H. for non-repair of a highway a prior Judgment of Quarter Sessions upon a presentment by a Justice under the "Highway Act, 1773," for non-repair of H. of the same highway was put in—The presentment alleged that the highway was in H., and that H. was liable for its repair—It also appeared by the Judgment that two inhabitants of H. had appeared and pleaded "Guilty," and that a fine was imposed—Held that this was conclusive evidence that the highway was in H. and that H. was liable—The presentment did not state how the Township was liable: Held, that having submitted to it the defendants were bound by it—The absence of proof of payment of the fine imposed did not prevent the Judgment from acting as an estoppel, no fraud being imputed—A recital in a repealed Local Act that the road in question was in D. held, not conclusive. (22 L. J., M. C., 89 : 1 E. & B, 501 : 6 Cox, C. C., 101.)

1862.   [2556]
Reg. v. *Hawkhurst Parish*. (2). Indictment for non-repair—Removal thereof by *Certiorari*—Held that an Indictment not being a Civil proceeding there cannot be an appeal to a Court of Error. (11 W. R., 116.)

18—.   [2557]
Reg. v. *Healaugh*. Highway crossing bed of stream — Indictment for non-repair — *Per* Martin, B. (to the Jury):—The way should be put in such a state of repair as that persons might walk dry-shod—Verdict for the Crown—Rule to set aside Verdict for misdirection, refused. (Glen, MS.)

1845.   [2558]
Reg. v. *Heanor Inhabitants*. "Highway Act, 1835," § 95—The power of a Judge to certify for Costs only extends to cases where there is a highway and the liability to repair the same is disputed—And therefore when on an Indictment for non-repair of a carriage-way the defendants were acquitted on the sole ground that the way was not a highway and the Judge certified for Costs under this

Section the Court set aside the Certificate. (14 L. J., M. C., 38 : 6 Q. B., 745 : 1 New Sess. Cas., 460.)

1863.   [2559]
Reg. v. *Heytesbury Inhabitants*. "Highway Act, 1835," § 95—Indictment for non-repair—Jury discharged because unable to agree on a verdict—Held that on this account the Judge had no power to award Costs against the Parish—Order of Justices held bad for not showing on its face that it was made at a Special Sessions for Highways held within the Division in which the highway complained of was situate. (8 L. T., 315.)

1845.   [2560]
Reg. v. *Hickling Inhabitants*. (2). "Highway Act, 1835," § 94—An order directing an Indictment for non-repair must show on the face of it that it was made at a Special Sessions, within the Division in which the road is situated—If it do not, it is void; and an Order for Costs made under § 95 by the Judge who tried the cause will be set aside on the ground of the defect in the Order of the Justices. (15 L. J., M. C., 23 : 7 Q. R., 880 at p. 890 : 2 New Sess. Cas., 117.)

1868.   [2561]
Reg. v. *Ipstones Inhabitants*. "Highway Act, 1835," § 95—An Indictment for non-repair when removed by *Certiorari* is no longer within § 95, so that if it is sent down for trial at *Nisi Prius* a Judge of Assize has no power to make an Order for payment of the Costs of the Prosecution—Costs in such a case are governed by 5 Will. & M., c. 11.—*Reg.* v. *Eardisland*, over-ruled. (37 L. J., M. C., 37 : L. R., 3 Q. B., 216: 9 B. & S., 106: 17 L. T, 497.)

1863.   [2562]
Reg. v. *James*. The "South Wales Highway Act, 1860," and "Highway Act, 1835," are to be construed together as one Act—Therefore, notwithstanding some alterations in the working of the earlier Act prescribed by the later Act, § 95 of the earlier Act remains in force in South Wales. (32 L. J., M. C., 211 : 3 B. & S., 901.)

1865.   [2563]
Reg. v. *Johnson* (3). "Highway Act, 1835 " § 95—Before directing an Indictment against a Parish for non-repair, where the liability is denied, the Justices must have some evidence that the *locus in quo* is a highway—If the existence of the highway is denied, *quære* whether the Justices have any jurisdiction. (34 L. J., M. C., 85: [*Reg.* v. *Askerton*] 13 W. R., 339 : 11 L. T., 706.)

1854.   [2564]
Reg. v. *Lambeth Surveyors*. An Order of Sessions for the payment of the Costs of a prosecution for non-repair is bad unless the amount of the Costs is ascertained and ordered by the same Sessions—The Sessions cannot refer the Costs to be taxed by their officer after the Sessions. (3 C. L. R., 35.)

1860.   [2565]
Reg. v. *Langley Inhabitants*. "Highway Act,

1835," § 95—When a Parish is indicted for non-repair and by two Surveyors pleads "Not Guilty," it is not competent to one only of such Surveyors to appear in person and retract such plea, the other Surveyor merely pleading by the Clerk of his Solicitor. (8 Cox, C. C., 366: 2 F. & T., 170.)

1876.   [2566]
Reg. v. *Lee* (3). "Highway Act, 1835," § 95—Summons for non-repair of a highway—Indictment ordered by Justices—Found at the trial that the way was only a foot-path and bridle-way, and Indictment amended accordingly, so as to be restricted to the limited obligation, which was not disputed—Held that the Judge's Order for Costs to be paid out of the Rates must be quashed, for the prosecution after such amendment was no longer "such prosecution" within § 95. (45 L. J., M. C., 54: L. R., 1 Q. B. D., 198: 34 L. T., 445.)

1886.   [2567]
Reg. v. *Lordsmere* (2). Indictment for non-repair of wall abutting on highway—Whether a wall belongs to highway or not is a question for a Jury—Evidence. (54 L. T., 766: 51 J. P., 86.)

1857.   [2568]
Reg. v. *Manchester, Mayor* (1). 16 & 17 Vict., c. 30, § 5—The prosecutor of an Indictment against a Corporation for non-repair of a highway, which is removed by *Certiorari* at his instance, is not required to enter into recognizances to pay the defendant's Costs in case of acquittal, Indictments against Corporations being excepted from this Act. (26 L. J., M. C., 65: 7 E. & B., 453: 28 L. T., (o. s.), 369.)

1843.   [2569]
Reg. v. *Martin.* "Highway Act, 1835," § 91—In an Order by Justices at Special Sessions for the Indictment of a highway it should be distinctly stated that such highway is within the Division for which such Sessions are held: if this is not stated an Order for payment of Costs made at Quarter Sessions is void, notwithstanding that it may appear, on the face of the proceedings at Quarter Sessions that the highway was within the jurisdiction of the Special Sessions. (13 L. J., M. C., 45: 2 Q. B., 1037: D. & M., 386.)

1843.   [2570]
Reg. v. *Milton Inhabitants.* Indictment for non-repair—Evidence of Boundaries—A Parish map produced from the Parish Chest, made under a private Inclosure Act (not printed) is not evidence of boundaries without proof of the Act—But it being proved by the Surveyor who made the map 34 years previously that he laid down the boundaries from the information of an old man of 60 who went round with him; held, that this would have been evidence of reputation, on proof, further, that the old man was not alive at the trial; but that without proof of his death it was not evidence. (1 C. & K., 58.)

1869.   [2571]
Reg. v. *Newbold Inhabitants.* It is not necessary, in order to support a conviction for the non-repair of an ancient common highway, to prove that the parish has ever actually repaired it. (19 L. T., 656: 17 W. R., 295.)

1840.   [2572]
Reg. v. *Paul.* "Highway Act, 1835," § 95—On an Indictment in the ordinary form for the non-repair of a highway a Parish cannot be convicted for not rebuilding a sea-wall washed away, along the top of which the alleged highway used to run—On a Parish being acquitted on such an Indictment on the ground of no highway the Court is not bound to award Costs—A Judge who tries at *Nisi Prius* an Indictment for non-repair removed by *Certiorari* has no power to award Costs under the above Section. (2 Mood. & R., 307.)

1843.   [2573]
Reg. v. *Pembridge Inhabitants.* "Highway Act, 1835," § 98—Where a Certificate has been granted that the defence to an Indictment removed by *Certiorari* into the Queen's Bench is frivolous and Costs have been awarded against the defendants the payment thereof may be enforced by attachment for contempt —6 Geo. IV., c. 50, § 34, authorising the Judge before whom the "Cause" is tried to certify for the Costs of a Special Jury, applies to criminal cases. (12 L. J., Q. B., 47: 3 G. & D., 5 and 503: 3 Q. B., 901.)

1887.   [2574]
Reg. v. *Poole, Mayor.* "Public Health Act, 1875," § 144—Form of Indictment—An Urban Sanitary Authority is not liable for non-repair of a highway in the same sense in which a Parish or persons liable *ratione tenuræ* are liable—*Quære,* whether an Indictment would lie if the preliminary steps before Justices required by the "Highway Act, 1835," § 20, were taken. (56 L. J., M. C., 131: L. R., 19 Q. B. D., 602: 57 L. T., 485: 52 J. P., 84.)

1830.   [2575]
Reg. v. *Preston Inhabitants* (2). "Highway Act, 1835," § 98—Indictment preferred at Quarter Sessions but removed by *Certiorari*—The Queen's Bench has power to award to the prosecutor Costs incurred previously to the removal of the Indictment if the defence has been in the opinion of the Judge frivolous or vexatious. (7 Dowl., P. C., 593.) [An application for Costs had been refused by the Judge who tried the case at Assizes, on the ground of want of authority to grant them. —See S. C. at *Nisi Prius,* 2 Mood. & R., 137.]

1854.   [2576]
Reg. v. *St. Mary, Lambeth, Highway Surveyor.* "Highway Act, 1835," § 95—Indictment for non-repair tried at Michaelmas Sessions and Costs of the prosecution allowed—No amount specified and nothing done on the Order till March following when the Costs were taxed —Held that the Order could not be enforced as the Sessions which tried the case alone had power to award Costs, and that Sessions had been superseded by the intervening Epiphany Sessions before the taxation. (24 L. T., (o. s.), 145.)

1854.   [2577]
Reg. v. *Sandon Inhabitants.* "Highway Act, 1835," § 95—An Indictment for non-repair preferred at the Assizes by an Order of Justices, whereon a true Bill has been found, may be removed by *Certiorari.* (23 L. J., M. C., 129 : 3 E. & B., 547 : 2 C. L. R., 1699 : 23 L. T., (o. s.), 64.)

1858.   [2578]
Reg. v. *Stainhall Inhabitants.* "Highway Act, 1835," § 95—Indictment for non-repair—Plea "Guilty"—Practice as to pleading by inhabitants—On the suggestion of Pollock, C.B., two of the inhabitants present pleaded to the Indictment, and 3 gentlemen entered into a bond to see the road repaired—No costs were ordered. (1 F. & F., 363.) [See Judgment in *Reg.* v. *Haslemere.*]

1843.   [2579]
Reg. v. *Steventon Inhabitants.* An Indictment stated a highway for carriages "leading from the town of A. in the county of B. towards and unto the village of E. in the same county" a part of which was out of repair—The part charged to be out of repair was a part of F. lane—It was proved that to go from A. to E. in a carriage a person must first go 4 miles along the C. turnpike road, then all along F. lane, and then cross the W. Turnpike road and for a short distance go along a road running from the W. Turnpike road to E.—Held that the road was not misdescribed—A road is not the less a highway because part of it is Turnpike. (1 C. & K., 55.)

1890.   [2580]
Reg. v. *Stockport Parish.* Indictment for non-repair—Application for new trial—Question whether since 53 & 54 Vict., c. 44, such application ought not to have been made to the Court of Appeal instead of to a Divisional Court—Held that the new Act referred to does not apply to Crown Cases, the practice as to which remains unaltered. (*Times,* Oct. 28, 1890.)

1852.   [2581]
Reg. v. *Surrey JJ.* (1). "Highway Act, 1835," § 95—Highway out of repair—Surveyor summoned before Justices—Liability denied—Order by Justices that Parish should be indicted—Indictment preferred but trial adjourned—Plea, that a private person was liable *Ratione tenuræ*—Verdict for the Parish—The lands were owned by one of the Justices who had signed the Order to indict : there was no evidence of collusion between him and the prosecutor—The Quarter Sessions having refused to allow the Costs out of the Highway Rate on the ground that the Order was void, because one of the Justices making it was interested, *Mandamus* granted to compel the allowance of Costs—The Order to indict was valid : The Quarter Sessions had jurisdiction to order Costs though the trial had been adjourned : and had no discretion to refuse Costs. (21 L. J., M. C., 195 : 1 B. C. C., 70 : 19 L. T., (o. s.), 171.)

1850.   [2582]
Reg. v. *Turneston Inhabitants.* Indictment for non-repair alleging an immemorial highway, and that it was out of repair—The first allegation not proved as regards immemoriality—Held that the averment might be neglected as surplusage, and that proof having been given that the road was a highway and out of repair the verdict of "Guilty" should be allowed to stand—It is not material to the liability of a Parish to show how a road became a highway provided that it is such—The way from T. to E. referred to in the Indictment led from T. into a Turnpike road; then lay for a short distance along that road; then branched off to E.—This was the direct way from T. to E.—Held that the way was properly described as from T. to E. (20 L. J., M. C., 46 : 16 Q. B., 109 : 4 Cox, C. C., 349.)

1847.   [2583]
Reg. v. *Upton St. Leonard's Inhabitants.* Indictment for non-repair of a highway preferred at the Assizes—Bill thrown out by Grand Jury—Two Jurymen, landowners in the parish, and taking part in opposing the finding of the Indictment—On proof of these facts the Court granted a criminal Information against the Parish for the alleged non-repair. (16 L. J., M. C., 84 : 10 Q. B., 827 : 2 New Sess. Cas., 582.)

1846.   [2584]
Reg. v. *Vowchurch Inhabitants.* "Highway Act, 1835," § 95—Indictment for non-repair—Plea, "Guilty." (2 C. & K., 393.) [See Judgment in *Reg.* v. *Haslemere.*]

1840.   [2585]
Reg. v. *Walton Inhabitants.* Indictment for non-repair—Verdict "Guilty" — Affidavit that little progress had been made with the repairs—The Court refused a Rule *absolute* for a fine, but enlarged the Rule *nisi* on the ground that it was not reasonable to expect repairs to be executed with speed in the winter. (4 Jur., 195.)

1847.   [2586]
Reg. v. *Watford Inhabitants.* "Highway Act, 1835," § 95—Indictment for non-repair—A Judge's Certificate for payment of Costs should state on the face of it out of what funds the Costs are to be paid ; where a Certificate did not do so the Court set it aside—*Semble,* that the Certificate was bad for not specifying the amount—The Certificate was made to pay the Costs to G. H. A. [the prosecutor] or his attorney—*Semble,* that it was not bad because G. H. A. was dead when it was made—*Semble,* that it suffices if it may be gathered by reasonable implication that the road is within the Division for which the Justices were sitting. (4 D. & L., 593 : 1 Saund. & C., 336 : 9 L. T., (o. s.), 59.)

1851.   [2587]
Reg. v. *Waverton Inhabitants.* Indictment for non-repair stated that a part of the highway from W. to M. at a place called A. and extending thence to L. highway was out of repair—Evidence that the place mentioned

as A. was in fact a place called B.—Held, no material variance, the erroneous description relating to the *terminus* not of the road but of the dilapidated portion thereof—Consideration of the circumstances under which the allegations of one count will be deemed sufficiently averred by reference in other counts. (21 L. J., M. C., 7 : 17 Q. B., 562 : 2 Den., C. C., 340 : 18 L. T., (o. s.), 136.)

1839.   [2588]

Reg. v. *Yarkhill Inhabitants.* "Highway Act, 1835," § 95—Indictment for non-repair preferred by Order of Justices—Verdict "Guilty" —Prosecutor held entitled to his Costs out of the Highway Rate—The words of the Act are imperative, and leave no discretion to the Judge. (9 C. & P., 218.)

1834.   [2589]

Rex v. *Bishop Auckland Inhabitants.* An Indictment charged that the Inhabitants of Bondgate in A., Newgate in A., and the Borough of A., in the parish of St. Andrew A., were immemorially liable to repair a highway in the town of Bishop A., in the Parish of St. Andrew A., and no consideration was laid—Indictment held bad, in arrest of Judgment, as not showing that the highway was within the District of defendants—Held to be no objection that the inhabitants of the 3 Townships were charged conjointly. (1 A. & E., 744.)

1809.   [2590]

Rex v. *Bridekirk Inhabitants.* Indictment for non-repair—Plea that the Parish had immemorially been divided into 7 Townships each liable for the highways within it, and that part of the highway indicted was within A. Township and part within B., and that the respective parts ought to be repaired accordingly—Plea held bad because it did not specify which parts of the highway in question lay within the two Townships respectively. (11 East, 304.)

1793.   [2591]

Rex v. *Chadderton Inhabitants.* "Highway Act, 1773," § 65 [Repealed]—Any application for Costs under this Section on the trial of an Indictment for non-repair must be made to the Judge who tries the case, as the Statute only gives power to the Court "before whom the Indictment is tried." (5 T. R., 272.)

1794.   [2592]

Rex v. *Clifton Inhabitants.* If part of a Parish be in one County and part in another, and a highway in one part be out of repair, an Indictment against the inhabitants of that part only is bad—The Indictment must be against the whole Parish. (5 T. R., 498.)

1698.   [2593]

Rex v. *Dixon.* An Indictment for non-repair must always be against the Parish—An Indictment against Overseers, quashed—Overseers are not bound to repair roads, but only to give notice to the Parish, to repair. (12 Mod., 198.)

1835.   [2594]

Rex v. *Downshire (Marchioness of).* Where in an

Indictment for non-repair, the part out of repair was described as running from a certain Turnpike road "towards and unto the Parish Church" and the way proved was from the road to a Churchyard gate from which there was a public way inside the yard into a new way running at an acute angle to the Church, it was held that the way was well described. (5 L. J., K. B., 50 : 4 A. & E., 232 : 5 N. & M., 662.)

1810.   [2595]

Rex v. *Eardisland.* Indictment for non-repair against a Parish comprising 3 Townships, A., B., & C.—Plea on the part of C. that each Township has immemorially repaired its own highways separately—The Records of Indictment against the Parish generally for neglect to repair highways in A. and B. with general pleas of "Not Guilty," and convictions thereupon are *primâ facie* evidence to disprove the custom for each Township to repair separately; but evidence will be admitted that these pleas were pleaded by inhabitants of A. and B. without the privity of the inhabitants of C. (2 Camp., 494.)

1836.   [2596]

Rex v. *Eastington Inhabitants.* Indictment for non-repair—A Parish which pleads that it is not liable must by its plea also show who is liable—Plea that there was a township in a Parish liable by immemorial custom to repair the roads which, but for that custom, would be repairable by Parish—No averment that the road in question was one which but for the custom, the Parish would be liable to repair—Jury found Custom—Verdict for defendants—But plea held bad in arrest of Judgment. (6 L. J., M. C., 17 : 1 N. & P., 193 : 5 A. & E., 565 : 2 H. & W., 373.)

1818.   [2597]

Rex v. *Ecclesfield Inhabitants.* Indictment for non-repair—Plea that a particular District within the parish had immemorially repaired all highways within that district, of which the highway named in the Indictment was one—Plea held good, notwithstanding that it did not state any consideration for the liability of the inhabitants of the district —*Rex* v. *St. Giles, Cambridge,* distinguished; "There cannot be a custom in one place to do something in another." (1 B. & Ald., 348.)

1790.   [2598]

Rex v. *Gamlingay Inhabitants.* An Indictment against Parish B. for non-repair of a road from A. to B. is exclusive of A., and therefore bad—It is not aided by a subsequent allegation that a certain part of the same highway situated *in* B. is in decay. (3 T. R., 513 : 1 Leach, C. C., 528.)

1810.   [2599]

Rex v. *Great Canfield.* An Indictment for non-repair must distinctly state the precise *termini* of the road—The road must be direct. (6 Esp., 136.)

1779.   [2600]

Rex v. *Hartford Inhabitants.* In an Indictment for non-repair it must be alleged that the highway out of repair lies in the Parish indicted. (2 Cowp., 111.)

1606. [2601]
Rex v. Ireton Inhabitants. Upon an Indictment against a Parish for not repairing a highway the defendants can give nothing in evidence upon a plea of "Not Guilty," but that the way is in repair; but if the Indictment be against a particular person he may give evidence that others ought to repair it. (Comberbach, 396.)

1792. [2602]
Rex v. Kettleworth. 5 & 6 Will. & M., c. 11, § 3 —A Justice who indicts a road for being out of repair (the Indictment being afterwards removed by *Certiorari*) is entitled to Costs if the defendant be convicted. (5 T. R., 33.)

1827. [2603]
Rex v. Knight. Indictment for obstruction— Indictment charged defendants with removing a culvert in Parish S., opposite to a mill, in a highway leading from S. to H.—Held that it sufficiently appeared from this that the *locus in quo* of the culvert was in S.— The word "from" as applied to a Parish in the description of a road is not of necessity exclusive. (6 L. J., (o. s.), M. C., 19 : 7 B. & C., 413 : 1 M. & R., 217.)

1810. [2604]
Rex v. Lancashire JJ. "Highway Act, 1773," § 47 [Repealed]—Indictment for non-repair —Parish found "Guilty"—Delay of 8 years in an application on behalf of 2 inhabitants on whom a fine had been levied for a *Mandamus* to Justices to cause a Rate to be made to re-imburse such inhabitants—Application refused—It ought to have been made within a reasonable time before any material change in the inhabitants—Various applications to Justices to make a Rate did not avoid the laches. (12 East, 366.)

1816. [2605]
Rex v. Lincombe. An Indictment for non-repair will not be quashed on an affidavit that the way is now in repair, but the defendant must plead "Guilty" and pay a nominal fine. (2 Chit., 214.)

1802. [2606]
Rex v. Liverpool, Mayor. Indictment for non-repair of a highway within a certain District, alleging prescriptive liability to repair all highways within such District except such as were repairable under certain Statutes, held bad because it did not aver that the highway in question was not within any of the exceptions—A count stating the liability of defendants to arise by virtue of an agreement with the owners of houses alongside the highway is bad, for the Parish, which is *primâ facie* bound to repair all highways within its limits, cannot be discharged from such liability by any agreement with others. (3 East, 86.)

1806. [2607]
Rex v. Loughton Inhabitants. In order to be discharged from an Indictment for non-repair of a highway, parties convicted must produce an affidavit that the highway has been put in good repair since the conviction, and is likely to continue so. (3 Smith, 575.)

1815. [2608]
Rex v. Mann. After a verdict of "Not Guilty" on the merits in an Indictment for a misdemeanour (*e.g.*, a nuisance to a highway) no New Trial will be granted. (4 Maule & S., 337.)

1804. [2609]
Rex v. New Windsor Inhabitants. On a Rule to show cause why a presentment for non-repair should not be discharged, being discharged with Costs, and the Costs not being paid, the Court granted an attachment against the persons who had made the affidavits on which the Rule had been granted. (1 Smith, 168.)

1794. [2610]
Rex v. Old Malton Inhabitants. Indictment for non-repair—Fine—Fine expended and way still out of repair—The Court doubted their power to inflict a further punishment or fine on the same Indictment, but intimated that there might be a new Indictment and a new fine thereon. (4 B. and Ald., 470, n.)

1816. [2611]
Rex v. St. Giles, Cambridge, Inhabitants. Indictment for non-repair—Plea that another Parish has repaired and ought to repair— Plea held bad; it ought to have shown a consideration, for such an obligation could only arise upon a durable consideration. (5 Maule & S., 260.)

1817. [2612]
Rex v. St. John's, Margate, Inhabitants. Indictment for non-repair removed by the prosecutor—If the Judge at *Nisi Prius* certify that the defence was frivolous the prosecutor will have his Costs notwithstanding that the defendants have obtained a Rule *Nisi* to arrest the Judgment. (6 Maule & S, 130.)

1794. [2613]
Rex v. St. Pancras Inhabitants. An Indictment against a Parish for non-repair of one side of a road in a case where the other side lies in another Parish ought to state that each Parish is liable *ad medium filum viæ*, and not that a certain part so many feet wide is out of repair—A Record of Conviction on an Indictment against a Parish for non-repair is *conclusive* evidence of the liability of that Parish, so as to exonerate another Parish indicted for not repairing the same road. (1 Peake, N. P., 219.)

1833. [2614]
Rex v. St. Weonard's Inhabitants. (1). Indictment for non-repair—A road had been repaired by a Parish, and persons on horseback had used it, but there was no evidence that any carriage had ever gone along the whole length of it—Held that the Parish could not be convicted of non-repair on an Indictment alleging a way for carriages; there should have been a count charging it to be a way for horses. (5 C. & P., 579.)

1834.   [2615]
Rex v. *St. Weonard's Inhabitants.* (2). Indictment
for non-repair of a pack-and-prime way—If
it be proved that the way is a carriage-way,
then the Indictment contains a misdescription which entitles the defendants to an
acquittal—In an Indictment for non-repair it
is not necessary to state the *termini* ; but if
they are stated they must be proved. (6
C. & P., 582.)

1818.   [2616]
Rex v. *Southampton, County of, Inhabitants.* Indictment for non-repair of a bridge—The
Court is reluctant to stay Judgment on such
an Indictment, and will not stay it generally
but only till further order—If the trial of
another Indictment against some third party
is not proceeded with at once Judgment will
be given on the original verdict. (2 Chit.,
215.)

1833.   [2617]
Rex v. *Sutton* (1). Indictment for non-repair—Verdict "Not Guilty"—Motion for New Trial
on the ground of misdirection and improper
rejection of evidence—New Trial refused,
but Judgment suspended in order that a new
Indictment might be preferred. (5 B. &
Ad., 52 ; 2 N. & M., 57.)

1815.   [2618]
Rex v. *Taunton St. Mary Inhabitants.* Several
persons held entitled to Costs under 5 & 6
Will. & M., c. 11, § 3, as prosecutors of an
Indictment (removed by *Certiorari*) for not
repairing a highway ; one as Constable of
the Manor, the others as parties grieved,
they having used the way for many years
going from their homes to a market-town,
and being eventually obliged to use a more
circuitous route by reason of the direct
highway being out of repair—Upon an Indictment against a Parish for non-repair of
a highway the right to repair may come in
question so as to entitle the Parish to
remove it by *Certiorari*, though the parish
plead only "Not Guilty." (3 Maule & S.,
465.)

1802.   [2619]
Rex v. *Upper Papworth Inhabitants.* "Turnpike
Act, 1773," § 33 [Repealed]—The Court of
King's Bench may apportion a fine for non-
repair of a highway between a Parish and a
Turnpike Trust, even though the Indictment
has been removed by *Certiorari* from Assizes.
(2 East, 413.)

1833.   [2620]
Rex v. *Upton-on-Severn Inhabitants.* An Indictment for non-repair must state affirmatively
that the road is within the District bound
to repair it—Stating a road to be "*from* and
through" a place excludes the *terminus a
quo.* (6 C. & P., 133.)

1817.   [2621]
Rex v. *Wandsworth Inhabitants.* Indictment for
non-repair—Defendants acquitted—In such
a case the Court will not grant a New Trial
—Yet under very special circumstances the
entry of the Judgment will be suspended to

enable the question to be reconsidered on a
new Indictment without the prejudice of the
former Judgment—The carrying of gravel
over a road for the repair of admitted highways is *primâ faeie* evidence of the road
traversed being itself a highway. (1 B. &
Ald., 63.)

1821.   [2622]
Rex v. *Yorkshire W. R. Inhabitants* (5). Indictment
for non-repair — Plea by inhabitants of a
County that a particular Township has immemorially repaired the highway at the end
of a County bridge situate within the Township — Plea held good — In the case of a
bridge it is not necessary to state any consideration for the prescription — *Rex* v. *St.
Giles, Cambridge,* distinguished. (4 B. &
Ald., 623.)

1861.   [2623]
Townsend v. *Read.* "Highway Act, 1835," § 111
—Defence of an Indictment—Held that when
the expenses had been agreed to by the
Vestry, allowance by 2 Justices was not
necessary—"And" before "allowed" in the
early part of the Section should be read "or."
(30 L. J., M. C., 223 and 245 : 10 C. B.,
(N. S.), 308 and 317 : 5 L. T., 180.)

1879.   [2624]
Worthing L. B. v. *Lancing Surveyor.* "Highway Act, 1835," § 94-5—Part of road entirely washed away by sea—*Mandamus* to
Justices to hear the case or direct an Indictment refused, the facts showing that the
road at the *locus in quo* had absolutely ceased
to exist, and therefore the Sections of statute
cited not applicable. (*Times,* Dec. 9, 1879.)
[This case has not been followed in more
recent cases, *e. g. Reg.* v. *Halliday.*]

(5.) LIABILITY FOR NON-REPAIR.

1867.   [2625]
Reg. v. *Greenhow Inhabitants.* Indictment for
non-repair—Road carried away by landslip,
but the line of it still discoverable—Held
that there was no such total destruction of
the road as would extinguish the liability to
repair which ordinarily attaches to a parish
—*Reg.* v. *Hornsea* distinguished. (45 L. J.,
M. C., 141 : L. R., 1 Q. B. D., 703 : 35
L. T., 363.)

1854.   [2626]
Reg. v. *Hornsea Inhabitants.* A public highway
had run down a hill to the sea-shore ; by the
encroachment of the sea the sea end of the
way had been destroyed and the way ended
abruptly at the edge of a cliff 20 ft. high—
The surface of the road was in good repair
down to the point of destruction—Held that
as the substance of the road had disappeared there was nothing for the Parish to
repair, and it was not bound to form a new
communication with the shore—The obligation on a Parish in such cases is to make good
something which *exists.* (23 L. J., M. C.,
59 : 2 C. L. R., 596 : Dears & P., C. C.,
291 : 6 Cox, C. C., 299 : 22 L. T., (O. S.),
337.)

1864.   [2627]

Reg. v. *Rathmines Commissioners.* A trackway along a canal held a public highway repairable by the Commissioners though vested in a Canal Company and tolls levied by them in respect thereof. (16 Ir. C. L. R., 532: 11 L. T., 281.)

1888.   [2628]

Reg. v. *Wakefield, Mayor.* "Highways Act, 1878," —An Indictment for non-repair will lie against an Urban Authority. (57 L. J., M. C., 52: L. R., 20 Q. B. D., 810: 52 J. P., 422.)

1830.   [2629]

Rex v. *Mellor.* Road formed as a public highway and continuing such during the continuance of the Local Act under which it was formed—Held that when the Act expired the road ceased to be a public highway and that the duty of repairing it did not fall on the Parish by Common Law. 8 L. J., (o. s.), M. C., 109: 1 B. & Ad., 32.)

1829.   [2630]

Rex v. *Paddington Vestry.* Local Act providing that previous to the adoption of a new road it must be certified by Surveyors appointed by the owner and the Vestry respectively—Road duly formed and used by Public, but frontage only partly occupied by new houses—*Mandamus* to Vestry to appoint a Surveyor to certify, refused, as the road would for some time to come be chiefly a benefit to the owner only. (8 L. J., (o. s.), M. C., 4: 9 B. & C., 456.)

1805.   [2631]

Rex v. *Skinner.* If a person removes an encroachment on a highway and repairs once the part of the highway injured by the encroachment and then leaves it to the Parish to repair in future he shall not afterwards be liable—But if he being the adjacent owner has for any length of time repaired the highway which was encroached upon, it will be evidence of his liability to repair unless he can give positive evidence of encroachment and so rebut the presumption. (5 Esp., 219.)

8. MISCELLANEOUS HIGHWAY CASES.

1885.   [2632]

Ansterberry v. *Oldham Corporation.* A road intended to be "open to the public" subject to a toll, is not "dedicated," and does not become a "highway" under the "Public Health Act, 1875," § 150. (55 L. J., Ch., 633: L. R., 29 Ch. D., 750: 53 L. T., 543: 49 J. P., 532.)

1889.   [2633]

Booth v. *Howell.* Salvation Army—Municipal By-Law against noisy instruments being used in street—Concertina held such—By-Law held not invalid, and conviction affirmed. (53 J. P., 678: 5 *Times* L. R., 449.)

1865.   [2634]

Broughton L. B. H., In re. Highway Rate levied in part of a district when no public works of paving, &c., had been established ("Local Government Act, 1858," § 37, subs. 3) in the whole district—Rate quashed. (12 L. T., 310: 29 J. P., 324.)

1884.   [2635]

Dyson v. *Greetland L. B.* "Public Health Act, 1875," § 144, impliedly repeals "Highway Act, 1835," § 29, and therefore consent of Inhabitants not necessary before an Urban Authority can levy a Highway Rate exceeding 2s. 6d. (53 L. J., M. C., 106: 48 J. P., 596: *48 L. T., 636.)

1870.   [2636]

Hirst v. *Halifax L. B. H.* "Public Health Act, 1848," § 69: Local Acts—Paving expenses—Construction. (40 L. J., M. C., 169: L. R., 6 Q. B., 181.)

1890.   [2637]

Lee v. *Nixey.* Footway blocked at an illegal hour by a slide for unloading casks—A foot-passenger attempting to pass met with an accident—Held that he was entitled to recover damages. (63 L. T., 285: 54 J. P., 807.)

1878.   [2638]

Nutter v. *Accrington L. B.* "Public Health Act, 1848," § 144: "Local Government Act, 1858," § 41 [repealed]—Footway belonging to a Turnpike road raised by Local Board and injury inflicted on plaintiff—Held that damage done by a Local Board in repairing a Turnpike road which was also a "Street" can be compensated for by arbitration under the "Public Health Act, 1848." (48 L. J., Q. B. 710: 487: L. R., 4 Q. B. D., 375: 43 L. T., 43 J. P., 635.)

1882.   [2639]

Oxenhope L. B. v. *Bradford, Mayor.* "Public Health Act, 1875," § 206—300 yds. of stone kerbing held not to be "Public works of Paving" so as to render a Highway Rate invalid. (47 J. P., 21.)

1881.   [2640]

Reg. v. *Belper L. B.* "Public Health Act, 1875," § 216 (3)—Highway Rate levied in District where there existed some stone drains of old date used as sewers, and where some Paving had been done at the cost of the Rates—Held that these were public works of sewerage, &c., and therefore Highway Rate invalid. (46 J. P., 166.)

1885.   [2641]

Saunders v. *Brading Harbour Co.* Agreement that defendants should make a road across plaintiff's land according to a specification, with a view to road becoming a highway under "Public Health Act, 1875," § 150—Road made according to the agreement, but found when completed not to comply in all respects with conditions of § 150—Held that defendants had fulfilled their contract, and that if road was still defective and plaintiff wished it taken over by Local Board he must himself make good the deficiencies. (52 L. T., 426.)

1874.   [2641a]

St. Mary, Islington, Vestry v. *Barrett.* Paving expenses—Insufficient evidence of dedication—The expression "New Street" in the

N

"Metropolis Management Amendment Act, 1882," § 112, is not confined to streets dedicated to the public, and liability for paving expenses is imposed by the "Metropolis Management Act, 1855," § 105. (43 L. J., M. C., 85 : L. R., 9 Q. B., 278 : 30 L. T., 11 : 38 J. P., 198.)

1879.   [2642]
Swansea Improvement Co. v. *Glamorganshire County Roads Board.* "South Wales Turnpike Act, 1844," 7 & 8 Vict., c. 91 : "Public Health Act, 1848"—A road not repairable by inhabitants at large, held not vested in the Urban but in the County Authority— *Nutter* v. *Accrington* distinguished. (41 L. T., 583 : 43 J. P., 798.) ·

1881.   [2643]
Whittaker v. *Rhodes.* Local Act—Draper's goods exposed for sale on ground in front of shop which seemed to belong to footway—No right so to expose goods found to exist or to have been reserved when street was dedicated— Conviction good although defendant's predecessor had so used the footway for 30 years. (46 J. P., 482.)

1862.   [2644]
Willes v. *Wallington.* "Public Health Act, 1848," § 61 [Repealed]—Local Acts—Question as to whether on the facts, a certain street was or was not a "highway." (32 L. J., C. P., 86 : 13 C. R., (N. S.), 865 : [*Wallington* v. *White*]* 4 L. T., 399.)

1892.   [2645]
Wimbledon L. B. v. *Underwood.* "Public Health Act, 1875," §§ 256, 261 : "Bills of Sale Act, 1882," § 14—Held that the last-named Section does not apply where proceedings for the recovery of a Rate have been taken in a County Court instead of by Warrant of Distress, so that in such case the holder of the Bill of Sale does not lose the protection of his Bill of Sale, the execution under a County Court judgment for unpaid Rates not being a "distress under a warrant for the recovery . . . of Rates" within the said § 14. (65 L. T., 55.)

9. BRIDGES.

(1.) DEFINITIONS OF.

1857.   [2646]
Beaver v. *Manchester, Mayor.* A bridge may be so situated as to be a "street" within the meaning of a Statute. (26 L. J., Q. B., 311 : 8 E. & B., 44 : 29 L. T., (O. S.), 226.)

1872.   [2647]
North London Railway Co. v. *St. Mary's, Islington, Vestry.* A bridge may be a "street" within the "Metropolis Management Act, 1855," § 109, though it crosses a Railway, and though before its erection a footway alone existed— Railway bridge held to have been dedicated as a highway, and Company liable to a Paving Rate. (Metropolis.) (27 L. T., 672 : 37 J. P., 341 : 21 W. R., 226.)

1870.   [2648]
Reg. v. *Chart Inhabitants.* "Highway Act, 1835," § 5—A "Hundred bridge" is to be deemed a

"County bridge" and therefore is not a "highway" under the Act, repairable by the Parish, and the hundred is not relieved by the Act from liability to repair. (39 L. J., M. C., 107 : L. R., 1 C. C. R., 237 : 11 Cox, C. C., 502 : 22 L. T., 416.)

1841.   [2649]
Reg. v. *Derbyshire Inhabitants.* Structure, 1275 yards long, consisting of a bridge proper over a river and a causeway with numerous arches, under some of which another stream was always running and under most of which there was usually some water, and which as a whole had always been repaired by the County, held properly described as a "bridge" and repairable by the County—It is not essential to a "bridge" in the legal sense that it should be a structure under all the arches of which water flows at all times. (11 L. J., M. C., 51 : 2 Q. R., 745 : 2 G. & D., 97.)

1852.   [2650]
Reg. v. *Southampton County.* (1). Bridges in the Isle of Wight—Local Act providing for the repair of bridges out of a Rate analogous to a County Rate—A foot-bridge formed of 3 planks about 9 ft. long with a handrail, and carrying a public footpath over a stream held not a "bridge" repairable by the County. (21 L. J., M. C., 201 : 18 Q. B., 841 : 19 L. T., (O. S.), 245.)

1886.   [2651]
Reg. v. *Southampton County.* (2). Bridge built to open a communication with an existing highway held not a county bridge the County not having acquiesced, although both bridge and road approaching it were duly dedicated to the public. (55 L. J., M. C., 158 : L. R., 17 Q. B. D., 424 : 55 L. T., 322 : 50 J. P., 773.)

1887.   [2652]
Reg. v. *Southampton County.* (3). To render a County liable to repair a new bridge it is not sufficient to show utility and user ; on the other hand proof of overt acquiescence or formal dedication is not indispensable, and the County may be liable without these—Questions of this kind are for a Jury—*Reg.* v. *Southampton* (2) dissented from, in part. (56 L. J., M. C., 112 : L. R., 19 Q. B. D., 590 : 57 L. T., 261.)

1832.   [2653]
Rex v. *Derby, County of.* 43 Geo. III., c. 59, § 5— Turnpike Trustees are "individuals or private persons" within the meaning of this Section —Therefore a bridge erected by such Trustees after the passing of the Act, but not under the direction or to the satisfaction of the County Surveyor is not a bridge which the County becomes liable to repair. (1 L. J., M. C., 15 : 3 B. & Ad., 117.)

1830.   [2654]
Rex v. *Oxfordshire Inhabitants.* (3). The County is only bound by Common Law to repair bridges erected over water which answers the description of *flumen vel cursus aquæ, i.e.*, water

flowing in a channel between banks more or less defined, although occasionally such channel may be dry—Causeway with several arches passing between meadows which were occasionally flooded and reaching more than 300 ft. from end of main bridge, held not repairable by the County, so far as regarded the portion lying beyond the 300-ft. limit. (8 L. J., (o. s.), K. B., 354 : 8 B. & Ad., 289.)

1835.   [2655]
Rex v. *Whitney.* On an Indictment for non-repair a plea of "Guilty" to a former Indictment against the same Parish for non-repair of the same highway is conclusive evidence that the way is public—Evidence that a Parish did not put guard fences at the side of a road is not receivable on an Indictment which charges that the King's subjects could not pass as "they were wont to do," if no such fences existed before—A structure is not necessarily a "bridge" because it is *super flumen seu cursum aquæ*—Though there cannot be a County bridge where there is no *cursus aquæ,* yet it is a question for a Jury in each case whether an arch over a *cursus aquæ* is such a bridge or not—It is not to be inferred from the absence of parapets that the bridge is not a County bridge. (4 L. J., M. C., 86 : 3 A. & E., 69 ; 4 N. & M., 594 : S. C. at *Nisi Prius,* 7 C. & P., 208.)

1865.   [2656]
Ward v. *Gray.* A "floating bridge" drawn by chains is, in spite of its name, a "ferryboat," and not a "bridge" in such a sense as to bring it within the "Mutiny Act, 1864," § 72. (34 L. J., M. C., 146 : 6 B. & S., 345 : 12 L. T., 305.)

(2.) APPROACHES TO.

1838.   [2657]
Reg. v. *Lincoln, Mayor.* A party liable by prescription to repair a bridge is also *primâ facie* liable to repair 300 ft. of highway at each end—Such presumption is not rebutted by proof that the party has been known only to repair the fabric of the bridge, and that the only repairs known to have been done to the highway have been performed by Turnpike Commissioners. (7 L. J., Q. B., 161 : 8 A. & E., 65 : 3 N. & P., 273 : 1 W. W. & H., 260.)

1864.   [2658]
Reg. v. *Middle Level Commissioners.* Bridge erected by Commissioners under a Local Act and also part of the approaches washed away—Commissioners required by a subsequent Act to rebuild the bridge—Held that their obligation was limited to rebuilding the bridge, and as no provision was made for restoring the necessary approaches, Judgment was given for the defendants, the Court having no power to supply a *casus omissus* in the Act. (10 L. T., 375.)

1811.   [2659]
Rex v. *Devon, County of, Inhabitants.* (1). 22 Hen. VIII., c. 5—Part of road repairable by Dorsetshire by reason of being within 300 ft. of a county bridge—Within these limits on the Devonshire side a stream crossed the road with a ford at the point of intersection—Subsidiary bridge constructed to take the place of the ford—Held that though this subsidiary bridge was less than 300 ft. from the Dorsetshire bridge it must be repaired by Devonshire, within which it lay, otherwise a new burden would be thrown on Dorsetshire. (14 East, 477.)

1813.   [2660]
Yorkshire, W. R. v. *Rex* [In Error]. By the Common Law as declared by 22 Hen. VIII., c. 5, and subsequent Bridge Acts, where the County is liable to repair a bridge it must also repair the highway at each end thereof to the extent of 300 ft.—If indicted for non-repair the County can only exonerate itself by showing that some one else is liable by prescription or tenure. (2 Dow., 1 : 5 Taunt., 284.)

(3.) LIABILITY TO REPAIR.

1842.   [2661]
Baker v. *Greenhill.* At Common Law the liability to repair bridges *Ratione tenuræ* is thrown ultimately on the owner of the land, though so far as the Public are concerned the occupier may be primarily liable—A covenant in a lease to pay "all taxes and deductions Parliamentary and Parochial imposed on the premises or on the lessor in respect thereof" held not to include payments made for such repairs, and lessee held entitled to recover from lessor the charge imposed upon him in consequence of the lessor's default in repairing. (11 L. J., Q. B., 161 : 3 Q. B., 148 : 2 G. & D., 435.)

1836.   [2662]
Dimes v. *Arden.* Where a Lord of a Manor repairs a bridge which is repairable *Ratione tenuræ* he may recover contribution from a person who holds lands which were parcel of the demesnes at any time whilst the Manor was so charged ; and in proportion to the value of the lands so held—Unless there is evidence that the demesne lands were severed from the Manor before the liability in respect of the Manor arose. (5 L. J., Q. B., 158 : 6 N. & M., 494.)

1626.   [2663]
Huntingdon, County of, Case. If no man by reason of tenure or otherwise ought to repair a bridge the County ought to do it. (Pop., 192.)

1889.   [2664]
Lancashire & Yorkshire Railway Co. v. *Bury, Mayor.* "Railways Clauses Act, 1845," § 46—An obligation to make and maintain a bridge includes the duty to maintain the metalling of the roadway over the bridge. (59 L. J., Q. B., 85 : L. R., 14 App. Cas., 417 : 61 L. T., 417 : 54 J. P., 197.)

1879.   [2665]
Metropolitan B. W. v. *South Eastern Railway Co.* "Metropolis Bridges Act, 1877," 40 & 41 Vict. c. 99—Bridge freed of tolls by pecuniary compensation, Company to retain

N 2

ownership and to repair—*Mandamus* to repair
granted. (*Times*, Nov. 11, 1879.)

1884.   [2666]
North Brierly L. B. v. *Lancashire & Yorkshire Railway Co.* " Railways Clauses Act, 1845," § 46 ;
Special Acts—Company held under the circumstances not liable to repair roadway over
bridge. (*Times*, Oct. 27, 1884.)

1843.   [2667]
Reg. v. *Adderbury, East, Inhabitants.* Indictment
for non-repair of an ancient bridge situated
partly in Township A. and partly in Township B.—Allegation that the former part was
out of repair and that Township A. was liable
by prescription—Evidence that so much of
the centre arch as was in A. had within
living memory been widened by 6 ft.—Held
that the Indictment against A. was sufficient and that there was no variance between
it and the evidence, as at all events the Township remained liable for the ancient portion
—*Quære*, whether the widening was anything
more than a mode of repair, so that the prescriptive liability extended over the added
part ? (13 L. J., M. C., 9 : 5 Q. B., 187 : 1
Dav. & Mer., 324.)

1855.   [2668]
Reg. v. *Bedfordshire Inhabitants.* Indictment for
non-repair of a bridge—Plea that A. was
liable, *Ratione tenuræ*—Hearsay evidence or
evidence of reputation is admissible in questions relating to matters of public and general
interest notwithstanding that private matters
might be involved ; therefore evidence of
reputation that A. was liable was admissible.
(24 L. J., Q. B., 81 ; 4 E. & B., 535 ; 3 C. L. R.,
442 ; 24 L. T., (o. s.), 268.)

1850.   [2669]
Reg. v. *Brecknock Inhabitants.* Indictment for
non-repair of half of a County bridge—Transfer of a District on one side of a stream from
one County to another specially for Parliamentary purposes held to involve the transfer
of the liability to repair half of a bridge
therein situated—In the absence of words
in the Act determining the boundary, the
ordinary rule of *medium filium aquæ* held to
apply. (19 L. J., M. C., 203 : 15 Q. B., 813
at p. 817 : 4 New Sess. Cas., 272.)

1878.   [2670]
Reg. v. *Buckinghamshire Inhabitants.* County
bridge lengthened by Turnpike Trustees on
account of Floods—No authority for this—
The Trustees repaired the extension whilst
individuals repaired the older part, *Ratione
tenure*—Held that on the expiration of the
Trust the repairs of the addition devolved on
the County, under 33 & 34 Vict. c. 73, § 12.
(43 J. P., 175.)

1704.   [2671]
Reg. v. *Bucklugh (Duchess of).* If a manor be
held by the service or tenure of repairing a
common bridge or highway and the Manor
be divided, the tenant of any parcel either of
the demesnes or services is liable to the whole
charge but may recover contribution — An
agreement by the Lord to discharge the pur-

chasers would only bind him and those who
claim under him; and will not affect the
remedy of the Public—Though the Manor
comes into the hands of the Crown yet the
duty continues as against every person claiming under the Crown. (1 Salk., 358.)

1702.   [2672]
Reg. v. *Bucknall,* A man cannot be charged with
the repairs of a bridge merely because he is
Lord of a particular Manor—There must be
proof of liability by prescription ; or *Ratione
tenuræ*—If a man liable *Ratione tenuræ* aliences
any part of the land the alience is liable to
contribute whenever the bridge is out of
repair, and the Information or Indictment
may be against one liable to contribute.
(2 Ld. Raym., 792 : 7 Mod., 55.)

1881.   [2673]
Reg. v. *Dorset Inhabitants.* Toll Bridge built
within Municipal Borough—On expiration of
Turnpike Trust held that, under 33 & 34 Vict.,
c. 73, § 12. the County became liable to repair the bridge, unless it could be shown that
the Borough was liable by immemorial usage
to repair all bridges within its boundaries.
(45 L. T., 308.)

1888.   [2674]
Reg. v. *E. & W. India Dock Co.* A statutory duty
to build bridges over the cuts of a dock company held to mean, bridges adequate for the
then existing traffic, not for future heavy
and extraordinary traffic. (60 L. T., 232 ;
53 J. P., 277.)

1850.   [2675]
Reg. v. *Ely Inhabitants.* The general rule as to
bridges built by private persons prior to
43 Geo. III., c. 59, is that if such bridges are
used by the public the County is liable to
repair them. (19 L. J., M. C., 223 : 15 Q. B.,
827 : 4 New Sess. Cas., 222 : 15 L. T., (o. s.),
412.)

1842.   [2676]
Reg. v. *Gloucestershire Inhabitants.* 43 Geo. III.,
c. 59, § 5—Bridge over a Stream running
through a sheet of water dammed up to protect adjacent meadows—If a bridge has been
erected for the convenience of the Public
passing over a stream the County must repair
it, even though the bridge might not have
been necessary when built. (Car. & Marsh.,
506.)

1845.   [2677]
Reg. v. *New Sarum Inhabitants.* Borough enlarged under the " Reform Act, 1832 " and
the " Municipal Corporations Act, 1835," by
the addition of Parish which contained a
County bridge—Held that the Borough did
not by the enlargement of its boundary become liable to repair the bridge—The liability remained with the County. (15 L. J.,
M. C., 15 : 7 Q. B., 941 : 2 New Sess. Cas.,
133.)

1704.   [2678]
Reg. v. *Saintiff.* An Indictment does not lie for
not repairing a bridge unless it be in a highway—" Highway is a general term for all
public ways, as well cart, horse, and footways,

and Indictment lies for any one of these ways, if they are common to all the Queen's subjects—If a way be in decay an Indictment must of necessity lie, for an Action on the Case will not lie, without special damage—By Common Right the County are bound to repair public bridges. (6 Mod., 255: Holt, 129 : [*Reg.* v. *Sainthill*] 2 Ld. Raym., 1174.)

1878.   [2679]
Reg. v. *Somersetshire.* 43 Geo. III., c. 59, § 5—
—Bridge in the course of a Turnpike road raised by a Canal Company—Road disturnpiked—Held that the interference with the bridge by the Canal Company did not release the County from its ordinary liability, which accrued on the termination of the Turnpike Trust. (38 L. T., 452: 42 J. P., 501.)

1876.   [2680]
Reg. v. *South Eastern Railway Co.*(2). Private Act —Obligation to maintain and repair a bridge held to include a duty to repair the roadway of the bridge, even though such roadway had been habitually repaired by the Parish. (32 L. T., 858.)

1838.   [2681]
Reg. v. *Sutton.* Indictment for non-repair of a bridge *Ratione tenuræ*— A Record dated 20 Ed. III. of a trial whereat a Jury found that there was no evidence of any person being liable *Ratione tenuræ*, and a subsequent grant of Pontage, both held admissible evidence to negative a prescriptive liability in any person, and therefore the liability of the present defendant. (7 L. J., Q. B., 205: 8 A. & E., 516: 3 N. & P., 569.)

1815.   [2682]
Rex v. *Buckingham (Marquis of).* A bar across a bridge kept locked except in times of floods is conclusive evidence that the public have only a limited right to use the bridge at such times, and an Indictment for non-repair stating it to be used by the public "at their free will and pleasure" is faulty. (4 Camp., 189.)

1810.   [2683]
Rex v. *Bucks, County of, Inhabitants.* A county is bound to repair every public bridge within it unless it can show that some person, or Body Politic or Corporate, is liable—Every bridge in a highway is, by 22 Hen. VIII., c. 5, to be deemed a public bridge for this purpose. (12 East, 192.)

1824.   [2684]
Rex v. *Devon Inhabitants.*(2). A bridge used only on occasion of floods, and lying out of and alongside the road commonly used, held a public bridge which the County was liable to repair. (Ryan & M., 144.)

1825.   [2685]
Rex v. *Devon County, Inhabitants.*(3). Liability on the part of a County to *repair* a bridge does not carry with it any liability to *widen* the bridge—*Rex* v. *Cumberland,* overruled. (4 L. J., (o. s.), K. B., 34: 7 D. & R., 147: 4 B. & C. 670.)

1833.   [2686]
Rex v. *Devonshire Inhabitants.*(4).43 Geo.III.,c.59, § 5—County bridge partly washed away and rebuilt by the Parish with the old materials, somewhat wider, but in the same line of passage, and placed on the old abutments—Held that though the bridge had been rebuilt without the privity of the County Surveyor it was nevertheless not a "new" bridge, and that the County was liable for its repair. (2 L. J., M. C., 74 : 2 N. & M., 212 : 5 B. & Ad., 383.)

1802.   [2687]
Rex v. *Glamorgan County.* Bridge erected in a highway across a river by a private individual for his own benefit but used by the public for 40 years—Held that the County was bound to repair. (2 East, 356, n.)

1833.   [2688]
Rex v. *Hendon Inhabitants.* A Parish may be indicted for non-repair of a bridge, without stating any other ground of liability than immemorial usage. (2 L. J., M. C., 55 : 4 B. & Ad., 628.)

1811.   [2689]
Rex v. *Kent Inhabitants.* (1.) Indictment for non-repair of a bridge—Bridge built by a Navigation Company as a substitute for a ford which they had destroyed by deepening a river—Held that the Navigation Company and not the County were liable to repair the bridge. (13 East, 220.)

1814.   [2690]
Rex v. *Kent Inhabitants.* (2.) Mill and dam erected on a stream with the result that a public ford through a river was rendered impassable—Bridge erected by millowner and used by the public—Held that the County and not the millowner must repair it, the public having derived benefit by the substitution of a bridge for a ford. (2 Maule & S., 513.)

1813.   [2691]
Rex v. *Kerrison.* (1.) An indictment charging an individual with the repair of a bridge by reason of his being the owner and proprietor of a certain Navigation is not equivalent to charging him *Ratione tenuræ.* (1 Maule & S., 435.)

1815.   [2692]
Rex v. *Kerrison.* (2.) Highway cut by Navigation Commissioners, who thereupon built a bridge over the cut—Held that the Navigation, and not the County must keep the bridge in repair, there being no benefit derived by the public from the substitution of the bridge for the highway. (3 Maule & S., 526.)

1831.   [2693]
Rex v. *Lancashire Inhabitants.* 43 Geo. III., c. 59, § 5—This section only applies to bridges newly built, not to bridges merely widened or repaired since the Act—Turnpike Trustees having built a bridge where a culvert would have sufficed but a bridge was preferable, held that the County could not refuse to repair such bridge on the ground that it was not absolutely necessary. (1 L. J., M. C., 1 : 2 B. & Ad. 813.)

1811. [2694]

Rex v. Lindsey Inhabitants. Highway crossed by a fordable stream—Bed of stream deepened by a Canal Company whereby a bridge was rendered requisite which they duly built—Company, not the County, held liable to repair the bridge. (14 East, 317.)

1821. [2695]

Rex v. Machynlleth and Penegoes Inhabitants. (1). The Quarter Sessions cannot impose more than one fine for non-repair of a bridge—A fresh Indictment is requisite if the first fine is inadequate. (4 B. & Ald., 469.)

1823. [2696]

Rex v. Machynlleth and Penegoes. (2). Indictment stating that an ancient bridge within two Parishes was out of repair, and that the inhabitants of the Parish and Town aforesaid, from time immemorial, by reason of the tenure of certain lands in the Parish and Town had repaired the bridges—Indictment held bad, for it did not appear that the bridge was within the Town, and therefore the inhabitants of the Town were not liable unless a special consideration were shown, inasmuch as the inhabitants not being incorporated could not hold land, and therefore the Common Law liability did not attach. (2 B. & C., 166 : 3 D. & R., 388.)

1832. [2697]

Rex v. Middlesex Inhabitants. Ancient bridge repairable *Ratione tenuræ*—Separate foot-bridge constructed, about a century before the Indictment, outside the ancient bridge but attached to it—Held that the foot-bridge was not part of the ancient bridge, and that he who was liable to repair the ancient bridge *Ratione tenuræ* was not liable for the foot-bridge, and therefore that the County must repair it. (1 L. J., M. C., 16 : 3 B. & Ad., 201.)

1814. [2698]

Rex v. Northampton County. A bridge may be a public bridge which is used by the public at all times when it is dangerous to pass through the river—In support of a plea of "Not Guilty" the defendants may give evidence, *quantum valeat*, of the bridge having been repaired by private individuals. (2 Maule & S., 262.)

1817. [2699]

Rex v. Oswestry Hundred. A Hundred may be charged by prescription with the repair of a bridge ; and this although it appears that by a Statute within legal memory one of the Townships, parcel of the Hundred, was then annexed to it. (6 Maule & S., 361.)

1812. [2700]

Rex v. Oxfordshire Inhabitants. (1). Indictment for non-repair of a bridge—Plea, that M. was liable, *Ratione tenuræ*—The plea is not sustained by evidence that M.'s estate was part of a larger estate which part he purchased, the rest remaining in the hands of the former owner, who as well before the sale as after had repaired the bridge in question—Where in such a case the County was found "Guilty"

the Court gave leave to stay the Judgment on payment of Costs, until another Indictment was preferred to try the liability. (16 East, 223.)

1825. [2701]

Rex v. Oxfordshire. (2). Indictment against a County for non-repair of a bridge erected by Turnpike Trustees in a road where there had not previously been a bridge—Held that the County was liable, the bridge having been built for public purposes in a public highway, and this notwithstanding that the Trustees possessed available funds—County might have a remedy over against the Trustees. (3 L. J., (o. s.), K. B., 198 : 4 B. & C., 194 : 6 D. & R., 231.)

1810. [2702]

Rex v. Salop Inhabitants. The County is *primâ facie* bound to repair all public bridges within it, whether foot, horse, or carriage bridges, unless it can be shown that others are bound to repair particular bridges. (13 East, 95.)

1812. [2703]

Rex v. Somerset Inhabitants. Local Act empowering Turnpike Trustees to replace an old by a new bridge and to take tolls and lay out the money thereby received in building the new bridge, and providing that when the powers of the Act ceased, the new bridge should be repaired by such persons as were liable by law to repair the old bridge—Held that during the time the powers of the Act were being exercised by the Trustees, the County was not liable to repair the new bridge. (16 East, 305.)

1811. [2704]

Rex v. Stratford-on-Avon, Mayor. A Corporation by prescription held liable by prescription and not *Ratione tenuræ* to repair a bridge—An Indictment charging the Corporation as *immemorially* bound to repair held sustainable. (14 East, 348.)

1810. [2705]

Rex v. Surrey Inhabitants. Parish bound by prescription to repair a wooden foot-bridge used by carriages in times of flood only—Wider bridge built of brick by Turnpike Trustees on same site and constantly used by all carriages for the 40 years since its erection—Indictment against County for non-repair—Plea, that Parish had immemorially been liable—Held that such plea was not supported by evidence of the above facts ; and that County was liable. (2 Camp., 455.)

1835. [2706]

Rex v. Sutton. (2). An infant seised of lands in the actual possession of his Guardian "in socage" is not indictable for the non-repair of a bridge *Ratione tenuræ*, but the Guardian is—*Quære*, whether an owner, who is not the occupier, of lands charged with the repair of a bridge can be indicted for non-repair? (4 L. J., K. B., 215 : 5 N. & M., 353 : 3 A. & E., 597.)

1770. [2707]

Rex v. Yorkshire, W. R., Inhabitants. (1). The County are of commonright bound to repair a new bridge built by a private person if it be of public utility. (5 Burr. 2594: 2 W. Bl., 685.)

1773.   [2708]
Rex v. Yorkshire, W.R., Inhabitants. (2). When it does not appear who ought to repair a bridge it is certain in such a case that, at Common Law, the duty is on the County. (Lofft, 238.)

1788.   [2709]
Rex v. Yorkshire, W.R. (3). Foot-bridge enlarged to a carriage bridge—Held that a Township liable to repair the foot-bridge continued liable *pro ratâ*, but no further. (2 East, 353, n.) [But see *Rex v. Surrey.*]

1802.   [2710]
Rex v. Yorkshire, W.R., Inhabitants. (4). If a bridge be of public utility and used by the public, the County must repair it, though built by Trustees under a Turnpike Act or by an individual—*Aliter* if built by an individual for his own benefit, and so continued without public utility though used by the public—A bridge built in a public way without public utility is indictable as a nuisance—And so, if built colourably, in an imperfect or inconvenient manner, in order to throw the onus of reconstruction or repair on the County. (2 East, 342.)

1840.   [2711]
Surrey Canal Co. v. Hall. Canal Act requiring Company to maintain bridges over their canal where it intersected highways—Bridge available for carriages erected in compliance with the Act at a spot where there had been only a bridle-way—Such bridge long used by carriages generally though designed only for carriages belonging to the tenants of a particular estate—Toll subsequently imposed, the traffic having become heavy as the neighbourhood became populous—Trespass for passing without paying toll—Direction by the Judge that supposing the bridge in question to have been originally erected for certain tenants in particular, yet if in consequence of the acts of the Company an idea grew up that the road had been dedicated the Jury might find such dedication—Held that this was not a misdirection and that the evidence warranted the Jury in finding a dedication. (9 L. J., C. P., 329 : 1 Scott, N. R., 264: 1 M. & G., 322.)

(4.) LEGAL PROCEEDINGS CONNECTED WITH.

1889.   [2712]
A. G. v. Newcastle, Mayor. Right held good of Municipal Corporation to negociate for freeing for a term of years a toll-bridge whereby the owners of another toll-bridge were pecuniarily injured—Restrictions on the financial operations of a Municipal Corporation, stated. (58 L. J., Q. B., 558 : L. R., 23 Q. B. D., 492 : 54 J. P., 292 : *60 L. T., 791.)

1805.   [2713]
Harrison v. Parker. Bridge built by private individual but dedicated to the public—Held that the property in the materials so far continued in him that he could maintain an

Action against a person who wrongfully removed them. (6 East, 154 : 2 Smith, 262.)

1854.   [2714]
Mackinnon v. Penson. No Action for damages will lie against a County Surveyor for personal or pecuniary injury resulting from non-repair of a County bridge. (23 L. J., M. C., 97 : 9 Ex., 609 : 22 L. T., (o. s.), 318.)

1858.   [2715]
Manley v. St. Helen's Canal Co. Highway intersected by Canal and gap made good by a swing bridge—The Canal Act authorised the Company to take tolls and gave a public user—Bridge opened for a boat in the dark and a person coming along the road drowned—Action under "Lord Campbell's Act" against the Company held maintainable on the grounds that the Company had a beneficial interest in the tolls, and that the bridge was improperly left unfenced—Held also that even if a bridge were sufficient at the time of construction the Company were bound to alter it so as to adapt it to increased traffic—The Jury were warranted in finding a bridge insufficient which when open left an unfenced gulf in the highway. (27 L. J., Ex., 159 : 2 H. & N., 840.)

1859.   [2716]
Newport Bridge, In re. 43 Geo. III., c. 59, § 2—*Mandamus* to Justices to order a bridge to be widened, refused, the enactment being permissive and not imperative—A presentment is a condition precedent to making such an order. (29 L. J., M. C., 52 : 2 E. & E., 377 : [*Reg. v. Monmouthshire*] 1 L. T., 131.)

1862.   [2717]
Nicoll v. Allen. Bridge erected by a private individual under a Private Act—Tolls leviable —Power to levy Ferry Tolls whilst bridge was under repair—The bridge having become ruinous and impassable, the proprietor (the defendant) established a Ferry service and took no steps to repair the bridge—*Mandamus* to defendant to rebuild the bridge refused, but held that he was liable to an Action at the suit of a person suffering special damage by reason of the bridge remaining impassable, while the defendant was in receipt of the Tolls. (31 L. J., Q. B., 283 : 1 B. & S., 934 : 6 L. T., 699.)

1850.   [2718]
Reg. v. Betts. Building a bridge partly in the bed of a navigable river is not necessarily a nuisance—The question is one of fact for a Jury whether or no the navigation is thereby impeded. (16 Q. B., 1022 : 4 Cox, C. C., 211.)

1849.   [2719]
Reg. v. Brecknock Inhabitants. (1). The "Highway Act, 1773," made applicable to bridges by the "County Bridges Act, 1803," is still so applicable notwithstanding that it is repealed as to highways by the "Highway Act, 1835" —Therefore one Justice may still present a County bridge which is out of repair. (18 L. J., M. C., 123 : 15 Q. B., 813 : 3 New Sess. Cas., 434.)

1844.   [2720]
Reg. v. *Merionethshire Inhabitants.* The "Highway Act, 1773," § 64, is kept alive as regards bridges by the effect of the "County Bridges Act, 1803," § 1, though repealed generally by the "Highway Act, 1835," § 1—Therefore the power of a Judge who tries an Indictment for non-repair, removed by *Certiorari*, to certify for Costs in the case of a frivolous defence continues. (13 L. J., M. C., 158: 6 Q. B., 343: 1 New Sess. Cas., 316.)

1828.   [2721]
Rex v. *Buckingham JJ.* Pending an Indictment at the instance of a Parish against a County for non-repair of a bridge, the object being to determine whether the County or the Parish was liable, the Court refused to grant the defendants an inspection of Parish books and documents relating to former repairs of the bridge. (6 L. J., (o. s.), K. B., 346: 2 M. & R., 412: 8 B. & C., 375.)

1788.   [2722]
Russell v. *Men of Devon.* No Civil Action lies against a County at the suit of an individual for an injury sustained in consequence of a County bridge being out of repair—Where an Action is brought against a Corporation for damages, the damages are to be recovered out of the corporate estate, and not against the individual corporators; and even if a County can in any sense be considered a corporation, there is no corporate fund out of which a claim can be satisfied. (2 T. R., 667.)

1828.   [2723]
Wiggins v. *Boddington.* Swing bridge on public highway—The owners of such a structure are bound, in the passing of vessels, to use all reasonable means (including number of men employed to assist and number of ships passed at a time) to prevent unnecessary delay—If they do not do all which can reasonably be expected, any person obstructed may recover damages for injury sustained. (3 C. & P., 544.)

PART III.—COUNTY COUNCILS.

1. ELECTION BUSINESS.

1892. [2724]
Crone v. *Waugh.* County Council Election—Tie—Deputy Returning Officer declined to give a casting vote—*Mandamus* granted at suit of a voter to Returning Officer to hold another election. (*Times,* June 3, 1892.)

1889. [2725]
Darlington, Ex parte. "Municipal Elections (Corrupt Practices) Act, 1884," § 13 : "Local Government Act, 1888," § 20—Relief granted where a. candidate had employed 12 messengers at 1s. 6d. each to distribute circulars. (53 J. P., 71.)

1890. [2726]
De Souza v. *Cobden.* "Local Government Act, 1888 :" "Municipal Corporations Act, 1882," §§ 41, 73—A woman being an unqualified person is subject to the penalty prescribed on such persons even though her election has for 12 months not been called in question. (60 L. J., Q. B., 533 : L. R., [1891] 1 Q. B., 687 : 65 L. T., 130 : 55 J. P., 565.)

1889. [2727]
Hope v. *Sandhurst (Lady).* "Local Government Act, 1888," § 2 : "Municipal Corporations Act, 1882," §§ 9, 63, 93 (7)—A woman is not eligible for election as a member of a Municipal Corporation or of a County Council—Votes given to an unqualified candidate are thrown away, and the seat will be awarded to the highest on the poll of the qualified candidates. (58 L. J., Q. B., 316 : L. R., 23 Q. B. D., 79 : 61 L. T., 150 : 53 J. P., 805.)

1890. [2728]
Knill v. *Towse.* "Local Government Act, 1888," §§ 2 (1, 4), 75—At an Election of County Councillors no person is entitled to vote in more than one electoral division of the same county. (59 L. J., Q. B., 455 : L. R., 24 Q. B. D., 697 : 63 L. T., 47 : 54 J. P., 789.)

1889. [2729]
Lenanton, Ex parte. "Municipal Elections (Corrupt Practices) Act, 1884," §§ 13, 14, 16 : "Local Government Act, 1888," § 75—"Inadvertence" means negligence or carelessness where the circumstances show an absence of bad faith—Notice of intended application for relief should be given (a) to opposite candidate, (b) to Returning Officer, (c) by posting about the district, and by newspaper advertisement — Need not be given to Attorney-General—The Court has no power

to grant relief to a printer who has been guilty of an offence against § 14. (53 J. P., 263.)

1889. [2730]
" *Loc. Gov. Act,* 1888," *In re* ; *Thomas, Ex parte.* "Municipal Elections (Corrupt Practices) Act, 1884," §§ 13, 20—A Divisional Court refused to make an Order allowing the employment of paid canvassers to be an exception from the provisions of the Act which would otherwise make the same illegal—Held that such a matter was within the discretion of the Divisional Court, but inasmuch as the election had since taken place and the applicant had been defeated, there had been a change of circumstances which the Court of Appeal would take into consideration and make the Order. (60 L. T., 728.)

1889. [2731]
Marton v. *Gorrill.* Nomination paper complete in all particulars except that name of Electoral Division had not been filled in—Nomination held good, the omission falling within and being cured by § 72 of the "Municipal Corporation Act, 1882." (58 L. J., Q. B., 329 : L. R., 23 Q. B. D., 139 : 54 J. P., 151.)

1889. [2732]
Walker, Ex parte. "Municipal Elections (Corrupt Practices) Act, 1884," §§ 13, 17, 20 : "Local Government Act, 1888," § 75—An appeal lies to the Court of Appeal against the refusal of the High Court to relieve a candidate from certain penalties—When a candidate incurred a penalty and the High Court refused relief, the Court of Appeal allowed it under the circumstances shown. (58 L. J., Q. B., 190 : L. R., 22 Q. B. D., 384 : 60 L. T., 581 : 53 J. P., 260.)

[During the few months immediately succeeding the first elections under the "Local Government Act, 1888," there were an immense number of applications to the High Court for relief from penalties unwittingly incurred by candidates at those elections. The cause of this lay in the fact that the "Municipal Corporations Act, 1882," then for the first time applied to the counties, was altogether unknown outside the previously existing Municipal Boroughs. Except in very rare instances these applications really disclosed no new points of Law, and an exhaustive digest of them in this work would be altogether unprofitable. Such of them as have not been dealt with previously in these pages will now be briefly referred to.

The applications were reported in considerable detail in the *Times* newspaper, and the columns of that journal must be consulted for details. See especially the numbers of the following dates :—1888: Dec. 21, 22; 1889: Jan. 12, 16, 17, 19, 22, 24, 25, 26, 29, 31; Feb. 1, 7, 8, 12, 28; Mar. 5.

The points raised in the various applications reported in the *Times* of the above dates may be succinctly and sufficiently stated as in the following paragraphs.

Failure to attach to Bills, etc. the Names and Addresses of Printers and Publishers.—In connection with this it was decided that an application for relief to a candidate could not be extended to include his printer. (Dec. 21). A circular printed on paper of note-paper size, to be sent by Post or hand, and asking for "vote and interest" is not a "bill, poster, or placard" requiring a printer's name. (Dec. 21). Circular address sent by Post having no printer's name. No Order made, relief not being necessary as there was no offence (Dec. 22). Application for relief made on eve of election; allegations that there had been no time to prepare affidavits. Application refused, *Per* Denman, J. :—"He was not aware of anything preventing the application being made even after an election." (Jan. 16).

Election Meetings held at Public-houses.—("Municipal Elections, Corrupt Practices, Act," 1884," § 16). Many such cases, *e.g.*, farmer stopping at public-house, some of his friends came in and discussed the election at an impromptu meeting; relief granted. (Dec. 22). Meeting at a place called the "Kilburn Town Hall," a place licensed for stage-plays with a license to sell liquor during the performances; relief granted. (Dec. 22). Meeting on village green interrupted by sudden storm, persons present had taken shelter and continued the meeting in a malt-house which formed part of licensed premises. (Jan. 19). In another case where licensed premises were used, application for relief adjourned because a doctor's certificate, not on oath, of candidate's illness and incapacity to make an affidavit was sought to be used. (Jan. 26). In another application with respect to a meeting on licensed premises, Denman, J., said :—"The Court was not sanctioning meetings on licensed premises or premises adjoining and connected therewith. There was here a *bonâ fide* mistake at a first election under the Act, and the offence would be excused, but it must not be treated as a precedent." (Feb. 7). Meetings in a room attached to a tea and coffee shop, which room was used in summer for the sale of refreshments; relief granted, but Huddleston, B., seems to have refrained from saying that an offence had been committed in this case. (Feb. 1). Application for relief for holding meeting on licensed premises. Relief granted, but costs granted to opposing Candidate. (Jan. 19).

Illegal employment of agents. ("Municipal Elections, Corrupt Practices, Act, 1884," § 13). Solicitor employed as paid election agent, but he resigned so soon as he found out the illegality. Relief postponed. (Dec. 22).

In another case Lord Coleridge said :—"The Act is plain enough—that paid agents must not

be employed—and if parties will not take the trouble to read the Act they must take the consequences." (Jan. 24).

Paid canvassers. Relief granted in a case where the man employed though a canvasser and though paid was paid in a method said not to be likely to influence the election. (Jan. 26). "Election agent" employed. Relief granted. (Jan. 22). Paid "Messengers" employed to deliver circulars but not to canvass. Held that no offence had been committed. (Jan. 19).

Notices as to applications for relief. Per Huddleston, J. :—"We laid it down that there should be notice to the returning officer, to the opposing candidate, and also, either posters put up in the locality or public advertisement in the local papers." (Jan. 19). In a case where it was shown that there was only one local paper and as that was published only once a week the notice would have been too late, a newspaper notice was dispensed with.

Committee Rooms. Using two Committee rooms 10 miles apart, only one being allowed. Relief refused as a petition was likely to be presented. (Jan. 26).

Election Expenses. ("Municipal Corporations, Corrupt Practices, Act," 1884, § 5) Joint candidates issued joint address, and worked together. Statutory maximum for expenses exceeded by inadvertence. Relief granted. (Feb. 8). "Profuse" expenditure, and employment of paid canvassers and of an illegal number of messengers by an Agent without the authority of and in defiance of the instructions of Candidate. Relief granted. ([2733], *Stopes, Ex parte.* March 5.)

Practice as to applications for Relief. [2734] In *Birtwistle, Ex parte,* a complicated controversy between two Candidates opposing one another, and going even to the Court of Appeal, is disclosed. (Feb. 28.) A candidate elected during his absence in India was allowed relief for not returning his expenses in due time. (March 5.)]

2. FINANCIAL MATTERS.

1890.   [2735]
Durham C. C. v. Chester-le-Street Union. A certified Industrial School under 29 & 30 Vict., c. 118, is rateable notwithstanding that it is in the hands of a County Council. (L. R., [1891] 1 Q. B., 331: 63 L. T., 461: 54 J. P., 759.)

1891.   [2736]
Howlett v. Maidstone, Mayor. "Local Government Act, 1888," §§ 62, 86 (4)–Visitors of County Lunatic Asylum have no longer the power of fixing charges for pauper lunatics sent from a borough which has not contributed to the building of the asylum—If differences arise Borough may demand settlement by arbitration. (60 L. J., Q. B., 570: L. R., 2 Q. B., 110: 65 L. T., 448: 55 J. P., 549.)

1892.   [2737]
Proctor v. Cheshire C. C. Profits arising from Management of Lunatic Asylum held under

the circumstances to belong to the County Council. (56 J. P., 523.)

1890. [2738]
Salford Mayor v. *Lancashire C. C.* "Contagious Diseases (Animals) Acts, 1869, 1878:" "Local Government Act, 1888"—Right of Borough to be recouped proportionate amount contributed to expenses of working the first named Acts—Liability of County Council to be sued. (59 L. J., Q. B., 576: L. R., 25 Q. B. D., 384: 63 L. T., 409: 55 J. P., 85.)

1891. [2739]
Salop C. C., In re. "Local Government Act, 1888," §§ 29, 38, 62, 124—Lunatic Asylum for paupers provided jointly by County and certain Boroughs—Agreements by Boroughs to pay annual rent for use of Asylum—Quarter Sessious Boroughs with less than 10,000 inhabitants—Transference of liability of Borough to County Council—Held that the Court has no jurisdiction under § 29 to decide questions of adjustment of liabilities under § 62. (65 L. T., 416: 56 J. P., 213.)

1889. [2740]
Somerset C. C., Ex parte: "Local Government Act, 1888." In re. "Local Government Act, 1888," § 30 (3)—The Standing Joint Committee has exclusive control of buildings and premises connected with Quarter Sessions and Police business—The County Council as such has no power to veto the requirements of the Joint Committee and must raise and pay such sums as the Joint Committee deem it necessary to spend. (58 L. J., Q. B., 513: 61 L. T., 512: 54 J. P., 182.)

1889. [2741]
Staffordshire Q. Sess. Chairman, Ex parte: "Local Government Act, 1888," In re. "Local Government Act, 1888," § 29: Local Act—Stipendiary Magistrate's District created under last named Act which authorised the Justices in Quarter Sessions to levy County Rates on the District—Now two County Boroughs in the said District—Held on case stated that County Council could only levy Rates on the part of District outside the limits of the County Boroughs and that the liability of the County Boroughs must be redeemed under § 32 of the Act of 1888. (54 J. P., 72.)

1890. [2742]
West Riding C. C., In re. "Local Government Act, 1888," § 24—County Council held bound in substitution for the Exchequer to pay out of County Fund local grants in respect of half year previous to the Council coming into existence. (54 J. P., 533.)

3. HIGHWAYS AND BRIDGES.

1890. [2743]
Curtis v. *Kesteven C. C.* "Local Government Act, 1888," § 11, (1, 6)—Strips of grass bordering the metalled part of a main road are "roadside wastes," and the herbage thereon is not vested in the County Council. (60 L. J., Ch., 103: L. R., 45 Ch. D., 504: 63 L. T., 543.)

1891. [2744]
Essex C. C. v. *Chelmsford Union.* Bridge washed away before the passing of the "Local Government Act, 1888"—Temporary bridge erected by Highway Authority—Held that the County Council was bound at its own expense to rebuild the bridge. (55 J. P., 84.)

1891. [2745]
Reg. v. *Norfolk C. C.* "Highways Act, 1878," §§ 13-15: Special Acts conferring certain powers on Fen Drainage Commissioners—Application that certain roads should be declared main roads—Held that the Commissioners though managing highways were not a Highway Authority within § 38 of the "Highways Act, 1878," and could not declare the roads to be main roads. (60 L. J., Q. B., 379: 65 L. T., 222: 56 J. P., 7.)

1890. [2746]
Staffordshire & Derbyshire C. C., In re. "Local Government Act," 1888, §§ 12, 29, 50: Local Act—Bridge formerly in two counties now in one county—Question whether the two counties were to continue sharing the expense or one to bear the whole—Held that the saving clause of the general Act (§ 12) kept alive the Local Act. (54 J. P., 566.)

1891. [2747]
Stockport and Hyde H. B. v. *Chester C. C.* Agreement for repair of Council's main roads by the Board—Held, nevertheless, that the Council continued to be the Road Authority so as to be able to claim as its perquisites surplus material created by a Tramway Company. (61 L. J., Q. B., 22: 65 L. T., 85: 55 J. P., 808.)

1891. [2748]
Warminster L. B., In re, and Wiltshire C. C. "Local Government Act, 1888," § 11—A road may include a footpath, and a duty to maintain a road carries with it the duty to maintain a footpath adjacent if there is one. (59 L. J., Q. B., 431: L. R., 25 Q. B. D., 450: 62 L. T., 902: 54 J. P., 375.)

4. LEGAL POINTS.

1891. [2749]
County Council of Kent and Councils of Boroughs of Dover, and of Sandwich, Ex parte. "Local Government Act, 1888," § 29—There is no right of appeal to the Court of Appeal from decisions of the High Court, under this Section. (60 L. J., Q. B., 435: L. R., 1 Q. B., 725: 65 L. T., 213: 55 J. P., 647.)

5. OFFICERS.

1891. [2750]
"*Local Government Act* 1888," *In re: London C. C., Ex parte.* "Local Government Act, 1888," §§ 3, 5: "Coroners Act, 1844 and 1887"—The appointment of franchise coroners not having formerly appertained to Justices in Quarter Sessions is not business transferred to County Councils; nor does the Act give the power of appointing any class of coroner

except those formerly elected by the Freeholders. (61 L. J., Q. B., 27 : L. R., [1892] 1 Q. B., 33 : 65 L. T., 614 : 56 J. P., 279.)

1890.   [2751]

Reg. v. *Hereford C. C.* "Lunatic Asylums Act, 1853"—A Chaplain who did not reside in the Asylum but at his benefice 2 miles off applied for a superannuation allowance being of the necessary age and service—Visiting Justices granted the allowance but County Council thinking him not an officer in the Asylum and not incapacitated as regards health and merely desirous of giving more time to his benefice, refused to pay the allowance—Held that though not resident he was an officer of and in the Asylum within the Act—*Mandamus* to enforce payment of allowance granted. (63 L. T., 245 : 55 J. P., 72.)

6. POLICE.

1890.   [2752]

Bootle-cum-Linacre, Mayor v. *Lancashire C. C.* "Municipal Corporations Acts, 1835," §§ 76, 82 : 2 & 3 Vict., c. 93, § 24 : 3 & 4 Vict., c. 85, § 14 : "Local Government Act, 1888," §§ 3, 64, 79—Police provided for a Borough by the County Justices — Separate Borough Police force established after a while—Moneys raised by Rate and in the hands of the County at the time of the change held not repayable to the Borough — Under such circumstances the Mayor and Corporation held not to represent the Borough ; and

no method available for allocating the moneys. (60 L. J., Q. B., 323.)

1890.   [2753]

Cardigan C. C., In re. "Local Government Act, 1888," § 29—Case stated by Chairman—Questions as to relations between Justices, the Standing Joint Committee and the Chief Constable respecting orders given to the Police—Held that the questions as stated were too vague and speculative to be answered by the High Court. (54 J. P., 468 : *Times*, July 18, 1890.)

1890.   [2754]

Leicestershire C. C., Ex parte. "Police Act, 1840," §§ 3, 27—The powers here conferred on Justices now belong to the Standing Joint Committee. (60 L. J., M. C., 45 : L. R., [1891] 1 Q. B., 53 : 64 L. T., 25 : 55 J. P., 87.)

7. GENERAL POWERS.

1890.   [2755]

Huth v. *Clarke.* Rabies Order under the "Local Government Act, 1888"—A public body by delegating some of its powers to a sub-committee does not necessarily lose its own right to exercise those powers—*Per* Coleridge, C. J.:—"The delegation, unless, of course, it is controlled by Statute, of any power by one person to another, does not contemplate the abandonment of the power. The power may always be resumed." (59 L. J., M. C., 120 : L. R., 25 Q. B. D., 391 : 62 L. T., 348 : 55 J. P., 86.)

(189)

ADDITIONAL CASES.

₊ *These Cases are not indexed. The second number attached to each of them indicates the place in the main text of this work where these "Additional Cases" should be inserted in noting-up.*

2756

1892. **[2756 = 13a]**
Barnes v. *Rider.* "Sale of Food Amendment Act, 1879," § 10—No particulars of the offence intended to be charged stated in Summons, and no statement made as to how the milk had been adulterated—Conviction quashed. (56 J. P., 709.)

1892. **[2757 = 131a]**
Reg. v. *De Rutzen.* "Housing of the Working Classes Act, 1890"—Orders made, first for closing (§ 32), then for demolition (§§ 33, 35) —Appeal by owner dismissed—Subsequent application to Magistrate to determine the Closing Orders on the ground that the premises had been made fit for habitation— Magistrate decided that the application was too late, and that so far as his jurisdiction was concerned the Demolition Order issued by the Vestry was final—The High Court held that the Magistrate was right; therefore Rule Nisi to the Magistrate to state a Case for the High Court discharged. (*Times,* Nov. 4, 1892.)

1892. **[2758 = 175a]**
Ellis v. *London County Council.* "Metropolitan Building Act, 1878," § 6—Houses with forecourts afterwards built over—Boundary wall nearest road then pulled down and replaced by fence—Saving for an "existing" street— Order by Magistrate to pull down and set back this new fence, held bad. (56 J. P., 740 : *Times,* Nov. 8, 1892.)

1892. **[2759 = 208a]**
Leicester Corporation v. *Brown.* "Public Health (Buildings in Streets) Act, 1888"—Wooden building erected by a photographer, 9 ft. long 3 ft. wide and 7 ft. high, with glass front and a door, the corner posts let into the ground, held within the Act, as a "building" and an "addition," and not having been sanctioned as required by the "Public Health Act, 1875," § 166, Conviction confirmed. (56 J. P., 708.)

1892. **[2760 = 259a]**
London County Council v. *Carwardine.* "Sky Signs Act, 1891," § 2—Timber Tower 50 ft. high fitted up as a Windmill and capable of grinding a small quantity of corn : Mill also used for hoisting weights, and for driving a Dynamo Machine—Held nevertheless that the structure was primarily intended to serve as an advertising expedient, and that the above-named uses were only colourable. (56 J. P., 725 : *Times,* Nov. 2, 1892.)

2766

1891. **[2761 = 266a]**
Odwell v. *Willesden L. B.* Building By-Laws— Coffee Stall, colourably resting on wheels but really on wooden supports standing on the ground, pulled down by Board because no building plan submitted—Action for Trespass —Held that the structure was a "new building"—Judgment for defendants. (*Loc. Gov. Chron.,* Nov. 28, 1891.)

1892. **[2762 = 290a]**
Tussaud v. *London C. C.* "Sky-Signs (London) Act, 1891"—Open iron trellis-work braced to a dome surmounting a building held not a "sky-sign" within the Act notwithstanding that the sky could be seen through the trellis-work — Though the structure was attached to a house yet it was not "over" the house within the meaning of the Act. (56 J. P., 740 : *Times,* Nov. 11, 1892.)

1891. **[2763 = 323a]**
Smith v. *Fovargue.* Local Act—By-Law prohibiting the cleaning of fish on the Sea Beach held valid notwithstanding a claim of right to do so by custom. (MS.)

1892. **[2764 = 579a]**
Paterson v. *Blackburn, Mayor.* "Gasworks Clauses Act, 1871," §§ 15, 38—Accident— Man killed—Action under "Lord Campbell's Act"—Corporation had announced its intention of cutting off the supply, and did so, leaving in a cellar an odd piece of pipe, stopped only by a plug—Consumer entered to carry away his meter which was his private property, and accidentally broke the odd piece of pipe, whereupon explosion and seven persons killed — Corporation held liable for the negligence, the consumer having ceased to be a "consumer" by the action of the Corporation, and therefore not within the prohibition of § 38. (*Times,* Nov. 9, 1892.)

1892. **[2765 = 584a]**
Richmond Gas Co. and Richmond, Mayor, Arbitration, In re. "Gasworks Clauses Act, 1847, 1871"—Local Gas Acts—Supply of Gas very deficient on many nights owing to a long continuance of frost—Held that as the Gas Company had made every endeavour to keep up the circulation of the gas through the mains, they were entitled to be paid the full contract price. (*Times,* Oct. 26, 1892.)

1892. **[2766 = 653b]**
Bettingham, In re. Melhado v. *Woodcock.* Premises held on lease — Repairs to drains needed to comply with the "Public Health

(London) Act, 1891"—Friendly summons taken out by Landlord—Tenants held liable, they having covenanted to discharge "all rates, taxes, assessments, and outgoings." (*Times*, Nov. 7, 1892.)

1889.   [2767 = 712a]
Howard v. *Metropolitan B. W.* "Lands Clauses Act, 1845"—Diversion of street—Erection of bridge—Compensation for injury to house. (*Times*, Aug. 10, 1889.)

1892.   [2768 = 805a]
New Romney, Mayor v. *Commissioners of Sewers.* Question as to whether certain scheduled buildings were or were not within the taxable area—Map made in 1832 for the Commissioners which showed that they were not—Held that such map was sufficient evidence that the buildings in question were never within the taxable area. (56 J. P., 662.)

1892.   [2769 = 1023a]
Reg. v. *Rochester Corporation.* "Public Health Act, 1875," § 299 — Default in providing sewerage — Rule *Absolute* for *Mandamus.* (*Times*, Nov. 22, 1892.)

1892.   [2770 = 1024a]
Reg. v. *Worcester, Mayor.* "Public Health Act, 1875," § 299—Default in providing sewerage—Rule *Absolute* for *Mandamus*, but issue of writ to be suspended for a short time to enable the Corporation do something to meet it. (*Times*, Nov. 22, 1892.)

1891.   [2771 = 1092a]
Brydges v. *Dix.* "Public Health Act, 1875"—The signature of a Clerk to a notice under § 150 may be printed. (*Loc. Gov. Chron.*, Feb. 7, 1891 : 10 *Law Notes*, 43.)

1892.   [2772 = 1109a]
Monmouth, Mayor v. *Lang.* "Public Health Act, 1875," §§ 211, 256—Notice on occupier of a dry dock to pay a Rate—Notice served at Dock Head-Office and not at the Dock—Dock being 1½ miles away, through fields, derived no benefit from the roads and lighting—Held that Justices were wrong in deciding (1) that the Notice was not duly served; and (2) that the premises were not liable by reason of their remoteness. (56 J. P., 725.)

1892.   [2773 = 1637a]
Stanley v. *Farndale.* Local Act — Newsboy bawling in street the name of a paper—By-law rendering this an offence if done to the "annoyance" of residents and passengers—Magistrate held that proof of the fact of bawling was proof of "annoyance"—Held that he was wrong — Conviction quashed. (56 J. P., 709.)

1892.   [2774 = 1683a]
East London Waterworks Co. v. *Foulkes.* "Waterworks Clauses Act, 1847," § 68—Action for arrears of Water Rates—Defence that defendant was not owner of all the houses assessed;

that annual value was excessive, and that certain of the charges for empties and baths were excessive—Certain of the matters in dispute ordered to be inquired into by an official Referee. (*Times*, Nov. 9, 1892.)

1867.   [2775 = 1830a]
Chadwick v. *Marsden.* Lease reserving "the free running of water and soil coming from any other buildings or lands contiguous to the premises hereby demised, in and through the sewers and water-courses" of the said premises—Tan-yard established after the demise on contiguous premises—Held, that the words of the reservations did not authorize the discharge of water and refuse from the tan-yard into and through a water-course traversing the demised premises. (31 J. P., 535.)

1884.   [2776 = 1836a]
Goodhart v. *Hyett.* Owner of house entitled as of right to receive a supply of water from spring through pipes running through neighbour's land and the right to enter such land to repair the pipes from time to time—Building commenced on land over line of pipes whereby repair of latter would become difficult—Injunction to restrain such building granted. (53 L. J., Ch., 219 : L. R., 25 Ch. D., 182 : 50 L. T., 95 : 48 J. P., 293.)

1874.   [2777 = 2221a]
Oliver v. *North Eastern Railway Co.* Level crossing—Duty to repair—A highway was crossed by a railway on a level and had been allowed to fall into disrepair so that the rails projected above the highway, and the plaintiff in driving across them was upset and suffered injury—Held, that Railway Company was bound to keep the highway in repair at the *locus in quo*, and was liable to plaintiff for the injuries he had sustained. (38 J. P., 709.)

1892.   [2778 = 2408a]
A.-G. v. *Talbot.* Trust Funds of ancient date (*temp.* Henry VIII.) for mending highways at Leeds—Altered circumstances—Scheme propounded by A.-G. and approved, for reconstituting the Board of Trustees and for spending the Charity Funds in providing open spaces in the Borough—Counter-scheme of Municipal Corporation to give the members of the Corporation a majority of votes on the Board, and to employ the Funds in widening Streets, rejected. (*Times*, Nov. 7, 1892.)

1892.   [2779 = 2408a]
Story v. *Sheard.* "Highways Act, 1878," § 23—The summary procedure provided by this Section is founded on Tort and proceedings under this Section fall to the ground on the death of the person in whose lifetime and by whose order the damage was caused. (61 L. J., M. C., 178.)

INDEX OF NAMES OF CASES.

₊ In order to save space, the names of the Cases are, in this Index, generally abbreviated, but not so much as to cause any obscurity.

₊ The names in italic are alternative names of Cases which are otherwise indexed.

₊ The "Additional Cases" on p. 189 are not indexed.

O

P

INDEX OF SUBJECTS OF CASES.

** The Main Titles under which the Cases are classified in the Text of the Digest of Cases are, in the following Index, for the sake of distinctness, set in small capitals.

LONDON : PRINTED BY WILLIAM CLOWES AND SONS, LIMITED, STAMFORD STREET
AND CHARING CROSS.

www.ingramcontent.com/pod-product-compliance
Lightning Source LLC
Chambersburg PA
CBHW030315270326
41926CB00010B/1381